ALGONQUIAN SPIRIT

Algonquian Spirit

Contemporary Translations of the Algonquian Literatures of North America

Edited by Brian Swann

UNIVERSITY OF NEBRASKA PRESS
LINCOLN & LONDON

Library of Congress Cataloging-in-Publication Data

Algonquian spirit : contemporary translations of the Algonquian literatures of North America / edited by Brian Swann.

p. cm.

Includes bibliographical references and index.

ISBN-10: 0-8032-4314-6 (cloth : alk. paper)

ISBN-13: 978-0-8032-4314-9 (cloth : alk. paper)

ISBN-10: 0-8032-9338-0 (pbk. : alk. paper)

ISBN-13: 978-0-8032-9338-0 (pbk. : alk. paper)

1. Algonquian literature—North America.
2. Algonquian mythology—North America.
3. Algonquian Indians—Songs and music.
4. Algonquian languages—Texts. 5. Legends—North America. 6. North America—Folklore.
I. Swann, Brian.

E99.A35A454 2005

897'.3—dc22 2005008091

Set in Quadraat by Tseng Information Systems, Inc. Designed by A. Shahan.

Printed by Edwards Brothers, Inc.

This book, like all the others, is for Roberta, with love.
None would have been possible without her.

Contents

Introduction xi
Brian Swann

PART 1 | East 1

The Tale of a Hoax:
Translating the Walam Olum 3
David M. Oestreicher

EASTERN SEABOARD COMMUNITY
Fair Warning 42
Alex MacKenzie Hargrave

LENAPE
The Arrival of the Whites 49
Jim Rementer
Told by Captain Pipe, Willie Longbone, Bessie Snake, and Nora Thompson Dean

MUNSEE
The Delaware Creation Story 62
John Bierhorst
Told by John Armstrong

PASSAMAQUODDY
Two Animal Stories 72
Robert M. Leavitt and Jennifer Andrews
Written by Lewis Mitchell
Translated by Robert M. Leavitt
Social and Ceremonial Songs 84
Ann Morrison Spinney
Sung by Blanche Sockabason, Wayne A. Newell, Joseph A. Nicholas, and Lewis Mitchell
Translated by Wayne A. Newell, Joseph A. Nicholas, and David A. Francis

MALISEET

Traditions of Koluskap, the Culture Hero 99
Philip S. LeSourd
Told by Peter Lewis Paul
Translated by Philip S. LeSourd

MI'KMAQ

The Great Fire 112
Franziska von Rosen
Told by Michael William Francis
Translated by Lorne Simon

PART 2 | Central 119

NASKAPI

Two Wolverine Stories 121
Julie Brittain and Marguerite MacKenzie
Told by John Peastitute
Translated by Julie Brittain, Alma Chemaganish, Philip Einish, Marguerite MacKenzie, and Silas Nabinicaboo

OJIBWE

Waabitigweyaa, the One Who Found the Anishinaabeg First 159
Jennifer S. H. Brown and Roger Roulette
Told by Charlie George Owen (Omishoosh)
Translated by Roger Roulette

The Origin of War 170
J. Randolph Valentine
Told by Waasaagoneshkang
Translated by J. Randolph Valentine

That Way We Should Be Walking 185
Mary Magoulick
Told by Oogima Ikwe

POTAWATOMI

Three Tales 201
Laura Buszard-Welcher
Told by Alice Spear and Jim Spear
Translated by Laura Buszard-Welcher

EASTERN CREE

Louse and Wide Lake 215
Richard J. Preston
Told by George Head
Translated by Gerti Diamond Murdoch

A Pair of Hero Stories 230
Susan M. Preston
Told by John Blackned
Translated by Anderson Jolly

OMUSHKEGO (SWAMPY CREE)

Omushkego Legends from Hudson Bay 247
Paul W. DePasquale
Told and Recorded by Louis Bird (Pennishish)
Transcribed by Paul W. DePasquale

MIAMI-ILLINOIS AND SHAWNEE

Culture-Hero and Trickster Stories 292
David J. Costa
Told by George Finley, Elizabeth Vallier, and an Unknown Shawnee Speaker
Translated by David J. Costa

MESKWAKI

Winter Stories 320
Ives Goddard
Written by Sakihtanohkweha and Charley H. Chuck
Translated by Ives Goddard

Three Winter Stories 368
Lucy G. Thomason
Written by Maggie Morgan, Pearl Leaf, and an Unknown Author
Translated by Lucy G. Thomason

MENOMINEE

The Origin of the Spirit Rock 411
Marianne Milligan
Told by Charles Dutchman (Naehcīwetok)
Translated by Marianne Milligan

PART 3 | West 429

PLAINS CREE

Pine Root 431
Stan Cuthand
Written and Translated by Stan Cuthand

ARAPAHO

Ghost Dance Songs 448
Jeffrey D. Anderson
Translated by Jeffrey D. Anderson

Three Stories 472
Andrew Cowell
Told by Richard Moss
Translated by Andrew Cowell and Alonzo Moss Sr.

BLACKFEET

Scarface 495
Theresa Schenck
Written and Translated by Pauline Running Crane

CHEYENNE

The Rolling Head 501
Wayne Leman
Told by Laura Rockroads
Translated by Wayne Leman and Josephine Stands in Timber Glenmore

Contributors 511
Index 523

Introduction

Brian Swann

While not many words in English are of Native North American origin, a good proportion of those that are derive from the Algonquian family of languages. The stirrings of an Algonquian presence can still be heard in the more obvious words, all nouns, such as "powwow" (originally meaning a priest, a "medicine man"), "sachem," "sagamore," "wampum," "wigwam," "wickiup," "pemmican," "moccasin," "tomahawk," "manitou," "totem," "kinnikinnik" (a tobacco mixture), "papoose," "squaw," and the less obvious such as "squash" (the vegetable), "musquash" (the animal), "musky," "scup," and "menhaden" (fish), "caribou," "moose," "wapiti," "hominy," "pone," "samp," "succotash," "persimmon," "saskatoon," "pipsissewa," "muskeg," "hickory," "pecan," "chinquapin," "tamarack," "tuckahoe," "quahog," "scuppernong," "toboggan," "mackinaw," "cushaw" (a crookneck squash), "whiskey jack" (the Canada jay, which bears the same name as the Cree "trickster," Wiskatjan).[1] To these we can add "terrapin," "skunk," "woodchuck," "opossum," "chipmunk," "raccoon," "Eskimo" (as well as its derivative "husky," the dog), and probably "caucus." There are several possible origins of the word "Yankee," but the *Oxford English Dictionary* calls the following etymology the "most used," and many Algonquinists, agreeing with Henry David Thoreau, believe it to be the correct one: it is northeastern Algonquian for "English" (compare the Massachusett "Yengeese").[2] The names of a number of towns and cities, such as Chicago, Milwaukee, Winnipeg, and Ottawa, are Algonquian in origin, as are the names of many states and provinces, from Massachusetts, Connecticut, Michigan, Wyoming, Wisconsin, Illinois, Mississippi, Missouri, and Oregon to Manitoba, Saskatchewan, and Quebec, as well as the names of many rivers, lakes, and mountains.

Early writers used the name "Algonquian" (and variants) to denote a variety of closely related Ojibwayan languages first encountered in the French missions near and along the Ottawa River valley in the first half of the seventeenth century. It was the language most familiar to Jesuit linguists, and the term "Algonquian" was adopted very early into French. It cannot be traced to a specific meaning, however, despite many attempts. Eventually it gave its name to the whole language family. Although in the same century the English in New England and the French in New France recognized the affinities of the languages spoken there, Alfred Gallatin in 1836 was the first to create the linguistic classification of the Algonquian family, which he called Algonkin-Lenape. Subsequently scholars have extended Gallatin's schema. Known now as the Algic family of languages, it is one of the most widespread language families in North America, stretching as far south as North Carolina and up into northern Canada. With Yurok and Wiyot in California, it reaches right across the continent, coast to coast, spanning two countries. It comprises some three dozen languages, many of which are still in existence today and are represented in this volume.[3]

The Proto-Algonquian language has a time depth of about three thousand years. From a center probably in the Great Lakes region, it diversified into eleven independent languages that developed into the groups knows as Blackfeet, Cheyenne, Arapahoan, Cree-Montagnais, Ojibwa, Potawatomi, Menominee, Sauk-Fox-Kickapoo, Miami-Illinois, Shawnee, and an ancestor of the eastern languages (Proto-Eastern Algonquian) that spread east and then south. Breaking down this family further, we have Cree (which comprises some nine languages, including Montagnais/Innu and Naskapi as well as the French-Cree creole Michif), Ojibwe (which contains seven), Kickapoo, Menominee, Meskwaki Sauk (Sac and Fox), Miami-Illinois, Potawatomi, Shawnee, Abnaki-Penobscot, Delaware (Munsee and Unami), Maliseet-Passamaquoddy, Mi'kmaq, Arapaho, Gros Ventre, Blackfeet, and Cheyenne, as well as Wiyot and Yurok and the extinct eastern languages such as Virginian and Carolinian Algonquian, Mohegan-Pequot, Mahican, Massachusett-Narragansett, and Wampanoag.

The health of these languages varies. Some, such as Ojibwe and Cree, are spoken by a significant number of children, and therefore the future is quite bright. For others, spoken by adults but few children, the future is not so assured. These languages include Arapaho, Blackfeet, Cheyenne, Maliseet-Passamaquoddy, Mi'kmaq, Michif, and Sauk-Fox. Sadly, it seems that those spoken by only a few adults (Abenaki, Gros Ventre, Menominee, Munsee and Unami Delaware, Potawatomi, and Yurok) might well join the many extinct languages.

While records were made of Algonquian languages in the sixteenth century, such as the list of names for birds and fishes, placenames, and personal names compiled by Thomas Harriot, a member of Raleigh's 1585 colony in North Carolina, Marc Lescarbot was the first European to record Algonquian literature when, between 1601 and 1607, he collected some Mi'kmaq songs in Acadia (Nova Scotia). He wrote down the words and set out the music in the tonic system.[4] The oldest surviving text from what is now the United States is a Powhatan "scornful song" recorded by William Strachey in his *Historie of Travail into Virginia Britannia*, published in 1612.[5] From the early sixteenth century, we have ethnographic texts made by the Jesuit missionaries in New France, which are collected in *The Jesuit Relations*.[6] Other missionaries to the south made attempts to record what they heard. For instance, Father Marquette gave the words of an Illinois, or Peoria, song in his account of his first voyage of 1674.[7] Unfortunately the words are mostly meaningless.[8] There are speeches reported in the Virginia records, and in 1632 Thomas Morton of the Plymouth Colony reported a speech of the sachem Chautawback, whose mother's grave had been desecrated by the settlers, a speech that also contains an account of the sachem's dream.[9] In New Amsterdam in 1679, one of the remaining Munsees, Tantaque, a man over eighty years of age, told a story of the creation of the world to Jasper Danckaerts and Peter Sluyter. Sluyter recorded this story, a version of the widespread "world on Turtle's back," in his journal.[10] There are materials from the eighteenth century, such as those collected from the Delawares and the Mahicans by the Moravian missionary David Zeisberger, but, as with many Native American languages, it was the nineteenth century that saw serious efforts at collecting, studying, and translating, notably by John Heckewelder, an important source for the novels of James Fenimore Cooper, and Henry Rowe Schoolcraft, whose work Henry Wadsworth Longfellow utilized for his "Song of Hiawatha" (1855).[11] In the twentieth century, some of the most important names are William Jones, Frank Speck, Frank Siebert, Edward Sapir, Carl Voegelin, Leonard Bloomfield, Frances Densmore, Charles Hockett, and Alanson Skinner.[12] In the twenty-first century, the field is in the capable hands of those who have contributed to this volume and of others who have not. For over thirty years, the Algonquian Conference has met annually, while the newsletter *Algonquian and Iroquoian Linguistics* is published quarterly.

In addition to this recording by both non-Native and Native, people of Algonquian descent were the first Native Americans to write and publish in English, a tradition continued in this volume. The first Native American autobiography, for instance, was written by the Reverend Samson Occum, a Christianized Mohegan, in 1768.[13] In 1791 Hendrick Aupaumut, a Mahican, wrote a narrative of a journey that included autobiographical elements.[14] Neither of these books was published during the authors' lifetime. That honor went in 1829 to the Reverend William Apess, a Pequod and a Methodist minister, for *A Son of the Forest*.[15]

This book has been a long time building. After specializing in medieval literature at Cambridge, in 1964 I won a Proctor Fellowship to Princeton to study American literature. As I read, I became aware of that "scattering of savages, noble and ignoble" noted by Roy Harvey Pearce.[16] But at the time the phenomenon didn't engage me much, even after I understood why Melville named his doomed ship the *Pequod* after an Algonquian-speaking people from what is now Connecticut, victims of a brutal massacre by the English in 1637 (and now proprietors of the world's largest casino). Gradually, however, it became clear to me that Indians were part of our origin story, a continual engagement. They slipped through our literature carrying all sorts of symbolic freight, from the founding myth of Virginia and the southern Algonquians, to the Puritan battle against the demonic Algonquians of the northeast, a battle that, if we follow the argument of Richard Drinnon, carried on in American history through the twentieth century.[17] I became aware of items derived from experiences among Indian, most likely Algonquian, cultures, such as the phrases "Indian giver," "Indian summer," and maybe even the nursery rhyme "Hush-a-Bye-Baby."[18] I also began to hear Algonquian names, filtered through English ears and orthography, echoing down the centuries, in many contexts and manifestations: Squanto, Powhatan, Pocahontas, Uncas, Metacomet (King Philip), Pequods, Mohegans, Mahicans, Narragansetts, Massachusetts, and so on. As the years went on, I began to realize that it was among the eastern Algonquians that English ideas and attitudes toward the natives and the land were first formulated, later to be carried all over North America and down through history.[19]

But, as I said, as a graduate student I didn't pay that much attention to the Indian component of American literature, even though I had been interested in "the oral tradition" for as long as I could remember. In fact, the first time I remember noticing the word "Algonquian" was when, a couple of years after my arrival, during an Easter break I checked into the Algonquin Hotel on West 44th Street, intending to spend time in the New York Public Library. Here I learned more about the famous Round Table but don't recall being interested in digging deeper into what "Algonquian" (or "Algonquin") meant, even though back in New Jersey I was surrounded by Algonquian-derived placenames such as Rahway, Parsippany, Moonachie, and Weehawken, and rivers with such names as Raritan, Manasquan, Passaic, Ramapo, Nevesink, and Rancocas. I didn't start to take a real interest in Indian America until about 1972, when, after I decided I wanted to make my home in the United States, I moved to Manhattan to teach. In this huge, anonymous, and constantly changing city, I began to understand the Crèvecoeurean desire to become a "new man" in a new land and to sense "the genuine need of taking root."[20] I missed the "spirit of place," such as I had had growing up in Northumberland, in the northeast of England.[21] And this, for me, meant finding some sort of aboriginal contact.

I was born in Wallsend, my mother's hometown, which had started life as a Roman station named Segedunum, right at the end of the wall built from sea to sea by the Emperor Hadrian in the second century AD. A part of this wall had been removed from its original position to accommodate a shipyard's expansion and placed in a public park, where we children clambered all over it. Trips inland included walks along the wall's extensive remains and visits to forts with resonant names such as Vindolana, Vindobala, Cilernum, Corstopitum, Aesica, Borcovicum, and Bricolitia. There were visits to Flodden Field, where King James IV of Scotland was killed in 1513, and to Chevy Chase, where Sir Henry Percy, Hotspur, killed the Earl of Douglas in 1388 ("Chevy Chase," most famous of the border ballads, tells the story of this battle). Excursions into the Cheviot Hills revealed ancient earthworks, stone circles, and burial cairns. Days were spent along the coast at such places as Lindisfarne, cradle of English Christianity, the home of Saint Cuthbert and the Lindisfarne Gospels, and at Alnwick, seat of the Percy family. Jarrow, just across the river Tyne from Wallsend, was home of the Venerable Bede (ca. 673–735). All this made history tangible and immediate.

I was ten years old when my family moved to Cambridge, my father's hometown, where I wandered around the colleges, many over five hundred years old. A mile or two from our house, in the Gog Magog hills, was an Iron Age earthworks or "fort" named Wandelbury, probably built by the Iceni, Queen Boudicca's people, though some claim it is much older. A prehistoric roadway, the Icknield Way, still passed close by, as well as a Roman road. I spent much time there and read all I could about the place, which had many legends attached to it. Meanderings by foot and bicycle led to all sorts of corners and discoveries, from places like Wicken Fen, still in its medieval state, undrained and unfarmed, to the Neolithic flint mines at Grime's Graves (Grime, or Grim, was a by-name of Woden), whose narrow shafts and tunnels I crawled through. Once, digging fossils from an old chalk pit nearby, a friend and I discovered a skull that turned out to belong to an Anglo-Saxon boy of about our age. The past was something I lived, not just something to study. When I learned Latin in high school, it was not a dead language to me. Later, as an undergraduate at Queens' College, studying, among other subjects, Anglo-Saxon and Old Norse, I found myself part of an institution whose patrons had included medieval queens as well as King Richard III, and whose walls had housed Erasmus and Dr. John Hall, Shakespeare's son-in-law and, in all likelihood, his physician.

So, starting with my move to Manhattan in 1972, I found myself becoming intrigued with New York's Indian past, a past stretching back eleven thousand years. First, there was the name of the island itself with its various translations: "hilly island," "the island," "small island," "clusters of islands with channels everywhere," "the place where we all became intoxicated." And then close at hand were Rockaway, Canarsie, and Jamaica. Trips to Long Island revealed Mamaroneck, Massapequa, Patchogue, Ronkonkoma, Quogue, and many more towns with Algonquian names until, at the very tip, sat Montauk. Soon, maps in hand, I was able to discover an older, deeper Manhattan, a shadow geography, starting with the fact that the brownstone whose basement I occupied near the Hudson River was a stone's throw from the cove near Gansevoort Street (a street named for Melville's mother's family), where there had been a landing place and a settlement named Sapohanikan (possibly "tobacco plantation"). I began to evoke a presence from before the flattening of Manhattan's hills and the filling in of marshlands both on the island and all around it; before streams like the Minetta Brook (whose name might sound Italian but is probably derived from "manitou," a word applied to anything remarkable, strange, or wonderful, a word embedded in "Manitoba") were diverted into the sewer system. I began to sense a time when such nearby places as Gramercy Park and Washington Square Park were swamps and Tompkins Square Park a salt meadow, and a great council tree grew in Astor Place, where I now type these words, at the intersection of three important paths, close to the main north-south path that became the Bowery. Each day when I walk to and from my apartment, I pass in front of Saint Mark's Church at Second Avenue and 10th Street, built on the site of the garden chapel of New Amsterdam's fourth and final governor general, Peter Stuyvesant, the original Peg-Leg Pete (1592–1672), who retired here to his sixty-two-acre farm known as the Great Bouwerie and who is buried in the family vault in the church graveyard. This land had once belonged to the Schepmoes, a branch of the Canarsies, who had a village close by. In the front courtyard, across from each other, heads raised, are the life-size statues of two Indian men: gray ghosts.[22]

When I look south out of my apartment window, I know that close to where the World Trade Center towers once stood is Corlaer's Hook. Here, in 1643, over one hundred Weckquaesgeek refugees were massacred on the orders of Willem Kieft, New Amsterdam's director general, after having been driven south by Mohawks from their homes around what is now White Plains.[23] Although thousands of Native Americans from all over the Americas live in New York City today (the American Indian Community House that serves them is on Lafayette Street, just across the street from my office), the Native peoples of this island and its surroundings had disappeared by the mid-nineteenth century. Not one aboriginal word of the Natives was recorded before most of them retreated to Staten Island and then to New Jersey toward the end of the seventeenth century. By the end of the Seven Years War in 1763, the surviving Munsees in Lenapehoking (Land of the Lenape, "the People") began heading west; their diaspora had begun. We can trace them as they moved west and north: Delaware, Ohio; Muncie, Indiana; Lenepah, Oklahoma; Muncietown, Ontario.[24] A few enclaves were left in Brooklyn, the Bronx, and Staten Island through the eighteenth century, but they had disappeared by the first decade of the nineteenth.[25] Today the principal Delaware communities are in southern Ontario and Oklahoma, but people of Delaware descent live all over the United States and Canada.

As the seventies rolled on, and the "Native American renaissance" hit its stride, my interest grew wider than local. After becoming a U.S. citizen in 1980, I felt the need to know more about my adopted country, especially its ongoing relations with the indigenous inhabitants. What I learned both disturbed and intrigued me. I was disturbed by our origins, by our history of mistreatment of Indians, and by still unresolved issues and injustices, as well as by widespread lack of knowledge, misunderstanding, or plain indifference.[26] I was intrigued by cultures rich and resilient, trying to retain contact with traditions and values and at the same time finding ways to live in the modern world.

As for the Algonquian-speaking peoples of North America, in the mid-nineties my desire to know more about them was sharpened when my wife and I bought a house and land in Delaware County's Vega Valley. This lovely part of the western Catskills had few Indian settlements, being used mostly as hunting territory by the Esopus Indians, or Waranawonks, a Munsee-speaking group. The Esopus were roughly handled by the Dutch in hostilities from 1659 to 1663 and in the years following dispersed to the west. By the time settlers moved into the area in the late eighteenth century, few Indians were left. After the American Revolution, a few Indian families lived on as squatters, and one named Tunis gave his name to the lake he lived beside, which still bears that name.[27] Although groups of mixed race developed, such as the Schoharies, by the mid-1800s the only Indians in the area came down from Canada as part of the major summer resort business.

Henry Rowe Schoolcraft was born near Albany in 1793. He became dissatisfied with the name of the mountains in his backyard and came up with a more Indian-sounding name for the Catskills, "On-ti-ora," which he said meant "Land in the Sky." He made up a legend about giants to go with the new name. The only Indian stories told in this land in the sky were those composed to bolster the taste for the quaint and the romantic and to lure summer boarders.[28] There is the saga of Winnesook, for example, the "Big Indian" for whom a hamlet is named near Slide Mountain. This story may have had some older historical components, but by the turn of the nineteenth century, it could be read in various literary versions. Another story, composed by a native of Stamford while a student at Yale, is centered on Utsayantha Mountain and concerns a tragic Indian maiden, Utsayantha, who drowned herself in the lake at its foot. This tale helped turn Stamford into a summer resort.

The idea of the Indian as proud revolutionary was used by the Calico Indians, taking their cue from the Mohawk disguises used at the Boston Tea Party. During the Antirent War of 1839–45, rioters dressed up in masks, feathers, scraps of tin, and gowns of flowered calico.[29] They even took Indian names. Asa Bishop, a Calico Indian who hid out in Delaware County, called himself "Black Hawk," presumably after the great Sauk chief whose revolt was crushed in 1832 and who died in 1838.[30] Ironically, the Mahican neighbors of the Esopus held their last gathering, the Great Council, on July 4, 1854, at Renselaerswyck, near Albany. At this gathering a real oppressed Indian, the Mahican chief Waun-nau-con, also known as John W. Quinney, or Quinnauquant, addressed a large crowd of Antirenters, who regarded themselves as oppressed Indians.[31]

Once the real inhabitants were forced out, then, imitation Indians and "invented traditions" were imported to these beautiful mountains.[32] In truth, not much memory of the original people remains, despite the powwows each summer at Hunter Mountain, Belleayre, and Big Indian. There are a few aboriginal-derived names such as Esopus, Shokan, and Pepacton, and the mountain above Margaretville, named Pakatakan, takes its names from the flats below. But many names are the result of the nineteenth century's enthusiasm for Indian or Indian-sounding appellations to attract and beguile summer tourists. Often perfectly good Dutch or English names were transformed. So, for instance, while Schoolcraft's "Onteora" didn't supplant "Catskill," near Woodstock Ohayo Mountain did take the place of Beaverkill Mountain.

Today most people can identify only a few of the mountains by name (which is not surprising, since as the older families sell and move to warmer climes, they are replaced by newcomers for whom nature is little more than playground or real estate). There are no myths; there are no storied or "symbolic landscapes," "narrated place-worlds" such as those inhabited by aboriginal peoples and, perhaps, my own ancient European ancestors.[33] Having said which, even though I may be a kind of deracinated postmodernist in a "condition of off-centeredness," I do not wish to sound like one.[34] Nor do I mean to sound like Henry James lamenting what he regarded as the American cultural vacuum and historical wasteland.[35] Clearly, different stories are told now, to go with a different attitude toward the land and toward reality itself. But with the collapse of the dairy industry, the forests are coming back, as are many of the animals, including the wolf.[36] I like to imagine the place as it once might have been, create a few echoes, give those echoes substance.[37] As I stand in our high back field, flat-top Bearpen behind me, looking all around I see forested mountains whose outlines have not changed since the Waranawonks looked at them. In addition, perusing signatures on old documents and treaties, I have come up with the Native names of people who could have known these parts. Using information on the life ways of closely related peoples, I have tried to imagine how they lived, or find out what they believed. I want to know the kind of stories they told, hear the kind of sounds they used in their language, try to get some sense of how linguistic habits and structures shaped their world (though my efforts to learn Delaware have been desultory, at best). John Bierhorst, my neighbor in the county to the east, has experienced the same desire. He has said that his own wish to know Delaware literature comes simply from living in Ulster County, within Lenape territory. "I wanted to know what stories had been told—or might have been told—here."[38] Perhaps it is mere sentimental fancy, but stories such as "The Naked Bear," "The Giant Squirrel," or "The Wood Dwarf" seem to change the way I look at things—I sometimes cannot see a squirrel at our feeder without thinking of its giant relative that ate everything in sight or watch quail without thinking of "The Boy Who Became a Flock of Quail."[39] Still it is hard to imagine a world full of manitous, a world understood as spirit and "person," a set of relationships, interwoven existences alive at many levels.

Over the years, from this intensely local interest in the Algonquian-speaking peoples of where I live, my interest in all things Native American has grown. The creation of this volume has been something very personal for me, and with it my involvement in American Indian literatures comes full circle, since it is in all likelihood the final volume in a series that began twenty years ago with *Smoothing the Ground: Essays on Native American Oral Literature*.[40]

There are many people to thank for their help and support over the years and for making possible not only this book but the others that have preceded it. First, of course, is my wife, Roberta. Then my friends Arnold Krupat, Dell Hymes, Julian Rice, and the late Alfonso Ortiz. I would also like to thank Gary Dunham, director of the University of Nebraska Press, and the anonymous reviewers of this book in its manuscript stage (who turned out to be Herb Luthin and Blair Rudes). Finally, I would like to express my gratitude to all the contributors whose skills, generosity, and enthusiasm for the project have created this volume, which completes a trilogy started in 1994 with *Coming to Light: Contemporary Translations of the Native Literatures of North America* and followed in 2004 by *Voices from Four Directions*. Each of these volumes contains Algonquian translations. In the former there are Delaware, Ojibwe, Passamaquoddy, Rock Cree, Menominee, and Sauk/Fox, while in the latter we have Mi'kmaq, Maliseet, Menominee, Ojibwe, Meskwaki/Fox, and Naskapi. So far as I am aware, however, while the present volume may not be the first to be devoted to the literature of one Native North American family of languages, it is the widest ranging. If some languages seem overrepresented and others underrepresented, and if one or two are not represented at all, it is not due to any lack of effort on my part. I tried to have every Algonquian language present, but I was dependent on a number of factors, including the state of the languages themselves, the kind of study and attention given to them, as well as the willingness of specialists in those languages to involve themselves in this venture. I was also dependent on the attitude of Native peoples toward promulgation of materials that in some cases are considered sacred, even if they have previously been published in anthropological treatments.

Finally, I would like to make two points. First, a note on this book's subtitle. "Contemporary translations" should be understood somewhat widely. It means, of course, that the great majority of the work is, in fact, newly translated from a Native language for this collection, though there are some contributions told or written in English. The focus of this volume is on translation of songs, stories, and oratory, from the famous translation hoax the Walam Olum and a translation of a speech from an unknown Algonquian language, to retranslations of "classic" texts, to translations of stories written or told by Native storytellers today or in the past, and songs that are still sung today. These texts span the centuries, from the seventeenth and the eighteenth into the twenty-first. As for the book's organization, reversing probable migration routes, I have started from the east, close to home, and meandered west, grouping the languages into Eastern Algonquian, Central Algonquian (Cree and Ojibwe are here, although they range from the Atlantic to Alberta), and Western Algonquian. And as for the book's aim and purpose, I hope that, with the essential help provided by the introductions, and with the aid of the suggested reading lists, the reader will be able to appreciate fascinating indigenous languages and wonderful indigenous literatures. For this book is intended for anyone interested in *literature*, in all its variations and manifestations.

The second point to be made is that the reader of this book will find a certain diversity of styles and approaches. This is what one should expect in a discipline, Native American studies, which is really an umbrella term for a set of subdisciplines such as anthropology, linguistics, folklore, and literature. The contributors come from a number of backgrounds and fields. There are not only anthropologists and linguists but also storytellers, singers, educators, and language activists. Some introductions may be more technical than others, but the aim is always to demonstrate the skill and particularities of the original. I have chosen to celebrate this variety while at the same time creating a uniform pattern of overall structure.

This volume is only a small selection from the riches that constitute the literary traditions of the Algonquian-speaking peoples of North America, a heritage that lives on, not only via oral transmission and creation in the Native languages but also in English, which in a number of cases has become the language of transmission. It continues also in the writings of authors with Algonquian heritage such as Louise Erdrich, Gerald Vizenor, the late James Welch, Ray Young Bear, Joseph Bruchac, Jack Forbes, Winona LaDuke, Barney Bush, Kim Blaeser, and Gordon

Henry in the United States, and in Canada Thomson Highway, Basil Johnston, Rita Joe, Beth Cuthand, Armand Garnet-Rutto, Drew Hayden Taylor, Kateri Akiwenzie-Damm, and others at the forefront of contemporary Native American and First Nations literature.

Notes

1. A controversy has grown around the word "squaw," which has been used as an insult supposedly deriving from its meaning "female genitalia." The word, however, simply means "woman," as both the Abenaki storyteller Marge Bruchac and the linguist William Bright have pointed out. See Marge Bruchac, "Reclaiming the Word 'Squaw' in the Name of Our Ancestors" (www.nativeweb.org), and William Bright, "The Sociolinguistics of the 'S-Word': 'Squaw' in American Placenames" (www.ncidc.org/bright).
2. "This is New Angleland, and these are the New West Saxons whom the Red Men call, not Angle-ish or English, but Yengeese, and so at last they are known for Yankees," from *A Week on the Concord and Merrimack Rivers* (1848; repr., New York: Holt, Rinehart & Winston, 1963), 42. The other main candidate is Dutch. See, for example, David L. Gold, "A Final Word on 'Yankee'," SSILA *Newsletter* 22, no. 2 (July 2003): 4.
3. For information on the earliest recordings of Algonquian languages, consult Ives Goddard, "The Description of the Native Languages of North America before Boas," in *Languages*, vol. 17 of *Handbook of North American Indians* (Washington DC: Smithsonian Institution Press, 1996), 17–42. In the same volume, see Michael K. Foster on "Algic" in "Language and the Culture History of North America," 97–100. See this volume also for information on other Algonquian languages and cultures, as well as vol. 15, *Northeast* (1978). Also, Richard A. Rhodes and Evelyn M. Todd, "Subarctic Algonquian Languages," in vol. 6, *Subarctic* (1981).
4. Marc Lescarbot, *Nova Francia: A Description of Acadia, 1609*, trans. P. Erondelle (London: Routledge & Sons, 1929).
5. William Strachey, *The Historie of Travaile into Virginia Britannia, 1612*, ed. R. H. Major (London: Hakluyt Society, 1849).
6. Reuben Gold Thwaites, ed., *The Jesuit Relations and Allied Documents* (New York: Pageant, 1959).
7. The text is in *The Indians of North America*, ed. Edna Kenton (New York: Harcourt, Brace, 1927), 551–52.
8. In correspondence Michael McCafferty notes that Marquette's original recording probably got transcribed in Quebec and then sent to France. He suggests that in France it was transcribed again and in that process lost most of the clarity it had.

He did, however, find two or three meaningful morphemes, one of which might have something to do with sandhill cranes.

9. Thomas Morton, *New England Canaan; a New Canaan, Containing an Abstract of New England* (1632; repr., New York: Peter Smith, 1947), 72–3. A book that covers the Algonquians of New England, their history, worldview, and literature is William S. Simmons, *Spirit of the New England Tribes: Indian History and Folklore, 1620–1984* (Hanover NH: University Press of New England, 1986).
10. Ann-Marie Cantwell and Diana diZerega Wall, *Unearthing Gotham: The Archeology of New York City* (New Haven CT: Yale University Press, 2001), 36.
11. John Hechewelder, *An Account of the History, Manners, and Customs of the Indian Nations*, 1819. Reprinted as *History, Manners and Customs of the Indian Nations Who Once Inhabited Pennsylvania and the Neighboring States* (Philadelphia: Historical Society of Pennsylvania, 1876; New York: Arno Press, 1971); Henry Rowe Schoolcraft, *Algic Researches* (New York: Harper & Brothers, 1839). Schoolcraft married Jane Johnston, daughter of an Irish trader and Oshanguscodaywayqua, daughter of Waubojeeg, chief of the Ojibwe at La Pointe, Wisconsin. Mother and daughter were largely responsible for compiling and translating the material Schoolcraft used, since his command of the Ojibwe language was weak. The published versions, however, were Schoolcraft's creation, reflecting his desire to "civilize" the Indian. For more on the subject, see William M. Clements, *Native American Verbal Art: Texts and Contexts* (Tucson: University of Arizona Press, 1996), 111–28.
12. For a survey of the history of the translation of Native American literature, see my introduction to *Coming to Light: Contemporary Translations of the Native Literatures of North America*, ed. Brian Swann (New York: Vintage Books, 1996), as well as Arnold Krupat's "On the Translation of Native American Song and Story: A Theorized History," in *On the Translation of Native American Literatures*, ed. Brian Swann (Washington DC: Smithsonian Institution Press, 1992), 3–42. For a brief description of the problematic nature of translation, I refer the reader to my introduction to *Voices from Four Directions: Contemporary Translations of the Native Literatures of North America*, ed. Brian Swann, (Lincoln: University of Nebraska Press, 2004), xiv–xix.
13. Samson Occum, "A Short Narrative of My Life," in *The Elders Wrote: An Anthology of Early Prose by North American Indians*, ed. Berndt Peyer (Berlin: Dietrich Reimer Verlag, 1982), 12–18.
14. Hendrick Aupaumut, *A Narrative of an Embassy to the Western Indians*, Pennsylvania Historical Society Memoirs (1827), 61–131.
15. *On Our Own Ground: The Complete Writings of William Apess*, ed. Barry O'Connell (Amherst: University of Massachusetts Press, 1992). It should be noted that Occum, Aupaumut, and Apess have antecedents. The uses of literacy in English among

the Christianized natives of New England in the seventeenth century is discussed by Kathleen J. Bragdon in her essay "The Interstices of Literacy: Books and Writing and Their Use in Native American Southern New England," in *Anthropology, History, and America Indians: Essays in Honor of William Curtis Sturtevant*, ed. William L. Merrill and Ives Goddard, Smithsonian Contributions to Anthropology, no. 14 (Washington DC: Smithsonian Institution Press, 2002), 121–30.

16. *Savagism and Civilization: A Study of the Indian and the American Mind* (Berkeley: University of California Press, 1988), 197. This book was originally published in 1953 as *The Savages of America: A Study of the Indian and the Idea of Civilization.*

17. *Facing West: The Metaphysics of Indian-Hating and Empire Building* (Minneapolis: University of Minnesota Press, 1980). As active and powerful agents of Satan, Algonquians played an unwitting role in the American Revolution. As Northrop Frye writes: "The Revolution itself built a good deal on the New England Puritan feeling that their colony was an attempt to construct a new society in spite of the devil, so to speak, and was consequently exposed to his greater malice" (*The Great Code: The Bible and Literature* [San Diego: Harcourt Brace Jovanovich, 1983], 118). Richard Slotkin makes similar points in *Regeneration through Violence: The Mythology of the American Frontier, 1600–1860* (Middletown CT: Wesleyan University Press, 1973), and in his 1992 study *Gunfighter Nation: The Myth of the Frontier in Twentieth-Century America* (New York: Harper Collins), where he notes how the myth of the frontier began with the Puritan colonists' "spiritual regeneration" (11) via "savage war" (12) against the Algonquian-speaking people of the East Coast.

18. "Indian gift" is first noted in the mid-eighteenth century and "Indian giver" about a hundred years later. Both derive from a misunderstanding of Indian land use. "Indian summer," first noted in the mid-eighteenth century, also contains the idea of deceit and falsehood (an Indian summer is a false summer). As for "the best-known lullaby in English," "Hush-a-Bye-Baby" (or "Rock-a-Bye Baby"), it first appeared in print in 1765, but there is a strong tradition that it was composed by someone who sailed on the *Mayflower* and who was impressed by the way Indian women near the colony hung birch-bark cradles from tree branches. See William S. Baring-Gould and Ceil Baring-Gould, *The Annotated Mother Goose* (New York: World Publishing, 1971), 224.

19. See, for example, William Cronon, *Changes in the Land: Indians, Colonists, and the Ecology of New England* (New York: Hill & Wang, 1983).

20. "The genuine need of taking root" is from a regionalist manifesto of 1929, quoted in Robert L. Dorman's *Revolt of the Provinces: The Regionalist Movement in America, 1920–1945* (Chapel Hill: University of North Carolina Press, 1993), 110. In chapter 1, Dorman discusses Crèvecoeur.

21. The phrase "spirit of place" is from D. H. Lawrence, *Studies in Classic American Lit-*

erature (1925; repr., New York: Viking, 1961), 5–6: "Every continent has its own great spirit of place. . . . The spirit of place is a great reality."

22. These two statues were erected in 1920 and designated "Aspiration" and "Inspiration" by their sculptor Solon Borglum (whose brother, Gutzon, was the carver of the faces on Mount Rushmore). Borglum was born in Utah in 1868 and traveled widely in the West. He made his considerable reputation as a depicter of the mythical vanished frontier and its "vanishing" Native inhabitants. The statues were erected during the pastorate of William Norman Guthrie, a progressive clergyman who had worked out a ritual based on the theory of the essential unity of all religions. For Borglum, see A. Mervyn Davies, *Solon H. Borglum: "The Man Who Stands Alone"* (Chester CT: Pequot Press, 1974), and for Guthrie, see *The WPA Guide to New York City* (New York: Pantheon Books, 1939), 123.
23. For information on New York City, see R. P. Bolton, "New York City in Indian Possession," in *Indian Notes and Monographs*, vol. 2, no. 7 (New York: Museum of the American Indian, Heye Foundation, 1920); R. P. Bolton, "Indian Paths in the Great Metropolis," *Contributions from the Museum*, vol. 23 (New York: Museum of the American Indian, Heye Foundation, 1922); Robert Steven Grumet, *Native American Place Names in New York City* (New York: Museum of the City of New York, 1981).
24. *Unearthing Gotham*, 148. Today there are two federally recognized Delaware groups: the Delaware Tribe of Indians, of Bartlesville, Oklahoma, and the Delaware Tribe of Western Oklahoma of Anadarko, Oklahoma. The first group, numbering about ten thousand, are descendants of the main body of the tribe that migrated from Indiana to western Missouri in the early nineteenth century and thence to Kansas and Cherokee territory. The second group, the "Absentee" or Western Delawares, numbering about twelve hundred, are descendants of those who broke away from the main body in the eighteenth century, migrating through Missouri, Kansas, and Texas and finally removing to the Wichita Agency in Anadarko. There are other Delaware descendants, including the Kansas Delawares and the Idaho Delawares, and those living among the Stockbridge-Munsees of Wisconsin and even among peoples of the North and the West, including the Nez Perces. In Ontario Delawares reside at Moraviantown, at Muncey Town, and on the Six Nations Reserve (Deborah Nichols, introduction to *Legends of the Delaware Indians and Picture Writing*, by Richard C. Adams, ed. Deborah Nichols [Syracuse NY: Syracuse University Press, 1995], xvii–xviii. This book was originally published in 1905.)
25. Theodore L. Kazimiroff, in *The Last Algonquian* (New York: Dell, 1983), tells the story of Joe Two Trees, "last known member of the Weckquaeskeg tribe of the Algonquin Nation" (xxv), "last of the Turtle clan" (46), whom the author's father met in 1924 on Hunter's Island on Long Island Sound in the Bronx. I have been

unable to authenticate this story, which has elements of Black Elk, Ishi, and Sealth and reads like a novel, so perhaps skepticism is in order.

26. "I blush to think of our origins—our hands are steeped in blood and crime" (Henry Miller, *Tropic of Capricorn* [New York: Grove Press, 1961], 287). "History, history! We fools, what do we know or care? History begins for us with murder and enslavement, not discovery" (William Carlos Williams, *In the American Grain* [Norfolk CT: New Directions, 1925], 39).
27. This might have been a Dutch name the man adopted, since on page 204 of her *Mohicans and Their Land, 1609–1730* (Fleischmanns NY: Purple Mountain Press, 1994), Shirley W. Dunn mentions a dispatch sent to the Dutch living on Catskill Creek via one Jan Dereth and an Indian named Teunis, whose Mohican name was Sickaneek.
28. This taste infected even the Catskill's most famous naturalist-writer, John Burroughs, (1837–1921), whose grandparents had cut a road through the wilderness to settle near Roxbury in 1795. In his essay "Wild Life about My Cabin," he compares Black Pond, near the Hudson River, to "an Indian maiden" in a passage Freudians and feminists could have a field day with: "Here I get the moist, spongy, tranquil, luxurious side of nature. Here she stands or sits knee-deep in water, and wreathes herself with pond-lilies in summer, and bedecks herself with scarlet maples in autumn. She is an Indian maiden, dark, subtle, dreaming, with glances now and then that thrill the wild blood in one's veins" (*The Birds of John Burroughs*, ed. Jack Kilgerman [Woodstock NY: Overlook Press, 1988], 134).
29. Much of my information on the Catskills is drawn from Alf Evers, *In Catskill Country* (Woodstock NY: Overlook Press, 1995), and *The Catskills* (New York: Doubleday, 1972), as well as from Arthur G. Adams, *The Catskills* (New York: Fordham University Press, 1990.) James Fenimore Cooper's 1846 novel, *The Redskins*, is concerned with Antirent sentiment.
30. Black Hawk's war was covered widely in the press, and J. B. Patterson had published *Blackhawk: An Autobiography* in 1833. It was republished by the University of Illinois Press in 1955.
31. Dunn, *Mohicans and Their Land*, 34. After the violence of 1839–45, by 1854 Antirent excitement had lessened but was not to disappear for many years. The text of Quinney's speech can be found in *The World Turned Upside Down: Indian Voices from Early America*, ed. Colin G. Calloway (New York: Bedford/St. Martin's, 1994), 40–41. The book includes other speeches by Algonquians from the seventeenth and eighteenth centuries.
32. The phrase "invented traditions" is from *The Invention of Tradition*, ed. Eric Hobsbaum and Terence Ranger (Cambridge: Cambridge University Press, 1983). From the late eighteenth century into the nineteenth, attempts were made in Europe to

create new mythologies and new histories, especially in connection with the rise of nation states and the establishment of national identities.

33. For discussion of "symbolic landscapes," land as an integrative concept in which active relationships pervade and where all elements have the status of "persons," see the introduction to Susan Preston's contribution to the present volume. The term "narrated place-worlds" is from Keith Basso, *Wisdom Sits in Places: Landscape and Language among the Western Apache* (Albuquerque: University of New Mexico Press, 1996), 32. In chapter 5, "Anchoring the Past in Place: Geography and History", Peter Nabokov discusses "deep geography," the function of stories, dream narratives, songs and song-cycles in the creation of "place," (*A Forest of Time: American Indian Ways of History*, Cambridge: Cambridge University Press, 2000).
34. The phrase is from James Clifford, *The Predicament of Culture* (Cambridge: Harvard University Press, 1988), 9.
35. I refer, of course, to James's lament that in this almost "no state," there are "no castles, nor mansions, nor old country houses, no palaces, no castles," and so on in his 1879 book *Hawthorne* (Ithaca NY: Cornell University Press, 1963), 34. James was by no means the first to make this lament. In his journal Thoreau takes to task his contemporaries who ignore the Indian past all round them and complain "that we have no antiquities in America, no ruins to remind us of our past" (quoted by Edwin Fussell in his essay "The Red Face of Man," in *Thoreau: A Collection of Critical Essays*, ed. Sherman Paul (Englewood Cliffs NJ: Prentice-Hall, 1962), 148.
36. The Munsees had three phratries: Wolf, Turkey, and Turtle (or Bear). In the 1960s, according to Ives Goddard, two lineages were still recognized, the Red Ochre People and the Yellow Tree People, both of the Wolf phratry. See Goddard, "Delaware," in vol. 15 of the *Handbook of North American Indians*, 225.
37. Perhaps this desire to link to the aboriginal past is behind the continuing appeal of Chief Seattle's famous and largely fabricated speech, particularly the part where he says "the white man will never be alone": "At night when the streets of your cities and villages shall be silent, and you think them deserted, they will throng with the returning hosts that once filled and still love this beautiful land" (quoted by Rudolf Kaiser in "Chief Seattle's Speech(es): American Origins and European Reception," in *Recovering the Word: Essays on Native American Literature*, ed. Brian Swann and Arnold Krupat [Berkeley: University of California Press, 1987], 521). Alan Trachtenberg interprets the speech as nineteenth-century wish fulfillment whereby the Indian vanishes but remains as "disembodied genius loci," which suggests "a perverse desire for a haunted virgin land" ("Dreaming Indian," *Raritan* 22, no. 1 [Summer 2002], 63–64).
38. In *Coming to Light*, 490.

39. Heckewelder relates the Mohican story of a ferocious bear called "the naked bear," which they claimed once existed. The last one was killed at Hoosick. Mothers disciplined their children with warnings of this animal (Dunn, *Mohicans and Their Land*, 33). For "The Giant Squirrel" and "The Boy Who Became a Flock of Quail," see *The White Deer and Other Stories Told by the Lenape*, ed. John Bierhorst (New York: William Morrow), 1995, and for the Wood Dwarf, who looks like a small boy but is strong and powerful, see Gladys Tantaquidgeon's *Folk Medicine of the Delaware and Related Algonkian Indians*, Anthropological Papers no. 3 (Harrisburg: Pennsylvania Historical & Museum Commission, 1977).
40. *Smoothing the Ground: Essays on Native American Oral Literature*, ed. Brian Swann (Berkeley: University of California Press, 1984).

1 East

Translating the Walam Olum

The Tale of a Hoax

David M. Oestreicher

Some texts present scholars with problems beyond those generally associated with a typical translation process.[1] One such case is the Walam Olum, or "Painted Record," a document long regarded as a classic native account of Algonquian origins. Ever since its "discovery" in the early nineteenth century, the text had been widely accepted as genuine. It appears in numerous anthologies of American Indian literature, has been cited by leading scholars as support for various migration theories, and can be found to this day in school textbooks as an example of aboriginal literature and culture. In recent years it has even been accepted by some American Indian groups seeking to reclaim their tribal heritage.[2] Although a minority of scholars were long skeptical of the veracity of the document, a larger number had endorsed its authenticity, and as no studies were advanced providing definitive textual evidence either proving or disproving the alleged Algonquian epic, it remained an enigma.

The Walam Olum first emerged some 170 years ago, when the well-known naturalist Constantine Samuel Rafinesque (1783–1840) announced that he had deciphered an ancient pictographic record whose story revealed the long-lost history of North America. Engraved and painted on wooden tablets, it was an account of the peopling of the continent by the Lenape (Delaware) Indians that had presumably been passed down in the tribe for thousands of years. According to Rafinesque, the tablets were obtained in 1822 from "the late Dr. Ward of Indiana," who had originally received them from a grateful Lenape patient he had cured (Rafinesque 1954, 7; 1836 1:122, 151). The "original" tablets were inexplicably lost; Rafinesque's notebook "copy" is the sole record of the hieroglyphs.

Rafinesque claimed to have acquired not only the original wooden tablets but also a transcription in the Lenape language of near-forgotten songs that explained the pictographs and revealed their story.[3] "This m[anuscri]pt and wooden original . . . was inexplicable till a deep study of the Linapi enabled me to translate them, with explanations," Rafinesque wrote on the cover of his manuscript (1954, 7), informing us that the translation was completed by 1833 (1954, 7; Rafinesque 1836, 1:151), years after the Walam Olum was originally obtained.

The Walam Olum's 183 pictographs appeared to reveal an astonishing saga: they relate a creation myth, a flood myth, and an origin legend of the Delaware people. They allegedly document how the Lenape crossed the Bering Strait from Asia and migrated southeast across the North American continent. They describe the Lenape conquest of an advanced mound-building people who had already settled in the Midwest, the fracture of the Lenape into the numerous tribes of the Algonquian language family, and the Lenape's settlement along the mid-Atlantic coast. The epic concludes with the arrival of Europeans in the Lenape homeland during the 1600s.[4]

In 1994 textual evidence was advanced demonstrating that the Walam Olum is spurious and that Constantine Samuel Rafinesque, its alleged discoverer, was in fact its author (Oestreicher 1994). The so-called Delaware Indian pictographs are not Delaware at all but are in fact hybrid combinations of Egyptian, Chinese, Ojibwa, and even several Mayan symbols newly published at the time (Oestreicher 1994, 16–21; 1995b, 101–231). As for the accompanying "Delaware" text, it was fabricated by Rafinesque from the very sources he claimed to have used as translation aids: mainly, David Zeisberger's Grammar of the *Language of the Lenni Lenape Indians* (1827) and John Heckewelder's list of Lenape place and personal names (1834) (Oestreicher 1994, 3–12; 1995b, 10–72). (Heckewelder and Zeisberger were both Moravian missionaries who had lived among the Lenape during the eighteenth and early nineteenth centuries.)

Additional evidence demonstrated that Rafinesque had created the document in December 1834 through January and possibly February 1835 in hope of securing the prestigious Volney Prize offered by the Institut Royal de France and thereby attaining a lasting and long-coveted place in history (Oestreicher 1994, 12–15; 1995b, 73–88). As for his claim to have completed the translation by 1833, Rafinesque was simply attempting to predate some of the published sources from which the forgery was crafted (1994, 13–15; 1995b, 76–83).

Rafinesque failed to win the prize, but he refused to give up on the Walam Olum. In 1836 he published an English "translation" of the epic in his book *The American Nations*, unleashing a controversy that would endure for more than a century and a half. Convinced that Rafinesque should be given credit for the "discovery" of the Walam Olum but that his English translation and accompanying notes—filled with scenarios of ancient migrations from Atlantis and elsewhere—were unreliable, a host of leading scholars made new translations and studies. (These scholars were of course unaware that Rafinesque had also created the "original" Delaware text and pictographs.) More often than not, the new renditions mirrored the theories of whoever happened to be investigating, allowing us to trace the ever-changing march of scientific ideas in this disembodied, continually recreated epic.

The list of those who fell under the Walam Olum's spell is impressive. E. G.

Squier and Daniel G. Brinton, both seminal figures during the formative years of anthropology, each published his own translation and commentary (Squier 1849; Brinton 1885). Cyrus Thomas, who conducted the Smithsonian Institution's classic study of the mound excavations, regarded the Walam Olum as a critical piece of evidence in his determination of the identity and fate of the Ohio Valley mound builders (Thomas 1889, 1890). Horatio Hale, James Mooney, M. R. Harrington, Frank G. Speck, C. A. Weslager, and other noteworthy scholars endorsed the document's validity in their writings.

Among the most ambitious efforts to determine the credibility of the Walam Olum was an interdisciplinary twenty-year study funded and directed by the pharmaceutical tycoon Eli Lilly under the auspices of the Indiana Historical Society. Lilly employed a team of over a dozen scholars to authenticate the document based on linguistic, ethnographical, historical, and archaeological research. In 1954 the Lilly team published *Walam Olum, or Red Score: The Migration Legend of the Lenni Lenape or Delaware Indians*, a lavishly bound and gilded volume with a new translation by the linguist C. F. Voegelin and commentary by Erminie Voegelin, Glenn Black, Paul Weer, Lilly, and others, but this work, like its predecessors, proved inconclusive.

To be sure, an increasing number of scholars would question the Walam Olum's historical reliability and antiquity. The development of radiocarbon dating in the mid-twentieth century, for example, contradicted the time frame of ancient history presented in the epic. Most scholars, however, continued to accept the Walam Olum as genuine Lenape folklore, and new translations of the text continued to appear.

Of late, the Walam Olum has enjoyed a burgeoning popularity. Excerpted portions have appeared in anthologies of English literature, encyclopedias of world mythology, and in Native American collections (e.g., Gill and Sullivan 1992, 327; Leeming and Leeming 1994, 168–69; Spence 1986, 77–78; Velie 1991, 92–133; O. Williams 1948, 3–9) It has inspired several contemporary poets, who have rhapsodized over its verses and attempted recreations of the text (Hoffman 1981; Napora 1992), as well as an oratorio composed by Ezra Laderman, dean of music at Yale University, which was performed at Symphony Hall at the Philadelphia Academy of Music and at the Independence Seaport Museum's concert hall in 2001. One writer has declared that the Walam Olum "has a metaphysical profundity equal to any other sacred scripture" (Zolla 1973, 233), while others have turned to it for answers to problems facing modern society. Joe Napora's new translation, for example, assumes a decidedly Marxist approach in its argument that the Walam Olum preserves a record of a lifestyle and a manner of storytelling unspoiled by the advent of capitalism and literacy "with its necessary estrangement, alienation, and separation from community," allegedly characteristic of European literature and society (1992, 5).[5] David McCutchen's translation, *The Red Record*, endeavors to act as a "guiding thread that can lead us back . . . to rediscover our lost innocence in an age of wonder" (1993, 181), sentiments reminiscent of Rousseau's noble savage hypothesis.

The fascination with the Walam Olum in Europe is almost as great as it has been in America. The document has appeared in whole or in part in several European works, including recent translations in Dutch and French (Ankh-Hermes 1989; Brotherston 1979, 176–78; Delanoë 1996, 198–216, 14), and has even found its way into such masterpieces of scholarship as Hans Jensen's *Sign, Symbol and Script*—an analysis and history of writing systems across the globe, originally published in Germany and later translated into English (1970, 48–49).

The various renditions of the Walam Olum make clear that rather than confronting hard textual evidence that might have demonstrated the text fraudulent, the translators mainly rephrased the epic to conform to their own theories. Ironically, those theories often ran counter to those incorporated into the Walam Olum when it was first created. The different versions of the same Walam Olum verses presented in this study underscore the need for translators to put aside agendas and confront textual evidence squarely.

In the pages that follow, I will discuss four of the major renditions of song III of the Walam Olum: Rafinesque's original version (1834–36) and the subsequent translations of Squier (1849), Brinton (1885), and Voegelin (1954). I will review some specific examples of how the theories of investigators colored the translations and how the translators grappled with the text in general. Finally, the respective translations themselves are presented for comparison.[6]

WO III:3

The Great Migration: North or South?

Abundant evidence shows that investigators consistently phrased their translations to conform to preconceived ideas regarding American Indian migrations. For example, Rafinesque's "translation" of WO III:3, as published in his *American Nations*, reads: "To possess mild coldness and much game, they go to the northerly plain, to hunt cattle they go" (1836, 1:129). By contrast, Ephraim G. Squier later translated this same verse as follows: "From the Northern plain, they went to possess milder lands, abounding in game" (1849, 185). In short, Rafinesque has the Lenape immigrating *to* the North, while Squier (and later Brinton as well) has them emigrating *from* it. Why the complete change in direction for the migrating Lenape?

The answer has nothing to do with a deeper understanding of the Delaware text's literal meaning. Indeed, the mangled and ungrammatical Lenape words of the Walam Olum are virtually meaningless to start with.[7] Rather, the answer has everything to do with the theories of the investigators and of Rafinesque himself.

When Rafinesque first crafted the hoax, he wanted to demonstrate that humankind had originated in the mountains of Central Asia. The region had allegedly served as a refuge for humans and animals during the biblical flood, and it was from that place that life had eventually spread again across the world.[8] As Rafinesque declared in his *Atlantic Journal*:

> The learned had long disputed on the locality and habitation of the primitive progenitors of mankind . . . late uncontrovertible discoveries and proofs have proved that the cradle of mankind was unique and in the central mountains of Asia. The best biblists assent now to this evident historical fact, see Wells, Russell, &c. as well as all the philosophers who are not blinded by their systems.
>
> Bishop Heber has said that the Imalaya mountains were the centre, the cradle, the throne, and the altar of the earth. Therefore they were the cradle of mankind, from whence the various nations have spread like divergent rays throughout the surrounding lands and islands. (Rafinesque 1832–33, 101)

Such a scenario of human origins was important to Rafinesque because like most scholars of his time, he was a monogenist—that is, he believed that all humanity, and indeed all life, had emanated from a single creation as related in the Bible. He further contended that subsequent to the flood, humanity could trace its roots primarily to the family of Noah. Intent on demonstrating humanity's common origin in the Himalayas, Rafinesque even laced the Walam Olum's pseudo-Delaware text with alleged "archaic words" such as Talli, Tula, and Tulapi, words resembling or contorted to resemble Asiatic designations for the region.[9] As Rafinesque's own explanations relate, "the holy song of the real Linapi tribe, alludes clearly to a great flood in Asia: when their nations at least was [*sic*] partly saved in *Tula* (the turtle land) in Central Asia, by the help of a goddess, and Noah or *Nana-bush*" (1836, 1:92). (One should note that Nanabush was not a Lenape culture hero but an Ojibwa figure that Rafinesque drafted into the Walam Olum and whose name he believed was an American Indian designation for Noah.)

After cryptically informing us in the epic that the mountains of Central Asia were the cradle of humankind and indeed the starting point of all human migrations, Rafinesque provides a reason for the Lenape's trek from the region: "It freezes was there, it snows was there, it is cold was there" (WO III:2).[10] Accordingly, to escape the inhospitable Himalayan weather, the Lenape ancestors immigrate "to the northerly plain" [i.e., Siberia] to "possess mild coldness and much game . . . to hunt cattle they go" (WO III:3). To make certain that the cryptic references throughout his epic to various locations and peoples are not lost on his readers, Rafinesque's notes in *The American Nations* fully elucidate the meanings he intends.

The various Lenape migration routes presented in subsequent translations of the Walam Olum often differ from Rafinesque's because the theories of the translators contradicted his. Squier's rendition is a case in point. Squier subscribed to Samuel G. Morton's views of polygenism—the belief that multiple creations occurred in different parts of the world—which gained ground among leading scientists when Morton's *Crania Americana* appeared in 1839. A renowned archaeologist and excavator of Indian mounds, Squier would become one of polygenism's foremost proponents.

Squier believed the Indians had been created separately in America, so it was necessary for him to have the migration depicted in the Walam Olum begin somewhere in the New World. Since the Walam Olum indicated that the cold, snowy, frozen weather had sparked the migration (WO III:2) and that the Lenape were seeking a milder climate and better hunting grounds (WO III:3), it seemed logical to him to look for the Lenape's original homeland somewhere in what is now northern Canada. "The traditions . . . relate first to a migration from the north to the south," Squier concludes in his notes to the epic (1849, 184).

Daniel G. Brinton's rendition of this passage is similar to Squier's, but for different reasons. Brinton's translation and commentary, which appeared some three and a half decades after Squier's version, mirror the archaeological discoveries and theories of his own time. With the publication of Charles Darwin's *On the Origin of Species* in 1859 and the accumulating evidence that all life had a common origin and evolved over a vast period of time, polygenism was no longer a viable theory in respectable scientific circles. Neither was biblical monogenism with its limited time frame of several thousand years. Instead, insofar as humanity was concerned, scholars talked increasingly of a "paleolithic" period—an ancient Stone Age antedating any human chronology previously imagined and possibly stretching back tens of thousands of years. In New Jersey the pioneer archaeologist Charles Conrad Abbot argued that the "rude [stone] implements" he was unearthing were strikingly similar to those found in Europe and probably heralded from the same time period, while the French scholar G. de Mortillet, basing his argument on this same apparent evidence, proposed that humankind had reached the New World by way of an Arctic land bridge *from Europe* (Kraft 1993, 3).

Horatio Hale, from whom Brinton drew much information for his translation of the Walam Olum, brought philology into the debate. In Hale's landmark 1883 article, "Indian Migrations as Evidenced by Language" (which demonstrated for the first time the common origins, respectively, of the Tutelo and Dakota and the Cherokee and Iroquois languages), Hale attempted to garner evidence from American Indian languages and oral traditions that could throw light on Indian origins. He concluded that the earliest transcontinental migrations of the Indians had taken them not eastward but westward and southward from the northeastern portions of the New World and argued that the polysynthetic structure of America's aboriginal languages was evidence for an ultimate connection with the Basques of Europe, who also spoke a polysynthetic language (1883, 24–27).

Most ironic in Hale's article are the citations and reinterpretations of the fraudulent Walam Olum (1883, 19–21). Rafinesque, it will be recalled, devised the hoax in part to demonstrate that the Lenape, the Iroquois, and other tribes had emigrated first from *south to north in Asia* (i.e., from the Himalayas to Siberia), then crossed over into the New World, and finally migrated across the American continent from *west to east*. By contrast, Hale believed that he had uncovered linguistic evidence of American Indian origins in Europe and was convinced that the Walam Olum related a subsequent Algonquian migration in which the Lenape, already in North America, emigrated from *east to west* and *north to south*. In short, Hale's interpretations of the epic were virtually opposite to the theories that Rafinesque had clandestinely designed it to prove in the first place.

Hale did not believe the Walam Olum actually chronicled the emigration from Europe because he seems to have concluded that that emigration must have happened in a time too remote for any human memory to have retained. Instead, he asserted that the Walam Olum's migration account began somewhere between Hudson's Bay and the coast of Labrador—evidently the first homeland of the Algonquians following their arrival in North America—and then proceeded across America southward and westward.

This background brings us back to the discussion of Brinton's rendering of WO III:3. Like Hale, Brinton accepted the new time frame postulated for human origins and argued that American Indians were autochthonous—that is, they had been in America so long that they could not remember having come from any other continent. Brinton argued further that during that lengthy period the Indians had had adequate time to develop into a completely separate race—the "American Race." He also adopted Hale's view that the Walam Olum's migration account began somewhere on or near the coast of Labrador, the region Hale had postulated as the first American homeland of the Algonquians. Brinton fashioned his translation accordingly. In Brinton's rendition of WO III:3, the Lenape migration begins "[*a*]t this northern place" (emphasis mine) where the people dreamed of "mild, cool (lands), with many deer and buffaloes" in the south (Brinton 1885,

183)—again, quite the opposite of what Rafinesque had devised! As Brinton explained: "At some remote period their ancestors dwelt far to the northeast, on tide-water, probably at Labrador. . . . They journeyed south and west" (1885, 165).

Literarily speaking (and without any linguistic basis), C. F. Voegelin's rendition of WO III:3 perhaps takes the most dramatic departure from those that preceded it, adding in phrases and words quite liberally. Compare Rafinesque's original "To possess mild coldness and much game, they go to the northerly plain, to hunt cattle they go" with Voegelin's "There where the land slopes north and at the time when the wind was blowing and the weather was getting cold, they secured many big deer and pieces of buffalo meat."

While Voegelin and the rest of the Lilly team certainly did not subscribe to Rafinesque's scenario of the Indians emigrating north from the Himalayas, nonetheless, some of the views of Rafinesque and his contemporaries regarding a Siberian passage into America had now reemerged as the dominant paradigm of the scientific establishment. Squier's and Brinton's view that the migrations described in the Walam Olum had all taken place within the confines of North America had long since fallen out of fashion. As far as the Lilly team was concerned, WO III:3 could only be a description of a Siberian landscape. As Erminie Voegelin explained, the place "where the land slopes north" must surely refer to northern Asia: "The Ob, the Yenisei, the Khatanga, the Olenek, the Lena, the Yana, the Indigirka, and the Kolyma rivers in northern Asia all drain into the Arctic Ocean," that is, *northward* (Lilly et al. 1954, 55). By contrast, she argued, America could not have been the place "where the land slopes north" because "[i]n the northern part of the New World . . . the most westerly of the large rivers, the Yukon, flows across Alaska in a southwesterly direction to drain into Bering Sea" (55–56).

WO III:10

The Earth Divides, or Was It the People?

The manipulation of text to accommodate agenda is not an isolated instance but occurs repeatedly throughout the various Walam Olum translations. Let us consider Rafinesque's initial version of WO III:10, which refers to a group of ancient people, the Snakes, fleeing their Lenape enemies from the Old World into America. After the Snakes cross over, the two lands are torn apart, the present shapes of the continents are fixed, and the Lenape are temporarily left behind in Asia.

Rafinesque's translation reads: "Thus escaping by going so far, and by trembling the burnt land *Lusasaki* is torn and is broken from the snake fortified land. *Akomenaki*." In Squier's rendition this has been changed to "[t]hus escaped the snake people, by the trembling and burned land to their strong island, (*Akomenaki*)" (no mention of land being torn and broken), while in Brinton's version the words "trembling," "torn," and "broken" have been transferred entirely from descriptions of the landscape to descriptions of the human actors in this saga: "Split asunder, weak, trembling, their land burned, they went, torn and broken, to the Snake Island." C. F. Voegelin's version follows Brinton's lead, further deleting any reference to land being burned: "and they were weak and worried and trembling: tattered and torn, they went off to Snake Island" (Rafinesque 1836, 1:129; Squier 1849, 185; Brinton 1885, 185; C. F. Voegelin 1954, 63).

To understand what happened here it is necessary to once again understand the respective ideas regarding the peopling of America held by the various translators. (It must also be reiterated that *none* of the renditions of this passage is accurate, as all attempt to rephrase what is to begin with a senseless, ungrammatical jumble.)[11]

We have noted that Rafinesque was an ardent advocate of the monogenist worldview, the belief that humankind originated in a single place. This thesis, however, sparked a number of vexing questions. If, for instance, people were not created separately on separate continents but spread throughout the world following Noah's flood, how did primitive tribes (as well as plants and animals) reach corners of the world such as America that are completely surrounded by vast oceans? One of the most popular explanations was that several thousand years ago (again, in accordance with the biblical time frame), the world's continents and islands were connected, enabling major migrations of plants, animals, and peoples. Sometime after the deluge, however, and after the aforementioned global migration, a second natural catastrophe separated the continents, leaving the various flora and fauna stranded on isolated parts of the earth.

Various aspects of this scenario had long been championed by leading scientists: Comte de Buffon, for example, had argued for an original connection of the continents that allowed for the spread of life across the globe; Georges Cuvier claimed to have found in both the fossil record and the mythologies of various peoples evidence of multiple geological catastrophes (Greene 1996, 123–24, 151, 156–57, 236–38; Cuvier 1815, 7–23, 146–65). The erudite biblical commentator Adam Clarke appeared to have found a scriptural basis for the theory when he asserted that the phrase "in [Peleg's] days was the earth divided" (Genesis 10:25)—a verse traditionally interpreted as referring to the linguistic division of the world following the destruction of the Tower of Babel—instead referred to a stupendous geological catastrophe that had quite literally "divided" the earth (Clarke 1825–26, 1:84).

Rafinesque accepted the scenario set forth by Buffon, Cuvier, Clarke, and others and incorporated it wholesale into his Walam Olum. Indeed, the scenario sets the stage for several waves of American Indian migrations that take place in his epic. But Rafinesque also needed to explain *why* such great migrations halfway around the world had occurred. In WO III:7, he informs us that "the turtling true men" had come to inhabit "the white country *Lumonaki*, north of the turtle country." His accompanying commentary and other writings make clear that the "turtling true men" was his designation for various Asian Tartar tribes including the Lenape (the alleged ancestors of all the Algonquian groups), and that the "white country" that they had come to occupy was intended to signify the aforementioned snow-covered wastes of Siberia (Rafinesque 1824, 21; 1836, 1:146). It was this invasion that led to the exodus of other Tartar groups already living in the Siberian region—namely, the Snakes—whom, as we learn in WO III:8, felt threatened by the newcomers. Rafinesque's writings make abundantly clear that his alleged Snake tribes signified the purported ancestors of the Olmecs, the Aztecs, the Navajos, and numerous other American Indian groups (1824, 18–19).

In WO III:9, the Snake tribes flee "Easterly," and by WO III:10, "escaping by going so far," they reach the New World. Once they are safely in America, however, "the burnt land" (i.e., the land joining America and Asia) is "torn and broken from the snake fortified land" (America) in the great cataclysm that allegedly took place in the days of Peleg. As Rafinesque explains in his accompanying commentary:

> The Linapi annals or songs [the Walam Olum] allude to the second [cataclysm following Noah's], which broke by volcanoes the *Lusasaki* (burnt land) and separated America or *Akomenaki* (snake island) from Asia to Behring strait. . . . The *Linapi* tribes had not yet reached America, and dwelt in Asia; but by their account the Snake tribes *Akowi* went to America in that period, led by *Nakopowa* (the Snake priest); it is even hinted [in the Walam Olum] that they [the Snakes] caused [by magic] this cataclysm or at least the separation of Asia and America, at *Lusasaki* (burnt land), in order to escape their foes, the *Elowi-chik* (hunters) of the *Linnapewi*, the original manly people. (Rafinesque 1836, 1:95–96, 97–98).

For subsequent translators of the Walam Olum, Rafinesque's views of a continental breakup were simply unacceptable. Although Rafinesque was "[a] man of unparalleled industry, an earnest and indefatigable collector of facts," Squier wrote, "he was deficient in that scope of mind joined to severe critical powers, indispensable to correct generalization. While, therefore, it is usually safe to reject his conclusions, we may receive his facts" (1849, 275). In this case, receiving Rafinesque's "facts" meant accepting his Lenape text and pictographs, along with the more palatable portions of his "translation," but rejecting those parts that appeared ridiculous and unbelievable.

Squier's version of WO III:7–9 closely follows Rafinesque's original "translation," in which the Snake tribes flee eastward from the more aggressive and warlike Lenape groups. As we have seen, however, Squier's translation of WO III:10 has been altered to eliminate any references to continental separation, and the words "torn" and "broken" have been inexplicably deleted. For a polygenist such as Squier, who held that the various peoples of the world were created separately on separate continents, no migration from Asia and no initial continental connection or subsequent separation were required to explain the American Indian presence in the New World; again, all the migrations described in the Walam Olum must have taken place on the North American continent, where the native peoples were created.

Brinton also believed the Walam Olum's migration account referred entirely to events in North America and took even more liberties with this passage than Squier did. In Brinton's translation, the words "trembling," "torn," and "broken" refer to humans and not to geography, and any references to the Snake people in the prior verses have been curiously eliminated, thereby making all the action descriptive of the Lenape alone. According to Brinton, the only migration described in the Walam Olum was that of the Lenape. As he explains, "The verses 8, 9, 10, are referred in Rafinesque's free translation to the 'Snake people.' They seem to me to be descriptive of the grief of the Lenape on leaving their ancient home" (1885, 227). While Brinton preserved the designation "Snake Island," it could now just as easily suggest an island where snakes (i.e., reptiles, not people) were plentiful. As in Squier's earlier translation, "Snake Island" no longer signified the North American continent but some small island in an inland lake or river.

As for Voegelin's version of this passage, we have already noted how closely it resembles Brinton's. There is no Snake migration, there is no Peleg's flood or cataclysm dividing the continents, and all the action described in this verse relates to the Lenape.

WO III:17

Giant Ocean or Gentle Lake?

The manipulation of the word *kitahikan* is yet another example of how translations were crafted to accommodate scientific agenda. This Lenape word can only mean "ocean." Rafinesque inserted it several times into his Walam Olum, translating it accurately. The word first appears in WO I:24. Rafinesque's translation reads: "All this happened very long ago, at the first land *Netamaki*, beyond the great ocean *Kitahikan*" (1836, 1:127). This verse is telling us that all the action described in the first song of the Walam Olum took place in the old homeland in Asia, beyond the great ocean.

The word next appears in WO III:17. According to Rafinesque's translation: "It was wonderful when they all went over the smooth deep water of the frozen sea, at the gap of the Snake sea in the great ocean" (1836, 1:130). In his accompanying Delaware text, Rafinesque employed the word *kitahikan* because he was trying to show how the Lenape, still in pursuit of their old foes, the Snakes, arrived in America from Asia. The Snake tribes, it will be recalled, had already reached the New World in an earlier migration when the continents were still connected. Now that a great cataclysm had taken place and separated America from Asia, leaving America completely surrounded by water, Rafinesque needed to explain how subsequent immigrations to the New World were made. Accordingly, WO III:17 (along with the verses that immediately precede and follow it) shows how the Lenape emigrated across the frozen waters of Bering Strait, "the gap of the Snake sea in the great ocean."

Naturally, the word *kitahikan* in the Walam Olum's migration account presented a problem for polygenists or for anyone who believed that all the action in the text would have taken place within the confines of North America. For Squier and Brinton, the accepted translation of this word as "ocean" was difficult to fathom. Squier was also uncomfortably aware that the legend of the Lenape crossing the ice as presented in the Walam Olum bore remarkable similarity to current migration theories among some scientists, in which the Indians came to America from Asia across the ice of Bering Strait. Squier was so convinced that this view was false and that the Indians had been created separately in America that he feared other polygenists who read the epic's crossing-the-ice legend might come to regard the Walam Olum as a fabrication. Accordingly, he commented: "It may be suggested that the account of the second migration, across frozen waters, is so much in accordance with the popular prejudice, as to the mode in which the progenitors of the American race arrived in America, that it throws suspicion upon the entire record. It is not impossible, indeed, that the original tradition may have been slightly modified here, by the dissemination of European notions among the Indians" (Squier 1849, 186). In other words, for Squier the tradition of crossing the *kitahikan* either constituted a recent borrowing among the Indians from Europeans or signified the crossing of some inland body of water. He certainly would not entertain the third possibility—the very one he himself had suggested—that the text might be a fabrication.

Squier crafted his translation in accordance with his view that the crossing-the-ice legend in the Walam Olum referred not to a passage from Asia into America but only to the crossing of some inland body of water. Whereas Rafinesque had originally written in WO III:17: "It was wonderful when they all went over the smooth deep water of the frozen sea, at the gap of the Snake sea in the great ocean," Squier's version reads: "Wonderful! They all went over the waters of the hard, stony sea, to the open snake waters." The word "sea" has been preserved (an inland "sea," after all, need not be saltwater), but the phrase "in the great ocean" has been summarily dropped. This notwithstanding the fact that the Walam Olum uses the authentic Lenape word *kitahikan*—which again, can only be translated as "ocean."

Much like Squier had done before him, Brinton also dropped Rafinesque's gloss "the great ocean," which the latter had used to identify the frozen body of water the Lenape had allegedly crossed (WO III:17). Brinton replaced this phrase with "the great Tidal Sea." The change was subtle, but one that allowed Brinton to advance his version of the migration route. Brinton believed that the frozen body of water the Walam Olum described was in all likelihood "the Detroit River" or "the Saint Lawrence about the Thousand Isles" (1885, 165, 227). The Saint Lawrence, after all, *was* a tidal estuary. Moreover, Brinton argued that the Lenape word *kitahikan*, "ocean," was not confined to the ocean alone but was "[p]robably . . . applicable to all large bodies of water" (227). His argument is without factual basis.

We should note that both Brinton and Squier also altered the translation of *kitahikan* in WO I:24, a passage that we have observed was designed to inform readers that all the events in song I had occurred in Asia. In his interlinear translation of this verse, Squier simply translates *kitahikan* as "great waters," a rendering that could just as easily refer to Lake Superior or another of the Great Lakes (1849, 180), while his free translation entirely omits any references to water. As for Brinton, he once again renders this word as "great tide-water."

Voegelin's interpretation of *kitahikan* in verses WO I:24 and WO III:17 is difficult to comprehend. In fact Voegelin fails to make *any* connection with "water," let alone "ocean," translating *kitahikan* simply as "something which is very big" (C. F. Voegelin 1954, 71). This is all the more puzzling because Voegelin, unlike Brinton and Squier, had no theoretical differences with Rafinesque regarding a Bering Strait crossing and was convinced that the Walam Olum chronicled that very thing. That Voegelin, or perhaps his assistant, Joe E. Pierce, was unable to translate such a basic Lenape word is additional evidence that for the most part, Voegelin never reviewed the Walam Olum's Delaware text with living Lenape speakers as he claimed or consulted the linguistic materials assembled by the Moravian missionaries (see Oestreicher 1995b, 392–99). Consequently, Voegelin's free translation of WO III:17 reads: "Things turned out well for all those who had stayed at the shore of water frozen hard as rocks, and for those at the great hollow well" (C. F. Voegelin 1954, 71). Thus Voegelin rendered *kitahikan*, "great ocean," as an adjective, "great," Rafinesque's *pokhakhopek*, "the gap of the Snake sea," as "hollow well" (71).

Voegelin's mistranslation of *kitahikan* in WO III:17 did not in any way diminish the Lilly team's belief that song III of the Walam Olum mainly chronicled the Lenape migration out of Asia. Too many other passages in the song appeared to be descriptive of a Bering Strait crossing. As Erminie Voegelin enthusiastically proclaimed in her commentary to WO III:16:

> Since there are no large lakes in northeastern Asia, where the ancestors of the present-day Delaware may have been at this time, the "frozen water" which the groups propose to cross may refer to Bering Strait. If this reference is to Bering Strait, we must assume a relatively great antiquity; so great, indeed, that the whole account must antedate linguistic differentiation into Delaware, Ojibwa, Shawnee, and other recent and present-day Algonquian languages . . . in place of a specific Delaware tradition . . . we should have to assume a migrational account of generalized Algonquian groups, preceding the differentiation into Delaware, Ojibwa, Shawnee, and other tribes . . .
>
> The Delaware may have alone preserved the account of this early Algonquian migration and, incidentally, taken full credit for it. (E. Voegelin 1954, 70)

WO III:18

Misformed Words and Mistaken Migrations

Rather than confront anomalous Delaware words squarely in the Walam Olum's "original" Delaware text and acknowledge that such words might be evidence of fraud, translators—presupposing the text authentic—often sought to "correct" such words by replacing them with similar-sounding words that appeared to make more sense. Naturally this method of "correcting" the text would have an impact on all subsequent renditions of the Walam Olum.

On one occasion, for example, a transcription error in Rafinesque's published source (further bungled by Rafinesque in his presentation of the word) actually led investigators to reroute the alleged ancient Lenape migration!

In WO III:18, Rafinesque wished to insert into his pseudo-Delaware text the Lenape word for "in the dark" or "by night." He was attempting to prove that the migration across Bering Strait could only have happened "at night"—that is, during the long darkness of the Arctic winter when the Strait would have been frozen over. In Zeisberger's *Grammar*, Rafinesque found the word *nissahwi*, "by night"

(Zeisberger 1980 [1827], 177). He was unaware that *nissahwi* is a typographical error for *nipawhi*, "by night." In fact the word is spelled correctly only several pages later in the *Grammar* (179), but Rafinesque in his haste failed to note this. Instead, he copied down the erroneous version of the word and then further added to the confusion by mistakenly rendering the *ss* of *nissahwi* (again, wrong in itself) as ll, thereby creating the equally meaningless word *nillawi*. (Rafinesque seems to have made this error simply by being unable to read his own handwriting; in his manuscript his *l*'s and *s*'s sometimes look similar, and he was probably constructing the text of the Walam Olum from word lists he had already copied from Zeisberger and other sources in the nearby library of the American Philosophical Society.) Whatever the case, Rafinesque's "original" Lenape text now contained an alleged "Lenape" word that never existed: *nillawi*, "by night or in the dark." His English "translation" of the verse reads: "They were ten thousand in the dark, who all go forth in a single night in the dark, to the Snake island of the eastern land *Wapanaki* in the Dark, by walking all the people.—OLINI."[12]

Squier and Brinton accepted Rafinesque's translation without question, incorporating it into their own versions with only minor alterations of style. C. F. Voegelin, however, had difficulty with *nillawi*. Unable to find a translation for this anomalous word, he simply replaced the erroneous *nillawi* with the similar sounding *nalahíi*, "upstream" (1954, 72). "Ten thousand men went upstream," Voegelin's translation reads, "went right on upstream during a single day, upstream to the eastern lands of Snake Island: every man kept going along" (72). (In substituting the genuine Lenape word *nalahíi*, "to go upstream," for Rafinesque's *nillawi*, "by night or in the dark," Voegelin removed one of the verse's two references to the night. The other reference, *gutikuni*, which Rafinesque translates as "single night" and had grafted with slight erroneous modifications from Zeisberger's *Grammar* (see Zeisberger 1827, 46), is preserved in Voegelin's version. However, Voegelin renders the translation as "single day"—a gloss that is also accurate as the word can be translated either as a single day or a single night. Unfortunately for Rafinesque, his carefully laid references to the long Arctic night or winter were now eliminated from the text.[13]

Having "corrected" Rafinesque's initial description of a tribe marching across a frozen sea "in the dark" during "a single night" to that of a tribe traveling "upstream" during "a single day," Voegelin and the Lilly team were faced with new problems of a geographical nature. How could the verse still refer to Bering Strait if the Lenape were traveling *upstream*? What stream *did* the verse describe, and could the migration really have occurred during only "a single day"? Fortunately for the Lilly team, the several verses preceding WO III:18 seemed to account for the Bering Strait crossing itself. WO III:18, therefore, could be left free for a description of some other river the Lenape must have navigated *after* reaching America. As Erminie Voegelin explains: "If the 'frozen water' [previously described in WO III:16] refers to Bering Strait, the first large river encountered east of Bering Strait would be the Yukon. In its middle course the Yukon flows in a southwesterly direction; travel upstream would thus lead toward the east, into the interior of Alaska" (1954, 73). In other words, the Lenape of WO III:18 must already be in the New World, moving "upstream" along the Yukon River. Accordingly, the map of the Lenape migration route in the Lilly team's 1954 volume depicts the Lenape trekking upstream along the entire course of the Yukon River![14]

Naturally, the Lilly team was aware that no such journey could have taken place within "a single day." Erminie Voegelin rationalizes: "The 'single day' mentioned in this verse refers in all likelihood to a single year. In Shawnee mythology, as in that of many other American Indian tribes, the space of time encompassed by one year is often referred to as 'one day,' especially when the speaker is a supernatural being or deity" (1954, 73). Although Rafinesque would certainly have been upset with the various attempts to "improve" on his verses, he would doubtless have been flattered to find himself characterized as a "supernatural being or deity."

WO III:18 is endemic of one of the major flaws that riddle the translations of the Walam Olum. In their desire to authenticate the document and validate the paradigms of the period, the translators came to far-reaching conclusions about the scope of American prehistory based on the merest inference. We have here traced how a typographical error in a Lenape word in Zeisberger's *Grammar* (which rendered the word meaningless to start with) was further mangled by Rafinesque when he inserted it into the text of the Walam Olum and was ultimately replaced altogether with a similar sounding—but completely different—Lenape word by Voegelin when he attempted to resolve the anomaly. Finally, we have seen how that new word became the basis by which the course of ancient prehistoric migrations were charted.

WO III:8

Strange Agreements and Odd Improvements

As a final example of what went wrong with the translations of the Walam Olum, let us follow the various renderings of a single verse, WO III:8.

Rafinesque's polished free translation of this verse in his book *The American Nations* reads: "Meantime all the snakes were afraid in their huts, and the snake priest *Nakopowa* said to all, let us go." Turning now to Rafinesque's earlier manuscript rendition of this verse, which presents the "original" Delaware text with his word-for-word English "translation," we find that the first Delaware word and gloss he offers is "Wemiako all (the) Snakes" (Rafinesque 1954, 61). Rafinesque created this word by grafting "Wemi, all" from Zeisberger's *Grammar* (1980 [1827], 178) and combining it with *ako*, a senseless fragment he ungrammatically truncated from a much longer placename included in Heckewelder's list of Lenape names (1834, 373). Rafinesque was convinced that *ako*, the fragment he had inappropriately sliced from Heckewelder's "*gíschACHKOkwalìs*, the SNAKES have all got into their dens," could stand as an independent word meaning "snakes" (caps mine to show the portions Rafinesque appropriated).[15]

Squier accepted Rafinesque's translation of *wemiako* without difficulty, freely rendering the latter's "all the snakes" as "[t]he snake (evil) people" (1849, 185). Brinton's rendition is a bit more interesting. We have noted that Brinton did not believe a Snake tribe was described in the early portions of the Walam Olum, at least in the first three songs.[16] Accordingly, he reinterpeted *ako* (Rafinesque's false designation for "snake") as the similar sounding *aki*, "land," thereby correcting the phrase to refer to all the land (Brinton 1885, 183, 251). It must be pointed out, however, that Brinton had no problem translating *ako* as "snake" elsewhere in the Walam Olum when the same word appeared to refer not to a tribe but to a serpent deity or to reptiles. Thus we find *maskanAKO*, "mighty snake" (WO II:1, 2, 5), and *mattAKOhaki*, "a land without snakes" (WO V:22) (Brinton 1885, 176–79, 206–7, caps mine). In short, Brinton preserved Rafinesque's translation of the meaningless truncation *ako* when it did not impinge on his views of American Indian prehistory and rejected Rafinesque's translation of the very same truncation when it did. As for Voegelin, he simply copied Brinton's rendition, thereby correcting Rafinesque's *wemiako*, "all (the) snakes," to read *wéemi*, "all," and *-aaki*, "land" (C. F. Voegelin 1954, 61).

The next several words of this verse in Rafinesque's pseudo-Delaware text are "yagawan (in the) huts" and "tendki being there" (Rafinesque 1954, 61). Rafinesque found the word *yagawan*, "a hut," in Zeisberger's *Grammar* (1980 [1827], 41) but was uncertain how to affix the locative, -ink, as reflected by his insertion of "(in the)" in parentheses. He ought to have written *yagawanink*, "in the hut/in the huts." He also grafted *tendki* from the *Grammar* (again altering the spelling from the original *tendchi*), but the translation he arrived at, "being there," makes no sense because Rafinesque, evidently in haste, accidentally copied that definition from the wrong Delaware word! "Epit, he who is there, BEING THERE" (caps mine) can be found in Zeisberger's *Grammar* several pages after *tendchi*, a participle signifying "many" or "so many" (1980 [1827], 47, 51).[17]

Squier accepted the veracity of Rafinesque's translation (including the impossible *tendki*, "being there," which he rendered simply as "being" and in an unjustified literary flourish, upgraded Rafinesque's "huts" to "cabins" [1849, 185]). Brinton, in turn, duplicated Squier's "cabins" but added a touch of his own. Unable to make sense of *tendki*, Brinton replaced it with the similar sounding *tindey*, "fire" (1885, 248), thereby creating the combination "cabin fires" in his own translation (182–83).

Voegelin accepted Brinton's rendering of Rafinesque's "tendki, (in the) huts, being there," as *yagawan tindey*, "cabin-fires," but not without slight modification. Voegelin *was*, after all, supposed to be creating "a new and brilliant translation of the songs of the *Walam Olum*," as the introduction to the Lilly volume claimed, "that smoothed out many of the obscure passages in the translation by Brinton" (Lilly et al. 1954, xi–xii). Evidently wishing to disguise the fact that he was once again incorporating one of Brinton's definitions and probably aware that Brinton's "cabin-fires" also sounded too civilized, Voegelin replaced "cabin-fires" with "hearths" (C. F. Voegelin 1954, 61). Exchanging one synonym for another, however, did nothing to improve the faulty Lenape grammar that remained in the sentence; as always, Voegelin obscured the existence of these problems by cloaking the Lenape words in a new, modern phonetic rendering.

The next Delaware word we find in Rafinesque's manuscript version of WO III:8 is "lakkawelendam troubled or afraid" (1954, 61). The word and its gloss, derived mainly from "LACHAUWELENDAM, to be TROUBLED in mind," in Zeisberger's *Grammar* (1980 [1827], 94, caps mine), were repeated by all the subsequent translators with slight modifications.[18]

Among the most problematic words in WO III:8 is *nakopowa*, which Rafinesque translated as "the snake priest." He concocted this compound by first inappropriately truncating initial *n* (which he mistakenly believed meant "the") from such forms as "Nigani, N'hitam, Netamiechink, first, in THE first place" in Zeisberger's *Grammar* (1980 [1827], 175, caps mine).[19] The truncation *n*, "the," was then attached to *ako*, "snake," another meaningless truncation we have examined, to form the equally meaningless compound *nako*. This in turn was attached to the non-Lenape word, "POWWÁw, a PRIEST" (caps mine), which Rafinesque found in Roger Williams's work on Narragansett, *A Key into the Language of America* (1973 [1643], 192).[20] Thus was born Rafinesque's impossible *nakopowa*, "the Snake priest."

Squier was unperturbed by Rafinesque's rendition and simply kept "the snake priest (*Nakopowa*)" in his translation (1849, 185). Brinton had more reservations. "*Pawa*, priest," he wrote by way of explanation. "The prefix [to *nakopowa*] doubtful" (Brinton 1885, 243). Again, the translation of "the prefix" *nako* as "the snake" apparently ran counter to Brinton's belief that the early portions of the Walam Olum do not refer to any snake tribes. Therefore, he rejected the first part of Rafinesque's translation, which referred to a snake, but accepted Rafinesque's definition of *-powa* as "priest," never questioning how a Narragansett word should end up in the Lenape text in the first place. In his final rendering of the word, Brinton simply translated *nakopowa* as "priest" (1885, 182–83).

Voegelin's translation of *nakopowa* is both flawed and startling. The word has been rendered by Voegelin into modern phonetics (*naxappóowe*) and translated as "pipe bearer" (C. F. Voegelin 1954, 61). Readers are informed that it is also to be compared to *hupóokkan*, "smoking pipe" (61), but even the similarly sounding subjunctive form *énta xupówa*, "when I smoke," is not equivalent to *naxappóowe*, "pipe bearer" and, at any rate, makes even less sense in relation to the rest of the sentence. The late Lucy Blalock, one of the last fluent speakers of Lenape, stated that she had never heard of *naxappóowe* and that it was meaningless to her (Blalock and Oestreicher, July 1993, tape 8, side B) as did the late Charles Webber, Frank Speck's Lenape informant. Webber simply places a question mark next to *nakopowa* in his own unpublished attempt with Speck to translate the Walam Olum, a translation that the Lilly team was in possession of (Speck and Webber, n.d., n.p.). Bruce Pearson and James Rementer, linguists competent in the Delaware language, likewise had no knowledge of this word (personal communications with author, December 2002). Indeed, the word is not only foreign to the Delaware language but so is the very role of a "pipe bearer," a custom that has not been recorded among the Delaware people.[21]

In contrast to what we are led to believe in the Lilly volume, Voegelin's gloss for *naxappóowe* as "pipe bearer" was not derived from the Delaware language at all. Instead, it has been "borrowed" from Brinton—not from the latter's translation of *nakopowa* but, incredibly, from another word Brinton translated elsewhere in the Walam Olum! And, Brinton's gloss was itself derived not from Delaware sources but from his own exaggerated rendering of a Narragansett word.[22]

In short, Voegelin's gloss, "pipe bearer," has been borrowed from Brinton's inflated translation of a non-Lenape, Narragansett word. The cultural elements are foreign to the Lenape Indians and to eastern woodlands Indians in general, and the gloss was then attached to a completely unrelated and meaningless word, Rafinesque's *nakopowa*, which does not exist in the Delaware language, but which Voegelin has recast into modern phonetic script. Both the word *naxappóowe* and its translation "pipe bearer" as Voegelin presents them are as much a fabrication as Rafinesque's original.

The remaining portions of WO III:8 require only brief comment. *Wemiowen*, derived from "Wemi auween, every man" in Zeisberger (1980 [1827], 178), has been accurately rendered and translated by Rafinesque, Squier, Brinton, and Voegelin as "all" or "everyone." The next word, *luen*, originally obtained by Rafinesque from Zeisberger (1980 [1827], 133), is simply an uninflected verb stem meaning "to say or tell," but Rafinesque and all the subsequent translators have presented this word as though it were fully conjugated. Last, *atam*, "let us go," was also originally grafted by Rafinesque from Zeisberger (1980 [1827], 80). Although Zeisberger presents the form as though it were complete in itself, *atam* is actually a second-person singular imperative that cannot stand independently, as for example, *uténink átam*, "let us go to town," *kámink átam*, "let us cross the river," and so on. Rafinesque, Squier, Brinton, and Voegelin all inappropriately present the form independently and without comment.

The widely divergent translations of song III of the Walam Olum presented here demonstrate that the translators shaped their renditions to accommodate prevailing scientific paradigms regarding American Indian and even global prehistory; that when theoretical issues were not at stake, the translators tended to agree with and even borrow from one another; that not only Rafinesque, the author of the hoax, but also its subsequent translators sometimes fudged their data; and that incredibly the entire "original" Delaware text the translators were working from (i.e., the text invented by Rafinesque) is virtually meaningless to begin with. It cannot be overemphasized that none of these or other translations of the Walam Olum justify their interpretations with solid linguistic evidence—a more accurate rendering of the pseudo-Delaware words in the document. Instead, when the translators were at a loss to comprehend the nonsensical grammar of the original or wished to underscore their historical views, they simply created new translations in accord with their beliefs.

In a sense the "original" Delaware text was sometimes irrelevant to the various translations. When confronted with the genuine Lenape word *kitahikan*, for instance, which can only mean "ocean," some of the translators disregarded its meaning. Yet when confronted with the nonexistent pseudo-word *nillawi*, some of these same translators accepted it without question, along with Rafinesque's translation. And why? When a word—even a genuine and well-known word—challenged the theories of these translators, they felt the need to reinterpret or alter it. When a word didn't challenge their theories, they often failed to investigate, even if the word did not exist in the language. Consequently, the new translations of the Walam Olum generally had nothing to do with a superior understanding of the Delaware language. Rather, they reflect the shifting perspectives in science in the century and a half that elapsed between Rafinesque's time and our own.

Notes

1. The writer is grateful to Bruce L. Pearson and James Rementer for their comments and constructive criticism; to Brian Swann for his patience, review of the materials, and suggestions; to Barbara Wojhoski for her painstaking editorial work; to Robin Fox, who has remained a constant source of encouragement and aid since my Walam Olum studies first began more than a decade ago; and most especially, to Paul J. Oestreicher, the writer's brother, whose steadfast editorial assistance and careful criticism were of immeasurable value.
2. Despite its recent popularity among some Lenape, the Walam Olum was unknown to tribal elders until it was introduced to them by non-Indian scholars and enthusiasts. Puzzled by the nonsensical linguistic text but recognizing some genuine Lenape words in it, some elders rationalized that the text might have been communicated in an extinct dialect or by someone with a poor knowledge of the language. Others, such as the late traditionalist Nora Thompson Dean, discounted it outright, stating that the text was a "hodgepodge" and that she had never heard of it. The late Lucy Blalock, who reviewed every Lenape word in the Walam Olum with this writer, also concluded that it was spurious. On February 11, 1997, after a review of the evidence that the Walam Olum is a hoax, the Delaware Tribe of Eastern Oklahoma formally withdrew its earlier endorsement of the document.
3. Rafinesque's account of how he received the Delaware language text of the Walam Olum is as deliberately vague as his account of the origin of the pictographs. He merely states that the "songs annexted thereto [to the pictographs]" were "obtained from another individual" (1836, 1:151); he does not tell us whether he personally was the one who obtained them nor does he reveal the identity of the "individual" from whom they were obtained.
4. Rafinesque further claimed to have obtained a sort of epilogue to the Walam Olum: a "fragment on the subsequent period," "translated from the Linapi" by an equally mysterious person, one John Burns (1836, 1:141; 1954, 208). Conveniently, the Burns "fragment" begins where the Walam Olum concludes—with the arrival of Europeans in North America—and it continues until about 1820, when the Delaware Indians were relocated from Indiana into Missouri. Thus, the Walam Olum, when placed together with the Burns account, forms an unbroken narrative spanning the millennia—from human origins in Central Asia to but a few years before Rafinesque announced his "discovery" of the document.
5. Shortly after the publication of "Unmasking the Walam Olum" in the *Bulletin of the Archaeological Society of New Jersey* (Oestreicher 1994), the writer received a gracious communication from Napora indicating that he had reviewed the refutation in the *Bulletin* and that he now recognizes that the Walam Olum is indeed

a hoax. Napora was dismayed that the sources upon whom he relied had been so negligent in their investigation of the document and that the hoax should have continued as long as it has.

6. Rafinesque has left us two translations to choose from: the more "literal" version presented in his manuscript, where, in interlinear fashion, his English glosses are juxtaposed against the phrases of his pseudo-Delaware text, and the more polished "free" translation, which appears in his published *American Nations*. As the former is stilted and difficult to follow, and as his intended meanings are best expressed in his published text, I have reproduced the version of song III that appears in *The American Nations* (1836, 1:129–30).
7. Rafinesque's pseudo-Delaware text and interlinear translation of WO III:3, as they appear in his manuscript, are as follows:

> *~~kwami~~ Lowankwamink* in Northerly plain
> *Wulaton* to possess~~ing~~
> *Wtakan* mild
> *tihill* coolness
> *kelik* much
> *meshautang* game
> *Sili* cattle
> *ewak* they go.

Note how Rafinesque first wrote *kwami*, changed his mind and replaced *kwami* with *lowan*, then placed *kwamink* after *lowan*.

Contrary to Rafinesque's claim, *lowan* means "winter", not "north". Rafinesque inadvertently fashioned this term because his source, Zeisberger's *Grammar*, only presented the form "Lowaneu, northerly" (Zeisberger 1980 [1827], 164). Rafinesque truncated *lowan* from *lowaneu* in an effort to convert "northerly" to "north," unwittingly creating the word "winter" instead. *Lowan*, "winter," was then ungrammatically attached to *kwamink*, another truncation inappropriately grafted from another of his published sources, John Heckewelder's list of Lenape personal and placenames. *Kwamink* is derived from Heckewelder's breakdown of the name "Wyoming." Heckewelder's analysis of Wyoming (with caps and brackets added to show the portions from which Rafinesque appropriated) is as follows:

> wyOMING . . . . m'CHEUÓMI, or m'CHeuWÁMI [= KWAMI], which signifieth EXTENSIVE LEVEL FLATS [= PLAIN]. In consequence of the large falls on this river it is called "m'CHWeuWAMI [= KWAMI] sipu" by the Delawares and by

the Six Nations; it is for the same reason called "Quahonta," which two words or names signify *a river having* LARGE FLATS [= PLAIN] *on it* [Heckewelder 1834, 361]

In fashioning *-kwamink*, Rafinesque truncated *m'cheuwami* to *chwami* and then changed the spelling to *kwami* in accordance with the orthographic system he employed consistently throughout the Walam Olum (in this case that meant converting Heckewelder's *ch* to *k*). Heckewelder's gloss, "extensive level flats," was also converted by Rafinesque to "plain." As it stands, the misspelled truncation *kwami* is meaningless, and the only reason it was translated by Squier and Brinton as "plains" is because that is how it appears in Rafinesque's earlier translation. Rafinesque then attached his ungrammatical *kwami-* to the locative *-ink*, having read in Zeisberger that "[i]t [the local case] is formed by means of the suffixes INK and UNK, and expresses IN, IN *the, on, out of*" (1980 [1827], 37, my caps].

While the locative case *-ink* can indeed mean both "to" and "from," the compound it has been attached to, *lowankwami-*, is meaningless to Lenape speakers. Moreover, nearly all the other "Delaware words" in WO III:3 have been similarly ungrammatically truncated from Rafinesque's published sources and make no sense either in isolation or in relation to one another.

In short, while the "original" Delaware text of the Walam Olum is senseless, and Rafinesque's accompanying English "translation" is somewhat stilted, his intended meanings are best expressed in the "free translation" he included in his *American Nations*. A full exposition of the Walam Olum, its Delaware text, pictographs, and history, is scheduled to appear in a forthcoming book by the present writer, to be published by the American Philosophical Society.

8. Many scholars of Rafinesque's time considered the Himalayas to be the true site of Ararat, the mountain where Noah's ark landed. Building on Fabre d'Olivet's erroneous interpretations of biblical Hebrew (1815–1816), Rafinesque was convinced that the ark itself was a mere metaphor for the Himalayan Mountains, which allegedly had served as a "refuge" during the flood.
9. The Lenape word for "turtle," for instance, is *tulpe*. In Rafinesque's manuscript of the Walam Olum, *tulpe* has been contorted to "Tulapit At Tula or turtle land" (WO II:8); "Tulagishatten at Tula he is ready" (WO II:9); and "tulapewini turtle being" (WO III:1). That the Aztec Tula, the name of the mythical origin city of the Toltecs, sounded almost identical to the Lenape word *tulpe*, or turtle, constituted further "proof" for Rafinesque of the Indians' Asiatic origins. *Tula* and *tulpe*, he contended, both shared the alleged universal root "*Tal/tol/tul*," which he had read of in Court de Gébelin's popular *Monde Primitif* and which supposedly designated "lofty mountains" (Court de Gébelin 1779, 6: (xxxix–cxliii). As far as Rafinesque

was concerned, the Aztec Tula and Turtle Land (the giant turtle that carried the world on its back in Lenape legends) both signified Tibet. Placenames such as Turan or Thala in Asia appeared to comprise exact cognates to the Delaware and Aztec words; even the English words "turtle" and "tortoise" seemed to shared the same root *tal*, *tol*, and *tul*! (Most nineteenth-century philologists were cognizant that *r* and *l* are frequently interchangeable between different dialects; with this in mind, Rafinesque argued that "turtle," "tortoise," Turan, Tula, and *tulpe* were identical in meaning. But such facts, Rafinesque contended, were evident only to the learned.)

10. According to Rafinesque, author of the Walam Olum, WO III:1 reads: "After the flood, the manly men *Linapewi*, with the manly turtle beings dwelt close together at the cave house, and dwelling of *Talli*." In a typical attempt to demonstrate a word's supposed universal roots, Rafinesque has employed the Delaware word *talli*, "there," to simultaneously signify not only the Delaware word itself, but the designation Talli, the alleged original name of the "cradle of mankind," the mountains of Central Asia. Again Rafinesque obtained the "root" *talli* from Court de Gébelin's *Monde Primitif*, where it appears as the purported primitive root for "mountains" (Court de Gébelin 1779, 6:cxxxix–cxliii). In Rafinesque's English "translation" of the Walam Olum appearing in his manuscript, the gloss "there" has been crossed out and replaced with the definition "of Talli" (WO III:1), thereby demonstrating that he considered this word to be not only an adverb but also a placename.

11. For example, Rafinesque's "pikihil is torn" and "pokwihil is broken" have been ungrammatically truncated from Zeisberger's *Grammar*, wherein appear the verbs "Pikihhilleu, it is torn" and "Poquihilleu, it is broken" (1980 [1827], 165). Rafinesque tried to neutralize the verbs *pikihhilleu*, "it is torn," and *poquihilleu*, "it is broken," by deleting the final *-eu*, which he believed corresponded to "it." He mistakenly concluded that the truncations *pikihil* and *pokwihil* could now be translated as "is torn" and "is broken," but in fact, his truncations make no sense. Rafinesque's ungrammatical presentation also contains additional evidence regarding the fabrication of the Walam Olum: both verbs are not only adjacent to each other in Rafinesque's pseudo-Delaware text but are also found almost directly adjacent to each other in Zeisberger's list of adjective verbs (1980 [1827], 165).

12. By inserting the "Olini" into his narrative, Rafinesque hoped to demonstrate the Lenape's direct descent from certain tribal groups in the Old World. He had read in Samuel Mitchill that "the North American natives of the high latitudes" were "of the same race with the Samoieds [a Mongoloid people inhabiting the Arctic coasts of Siberia] and Tartars of Asia" (1820, 340). Thomas Nuttall had

also identified the North American Indians with the "Samoyades" (1821, 196–97). (We should note that the term "Tartary," as used by Rafinesque and his contemporaries, encompassed the entire region of Central Asia and Siberia, while the designation "Tartar" was loosely used to refer to any number of tribes from this vast region, including the Samoyeds.)

Rafinesque accepted the conclusions of his contemporaries concerning the Tartar ancestry of the Indians. However, he had to find some other way of expressing these thoughts in the Walam Olum. Certainly he couldn't overtly insert the phrase: "The Samoyeds and Tartars were the ancestors of the Lenape," which obviously would have betrayed the author of the document as a scholar rather than a traditional Lenape. Accordingly, Rafinesque needed to rely on other means to demonstrate the Asiatic lineage. He soon found what he was looking for in a series of philological "proofs." According to C. F. Volney, the versatile French scholar, the Miami Indian word for "man" was *helaniah*. In the related Delaware, Chippewa, and Shawnee languages, the same word was, respectively, *lenno*, *lennis*, and *linni*. "Why were the ancient Greeks called *Hellenes*?" Volney queried. "And a Tartar tribe *Alani*?" Volney concluded that the words demonstrated the common origin of all these tribes (1804, 495). Volney's arguments concurred with those presented by Benjamin Barton, who also argued for affinities between Samoyeds, Tartars, and Lenape (1798, lxxvi, 19–20, appendix: 18–19).

Further reading by Rafinesque revealed what appeared to be additional evidence of the Tartar lineage of the Lenape. He discovered in P. Du Halde's *General History of China* that a tribe of the Tungus family in eastern Siberia was known as the Orotchon, after the *oron*, a type of deer (1741, 4:149). In Samuel Purchas's *Pilgrimage*, another source Rafinesque drew from frequently, he learned that some Samoyed tribes similarly referred to a deer as *ollen* (1617, 4:488–90). *Oron* and *ollen* both sounded to Rafinesque like Alani, the Tartar tribe mentioned by Volney, and like the Lenape word *lenno*, "man." The resemblance seemed even more apparent when Rafinesque read Edwin James's comments in John Tanner's *Narrative* about the Algonquian words for "man." Explaining that *r*, *l*, and *n* were interchangeable in the different Algonquian languages, James pointed out that "[i]n the Cree dialect . . . the word E-RIN-NE signifies MAN; in the Ojibbeway it is E-NIN-NE; in some other dialect approaching the Delaware, it is IL-LEN-NI; in the Delaware, according to Zeisberger, LEN-NO; in the Menomonie E-NAIN, or E-NAI-NEW" (James, in Tanner 1830, 391, my caps).

Since a Tungus tribe had been named after the *ollen* or *oren* (whom Rafinesque equated with Volney's "Tartar tribe Alani") and since *ollen*, *oren*, and Alani sounded so similar to Cree *e-rin-ne*, Ojibwe *e-nin-ne*, Illinois *il-len-ni*, and Lenape *lenno*, Rafinesque concluded that Olini (his own hybrid form) was the original ancient name of the tribe. Accordingly, the designation of the Lenape in this verse of the Walam Olum is Olini. "Here the people begin to be called O-LINI," he explained in his commentary. "[T]his was probably their old name when coming to America. The tribes that used R for L must have said *O-rini*, those who have neither, as the Niniwas and Ottawas, say *O-nini*. This will afford matter for many philological enquiries and comparisons" (1836, 1:153).

In this manner Rafinesque linguistically "demonstrated" in his epic the descent of the Lenape from Tartars and Samoyeds.

13. Rafinesque's erroneous "gutikuni Single night" is mainly derived from Zeisberger's "nGUTTOKUNI, ONE NIGHT" (1980 [1827], 46) but is also modeled after other forms in the *Grammar*, including "nGUTTI gischuch, ONE month" (46); "nGUTTI gachtin, ONE year" (47); "nGUTTI, 1" (44); and "nekti, the only one, SINGLE" (177). (I have used capital letters to illustrate which portions of the words in his sources Rafinesque appropriated.) Voegelin interpreted Rafinesque's *gutikuni*, "single night," as Southern Unami *kwəttúukkwəni*, "one day or night," and in his free translation rendered the phrase as "a single day" (C. F. Voegelin 1954, 72). Cf. Munsee *ngwutóokwŭnii*, "one day" (O'Meara 1996, 435).

14. This is not to say that some migrating American Indian groups could not or did not travel along the Yukon Valley; we are only noting here how the mystery of the route was "resolved" by the Lilly team.

15. The name and explanation as it appears in Heckewelder's list (with the portions Rafinesque appropriated designated here in capital letters) are as follows: "gíschACHKOkwalìs, *the* SNAKES *have all got into their dens*. Made from the words 'gìschi,' already; 'ACHGOok,' SNAKE; 'walìcu,' *in holes, dens*" (Heckewelder 1834, 373; see also 374).

Because Rafinesque was uncertain as to the proper boundaries of the word for "snakes," instead of correctly separating *achkok*, "snake," from the placename "*gíschACHKOkwalìs*, the SNAKES have all got into their dens," he inaccurately truncated it as *achko*, deleting final *-k*. He then altered the spelling of *achko* to *ako*, in accordance with the rules of orthography he invented specifically for use in the Walam Olum (see Oestreicher 1995b, 439–42). In so doing, he cleverly disguised the words in his text to preclude association with the published sources from which the words were drawn and made it appear as though he had obtained the words himself, directly from a Delaware Indian, out in the field. Rafinesque's *ako*, or "snakes," however, is as meaningless in Lenape as the fragment *sna-* might be were it severed from the English word "snakes."

16. By contrast, Brinton did believe that a Snake tribe was described later in the text, notably in WO IV:6–7, and *there* he translated the very same Rafinesque truncation, *ako*, as "Snakes" and "Snake Tribe," just as Rafinesque had done. In other

words, when the meaning of a Walam Olum word conflicted with Brinton's ideas of prehistory, he substituted a new translation for it; when the very same word appearing elsewhere in the Walam Olum did not conflict with his ideas, he kept the original translation.

17. Searching through Zeisberger's *Grammar* for a Delaware word with which to convey the idea of being somewhere, Rafinesque came across the form *epit*, "he who is there, being there" (Zeisberger 1980 [1827], 51). He copied down the English gloss, "being there," most likely into a list of Delaware words he was compiling for construction of the Walam Olum's Delaware language text. However, evidently due to a disruption or simply to a later misreading of his own hastily transcribed word list, he affixed next to this gloss the wrong Delaware word, *tendchi*, which he also obtained from Zeisberger's *Grammar*. *Tendchi* appears in Zeisberger but several pages prior to "Epit, . . . being there," as part of the phrases: "newinachk TENDCHI gaghtinamo, he is forty years old," "newinachk TENDCHI gachtinamiyenk, we are forty years old," and so on. (1980 [1827], 47, caps mine). *Tendchi*, which Rafinesque respelled as *tendki*, is a participle expressing the idea of "many" or "so many" (cf. Southern Unami *ntə́ntxi kḗku lúwan*, "that's about all I can say"; Northern Unami *endchi*, "as many," in Whritenour 1995, 33; and Munsee *Ngwútaash ndúndxu-kundŭweewŭnáhke*, "I was gone for six weeks" [O'Meara 1996, 323]).

As he had done on a number of occasions in his construction of the Walam Olum, Rafinesque has here accidentally attached the wrong Delaware word to an English gloss, both of which he obtained from the same published source. In some cases both his "wrong" English glosses and the Delaware words that accompany them can be found in very close proximity to each other in the original published source from which they were drawn, sometimes only separated by an intervening word or two. Such evidence makes abundantly clear how the incongruous combinations (Delaware words with the wrong English definitions) ended up in Rafinesque's Walam Olum manuscript. What makes the evidence of fraud even more compelling is that only the English glosses—and not the supposedly original Delaware texts—make sense in the Walam Olum, proving yet again that the text was composed from English into Delaware, not the other way around, as Rafinesque claimed.

18. Rafinesque's "*lakkawelendam* troubled or afraid" was grafted from "LACHAUWELENDAM, to be TROUBLED in mind," in Zeisberger's *Grammar* (1980 [1827], 94, caps mine), although he also took the liberty of amending Zeisberger's definition to include the meaning "afraid." (In fact, Rafinesque carelessly began to spell the word precisely as he found it in Zeisberger but then penned *kk* over *ch* and omitted the *u* of Zeisberger's *au* so as to conform with the orthography he

had devised for the Walam Olum, which here meant avoiding the use of Moravian *ch* and sequential vowel signs.)

Squier's translation omitted Zeisberger's definition of *lachauwelendam*, repeating only Rafinesque's insertion, "afraid" (1849, 185). Brinton accepted Zeisberger's original definition "to be troubled in mind" (which he confirmed by consulting the Moravian linguistic materials [1885, 239]) but preferred to render the gloss as "disquieted" (183). Voegelin was uncertain what to do. He was unable to find *lachauwelendam* in the Southern Unami dialect of Lenape that he had studied and did not consult Zeisberger's *Grammar* and other Moravian materials written in the Northern Unami dialect, where the word appears. Consequently, he preserved Rafinesque's English definition, "troubled," but replaced *lachauwelendam* in his reconstructed Delaware text with another word (one found in all the Lenape dialects) bearing the same meaning—*sakkweelə́ntam*, "he is worried, troubled" (Lilly et al. 1954, 61). Although the two Delaware words are indeed synonyms, their roots are entirely different. In other words, Voegelin corrected Rafinesque's "original" Delaware text with words that appeared to conform with Rafinesque's English translation!

19. Zeisberger did not give an independent translation of "the" in the Delaware language, and Rafinesque was unaware that the Lenape article "that," presented in the *Grammar* on page 48, is, in fact, equivalent to "the." Consequently, Rafinesque searched for any appearance at all of "the" in the *Grammar*'s English glosses and finally happened on the gloss "first, in THE first place" (caps mine), which accompanied the Lenape words "Nigani, N'hitam, Netamiechink" (1980 [1827], 175). Rafinesque thereupon attempted to divest those portions of these Delaware words, which he believed corresponded to "the" and which he further believed could be siphoned into new Delaware compounds.

The entire text of the Walam Olum was constructed in just this manner, and as a result, the key to understanding how the epic's pseudo-Delaware text was constructed may be found in Rafinesque's English glosses. The Walam Olum, after all, was originally created by Rafinesque in English and then translated into Delaware. To accomplish this, Rafinesque searched the English glosses of his Delaware sources to locate Delaware words that best expressed the meanings he sought. As these Delaware words are generally in compound form, and Rafinesque did not know which part of the compounds corresponded with the parts of the English glosses he wished to graft into his text, he inaccurately truncated the compounds in an effort to isolate the desired parts. Consequently, the entire text of the Walam Olum is riddled with ungrammatical truncations that have been broken from larger compounds in Rafinesque's sources and then siphoned into new and artificial compounds in the hoax. In short, the only way of unscrambling these senseless and often unrecognizable compounds is by recreating the process by which they were made in the first place: matching Rafinesque's English glosses with the English glosses in Rafinesque's Delaware-language sources and then noting which parts of the corresponding Delaware words were inappropriately truncated by Rafinesque and inserted into the new and artificial compounds of the Walam Olum.

20. When Rafinesque could not find the Lenape words he needed, he frequently turned to non-Lenape sources for the words (see Oestreicher 1994, 8–9).

21. The Lenape certainly smoked and used tobacco for a variety of purposes. However, the role of an official "pipe bearer," let alone an official pipe belonging to the community, was unheard of.

Insofar as the construction and gloss of this alleged Lenape word is concerned, Voegelin seems to have concluded that *naxappóowe* can be broken down as *na xappóowe*, "the pipe bearer." *Na* is indeed the article "the" and *xappóowe* does resemble the subjunctive form *énta xupówa*, "when I smoke a pipe," and the probable though unrecorded form *énta xupówit*, "when he smokes a pipe." In fact, the existence of such similarly sounding forms may have encouraged Voegelin to rationalize that the anomalous *naxappóowe* could be translated as "pipe bearer." However, it must be reiterated that *naxappóowe* does not mean "pipe bearer," that none of the native speakers of Lenape questioned about the alleged term could translate it, that the subjunctive forms cited here make no sense in relation to the rest of this Walam Olum verse, that the English gloss "pipe bearer" was derived from Brinton (and from Brinton's translation of completely different words in the Walam Olum [see note 22]), and that the concept of a "pipe bearer" is foreign to the Lenape Indians.

22. In WO IV:2 and with slight variations in IV:37, 55, and V:2, the form *tamaganat* appears. Rafinesque derived both the word and the translation from Heckewelder's list of names, telling us that *tamaganat* means "Path Leader." As Heckewelder had explained: "Uttamaccomak . . . uchTAMAGANÂT means *a* PATH *maker, a* LEADER, *a warrior;* w'TAMAGANAT, *a* CHIEFTAIN, *a* LEADER *of a band*" (1834, 380, caps mine). Later, when Brinton set to work on his translation of the Walam Olum, he had difficulty making sense of *tamaganat*. He was unaware that *təmákan* is, in fact, a Lenape word meaning "path" and, consequently, turned to the related Narragansett language for clues as to its meaning. Ironically, he consulted the very source Rafinesque had used for his construction of *nakopowa*, Roger Williams's *Key into the Language of America*. There he came across the Narragansett word, "Wuttámmagon . . . A Pipe" (1973 [1643], 127; Brinton 1885, 228). Stretching the meaning and investing cultural elements that were foreign to Eastern Algonquians, Brinton explained "I take *tamagamat* [*sic*, read *tamaganat*]

to be the pipe-bearer, he who had charge of the Sacred Calumet" (1885, 228). Brinton thereupon translated the form as it appeared in WO IV:2, 37, 55, and V:2 as "Pipe-Bearer."

References and Suggested Reading

Ankh-Hermes, Uitgeverij. 1989. *Walam olum: Het heilige boek van de Delaware-Indianen.* Deventer, Neth.: Vertaald en toegelicht door Jelle Kaspersma.

Barton, Benjamin Smith. 1798. *New Views of the Origin of the Tribes and Nations of America.* The second edition, corrected and greatly enlarged. Philadelphia: Printed for the author by John Bioren.

Blalock, Lucy, and David M. Oestreicher. 1993. Taped conversations on the Walam Olum. Tapes 1–31, June–August 1993. Tapes on file with the author.

Brinton, Daniel G. 1885. *The Lenape and Their Legends; With the Complete Text and Symbols of the Walam Olum, a New Translation, and an Inquiry into Its Authenticity.* Brinton's Library of Aboriginal American Literature, no. 5. Repr., New York: AMS Press, 1969.

Brotherston, G. 1979. "Genesis according to the *Walam Olum*," In *Image of the New World: The American Continent Portrayed in Native Texts*, edited by G. Brotherston, 176–78. London: Thames & Hudson.

Clarke, Adam. 1825–26. *The Holy Bible Containing the Old and New Testaments: The Text Printed from the Most Correct Copies of the Present Authorized Translation, Including the Marginal Readings and Parallel Texts. With a Commentary and Critical Notes. Designed as a Help to a Better Understanding of the Sacred Writings.* Vols. 1–6. New York: N. Bangs and J. Emory, for the Methodist Episcopal Church.

Court de Gébelin, Antoine. 1777–1782. *Monde Primitif.* Nouvelle Édition. Vols. 1–9. Paris: Chez l'Auteur, rue Poupée, Maison de M. Boucher, Secrétaire du Roi; Boudet, Imprimeur-Libraire, rue Saint Jacques; Valleyre l'aîné, Imprimeur-Libraire, rue de la vieille Bouclerie; Veuve Duchesne, Imprimeur-Libraire, rue Saint Jacques; Saugrain Libraire, quai des Augustins, Ruault, Libraire de la Harpe.

Cuvier, Georges. 1815. *Essay on the Theory of the Earth. Translated from the French by Robert Kerr. F. R. S. & F. A. S. Edin, with Mineralogical Notes, and an Account of Cuvier's Geological Discoveries, by Professor Jameson.* Second edition with additions. Edinburgh: Printed for William Blackwood, Edinburgh; and John Murray and Robert Baldwin, London.

Delanoë, Nelcya. 1996. *L'Entaille Rouge: Des Terres Indiennes à la démocratie américaine, 1776–1996.* Nouvelle édition revue et augmentée. Paris: Albin Michel.

Du Halde, P. 1741. *The General History of China. Containing a Geographical, Historical, Chronological, Political and Physical Description of the Empire of China, Chinese Tartary, Corea and Thibet. Including an Exact and Particular Account of their Customs, Manners, Ceremonies, Religion, Arts and Sciences. The whole adorn'd with Curious Maps, and a Variety of Copper Plates.*

Done from the French of P. Du Halde. Vols. 1–4. 3rd ed., corrected. London: Printed for J. Watts and Sold by B. Dod. First ed. published 1735.

Fabre d'Olivet, Antoine. 1815–1816. *La Langue Hébraïque Restituée, et le véritable sens des mots hébreux rétabli et prouvé par leur analyse radicale.* Paris, Chez l'auteur, Barrois et Eberhart, 1815–1816. Vols. 1 and 2.

Gill, Sam D., and Irene Sullivan. 1992. *Dictionary of Native American Mythology.* New York: Oxford University Press.

Greene, John C. 1996. *The Death of Adam: Evolution and Its Impact on Western Thought.* Ames: Iowa State University Press.

Hale, Horatio. 1883. "Indian Migrations as Evidenced by Language, comprising The HuronCherokee Stock: The Dakota Stock: The Algonkins: The ChahtaMuskoki Stock: The Moundbuilders: The Indians." Paper read at a meeting of the American Association for the Advancement of Science, held at Montreal, in August, 1882. Reprinted from the *American Antiquarian* for January and April 1883. Chicago: Jameson & Morse.

Heckewelder, John. 1834. "Names which the Lenni Lenape or Delaware Indians, who once inhabited this country, had given to Rivers, Streams, Places, &c., &c., within the now States of Pennsylvania, New Jersey, Maryland and Virginia: and also Names of Chieftains and distinguished Men of that Nation; with the Significations of those Names, and Biographical Sketches of some of those Men." *Transactions of the American Philosophical Society,* n.s., 4:351–96.

Hoffman, Daniel. 1981. *Brotherly Love.* New York: Vintage Books.

Jensen, Hans. 1970. *Sign, Symbol and Script: An Account of Man's Efforts to Write.* Translated from the German by George Unwin. 3rd ed., revised and enlarged. London: Allen & Unwin.

Kraft, Herbert C. 1993. "Charles Conrad Abbot, New Jersey's Pioneer Archaeologist." *Bulletin of the Archaeological Society of New Jersey* 48:1–12.

Leeming, David Adams, with Margaret Adams Leeming. 1994. *A Dictionary of Creation Myths.* New York: Oxford University Press.

Lilly, Eli, C. F. and Erminie Voegelin, Paul Weer, et al. 1954. *Walam Olum, or Red Score: The Migration Legend of the Lenni Lenape or Delaware Indians, a New Translation.* Indianapolis: Indiana Historical Society.

McCutchen, David, trans. and annotator. 1993. *The Red Record: The Wallam Olum; The Oldest Native North American History.* Garden City Park NY: Avery.

Mitchill, Dr. Samuel. 1820. Letter no. VI. "Heads of that part of the Introductory Discourse delivered November 7, 1816, by Dr. Mitchill, in the College of Physicians at Newyork, which relates to the Migration of Malays, Tartars, and Scandinavians, to America." In *Archaeologia Americana: Transactions and Collections of the American Antiquarian Society* 1, 338–44. Worcester MA: American Antiquarian Society.

Morton, Samuel George. 1839. *Crania Americana; or A Comparative View of the Skulls of Various Aboriginal Nations or North and South America: to which prefixed an essay on the varieties of the human species*. Philadelphia: J. Dobson; London: Simpkin, Marshall & Co.

Napora, Joe, trans. 1992. *The Walam Olum*. Greenfield Center NY: Greenfield Review Press.

Nuttall, Thomas. 1821. *Journal of Travels into the Arkansa Territory, During the Year 1819. With Occasional Observations on the Manners of the Aborigines*. Illustrated by a map and other engravings. Philadelphia: Thomas H. Palmer.

Oestreicher, David M. 1994. "Unmasking the Walam Olum: A Nineteenth-Century Hoax." *Bulletin of the Archaeological Society of New Jersey*, no. 49:1–44.

———. 1995a. "Text Out of Context: The Arguments that Sustained and Created the Walam Olum." *Bulletin of the Archaeological Society of New Jersey*, no. 50:31–52.

———. 1995b. "The Anatomy of the Walam Olum: The Dissection of a Nineteenth-Century Anthropological Hoax." Ph.D. diss., Dept. of Anthropology, Rutgers University, New Brunswick NJ.

O'Meara, John Desmond William. 1996. *Delaware-English/English-Delaware Dictionary*. Toronto: University of Toronto Press.

Purchas, Samuel. 1617. *Purchas his Pilgrimage, or Relations of the World and the Religions Observed in Al Ages and Places discouered, from the Creation unto this Present*. In four parts. 3rd ed. London: Printed by William Stansby for Henry Fetherstone.

Rafinesque, Constantine Samuel. 1824. *Ancient History, or Annals of Kentucky; With A Survey of the Ancient Monuments of North America, And a Tabular View of the Principal Languages and Primitive Nations of the whole Earth*. Frankfort KY: Printed for the author.

———. 1832–33. *Atlantic Journal, and Friend of Knowledge. In Eight Numbers*. Philadelphia: C.S. Rafinesque.

———. 1836. *The American Nations; or, Outlines of Their General History, Ancient and Modern: including the Whole History of the Earth and Mankind in the Western Hemisphere; the Philosophy of American History; the Annals, Traditions, Civilizations, Languages, &c., of All the American Nations, Tribes, Empires, and States*. Vols. 1 and 2. Philadelphia.

———. 1954. "Pictographs and Lenape Text." (Photo duplication of Walam Olum manuscript [1834].) In *Walam Olum, or Red Score: The Migration Legend of the Lenni Lenape or Delaware Indians, a New Translation*, by E. Lilly et al., 5–215. Indianapolis: Indiana Historical Society.

Speck, Frank G., and J. C. Webber. n.d. Translation of the Walam Olum into modern Delaware. Voegelin Papers, box 5, folder 8; also in box 8. American Philosophical Society Library, Philadelphia.

Spence, Lewis. 1986. *North American Indians*. Myths and Legends Series. New York: Avenel Books.

Squier, Ephraim G. 1849. "Historical and Mythological Traditions of the Algonquins;

With a Translation of the 'Walum-Olum,' or Bark Record of the Linni-Lenape." *The American Review, a Whig Journal devoted to Politics and Literature*, no. 14, 273[sic]–193.

Tanner, John. 1830. *A Narrative of the Captivity and Adventures of John Tanner, (C.S. Interpreter at the Saut De Ste. Marie) During Thirty Years Residence among the Indians in the Interior of North America*. Prepared for the Press by Edwin James, M.D. New York: G. & C. & H. Carvill.

Thomas, Cyrus. 1889. *The Problem of the Ohio Mounds*. Washington DC: Smithsonian Institution, Bureau of Ethnology, GPO.

———. 1890. *The Cherokees in Pre-Columbian Times*. New York: N. D. C. Hodges.

Velie, Alan R., ed. 1991. *American Indian Literature: An Anthology*. Rev. ed. Norman: University of Oklahoma Press.

Voegelin, Charles F. 1941. "Word Distortions in Delaware Big House and Walam Olum Songs." *Proceedings of the Indiana Academy of Science*, no. 51:48–54.

———. 1954. "Walam Olum: Translation." In *Walam Olum, or Red Score: The Migration Legend of the Lenni Lenape or Delaware Indians*, 3–215. Indianapolis: Indiana Historical Society.

Voegelin, C. F., and Joe E. Pierce. 1954. "Validity of Translations of the Walam Olum." In *Walam Olum, or Red Score: The Migration Legend of the Lenni Lenape or Delaware Indians*, 216–25. Indianapolis: Indiana Historical Society.

Voegelin, Erminie W. 1954. "Walam Olum: Ethnological Observations." In *Walam Olum, or Red Score: The Migration Legend of the Lenni Lenape or Delaware Indians*, 3–215. Indianapolis: Indiana Historical Society.

Volney, C. F. 1804. *View of the Climate and Soil of the United States of America: To Which Are Annexed Some Accounts Of Florida, the French Colony on the Scioto, Certain Canadian Colonies, and the Savages or Natives*. Translated from the French of C. F. Volney, Member of the Conservative Senate and the French National Institute, and Honorary Member of the American Philosophical Society at Philadelphia, the Asiatic Society at Calcutta, the Athenaeums of Avignon, Alengon, &c. With maps and plates. London: Mercer & Co.

Whritenour, Raymond, ed. 1995. *A Delaware-English Lexicon of Words and Phrases*. Compiled by David Zeisberger and other missionaries of the United Brethren. Butler NJ: Lenape Text & Studies.

Williams, Oscar. 1948. *A Little Treasury of American Poetry*. New York: Charles Scribner's Sons.

Williams, Roger. 1973 [1643]. *A Key into the Language of America, or an Help to the Language of the Natives in that Part of America called New England; Together with Briefe Observations of the Customs, Manners, and Worships, etc. of the Aforesaid Natives, in Peace and Warre, in Life and Death. On all of Which are Added Spiritual Observations Generall and Particular*. Detroit: Wayne State University Press. Originally published in 1643 in London by Gregory Dexter. Extracts of the work were published by the Massachusetts Historical Society in 1794 and 1798, and the entire work was republished in 1827 by the Rhode Island Historical Society.

Zeisberger, David. 1980 [1827]. *Grammar of the Language of the Lenni Lenape or Delaware Indians*. Translated from the German manuscript of the author by Peter Stephen Du Ponceau. New York: AMS Press.

Zolla, Elemire. 1973. *The Writer and the Shaman: A Morphology of the American Indian*. Translated by Raymond Rosenthal. New York: Harcourt Brace Jovanovich.

WALAM OLUM SONG III

Rafinesque's "Translation"

1. After the flood, the manly men *Linapewi*, with the manly turtle beings dwelt close together at the cave house, and dwelling of *Talli*.
2. It freezes was there, it snows was there, it is cold was there.
3. To possess mild coldness and much game, they go to the northerly plain, to hunt cattle they go.
4. To be strong and to be rich the comers divided into tillers and hunters. *Wikhichik, Elowi-chik*.
5. The most strong, the most good, the most holy, the hunters they are.
6. And the hunters spread themselves, becoming northerlings, easterlings, southerlings, westerlings. *Lowaniwi, Wapaniwi, Shawaniwi, Wunkeniwi*.
7. Thus the white country *Lumonaki*, north of the turtle country, became the hunting country of the turtling true men.
8. Meantime all the snakes were afraid in their huts, and the snake priest *Nakopowa* said to all, let us go.
9. Easterly they go forth at Snakeland *Akhokink*, and they went away earnestly grieving.
10. Thus escaping by going so far, and by trembling the burnt land *Lusasaki* is torn and is broken from the snake fortified land. *Akomenaki*
11. Being free, having no trouble, the northerlings all go out, separating, at the land of Snow *Winiaken*.
12. The fish resort to the shores of the gaping sea, where tarried the fathers of white eagle and white wolf. *Waplanewa, Waptumewi*.
13. While our fathers were always boating and navigating, they saw in the east that the snake land was bright and wealthy.
14. The head-beaver *Wihlamok*, and the big-bird *Kicholen*, were saying to all, let us go to the Snake Island *Akomen*.
15. By going with us, we shall annihilate all the snaking people, *Wemaken*.
16. Having all agreed, the northerlings and easterlings, went over the water of the frozen sea to possess that land.

17. It was wonderful when they all went over the smooth deep water of the frozen sea, at the gap of the Snake sea in the great ocean.
18. They were ten thousand in the dark, who all go forth in a single night in the dark, to the Snake island of the eastern land *Wapanaki* in the Dark, by walking all the people.—OLINI.
19. They were the manly north, the manly east, the manly south; with manly eagle, manly beaver, manly wolf; with manly hunter, manly priest, manly rich; with manly wife, manly daughter, manly dog.
20. All coming there, they tarry at Firland *Shinaking*. But the western men doubtful of the passage, preferred to remain at the old turtle land.

Squier's Translation

1. After the flood the true men (*Lennapewi*) were with the turtle, in the cave house, the dwelling of *Talli*.
2. It was then cold, it froze and stormed, and
3. From the Northern plain, they went to possess milder lands, abounding in game.
4. That they might be strong and rich, the new comers divided the land between the hunters and tillers, (*Wikhichik, Elowichik*.)
5. The hunters were the strongest, the best, the greatest.
6. They spread north, east, south and west;
7. In the white or snow country, (*lumowaki*,) the north country, the turtle land and the hunting country, were the turtle men or *Linapiwi*.
8. The snake (evil) people being afraid in their cabins, the snake priest (*Nakopowa*) said to them, let us go away.
9. Then they went to the East, the snake land sorrowfully leaving.
10. Thus escaped the snake people, by the trembling and burned land to their strong island, (*Akomenaki*.)
11. Free from opposers, and without trouble, the Northlings (*Lowaniwi*) all went forth separating in the land of snow, (*Winiaken*,)
12. By the waters of the open sea, the sea of fish, tarried the fathers of the white eagle (tribe?) and the white wolf.
13. Our fathers were rich; constantly sailing in their boats, they discovered to the eastward the snake Island.
14. Then said the Head-beaver (*Wihlamok*) and the Great-bird, let us go to the snake land.
15. All responded, let us go and annihilate the snakes.

16. All agreed, the Northerlings, the Easterlings, to pass the frozen waters.
17. Wonderful! They all went over the waters of the hard, stony sea, to the open snake waters.
18. In vast numbers, in a single night, they went to the eastern or snake island; all of them marching by night in the darkness.
19. The Northerlings, the Easterlings, the Southerlings, (*Shawanapi*,) the Beaver-men, (*Tamakwapis*,) the Wolf-men, the Hunters or best men, the priests, (*Powatapi*,) the *Wiliwapi*, with their wives and daughters, and their dogs.
20. They all arrived at the land of Firs, (*Shinaking*,) where they tarried; but the Western men (*Wunkenapi*) hesitating, desired to return to the old Turtle land, (*Tulpaking*.)

Brinton's Translation

1. After the rushing waters (had subsided) the Lenape of the turtle were close together, in hollow houses, living together there.
2. It freezes where they abode, it snows where they abode, it storms where they abode, it is cold where they abode.
3. At this northern place they speak favorably of mild, cool (lands), with many deer and buffaloes.
4. As they journeyed, some being strong, some rich, they separated into house-builders and hunters;
5. The strongest, the most united, the purest, were the hunters.
6. The hunters showed themselves at the north, at the east, at the south, at the west.
7. In that ancient country, in that northern country, in that turtle country, the best of the Lenape were the Turtle men.
8. All the cabin fires of that land were disquieted, and all said to their priest, "Let us go."
9. To the Snake land to the east they went forth, going away, earnestly grieving.
10. Split asunder, weak, trembling, their land burned, they went, torn and broken, to the Snake Island.
11. Those from the north being free, without care, went forth from the land of snow, in different directions.
12. The fathers of the Bald Eagle and the White Wolf remain along the sea, rich in fish and muscles.

13. Floating up the streams in their canoes, our fathers were rich, they were in the light, when they were at those islands.
14. Head Beaver and Big Bird said, "Let us go to Snake Island," they said.
15. All say they will go along to destroy all the land.
16. Those of the north agreed,
Those of the east agreed.
Over the water, the frozen sea,
They went to enjoy it.
17. On the wonderful, slippery water,
On the stone-hard water all went,
On the great Tidal Sea, the muscle-bearing sea.
18. Ten thousand at night,
All in one night,
To the Snake Island, to the east, at night,
They walk and walk, all of them.
19. The men from the north, the east, the south,
The Eagle clan, the Beaver clan, the Wolf clan,
The best men, the rich men, the head men,
Those with wives, those with daughters, those with dogs,
20. They all come, they tarry at the land of the spruce pines;
Those from the west come with hesitation,
Esteeming highly their old home at the Turtle land.

Voegelin's Translation

1. After the flood, the Delaware turtle men were crowded together: they lived well and stayed with the turtle.
2. The water froze over where they stayed: snow came, the wind blew, and it was cold.
3. There where the land slopes north and at the time when the wind was blowing and the weather was getting cold, they secured many big deer and pieces of buffalo meat.
4. Those who were strong and those who had power came away, separating from those who remained living there.
5. The strongest, the gentlest, and the most religious did this: they were the hunters.
6. To the north, east, south, and west the hunters traveled.

7. In the land of long ago, the north land, the turtle land, there the Turtle Delaware were hunting.
8. All the other hearths in the land were troubled: everyone said to the pipe bearer, "Let us depart."
9. And all these went on in another direction to the Snakes in the east: they were in earnest and they were grieving . . .
10. . . . and they were weak and worried and trembling: tattered and torn, they went off to Snake Island.
11. There were still free people who were well cared for in the north: they were the next to go away from the snow country.
12. Where fish were in clear water in a hollow well by Snow Mountain, there were the fathers of Bald Eagle and White Wolf.
13. And while in a boat going upstream, our fathers dreamed of Snake Island to the east.
14. Head Beaver and Big Bird said to one another, "Let us all go to Snake Island."
15. All of them said they would go together to the land there, all who were free . . .
16. . . . the Northerners were of one mind and the Easterners were of one mind: it would be good to live on the other side of the frozen water.
17. Things turned out well for all those who had stayed at the shore of water frozen hard as rocks, and for those at the great hollow well.
18. Ten thousand men went upstream, went right on upstream during a single day, upstream to the eastern lands of Snake Island: every man kept going along.
19. The North Delaware, the East Delaware, the South Delaware; and the Eagle Delaware, the Beaver Delaware, the Wolf Delaware; and the hunting men, the shamans, the headmen; and Delaware women, Delaware daughters, Delaware dogs . . .
20. . . . all came from Snow Mountain and the forest country; the West Delaware came out of humor, for they preferred the old Turtle land.

Fair Warning

Introduction by Alex MacKenzie Hargrave

This speech was first posted on the SSILA web page by a Dutch linguist.[1] Its provenance is uncertain. Its current lack of identity, however, does not obscure the remarkable nature of the text, which readily affirms its classical Algonquian pedigree and essentially rules out a modern origin.

This speech was given by a powerful sachem presumably to the agent of a foreign viceroy at a time when the native hegemony appears on equal footing with the foreign forces. Unlike so many documents that have survived from the early contact period, it is neither a petition to a Crown commission seeking redress nor a document with Western legal notions such as "deed" intended for a clerk. It records a speech, a recitation of promises broken and sureties violated. The exasperation it reveals bespeaks prior unsuccessful attempts at conciliation. It warns that the next step is war. While addressed to a *ku.to.wé*, or lord, its true audience must have been the warriors themselves who were listening to it as it was given. It could not fail to stir them up. The time for action had clearly come.

One can only speculate on the circumstances that produced this ultimatum, though they were hardly unusual anywhere along the eastern seaboard in the seventeenth or the eighteenth century. Turning to the internal evidence of the text, however, one can draw some inferences. First, whoever initially dictated or transcribed this speech was evidently fluent. Subtle distinctions have survived intact in spite of the ad hoc orthography of the time. In this document alone, there are five ways of spelling the term for "land" or "territory": *ayka*, *owkhu*, *ahké*, *ahki*, and *ahka*. This is quite to be expected. In Massachusett texts known to date from this period, over thirty variant spellings of *ohke* are employed.[2] An odd form might cause some head scratching, but will usually yield its secret if parsed correctly. In the posted text, two terms, *ohw* and *sahki*, did not make much sense until it became clear a transcription error had merged three letters of the former with the latter somewhere along the way. Correcting this yielded *oh.wah.s*, a common Algonquian lexical form of "animal," and *ahki*, "land."

There are two references to a feast council and its attendant ceremonies. The word *me.tso.pah.wi* is a compound of "food," *me.tso*, and "council," *pah.wi*, now "powwow," itself a compound of "divide" and "talk." It was during these events that the major decisions of the tribal nations were reached and its treaties made.

Rituals leading up to them varied greatly depending on the occasion. At only the most important would the sacred fire be lit and solemnified with condolences for the deceased, whose names could be uttered only at such times. Ceremonies like this would commonly last from five days to two weeks. Evidently, much of this was lost on, or ignored by, the foreign antagonists. These rites, however, cemented the strictest of obligations in the mind of the speaker, for whom the promises exchanged during the solemnities equaled or exceeded the importance of any parchment with its legal embellishments, flourishes of calligraphy, and prepossessing seals of coat armor. That the terms of the treaty were ratified under native auspices as well as at their place of assembly further argues that this speech dates from a period in which the native culture and its traditions were in full flower. Nonetheless, Western influence on the dialogue is visible in the reference to the first Old Testament murder. Does this suggest the speaker was a Christian convert? Lacking protestation to the contrary, it shows no more than familiarity with the biblical story, one no doubt preached unendingly by missionaries and others eager to discourage like behavior. So saying, it probably also struck a chord in the native ear. To European settlers brotherhood was a nearly fungible concept, entirely apart from the Decalogue. To the Algonquians it was the very foundation of trust.

Nowhere is the integrity and sophistication of this culture more apparent than in the elegant diction the speech employs. The speaker relies on antithetical pairs to highlight his grievance: *si.so* . . . *pe.ko.ssih*; *ta.ché.ki* . . . *ha.hi.tje.kah*; *no.cho* . . . *wo.ch.to*; and culminating in *ma.hé.ha* . . . *ma.he.ya*. This is oratory that falls not far from poetry. At the heart of the speech is a veiled threat. The speaker inquires if the distant lord knows all the "boundaries." Boundaries were blazoned by the cuts of a knife. The literal word is "makes cuts," metaphorically "knives," and by extension the "warriors" who wield them. I doubt this was an idle analogy. It was entirely in keeping with woodlands rhetoric. Courtesy and self-respect would simply not allow more overt bellicosity. Nor was it needed. The speaker creates a Socratic interrogatory throughout by posing questions to his absent adversary, which he then forcibly answers himself. "Promises . . . broken promises," "Do you know how many? . . . I know how many." In the second stanza the questions are artfully inverted for even greater effect; "slaughter . . . Is this your wish?" and "killed by brother . . . must (we) die?" With certain irony, the orator reminds his recipient of the biblical treachery between brothers, as brothers he and his foreign counterpart both no doubt have pledged to be. These rhetorical questions set up the mirrored alternation of the penultimate and final exclamations: "*Ma.hé.ha* . . . *Ma.he.ya!*" "Dead! Never!" These words gained their strength from the natural tendency of Algonquian root stems to carry additional metaphorical freight,

-ma- being a strong prohibitive, "no, don't, not" as well as "end, dead" and its accessory extensions. But their purpose was to dramatize the speaker's conclusion. The words ring out just as chillingly today.

While the language is emphatically Algonquian, it is difficult to speculate on any tribal affiliations beyond the obvious clue that the speaker's tribe was located along the Appalachian chain. Southern Algonquian languages are sparsely attested. A number of usages are present in Lenape, which makes it a good point of comparison, if not the language in question. The form *e.k.hi.li* in the text has the same meaning as Lenape *e.quo.he.llen*, "to die," in a contracted form. Finding a usage characteristic only of Lenape is difficult among parlance that is shared so widely. The morpheme *-aske-*, "must," in the line "must Appalachia die," is a free morpheme in Lenape with this specific sense, though more often a prohibitive in neighboring languages—"don't!" Lenape evinces *th-* as in *thje*, also less usual, but possibly performance related. Many terms in the speech are found in far-flung Algonquian tongues, underlining the commonality of its word stems. *Wo.chw.to* has a parallel in Lenape *woa.to.n*, "to know," but is attested in Mahican even more closely as *wa.wa.ch.taw-*, "I am acquainted." *Sha.za*, *sa.si*, *shaz . . . zi* are variant orthographies meaning "to kill, murder" and would leave no doubt in the mind of any Algonquian what was intended. The stem *-sha-*, "to slay," extends from Menominee to Natick and Narragansett. *Oh.wah.s*, "animal," as *ooas*, *howaas*, *oowaas*, and so on, was noted in Narragansett by Roger Williams by 1643 and in Ojibwe as *awessi* by Bishop Frederick Baraga two hundred years later. *Ma.shew.ki*, "fort," has a direct parallel in Shinnecock-related names for Long Island, *mashomack*, there designating a palisaded fortification. "Boundary" or "cut" from *kuh*, often reduplicated as *kuh . . . kuh*, is basic Algonquian.[3] A term of particular interest, however, is *hwoh.i.sa.ti*, which I translate as "sacred fire." It employs the stem *-hwoh-*, showing clearly a rare, and possibly archaic, labialized velar for this form. Commonly lexicalized as *-hoo-* or *-hou-*, the form in the text accords with one given by John Eliot in 1663, *pu.ki.tta.u(oo)*, "it smokes."[4] Eliot's form employs the verbal compound *pu.ki*, "split apart, destroy," used with fire to denote the smoke and, metonymically, ashes. The identical compound appears in the text at hand as *pe.ko* and *poi.chow* to describe "broken" promises and "divided" land, respectively. The common form for "fire" points up the archaism, which in turn quietly argues for an early date to the text and, less sotto voce, its thorough legitimacy.

With the oratory of a Pericles—poetic, spare, reasoned, impassioned—the speaker narrows his images and argument down to one implacable word of defiance. Rare is this glimpse into the heart of an age fashioned at the hands of a master. In sixteen lines this chief condenses the diplomatic history of the Algonquian world and delivers its prophetic summation.

Note on Pronunciation

I have made no attempt to regularize the spelling, in part to give the flavor of the text, which issues from a period with no fixed orthography, and in part because Algonquian makes room for performance variations of the same set of sounds without loss of meaning. It is this latitude on which its metaphoric power reposes. The fastidious desire to abstract unruly lexical forms into proto-forms is a noble but perilous undertaking to the extent that it obliterates the underlying etymologies. For present purposes, the reader should be emboldened to sound out the words as best seen fit, attentive to the rhythm and sonority of the language.

Note on Word Division

All parsing of Algonquian words in text and examples is by the translator, as are the stanza breaks. Periods are used to divide word and phrase elements. Where word division is given in a contemporary source, it is observed and indicated by hyphens.

Notes

1. SSILA: The Society for the Study of the Indigenous Languages of the Americas (Initial posting: Peter Baaker, "Language identification sought," SSILA *Bulletin* 140.1 [2001]: ssila@uoregon.edu). Further inquiry established that the origin of the text was from a private individual who states he transcribed it from a public source in Holland years ago (Arnold de Lange, email correspondence with author, June–July 2001). An unnamed correspondent subsequently asserted, without further ado, that this text was "Kemosabe" language, presumably on a par with "he heap big no speakum" (Peter Baaker, "Language a hoax?" SSILA *Bulletin* 141.1 [2001]: ssila@oregon.uoregon.edu).
2. Ives Goddard and Kathleen Bragdan, *Native Writing in Massachusett*, vol. 2 (Philadelphia: American Philosophical Society, 1988).
3. Lenape: Daniel G. Brinton and Rev. Albert Seqaqkind, eds., *A Lenape-English Dictionary* (Philadelphia: Historical Society of Pennsylvania, 1888; New York: AMS Press, 1979).

   MAHICAN: Carl Masthay, ed., *Schmick's Mahican Dictionary*, Memoirs of the American Philosophical Society, vol. 197 (Philadelphia: American Philosophical Society, 1991).

   MENOMINEE: Leonard Bloomfield, *The Menomini Language* (New Haven CT: Yale University Press, 1962).

   NARRAGANSETT: Roger Williams, *A key into the language of America; or An help to the language of the natives in that part of America, called New England* (1643; reprint, Bedford MA: Applewood Books, 1997).

OJIBWE: Bishop Frederick Baraga, *A Dictionary of the Otchipwe Language*, ed. Albert Lacombe (1878, 1880; reprint, St. Paul: Minnesota Historical Society Press, 1992).

4. Natick: John Eliot, *Mamusse wunneetupanatamwe up-biblum God naneeswe nukkone testament kah wonk wusku testament* (1685), in *Natick Dictionary*, by James Hammond Trumbull, Bureau of American Ethnology Bulletin 25 (Washington DC: GPO, 1903).

FAIR WARNING

Translated by Alex MacKenzie Hargrave

I.tto.ki.wéh sa.lo ii me.tso.pah.wi!
Our realm was long ago assured to us at the feast council!

Si.so! Pe.ko.ssih.
Promises! Broken promises.

Ayka.si e moh.swa.ka wi.toh.
The land treaty has not been followed since.

Ku.to.wé, i.loh.we na.che owkhu e poi.chow thje.
My lord, long has this land been divided thus.

Ahké.wi—oh.wah.s, ahki, ma.shew.ki.
It was divided up—the animals, the land, the forts.

Ke.yo.ché!
There are many boundaries, (blazoned by many knives, many warriors),

Ta.ché.ki e no.cho! Wo.chw.to?
How many I know! Do you know?

Ha.hi.tje.kah!!
Vast numbers!!

Sha.sza.sa, e.k.hi.li, o moy.sa.si!
Slaughter, murder, and war!

E?
Yes?

Hwoh.i.sa.ti é ma.sha.sah!
The sacred fire was lit and condolence given for the dead!

Ahka.si mo.cho.wé!
The land treaty cannot be ended!

Able.tzse.ja 'owh sha.z.key.zi!
Abel was killed by his own brother!

Ma.hé.ha!
Dead!

A.pa.la.chja sy.aske.zi?
Must Appalachia die?

Ma.he.ya!
Never!

The Arrival of the Whites

Introduction by Jim Rementer

Many accounts and history books tell of the arrival of the Europeans in America from the viewpoint of the Europeans. In this account we will look at various stories told by the Lenape, or Delaware, Indians of the same event.

The people who called themselves Lenape lived originally in what is now New Jersey, eastern Pennsylvania, northern Delaware, and southeastern New York. Population estimates for the Lenape at the time of the arrival of the Europeans vary and range all the way from eight thousand up to twenty-five thousand. Two main divisions of the Lenape existed in the old homeland. In the northern area were found the speakers of the Munsee dialect; they ranged into the area of today's New York City and north into the Catskills. In the area generally south of the Raritan River were found the Unami speakers. The Unami dialect was divided into Northern Unami, the dialect mainly used by the people with whom the Moravian missionaries worked, and Southern Unami. The southern dialect was used by both Lenape groups in Oklahoma.

Storytelling always held an important place in the lives of the Lenape people. In the days before movies, television, radio, and the written word, it was not only a form of amusement but also the only means of passing down tribal history and legends. As Francis Pastorius wrote of the Lenape in 1698, "They are people of the forest who instruct and teach one another by means of tradition, from the aged to the young" (Pastorius 1912, 433).

Lenape stories can be divided into two major categories: *athiluhakàna* (wintertime stories) and *achimëwakàna* (stories that can be told at any time). Wintertime stories should only be told during that season because doing so at other times will cause the teller to have various insects and other pests go after him or her. The Lenape had a solution for this possible problem should they have to relate such a story in other seasons. The teller would precede the story with the Lenape statement, "Tèlën òk nisha shkakwxèsa ntapapi!" (I am seated on twelve skunk hides!). This was apparently a potent enough threat to keep the pests away.

The Lenape said there were people gifted in storytelling, even as recently as the 1900s. Most were men, but some women storytellers were also known. In fact many Lenape speakers, if asked to tell a story, would begin with the disclaimer,

"Well, I'm not a storyteller, but I will do my best." The following small scene gives an idea of how a story session might have taken place in precontact times:

> It is the middle of winter, and the night is cold. Somewhere in a village along what would later be known as the Delaware River, there is a gathering of Lenape people who have come together in a *wikëwam* to listen to an elderly man tell *athiluhakàna* (wintertime stories). Inside the *wikëwam* a fire is burning, and it is warm but there is very little smoke. People are sitting around waiting. Then the old man opens a small deerskin bag he carries with him. He reaches in and soon pulls out a small figure carved of bone. He looks at it and says, "Wèwtunëwèsi athiluhakàn" (The wintertime story of the mermaid). And so he begins, "Nìki lòmëwe wàni Lenape . . ." (Once a long time ago the Lenape people . . .). And his stories continue for several hours into the night. The stories are wonderful, the year is 1590, and the world of the Lenape is about to change forever.

Unfortunately, the earliest Europeans to arrive in the Lenape homeland had little interest in the traditional stories. Their main interest was in trading for furs or trying to acquire the land. As shown in the book *Mythology of the Lenape*, by John Bierhorst, only five stories were written down prior to 1760. From 1760 until 1825 only twenty-five additional stories or pieces of stories appear in manuscripts. One possible reason, other than lack of interest, is that a pidgin trade language had come into use for dealings between the Europeans and the Lenape. Such a pidgin language would not have been a good vehicle for relating complicated stories.

Pidgin Talk

Lenape pidgin was a contact language used between the Lenape and the Europeans during the colonial period. According to linguist Ives Goddard, "Pidgin Delaware developed in the 1620s, and almost all documentation of it dates from the seventeenth-century. . . . nearly all of its attested vocabulary has clear origins in Unami words and expressions" (1997, 43). As an example of pidgin Lenape or Delaware compared with proper Lenape, the word for "I love you" is *ktaholël*, (note that in proper Lenape the pronouns are attached to the verb), while in pidgin Lenape it is *nee tahottamen kee*, or literally, "I love-it you."

The early Europeans who came to America often concluded that the native languages were less developed than those of the Europeans. William Penn was of this mind. He stated that "[t]heir Language is lofty, yet narrow . . . one word serveth in the place of three, and the rest are supplied by the Understanding of the Hearer" (1970, 22) What Penn did not realize was that the "language" he had learned was simply a pidgin tongue that had come into use as a trade language between the

Lenape and the Dutch, the Swedes, and the English. The words in the pidgin were nearly all Lenape words, the grammar was extremely simplified, and the sentence structure was not unlike that used in Dutch, Swedish, and English.

Lenape Language Today

A few speakers fluent in the Munsee dialect live at Moraviantown, Ontario. There are no longer any fully fluent Unami speakers, that is, people who grew up with Lenape as their first language, in either group in Oklahoma. Some middle-aged and older speakers have a partial command of the language.

The Delaware tribe in eastern Oklahoma has over one thousand hours of language recordings and presently has people working under a grant from the National Science Foundation to have the recordings converted to digital format, from which teaching materials using the voices of native speakers will be produced. Language classes are just getting started. Language preservation efforts are also underway at Moraviantown, Ontario, for the Munsee dialect.

The Stories of the Arrival of the Whites

One early story is the Lenape account of the arrival of the Europeans. This story was first recorded in the 1700s and has been passed on by oral tradition up to the present. The different versions that follow were told by various raconteurs over the last two centuries.

This story contains several elements, one being the prediction of the arrival of the whites, the next being the actual arrival, then the gift exchange between the Lenape and the whites, and finally how the whites tricked the Lenape and took their land. One segment that occurs in at least two later versions of the story involves what might be called a folk etymology that explains how the Lenape came to be called "Delawares."

The first version of the story was related to the Moravian missionary John Heckewelder sometime in the latter 1700s. Heckewelder states, "I give it as much as possible in their own language," by which we assume he means his version written in English follows as closely as possible the Lenape account he heard.

The second version of the story was told by Captain Pipe to C. C. Trowbridge in 1824. This account was taken down by Trowbridge when he visited White River, Indiana, to do research on the language and customs of the Delawares as requested by Governor Cass.

The third version of this story was told in Lenape by Willie Longbone to linguist Carl Voegelin in 1939 and was recorded on phonograph records. These recordings have been preserved by the Archive of Traditional Music at Indiana University, and the story presented here is a rough translation of that rather scratchy recording.

A review of Voegelin's field notes at the American Philosophical Society Library shows a portion of this story, but it is markedly different from the recording. This version and version five add the statement that some Lenape wished to kill the newcomers.

The fourth version was told by Bessie Snake in Lenape in 1978. Bessie is a member of the Delaware Tribe of Western Oklahoma, which has been separated from the other Delaware group represented in Oklahoma since about 1795. This suggests great antiquity for the story. Bessie's version contains several new elements, such as "as long as the creek flows" and "the red flag," not found in other versions.

The fifth and final version was told by Nora Thompson Dean of the Delaware tribe in northeastern Oklahoma on several occasions in the 1970s and early 1980s. Because different features occurred in different tellings of the story, we have combined them into one so that we have the most complete version possible for this contribution.

Note

Throughout this paper, the terms "Lenape" and "Delaware" are used interchangeably. "Lenape" is the name that the people who speak the language use to refer to themselves. Many of the younger people whose language is English use the term "Delaware" more frequently.

I also use the term "Indian" with the full understanding that some people prefer the use of the term "Native American." I am guided by the fact that the main group of Delawares who now live in northeastern Oklahoma refer to their group as the "Delaware Tribe of Indians" and not the "Delaware Tribe of Native Americans."

Pronunciation Key

a like **a** in English "father"; à like **u** in "cup"; *e* like **a** in "fate"; è like **e** in "met"; *ë* like **a** in "sofa"; *i* like **e** in "she"; ì like **i** in "fit"; *o* like **o** in "nose"; ò like **o** in "north"; *u* like **oo** in "fool"; ù like **u** in "pull". *x* has no equivalent sound in English. It is pronounced like the **ch** in the German word "do**ch**," almost as if one is lightly trying to clear the throat.

Lenape Words Used in the Text

Achimëwakàn	a story
Athiluhakàn	a wintertime story
Ktaholël	I love you
Nìki lòmëwe	Once a long time ago

Ntapapi	I am seated
Shkakwxèsa	skunk hides
Tèlën òk nisha	twelve
Wàni Lënape	the Lenape (a plural form)
Wèwtunëwèsi'	of a mermaid
Wikëwam	a house (in early days they were mainly made of bark)

References

Bierhorst, John. 1995. *Mythology of the Lenape: Guide and Texts.* Tucson: University of Arizona Press.

Goddard, Ives. 1997. "Pidgin Delaware." In *Contact Languages: A Wider Perspective*, edited by Sarah G. Thomason. Creole Language Library, vol. 17. Amsterdam: John Benjamins.

Heckewelder, John G. 1876. *History, Manners, and Customs of the Indian Nations Who Once Inhabited Pennsylvania and the Neighboring States.* Philadelphia: Historical Society of Pennsylvania.

Pastorius, Francis Daniel. 1912. "Circumstantial Geographical Description of Pennsylvania, 1700." In *Narratives of Early Pennsylvania, West New Jersey and Delaware, 1630–1707*, edited by Albert Cook Myers. New York: Barnes & Noble.

Pearson, Bruce, and James Rementer. 1978. "Recordings of Lenape Stories Told by Bessie Snake." Unpublished taped stories in author's possession.

Penn, William. 1970. *William Penn's Own Account of the Lenni Lenape or Delaware Indians.* Edited by Albert Cook Myers. Somerset NJ: Middle Atlantic Press.

Rementer, James. 1961–2002. Notes and tapes made with Lenape speakers in Oklahoma.

Weslager, C. A. 1972. *The Delaware Indians: A History.* New Brunswick NJ: Rutgers University Press.

Suggested Reading

Most of these publications are available at Lenape Culture Studies, 5100 E. Tuxedo, Bartlesville OK 74006. This is the Delaware tribal gift shop. The publications can also be ordered online through the tribal Web site: www.delawaretribeofindians.nsn.us.

The Lenape-Delaware Indian Heritage: 10,000 BC to AD 2000, by Herbert C. Kraft (Stanhope NJ: Lenape Books at Lenape Lifeways, 2001). Kraft's full-length study of the Indians of Lenapehoking (the old Lenape homeland). Written in nontechnical language and intended for the general reader, this book corrects many myths and mistakes and presents new evidence concerning the origins, prehistory, and life ways of the people commonly called Lenape, or Delaware, Indians. The book has 695 pages, with 400 photographs, maps, illustrations, a comprehensive index, and a bibliography. Available in hardcover or softcover.

Lënapei Lixsëwakàn: The Lenape Language CD-ROM, by Jim Rementer with Jan Brown and David Motz, vol. 1 (Bartlesville OK: Delaware Tribe of Indians, 2000). A basic introduction to the Delaware, or Lenape, language to use on your computer. Each word is spoken by a native Lenape speaker and is illustrated by a photograph.

The Indians of North America: The Lenape (Wynnewood PA: Schlessinger Media, 1995). History of the Lenape people told by themselves. A thirty-minute documentary on VHS videotape on history, language, dances, and culture.

Legends of the Delaware Indians and Picture Writing, by Richard C. Adams, edited by Deborah Nichols (Syracuse NY: Syracuse University Press, 1997). Originally published in 1905 and highly valued by both scholars and general readers, this work has been out of print until this edition appeared. The stories teach lessons, such as the importance of keeping a promise. Four of these legends have been retranslated into the Delaware language by native Delaware speakers. Richard C. Adams (1864–1921), a Delaware, sought to preserve the culture and traditions of his people through his writings. 128 pages. Softbound.

Lenape Language Lessons, set 1, *Lessons One and Two*, by Nora Thompson Dean (Dewey OK: Touching Leaves Indian Crafts, 1979). The topics are the sounds of Lenape; greetings; common phrases; weather expressions; kinship terms; and the numbers in Lenape. Audiocassette and book.

Lenape Language Lessons, set 2, *Lessons Three and Four*, by Nora Thompson Dean (Dewey OK: Touching Leaves Indian Crafts, 1980). The topics are names for food; words used in prayer; more kinship terms; Lenape grammar; names of birds; the ages of men and women; and more numbers in Lenape. Audiocassette and book.

The Delaware Indians: A History, by C. A. Weslager (New Brunswick NJ: Rutgers University Press, 1972). The most comprehensive history of the Lenape. This book is a must for every Lenape and for every student of Lenape history, culture, and customs. 576 pages. Softbound.

Mythology of the Lenape: Guide and Texts, by John Bierhorst (Tucson: University of Arizona Press, 1995). This catalog of Lenape mythology features synopses of all known Lenape tales and complete texts of unpublished stories collected in the early twentieth century. 192 pages. Softbound.

The Delaware Language: Preliminary Edition, by Lucy Blalock, Bruce Pearson, and James Rementer (Bloomington IN: Yorkshire Press, 1994). A grammar prepared at the request of the Delaware Culture Preservation Committee, written for the student who wants to learn the language basics. 88 pages. Softbound.

THE ARRIVAL OF THE WHITES

Version 1: "Indian Account of the First Arrival of the Dutch at New York Island"

As told to John Heckewelder

The relation I am going to make was taken down many years since from the mouth of an intelligent Delaware Indian, and may be considered as a correct account of the tradition existing among them of this momentous event. I give it as much as possible in their own language.

A great many years ago, when men with a white skin had never yet been seen in this land, some Indians who were out a fishing, at a place where the sea widens, espied at a great distance something remarkably large floating on the water, and such as they had never seen before. These Indians immediately returning to the shore, apprised their countrymen of what they had observed, and pressed them to go out with them and discover what it might be. They hurried out together, and saw with astonishment the phenomenon which now appeared to their sight, but could not agree upon what it was; some believed it to be an uncommonly large fish or animal, while others were of opinion it must be a very big house floating on the sea. At length the spectators concluded that this wonderful object was moving towards the land, and that it must be an animal or something else that had life in it; it would therefore be proper to inform all the Indians on the inhabited islands of what they had seen, and put them on their guard. Accordingly they sent off a number of runners and watermen to carry the news to their scattered chiefs, that they might send off in every direction for the warriors, with a message that they should come immediately. These arriving in numbers, and having themselves viewed the strange appearance, and observing that it was actually moving towards the entrance of the river or bay; concluded it to be a remarkably large house in which the Mannitto (the Great or Supreme Being) himself was present, and that he probably was coming to visit them. By this time the chiefs were assembled at York island, and deliberating in what manner they should receive their Mannitto on his arrival. Every measure was taken to be well provided with plenty of meat for a sacrifice. The women were desired to prepare the best victuals. All the idols or images were examined and put in order, and a grand dance was supposed not only to be an agreeable entertainment for the Great Being, but it was believed that it might, with the addition of a sacrifice, contribute to appease him if he was angry with them. The conjurers were also set to work, to determine what this phenomenon portended, and what the possible result of it might be. To these and to the chiefs and wise men of the nations, men, women, and children were looking up for advice and protection. Distracted between hope and fear, they were at a loss what to do; a dance, however, commenced in great confusion. While in this situation, fresh runners arrive declaring it to be a large house of various colours, and crowded with living creatures. It appears now to be certain, that it is the great Mannitto, bringing them some kind of game, such as he had not given them before, but other runners soon after arriving declare that it is positively a house full of human beings, of quite a different colour from that of the Indians, and dressed differently from them; that in particular one of them was dressed entirely in red, who must be the Mannitto himself.

They are hailed from the vessel in a language they do not understand, yet they shout or yell in return by way of answer, according to the custom of their country; many are for running off to the woods, but are pressed by others to stay, in order not to give offence to their visitor, who might find them out and destroy them. The house, some say, large canoe, at last stops, and a canoe of a smaller size comes on shore with the red man, and some others in it; some stay with his canoe to guard it. The chiefs and wise men, assembled in council, form themselves into a large circle, towards which the man in red clothes approaches with two others. He salutes them with a friendly countenance, and they return the salute after their manner. They are lost in admiration; the dress, the manners, the whole appearance of the unknown strangers is to them a subject of wonder; but they are particularly struck with him who wore the red coat all glittering with gold lace, which they could in no manner account for. He, surely, must be the great Mannitto, but why should he have a white skin? Meanwhile, a large Hackhack (*Hackhack is properly a gourd; but since they have seen glass bottles and decanters, they call them by the same name*) is brought by one of his servants, from which an unknown substance is poured out into a small cup or glass, and handed to the supposed Mannitto. He drinks—has the glass filled again, and hands it to the chief standing next to him. The chief receives it, but only smells the contents and passes it on to the next chief, who does the same. The glass or cup thus passes through the circle, without the liquor being tasted by any one, and is upon the point of being returned to the red clothed Mannitto, when one of the Indians, a brave man and a great warrior, suddenly jumps up and harangues the assembly on the impropriety of returning the cup with its contents. It was handed to them, says he, by the Mannitto, that they should drink out of it, as he himself had done. To follow his example would be pleasing to him; but to return what he had given them might provoke his wrath, and bring destruction on them. And since the orator believed it for the good of the nation that the contents offered them should be drunk, and as no one else would do it, he would drink it himself, let the consequence be what it might; it was better for one man to die, than that a whole nation should be destroyed. He then took the glass, and bidding the assembly a solemn farewell, at once drank up its whole contents. Every eye was fixed on the resolute chief, to see what effect the unknown liquor would produce. He soon began to stagger, and at last fell prostrate on the ground. His companions now bemoan his fate, he falls into a sound sleep, and they think he has expired. He wakes again, jumps up and declares, that he has enjoyed the most delicious sensations, and that he never before felt himself so happy as after he had drunk the cup. He asks for more, his wish is granted; the whole assembly then imitate him, and all become intoxicated.

After this general intoxication had ceased, for they say that while it lasted the whites had confined themselves to their vessel, the man with the red clothes returned again, and distributed presents among them, consisting of beads, axes, hoes, and stockings such as the white people wear. They soon became familiar with each other, and began to converse by signs. The Dutch made them understand that they would not stay here, that they would return home again, but would pay them another visit the next year, when they would bring them more presents, and stay with them awhile; but as they could not live without eating, they should want a little land of them to sow seeds, in order to raise herbs and vegetables to put into their broth.

They went away as they had said, and returned in the following season, when both parties were much rejoiced to see each other; but the whites laughed at the Indians, seeing that they knew not the use of the axes and hoes they had given them the year before; for they had these hanging to their breasts as ornaments, and the stockings were made use of as tobacco pouches. The whites now put handles to the former for them, and cut trees down before their eyes, hoed up the ground, and put the stockings on their legs. Here, they say, a general laughter ensued among the Indians, that they had remained ignorant of the use of such valuable implements, and had borne the weight of such heavy metal hanging to their necks, for such a length of time. They took every white man they saw for an inferior Mannitto attendant upon the supreme Deity who shone superior in the red and laced clothes. As the whites became daily more familiar with the Indians, they at last proposed to stay with them, and asked only for so much ground for a garden spot as, they said, the hide of a bullock would cover or encompass, which hide was spread before them. The Indians readily granted this apparently reasonable request; but the whites then took a knife, and beginning at one end of the hide, cut it up to a long rope, not thicker than a child's finger, so that by the time the whole was cut up, it made a great heap; they then took the rope at one end, and drew it gently along, carefully avoiding its breaking. It was drawn out into a circular form, and being closed at its ends, encompassed a large piece of ground. The Indians were surprised at the superior wit of the whites (these Dutchmen were probably acquainted with what is related of Queen Dido in ancient history, and thus turned their classical knowledge to a good account), but did not wish to contend with them about a little land, as they had still enough themselves. The white and red men lived contentedly together for a long time, though the former from time to time asked for more land, which was readily obtained, and thus they gradually proceeded higher up the Mahicannittuck [Hudson River], until the Indians began to believe that they would soon want all their country, which in the end proved true. (Heckewelder 1876, 71–76)

Version 2: "First Acquaintance with the Whites"

As told by Captain Pipe to C. C. Trowbridge (1824)

The tradition of their first acquaintance with the whites has been minutely related by Mr. Heckewelder and agrees in substance with the account now given of that important event. Capt. Pipe says that in those days the Indians were accustomed to worship annually as they now do, in a large building prepared and kept for that purpose. At one of these meetings an old man prophesied the coming of some important and extraordinary events and a few days after a ship hove in sight and a boat with some of the officers came on shore. The Indians, supposing the crew to be inferior deities sent by the great Spirit, spread beaver skins upon the ground for them to walk upon. The whites refused to comply and pointed to their hats endeavouring to make them understand the value and proper use of the skins, but they were compelled to accept the politeness of their new acquaintances who surrounded them and drove them on the skins. When they arrived at the great council house or place of worship one of them took a cup and filling it with liquor drank of it and offered it to the astonished spectators. The cup passed around, refused by all. At length three brave men supposing the Deity would be offended by their stubbornness resolved to undertake the dreadful task, and having drunk the contents of the cup they were taken out of the lodge and seated upon a log. The effect of the liquor soon prostrated them to the ground, and their recovery was despaired of. However they were closely watched and at length one of them lifted up his head and demanded more of the poison. In time they all recovered and their account of its pleasing effects induced others to join, and its use soon became universal.

After becoming familiar with them the whites solicited them to give a small piece of land upon which they might build a fire to prepare their food. They demanded only a piece as large as a Bullocks hide and the request was readily granted, when to their great astonishment the bullocks hide was soaked in water and cut into a small cord with which the land was surrounded. However, they determined to overlook the deception and be more wary in future. They whites presented them with Axes, hoes etc. and departed, promising to revisit them the next year.

Upon their return they were not a little amused to see the Indians walking about with these things suspended from their necks as ornaments. They taught them their use, trafficked a little with them, and at length told them that they wanted more lands, because it was impossible from the smallness of the size of the first grant, to build a fire upon it without being incommoded with the smoke. It was therefore resolved to add to the first piece a quantity large enough to hold the chair of the whites, without the influence of the smoke. Upon this the bottom of the chair, which was composed of small cords, was taken out and like the hide, stretched around the lands. This second deception determined them never to give more lands without fixing some boundary understood by both parties distinctly. (Weslager 1972, 475–76)

Version 3: "The Coming of the Whites"

As told in Lenape by Willie Longbone in 1939 to Carl Voegelin

A long time ago when the whites came across the water the Lenape did not know that they were coming. One man said in his vision song, "Someone wants to come to see us. He will come across the water." A warrior said, "I'll kill him when I see him."

The next year they saw a ship coming in this direction, and the chief [who had the vision] said, "Now that's the one. The one coming is our elder brother," but the warrior said, "Not mine!" When the whites had arrived, the warrior began to say, "I want to overpower him," but the man [chief] said, "This one is our older brother, that's what I said! [Na nën ndëluwèn]" The white man said, "Oh, [repeating the Lenape word *ndëluwèn*], you must be a Delaware!" That is the reason they began to call the Lenape "Delaware." [At this point the sound on the record becomes very distorted, but then it resumes as] "What do you want?" He [the white man] said, "I want a little piece of land, only as much as a cowhide will cover. Will you give it to me?"

[The Lenape answered], "Oh yes, we can give you that much." Ah, but they did not use just the cowhide. They began to cut it into little thin strips so that when stretched out it encircled a large piece of land. [End of recording].

Version 4: "The White People Are Still Fooling Us"

As told in Lenape by Bessie Snake of the Delaware Tribe of Western Oklahoma in 1978 to Jim Rementer and Bruce Pearson

This one when he was first here, he wanted to fool us, our elder brother [white people]. They said, "We will treat you good for as long as the creek flows and our uncle, the sun, moves and as long as the grass grows every spring, for that long I will take care of you people and I will be friends to you people," he said. He just wanted to fool us, and it seems that he is still fooling us.

Then he said, "I will give you this red flag." He said, "As long as you keep this, you give us a little piece of land as much as [will be covered by] a cow we will kill and then skin him." Then they did not take the hide off but cut it into very small pieces. Then they [the Delawares] looked good at it. It was a big piece of land our Lenape ancestors of long ago gave to them. They thought that the land was only to be as big as the hide they put on the ground, but it was a big piece.

Then they said, "You did not say, 'I want to cut it up!'" Then he [white man] said, "Now you have already finished signing this paper!" Now that is where our money now comes from that we receive, and we are we are still fighting it. It was said at that time, "We will treat you good and you will be given everything." This is true, he does give us everything.

Then [to] those deceased chiefs they [the whites] gave to them an axe and a hoe for them to use. Then they [the chiefs] just put them on their necks. The white man told them, "That is not the way to use it putting it on your neck. I will give you something else to wear around your neck." Then they handed them back to him, and he took them. Then he put them on handles so they can take ahold of them.

Then the white man told him, "This is how it is used when you plant something to make rows. Now this axe is used to cut trees or to cut wood or to make a log house; that is what you use to make it." Then he [the Lenape] said, "All right!" Then from then on they always used it.

Then I told my daughter and my grandchildren that they are still fooling us.

Version 5: "Prediction of the Arrival of the White People"

As told by Nora Thompson Dean, 2002

Long ago there was a Lenape man who had remarkable powers. He would often go and meditate. He was able to foresee the future. One day he told his people, "Soon we will have visitors. They will be real white, fair-skinned people, and they will come from the east in a huge vessel. They are a people who will change our way of life."

Not many people believed him, but finally one day the Lenape people saw a ship coming in. And when these men got out of their boat, the Lenape people were much amazed as they had light skin, blue eyes, and light hair. They were very stunned and dumbfounded, but most of the Lenape were so glad that these visitors had come that they put down furs for them to walk on.

But some Lenape wanted to kill the white people and said, "We don't want these people here. We'll just kill them." But the powerful man said, "No, they came to me in a vision. We will not kill them. They might be our brothers. They might bring us good things. They are going to bring us good things, eventually. We want to treat them good."

And so they did. They put furs down for the white people to sit and walk on. They gave the white people seeds, food, and other things they needed. That's the way the prediction was told a long time ago about the arrival of the white people.

The Delaware Creation Story

Introduction by John Bierhorst

Under the heading "Work of Mr. Jeremiah Curtin"—referring to the philologist-folklorist and former diplomat who had come on staff during the previous twelve-month cycle—the annual report of the Smithsonian Institution's Bureau of Ethnology for the year 1883–84 states briefly: "On September 1, 1883, Mr. Jeremiah Curtin went to the Cattaraugus Reservation, New York, where he collected about one hundred and seventy myths and some texts. Many of these myths are long and were written out with full details." Not to be published for another thirty-five years, the myths in question were the traditional narratives comprising "the first serious attempt to record with satisfactory fullness the folklore of the Seneca."[1] Not mentioned in the 1883 notice, and here published for the first time, was a narrative of somewhat greater rarity, written out in the Munsee Delaware language, with English interlinear glosses, and provided with the title Mōskīm. This, a version of the Iroquoian-Algonquian creation story, including the descent of the sky woman, the establishment of the earth on the back of the turtle, and the birth of the culture hero, was obtained by Curtin on November 28, 1883, from the versatile traditionalist John Armstrong. The manuscript gives the location as Versailles, New York, which is in the northernmost part of Cattaraugus County, adjacent to the Cattaraugus Seneca Reservation.

At a later date Curtin's manuscripts passed into the hands of the Iroquoianist J. N. B. Hewitt, who recorded additional Seneca narratives at Cattaraugus in 1896 and who was inspired on that occasion to reelicit the Delaware Moskim text from Armstrong in a fuller version. In a prefatory note to a Delaware vocabulary obtained from Armstrong in October 1896, Hewitt described his informant as "a Delaware Indian, married to a Cayuga woman." A few years later, when publishing Armstrong's Seneca-language version of the creation story—as if to emphasize Armstrong's Seneca credentials—Hewitt described him as "of Seneca-Delaware-English mixed blood, an intelligent and conscientious annalist." Armstrong's photograph, submitted to the Bureau of Ethnology by Curtin in 1887, shows a man well past middle age, with penetrating eyes and almost a smile, holding an opened book in his hands and looking toward the camera. It is a portrait that calls to mind Hewitt's further description of Armstrong and other traditionalists at Cattaraugus as "patient, kind, and interested. They were men whose faith in the religion of their ancestors ennobled them with good will, manliness, and a desire to serve." Armstrong supplied Seneca stories, as well as Delaware stories, to both Curtin and Hewitt. Among his accomplishments he is said to have been an herbalist. From the dated photograph it can be conjectured that he was born about 1820 (in fact, according to Hewitt, "he was born about 1824"); he died between 1896 and 1903.[2]

The Munsee community at Cattaraugus, which we may assume had nurtured Armstrong, originated in the early 1790s at the time of the Delaware exodus from western Pennsylvania and Ohio. At least in part, the Munsee group that ended at Cattaraugus reached New York by way of the Allegheny River valley. As the main body of Delawares moved across Ohio and into Indiana, other Munsee groups immigrated to Ontario, settling at Moraviantown, Munseytown, and Six Nations Reserve near Brantford. Many Delawares continued on to Kansas and eventually Oklahoma; these were principally Unami Delawares, who had often banded with Munsees over the course of the westward trek. At the time of the American Revolution, the combined Unami and Munsee population is estimated to have been 3,200. At Cattaraugus, in 1800, the Munsee colony was censused as thirty cabins and 160 souls.

That same year of 1800 marked the beginning of a notorious series of events in which the Cattaraugus Munsees were accused of witchcraft by their Seneca hosts—an episode colorfully recreated by Anthony F. C. Wallace in his *Death and Rebirth of the Seneca*. According to some accounts, including Wallace's, the Munsees escaped persecution as witches by fleeing en masse to Canada, where they found refuge with their sisters and brothers already safely settled at Six Nations Reserve. Still, a document that can be dated to 1821–22 lists the Munsee settlement in Cattaraugus County as having a population of no less than fifty, including twenty "warriors." Thereafter Munsee culture at Cattaraugus declined—though at the end of the century it glowed brightly in Armstrong's dictations to Curtin and Hewitt, and as late as 1945 the ethnologist Frank G. Speck could report that "some Delawares, of the Armstrong family, reside there yet."[3]

Though removed by many generations from their seventeenth-century homeland of New Jersey, eastern Pennsylvania, Delaware, and southeastern New York, Delaware storytellers preserved memories of "the great water" and "the dense woods." Even in the twentieth century a traditional tale might begin, "Many long days ago, when the Lenape [i.e., Delawares] lived in the East." Armstrong himself set one of his stories on the Delaware River, and as recently as the 1970s a narrator at Morpeth, Ontario, south of Moraviantown, was able to tell a fragment of the creation epic, calling it "an eastern story."[4]

Armstrong, of course, was sought out by Curtin and Hewitt as a Seneca, not

Delaware, informant. His Delaware material, for them, must have been incidental. By far his best-known contribution is his Seneca-language version of the creation story, published by Hewitt in 1903 and treated for the past hundred years as a standard work of Seneca literature. On the surface this major text agrees quite well with other Seneca versions of the Creation and fits comfortably within the Iroquoian tradition. Yet on close inspection it reveals features that set it apart. Among these the most significant is the emotive Dying Brother episode, highly typical of Algonquian versions (Ojibwe, Cree, Montagnais, Menominee, Fox, Sauk, Blackfeet), in which the hero's brother is killed by evil beings, prompting the hero himself to weep inconsolably. In Menominee and Fox versions his sobs are answered by the trembling earth; in Armstrong's Seneca-language version, by the rumbling sky.[5]

Further, Armstrong slips in a hint that the hero had two additional siblings, echoing Algonquian tellings that specify triplets, quadruplets, or even a company of five (Ojibwe, Mahican[?], Potawatomi, Powhatan).[6] We also learn that the hero's mother had been impregnated by wind, another Algonquian feature.

In Armstrong's Delaware-language versions, the Algonquian affinity asserts itself unmistakably in the name given to the hero, Moskim ("hare" or "rabbit"), corresponding to the familiar Manabozho, Nanabush, Tschimammus, and others of Central and Eastern Algonquian lore, generally translated "hare." As understood in the second half of the twentieth century, the Munsee term is *móoshkiingw*, with the two vowels approximately as in "no" and "skim" and the final *ngw* trailing off into voicelessness. Since both Curtin and Hewitt wrote *s* for either /s/ or /sh/ (i.e., /š/), often missed the word-final /w/ when preceded by a consonant, sometimes wrote *m* for /n/ (and *n* for /m/), and could have put *m* for /ngw/, we may not conclude that Armstrong pronounced the term differently from modern speakers. In any case it is here assumed that readers of the English translation will have no objection to Curtin's "Moskim," rhymes with "no skim" (accented on the first syllable), wherever the word is used as a proper noun—saving the form *móoshkiingw* for the common noun "hare."

Linguistically the text is better than the preceding comments might imply. The opening sentence, as written by Curtin, reads:[7]

Nûl īn yok lennapewak monenawáuwûl yol hwatdjĕ míntgwûl

Which may be rewritten in modern orthography:[8]

Nál íin yóok lunaapéewak mahkŭnaawáawal yóol xwáchu-míhtkwal.

With the help of these English glosses added by Curtin in the manuscript:

> /Then/ /those/ /people/ /pull up/ /this/ /big/ /tree/

Minimally refined as follows:

> /Then/ /it is said/ /these/ /people/ /they pull it up/ /this/ /big/ /tree/

Freely translated:

> Then, it is said, these people pulled up this big tree.

And, finally, in the presentation that follows:

> Then these people pulled up this big tree.

Thus the Armstrong-Curtin text (though it is not without problems) is comprehensible in the light of modern language study.

Seemingly unobtrusive in the preceding example, Armstrong's "it is said"—always unobtrusive in the Delaware text—becomes an impediment in English. A further example, not atypical, should make the point:

> When Moskim, it is said, was born, it is said the old woman was very glad, it is said.

Here, incidentally, is another of Armstrong's non-Iroquoian touches. The old woman's pleasure over Moskim's birth belongs to Algonquian, not Iroquoian, versions of the creation story. In Iroquoian tellings the grandmother usually favors the hero's troublesome brother and is never said to be "glad" when the hero is born. The detail, interestingly, is not included in Armstrong's Seneca telling or in his 1896 Delaware version. It appears only in the 1883 manuscript, which is also the only version that explains how Moskim received his name ("As for you, you'll be called Moskim, because the *móoshkiingw* likes to jump right out and creep into its burrow. From now on you'll be Moskim").

Overall, however, the Delaware manuscript of 1896 is superior to the 1883 text.[9] Its forty pages more nearly follow Armstrong's well-developed Seneca version, carrying the story beyond the hero's birth, covering his various adventures and the death of his younger brother. The four-page 1883 version, much shorter, stops with the birth of the hero and the establishment of the path of souls, and it omits the opening mind-guessing episode in the sky world. Moreover, it fails to include the origin of Ursa Major ("the Bear Followers, or Chasers") and the autumn-appearing Pleiades ("the Bunched Ones"). These and other, lesser details that are helpful for a full understanding of the story have been supplied from the 1896 Delaware version and enclosed in brackets. Note that nothing has been suppressed or reordered in the 1883 text. The translation of Armstrong's 1883 version, presented here, is complete and in sequence.

A point that is somewhat obscure in all three of Armstrong's dictations (including the published Seneca-language variant) is that the sky woman takes her shawl, or blanket, in her teeth so that she will have both hands free to support herself as she looks down through the sky hole. The important shawl holds her infant daughter, who must accompany her in her descent to the world below—because it is the daughter who will become the mother of Moskim.[10]

Notes

1. J. N. B. Hewitt, ed., "Seneca Fiction, Legends and Myths," in *Thirty-second Annual Report of the Bureau of American Ethnology, 1910–1911* (Washington DC: GPO, 1918), 48. ("American" was added to the Bureau of Ethnology's title beginning in 1894.)
2. Scraps of information on Armstrong and on Curtin are in Hewitt, "Seneca Fiction, Legends and Myths"; Hewitt, "Iroquoian Cosmology, First Part," in *Twenty-first Annual Report of the Bureau of American Ethnology, 1899–1900* (Washington DC: GPO, 1903); William N. Fenton, *The Great Law and the Longhouse* (Norman: University of Oklahoma Press, 1998), 38; Jeremiah Curtin, *Seneca Indian Myths* (New York: Dutton, 1923); National Anthropological Archives (NAA), Smithsonian Institution, photographic catalog, no. 947–i; and NAA MS 15, "Vocabulary of Delaware taken October 1896." The quotation "patient, kind, and interested . . ." is from Hewitt, "Seneca Fiction," 50.
3. In addition to Anthony F. C. Wallace, *Death and Rebirth of the Seneca* (New York: Knopf, 1970), 254–61, the references are Frank G. Speck, *The Celestial Bear Comes Down to Earth* (Reading PA: Reading Public Museum, 1945), 9–12; Ives Goddard, "Delaware," in *Handbook of North American Indians*, vol. 15 (Washington DC: Smithsonian, 1978), 214, 223–24; Goddard, "The Delaware Language, Past and Present," in *A Delaware Indian Symposium*, ed. Herbert C. Kraft (Harrisburg: Pennsylvania Historical and Museum Commission, 1974), 105; and C. A. Weslager, *The Delaware Indian Westward Migration* (Wallingford PA: Middle Atlantic Press, 1978), 163, 205.
4. John Bierhorst, *The White Deer and Other Stories Told by the Lenape* (New York: Morrow,

1995), 14, 85, 99; and Bierhorst, *Mythology of the Lenape: Guide and Texts* (Tucson: University of Arizona Press, 1995), 71–72.

5. Hewitt, "Iroquoian Cosmology, First Part," 242–43; John Bierhorst, *The Mythology of North America*, rev. ed. (New York: Oxford University Press, 2002), 218–20, 259.
6. Hewitt, "Iroquoian Cosmology, First Part," 233; Victor Barnouw, *Wisconsin Chippewa Myths and Tales* (Madison: University of Wisconsin Press), 14–15; Adriaen van der Donck, *A Description of the New Netherlands*, ed. Thomas F. O'Donnell (Syracuse NY: Syracuse University Press, 1968), 107–9; Margaret W. Fisher, "The Mythology of the Northern and Northeastern Algonkians," in *Man in Northeastern North America*, ed. Frederick Johnson (Andover MA: Phillips Academy, 1946), 232; William Strachey, *The Historie of Travell into Virginia Britania* (1612; reprint, London: Hakluyt Society, 1953), 102.
7. Curtin's *monenawáuwûl* is here taken to be a slip of the pen for *mokenawáuwûl*. Hewitt's 1896 transcription of the corresponding passage clearly has *k*.
8. The writing system used here has been taken from John O'Meara, *Delaware-English / English-Delaware Dictionary* (Toronto: University of Toronto Press, 1996). The same system, without the stress marks, was used in the Delaware Nation Council's *Lunaapeew Dictionary: Basic Words* (Thamesville ON: Moravian of the Thames Band, 1992).
9. The 1896 Delaware version is National Anthropological Archives MS 16, Smithsonian Institution, Washington DC. A philological study of this text has been promised by Ives Goddard, who has an English translation prepared in the late 1960s in collaboration with Anderson Pheasant of Moraviantown (Goddard, personal communication). The 1883 text is NAA MS 2204.
10. My reading of MSS 16 and 2204 is indebted primarily to O'Meara's *Dictionary*, which incorporates most of John Armstrong's creation-story vocabulary; and to Ives Goddard's *Delaware Verbal Morphology* (New York: Garland, 1979), which permits the analysis of Munsee verb forms.

Suggested Reading

John Bierhorst. "Tales of the Delaware Trickster." In *Coming to Light: Contemporary Translations of the Native Literatures of North America*, edited by Brian Swann. New York: Random House, 1994.

———. *Mythology of the Lenape: Guide and Texts*. Tucson: University of Arizona Press, 1995.

———. *The White Deer and Other Stories Told by the Lenape*. New York: William Morrow, 1995.

Goddard, Ives. "Delaware." In vol. 15 of *Handbook of North American Indians*, edited by William C. Sturtevant, 213–39. Washington: Smithsonian Institution, 1978.

Grumet, Robert S., ed. *Voices from the Delaware Big House Ceremony*. Norman: University of Oklahoma Press, 2001.

Kraft, Herbert C. *The Lenape-Delaware Indian Heritage: 10,000 BC to AD 2000*. N.p.: Lenape Books, 2001.

Weslager, C. A. *The Delaware Indians: A History*. New Brunswick NJ: Rutgers University Press, 1972.

MOSKIM

Told by John Armstrong

[Above the clouds they lived. The chief had his lodge in the middle of the village. He had a wife, and he had a child, a little girl.

One day he began to brood. He declared there was something unclean. He was jealous. He desired something.

Everyone tried to enlighten him. No one could guess what this chief might desire.

After a while, a man spoke up. He announced, "Now I really believe this might be what he wants. Perhaps he's thinking, 'I ought to pull up this tree of mine, then I ought to set it over there.' "

Then everybody came.]

Then these people pulled up this big tree. Then the ground fell out through the opening. All the people saw how the ground opened up, right while everyone was looking at it.

And the chief, too. He told his wife—he said, "Come on, let's go over to this hole, where everybody's looking!"

[Then the woman picked up her child and put the little girl on her back.]

Then they set off at once. They got there, and right away the chief looked into the hole.

Then he said to his wife, "Come on! You look, too!"

The woman said, "Alas! I'm frightened." "Come on now, take a look!" So the woman stepped forward, and she looked.

The chief said, "Look closely, get down there!"

She put her shawl between her teeth. [Then she took hold of the ground there, on the far side and on the near side.] She took hold on both sides—closed her fists on some huckleberry bushes with soil attached.

[Then she bent her head far down.] Right away the chief grabbed his wife and pushed her all the way in. Then the woman was really flying.

While they were traveling through the clouds, she met the fire serpent. He said to her, "You poor thing! I'm the one he's jealous of. That's actually why he wanted to kill you."

He put his hand in his side and took out some corn, an ear of corn—just one.

And a bone, a beaver bone. And a little kettle. And a mortar. And a little corn pounder. That might be all.

Then the manitous and spirit powers held council and said, "Who will watch out for this poor one?" [They said, "Maybe the sunfish?"

And he spoke up: "I can take care of that person!"

Then the others declared, "The sunfish couldn't take care of anything. He's an ugly one."

They said, "The pike fish. He could be the one."]

Then the pike fish spoke up: "I'm a good man. I could take care of her forever." The manitous answered, "Not you. You couldn't do it. You're too silly, too ill-tempered. You couldn't do it at all!"

Then next, the turtle—the good one—spoke up: "I can take care of that person forever."

"You're the one who can do it, all right." Then in fact he came over and raised his back, and the woman landed there.

Then, as she wept, she said to her child, "My little one, truly we are poor."

Then she saw that she had some dirt in her hands, and she let it fall to the ground. What she spread out there grew larger.

The more she spread it, the more it grew, and eventually it got much bigger.

Then it kept on growing bigger and bigger. [And before long this woman saw everything growing.] Eventually trees grew, and potatoes, and grass.

[And whatever this woman might say, that's what would happen. Before long she thought, "The sun! There it is!" And immediately it came about.

So there it was, the light of day. It walks the road each morning, that light of day.

Then she spoke again. "Well," she said, "There are stars, too." Then it really happened.

Then she used her hand and pointed to where the stars are. And she declared, "Now these are the Bear Followers—the Chasers. And these are the Bunched Ones—in wintertime, thanks to them, people will know how much of the winter has gone by."

Well then, the little girl was now grown.]

Now, this girl, as she went out to play, found some woods where she could swing.

When she grew tired, she would lie down.

It felt very good, because of the wind. [Now really, the way the wind was blowing she enjoyed it, and it made her feel as if it might be inside her.]

One day the old woman took a good look at her and wondered. She thought, "This daughter of mine looks pregnant."

Then she questioned her. She asked, "Didn't you ever see anyone? No one at all?" asked the old woman. But then it must have been so.

[Indeed, later on, twins grew in the belly of this girl.]

It was not long before these two—these twins—began to quarrel, arguing over which one would be born first.

The one who was in position to be firstborn spoke up and asked his younger brother, "Which way would you come out?"

"Right here at my mother's navel," he answered. Moskim said, "You'll kill our mother," and then he said to him, "From now on you'll be called Flint."

"So be it," said Flint. "As for you, you'll be called Moskim, because the *móosh-kiingw* likes to jump right out and creep into its burrow. From now on you'll be Moskim."

When Moskim was born, the old woman was very glad.

And then another one. And so Flint was born. [In fact, when he was born, he went straight out. He was born through his mother's navel. He cut through it.]

When Flint was born, the young woman died. Then the old woman cried.

When she had quite finished crying, the old woman dug a grave. As she laid her daughter's head toward the west, she spoke to her encouragingly.

[She made her daughter hear her.] She told her, "You are the first to go. [You prepare the road to the cold winds above the clouds.] Everyone will go when they've finished living here.

"That's where they'll go. Now you go first. That's where all will go. It will be that way forever here."

Two Animal Stories

Introduction by Robert M. Leavitt and Jennifer Andrews

"Cihkonaqc: Turtle" and "Espons: Raccoon" both explore the power of transformation and the danger of deception through stories about animals.[1] The narratives not only teach about the origins of specific physical traits that characterize the turtle and the raccoon, respectively, but also show how destiny and fate play an important role in the lives of these animals.

Told and written down in Passamaquoddy by the Honorable Lewis Mitchell of Pleasant Point in the late 1800s and published by John Dyneley Prince in his *Passamaquoddy Texts*, the two stories are traditional Wabanaki legends, translated here from Passamaquoddy into English.[2] The English translation follows the Passamaquoddy sentence by sentence in order to reproduce the original narrative as accurately as possible. The English version may seem slightly stilted or awkward in places because our primary concern is to replicate the stories precisely rather than to create an idiomatic English narrative. Most of the animal names in these stories were in Mi'kmaq in Mitchell's texts and in Prince's published versions; we have changed them to Passamaquoddy here.

Both stories appear in previous collections of Mi'kmaq narratives. For instance, "The Origin of the Turtle" appears in Spicer's *Glooscap Legends*, which brings together a selection of the most significant stories about Koluskap (GLOO-skahb).[3] Spicer's version, written in the past tense, is an abbreviated account of how Koluskap, while out hunting in Nova Scotia, visits and transforms his poor and homely uncle, Mikjikj (MEEK-cheekch: "turtle" in Mi'kmaq), into a handsome young man so that his uncle may win the love of one of the chief's daughters. Turtle, however, eventually removes the belt Koluskap has given him to complete this physical transformation and resolves to roam the world; in response Koluskap promises him that he will live on land and in water, surviving no matter how many times others attempt to destroy him.

The translation for this volume offers a more detailed and complex description of Turtle's transformation and the challenges he faces after successfully marrying the chief's youngest daughter, a beautiful woman, who is frustrated by her husband's laziness. Spicer presents Turtle as a virtuous and selfless older man who is unwilling to deceive a potential bride and be revealed for what he really is—an old, ugly man. The Mitchell/Prince version is less explicit in its moral message. Koluskap comes a much longer distance, traveling by canoe from Newfoundland to Pictou, Nova Scotia, to visit his uncle, who is known by the locals as a lazy and slow man. Some members of the community actually speculate that these qualities are inherited from Koluskap, which can be read perhaps ironically as exposing the shortcomings of this prominent culture hero as well as those of his uncle. Koluskap has been traditionally regarded as a prophet and protector of the Wabanaki people. He is responsible for creating the land and its inhabitants, bringing innovations to the population, distributing key survival elements (fish, hares, tobacco) around the world, mediating the weather, and generally transforming those who occupy the earth into their present forms. In this story he provides Turtle with the means to win a bride by giving his uncle not only the right material goods to attract a wife but also the promise that he will change his personality—from sweet and lazy to hardy and resourceful.

As the legend describes it, the transformation of Turtle requires several steps. As in the Spicer version, initially Koluskap gives his uncle a belt to help the older man attract a spouse at a local gathering. The belt makes him wonderfully handsome and gives him the status to ask the youngest daughter of the chief at Pictou to marry him, a union that makes the other men in the village jealous. Yet despite this outer change in appearance, Cihkonaqc's character remains the same: he is a lazy man whose behavior angers his wife.

Ironically, Koluskap and Turtle's mother-in-law are the only characters who hold out hope that he will eventually become a man worthy of his beautiful wife. The much more dramatic physical transformation of Turtle comes when he faces a series of attacks by the jealous men of the village. Koluskap arranges it so that in the process of these attacks, his uncle becomes the chief of the turtles: his skin is dried and hardened, scorched by smoke, and most of his intestine is removed. Though Turtle is initially wary of such alterations, he soon realizes their value. With Koluskap's help, he outwits his attackers on several occasions, even when he is thrown into fire and water. In turtle form, he not only survives but also thrives, returning to his wife a changed man.

His transformation teaches about unique physical traits of the turtle—a hard shell able to withstand fire and water, a heart that continues to beat after it is removed from the body, and a body that survives even after the head is cut off. Turtle becomes a highly flexible and adaptable individual whose hardiness secures his survival and justifies his marriage to the chief's daughter. Further, the turtle, with its withdrawn head, hard shell, and dried skin, though ugly, is revealed as a thing of beauty and strength, much like the lazy and slow-moving uncle, who is initially overlooked by everyone but Koluskap.

The conclusion of the story adds a comic dimension to the turtle's character and his relationship to Koluskap. After Turtle returns, he and his wife have a child, who cries when Koluskap eventually comes to visit. Though the chief of the turtles does not know the significance of his child's cries, Koluskap claims that the infant, in calling "wah wah" is making the sound for egg (*wawon*—WAH-w'n—in Passamaquoddy), a linguistic double entendre that links babies with eggs. Koluskap uses this information to instruct his uncle to dig in the sand and look for eggs, which he uncovers. This egg hunt based on the child's cries mocks the reproductive naiveté of male turtles, who do not know where the female's eggs are laid, turning the last section of the story into an elaborate joke in which Koluskap has the last laugh.

"Cihkonaqc: Turtle" combines a cautionary tale about the tendency to judge individuals too quickly and overlook their virtues with a demonstration of the powers of inner and outer transformations. Certainly, becoming a turtle gives Koluskap's uncle the ability to survive and thrive despite his rivals and justifies his marriage and his place in the community. But the rationale for Koluskap's transformation of his uncle, the story's depiction of the brutal behavior of the other men in the village, and the roles of destiny and fate in Wabanaki society all remain unexplained. The final humorous twist in the narrative exposes the male turtle's ignorance, providing a reminder of the limitations of Cihkonaqc's transformation; it is Koluskap who possesses the ultimate power and knowledge.

Similarly, "Espons: Raccoon" combines humor and an account of certain physical traits that characterize raccoons with an often ambiguous moral message. Raccoon has the ability to transform himself into whatever he wishes and uses his skills of deception to outsmart and destroy those animals that pose a threat or disobey him. Raccoon is first preyed on by Bear, who wants to eat him. In an ironic twist, Raccoon skins Bear and makes mittens out of the fur, which he then dons, and continues walking. The brutality of Raccoon's survival strategies becomes much more apparent in his subsequent meeting with a group of baby fishers, who eat the mittens. Raccoon angrily strangles the group, leaving only the youngest one (who cannot speak) alive, and then taunts their mother by positioning the dead fishers on the path, mouths propped open, to greet her. The raccoon's cruelty and dismissive treatment of the youngest fisher come back to haunt him when the child identifies the perpetrator by circling its eyes and mouth with charcoal. However, Raccoon manages to escape and moves on to inflict his wrath on two groups of women.

In these subsequent encounters, he mocks the slowness of human efforts to raise children and sew leather pouches. In both cases, he uses a mixture of sly rhetoric and a mocking tone to convince the women to speed up these processes of creation. He tells nursing mothers to submerge their children in icy water to raise them more quickly and shows them that placing their fine skin pouches on the coals will complete them without further effort. Although Raccoon is able to use his magical powers to make these shortcuts appear effective, when the groups of women actually attempt them, the results are disastrous. Raccoon successfully thwarts the efforts of both groups of women; he seems to take delight in the acts of destruction, moving from one to the next in rapid succession.

But the grimness of much of Raccoon's story is countered by the ending, where he makes the mistake of eating rose hips. Despite being told that they will make him itch, Espons goes ahead and indulges his appetite, with humorous results. The scatological dimensions of the narrative are made explicit through this encounter—the Passamaquoddy word for rose hips is literally "itchy-anus berries" —and thus the cocky raccoon gets what he deserves. The story offers what are typically described as "verification elements" by providing a narrative description that explains the physical appearance of raccoons. More than that, Raccoon's suffering, while minor compared to the fate of the baby fishers and the human children, becomes reparation for the damage he has cunningly inflicted on others. His rebellious assertion that he wants to itch is a form of sweet revenge, as he must live with a permanent mark of his arrogance and stupidity.

Like "Cihkonaqc: Turtle," the story of Espons the Raccoon is a cautionary tale that, though it lacks a clear moral message, demonstrates the problems with possessing magical powers but not knowing how to use them effectively. Moreover, the raccoon's transformations, his ability to deceive, and his success in manipulating others do not save him from his destiny: to be branded for life by a hairless behind. In contrast with Turtle, whose metamorphosis provides him opportunities to better himself, Raccoon uses his transformative skills to exploit the naiveté of those around him. As a pair of stories, the narratives of the turtle and the raccoon offer contrasting perspectives on transformation, destiny, and fate; both are framed by humor and remain enigmatic in terms of justifying the brutality of human and animal behavior.

Notes

1. Cihkonaqc is pronounced JEEK-nahkwch; Espons, ESS-p'nss.
2. See John Dyneley Prince's *Passamaquoddy Texts*, Publications of the American Ethnological Association, ed. Franz Boas, vol. 10 (New York: G. E. Stechert, 1921). Earlier versions of the present translations, along with the original Passamaquoddy in modern orthography, were published for educational use by the Wabanaki Bilingual Education Program, Indian Township, Maine, in 1976. The

present versions are included by permission of Wayne A. Newell, former director of the Wabanaki Bilingual Education Program and great-grandson of Lewis Mitchell.

3. See Silas Tertius Rand's *Legends of the Micmacs* (New York: Longmans, Green, 1894), and Stanley T. Spicer's *Glooscap Legends* (Hantsport NS: Lancelot, 1991).

Suggested Reading

Prince, John Dyneley. *Passamaquoddy Texts.* Publications of the American Ethnological Society, edited by Franz Boas, vol. 10. New York: G. E. Stechert, 1921.

Rand, Silas Tertius. *Legends of the Micmacs.* New York: Longmans, Green, 1894.

Spicer, Stanley T. *Glooscap Legends.* Hantsport NS: Lancelot, 1991.

CIHKONAQC: TURTLE

Written by Lewis Mitchell
Translated by Robert M. Leavitt

When Koluskap[1] leaves Newfoundland, he goes by canoe. He paddles to Pictou. When he arrives at the people's village, there he finds his uncle Cihkonaqc.[2] Cihkonaqc is extremely lazy and slow in nature. They say, "He must indeed be Koluskap's uncle." Others, however, think that it is a result of Cihkonaqc's upbringing. Nevertheless, he is so good natured that Koluskap has a fondness for him. He decides to transform him into a man of strong character.

When Koluskap arrives at Pictou, those living there number more than one hundred wigwams. Koluskap is very handsome, twice as fierce looking as a chief would be. He is well loved. There are few women who do not like him. Each one desires him to visit at her wigwam, but he refuses to see them. He stays with his uncle, the eccentric.

There is going to be big gathering complete with games, but Koluskap does not think he will attend the festivities. Still, he asks Cihkonaqc to participate. He tells him, "All the young girls will be there." He asks him why he isn't married. "You should not live by yourself."

"I am so poor, I don't even have one bit of clothing good enough for the festival. It is far better for me to sit at home and smoke."

"If that is all that is wanted," Koluskap answers his uncle, "don't worry. He who possesses supernatural powers thinks it an easy task to change mere clothing."

"Yes, my child," says Cihkonaqc, "but is it possible for you to change the insides of a person?"

"Well, now," answers the chief, "that is a difficult task. Before I leave this little village, I will do that. But for now, you will attend the games. Here, put on my belt."

As soon as he has put it on, Cihkonaqc becomes so handsome that no man or woman has ever seen the like. Koluskap dresses him in the finest clothing. He promises him that to the end of his days he will be handsomest of all men.

And so Cihkonaqc goes to the gathering. Now the chief at Pictou has three

1. GLOO-skahb.
2. JEEK-nahkwch, "Turtle."

very beautiful daughters, especially the youngest. That's the one Cihkonaqc sees. He goes back. He says, "I see the one I want." Now the youths at Pictou all want this girl. They'll kill the one who wins her.

Taking wampum, Koluskap goes to negotiate on behalf of Cihkonaqc. The mother accepts Cihkonaqc, and so the young girl arranges a bed of new fir boughs, spreading out a big white bearskin. She goes to Cihkonaqc, and they eat an evening meal of dried meat. In this way the couple is married.

Cihkonaqc is extremely lazy. While the others hunt, he just lies around at home. One day his wife says to him, "If you don't do something, we'll starve soon."

So he puts on his snowshoes. The woman follows him as he goes hunting—she wants to see what he does. He does not go far before he trips and hurts himself. Quickly his wife returns to tell her mother: "Cihkonaqc is a good-for-nothing."

But her mother says, "Later on he'll accomplish something. Leave him alone."

One day Koluskap tells Cihkonaqc, "Tomorrow everyone is getting together for a big ball game. You also must participate. Since all the young men here hate you, they will try to kill you. They'll pile up on you and trample you. When that happens, you will be near your father-in-law's *wikuwam*.[3]

"You will be able to escape them. I'll give you the power of supernatural illusion so that you'll be able to jump over the *wikuwam* twice. The third time, however, it will go badly, but this is the way it has to be."

All he is told happens. The young men do try to kill him. In escaping them he jumps over the *wikuwam* as a bird would swoop, but on the third time, he is caught on the *wikuwam* poles. There he hangs, furious, in the smoke. He is dried and hardened by the smoke rising from below.

Now Koluskap is sitting inside. He says, "Uncle, I'm going to make you chief, the great chief of the turtles."

He continues to cure Cihkonaqc. At last his skin is shriveled and hard: the scorch marks can still be seen today. Also, he cuts out his intestine, leaving only one short piece.

And Cihkonaqc yells out loud, "You've nearly killed me!"

But Koluskap replies, "That's not true. I am giving you long life. From now on you will be able to roll in the fire; you will be able to live on land and in the water. Even if your head is cut off, still you will live for nine days. And even your heart will beat for a long time after it is taken out."

Cihkonaqc is very happy at this. All that has been done to him he can now use.

In the morning all the men go hunting. Koluskap informs him, "They will look for a way to kill you."

3. WEE-goo-wahm, "house."

The young men walk ahead, and Cihkonaqc hangs back. But all of a sudden, he makes a magic flight. He soars unseen over their heads. Deep in the forest, he kills a moose. He drags it to the snowshoe path. When his enemies come along, there he sits, on top of the moose, smoking and waiting.

So it comes to pass that they hate him all the more. They resolve to kill Cihkonaqc and Koluskap.

When Koluskap is going to leave, he tells Cihkonaqc what they will do. "First of all, they will build a great fire. And then they'll throw you in. Uncle, go happily; with my great powers you shall not suffer. Then they will talk about drowning you. At that, stop them, saying, *Don't let it happen!* They will want to do it even more. Fight them. However, it will still happen."

What he says comes to pass. Cihkonaqc is pleased. He says adieu to Koluskap. The youths grab him and throw him into the fire. There he rolls over and falls asleep—he is lazy, after all. When the fire burns out, he wakes up; he asks for more wood, because the night is cold.

Again they seize him; they tell him they are going to drown him. That he is terribly afraid of. He says, "Don't let it happen! Better you should cut me to pieces than throw me in the water."

That is why they decide to drag him away. Then he shouts and struggles desperately. He uproots trees. He tears up rocks and roots like a crazy man. They load him into a canoe and take him out into the middle of the water. There they throw him in and watch him until they can no longer see him sinking.

In the morning it is quite warm. They see something moving on a big rock near the horizon. Two youths take a canoe and paddle out to see what it is. As they arrive, the wind picks up. On some big rocks, barely sticking up out of the water, there lies Cihkonaqc, sunning himself.

He sees them coming, and he knows they are after him. He bids them adieu, disappearing into the water heels last. Even today, all turtles, when they see someone, disappear into the water heels last.

Cihkonaqc rejoined his wife. They lived happily, and they had a child. It happened after a time that Koluskap went to see his uncle. The child was crying. "Do you understand what he is saying?" Koluskap is reported to have asked.

"No." Cihkonaqc yawned. "Perhaps he is speaking *musikisq*.[4] No ordinary man can understand it."

At that point Koluskap said, "He is talking about eggs. He's saying, 'Wah, wah.' That's what the Passamaquoddies still call an egg—*wawon*."[5]

4. MOO-zee-geeskw, "sky (language)."
5. WɅH-w'n.

Cihkonaqc said, "Where are they?"

Koluskap instructed him to dig in the sand, and Cihkonaqc found many of them. He liked the way they looked and looked at them curiously. Still, even to this day, turtles lay their eggs in the sand. This is how Koluskap jested.

ESPONS: RACCOON

Written by Lewis Mitchell
Translated by Robert M. Leavitt

One fine morning, Laks starts walking, having assumed the shape of a raccoon. When he used to roam the earth, he could change himself into many things. As he is walking, all of a sudden coming toward him is a large bear, Muwin.[1] He is very happy to see Espons.[2] Right then and there Muwin decides to kill him, if only he can manage it. First he will punish him for the many ways he has behaved—and besides, he is hungry. But Espons immediately starts running away and dives into a hollow tree. Muwin starts uprooting it. Espons knows that the tree will fall, and then he will get away. He bursts into song as if he were not worried about Muwin at all. "However much you dig and however much you push on this tree, you will not catch me. If you back in where I did, then you will get me, and I will die. But that you cannot do while the hole in the tree is small." When Muwin hears this, he believes him. However, he sees that he can easily enlarge the hole. When he goes in, Espons grabs him; he holds on to him until he is dead. Then he crawls out; he makes little bearskin mittens. And then he resumes his walk.

While he is walking along, suddenly there in front of him is a *wikuwam*[3] with smoke rising out of the chimney. He enters; there, inside, is a family of baby fishers. He talks to them pleasantly. He says to them, "Children, comb me. I will pay you with these bearskin mittens of mine." Then the little fishers comb him. They part his hair, and they blow on his tail. They groom him until he falls asleep. The little fishers are so hungry that they eat Espons's mittens. Scraping off the meat, they cook them and eat them. When Espons wakes up, he glares at them and yells at them angrily. "Where are my bearskin mittens?" he says.

They are frightened. "We cooked them and ate them," they reply.

Then Espons goes after them. In no time at all, he strangles every one. The youngest is the only one he does not get, but he does not know how to talk anyway, and Espons thinks he won't be able to tell what happened. He picks up the little dead fishers, and propping their mouths open with twigs, stands them up

1. MOO-ween.
2. ESS-p'nss, "raccoon."
3. WEE-goo-wahm, "house."

on the path where the big fisher will come along, so that she will think, "My little children are coming so happily." She hurries toward them. "How happy the little ones are to see me!"

When she approaches, none of them moves. Then she becomes suspicious, something is wrong. Quickly her thoughts change; she is grief stricken. But all of a sudden the youngest one hears his mother. He jumps out from a little hole. He is still too young to be able to tell what happened, but he is very clever. Grabbing a piece of charcoal, he marks himself around the eyes and around his mouth. "Aha!" says his father, Pokomk,[4] "I know that one. That's Espons!" Immediately he starts chasing after him.

Soon Pokomk overtakes him, looking extremely angry. He swings a club as a man would. Espons looks at him. "Ah," he says, "but a club cannot kill me. A cattail is what will kill me."

Pokomk knows just where to go for them: he heads down toward the swamp, gathers a few, then strikes Espons as hard as he possibly can. The cattails break apart on impact, and the fuzz runs down over Espons's head and sticks where it is wet. But Pokomk thinks, "That is Espons's brain that I have splattered." Only then does he leave. Espons lies there perfectly still until Pokomk is gone; then he also leaves. He was a great *motewolon*,[5] but there were few he treated kindly.

As he goes on, he comes to a place where many women are nursing children. He tells them, "How terribly slowly you raise your children. Where I come from, we raise them fast."

The good women say to him, "How then are we to raise them?"

"Well, I will tell you what we do. When we want them to grow fast, we soak them in the water all night. Here, lend me one. I'll show you what to do if you want to raise them quickly."

They give him one. He takes it to the river. He chops away the ice and puts the child in. In the morning he gets him. When he pulls him out, the women are truly surprised at the wonder of his accomplishment. That night, every one of the women puts her little child into the river. At that point, Espons hurriedly departs. But the children's eyes turn white with the cold. They all die.

Again, he comes to another *wikuwam*, where there are many women. Using fine skins, they are making pouches. He says to them, "How very slowly you make these. In our homes, we roll them in ashes. Here, give me the material you are using, and I will teach you."

They give him one. He puts it in the hottest, glowing part of the ashes. After

4. b'-G'MK, "fisher."
5. m'-DEH-w'-l'n, "person with extraordinary powers."

a few breaths, he pulls it out. It is a well-made and beautifully designed pouch. Now they are tempted into doing it. So all of them roll theirs in the ashes too. When they take them out, every one is shriveled and burnt to a crisp. They have ruined them all. And again he goes on his way.

Eventually he comes to a big river. He does not know how he is to get across. Looking along the riverbank, he sees a giant slug, Wiwilomeq,[6] lying stretched out—he looks like a big alligator. He is blind. Espons says to him, "Grandfather, take me across."

"Of course, my grandson, get on my back." Then he starts swimming. The crows and the big ravens begin to laugh at him. "What are those birds saying?" asks Wiwilomeq.

"They say, 'Hurry, go fast with that raccoon if you want to save your life.'" Wiwilomeq does not see the land in front of him. Rushing along, he runs aground; he plunges halfway into the riverbank. Espons jumps off. He departs in great haste.

Going along, he comes to a blackberry patch. He says to them, "How would you affect me if I were to eat you?"

"We would affect you badly, Espons, because we are all chokeberries."

"Uh-oh, I don't want you."

Continuing on his way, he finds some rose hips. "How will you affect me if I eat you?"

"We will make you itch for sure; we are all itchy-anus berries."

"Ah, that is exactly what I want," he answers. He eats. At last he eats his fill. Off he goes. Suddenly he begins to feel sick, as if something were piercing him. And he starts to scratch himself, but it does not help. At last he finds a rough rock; there he rubs back and forth until all the hair comes off his backside. Still today it can be seen that the raccoon has no hair on his rear end.

And that's the end of him.

6. wee-WEEL-megw.

Social and Ceremonial Songs

Ann Morrison Spinney

The Passamaquoddy people are Eastern Algonquians, residing in the area that is now eastern Maine, part of their traditional homelands. There are two federally recognized Passamaquoddy reservations: Sipayik (Pleasant Point) near Perry, Maine, and Motahkomikuk (Peter Dana Point) near Princeton, Maine. Culturally, the Passamaquoddy people are very closely related to the Maliseet people, who reside further inland in what is now New Brunswick and Quebec; they share a language (Passamaquoddy-Maliseet), though there are dialect differences between Passamaquoddy and Maliseet communities. As the Eastern Algonquian identity suggests, the life ways of Passamaquoddy and Maliseet groups are (and historically seem to have been) similar to those of some of their neighbors, while distinct from those of the Iroquois nations. Historically, both Passamaquoddy and Maliseet communities have been politically allied with the Penobscots and the Abenakis to their west and with the Mi'kmaqs further east. These five groups were part of a historical Wabanaki Confederacy that is also an active political force today.

The confederacy, recognized by the French around 1700 but based on older alliance networks, established protocols for ceremonies of alliance that required chants, songs, and dances.[1] These protocols are shared among the member nations, but each nation has its own distinctive versions of the songs. Historical evidence suggests that the songs and dances may be older than the confederacy itself.

The ceremonies are described in the Wampum Records, a history of the confederacy and record of its protocols that was memorized by a designated person in each community. Mnemonic belts were woven of blue and white wampum beads both to preserve the general protocols and to commemorate particular historical occasions.[2] These Wampum Records were recited or "read" publicly on important occasions and at least once annually. The Passamaquoddy version of the Wabanaki Wampum Records has been translated and published by Robert M. Leavitt and David A. Francis (1990). The chants and songs for some of the ceremonies were included on field recordings made by William Mechling, Frank Speck, Nicholas Smith, and others over the course of the twentieth century.[3]

The wampum protocols are still used in the ceremonies of the Wabanaki Confederacy and on other political and social occasions in Wabanaki communities, such as the installation of a tribal governor and council, weddings, and intertribal meetings. The Passamaquoddy versions of the songs and dances have been maintained over the centuries and are presented in a public educational program at the annual Ceremonial Day (some call it Indian Day) at Sipayik and Motahkomikuk. The songs and dances are integral parts of the Wampum Ceremonies, so the singers and dancers enact the ceremonial function by performing them.

Five ceremonial dances are associated with the Wampum Ceremonies: the Welcome Dance between tribes, the Greeting Dance between leaders, the Peace Pipe Ceremony Dance and the War Club Dance performed by the councilors, and the Marriage Dance. The first four ceremonies form a sort of complex. Marriage was included in the Wampum Records protocols; marriage can be understood as a political ceremony, particularly when it takes place between persons of different communities, which helps to strengthen alliances. In addition, social dances typically are done between the ceremonial dances. Today these include old-style dances such as the women's shawl dance Tuhtuwas as well as round dances and other Intertribal-style dances.

Descriptions of ceremonial dances like the ones performed for the Wampum Ceremonies can be found in the earliest records of Europeans visiting Wabanaki areas, before the Wabanaki Confederacy had been recognized. Jacques Cartier described a welcoming protocol performed by people he encountered on the Gaspé Peninsula.[4] Champlain described dancing done by men at a war council supper during a campaign against the Iroquois in 1603 that is similar to the form of the modern Peace Pipe Ceremony Dance (Champlain 1922, 1:98–103).

Changing cultural circumstances and individual taste have introduced changes into the Passamaquoddy repertory of ceremonial songs and dances. The most common means of transportation between communities is now the car rather than the canoe—although for the past four years the Sipayik Ceremonial Day weekend has been opened by the arrival of canoes carrying visitors from Motahkomikuk who have paddled down the Saint Croix River and around Passamaquoddy Bay. Rather than being held outdoors, even the ceremonies involving the whole community are now frequently performed indoors in school gymnasiums and community centers during inclement weather and the colder months. But the songs remain remarkably consistent in key melodic formulas (e.g., opening motives) and in text to those recorded nearly a century ago. Since field recording was not available before 1890, and since few observers were inclined to notate the melodies of the chants and songs, we can only extrapolate from the past century of evidence the integrity of the wampum ceremonial tradition over the previous decades and centuries.

The songs have been adapted to several different performance styles. The old recordings include accompaniment with a shot-horn shaker, struck on the ground or a board to keep an underlying, flexible duple pulse over which the lyrics are sung—often freely and with a swinglike feel.[5] Singers agree that some sort of drummed accompaniment is needed for singing; some historical accounts mention striking birch-bark rolls or the ground. Today most singers in the traditional style use a hand-held frame drum with a single head, struck with a beater. Some traditional songs are also sung around the powwow-style stationary drum, beaten "in unison" by a group with beaters. This changes the rhythm, making it more deliberate. The traditional style of singing is with a relaxed, open tone, often in the lower range known as "chest voice." In this feature as well there is a marked contrast with powwow-style songs.

The versions presented here are traditional-style renditions from the repertory of Joseph A. Nicholas of Sipayik, Blanche Sockabason, and Wayne A. Newell, both currently residing at Motahkomikuk. Joseph Nicholas is a former Passamaquoddy representative to the Maine state legislature. In the mid-1960s Nicholas worked with Mary Moore to establish a group at Sipayik dedicated to maintaining the songs and dances and to presenting public cultural programs to educate surrounding communities. Working with the Catholic Diocese of Maine, he presented the first public Ceremonial Day in 1965. (Catholic missions began in the early 1600s, and the Native communities' subsequent demands for Catholic priests gave the church its first establishment in Maine.) Later Nicholas helped establish a tribal museum at Sipayik and has advised and taught generations of scholars. Blanche Sockabason is Joseph Nicholas's cousin and has been the lead singer at the Sipayik Ceremonial Day for the last ten years. She has participated in state and federal traditional-arts programs and has advised outside scholars. Wayne Newell was raised at Sipayik; he often sings with Sockabason and has been involved in documenting Passamaquoddy culture for decades. He has assisted scores of outside scholars researching Passamaquoddy culture. He is also an educator and primary school administrator at Motahkomikuk and has been elected to the tribal council several times. A former deejay, Newell is often asked to emcee events as well as to sing.

Passamaquoddy songs and ceremonies are a living tradition. Those presented here are used today within the community. It is from use that they derive their meanings, and this leads to several points. First, attempts at out-of-context representation will always be to some degree misrepresentations. Musical transcription and textual translation can never substitute for the performance. Further, every performance will be different due to contextual differences; the extemporization by singers to suit each occasion highlights this. Finally, the material here is not intended as directions or "scores" for outside performance. Misuse of traditional songs, chants, and ceremonies can be dangerous—as an elder once remarked, it would be like trying to say the Catholic Mass when you are not a priest. Anyone who works with musical transcription knows that it is a rough tool and is limited by its purpose. Our purpose here has been to give outlines that show the structures of the song melodies and that are graphically easy to apprehend even for those who do not read music. The meaning of these songs—whatever power or spirit or aesthetic pleasure a listener/reader gets from them—lies in the way that a singer literally brings them to life in each performance.

Despite many political and social pressures, many Passamaquoddy families and community leaders have taken steps to combat the loss of cultural traditions and of the language. Although some previous generations considered it a handicap to teach children the Native language, today many families encourage its use, and those adults who were not taught Passamaquoddy have learned it as a second language. Still, the majority of fluent speakers are over age forty. Passamaquoddy songs generally have lexical texts, and the placement of syllables in relation to pitch and rhythm is crucial to intelligibility and usefulness. Songs for children's games thus help to teach fluency in the language.

Ironically, one of the biggest challenges to traditional songs and dances today comes from the more widely popular Intertribal styles. Young people growing up in urban or mixed-heritage environments tend to have more exposure to these genres, which do not have language barriers and are less bound by specific traditional rules. In the Passamaquoddy community, Intertribal song and dance styles have been accommodated in some of the Wampum Ceremonies by including them in alternation with or following the prescribed songs and dances. A clear distinction between the two musical styles is maintained, however.

Many Passamaquoddy families who had to move away from the traditional homeland to make a living returned after federal recognition was achieved in the 1980s. The summer Ceremonial Days bring many others back to participate in the dances and traditional arts. The reservation schools incorporate Native language and cultural programs, and among the most successful and visible activities at the youth center are dancing and drumming groups. Amid the struggles for legal recognition, for sovereignty, for economic survival, for access to spiritual sites, for repatriation of ancestors' remains and ceremonial objects, the maintenance of traditional ceremonies with their dances and songs continues across generations.

Songs for the Greeting Dance of the Wampum Ceremonies

"E, Qanute" is a version of the formal Greeting Chant, sung and danced between the host governor (*sakom*) and a visiting tribal governor. Like many Passamaquoddy ceremonial chants, it is in two sections: a slow first section during which the ceremonial action is accomplished, then a fast section in which the leaders dance to celebrate their greeting.

The Passamaquoddy Wampum Records describe this ceremony as follows, from the perspective of a Passamaquoddy delegation going to a Mi'kmaq community:

> When the messengers come to the country of the Micmacs, and the Micmacs see a canoe coming carrying a flag, they understand what it means. Then the chief gathers his soldiers. He says to them, "Those who are coming arrive here as messengers."
>
> Then all of them—children and women and men—walk down the hill to greet them. At last they land. Then one of the messengers steps ashore and immediately sings a greeting song to them. Then he walks back and forth between their lines greeting them. Finally, he finishes singing. Then the Micmacs—one of their councillors goes out from shore and answers his brother, and he makes a greeting. (Leavitt and Francis 1990, 41)

The choreography of the dance done today is as follows: host and visiting delegations line up facing each other, then dance forward and backward in line during the Welcome Dance, while the *sakomak* stand one at each end and dance in place. During the Greeting Dance, the delegations stand or sit down, still in line, while the host *sakom* dances slowly toward the visitor. The step is of the "stomp dance" type: each foot is lightly touched to the ground once or twice before the dancer steps out on it. The host speaks a formal welcome, bestows a gift, then dances slowly backward to his place at the end. Then the visitor dances slowly toward the host, repeats the formal greeting, and may bestow a reciprocal gift. After he dances slowly backward to his place, the singers begin the fast section, and the two *sakomak* dance in the center in celebratory freestyle.

The current Passamaquoddy form of the Greeting Dance is remarkably similar to that described by Speck's elderly Penobscot informants as part of intertribal visits in the nineteenth century (Speck 1997, 289–91). Descriptions by other ethnographers of intertribal welcoming protocols in Mi'kmaq and Maliseet communities are also consistent.[6]

The contemporary Passamaquoddy chant for the slow section is quite similar to Greeting Chants recorded by Speck and others among the Penobscots and the Maliseets nearly one hundred years ago.[7] The melody takes the form of a verse, repeated as necessary. It is in two parallel phrases or sections, descending overall (fig. 1). The version given here is one sung by Blanche Sockabason. Some singers

Greeting Dance: First (Slow) Section

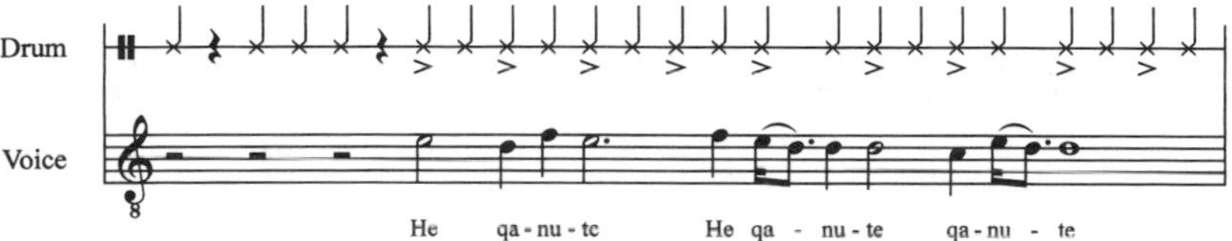

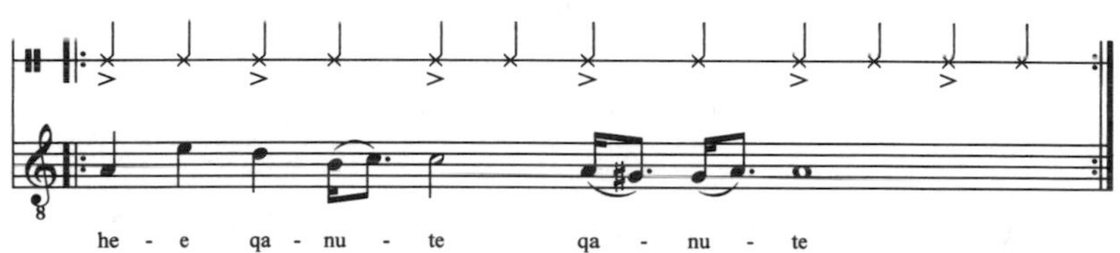

The whole song repeated as necessary to accompany the Dance.

1. Greeting Dance: First (Slow) Section

add elaborations to the ending phrase. Nicholas Smith (1955, 32) reported that the *sakom*'s ceremonial songs could be sung by a proxy, which is often how this chant is handled today. Its slow speed and the many repetitions seem to be markers of the prestige of the participants and the solemnity of the occasion.

The text of the Greeting Chant repeats the phrase, "He qanute, qanute." The word *qanute* is described by singers as "not a real word" or "a chant word." It seems to be an archaic ceremonial word but also can be parsed as something like "let's do the Welcoming Dance." This same word, or particle, is also found in some chants associated with the Longhouse Ceremonies of the Seneca.[8] It may be associated with political interaction between the Wabanaki and Iroquois groups.[9]

2. Greeting Dance: Second Section

The songs for the celebratory dancing in the second section are typically extemporized to existing dance melodies. The example presented here is an excerpt from a performance by Wayne A. Newell, who provided the translation. In performance several songs are strung together to form a suite, lasting as long as is necessary or desired (fig. 2).

Memkiskahk maqayapasuwok skicinuwok
Qe ha wa ni ho
Psiteya wolapewultowok
Qe ha wa ni ho, qe ha wa ni ho.

Translation:

> Today all the Native people are gathered
> *Qe ha wa ni ho*
> Everyone looks good
> *Qe ha wa ni ho, qe ha wa ni ho.*

According to Joseph Nicholas, the melody often used (given here) is also associated with a song about an important historical event: the forced removal of the Passamaquoddy people from Saint Andrews, New Brunswick. His grandmother used to sing it:

> Qonasqamki monihkuk, weci macehay,
> *qe ha wa ni hu, qe ha wa ni hu, qe ha wa ni hu*

Nicholas's translation:

> Saint Andrews Island they left, because . . . (phrase left unfinished)
> *qe ha wa ni hu, qe ha wa ni hu, qe ha wa ni hu*

The text is cryptic and fragmentary; it seems to be a coded reference that members of the community would understand, but outsiders would not. This melody is often used to extemporize new words for dance songs (i.e., to make contrafacta). Although it is not possible to determine whether the melody is older and the short lyrics about Saint Andrews were set to it, or whether the melody and lyrics came about together, the association of this melody with the Saint Andrews lyrics keeps the memory of removal in the minds of ensuing generations of dancers. Turning a song about a community tragedy into a dance melody accomplishes a kind of poetic resistance to the injustice.

Tuhtuwas (Little Pine Tips)

Tuhtuwas is a women's dance song (fig. 3). Today it is used at formal events such as the installation of a tribal governor (Sakomawkan) as well as at social events; at a Sakomawkan, the women's dance signifies their approval of the leader. This was a feature of historical installations as well.[10] The melody given here is strongly identified with the Passamaquoddy communities and has been used to set other texts about contemporary issues (to create contrafacta). The dance is typically performed with a shawl draped over the shoulders and seems to belong to the general category of women's shawl dances that are found throughout Native North

Tuhtuwas Dance Song

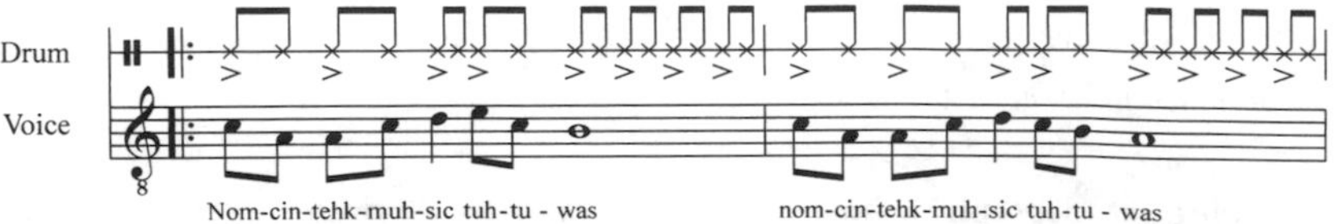

3. Tuhtuwas Dance Song

America. It is performed by women, who move in line tracing a circle clockwise around the dancing area. The step is of the "stomp dance" type, which is here somewhat of a misnomer as each foot is lightly touched to the ground before the dancer steps out on it. As is traditional with Passamaquoddy women dancers, the movements are conservative.

The tune again takes the form of paired phrases forming each verse and each refrain. The melody is repeated but can be altered slightly at the singer's preference. Sometimes on subsequent verses, Blanche Sockabason has altered the intervals on the syllables *-tehkmusic* to move the song into a European major modality from the minor modality. (The European major and minor modes are not functional in Passamaquoddy songs; we are only drawing an analogy.)

The lyrics to this song give the dancers directions; thus in order to dance well, the dancers must understand the language. The name indicates that the women in their shawls look like the tufted tips of pine branches dancing in a breeze. Rather than giving direct commands to the dancers ("dance sideways"), the singer asks them to create the illusion of pine tufts dancing. This version is sung by Joseph Nicholas, who also provided the translation.

Tuhtuwas is a very graceful dance, unless the singers sing very fast for the verse "Have it dance faster!" when confusion and hilarity can ensue. As with other traditional Passamaquoddy social dances, the lyrics are partly extemporized and often respond to the dancers and what they are doing. In *Penobscot Man*, Frank Speck (1997, 183) described a game of bouncing pine tufts on a board that had a similar song. However, the women's dance seems to have been used in ceremonies when their presence was important, such as immediately after the installation of a tribal governor. It is almost an Honor Song, honoring Passamaquoddy women.

Typical lyrics for the Tuhtuwas Dance might go:

Verse 1: Nomcintehkmuhsic tuhtuwas
Nomcintehkmuhsic tuhtuwas
Refrain: Qe he wa ne hu, qe he wa ne hu,
Qe he wa ne hu, qe he wa ne hu (vocables)
Verse 2: Kiwtahqessossic tuhtuwas . . .
Verse 3: Wiwonihtehkmusic tuhtuwas . . .
Verse 4: Sehtahtehkmuhsic tuhtuwas . . .
Verse 5: Kakawtehkomusic tuhtuwas!

Translation:

Verse 1: Have it dance sideways, the little pine tip tuft
(Refrain)
Verse 2: Have it spin from side to side, the little pine tip tuft
(Refrain)
Verse 3: Have it dance around in a circle, the little pine tip tuft
(Refrain)
Verse 4: Have it dance backward, the little pine tip tuft
(Refrain)
Verse 5: Have it dance FASTER, the little pine tip tuft!
(Refrain)

Song of the Drum

"The Song of the Drum" seems to be associated with a *motewolon*, a person with spiritual power. It was originally published by John Dyneley Prince in 1901, from the collection and perhaps the repertory of Lewis Mitchell, a prominent and learned Passamaquoddy elder. Prince published the song text without any musical notation, though he used notation for some other songs. If he knew of a melody, he may have opted to protect it, as this is a powerful text. One singer expressed the opinion that this is the traditional Passamaquoddy concept of drumming, comparable to the "heartbeat of Mother Earth" that is popularly referenced today. Anthropologists would class a *motewolon* as a shaman, a human being who can use power but is not himself good or evil. Speck translated the term as "Drum Sound Person" (1919, 241). Passamaquoddy elder and linguist David A. Francis points out that the particle *-ol-* or *-ul-* literally means "beaten hollow thing." The distinction between drums and drumming (with hands or other instruments) is important, as the historical and oral records show that in Passamaquoddy communities drumming was often performed by striking shakers on the ground, by beating on a roll of birch bark, a board, or some other resonant object. Francis corrected and updated Prince's transcription, producing the modern Passamaquoddy version and its translation presented here.

Pronunciation Guide for Passamaquoddy Transcriptions

A, AH as in English "father"; AY as in "aye"; AW like *ow* in "owl"
C voiced as English J; unvoiced as *ch* in "chop"
E as in "bed"; EH as *a* in "apple"; EW like "elder"
H as in English
I, IH as in "ski"; IW like *ew* in "dew"
K voiced as English G; unvoiced as K
L as in English
M as in English
N as in English
O is the schwa sound, as in "apron"; OH as in "go." The appearance of in the middle of words is dictated by the grammar.
P voiced as English B; unvoiced as P
Q voiced as English GW; unvoiced as KW
S voiced as English Z; unvoiced as S
T voiced as English D; unvoiced as T
U, UH as in "blue" (without diphthong)
W as English, except in combination with vowels as listed here
' (apostrophe) makes an initial consonant voiceless; otherwise, initial and single consonants are voiced, and consonants next to other consonants are unvoiced.

SONG OF THE DRUM

By Lewis Mitchell
Translated by David A. Francis

Nil nulopin naka ntotolitehmen pokuhulakon.
Nil ntotoli wiqtahan weyossisok . . .
pemotonek naka ona peciw wucowsonol n'ciksitmakon n'pokuhulakon.

Nulopin naka ntotolitehmen pokuhulakon.
Peciw mecikiskak petagik ntasitemgok pokuhulakonok
naka na kci Apolahsomwehsit cenisu 'ciksotomon npokuhulakon.

Nulopin naka n'pokuhulakon.
Nitte Cipelahq naka n'ciksotomakun npokuhulakon.
Eltaqak pecite kci Wocawson 'conekehla unoski
naka 'ciksitomon eltaqak npokuhulakon.

Nulopin naka n'tokotomon npokuhulakon.
Peciw te Lumpeqinuwok moskapasuwok naka 'ciksotomoniyia
    npokuhulakon
naka na Atwosskonikess conaqtihike naka 'ciksotomon n'pokuhulakon.

Nulopin naka ntokotomon npokuhulakon
naka kci Aputamkon
muskessin tehna nekom 'ciksotomon npokuhulakon.

Pesahqetuwok, petakiyik, wucowsonol, mecikiskakiyil,
Atwosskonikess, Apolahsomwehsit, Lumpeqinuwok, Cipelahq,
nipsiu macc petapaouwok naciciksotomoniya eltaqahk npokuhulakon.

Translation:

I sit down and I am beating the drum.
I am drawing[11] them in . . .
and even the winds listen to my drum.

I sit down and I am beating the drum.

Even storm clouds[12] and thunder reply with their drums;
and more, Apolahsomwehsit the great whirlwind stopped and listened to my drum.

I sit down with my drum.
And Cipelahq (that great monster) listened to my drum.
The great Wind Bird, making noise, suddenly stopped moving its wings
and listened to the sound of my drum.

I sit down and I am striking my drum.
Even the water creatures[13] rise out[14] of the water and listen to my drum
and more, Atwosskonikess[15] stops chopping and he listens to my drum.

I sit down and I beat my drum and the great sea serpent Aputamkon[16]
he also comes out, he listens to my drum.

Lightnings, thunders, winds, storm clouds,
Atwosskonikess, whirlwind, water creatures, Cipelahq;
they begin to come to me, following[17] the sound of my drum.

Notes

1. Regarding the history of the confederacy, see Bourque (2001, 173–75, 235–44).
2. See Speck (1919).
3. See Mechling (1911); Speck (ca. 1905–11); Smith (1951–59).
4. See Biggar (1924, 49–53).
5. See the description of rhythm in Speck (1997, 274).
6. See Wallis and Wallis (1955, 184–89).
7. Speck collection PR 66b, PR 72, PR 18.
8. See Fenton (1942).
9. See Bourque (2001, 173–75, 235–44).
10. See Brown (1892); and Speck (1997, 240–42).
11. *wiqtahan:* lit., "hooking them in."
12. *mecikiskak:* lit., "bad weather."
13. *lumpeqinuwok:* lit., "creatures that live under water."
14. *moskapasuwok:* lit., "they start coming out."
15. Prince says this is "an invisible being who roams the forest armed with a stone hatchet with which he occasionally fells trees with a single blow" (1901:386n4). David Francis says the word means "caterpillar" or "inchworm." Wayne Newell suggests it is an earth creature that is coming out like the water creatures in the previous line.

16. David Francis says the name means "his face is turned inside out," i.e., is concave. Prince says this is a "bugaboo" with long red hair that lived under the water, invoked to frighten children (1901:386n4).
17. "mace petapasuwok naciciksotomoniya": lit., "they start walking over here, they change direction [to] listen to it."

References and Suggested Reading

Bourque, Bruce. 2001. *Twelve Thousand Years: American Indians in Maine.* Lincoln: University of Nebraska Press.

Biggar, H. P. 1924. *The Voyages of Jacques Cartier.* Publications of the Public Archives of Canada, no. 11. Ottawa: F. Acland.

Brown, Mrs. W. Wallace. 1892. "'Chief-Making' among the Passamaquoddy Indians." *The Journal of American Folklore* 5, no. 16:57–59.

Champlain, Samuel de. 1922. "Des Sauvages." In *The Works of Samuel de Champlain, in Six Volumes,* ed. H. P. Biggar, vol. 1: 1599–1607, trans. and ed. H. H. Langton and W. F. Ganong, 83–189. Toronto: Champlain Society.

Fenton, William. 1942. *Songs from the Iroquois Longhouse: Program Notes for an Album of American Indian Music from the Eastern Woodlands* (booklet and audiocassette). Smithsonian Institution Publication 3691. Washington DC: Smithsonian Institution.

Fewkes, J. Walter. 1890. "A Contribution to Passamaquoddy Folk-lore." *The Journal of American Folklore* 3, no. 11:257–80.

Havard, Gilles. 1992. *La Grande Paix de Montréal de 1701: Les voies de la diplomatie franco-amérindienne.* Montréal: Recherches Amérindiennes au Québec.

Leavitt, Robert M., and David A. Francis. 1990. *Wapapi Akonutomakonol / The Wampum Records: Wabanaki Traditional Laws.* Fredericton: Micmac-Maliseet Institute, University of New Brunswick.

Mechling, William Hubbs. 1911. Field recordings. Saint Mary's NB, Collection III-E-1.1-46, Canadian Museum of Civilization

Prince, John Dyneley. 1901. "Notes on Passamaquoddy Literature." *Annals of the New York Academy of Science* 13:381–86.

Smith, Nicholas. 1951–59. Penobscot, Passamaquoddy, and Maliseet songs, recorded at Woodstock, Tobique, Kingsclear NB, Old Town ME. Collection III-E-2, Canadian Museum of Civilization.

———. 1955. "Wabanaki Dances." *Bulletin of the Massachusetts Archeological Society* 16, no. 2:29–37.

Speck, Frank. Ca. 1905–11. Field recordings. Cat. no. 60-018-F, Archives of Traditional Music, Indiana University.

———. 1919. "The Functions of Wampum among the Eastern Algonquian." *Memoirs of the American Anthropological Association* 6, no. 1:3–71.

———. 1997. *Penobscot Man.* Philadelphia: University of Pennsylvania Press, 1940. Repr., Orono: University of Maine Press.

Wallis, Wilson D., and Ruth Sawtell Wallis. 1955. *The Micmac Indians of Eastern Canada.* Minneapolis: University of Minnesota Press.

Traditions of Koluskap, the Culture Hero

Introduction by Philip S. LeSourd

The best-known figure in the oral literature of the Maliseet Indians of New Brunswick and Maine is undoubtedly Koluskap, who shaped the landscape, tamed the wind, reduced the size of the once ferocious beaver and squirrel to manageable proportions, and generally served as a benefactor to all the Wabanakis, the Algonquian peoples of northern New England and Maritime Canada. Long ago Koluskap left to establish a home for himself at the end of the earth. It is said that he lives there today, but that he will return to help the Wabanakis if the need should arise.

Koluskap is a figure of the type that anthropologists call a culture hero: a character whose exploits have formed the basis for a large number of tales that have been told and retold in countless versions, sometimes with a moral or instructional purpose, sometimes just for fun. As is typical for such characters in Algonquian traditions, however, Koluskap is not always portrayed as heroic in the conventional sense of the term. In particular, he can be a trickster. Indeed, the literal meaning of his Maliseet name is "Liar."

Traditions of the Wabanaki culture hero among the Mi'kmaqs, the northern and eastern neighbors of the Maliseets, were documented in the nineteenth century by Silas T. Rand in his *Legends of the Micmacs*.[1] Specifically Maliseet accounts were collected in New Brunswick in the early years of the twentieth century by W. H. Mechling.[2] The story of Koluskap is known to the general public, however, primarily through the collection of Wabanaki legends published by Charles G. Leland in 1884, which includes both Mi'kmaq material that Leland obtained from Rand and tales that he collected himself among the Passamaquoddies of eastern Maine, who speak essentially the same language as the Maliseets, and among the Penobscots, a linguistically distinct group whose territory lies to the southwest of Passamaquoddy country in Maine.[3]

Leland's work is still of considerable value, since he recorded many tales that might otherwise have been lost. He had little personal knowledge of the languages and cultures of his consultants, however, and his accounts of Koluskap's adventures are not always reliable. As Thomas C. Parkhill has demonstrated in detail, some of the narratives that Leland presents as if he had taken them down directly from his Indian consultants are actually compilations of material derived in part from secondary sources, and Leland reshaped a number of the stories to fit his own conceptions of what an Indian tale should be.[4] He was also convinced that the traditions of the Wabanakis were historically connected with those of the Norse. Not surprisingly, then, the style he adopted in recounting Koluskap's adventures sometimes owes more to the Norse sagas than it does to the Wabanaki oral tradition.

John Dyneley Prince's *Passamaquoddy Texts*, published in 1921, includes several accounts of Koluskap's adventures in the Passamaquoddy language, together with English translations.[5] Prince's Passamaquoddy consultant was Lewis Mitchell (1847–1931), a well-respected member of his community with extensive personal knowledge of Wabanaki traditions. As it happens, however, all the manuscripts that Mitchell originally wrote for Prince were destroyed in a fire at Prince's home in 1911. Mitchell then recreated the texts at Prince's request. Mitchell had in fact served as one of Leland's consultants and was clearly familiar with his work. When he was called upon to rewrite his accounts of Koluskap's exploits, he appears to have turned to Leland's published accounts as his guide. As a result, many of the texts that Prince ultimately published are essentially translations into Passamaquoddy of Leland's English renderings of Wabanaki tales.[6]

The Maliseet language is spoken today on five reserves in New Brunswick, located along the Saint John River at Tobique (near Perth-Andover), Woodstock, Kingsclear, Saint Mary's (opposite Fredericton), and Oromocto. Another small reserve, known as Saint Basile, is located at Edmundston, New Brunswick; but there are reportedly no Maliseet speakers living there today. An additional reserve at Viger, Quebec, is now depopulated. The language continues to be spoken, however, by members of the Houlton Band of Maliseet Indians in Aroostook County, Maine, and by Maliseet residents of the Penobscot reservation at Old Town, Maine. Passamaquoddy is spoken on two reservations in Washington County, Maine: Pleasant Point, near Eastport, and Indian Township, adjacent to Princeton. English has made inroads into the use of the traditional language in all the Maliseet and Passamaquoddy communities, however, and most of the fluent speakers of either dialect are now over forty years old. Recent estimates place the total number of speakers at around five hundred, a minority of the population.[7]

The four stories included here reflect Maliseet traditions concerning Koluskap as these were recounted in the 1960s and 1970s. All of them were told in Maliseet by Peter Lewis Paul of the Woodstock reserve, who was born in 1902 and died in 1989. Paul recorded three of the tales, given here as "Jack-in-the-Pulpit," "Koluskap and Baby," and "Wishes Granted," for the linguist Karl V. Teeter during the summer of 1963. He recorded "Koluskap and Turtle" and a second version of "Wishes Granted" for the present writer at Indian Township, Maine, in 1976.[8]

Paul was widely recognized in his community as an expert on the traditions of the Maliseets.[9] Both his mother and a twin brother died shortly after his birth. His father then left him in the care of his maternal grandmother, who was still nursing a child of her own. As Teeter has noted, Paul's upbringing gave him a knowledge of the language and the customs of the Maliseet people that was "a generation deeper than that of his contemporaries."[10]

Paul's paternal grandmother was white, and his relatively light complexion earned him the nickname "White Pete," by contrast with his uncle Peter Polchies, who was known as "Black Pete." Despite the nickname, however, he never regarded himself as anything but Maliseet. At an early age, he developed an avid interest in the history and culture of his people and an intense affection for the Maliseet language. He generously shared his knowledge of Maliseet traditions with several generations of linguists, anthropologists, and historians. In honor of his efforts to preserve knowledge of the language and culture of the Maliseets, he was awarded an honorary doctorate by the University of New Brunswick in 1970 and was elected to the Order of Canada.

The translations given here for the stories that Paul recorded for Teeter are based on the latter's notes from his subsequent work on the texts with Paul, carried out at intervals between 1963 and 1978, and on additional material provided by Paul's daughter Carole Polchies of Woodstock. The two texts that Paul recorded in 1976 have been translated in consultation with Anna Harnois and Estelle Neptune of Indian Township, Maine.

Paul's stories presuppose a traditional Maliseet view of the world, one that recognizes the existence of many beings of great power. Some of these can be helpful, like the *kiwolatomuhsísok*, or "little people." It is these creatures, Paul explained, who fashion the clay concretions that one finds along the banks of streams, forming them into shapes that provide signs of things to come. Other powerful beings are dangerous. Among these are the *kiwahqíyok*, or cannibal giants of the northern forests, who have ice around their hearts and shriek as they travel.

Certain individuals (by some accounts, all indigenous people) are endowed with a power that allows them to accomplish extraordinary feats. A man or a woman who has learned to wield this power is known as a *motewolòn* (pl. *motewolònuwok*). Such individuals can use their power to clear the sky of clouds or to call up a storm. They can help their friends or injure their enemies by thought alone. *Motewolònuwok* will typically walk off out of sight before employing their power, however, with the result that their methods remain shrouded in mystery. On the other hand, a *motewolòn* may choose to display his or her power by walking along stepping ankle-deep in the ground. Paul noted that a sufficiently powerful *motewolòn* can even leave tracks in solid rock. "I suppose he gets heavy with power," Paul remarked.

The most powerful *motewolòn* who has ever lived is Koluskap. Even Koluskap's power is not without limit, however. Like any *motewolòn*, Koluskap will sometimes exhaust his resources. He must then rest and wait for his power to return. At such times, he is vulnerable to attacks by his enemies. One of the most formidable opponents that he ever faced is the evil Pukcinsqehs, or Jug Woman, who figures prominently in Paul's story "Jack-in-the-Pulpit." She was a powerful *motewolòn* in her own right, capable of transforming herself at will into any of variety of shapes. Although Koluskap was ultimately able to defeat her, he could not destroy her. Instead, she transformed herself into the mosquito so that she could continue to torment humanity.[11]

The stories presented here were among Paul's favorites, and he clearly took great pleasure in telling them, even for visiting linguists. Several of them include slightly off-color elements, in which Paul took particular delight. It should not be supposed, however, that Paul intended his stories solely as entertainments, even though he found it hard to keep from laughing out loud as he delivered some of the lines. Indeed, all but one of the texts ends with a statement of a lesson that the tale is meant to teach. Paul commented explicitly on this point (in Maliseet) after he told the last story given here: "Young people are to learn from this that you shouldn't ask for something that won't do you any good."

A final word is in order on the nature of these stories as performances. A comparison of the two versions of the last tale included here, "Wishes Granted," is instructive in this connection. The first version, which Paul recorded for Teeter in 1963, provides little more than a summary of the main incidents of the narrative. Events are presented in a straightforward, linear fashion. Paul is also somewhat circumspect here about the more off-color parts of his story, very likely as a reflection of the fact that he recorded this text during his first season of work with Teeter, whom he did not yet know well. The second version, which Paul recorded for me in 1976, includes more descriptive detail and a more elaborated account of the action of the story. The narrative shifts back and forth among the characters in a way that serves to build suspense. Paul is less circumspect here as well, perhaps because he had already known me for some time as one of Teeter's students. Thus the second version of this tale probably provides a closer approximation to the way Paul would have told it in a more natural setting. Even so, when he and I were discussing the story after he had recorded it, he indicated that he had toned down the ending to make it more respectable for anyone that I might have occasion to play the recording for. It did not take much persuading to convince him that there was real value in recording the story as he had actually heard it. So he recorded the ending a second time the way it should *really* be told, chuckling all the while. I have appended this second ending after the first. I would like to think that this final passage brings us one step closer to hearing Paul's voice the way his family and friends were privileged to hear it.

A Note on Pronunciation

Maliseet words are given here in their usual spellings in a practical writing system that is now widely used by native speakers. The vowels of the language are *a* (as in "father"), *e* (as in "bed"), *i* (as in "machine"), *o* (as in "apron," or like the *a* in "about"), and *u* (as in the American pronunciation of "sue"). The letter *c* is pronounced much like the *ch* in "church," while *q* has the sound of *qu* in "squeal." Between vowels, however, *p*, *t*, *k*, and *q* are pronounced like *b*, *d*, *g*, and *gw*. Maliseet is a pitch-accent language, in which each word must be pronounced not only with the proper pattern of stressed and unstressed syllables, but with the right "tune." The acute written over a vowel letter indicates that the corresponding syllable is stressed and pronounced at a higher pitch than surrounding syllables. The grave accent indicates a relatively low-pitched stressed syllable. Koluskap's name, for example, is pronounced *Koluskàp* in Maliseet, with stress and low pitch on the word-final syllable.

Notes

1. Silas Tertius Rand, *Legends of the Micmacs* (New York: Longmans, Green, 1893).
2. W. H. Mechling, *Malecite Tales* (Ottawa: Government Printing Bureau, 1914).
3. Charles G. Leland, *The Algonquin Legends of New England or Myths and Folk Lore of the Micmac, Passamaquoddy, and Penobscot Tribes* (London: Sampson Low, Marston, Searle & Rivington, 1884).
4. Thomas C. Parkhill, *Weaving Ourselves into the Land: Charles Godfrey Leland, "Indians," and the Study of Native American Religions* (Albany: State University of New York Press, 1997).
5. John Dyneley Prince, *Passamaquoddy Texts* (New York: G. E. Stechert, 1921).
6. Prince gives an account of the loss and re-creation of Mitchell's manuscripts in the introduction to his *Passamaquoddy Texts* (2–3), but he does not seem to have recognized the relationship between Mitchell's reconstructed manuscripts and the texts that Leland had published, claiming instead that Mitchell's texts had been "reproduced at my request from memory."
7. Robert M. Leavitt, *Passamaquoddy-Maliseet* (Munich: Lincom Europa, 1996), 1.

8. The titles, it should be noted, have been supplied by the present writer. Maliseet storytellers often begin their tales with an indication of the nature of the material to follow, but they do not ordinarily give titles to their stories.
9. Much of the information concerning Peter Paul's life that is given in this paragraph and the next is taken from an interview recorded by Harald Prins and Bunny McBride, included in Karl V. Teeter, ed., *In Memoriam Peter Lewis Paul, 1902–1989* (Hull QC: Canadian Museum of Civilization, 1993), 7–18, or from other contributions to the same volume.
10. Teeter, *In Memoriam*, 3.
11. A version of the story of Pukcinsqehs derived from Passamaquoddy sources is given by Leland (*Algonquian Legends*, 44–50).

Suggested Reading

Leland, Charles G. *The Algonquin Legends of New England or Myths and Folk Lore of the Micmac, Passamaquoddy, and Penobscot Tribes*. Boston: Houghton, Mifflin, 1884.

LeSourd, Philip S., ed. *Tales from Maliseet Country: The Maliseet Texts of Karl V. Teeter*. Lincoln: University of Nebraska Press, forthcoming.

Mechling, W. H. *Malecite Tales*. Canada Department of Mines and Geological Survey Memoir 49. Ottawa: Government Printing Bureau, 1914.

Parkhill, Thomas C. *Weaving Ourselves into the Land: Charles Godfrey Leland, "Indians," and the Study of Native American Religions*. Albany: State University of New York Press, 1997.

Prince, John Dyneley. *Passamaquoddy Texts*. Publications of the American Ethnological Society 10. New York: G. E. Stechert, 1921.

Teeter, Karl V. *In Memoriam Peter Lewis Paul, 1902–1989*. Canadian Ethnology Service Mercury Series Paper 126. Hull QC: Canadian Museum of Civilization, 1993.

TRADITIONS OF KOLUSKAP, THE CULTURE HERO

Told by Peter Lewis Paul
Translated by Philip S. LeSourd

Koluskap and Turtle

Long ago, they say, a festival was going to be held somewhere. It was going to be quite an event. All the Indians were getting together. They were going to play ball and even hold races and jumping contests—just about everything. It would be lots of fun. Finally Koluskap wanted to go, too. He wanted to go and look on. But then Turtle wanted to tag along as well.

For Turtle, after all, is Koluskap's mother's brother. And it is because Turtle is Koluskap's mother's brother that the turtle carries the months of the year on his back. There are thirteen new moons in a year. The way the Indians count out a year is thirteen moons. So on a turtle's back there are thirteen round bones. Five are grouped together in the middle, and there are four on either side. So there are thirteen in all.

So Koluskap and Turtle set out to go and look on with the others. Koluskap said to Turtle, "Are you going to join in? You can join in the races, or the jumping, or anything else you would like to take part in. And I'll help you. But don't go beyond what I give you the power to do."

"Of course not," he replied.

So then they arrived at the place where everything was going on. When they first saw the place, it seems that the Indians there had killed a whale. They were wondering how they were going to be able to drag it ashore. There weren't enough people there to move this whale.

Now Turtle was always trying to act like a tough guy. So he told them, "Oh, I can carry it up the hill all by myself."

One of the Indians said, "Who the . . . Oh, sure you can! When you're so small!"

"Oh, but I can! Just wait for me for a little while."

So then he left for the place where Koluskap was staying. "What is this that you're going to do?" Koluskap asked him. "You're going to carry this whale up a hill?" Then he told him, "*Well*,[1] you'll be able to do that. But don't carry it any

1. Paul slipped into English momentarily here. Annoyed with himself, he muttered, "'Well' again!"

farther than I tell you. And I'll tell you how far you should carry it. Don't go any farther."

Then he told him how far he should carry it. After that, Turtle went back. When he arrived, they were waiting for him. How could he carry it, when he was so small? It was so big!

But then he crawled in under the whale. And he started to carry it, and everyone was cheering. They were really impressed with him for being so strong.

After that, he forgot where he was supposed to put the whale down. He went farther than he had been told to go. And then, because the whale was too heavy for him, it pinned him right here on the ground.

The people were waiting for him to come out. But he didn't come back out into sight, this vanished turtle. Finally they slid the whale off at one end. Here he lay, sticking out from beneath it. "What happened to you?" someone asked him.

"All of a sudden," he said, "as I was going along carrying the whale—all of a sudden I started to feel sleepy. So I thought, I'll just doze off for a moment."

The people believed him. But as for Koluskap, he just wanted to laugh. He knew that Turtle was lying.

Next some of the other Indians were taking part in other contests. Turtle went to watch the people who were jumping hurdles. Nearby Koluskap was sitting in the lodge where he was staying.

Once the jumping was finished, Turtle went over to the site of the contest. As for him, he could jump over whatever they had not been able to jump. "Even if it were twice as high as that," he told them, "I could jump over."

Then they raised the bar where they had been jumping. Sure enough, he sailed right on over. "That wasn't worth it," he said.[2]

He wanted to do something even more impressive. So he told them, "I can jump over this lodge here."

"So jump over, then!" someone told him.

"Just a moment while I go inside here," he replied. Then he went in where Koluskap was sitting.

Koluskap told him, "This is what you've done. You've told these people that you'll jump over the lodge where you were. I've told you not to do it, not to try to jump over." Then he told him, "Well, go ahead and jump. But don't jump over right in the middle. Along the side somewhere."

2. The meaning of the quoted material here is uncertain. Other consultants translate the verb that Paul uses in this sentence as "he hasn't been paid" and attribute this statement to one of the onlookers, rather than to Turtle. This interpretation does not appear to fit the sense of the story, however.

So Turtle was very happy, and out he went. He went on back. He ran. And then he jumped. But he chose exactly the point where the lodge was highest. And these poles were sticking out. He jumped up right toward that point. In the end, he didn't jump high enough. This one pole that was sticking up speared him right in the butt. He just hung there wiggling his legs. They finally had to take the lodge apart pole by pole to get him off.

"What happened to you?" someone asked him.

"Just as I was about to jump," he told him, "a dog ran across my path, and I tripped over it. That's why I got myself stuck on the pole here when I landed."

Koluskap just wanted to laugh. He knew that Turtle was lying again. Koluskap told him, "This should teach you not to do more than you've been told that you can."

Jack-in-the-Pulpit

Long ago, after he had been traveling around and helping the Indians, Koluskap grew tired. Then he went to take a nap on an island, to rest. But Pukcinsqehs (Jug Woman) was always watching him wherever he went, and she envied him.

"Now I'll get the best of him," she thought. So she stole his canoe and paddled across to the mainland, leaving Koluskap behind on the island. As she hurried away, she was thinking, "Now I'll be able to turn the people against him, these people who think so highly of him."

When Koluskap woke up and looked around, his canoe was gone. Someone had stolen it. Right away, though, he knew it was her work. "It's that Pukcinsqehs. She is always out to get me, and she's the one who has stolen it from me."

So he called a fox to him. "Help me to get across," he told him. He grabbed the fox by the tail, and the fox swam across. Koluskap held onto his tail. At last they arrived on the other side. There was his canoe. From there he set out to track Pukcinsqehs.

So then he pursued her. He traveled on and on. Finally, she must have sensed him as she walked on, up ahead. Then Pukcinsqehs had to run, leaving her children behind. So Koluskap found them first.

"I had better burn them up," he thought to himself, "so that they will never again go about doing evil in the world."

Sure enough, he burned up Pukcinsqehs's children. That is why Pukcinsqehs-child (jack-in-the-pulpit root) is a good medicine now, when it is cooked. But if it is eaten raw, it will kill you.

Koluskap and Baby

Long ago, they say, Koluskap had stretched out to sit on the ground. Through his superior power, he had conquered all his adversaries, the cannibal giants and the *motewolònuwok*, even the wind. He had defeated them all. So as he sat there by the fire, he said to himself, "I guess there just isn't anything that I wouldn't be able to conquer."

A woman heard him, they say. "Oh, but there is," she told him. "There is still one adversary whose power you have not overcome. And you never will."

"Tell me about it, then," he said. "What is it? Or who is there who has such great power?"

"It is Baby," she told him. "Baby you will never conquer. Just try your strength with him."

So then Koluskap said to Baby, "Come here. Come to me."

Baby was sucking on a bit of maple sugar. He went on sucking at it and just looked at him. Then he laughed.

Again Koluskap said, "Come here. Come over here where I am."

Baby paid no attention to him. He just laughed a little, all the while sucking on the maple sugar.

Then Koluskap did his best to make his voice sound like a baby's. He tried to sound nice, so that Baby would mind him. Still Baby just looked at him. He wouldn't mind him.

By this point Baby was making Koluskap a little angry. So he shouted a little. He hollered at him. Then Baby cried. He made a great noise with his crying.

Then Koluskap tried to calm him. But no, he couldn't do anything with him. Finally he thought, "I'll try a little of my power on this Baby, so that—so that he'll mind me." In the end, oh, he tried all kinds of things. But Baby just looked at him and laughed. Instead of minding him, he just looked at him as if he thought we were funny.

Koluskap tried everything, even the power that he had used when he conquered the great *motewolònuwok*, the cannibal giants, the wind, and the fierce storms. Nothing worked with Baby. He just sat there and laughed.

"This Baby seems to have defeated me," said Koluskap. "I don't know how to take care of a baby, since I've never been married." Indeed, a baby will always get the best of us.

Wishes Granted (first version)

They say that Koluskap lives at the end of the earth, wherever that may be. You can ask him for anything, they say, and your wish will be granted. Once three men decided to go. They went to ask him for favors. One wanted to live forever. Another wanted to be a lucky man all the time. Another wanted women to love him.

Finally they set out. It took them seven years to get there. When they came to their destination, where Koluskap lived, they stopped. One walked up to the house. As he walked up to the door, he heard someone say, "Why have you come, wanting to see me?"

"I want to live forever," he answered.

"Then so shall you receive."

When the next one went up to the door, he was asked, "What is it that you want?"

"I want to be a lucky man at all times," he replied.

"Just so shall you receive."

Then the next one . . .[3] When the next one came to the door, he was asked, "What will it be for you?"

"I want women to love me all the time," he answered

"So shall you receive."

Then out came Koluskap. His face looked just like rock, like ancient rock, covered with moss.

To the one who wanted to have a long life, he said, "You come with me." So the man went with him, the one who wanted to live forever. As they walked out onto a point of land, Koluskap told him, "Stand right here." Then he took him by the neck and by the leg, and he twisted him. And there stood a huge tree, the sort of tree that has an exceedingly twisted grain. "There," he told him. "No one will ever cut you down. You will never be of any use. You will just go on growing."

Then he went back again and told the others, "You two go on now." So then they started off. And they had traveled only seven days, they say, when they were home again.

When they got to their homes, one went out hunting right away, the one who had wanted to be lucky. He just walked out in back of his home, and there stood a deer. He shot it right there. From then on, he could shoot game right there in back. Right in back of his house.

As for the one who wanted women to love him, just as soon as they walked into their village, the women ran right out to him. They threw their arms around his neck. He could not even sit down. The women struggled together over him, each trying to pull him away from the others.

Time went on, and the women went right on treating him this way. He couldn't

3. Here Paul was interrupted for a moment when the telephone rang.

even go off anywhere by himself to shit or to piss. No matter where he went, the women pursued him. In the end, he didn't live very long. They killed him, those women of long ago.

Wishes Granted (second version)

Once, long ago, three men went to look for Koluskap. They went to seek his help. For they say that when Koluskap was leaving, he said, "If someone among you ever truly desires my help, have him look for me, and you will find me."

Finally, they say, three men set out to make the trip. They traveled and traveled, until finally seven years had passed. Then they came to a place where the land stretched out into the sea. There, off in the distance in an open area, stood a little house. When they came close to it, they stopped, and then they called out to whoever might be there inside. "Hello!"

In just a little while, out stepped some person. His whole face was like something made of rock, and there were even strands of moss growing out from a crack in the rock. This, they say, was Koluskap.

"I know why you have come," he told them. "Would I be able to help you in some way?"

"Yes," they told him.

One of them stepped forward. "I want to live forever," he told him.

"Certainly," Koluskap told him. "So shall you receive. Come. Come with me."

He led him off to a point of land. "So! Stand right here!"

He took him by the head, and then here, about where he wore his belt. And at that point he twisted him. And when he let go of him, here stood a tree, one that was terribly crooked. Its grain was bad, and it was full of knots. No one would cut it down for any purpose. Nor would you be able to get anything useful from it if you wanted to use it for firewood. That's what this big tree was like. "Well!" he told him. "This is where you will stand now. You will be here forever. You will never die."

Then he went back to where the other two were standing. Another of the men stepped forward. "As for me," he told him, "I want all women to love me."

"Oh," Koluskap told him, "that's easy. So shall you, too, receive. What about you?" he asked the third one, still standing at a distance.

"As for me," he told him, "I want always to be lucky. Whenever I go out hunting, I want to be lucky. That is what I want."

"That, too, is easy," he told him. "You shall both receive just as you have wished."

"When you go back," he told them, "do not walk in the direction from which you came." Then he pointed off in the distance. "You should go in that direction. Then you will arrive at the place from which you set out."

Sure enough, they started out. Then, they say, after seven days, they suddenly came walking in, here where they had set out seven years before. As soon as someone saw them coming, all the women came out in a mob from the village. Right away they ran up to greet him, the one who had wanted to be loved. They surrounded him, kissed him all over, and even made love to him fiercely.

But the other man walked straight on. He finally arrived at his home. There had been no food there for a long time. His relatives could scarcely live. So he picked up a gun . . .[4] Then he went out to hunt for meat. As soon as he stepped out behind his little house, there stood a deer. He shot it right there, and it fell down. Then he skinned it. It had a lot of meat on it. From that time on, whenever he went hunting, he made a kill right away. It was just the same when he went trapping. He soon collected a lot of hides.

But as for the other man, the women still loved him passionately. He couldn't go anywhere by himself. They would always follow him around. Finally, as time went on, he grew weary of them. He just couldn't get them to stop. They still loved him just as intensely as before. Eventually he began to grow ill. He couldn't go anywhere alone. He always had a crowd of women around him. As time went on, they finally did him in. The mob of them rode him to death, these women did. That was the end of him.

≈≈≈

Now this is how I heard the story told about the third man, the one that the women loved to death. Wherever he went, they say, that's where the women went. They followed him, and he couldn't go anywhere to take a shit or to take a piss. He couldn't get rid of the women. After some time, he finally died from needing to shit or died from needing to piss!

4. Realizing that the man in question could not have owned a gun at the time when his story is set, Paul stopped the tape recorder for a moment here, muttering that he should have indicated instead that the man had arrows and a bow.

The Great Fire

Introduction by Franziska von Rosen

It was a July afternoon in 1991. During a filming session for *Micmac Storyteller: River of Fire*, Michael William Francis (1923–95) spoke about the importance of the environment for lending credibility to his stories. Mike, a Mi'kmaq elder, was sitting on the beach looking out at the calm waters of the Northumberland Strait. Flocks of tiny sandpipers were darting among the flotsam and jetsam, while in the distance gannets hovered, eyeing the waters below for signs of mackerel.[1] "They'll want to see the atmosphere," he said, "see the environment, such as water, sun and all that stuff, goes along with the story; that's what they want: to prove what I am saying" (von Rosen and Francis 1991, videocassette). For Mike place and stories are indivisible: the land gives his stories their authority, the stories in turn re-create the land, as he experiences it.

From 1985 to 1993 I spent a few months each year working with Mike and members of his extended family on documenting stories. Mike was born in Big Cove, New Brunswick, the fifth child of a family of seven. At age five, Mike and his two remaining siblings (others had died) left the reserve to live in transient work camps with his father, grandfather, and a few other men from Big Cove. The men were making axe handles for the Canadian National Railway. Mike's grandfather did all the cooking in camp, and at night he would tell stories around the campfire. Sometimes drifters would stop at the camp and bring stories as well.

Here Mike learned his wealth of stories.[2] They included the myths about the origin of the Mi'kmaqs and the initial birth and deeds of some of the powerful spiritual beings (Mi'kmwesu, Tune'l, Kluskap). There were also stories that tell of the Vikings, of tribal and intertribal histories (wars with the Mohawks and the Wabanaki Confederacy), of contact and conflict with the Europeans, of local histories (hunting, shipbuilding, working in lumber camps; stories about gatherings and celebrations).

Then there were the family or personal histories (life stories and family anecdotes). Mike's memory encompassed five generations (including his own) of the Francis family. He knew of Brown's Yard, just up the Richibucto River, where great-great-grandfather Peter Andrew Francis (born circa 1780) freed the Mi'kmaq "slaves" from the British "pirates." He also learned humorous and satirical stories, ghost stories, devil stories, and spiritual experience stories. Finally there were the stories inspired by radio, television, or books that Mike retold in ways that reflected his personal values and philosophy.

In Big Cove the telling of stories was a family event, and stories would be passed on from one generation to the next within the extended family circle. Ektaanuk, the sand-dune island at the mouth of the Richibucto River, was Mike's favorite place for storytelling. There, in a simple shelter made of driftwood and seaweed, Mike and his family would often spend their summer months. Evenings they would sit around the campfire and listen to Mike tell his stories. Jesse Simon, Mike's great nephew, remembered one such event:

> Most of the legends that I heard were from Uncle Mike. In one particular moment we were at Ektaanuk, a little island right off the Atlantic Ocean, and all seventeen of us [Simons] were there. One moment I remember is near a fire; we were all sitting on the rocks. Everybody was quiet. We could hear the waves crashing between the rocks and Uncle Mike talking in pitch darkness. His cigarette lighting up every time he takes a puff. And one [story] in particular is the Lobster and the Eel. It was so cool 'cause we were by the ocean, hearing the crashing, and I was visualizing the lobster flapping his tail and making that big noise. And today I try and remember that legend, and I even tell it to my nephews and nieces. (von Rosen and von Rosen 1995, videocassette)

The Great Fire story had a special significance for Mike. At the time we recorded it in the summer of 1991, I had not heard him tell it before, nor did I find any written records of it. In the introduction to his English translation of the Great Fire story, Lorne Simon, Mike's nephew explained the importance of this tale.

> The [Great Fire] story is of particular importance to the people of Big Cove because it deals with a mystical aspect of our heritage.[3] Also it should be of interest to all people who live within the Richibucto River area. The story explains the origin of the name Richibucto. The French pronunciation of the word is a corruption of the original Mi'kmaq place name, Lsipogtog, which means "The River of Fire." The river is named after Egjipogteo, the Great Fire.

When we discussed the making of the *River of Fire* video, Mike suggested that it should start with a sunset followed by the telling of the Great Fire story. Both suggestions were surprising for me. I had thought that Mike would want to start with a sunrise,[4] but as he explained to me, in the beginning there are no stories. First there has to be experience, and then there are stories for people to tell.

So in the summer of 1991, Mike sat on the beach in his blue and green plaid shirt with a baseball cap pulled low over his curly head of hair, faced our video camera, and told the Great Fire story in Mi'kmaq. He would have preferred to tell it in English.[5] Mike's first concern was with passing on the stories to the next generations. In Big Cove in the 1990s very few young people, including Mike's own grandson, were fluent in their Native tongue. Mike wanted his grandson, Cory, to carry on the storytelling tradition, so communication became more important for him than maintenance of the language. The other difficulty was that none of us on the beach that day understood Mi'kmaq, neither the film crew nor the members of his family. Mike liked having a responsive audience to perform for. He spoke of "polishing" his stories to make them "go right," to make them "sound good" (*welta'q*). This meant that he consciously varied his tempo, intonation, pitch, and dynamics over a wider range than during normal speech. He also used repetition and parallelisms to emphasize key passages and miming of different voices and actions to make his characters come alive.[6] So Mike was somewhat reluctant to tell the story in Mi'kmaq that day.[7]

Having the Great Fire story translated into English proved to be a difficult task. We asked Mike to help, but he was too much of a storyteller. Instead of translating the old story, he always launched into new ones. We then engaged the help of a Mi'kmaq translation service. They had a great deal of difficulty with the text, not only because Mike had a slight speech impediment, which made him difficult to understand, but also because he used words that were not familiar to them.[8] Finally it was Lorne Simon, Mike's nephew, who offered to translate the story. Not only had Lorne grown up hearing Mike's stories, but he was also a storyteller and writer.[9]

Here then is the story of the Great Fire as told by Michael W. Francis and as translated into English by his nephew, Lorne Simon.

Notes

1. See von Rosen (1992) for a more detailed analysis of the making of *Micmac Storyteller: River of Fire*.
2. The Mi'kmaq have two kinds of stories: the *a'tnutmaqn*, which are the old legends as they have been passed through the generations, and the *aknutmaqn*, which are historical events or news (Michael W. Francis, conversation with the author, July 15, 1989).
3. The Big Cove reserve is situated approximately thirty-two kilometers upstream from the mouth of the Richibucto River.
4. The Mi'kmaqs are also known as the Wapanaki, meaning people of the sunrise.

5. I asked Mike to tell the story in Mi'kmaq, for language educators had made me aware of the need for Mi'kmaq language material in the schools.
6. See von Rosen (1994) for a more detailed analysis of Michael W. Francis's storytelling style.
7. The next story that we recorded that day was in English, and Mike gave a more animated performance knowing that we understood what he was saying.
8. The Mi'kmaq translation service in Truro, Nova Scotia, suggested that the difficulties they encountered could have been due to regional language difference as well as the use of specialized vocabulary for storytelling.
9. Lorne died in a fatal car crash in 1994 just when his first novel *Stones and Switches* was being published by Theytus Books.

References and Suggested Reading

Parsons, Elsie C. 1925. "Micmac Folklore." *Journal of American Folklore* 38:55–133.

Rand, Silas T. 1894. *Legends of the Micmacs*. New York: Longmans, Green.

Simon, Lorne. 1994. *Stones and Switches*. Penticton BC: Theytus Books.

von Rosen, Franziska. 1992. "Micmac Storyteller: River of Fire—The Co-creation of an Ethnographic Video." *Canadian Folk Music Journal* 20:40–46.

———. 1994. "Thunder, That's Our Ancestors Drumming." In *Canadian Music as Culture: Issues of Hegemony and Identity*, 557–79. Toronto: Canadian Scholars' Press. Revised Master's paper.

von Rosen, Franziska, and Michael Francis. 1991. *Micmac Storyteller: River of Fire*. Thirty-four-minute 8mm videocassette. Lanark ON: Franziska von Rosen.

von Rosen, Franziska, and Douglas von Rosen, dirs. 1995. *River of Fire Festival: Celebration of Life*. One-hour 3/4" videocassette. Ottawa: Pinegrove Productions.

Wallis, Wilson D., and Ruth Wallis. 1955. *The Micmac Indians of Eastern Canada*. Minneapolis: University of Minnesota Press.

Whitehead, Ruth Holmes. 1988. *Stories from the Six Worlds: Micmac Legends*. Halifax: Nimbus Press.

THE GREAT FIRE

Told by Michael William Francis
Translated by Lorne Simon

Long ago the Mi'kmaqs had camps all along the Richibucto River, from the place today known as Big Cove to the breakwaters. One day a young man left his camp. After nightfall he walked to the river and followed the shore. As he walked along, he saw a fire glowing in the distance. The fire was extremely bright. He walked to the fire. He intended to play with the fire.

When he got to the fire, he found that it was actually a glowing rock. The rock was so radiant that it almost blinded him. He seized the rock and held it in his hands for a long time. Then he decided to take it home.

An old man sat inside a birch-bark wigwam. The elder told the people around him, "A boy is coming toward us. He is bringing something that is extremely bright. It is dazzling."

When the young man got close, the rock illuminated the whole village.

One youth sprang to his feet and said to himself, "Let me seize that fire! Let me steal it from him!" When the youth grabbed the rock, fire consumed his hands and almost entirely burned his garments. The rock dropped to the ground. The young man who had first found the glowing rock raised the rock from the ground and held it high in his hands again.

The elder told the young man, "Dim the fire a bit, for it is too brilliant." The young man cupped the rock with one hand and covered it with the other hand so that it seemed like the fire was extinguished. Only the young man could master this flaming rock.

The elder said, "This is Egjipogteo. This is the Great Fire. I have heard of it before. I was told that it existed somewhere. This boy has found it. He has found it."

The young man took the Great Fire to an old and crippled man. The young man placed the glowing stone in the hands of the old cripple. Instantly the old cripple's legs healed. The old man who had been crippled stood up and walked. He said, "Oh, my legs are restored wonderfully, my son! Now I can move around in good health again." Then he told the people, "It is medicine that the boy is carrying, medicine!" and the medicine was so bright that nobody could look at it. The man who had been a cripple told the young man, "Shield it from our eyes."

The young man set the rock on a pole and covered it with skins. It became dark. Only a faint glow came from the pole.

From then on the Mi'kmaqs could work through the nights. Whenever the rock was unveiled, it lit the entire village. The rock was very good medicine for the people.

One day an Indian from another nation arrived. He said, "What's the big deal here? I can control this fire. I'm the one who is the boldest!"

So he grabbed the pole. He intended to steal the Great Fire. He took down the rock. When he seized the rock, he burst into flames. All that remained were his ashes.

The elder said, "Nobody can master this fire except one man. Only he can master it. Often people try to steal it, but the fire always kills them."

The Great Fire illuminated the entire river. The region glowed like a city. The people took the Great Fire to the mouth of the river. The Great Fire could be seen from Prince Edward Island.

The elder told the young man who had mastered the Great Fire, "Son, the Great Fire has killed people. The people do not know how to properly care for the Great Fire. Bury the Great Fire. Take it out only when you need it for medicine."

The elder and the young man went off with the Great Fire and buried it under dirt and mud.

The elder said, "I just want a little beam of light to shine from it."

The elder took a little piece of wood and drilled through the dirt and mud. The hole was small. The rock glowed from the tiny hole.

The elder said, "If a person should want to heal himself and should that person have great reverence for this fire, then let him come here and heal himself."

Indians came from everywhere. They heard about this Great Fire. They came from the north. They came from the south. They came from where the sun rises and from where the sun sets.

One man was sick. Nothing could cure his hands, and nothing could cure his face.

The elder told him, "Take a piece of wood and make a small opening through the earth to bare a piece of the fiery rock."

So the sick man opened up a small part of the Great Fire.

The elder told him, "Place your head there for a moment, right there where the light of the Great Fire is shining through."

The sick man's face completely healed. To all appearances it seemed like there had never been a scar on his face.

The same miracle happened to an old woman. Her hands healed. Her feet healed. Whatever ailed the Mi'kmaqs, they were cured by the Great Fire.

The elder told the people, "From now on, whenever you travel at night along this river, you will be haunted by visions of the fire. A ball of fire will glow over the waters. And it will glow in the sky. The Great Fire comes from the sky. It descends to the earth, where it shines. The fire comes from the holy place."

So to this day, this ball of fire can be seen. Even white people believe this. They have seen fiery balls floating over different spots along the Richibucto River and out to the breakwaters.

2 Central

Two Wolverine Stories

Introduction by Julie Brittain and Marguerite MacKenzie

The two stories we have selected to contribute to this anthology—"Wolverine and the Ducks" and "Wolverine and the Geese"—are from the Naskapi community of Kawawachikamach, which is near Schefferville in northern Quebec, Canada.[1] Both stories belong to a genre of Algonquian oral literature referred to (in Naskapi) as *âtiyûhkin* (traditional tale) and take as their main character the trickster figure, Wolverine.[2] Kwâhkwâchâw, as he is known in Naskapi, is the quintessential Native North American trickster figure—scandalous, sneaky, disruptive, amusing, quick to humiliate or be humiliated, and not infrequently on the lookout for a good plan to get some unsuspecting creature into his cooking pot. He is also ruthless, as these two stories attest.

"Wolverine and the Ducks" and "Wolverine and the Geese" were narrated at a single sitting, in the same order as they appear here, by the late Naskapi elder and renowned storyteller John Peastitute. They were recorded in the summer of 1967 by students working with the Laboratoire d'anthropologie amérindienne, under the supervision of anthropologist Rémi Savard. Five of Peastitute's Kwâhkwâchâw stories were recorded that year. The following summer, in 1968, Savard and his students recorded Peastitute's "non-trickster" *âtiyûhkina* and his historical narratives (*tipâchimuna*).[3] A total of forty-six stories were recorded over these two summer periods. Although the presence of the anthropologists may have been the catalyst for the telling of these stories, the sounds of audience participation confirm that they were authentic performances in the sense that they were performed before a live audience. At various points in the stories, the narrator steps outside his narrative world to provide his audience with additional pieces of information.[4]

In 1994 the Laboratoire d'anthropologie amérindienne made the tapes available to the Naskapi community for transcription, translation, and publication.[5] While publication of the collection in Naskapi is a high priority for the Naskapi people, they are also keen to see the stories published in translation so that non-Naskapi speakers can read them. Thus, the stories will be published in Naskapi and in (English and French) translation. Preparation of the texts for publication is one of the many ongoing language-related responsibilities of the Naskapi Grammar, Lexicon and Translation (NGLT) project, which is based at Kawawachikamach.[6] Alma Chemaganish, Silas Nabinicaboo, and Philip Einish work for the NGLT project. They carried out the transcription and preliminary English translations of both the stories we present here, under the supervision of Bill Jancewicz.[7] The work of transcription and translation is time consuming and painstaking, and the driving force behind the productivity of the staff of the NGLT project is their commitment to preserving their language and culture.[8]

John Peastitute's 1967 narrative performances of "Wolverine and the Ducks" and "Wolverine and the Geese" have been published previously in fairly free translation—in English (Desbarats 1969) and in French (Savard 1971). The translations we present here are the first to be based on meticulous analysis of the Naskapi text. We have also endeavored to reproduce the elegance and style of John Peastitute's language as well as the skill with which he varies the pace and the tone of his voice in the telling of the stories. Wolverine comes across as a decidedly sinister character when you hear John Peastitute play the part. We employ the formatting conventions introduced by Anthony C. Woodbury and Leo Moses in their translation of "Mary Kokrak: Five Brothers and Their Younger Sister" (in Swann 1994, 15–36).[9] Distinct typefaces correspond to the narrator's various tones of voice, and pauses are represented in the manner indicated in the following table:

Line break	Pause averaging slightly less than one second.
Line space	Long pause within sentence or drop to low pitch to mark end of sentence/sentence group.
Large capital	Episode break, marked by pitch range reset and other vocal features, or determined by content.
Small caps	Impressionistically harsh (breathy, raspy) voice quality, sometimes in unusually low pitch.
Italics	Impressionistically mild voice quality or higher pitch register.
Italic small caps	Impressionistically mild voice in low pitch.
Bold	Menacing voice, slow, soft, frequently employed when Wolverine is speaking to other characters.

Savard includes both "Wolverine and the Ducks" and "Wolverine and the Geese" in his 1971 French translation.[10] Savard's Innu collaborator, Matthew Rich of North West River (Labrador), listened to the audio recordings and made English translations of the stories, on which Savard then based his French translations. Desbarats's 1969 collection, *What They Used to Tell About: Indian Legends from Labrador*, includes an edited version of Matthew Rich's English translation of "Wolverine and the Geese."[11] We will refer to these earlier publications of John Peastitute's recordings (and to Savard's alternative versions of "Wolverine and the Ducks") as they become relevant to our discussion. Versions of both stories we present here also appear in English translation in Lucien Turner's 1894 account of the time he spent with the Naskapis.[12] The stories, told to Turner in Naskapi and translated by him into English, are titled "Story of the Wolverine" (i.e., "Wolverine and the Ducks") and "Story of the Wolverine and the Brant" (i.e., "Wolverine and the Geese"—a "brant" is the type of goose found in the Naskapi homeland). We will refer to Turner's versions of the stories as they become relevant.

Neither of these two stories is uniquely Naskapi except in the details of its telling. Versions of both stories are told throughout the Algonquian-speaking world. For example, Leonard's Bloomfield's 1930 collection of Cree stories, *Sacred Stories of the Sweet Grass Cree*, includes a version of "Wolverine and the Ducks" (better known as "The Shut-Eye Dance"). Two more Cree versions of the story appear in Douglas Ellis's 1995 collection of stories from the west coast of James Bay, *Âtalôhkâna nêsta tipâcimôwina: Cree Legends and Narratives from the West Coast of James Bay*.[13] And the present volume includes a version of this much-loved story (see the Omushkego/Swampy Cree chapter). Versions of "Wolverine and the Geese" are less common but are also attested in the published literature; for example, Ellis (1995) includes two versions of it, and there is a version in E. Ahenakew's "Cree Trickster Tales" (1929).

Nor are these stories restricted to the Algonquian-speaking world; they have passed across the linguistic borders to become part of the narrative worlds of neighboring Aboriginal communities whose cultures and languages are different. Many Native American stories are now available on the World Wide Web; at the time of writing, we found at least two versions of "Wolverine and the Geese" told by Siouan-speaking people in Canada and the United States. One of these is a Hotcâgara (Winnebego) story from Wisconsin in which the Hotcâgara trickster Wak'djûk'aga is the main character.[14] The Assiniboine people tell a version of this story with their trickster figure, Iktome, as hero.[15]

The Trickster Kwâhkwâchâw

The unifying theme in these two stories is the personality of the trickster, Wolverine. His desires, his cunning, and his stupidity drive the plots in characteristic trickster manner. The trickster is a universal figure and, as such, has been discussed widely in the literature. While it lies outside the scope of our aims, as well as our expertise, to discuss the figure of the trickster in any detail here, we will say something about this particular manifestation of the trickster, Kwâhkwâchâw.[16]

Kwâhkwâchâw is found in the stories of a subset of the Algonquian-speaking peoples of the Quebec-Labrador peninsula. We can best characterize this group in linguistic terms. The "Cree-Montagnais-Naskapi dialect continuum" is the term used to refer to the most widely spoken Aboriginal language in Canada.[17] It is spoken from Labrador in the east to the Rocky Mountains in the west and is comprised of numerous dialects that are broadly classified (on the basis of linguistic characteristics that do not concern us here) as Cree, Montagnais, or Naskapi. Wolverine is the trickster figure for speakers of dialects of Montagnais and Naskapi. These communities are all on the Quebec-Labrador peninsula, but speakers of Cree who live in this region have Mâsw rather than Wolverine as their trickster figure.[18] Further west still, along the west coast of James Bay, the Cree trickster is Weesakechahk. Thus, a Wolverine trickster only appears at the eastern extreme of Algonquian territory.

The Innu community at Sheshatshiu speak a Montagnais dialect; the communities of Kawawachikamach and Davis Inlet speak Western and Eastern Naskapi, respectively. It is important to note, however, that the term "Montagnais" has largely been replaced now by the terms "Innu," which refers to the people, and "Innu-aimun" (literally, "person-word"), which refers to the language. Likewise, as we mentioned earlier (note 1), the term "Naskapi" is no longer used to refer to either the people or the language of the Davis Inlet community. Thus, the Sheshatshiu and Davis Inlet communities are "Innu" and their language is "Innu-aimun." The Naskapis of Kawawachikamach, however, prefer that the term "Naskapi" be used to refer both to them as a people and to their language. Despite the difference in terminology, clearly Davis Inlet Innu-aimun is more closely related to Kawawachikamach Naskapi than it is to Sheshatshiu Innu-aimun. Speakers of all three dialects can, however, understand one another with relative ease.[19]

The real-life wolverine (*Gulo gulo*) is indigenous to many parts of Canada. Why, one might ask, is it only the Innu and the Naskapis who have chosen the wolverine as their trickster figure? This is not a question we would like to attempt to answer; it is of some interest, however, to consider the fact that wolverines seem, at least to an outsider to Naskapi/Innu culture, to share certain characteristics with the mythical Kwâhkwâchâw. When we asked some of the elders from Kawawachikamach how they felt about wolverines, without exception, they told us that they don't like them. Wolverines have sharp claws and teeth and are reputed to be ferocious fighters, taking on animals many times their size. Although it may resemble a small bear more than anything else, the wolverine is in fact the largest member of the weasel family (*mustelidae*), with some males weighing as much as sixty pounds. We will see from these two stories that Kwâhkwâchâw is without doubt a vicious fellow. Apart from this, the real-life wolverine lives in borrowed homes and feeds on carrion; it is a highly intelligent animal that lives by its wits and benefits from the hard work of others. For humans the wolverine is a destructive nuisance. Elders told us stories of wolverines breaking into caches of food—supplies of meat, for example, hidden for a return trip through the bush, were raided and eaten by greedy wolverines.[20] These feelings are echoed in Turner: "The Indian conceives the wolverine to be an animal embodying all the cunning and mischief that can be contained in the skin of a beast. To its cunning is added great bodily strength, enabling this medium-sized animal to accomplish destruction apparently much beyond its strength" (1979, 63). With this image in mind, one can more easily appreciate the full sinister quality of some parts of these stories. Before we turn to discussion of the stories themselves, however, we must make brief comment on some of the more technical linguistic issues that are of relevance.

Guide to Naskapi Pronunciation

Naskapi people read and write their language using a syllabics system that was developed for the Crees and the Ojibwes in the first quarter of the nineteenth century (by James Evans); the roman representation we use here tends to be used by a non-Naskapi readership only. A description of Naskapi syllabics appears in the *Naskapi Lexicon* (MacKenzie and Jancewicz 1994, xvi–xxii). The pronunciation guide we provide here is based on the guide provided in the *Naskapi Lexicon*.

Vowels

There are six vowel sounds in Naskapi, three long (*î*, *û*, *â*) and three short (*i*, *u*, *a*). The following provides an approximation of their English counterparts:

Naskapi	English sound
î	*ee* as in "feet"
i	*i* as in "bit"
û	*oo* as in "boot"
u	*oo* as in "book"
â	*a* as in "hat"
a	*a* as in "about"

Consonants

In order to discuss consonants, we have divided them into three sets. Each set requires a slightly different explanation:

Set 1: *m*, *n*, *s*, *y*, *w*, *h*
Set 2: *p*, *t*, *k*, *ch*, *kw*
Set 3: *hp*, *ht*, *hk*, *hch*

Set 1 consonants are pronounced much like their English counterparts in the examples given here. Note, however, that *s* is sometimes pronounced as English *sh*.[21]

Naskapi	English
m	*m* as in "*m*itten"
n	*n* as in "*n*eat"
s	*s* as in "*s*eat" or *sh* as in "*sh*eet"
y	*y* as in "*y*ear"
w	*w* as in "*w*eed"
h	*h* as in "be*h*ind"

Set 2 consonants vary in their pronunciation, depending on the context in which they occur. In English the graphemes *p*, *t*, *k*, and *ch* represent voiceless consonants (sounds made without any vibration of the vocal cords). The voiced counterparts of these sounds are, respectively, *b*, *d*, *g*, and *j*. The feature of voice distinguishes the meaning of the following pairs of English words:

Voiceless initial consonant	Voiced initial consonant
*p*it	*b*it
*t*in	*d*in
*k*ill	*g*ill
*ch*ar	*j*ar

In dialects of the Cree-Montagnais-Naskapi continuum, voice is not a feature that distinguishes one sound from another. Set 2 consonants are by default voiceless; they are only voiced in intervocalic position (between two vowels) and in word-initial position. Thus, the Naskapi word for "man," which is written *nâpâw*, is pronounced "*nâbâw*," and the word for "ptarmigan," which is written *piyâw*, is pronounced "*biyâw*." The Naskapi alphabet has no need to represent the voiced variants of *p*, *t*, *k*, and *ch* because voicing occurs in entirely predictable environments. Thus, the reader should pronounce *p*, *t*, *k*, and *ch* as (respectively) *b*, *d*, *g*, and *j* where they occur in intervocalic or word-initial position.

Naskapi	English	Example
p	*p* as in "*p*it"	is*p*imîhch, "above"
	b as in "*b*it"	nâ*p*âw, "man"
t	*t* as in "*t*in"	âs*t*im, "come here!"
	d as in "*d*in"	â*t*iyûhkin, "traditional tale"
k	*k* as in "*k*ill"	is*k*wâw, "woman"

	g as in "*g*ill"	ku*k*imâs, "lake trout"
ch	*ch* as in "*ch*ar"	uski*ch*, "first time"
	j as in "*j*ar"	kwâhkwâ*ch*âw, "wolverine"

The final sound in set 2 is the sequence *kw*, which occurs in English words like "*qu*ick" and "e*qu*al." This sound sequence never occurs in word-final position in English. In Naskapi the sequence *kw* can occur in any position in the word, and it follows the same pronunciation rules as the rest of the sounds in this set; it is voiced only in word-initial position and in intervocalic position.

Naskapi	English	Example
kw	*qu* as in "*qu*ick"	kâ*kw*, "porcupine"
	gw as in "*Gu*am"	*kw*â*kw*âpisîs, "butterfly"

Set 3 consonants are the preaspirated set. There is no equivalent sound in English. Preaspiration means that a small release of air (represented by *h*) precedes the pronunciation of the consonant. This set occurs in the following Naskapi words: akû*hp*, "coat"; mî*ht*, "piece of firewood"; kû*hk*ûs, "pig"; and kâsû*hch*ît; "loader/grader."

Reduplication as a Narrative Device

In both translations the reader will notice the repetition of certain verbs. Sometimes this is a threefold repetition ("run-run-running" in the opening line of "Wolverine and the Ducks"), and in other cases it is a twofold repetition ("wiggle-waggled" in paragraph 5 of "Wolverine and the Geese"). This indicates that in the Naskapi text the narrator has employed a linguistic device referred to as "reduplication." Reduplication refers to the replication of all or part of a word. In Algonquian languages, generally only the first one or two syllables of the word are repeated. Reduplication is a highly productive process in Naskapi and related dialects, and John Peastitute uses it playfully and to great literary effect in his stories.

The effect of reduplication is to modify the meaning of the verb in a variety of ways, depending on the semantics of the verb to which it is applied. For example, in line 1 of "Wolverine and the Ducks," the narrator creates a reduplicated form of the Naskapi verb *pimipâhtât*, "she/he runs," by changing the initial vowel (from i to *a*) and copying the initial syllable to produce *pâpâmipâhtât*.[22] The reduplicated form means something like "running here, there and everywhere/all over the place." In "Wolverine and the Geese," on the other hand, the verb *wâtipich*, "they wriggle," which is reduplicated to produce the form *wâwâtipich*, conveys the sense of doing something repeatedly—the old ladies wriggle around repeatedly in order to get themselves comfortable.

English lacks the means to precisely capture the formal and semantic properties of Algonquian reduplication, but we have sought to reproduce the process as best we can. We have translated the Naskapi word *pâpâmipâhtât* by means of the phrase "he was run-run-running around here, there, and everywhere." Although a twofold repetition of "run" (i.e., "run-running") would be more faithful to the formal properties of the Naskapi reduplicated verb, the prosodic rules of English prefer a threefold repetition of "run."[23] In order to capture the semantic properties of the Naskapi reduplicated verb, we have modified "run-run-running" with the English phrase "here, there, and everywhere."

Sometimes, however, it is possible to provide a closer approximation of the Naskapi reduplicated verb. In translating *wâwâtipich* as "they wiggle-waggled," we have been able to capture the form of the original Naskapi word quite closely by copying the base form twice. As well, in this case the duplicated English form actually conveys the idea of repeated action, so we did not need any additional modifying phrases to translate the Naskapi reduplicated form. Our aim in attempting to represent Naskapi reduplication has been to remain as faithful as possible to the formal properties of the original text. We also hope that we have transferred into English some of the fun that John Peastitute had with language.

Wolverine and the Ducks

This story opens with Wolverine, in characteristic fashion, running around all over the place. In the opening line of the story, the narrator uses the reduplicated form of the verb meaning "run" (as discussed earlier). Use of this form of the verb conveys not just the idea that Wolverine is covering a lot of different territories as he runs but also that he is running in a frenzied, disorganized manner. He is on the lookout for some mischief to get into, which the audience assume because they know him so well. And he finds it—a group of his "younger brothers" (ducks) gathered at the shore of a lake.[24] The ducks are enjoying the mud, from which we can conclude that the story is set in warm weather. Wolverine sees an opportunity to have himself a good meal, if he can only work out how to gain their trust. He knows that if he simply goes over to them, they will fly away, so he comes up with a plan to approach them without scaring them away. He pulls up some moss and folds it into a little parcel so that it looks like a gift. He refers to this moss parcel as *âmûn*. He shouts to the birds:

"Younger brothers!"
"I've brought you some 'âmûn'!"

The Naskapi people we consulted about this explained that ducks and geese are curious birds. This is why, for example, geese can be lured from the air by a decoy on the ground. Wolverine is exploiting this curiosity by making a fake gift, which is really "nothing at all," and using it to allow him to approach them. The birds are curious enough to want to find out more about the parcel he has brought them.

Our consultants at Kawawachikamach were unable to translate *âmûn*, and initially we all concluded that it must be an archaic term referring to moss. In the Davis Inlet version of this story that appears in Savard (1971), Wolverine also uses moss to make a parcel, which he then refers to as *âmûn*. However, in Savard's North West River version of the same story, Wolverine makes a parcel from old clothes and calls that *âmûn*. Thus it seems that *âmûn* is the name Wolverine gives to his decoy gift, regardless of what he uses to fabricate it.[25] In our translation we have left *âmûn* in Naskapi to indicate its special status as a term that has variable reference.[26]

Using the *âmûn*, Wolverine is able to get close to the ducks. One of them comes forward and asks him what the significance of his gift is—what happens when Wolverine brings *âmûn*? Wolverine replies: "I sing and everyone dances with their eyes closed." The birds proceed to dance with their eyes closed while Wolverine sings—this is "the shut-eye dance," although in this version of the story the term is never used. In this story, unlike in the following story, "Wolverine and the Geese," the narrator doesn't sing the song.[27] However, he does tell us that Wolverine sings a song about the *âmûn*.

While the birds dance with their eyes closed, Wolverine sets about killing them by pulling off their heads. He makes a pile of heads off to one side and lays out the bodies separately.[28] One of the birds, a loon, begins to realize that the dance floor is emptying because he can't feel the other birds around him anymore: "How come no one seems to be bumping into me anymore?" Suspicious, Loon disobeys Wolverine's instructions and opens one eye to take a peek at what's going on. He sees the bodies laid out and decides that he should save himself. Trying not to alert Wolverine to the fact that he intends to escape, Loon continues dancing but dances toward the lake. Before leaving, Loon shouts to warn the remaining birds: "Fly away! Our elder brother is killing us all!" Wolverine hears Loon's shout and runs down to the water's edge, but not in time to catch him. Loon dives into the water and doesn't resurface until he's well out into the lake.

Wolverine, his killing spree brought to a halt by Loon, returns to the pile of dead birds and begins to think about how to cook them. At this point in the story, a new character is introduced—Nâstûch, the name Wolverine uses to address his anus.[29] The trickster's ass is often a character in the stories, and, as we see here, it frequently gets the better of him.[30] Nâstûch appears in a number of other Wolverine stories in John Peastitute's 1967 collection. In Savard's Davis Inlet version of "Wolverine and the Ducks," the ass is called Nishtut—this is a variant pronunciation of the Kawawachikamach word Nâstûch. In the North West River version, the ass appears as a character, but its name is not used.

The name Nâstûch requires some comment. At a slightly later point in our story, Wolverine's ass uses the term "Nâstûch" to call out to Wolverine. Thus, it would seem, the word can vary in reference and does not have a specific meaning; it does not mean "ass," for example. Our consultants guessed that the term could be translated as something approximate to "old buddy" or "old friend"; no one knew exactly what it meant. However, a more intriguing possibility exists. Luci Bobbish-Salt of the East Cree community in Chisasibi, Quebec, told us that the East Cree trickster Mâsw calls his ass Nistuch—this is a variant pronunciation of the Naskapi word Nâstûch.[31] Bobbish-Salt offers the following possible explanation of how the ass came by this name: In one of the East Cree trickster stories, the ass farted three times and was thereafter given the name Nistuch, which is comprised of the root for "three" (*nistu* in East Cree and Naskapi) and a suffix *-ch*.[32] If Nâstûch is in fact the ass's name, when it calls Wolverine Nâstûch, it is making a joke at Wolverine's expense—it is calling him an ass. The ass calls Wolverine Nâstûch immediately following the part of the story where some humans have stolen Wolverine's ducks right from under his nose:

> His ducks got scooped out of the pot and eaten.
> The bones were dropped back into the broth.

Use of the term "ass" would certainly be appropriate, given the context. The ass explains to Wolverine how the thieves came and stole his ducks while he was asleep: "[T]hen, the ass called out to Wolverine, 'Nâstûch, some people were here, they came paddling up to us in a canoe,' it said to him."[33]

Returning to our story, Wolverine tells Nâstûch that they are going to have a good meal and then sets about plucking the ducks and putting them into his cooking pot. He settles down to sleep, leaving Nâstûch, who never sleeps, to guard the food against thieves. But the ass only calls Wolverine after the ducks have been stolen. Wolverine looks into his pot and finds only bones, broth, and fat left. He scoops out the bones and, desperate for something to show for all his hard work and hungry, sets off with the pot in search of Muskrat. We are told that the pot contains fat.

Wolverine asks Muskrat, who is a good swimmer, to take the pot with its contents of bird fat and swim around in the cold water until the fat hardens. (We assume either that the fat is more palatable if it is solidified, or that Wolverine's pot contains broth and fat and that putting it in the cold water will separate the fat from the broth.) Wolverine tells Muskrat that if he does this favor for him, he will share his fat with him. Muskrat swims around for a while and then returns to shore with the pot. Wolverine checks the fat—it's not quite done to his liking yet. He says to Muskrat: "A little more, a little more, O younger brother, swim out into the water with it again." Muskrat goes off again, but this time he decides to sit on a rock in the middle of the lake and eat all the fat for himself. Wolverine begs him to stop, but Muskrat finishes the lot, returning Wolverine's empty pot to him at the end of the story. Thus, out of his entire adventure Wolverine gets nothing except the empty pot he had at the start—he has been duped, yet again, and he's still hungry.

Wolverine and the Geese

"Wolverine and the Geese" was told immediately after John Peastitute had finished telling "Wolverine and the Ducks," and he begins the second story by referring back to the opening scene of the first story: "The same thing happened yet again." Wolverine came across a group of his younger brothers at the water's edge. This time, the birds are "molting geese" (*apistikich*), geese that are losing their feathers.[34] Geese begin to lose their feathers in late summer, so use of the term *apistikich* provides a precise temporal setting for the story. Wolverine approaches the geese and asks them for their wing feathers—presumably since they are molting anyway, he has the idea that he can use their feathers to make himself some wings. The oldest goose in the group asks his fellow geese to give Wolverine some feathers, and each bird donates one wing feather. Wolverine attaches the feathers to his rear end, and he's ready for flight. He's pleased with this new ability to fly; as he explains to the oldest goose (i.e., the leader), he has so much traveling to do, it will be a lot faster now that he can fly.

The oldest goose tells Wolverine that all the geese are about to leave, and he invites him to join them on their flight. Wolverine accepts. In this version of the story, we are not told where the geese are headed, but in other versions they are flying south.[35] In Savard's French translation of John Peastitute's performance of this story (1971, 41), the oldest goose says they are about to leave for somewhere far away ("La vielle outarde lui dit: 'nous sommes sur le point de partir pour aller loin d'ici'"); Savard adds a footnote, based on interviews with the storytellers, that the geese were preparing to migrate south. After the geese have lost all their old feathers, and before new ones have fully grown in, geese cannot fly. This period of several weeks is not referred to in the narrative; immediately after Wolverine has made his wings, they all fly off together, presumably during the fall migration period. Although time must have elapsed between the molting period and the geese migrating, we must assume that in this magical world, strict time lines don't matter.

As they are flying along, the oldest goose tells Wolverine that they are going to be flying over some camps and that the people on the ground are going to be calling to them. The oldest goose warns Wolverine that if he doesn't close his eyes, he will fall from the sky: "Don't look at them, close your eyes . . . [or] you will fall to the ground." We wondered why Wolverine should be told to close his eyes. If he shouldn't listen to the people calling, it would surely make better sense to plug up his ears. In the Hotcâgara version of this story (see note 14), "Trickster and the Geese," the leader of the geese says to the trickster "concentrate your mind on flying as we pass over this land, and every now and then give a honk." We speculate that the geese close their eyes in order to concentrate on flying, to more effectively ignore the calls of the people below. The people calling to the geese is a reference to the goose calls that hunters make to lure geese to within shooting range.[36] In the Hotcâgara story the geese are all encouraged to honk in order to drown out the calls of the people.

We noted that the time line is not strictly adhered to in this magical world. With this reference to the goose hunt, however, we run into a still more serious mismatch between the real world and the fictional world. Naskapi people hunt geese in the spring only because it is the only season in which the birds fly over the Naskapi homeland. When the birds fly south in the fall, they take a different route, and the Naskapis don't see them. It was the same in Turner's day, as he notes in his discussion of this story: "These birds [geese] are only seen in the spring migrations and then in great multitudes, while in the fall it is rare to see even a single individual, as they have a different return route than in spring" (1979, 163n1). In spite of this, the story does seem to be set in late summer, which precedes the fall migration, perhaps indicating that the story originated in a part of the country that has a fall goose hunt.

Returning to our story, Wolverine begins to sing "his two songs" just as the birds are approaching the community: "Now, when he guesses they have reached the place where the people are, Wolverine will start to sing his songs." John Peastitute sings the songs for his audience, clapping in time to the beat. (The underlined syllables are where he claps.)

Wolverine's first song:

Nîsîmich îyâ-nûwâ-kwâ-u-âna.
Nîsîmich îyâ-nûwâ-kwâ-u-nih!

And his second song:

kâ-ukuskwinîtâ-kâ-shîshichîyâ
kâ-ukuskwinîtâ-kâ-shîsh!

Except for the first three syllables of each line of the first song, we were not able to make out the words of the songs—we just transcribed what we heard.[37] The hyphens indicate slight rests between syllable groups, not word boundaries. We think that the first three syllables of song 1 is the word *nîsîmich*, "my younger brothers" (*nîsî* = younger sibling; *-m* = possessive; *-ich* = animate plural). Savard's translation of this text describes Wolverine (Carcajou) singing the line "Mes jeunes soeurs m'accompagnent!" (My younger sisters are coming along with me) to two different tunes.[38] This lends support to our analysis of the initial syllables of song 1 as *nîsîmich*.

In our story John Peastitute has different words for each song, and so the number of beats per line differs in each song: five beats per line in the first song, and in the second song, there are three beats in line 1 and four beats in line 2. Savard (1971, 62) speculates that Wolverine's two songs are the two distinct calls the goose makes as it flies: a honking and a barking.[39] Lending support to this suggestion is the fact that in some versions of the story the trickster actually seems to turn into a goose. In "Weesahkwecahk Flies South with the Waveys" (Ellis 1995), the trickster actually transforms himself into a goose; he does not borrow feathers, he does not merely "dress up" as a goose so that he can fly—he becomes a goose. If he literally became a goose, we would expect him to "honk" and "bark" like a goose. In another version of this story (Ahenakew 1929, 351), the trickster honks like a goose as he swoops down into the people's camp ("Wesakaychak, . . . flew right straight for a camp, crying: 'Honk! Honk! as he approached it' ").

It indeed seems that Wolverine, in all these versions of the story, including the one we present here, has assumed the characteristics of a goose. The people in the camp recognize Wolverine's singing and shout louder to try and draw him to the ground. Along with the geese, he is circling the camp, flying lower and lower, lured to the ground by the calls of the people. Then, just like the curious birds who couldn't resist coming to see what the *âmûn* was, Wolverine can't resist taking a peek to see where the calls are coming from. He has fallen prey to a goose-like weakness—curiosity. Had he not been curious, he would have simply flown on and not gotten into trouble. But he doesn't. He can't resist having a peek; he opens his eyes and falls to the ground.

He lands not at the camp but some distance from it. The people run over to find him, so that they can defecate on him. The story from this point onward is about the people at the camp and the delight they take in having an opportunity to defecate on Wolverine.[40] Savard (1971, 62) speculates that the people in this story might want to shit on Wolverine to get even with the real-life wolverine. Wolverines have musk glands in their anuses and mark the food they don't eat by rubbing their anuses against the food. They will break into a food cache, eat what they want, and soil the rest with liquid from their anal glands. Savard (1971, 42) has a story about two old women who want to shit on Wolverine. They say "Nous venons déféquer sur toi; nous désirons excréter sur l'excréteur" (We have come to shit on you; we want to shit on the shitter).[41]

In John Peastitute's telling of "Wolverine and the Geese," Wolverine gets his revenge. Two old women, whom the narrator tells the audience "weren't very smart," went off to find Wolverine to tell him they hadn't had their turn to shit on him yet.[42] Wolverine agrees to give them their turn, so long as they each go home and get their *apwânâskw* (roasting stick). A roasting stick is a long stick sharpened to a point at each end. It is used for roasting various kinds of meat over a fire and can also be used for roasting bannock dough. The food is skewered on one end, and the other end is driven into the ground at an angle placing the food over the fire. Wolverine says to the old women: "It seems that you two ladies don't have your sticks. Don't people carry their sticks whenever anyone shits on me?" Why would people take a roasting stick to the latrine? We wondered if it could be used as a weapon, for protection from wild animals. Our consultants said, "Yes, it could, but no one would ever use it that way—no one would ever take their stick with them to the latrine." So we wondered what to make of this part of the story. What we are told about the old women is that they are not very smart. Evidence of this, we think, is the fact that Wolverine only has to make some absurd suggestion to them (bringing their roasting sticks to the latrine) and they run off and do it. Why does he tell them to do this? We find out shortly.

The old women fetch their sticks and meet Wolverine at the latrine (literally, "the shitting place"). Wolverine lies down and tells the old women to stand one stick on either side of him (by forcing one of the sharpened ends into the ground so that it stands upright). Then he tells them to go ahead and shit wherever they want. As they are getting comfortable on top of him, he grabs a stick and skewers one of the old women. Then he takes the second stick and uses it to kill the other one. He had asked them to bring their sticks so that he would have a weapon to hand to kill them. Having killed the old women, he arranges the bodies in a sitting position, securing them with the sticks, which, in other versions of this tale, he runs through them lengthwise, from anus to mouth. Thus, it looks as if they are sitting, using the latrine. From a distance no one realizes they are dead, and this gives Wolverine an opportunity to make his getaway. He had been humiliated by the people of the camp, and this has been his act of revenge.

Eventually, the rest of the people in the camp get suspicious. The two old women have been at the latrine too long. They go over to investigate and only then discover the awful truth. They realize that Wolverine was responsible and, horrified by this latest evidence of his cruelty, sneakiness, and general underhandedness, they run back en masse to the security of their camp.

We note that in neither of these two stories, nor indeed in any of John Peastitute's *Kwâhkwâchâw* stories, is there any attempt to link the events of the narrative with the occurrence of natural-world phenomena. This is quite unusual; in both versions of the shut-eye dance included in Ellis 1995, for example, we are told that Loon is kicked out of the dance, which is how the loon came to have a flat back. Text 55 of Ellis's 1995 collection, "Weesakechahk and the Birds, and Why the Trees Have Scabs" (a Cree version of "Wolverine and the Geese"), explains why there are sticky black patches on the bark of willow trees. Whether the absence of these "just so" stories is characteristic of our narrator or of "Naskapi" oral literature in general remains to be determined by future investigations.

Finally, we would like to thank everyone at Kawawachikamach who has helped us understand these stories. In particular our thanks go to the community elders whose advice on matters of Naskapi language and culture has been of particular importance to us. We hope that we have understood you well—if we have not, the fault is entirely our own.

Notes

1. The Naskapi people were originally nomadic caribou hunters. By the mid 1950s, they had divided into two more or less sedentary groups—the Western Naskapi, who are now resident at Kawawachikamach, and the Eastern Naskapi, who until recently lived at Davis Inlet, Labrador. (The Davis Inlet community has relocated to Natuashish, Labrador; for the sake of simplicity, we continue to refer to the Natuashish community as the "Davis Inlet" community.) It is important to note that the people of the Davis Inlet community refer to themselves as Innu and to their language as Innu-aimun. The community at Sheshatshiu, Labrador, also use the terms Innu and Innu-aimun. The issue of terminology is discussed in more detail in the section "The Trickster Kwâhkwâchâw." The people of Kawawachikamach moved to Schefferville in 1956 and relocated to their present home at Kawawachikamach in the early 1980s. Both communities have adopted English as their second language. For further information on the history of the Naskapi people, the reader is referred to Henriksen 1973. For a brief overview of the history of the Naskapi people and their language, see Brittain and MacKenzie (2004).
2. See section "Guide to Naskapi Pronunciation."

3. *Âtiyûhkina* is the plural of *âtiyûhkin*, "traditional tale." The plural of *tipâchimun*, "historical narrative," is *tipâchimuna*. In Naskapi, as in all Algonquian languages, nominals are either animate or inanimate. The suffix *-a* is the inanimate plural; *-ich* is the animate plural.
4. Although the student anthropologists who were recording the stories could not speak Naskapi, we have noticed that the explanations that John Peastitute provides often seem to be directed toward a non-Naskapi member of the audience. These explanations cover, for example, typical Naskapi customs involving food or clothing, information that a Naskapi person would not need to have explained to him or her. For example, in "Umâyichîs: A Naskapi Legend from Kawawachikamach" (Brittain and MacKenzie 2004), John Peastitute provides a description of Naskapi leggings as an aside to the audience. Presumably he includes cultural information as a courtesy to non-Naskapi listeners, knowing that his stories would eventually be translated into a language they will understand.
5. One of John Peastitute's 1968 traditional tales ("Umâyichîs: A Naskapi Legend from Kawawachikamach") appears in English translation with commentary in Brittain and MacKenzie (2004).
6. The NGLT project operates under the auspices of the community-funded Naskapi Development Corporation.
7. Bill Jancewicz works for the NGLT project on behalf of SIL International. Although his name does not appear in the bylines, he has been the indispensable hub of all the work that has culminated in this chapter.
8. Many people have contributed over the years to the translations that appear here. Thomas Sandy was involved in making the initial Naskapi transcription. Noat Einish, who presently works for the NGLT project, assisted us in many of the work sessions during which we listened repeatedly to parts of the recordings that required further clarification. Community elders Joe Guanish and George Chemaganish also attended many of these work sessions and have over the years given us valuable advice on matters of both Naskapi language and culture.
9. We have made some additions to Woodbury and Moses's conventions in order to capture the full range of our storyteller's repertoire. Note that we use these conventions in our translations only and not in the portions of text cited in this introduction.
10. Savard's 1971 book is a collection of Quebec-Labrador Innu/Naskapi Wolverine stories. It also contains two Labrador Innu versions of "Wolverine and the Ducks"—one from the community of North West River (which is now known as Sheshatshiu) and one from the community of Davis Inlet.
11. Debarats's version of "Wolverine and the Geese" differs in detail from our version in spite of the fact that both translations are based on the same Naskapi

performance (by John Peastitute in 1967). Since our translations are faithful to the Naskapi original, we have looked to neither Debarats nor Savard to clarify our translation work. Savard, however, supplements his collection with ethnographic detail pertaining to the stories, obtained from the storytellers themselves, which has been of great help in understanding the two stories.

12. Turner's book was republished in 1979. It is also an account of time he spent with the Inuit of the Quebec-Labrador peninsula.
13. Ellis 1995. In text 18 of this collection, "Weesakechahk Carries around His Song Bag" (pp. 120–27), the trickster sings a song in which the phrase "a Shut-Eye Dance" appears. Several versions of this popular Algonquian story can, at the time of writing, be found on the World Wide Web.
14. This story, "Trickster and the Geese," appears on the World Wide Web as part of a comprehensive collection of Hotcâgara myths and legends. At the time of writing, the Web site is called "The Encyclopedia of Hotcâk Mythology," and it is edited and compiled by Richard Dieterle. The Hotcâgara were surrounded by Algonquian-speaking peoples (Algonquins, Menominees, Anishinaabe, Potawatomis, and Fox Indians).
15. This story is called "The Trickster Who Wanted to Fly." Like the Hotcâgara, the Assiniboines (Montana and western Canada) have Algonquian-speaking (Plains Cree) neighbors.
16. The reader is referred to Bright (1993) for a collection of diverse portraits of the Native American trickster. For a discussion of Wolverine as trickster, the reader is referred Savard (1971, 13) and to Millman ("Wolverine: An Innu Trickster," in Swann 1994, 208–24). Millman discusses the figure of Wolverine in his introduction to the English retelling of nine Innu trickster stories from Labrador (Sheshatshiu and Davis Inlet). It should be noted that Millman refers to the trickster as Kwakwadjec (208) rather than by the more commonly used name Kuekuatsheu (which is pronounced as *Kwâhkwâchâw* in Kawawachikamach).
17. For discussion of the Cree-Montagnais-Naskapi continuum from a technical linguistic perspective, the reader is referred to MacKenzie (1980).
18. East Cree speakers live in Quebec, on the east coast of James and Hudson bays.
19. Readers who are interested in more technical linguistic issues pertaining to dialects of Naskapi may consult chapter 1 of Brittain (2001). Also see MacKenzie (1979).
20. Naskapi elders also told us it has been years since they have had a face-to-face encounter with a wolverine. In 1989 the eastern Canadian wolverine was placed on the endangered species list (Committee on the Status of Endangered Wildlife in Canada). Commercial hunting in the area is seen as the major contributing factor in the species' decline.

21. Within the Naskapi speech community at Kawawachikamach, there is a small amount of dialect variation because people come from different linguistic backgrounds. The *s/sh* alternation occurs under the influence of neighboring dialects. The Naskapi word *sîsîp*, "duck," for example, may be pronounced "*shîshîp*" by some speakers.
22. The initial vowel is not always changed in cases where the verb undergoes reduplication.
23. This is due to the fact that "run" is a one-syllable word. Notice that "he was run-running" does not work as well prosodically as "he was run-run-running."
24. Although the word "duck" does not appear until about halfway through the story, we assume from the title of the story that the birds are ducks.
25. It is interesting to note that in Turner's account (1979, 163) Wolverine says to the ducks, "Come here, Brothers. I have found a pretty bees' nest. I will give it to you if you will come on shore and have a dance." We do not know, however, if the word *âmûn* appears in Turner's text. In both versions of this story that appear in Ellis's compilation (1995) (text 18, "Weesakechahk Carries around His Song Bag," and text 55, "Weesakechahk and the Birds, and Why the Trees Have Scabs"), the trickster uses moss to make what he calls his "song bag." With this he lures various aquatic birds from the lake into his tent. The lure in these stories is referred to as *otaskiiwat*, literally, "his moss bag."
26. For further discussion of the term "*âmûn*" in the Quebec-Labrador stories, the reader is referred to Savard (1971, 50–54).
27. Turner (1979, 163) transcribes the syllables of the (Naskapi) shut-eye dance (since he does not translate them, we assume that he was unable to): "The Wolverine said, 'Let us have a dance and I will sing. Shut your eyes and do not open them until we are done dancing.' He began to sing, 'A-ho'u-mu-hou-mu'-mu'-hŭm'.' "
28. In Ellis (1995), the shut-eye dance is performed inside a tent. In this story we are not told where Wolverine has the birds dance.
29. We decided to use the more colloquial (though less anatomically specific) term "ass" in our translation of *-skichisiy*, which literally means "anus."
30. The trickster's ass appears as a character in a different version of this story (text 55, Ellis 1995). Coyote's "butt-hole" is a character in Thomas King's modern trickster story, "The One about Coyote Going West" (in King 1990, 95–106).
31. The initial vowel is frequently modified in Naskapi vocative forms. Thus, East Cree Nistuch and Naskapi (vocative) Nâstûch.
32. Assuming this to be the correct morphological breakdown of Nâstûch/Nistuch, we are not at the present time able to account for the suffix *-ch*.

33. Savard (1971, 55–56) records an alternative explanation of the etymology of Nâstûch, offered by Matthew Rich, to which we refer the interested reader.
34. *Apistikich* is a plural form (*apistik* = "molting goose" and *-ich* = animate plural).
35. Text 20, "Weesakechahk Flies South with the Waveys," in Ellis (1995, 138–43). A wavey is a type of goose.
36. However, Turner's 1894 discussion of the text "Story of Wolverine and the Brant" offers the following more spectacular explanation for the shouting: "When the Indians perceive a flock of these brant [geese] they make a loud clamor, which frightens the birds so much that they lose their senses, fall to the ground and are thus killed" (Turner 1979, 163n1).
37. The elders who listened to the songs many times for us said that, although they couldn't make out the words, they found them humorous nevertheless.
38. Savard says Wolverine sings "dans deux tons," which may translate as "two tunes" or "keys" or "pitches." It is not clear why the geese in Savard's translation are referred to as "sisters"—the Naskapi word *nîsî* is in fact genderless (see the discussion in the text), meaning "my younger sibling." Desbarats (1969, 86) refers to only a single song or tune, the words of which he translates as "My brothers are coming with me."
39. While we may find some explanation of what Wolverine is up to here by looking to the natural world, we do not want to dismiss the possibility that he is singing to bring about some kind of trickster magic. Wolverine often seems to use song to make magic. In "Wolverine and the Ducks," for example, he uses song to enchant the ducks.
40. In the translation we have used the more colloquial verb "shit," as it fits the register of the story better—we will use this word henceforth in the introduction.
41. If this is the explanation, we would not expect to find reference to people shitting on the trickster in versions of the story told outside the area in which Wolverine is the trickster. Indeed, as far as we can determine at present, this episode is unique to the Innu/Naskapi versions of these stories.
42. We suppose that the story of two old women wanting to shit on Wolverine in Savard's book (1971) is related to, or the same as, the story included in John Peastitute's version of "Wolverine and the Geese."

References and Suggested Reading

Ahenakew, E. 1929. "Cree Trickster Tales." *Journal of American Folklore* 42:309–53.

Bloomfield, Leonard. 1930. *Sacred Stories of the Sweet Grass Cree.* Musée national du Canada, Bulletin 60, Série anthropologique 11. Ottawa: Ministère des mines.

Bright, William. 1993. *A Coyote Reader.* Berkeley: University of California Press.

Brittain, Julie. 2001. *The Morphosyntax of the Algonquian Conjunct Verb: A Minimalist Approach*. Outstanding Dissertations in Linguistics Series. New York: Garland.

Brittain, Julie, and Marguerite MacKenzie. 2004. "Umâyichîs: A Naskapi Legend from Kawawachikamach." In *Voices from Four Directions: Contemporary Translations of the Native Literatures of North America*, ed. Brian Swann, 572–90. Lincoln: University of Nebraska Press.

Chamberlain, A. F. 1891. "Nanobozhu amongst the Ochipwe, Mississagas, and Other Algonkian Tribes." *Journal of American Folklore* 4:193–213.

Desbarats, Peter, ed. 1969. *What They Used to Tell About: Indian Legends from Labrador*. Toronto: McClelland & Stewart.

Ellis, Douglas C., ed. 1995. *Âtalôhkâna Nêsta Tipâcimôwina: Cree Legends and Narratives from the West Coast of James Bay*. Algonquian Text Society 4. Stories told by Simeon Scott et al. Winnipeg: University of Manitoba Press.

Henriksen, Georg. 1973. *Hunters in the Barrens: The Naskapi on the Edge of the White Man's World*. Newfoundland Social and Economic Studies 12. Saint John's: Institute of Social and Economic Research (ISER), Memorial University of Newfoundland.

King, Thomas, ed. 1990. *All My Relations: An Anthology of Contemporary Canadian Native Fiction*. Toronto: McClelland & Stewart.

MacKenzie, Marguerite. 1979. "Fort Chimo Cree: A Case of Dialect Syncretism?" In *Papers of the Tenth Algonquian Conference*, ed. William Cowan, 227–36. Ottawa: Carleton University.

———. 1980. "Toward a Dialectology of Cree-Montagnais-Naskapi." PhD diss., University of Toronto.

MacKenzie, Marguerite, and Bill Jancewicz. *Naskapi Lexicon*. Kawawachikamach QC: Naskapi Development Corporation.

Mailhot, José. 1997. *The People of Sheshatshit: In the Land of the Innu*. Trans. Alex Harvey. Social and Economic Studies 58. Saint John's: Institute of Social and Economic Research (ISER), Memorial University of Newfoundland.

Savard, Rémi. 1971. *Carcajou et le sens du monde: récits montagnais-naskapi*. Collection Civilisation du Québec, série cultures amérindiennes 3. Québec: Ministère des affaires culturelles.

Swann, Brian, ed. 1994. *Coming to Light: Contemporary Translations of the Native Literatures of North America*. New York: Vintage Books.

Tanner, Vaino. 1944. "Outlines of the Geography, Life and Customs of Newfoundland-Labrador (the Eastern Part of the Labrador Peninsula)." *Acta Geographica* 8:1–907.

Turner, Lucien M. 1979 [1894]. *Indians and Eskimos in the Quebec-Labrador Peninsula Ethnology of the Ungava District*. Inuksiutiit Association. Québec: Presses COMÉDITEX.

WOLVERINE AND THE DUCKS

Told by John Peastitute
Translation by Julie Brittain, Alma Chemaganish, Philip Einish, Marguerite MacKenzie, and Silas Nabinicaboo

Now then, Wolverine was run-run-running around here, there, and everywhere.[1]

AND THEN HE SPOTTED HIS YOUNGER BROTHERS[2]

over there by the shore.
By this great expanse of water, where it was so pleasant, right there was where they were.
Right there in the mud, there were indeed lots and lots of them.

"NOW THEN, *HOW AM I GOING TO SNEAK UP ON THEM?*" WOLVERINE THOUGHT TO HIMSELF.

What he's really good at is tricking people.[3]

Now then, there's a kind of moss, a moss;[4]

1. The repetition of "run" (i.e., "run-run-running") indicates that in the original narrative the narrator employs a linguistic device known as reduplication. Reduplication refers to the replication of all or part of a word. This is discussed in more detail in the introduction (see "Reduplication as a Narrative Device").

2. Wolverine's "younger brothers" are probably understood by the audience to be ducks, since the title of the story is *Wolverine and the Ducks*. In Ellis's (1995) Cree versions of this story, a variety of aquatic birds are listed, including ducks. John Peastitute does not refer to a specific type of bird until about halfway through the story, when Wolverine plucks the birds (he refers to *sîsîp*, which is a generic term meaning simply "duck"). The creatures with whom Wolverine interacts address him respectfully as "elder brother." He in turn acknowledges this relationship by referring to any creature he meets as "younger brother." In Algonquian culture there is an avoidance of using personal names in favor of more respectful kinship terms.

3. Aside to the audience.

4. A generic word for moss is used here: *aschiy*, literally, "land" or "earth," something that covers the ground one walks on.

he tore up a piece of that moss and folded it into a little parcel.
Really, it's nothing at all.[5]
He approached them and called out to them:

"Younger brothers!"

"I've brought you some 'âmûn'!"[6]

WOLVERINE SAID.

"Âmûn" is what he called this moss.[7]

"That must be our elder brother." [said the ducks.]

Wolverine went over to them.

He went right up close to them.

Now then, he walked right up to them,

and they didn't fly away when approached.

"Younger brothers," said Wolverine,
"I've brought you this 'âmûn.'"

Wolverine showed them this little moss parcel he had made.
"Look at this 'âmûn' I've brought," he said to them.

"O my elder brother, what should people do when you bring 'âmûn'?"[8]

5. Aside to the audience. Wolverine is fixing a little parcel of moss so that it looks like a gift, but it is an empty parcel, containing nothing.

6. This is the name he gives to his little moss parcel. See the introduction for further discussion of the term *âmûn*.

7. Aside to the audience.

8. It is clear from the Naskapi text that only one of the birds speaks to Wolverine at this point, presumably the leader. The singular form of address *nistâsa* is used ("My elder brother"); if all the birds spoke together, we would expect the plural form *nistâsukw*, "Our elder brother." The bird asks, "What should people do when you bring *âmûn*?" Literally, this means something like "What happens now?"

"What should people do? said Wolverine.
Well of course, people are happy,
whenever I bring 'âmûn.'
Everyone dances.

Now then, I sing and everyone dances with their eyes closed. People always dance.

They dance.
They're happy."

Wolverine said to his younger brothers.
"Well now, younger brothers,
You all dance! Dance!"
And I will sing." **He sang, he sang, he sang about this moss that he had brought.**
'Âmûn' is its name, this moss that he had wrapped up in a little parcel.

[A child in the audience laughs.]

Now then, they did exactly what Wolverine had told them to do.
They didn't open their eyes, they danced with their eyes shut,
they danced.
Well now, those younger brothers,
Wolverine grabbed hold of their heads one after the other.
He pulled off their heads and made a pile of them to one side, over and over again he did this.[9]
That's all he did, again and again; he kept on throw-throw-throwing away their heads.

After a while, he had killed lots of them.
He had just kept on throw-throw-throwing away their heads.

Then, Loon,[10]

9. It seems that Wolverine is making a pile of the birds' heads rather than their bodies. This is indicated in the following sentence.

10. A specific type of bird is now introduced as a character in the story: the common loon (Naskapi *mwâkw*), or great northern diver (*Gavia immer*), which is ubiquitous in Canada and the northern United States.

who had been bump-bump-bumped into over and over again as the dancing was going on,

"How come no one seems to be bumping into me anymore?"

Loon thought to himself as he kept on dancing.[11]

Then Loon saw Wolverine.

He had looked around for Wolverine by peeping through one eye. Loon had taken a peek at him.

And Loon saw that Wolverine had killed all the birds. Wolverine had thrown them away to one side.
There were already lots of them laid out over there.[12]

Now then, Loon started to move like so, inching his way as he danced away from Wolverine; away, over there, he started dance-dance-dancing.[13]
He danced toward the water's edge, over there.
Now then, he had almost reached the water.

WELL NOW, "I COULD JUMP INTO THE WATER,"
LOON THOUGHT TO HIMSELF.

LOON CALLED OUT TO THOSE WHOM HE TRULY REGARDED AS HIS KIN.[14]

"Fly away! Our elder brother is killing us all," he said.

AND THEY TOOK OFF INTO THE AIR.

11. Up to this point the dance floor had been so busy that the loon was constantly being bumped into by the other ducks.

12. Most likely the phrase "over there" is accompanied by a gesture from the narrator (away to one side).

13. We assume that the narrator accompanies this line with a gesture to show the direction in which Loon begins to dance away from the scene of slaughter. Perhaps the narrator also shows the manner in which Loon dances.

14. Loon wants to warn the rest of the birds about the danger. We do not know if these other birds are loons, but they are a type of aquatic bird and are thus regarded by Loon as his kin.

Then Loon waddled down to the water's edge,
And he jumped into the water.
Wolverine began to run toward him, but even though he tried hard to grab him, he wasn't able to.

[Narrator and child both laugh.]

So now, Loon could be seen over there, way out there on the water.[15]

Now then, Wolverine went over to those younger brothers of his that he had killed,
"Oh my goodness!" [said Wolverine.]

It seems that you and I are going to have ourselves a good meal!"
That's his ass he's talking to, and his ass talks back to him.
Everything
talks to Wolverine,
because he is Wolverine.[16]
"Well then, I will sit here and do some plucking," said Wolverine to himself.
WOLVERINE PLUCKED THE DUCKS; HE PLUCK-PLUCK-PLUCKED THEM."

And after he had finished plucking them all,
well then, he dropped *his ducks* into a pot of water,

"So then!"

"What are we going to do now,
Nâstûch?"[17]

"WHAT ARE WE GOING TO DO?"

"*Well now*," [the ass replied.]

15. Loon has dived under the water close to the shore to escape and does not resurface until he is out in the middle of the lake. This is typical loon behavior.

16. All living creatures talk to Wolverine because of his special status as Trickster.

17. Nâstûch is the name Wolverine uses to address his anus, with whom he converses for the remainder of the story. See the introduction for further discussion.

"We will go to sleep
after we have put our ducks into our pot of water."

"Yes, yes, of course," Wolverine said. "I had already thought of that," he said.
That's what Wolverine always says back to his ass. No matter what it says to him, Wolverine replies, "*I thought of that ages ago.*"[18]
[Wolverine said to his ass,] "I thought that once we had dropped the ducks into our pot, well then, I would be able to go straight to sleep. That's what I had thought of doing," Wolverine said.
"So then, if you and I got hungry while we were resting, well now, we would be able to eat.
I had already worked all that out," Wolverine said.

Wolverine was really annoying his ass.
The ass didn't want to respond to Wolverine.[19]

THEN WOLVERINE WENT TO SLEEP.

"*Nâstûch, call me if anyone goes near our food.*
Our pot will be stolen from us. Watch out for them if you aren't going to go to sleep,"[20] said Wolverine.
It never sleeps;
Wolverine's ass never sleeps.[21]

[A child in the audience laughs.]

Some people came paddling over to where Wolverine was.[22]

18. Aside to the audience.

19. It is not clear from the story why Nâstûch is annoyed with Wolverine, except that we are given the impression Wolverine always has to be right, always has to be the one who comes up with the good ideas. Nâstûch, perhaps, is offended that Wolverine has appropriated yet another good idea.

20. The narrator does not specify who Nâstûch should keep an eye out for. Anyone who might want to steal their pot of birds, presumably, is the potential culprit.

21. Aside to the audience.

22. We have translated the Naskapi word *iyûch* as "people," and that is literally what the word means (*iyiyuw* = "person" and *-ch* = plural suffix). However, in the context of a Naskapi story, it should be understood to refer to Naskapi people. The early translations of this story (made by Naskapi speakers) had this word translated as "Indians" or "natives," which clearly shows who the people in this narrative world are.

They got out of their canoe, and they began searching around for the pot of ducks.

And the very thing that Wolverine had said might happen to him happened. The contents of his pot got completely eaten up.[23]

His ducks got scooped out of the pot and eaten.

The bones were dropped back into the broth.

Now then, the people spoke to the ass.

"Right here, there is a point of land.[24] Just as we start to disappear from view behind it,

then call out to Wolverine."

That's what the ass was told.

When those people were almost out of sight,

almost,

then, the ass called out to Wolverine, "Nâstûch, some people were here; they came paddling up to us in a canoe," it said to him.

Quickly, Wolverine started to get up; he started to go off and look for them.

It seemed to him that the people in the canoe were starting to paddle backward; that's what he thought.[25]

They seemed to be paddling out into open water, away from the point of land. It looked to him as if they were indeed people. They had already got far away from him; they had already paddled far away,

[Audience laughs.]

and everything that was in Wolverine's pot had been eaten.

Wolverine said, "Nâstûch, *after they had gotten out of the canoe,*

you should have woken me up then.

That way, we would have known what kind of people they were.[26]

23. Why doesn't Nâstûch wake Wolverine up at this point? One possibility is that he doesn't because he is annoyed with Wolverine and sees no reason to comply with his instructions.

24. The first word the narrator uses in this sentence is *mâwa*, which means "here" and is always accompanied by a hand gesture. The narrator thus gestures at this point in the story to show the audience where there is a point of land protruding into the water next to which Wolverine is camped.

25. It was not clear to any of the Naskapis consulted about this part of the story why the people in the boat should be paddling backward. We checked the translation carefully; there is no doubt that the verb means "backward" and not "back the way they had come," for example.

26. Literally, "we would have known what their intent was."

Those people who came to us in their canoe have already stolen from us and are long gone."

[Child and narrator both laugh.]

Now then,

Wolverine dished out his bones from the pot,

and yet, yet,
he couldn't eat; he wasn't able to eat
his own cooking. All his ducks had already been eaten.

Now, all that was left there in the pot was some fat; that's how it seemed to Wolverine.
So, here's what he did next with that fat of his.
Aha, he went off look-look-looking here, there, and everywhere for Muskrat.
And still, because of his searching, he wasn't able to eat that fat of his.
Still, Wolverine search-search-searched all over the place for Muskrat.

"*O younger brother*," Wolverine said to Muskrat. "Swim around with this fat of mine," he said to him.
"It should freeze and become quite solid," said Wolverine.
"When it is quite solid, then you and I will eat it. I'll share it with you," said Wolverine to Muskrat.

Then Muskrat swam out into the open water carrying Wolverine's fat.

Aha, and when he brought it back, it seemed that the fat was beginning to harden; that's how it seemed.

"*A little more, a little more, O younger brother, swim out into the water with it again.*"
And Muskrat swam out with the fat, swam away from the shore, one more time.
Now then,

there was a rock out there,
AND THAT'S WHERE MUSKRAT GOT OUT OF THE WATER,

THAT'S WHERE HE SAT, THAT'S WHERE
HE ATE THAT FAT.

"OH MY GOODNESS, YOUNGER BROTHER!" said Wolverine to Muskrat. "YOU'RE GOING TO EAT UP ALL MY FAT!" he said to him.
"*Bring it here! I told you I would share it with you when I eat!*" Wolverine said.

Now then,

when Muskrat had eaten all the fat, he gave Wolverine his bowl back.
"Here's your bowl back, elder brother," said Muskrat.

Wolverine hadn't even had a bite of those ducks of his, not even after all that work.
He couldn't do a thing about it; someone else had played a trick on him.

That's the end of the story about Wolverine.

WOLVERINE AND THE GEESE

Told by John Peastitute
Translated by Julie Brittain, Alma Chemaganish, Philip Einish, Marguerite MacKenzie, and Silas Nabinicaboo

The same thing happened yet again.[1]
Wolverine saw his younger brothers, there at the water's edge.
There were lots of molting geese, aha, molting geese, "apistisk" is what people call them.[2]

He went toward them.

He went right up to them.

"Younger brothers," he said, "I want you all to do me a favor."

"What favor?"

"Your wing feathers," said Wolverine. "All of you should give me your wing feathers," Wolverine said.

Now then, he had said all this to a certain molting goose who was older than the rest.

"All of you," said the oldest molting goose, "give your wing feathers to our elder brother."
Now then, each one of the geese plucked out one of his wing feathers.

1. This is a reference to the beginning of the previous story, where Wolverine sees birds at the water's edge.

2. The narrator's choice of the word *apistisk*, "molting goose," sets the story in late summer—several weeks before the fall migration. The narrator most likely addresses the phrase "*apistisk* is what people call them" to the anthropologist recording the session. We have left *apistisk* untranslated to indicate that the narrator is explaining the meaning of the word.

Wolverine made himself some wings; he made himself some wings, and he hung them here and there on his ass. He'll hang those little feathers just like so.[3]

[A child laughs.]

Now then,

That little one [Wolverine] took off into the air. He and his ass flew around in the air,
and then he landed.
"Younger brother," said Wolverine to the oldest molting goose, "I'm going to be very happy with these wings.
I'm always doing too much running around here and there," said Wolverine.
"Now, I will take off into the air and go wherever I please."

Now then, that oldest molting goose, that goose, that goose, he said to Wolverine,
"Elder brother, let's all fly away," he said to Wolverine.
"Far from here, we'll all fly like so. We can all take off into the air.
You can come along, if you want to," he said to Wolverine.

"Okay," said Wolverine, "I'll come along with you."

And then Wolverine's younger brothers took off into the air.

Now,
Wolverine flew; he flew along.

And while he was flying along,
Goose said to Wolverine,
"There will be people at the place we are flying to," Goose said to him.
They'll call to us when they see us flying," he said to Wolverine.[4]

3. The change of tense at this point in the narrative (from past to future) and the audience response (laughter) indicate that the narrator has stepped out of the narrative to show how Wolverine attaches the feathers to his rear end.

4. This is a reference to a strategy used by hunters to lure flying geese to within shooting range. Hunters make goose calls that attract the birds.

"They won't see me . . ."[5]

"Don't look at them, close your eyes."[6]

Now then,

"You will fall to the ground,

if you see them, if you close your eyes . . . if you don't close your eyes," he said to Wolverine.[7]

"**Okay,**" said Wolverine.

So now Wolverine realized that they would be flying to a place where there would be people.

"Okay," said Goose, "right here," he said, "here's the place, right here. The people are here,"

Goose said to Wolverine, as they were flying, flying around.

Now then, Wolverine began to sing,
and on and on he sang,
because he has two songs.
His songs, he will sing his songs; he will sing his songs.[8]

Now, when he guesses they have reached the place where the people are, Wolverine will start to sing his songs.

[Narrator sings these next two lines, marking the beat by clapping.][9]

5. The narrator makes a false start here. He begins a sentence and then changes his mind and abandons it, starting over again with "Don't look at them."

6. In the Hotcâgara version of this story (see the introduction), the goose tells the Trickster that they have to concentrate their minds as they fly in order not to be distracted by the calls of the hunters below. Presumably this is why he suggests they all close their eyes. In addition to calling, Cree hunters place decoys on the ice to lure the birds. It could also be the case that the birds are advised to close their eyes so as not to see the decoys.

7. The narrator makes a mistake here, saying, "You will fall to the ground, if you see them, if you close your eyes." He corrects himself in the next phrase: "if you don't close your eyes."

8. The switch to future tense suggests that the narrator is addressing the audience here, explaining what Wolverine does with the two songs he knows.

9. The underlined syllables of the song are where the beat is and also where John Peasti-

"Nîsîmich-îyâ-nûwâ-kwâ-u-âna
Nîsîmich-îyâ-nûwâ-kwâ-u-nih!"

Everyone could hear him as he approached![10]
He could be heard coming closer and closer.

"Don't you think that must be Wolverine, that sly-sneaky-underhanded-guy?"[11]
the people said.
"All of you, call to him and he'll start to fall." That's what the people said.

"Not long now [until he falls]."

[Narrator sings the next line. A child in the audience laughs as he sings.][12]

"kâ-ukuskwinîtâ-kâ-shîshichîyâ
kâ-ukuskwinîtâ-kâ-shîsh!"

Not long afterward he sang his song, . . . his song.
His songs that he sings are two in number,
he sings.

Wolverine was getting closer and closer. Someone was calling to him.

Now then,

Wolverine closed his eyes;
HE CLOSED HIS EYES.

---

tute claps. The hyphens indicate slight rests between syllables, not word boundaries. Only the first word, *nîsîmich*, could be translated—it means "my younger brothers." Both songs are discussed in more detail in the introduction.

10. "Everyone" refers to the people below on the ground. From their reaction to his approach (they want to make him fall), we can assume he is not a welcome guest.

11. We have hyphenated "sly-sneaky-underhanded-guy" because it corresponds to a single word in Naskapi: *âsititikisihtit*, which literally means something like "she/he misbehaves in a sneaky way."

12. This is the second of Wolverine's two songs. These syllables could not be translated. Again, hyphens represent not word boundaries but slight rests between syllables.

Goose was flying, circling, circling as he flew.[13]
He was indeed, for a goose flies in circles whenever he is called to, all geese do this.[14]

Wolverine's younger brother Goose was circling just like so.

"*Close your eyes!*" That's what people had told him to do.[15]
Wolverine closed his eyes as the rest of them circled around.

Now then, on their next circle,
Wolverine went to see where the people were calling him from.[16]
He was flying along, and he was looking for them;
he was looking for them.

Then he saw tents were pitched there, and then he dropped to the ground.[17]

Now then, at a different spot from where the tents were pitched, that's where he fell.

"*That must be Wolverine!* All of you, go and find him; all of you go and see if you can find him!"

Now then, the people set out to look for Wolverine. That's exactly who it was. Wolverine was indeed lying there.

So, "*It's that sly-sneaky-underhanded guy,*" the people said.

13. Hunters confirm that geese will circle an area as they prepare to land, if the landing space is limited. This line is a reference to the geese being lured to the ground by the hunters who have been making goose calls to them. Savard (1971, 62) confirms that geese circle before landing (flying at an altitude of 100 to 120 feet) and that they prepare to land when they hear hunters imitating geese.

14. An explanatory aside to members of the audience who are not familiar with the behavior of geese.

15. It is not clear here who is speaking. It could be Wolverine talking to himself, reminding himself to keep his eyes closed. It could also be the narrator, stepping out of the narrative to offer advice to Wolverine.

16. At this point in the story, Wolverine disregards the advice of the goose. Overcome with curiosity to see who is calling to him, he opens his eyes and looks down.

17. Exactly what the goose warned him about has just happened.

"Whenever we want to take a shit," they said,
"Let's go and find Wolverine!"[18]

"All of you shit right there on top of Wolverine! Shit on him right there where he lies!"

Now then, these people went to Wolverine; they went to where he was lying whenever they wanted to take a shit.
AND THE PEOPLE SHIT-SHIT-SHIT ON WOLVERINE.

Now, there were these two old ladies, these old ladies.
"My fellow old lady!" said one to the other, "let's go off and find Wolverine, aha, just us two, and let's shit on him," she said.

"We haven't had a chance to shit on him yet," she said to her fellow old lady.

So, off they went to see Wolverine.
They weren't very smart, those old ladies; they weren't very smart.

That Wolverine, he's going to talk to those old ladies, aha.[19]

"What are you up to?" Wolverine said to them.

"*We want to shit on you*," they replied.

"We want to shit at the shitting place."[20]

"*Okay*," he said to them.

"*Okay*," they replied.

"Well now," said Wolverine, "*it seems that you two ladies don't have your sticks. Don't people carry their sticks whenever anyone shits on me?*"

18. The narrator must assume his audience understands why the people want to do this—we are given no introduction to this new turn in the narrative.

19. Aside to the audience.

20. Camps always have a designated latrine area. If the ground is not frozen, it may be a pit. This is what the old women refer to when they say "shitting place."

"My fellow old lady," said one to the other, "my fellow old lady, let's go get our sticks."

So off they ran to get their sticks, "apwânâskw" is what this stick is usually called.[21]

Then they went back to Wolverine.

Now then, indeed, Wolverine lay down; he lay down like so.

"Both of you stand your sticks upright," Wolverine said to the old ladies. **"Put one stick on either side of me,"** he said to them.

They stuck their little roasting sticks into the ground.

The sticks stood up straight.

"Now then," said Wolverine. "You two shit anywhere you want." He said this to them as he was lying there.

Then the old ladies wiggle-waggled themselves around into a comfortable position so they were ready to shit on him.

They were ready to shit on him.

Now, when Wolverine knew that they were really ready to shit on him, he grabbed one of them and

he skewered her with her very own stick.

And again,
he grabbed the next old lady.

They were sitting here like this,[22]

[Laughter from audience.]

AND HE SKEWERED THEM BOTH.

21. An *apwânâskw* is a stick for roasting meat or bannock. This is an aside to the audience, perhaps for the benefit of the anthropologists. We have left the word untranslated to indicate that the narrator is highlighting a Naskapi word for the audience.

22. We assume that here the narrator mimes the position of the women.

So, they were seated like so, and away trot-trot-trotted Wolverine.

"They really wanted to make fun of me," he says, "they were making fun of Wolverine," he said to himself.

And away trot-trot-trotted Wolverine!

Now then, for a long time it seemed that the elderly women were just having a little sit down.
It looked to everyone as if they were still alive.

This was because Wolverine had impaled them with the sticks.
"LET'S GO OVER THERE AND SEE THEM.
Those old ladies have been sitting like that for too long.
They were shitting; they were shitting at the shitting place," people said.

They all ran over there,
toward these old ladies, and saw that Wolverine had run them through with their own roasting sticks,
they saw that he had killed them.

And then the whole lot of them ran back home together!

"It seems that Wolverine killed those old ladies who are no more," they said.
"He's gone, that Wolverine has," they said.

It seemed that Wolverine had skewered those old ladies
with their own roasting sticks that they had been carrying.

THAT'S WHAT EVERYONE SAID HAD HAPPENED.

"Now then," said the people,
"It looks like the old ladies were not simply sitting there.
It looks like Wolverine killed them,
and then he must have trot-trot-trotted off," they said.

"He's *gone*."

Now then, "All of you see

what a sly-sneaky-underhanded guy he is,
that Wolverine."
THAT'S WHAT THOSE PEOPLE SAID ABOUT HIM.

And away trot-trot-trotted Wolverine!

That's the end of the story people tell about Wolverine.

Wolverine, he's the only one that people tell stories about.

Waabitigweyaa, the One Who Found the Anishinaabeg First

Introduction by Jennifer S. H. Brown and Roger Roulette

The narrative presented here was told by Charlie George Owen (Omishoosh) in February 1996 at Pauingassi, Manitoba, a small Ojibwe reserve in the upper Berens River watershed, just west of the Ontario border. It was recorded by CBC Radio documentary journalist Maureen Matthews during one of our numerous visits to Pauingassi over the last decade. We had first been drawn to the community in 1992 in connection with our researches on the drum ceremony of Charlie George Owen's grandfather, Fair Wind (Naamiwan), a renowned medicine man. In turn, that interest had arisen from Jennifer Brown's studies of the anthropologist A. Irving Hallowell, who in his field work along the Berens River in the 1930s, met both Naamiwan and Owen and many of their relatives and wrote about Naamiwan's ceremonies. Charlie George Owen, whom we got to know during this work, was highly respected in his community for his deep knowledge and long life experience (he died in his late eighties on December 30, 2001). Monolingual in Ojibwe, he spoke his language with a sophistication and richness of vocabulary that are now rarely found.

The transcription and translation of the text are by Ojibwe linguist Roger Roulette. The English format used here echoes the Ojibwe speech and sentence patterns and pauses of Charlie George Owen to the extent possible. The story forms part of a long conversation in which Owen talked in depth on many subjects. We are still working through the more than fifty hours of audiotapes that preserve his voice; this text conveys a small sample of their richness and content.

Ojibwe is one of the major languages in the Algonquian language family and is still widely spoken in northern Ontario, Manitoba, Michigan, Wisconsin, and Minnesota, and in some northern Plains communities. Linguists often prefer the spelling "Ojibwe" to the more common "Ojibwa" or "Ojibway" because it more closely approximates the pronunciation of the word in the Ojibwe language. The term "Chippewa," widely used in the United States, is a more removed English variant of "Ojibwe." The Ojibwe term of self-reference is "Anishinaabe" (pl. Anishinaabeg), meaning "human being." When used in contradistinction to outsiders such as white men, the term has the sense of "our people" or may be translated by some as "Indian." In Canadian Algonquian homelands, "Anishinaabe" has entered English as a standard term often preferred over other names.

The common Ojibwe term for Europeans in many northern communities is "Wemitigoozhi," a cognate of the James Bay Cree term for "white man," *wemistikosiw*, which linguist C. Douglas Ellis analyzes as "one having a wooden boat."[1] The term encodes the powerful first impression that the wooden ships of the European newcomers made on those who first saw them. The ship motif, prominent in this story, is common in the oral traditions of the region (as also elsewhere) and became the core element in the name that both the Hudson Bay Cree and the northern Ojibwe applied to these unfamiliar people.[2]

First-contact stories from Aboriginal people seem to hold special interest for outsiders curious about how their ancestors were received and eager to find new angles of vision on those experiences. It is likely that the outsiders' questions often provoked the telling of such stories. The French at Port Royal (Nova Scotia) liked to suppose in 1610–11 that the elderly Mi'kmaq chief Membertou had met Jacques Cartier on his first voyage back in 1534. Euro-Canadians have for quite a long time been interested in whether Native people on Vancouver Island had oral traditions about Captain Cook's visit in 1778, and indeed it appears some memories go back to that event.[3] But in these and other instances, we must wonder whether leading questions were sometimes asked and were answered with polite but inconclusive affirmatives echoing what the questioners wanted to hear. Actual first European-Native contacts may often have been fleeting, not even of great significance to Native observers—at least, until later, with hindsight, and when questions arose. And as in Owen's story presented here, Native people also assigned names of their own fashioning to the visitors; monikers such as Cartier and Cook did not enter their lexicon. Indeed, the name of the anthropologist Hallowell means nothing to Ojibwe-speakers on the upper Berens River; two communities that he visited each gave him a distinct Ojibwe name by which they still remember him.

It is interesting, then, that Owen launched into the telling of this first-contact story without any prompting or questioning; it simply seemed an important tradition to share, among others. He knew, too, that it would be recorded and preserved by us as listeners, even though some of us could not understand the story until Roger Roulette made it accessible. He graciously consented to the publication of this and his other stories; in fact, he requested that they be made available both in English and in the Ojibwe language to the fullest extent possible, to teach about the history of his family and community. We gratefully acknowledge his contributions and his generosity.

As Owen makes clear in his opening lines, this is a very old story, *aadizookewin*, like the Bible, from long ago: "I speak about it like a legend." Such stories may have historical elements, but with the passing of the generations, they shade into what Anglophones call myth, and their personages may assume remarkable spiritual or magical powers, as implied in the case of the Anishinaabe man who here crosses the ocean to Europe and then returns after a remarkable escape.

To date we have not found any close parallels to this story. Other contact tales mention ships, first encounters with trade goods and liquor, silent trade (items being left behind and then picked up by the other party), and efforts to name the new items, to define their purposes, and to learn how to use them. But the darker themes of conflict, rejection and dirtiness, attempted murder and remarkable escape weave a powerful story that so far stands alone among recorded contact legends in the region.

If we try to localize the legend in real geography and historical time, it would seem perhaps to echo happenings in James Bay in the 1600s. James and Hudson bays provided the only northern access for sailing ships, and several European expeditions touched land in the period from Henry Hudson (1610–11) to the founding of the Hudson's Bay Company in 1670. Ojibwe traditions link the origins of the people of the upper Berens River to points farther east, north of Lake Superior, and old travel and trade routes connected the Pauingassi region to two major rivers, the Albany and the Severn, which flow into James Bay and Hudson Bay, respectively. The presence of the flintlock gun also points to the late 1600s, as the flintlock was increasingly used and traded in that period.[4]

Of deeper interest, however, are the core themes of the story. It develops into a triangle of actors and agents. A certain white man and his companions become aware of people living on the land they have reached ("footprints on the sand") and leave some items for exchange in silent trade. For the Anishinaabeg, the arrival of these items is foreshadowed by the knowledge that certain old men already have of guns, axes, and knives and how to use them, even as they give them names that index first efforts at description and do not become the standard terms. Then come the white men's building of a house, first meetings, the first trial of liquor, the giving of gifts, and the visitors' departure across the water.

Halfway through the story, the white man, the leading trader, is identified by an Ojibwe name, Waabitigweyaa, which Roger Roulette suggests could be translated as "sandy white water" (like waves breaking and washing the sand about).[5] Then immediately another entity comes onstage—Kwampanii. This is a borrowed word—"Company"—which appears in other contexts as the term for the Hudson's Bay Company. In this story, however, its significance expands and its meaning darkens; it is the locus of powerful people in Britain who hate the Anishinaabeg, see them as dirty, and do not want them to come to their land. When one man goes across the ocean in spite of the consequences, he faces a dire fate. But then appear the magical, legendary elements of the story. Though his power, in true Ojibwe fashion, is left unstated, the man by his escape shows himself to be *mide*, to have strong spiritual qualities.[6] With the help of Waabitigweyaa, the trader, he returns to his own land.

In the finale, however, the Kwampanii subverts and defeats the trader—whereupon it must itself begin to provide for the Anishinaabeg and becomes equated with the (Canadian) government, which has appropriated the wealth of the people. The story speaks on several levels. One element of context, however, may offer partial understanding. Charlie George Owen's grandfather, Fair Wind, the medicine man, himself challenged the Kwampanii and other outside powers, such as church missions, that tried to claim authority over his community. Our writings on him, cited among the suggested readings, trace the ways in which he maintained independence, frustrating the local Hudson's Bay Company managers by trading with independent traders (comparable to the friendly one in the story), and frustrating missionaries by appropriating the Cree syllabic Bible and a church bell to his own ceremonial purposes at Pauingassi. Ultimately, the Kwampanii, a remote blend of corporate and governmental power, dominated. But the story preserves themes of challenge, resistance, and an element of independence and agency well exemplified in Owen's family history and provides a subtle narrative critique, in microcosm, of the dealings of British and Canadian authority figures with Aboriginal people.

Notes

1. Cited by John S. Long, "Treaty No. 9 and Fur Trade Company Families," in Jacqueline Peterson and Jennifer S. H. Brown, eds., *The New Peoples: Being and Becoming Metis in North America* (Winnipeg: University of Manitoba Press, 1985), 162n62.
2. For discussions of Cree oral accounts of first encounters with white men and their ships in James and Hudson bays, see John S. Long, "Narratives of Early Encounters between Europeans and the Cree of Western James Bay," *Ontario History* 80 (3): 227–45; and Toby Morantz, "Plunder or Harmony? On Merging European and Native Views of Early Contact," in *Decentring the Renaissance: Canada and Europe in Multidisciplinary Perspective 1500–1700*, ed. Germaine Warkentin and Carolyn Podruchny, 48–67 (Toronto: University of Toronto Press, 2001).
3. Daniel Clayton, "Captain Cook and the Spaces of Contact at 'Nootka Sound',"

in *Reading beyond Words: Contexts for Native History*, ed. Jennifer S. H. Brown and Elizabeth Vibert, 95–123 (Peterborough ON: Broadview Press, 1996).

4. Brian J. Given, *A Most Pernicious Thing: Gun Trading and Native Warfare in the Early Contact Period* (Ottawa: Carleton University Press, 1994).

5. Further discussions in 2003 by Roger Roulette and Louis Bird, Omushkego Cree historian from Peawanuck, Ontario, suggest that this term relates to an old word, Waabistikweya, meaning “narrow place in a river” or “place where the river narrows”; it could even evoke the Saint Lawrence River at Quebec. This idea hints that Waabitigweyaa was French and that the story goes back to early French–Hudson’s Bay Company competition in the late 1600s. The French indeed were the Europeans who “found the Anishinaabeg first,” in the 1640s at Sault Sainte Marie, another place where the waters narrow (between Lakes Superior and Huron). In the 1680s the French were sailing into Hudson and James bays to trade and compete with the English Hudson’s Bay Company, and Anishinaabeg probably met them in the James Bay area, in a trade situation in which the HBC prevailed.

6. *Mide*, with the final *e* pronounced like the French *é*, is difficult to translate because all the diverse English words used for it—“shaman,” “medicine man,” “conjuror,” “priest,” and others—carry their own baggage and connotations. *Mideg* (pl.) may officiate at Midewiwin, or Grand Medicine Society, ceremonies held for healing and initiation of new members at different levels, but more generally, *mideg* are persons who have received special powers and skills through spirit visitors in dreams and visions (see, e.g., Michael Angel, *Preserving the Sacred: Historical Perspectives on the Ojibwa Midewiwin* [Winnipeg: University of Manitoba Press, 2002]). These gifts are manifested not by talking about them but through remarkable acts that may become still more magical and amazing as their stories are passed down the generations; see the suggested readings for further examples.

Suggested Reading

Brown, Jennifer S. H. “Ojibwa.” In *Encyclopedia of World Cultures, Supplement*, edited by Melvin Ember, Carol R. Ember, and Ian Skoggard, 249–53. New York: Macmillan Reference USA, Gale Group, 2002.

Brown, Jennifer S. H., with Maureen Matthews. “Fair Wind: Medicine and Consolation on the Berens River.” *Journal of the Canadian Historical Association* 4 (1994): 55–74.

Hallowell, A. Irving. *The Ojibwa of Berens River, Manitoba: Ethnography into History*. Edited with introduction and afterword by Jennifer S. H. Brown. Fort Worth TX: Harcourt Brace Jovanovich, 1992.

Matthews, Maureen, with Jennifer Brown, Margaret Simmons, and Roger Roulette. "The Search for Fair Wind's Drum." *Ideas*. Toronto: CBC Radio, 1993.

Matthews, Maureen, and Roger Roulette. "Fair Wind's Dream: *Naamiwan Obawaajigewin*." In *Reading beyond Words: Contexts for Native History*, edited by Jennifer S. H. Brown and Elizabeth Vibert, 330–59. Peterborough ON: Broadview Press, 1996.

WAABITIGWEYAA, THE ONE WHO FOUND THE ANISHINAABEG FIRST

Told by Charlie George Owen (Omishoosh)
Translated by Roger Roulette

This is very similar to the telling of the Bible.

This is the same thing with the white man [*wemitigoozhi*]. What happened long ago with the Anishinaabeg's land, the story of it.

Consider. I will tell you one more thing. I often tell this story. I speak about it like a legend, *aadizookewin*.

This land. This land was given to the Anishinaabeg. No one [else] owns this land. Over in the land across the water [Europe], what the white people did, they didn't know there was land here. Nevertheless, one white man sailed this way from their land.

And so, they found land, this land. Here. A huge ship, that's what they called it, "Gichi-naabikwaan." It sailed.

They landed on the shore of this land. They landed on the sands, it was said. This is where they must have seen someone's footprints on the sand.

The white man has the same type of feet. His feet left the same kind of footprints in the sand. At that time, they [the white men] knew there was someone living on this land.

They proceeded, with all their supplies in their possession, food, all kinds of things. They deposited them there; that's what they did. To see if someone might take the supplies when they return. They sailed off again. Off to wherever they came from. This is what was told again.

The Anishinaabeg who arrived at the open area toward the water, they saw, they found things left behind. They didn't know what those things were. They apparently went home. I don't know exactly where they were from. They wanted to tell of their findings.

They left for home after they'd seen everything. They didn't know about guns, axes, anything. Wearing apparel.

One old man knew of the gun. Apparently, he called it "Gaa-madweweg" [a reverberating noisemaker]. He also knew about gun powder, pellets; that's how the old man was aware of the gun. This is probably the use of this, he apparently said. They watched him inserting the black powder. They'd put something fibrous inside. Closing it up. Also the pellets.

Something, a package, came untied, where the heap of supplies was. Something curved. He proceeded to place a brownish flint. For, he knew, no one had told him.

"Could you, please, go hang up this piece of birch bark, do you mind?" It [the gun] discharged. Ah, when they had hung the birch bark, that's what he apparently had done when he discharged it. Sure enough, it reverberated. The birch bark instantly became full of holes, like a net. See, that's the noisemaker.

Another old man, apparently, knew the use of the axe. I guess he said, "The thing that makes a noise on impact, this is probably what it is called." Ah, let me see. Certainly, observe, he went to retrieve a log. Observe, he struck the log. The log split.

The log he struck, that's what split. Nonetheless, that's what they called it according to its use. They knew then.

Another old man took a knife. "Ah, what is the purpose of this? What is its use?" they had said. However, one old man knew. "This is probably called 'Gaa-daashkiiwagiseg' [flesh cutter]," he said, apparently. "If you intend to cut something, you'd be able to cut it. This is what it shall be called, 'Gaa-daashkiiwagiseg'," he said of the knife.

So, they tried it again. The old man started to cut birch bark. He cut it quickly. They knew then what it was for.

However, I couldn't say all the things that were there. But they didn't know what was there. The food that was inside a metal container. They didn't know what kind of food was there.

They [the white men] did take a lot of things with them. They did recognize clothing because it was made of furs. Caribou leggings, they [the Anishinaabeg] made clothing from any fur. They also covered themselves in rabbit fur.

When the white men sailed [here] again, they found only a few things left that weren't taken away. The white men knew there were Anishinaabeg [human beings] living here.

The many things the Anishinaabeg took. They [the white men] said they were going to build a house. So, they proceeded to make a house. Again, the Anishinaabeg went over. It was said there were four of them. They went to look around where they had found the things.

Ah, they heard the activity. Hammering. They peeked. Spying on them. They [the white men] were working away. They [the Anishinaabeg] were afraid of them. One man apparently said, "I'll go over." The other three were afraid. So, the man proceeded to leave and go over.

He saw a white man coming. He saw poles standing. The man came closer and closer. Suddenly, the white man caught a glimpse of him. He waved his arm and approached him. Shook his hand. He proceeded to take the Anishinaabe to where he was.

At this point, I'm not quite sure how they communicated with the white men, having a different speech.

Apparently, that's what they had done; they wanted all [the Anishinaabeg] to go over where they were. All of them. "Don't be afraid for us to take a look at you," was said to them.

Surely, they [the Anishinaabeg] went home to where their people lived to tell of the news. That's what the old men had said as they came down the shore. That's where they met them. They [the white men] treated them well, for they pitied them. They showed the Anishinaabeg everything they had.

You see, they apparently had liquor. It was said it was in a box. That was probably what they gave them. When the women started to get drunk, they started crying because they were afraid. Eventually, some of them went to sleep. They were covered up so they would not be exposed. That's what was said. The old men also were drunk.

When they sobered up, they were allowed to leave. They were given things. Whatever they could take with them, they took. Tools. That's when the Anishinaabeg were rich with things. They [the white men] started to be aware of the Anishinaabeg.

Again, they sailed off home to the land across the water. So it was said. The white man was called Waabitigweyaa. That was the name given to him. That's the one that found the Anishinaabeg first.

It was said, the news in Europe was, this land was peopled by human beings [the Anishinaabeg]. The Kwampanii [leader], the one getting rich off this land, said, "If there are human beings on that land, I never want them to come over here. They are dirty [impure]; they'll pollute my land." Apparently, that's what was said to the Anishinaabe. That's how much the Kwampanii hated the Anishinaabeg. That was the beginning of relationships.

Thus, that's probably how they came to that decision. The conclusion the Anishinaabeg made when they met the white man. They'd confer with one another and bartered for all the things that were traded in exchange for the fur clothing they gave the white man.

This was the reason for acquiring furs, to barter with the white man. That was probably the beginning of the fur trade. This was what was said.

That's when the white man, Waabitigweyaa, started to become very wealthy in his land. This was due to trading with the Anishinaabeg with furs from this land.

However, when word went out, when they were told that the Kwaampanii didn't want Anishinaabeg in their land because they thought they were dirty, one man apparently said he intended to go to Europe by ship. Even though he was told of the consequences, he embarked anyway.

When he disembarked in the land across the water, he was told not to go to the Kwaampanii. He, apparently, said he intended to go to the Kwampanii leaders' land.

When the Kwampanii leaders saw him, he was told he wasn't welcome. The leader called to his staff, "Could you make a wooden crate? Make it heavy on one side and place him inside. Throw him far out into the ocean; I don't want him remaining here," said the leader apparently. Thus, that's what they did with the wooden crate.

It was fashioned in a specific way. Lead was placed inside to make it heavy. The leader's assistants proceeded to carry the man off while he was inside the wooden crate. This is how much he detested him. Sure enough, the crate was tossed in the midst of the big waters. That was that. It didn't sink; it was said it stood upright.

While it was adrift, a white man fished it out of the water onto an island in a river. That's where it [the crate] came ashore and opened up. The man was in the crate. Afterward, they fed him so he wouldn't be hungry and he wouldn't be in need of anything.

Traveling by was his large ship [that he had come on]. The one who had given him a ride [to Europe] noticed him. He proceeded to give him a ride, whereupon he returned to his own land.

When the Kwampanii heard of the Anishinaabe trading—trading furs with Waabitigweyaa and getting wealthy from it—when the leader of the Kwaampanii heard what was going on, this is when he attempted to war with the white man, Waabitigweyaa.

He realized the traders discovered wealth in Anishinaabe land. This is probably why the wars came to be. The reason why the Kwaampanii fought for the wealth of the Anishinaabeg. However, the Kwaampanii defeated the white man; he killed him. The Kwaampanii then accepted to provide for the Anishinaabeg.

Consequently, the appropriation is very evident today. The wealth of *kwaampanii* [government]. That's the government's wealth. This was what was said of what I am telling you people. He [the government] continues to buy furs today. He has amassed his wealth as well as his abhorrence toward the Anishinaabeg visiting his land.

The Origin of War

Introduction by J. Randolph Valentine

Veterans are accorded great respect in Ojibwe communities. Early in every powwow, a special dance is performed to honor them. Native American communities have historically shown rates of volunteerism in times of war that are unmatched by any other ethnic group in the United States. There is nothing new about this willingness to protect one's community and to distinguish oneself through acts of bravery. When William Warren, a mixed-blood Ojibwe living in the early nineteenth century, sought to record the oral history of the Ojibwes of Minnesota and Wisconsin by directly interviewing prominent elders, the stories he gathered were overwhelmingly accounts of battle. Warren's work has been criticized as reflecting a Western historicism in its emphasis on such military events, but there is no compelling evidence that his account does not in fact reflect history as perceived by the elders whom Warren interviewed and whose perspectives he ardently sought to document and publicize. And on this basis, too, one should not be surprised that among the foundational acts of the culture hero/trickster Nenabozho recounted in Ojibwe mythology is the invention of war and practices associated with it. Yet the myth associated with the establishment of these institutions does not present the culture hero's act in terms of glory, though initially that is Nenabozho's assessment when he invents them. Rather his deed is portrayed as a consummate act of stupidity, which he readily acknowledges when confronted with the wisdom of his grandmother, who gently explains to him that the most significant effect of war will reside not in the glory it brings to warriors but in the inestimable sorrow and loss that it brings to the lives of children.

This account of the invention of war represents another installment of the gifted storyteller Waasaagoneshkang, "He Who Leaves the Imprint of His Foot Shining in the Snow," who was recorded by a young Fox anthropologist named William Jones at the dawn of the twentieth century, as part of Franz Boas's program to document the indigenous languages of North America. Jones recorded celebrated Ojibwe storytellers living on the shores and inland regions of western Lake Superior, using a simple process of dictation, transcription, and translation. Other stories by Waasaagoneshkang in the same cycle of Nenabozho myths appear in *Voices from Four Directions*, including an account of Nenabozho's birth, his theft of fire, and his learning the art of hunting as he travels with a pack of wolves.

Waasaagoneshkang lived at Pelican Lake, near the Bois Fort Reservation, in Minnesota, and had grown up nearby, on Rainy River, Rainy Lake, and the Lake of the Woods. Because of Jones's tragic and untimely death in the Philippines shortly after he carried out his Ojibwe work, little is known of those whom he recorded, nor do we have any but the scantest details of the social contexts in which the stories were told.

Waasaagoneshkang's accounts of episodes in the Nenabozho mythological suite often show similar thematic structures and motifs, particularly the stories of Nenabozho's battles with his brothers, who destroyed their mother during birth in a dispute over who would be firstborn. Raised by his maternal grandmother, Nenabozho embarks on a program to revenge his mother's death, though his own part in the act is decidedly ambiguous. The net result of these exploits is the establishment of various institutions among humans, animals, and the physical world, sometimes with consequences that Nenabozho does not foresee. He is consistently portrayed by Waasaagoneshkang as bold and impetuous to the point of cockiness, as a consummate schemer, the ultimate enfant terrible, having an audacity that allows him to prevail over more powerful opponents even though they are deeply suspicious of him from the moment they set eyes on him. Yet he rarely accomplishes his goals on his own. Typically his grandmother provides him with crucial details pertaining to whatever adversary he is about engage, explicitly defining the challenges before him but also providing intelligence critical to his success. It is also common for him, once engaged in his mission, to be aided at a moment of crisis by some small creature that reveals a crucial mortal weakness in Nenabozho's adversary. Armed with this information, Nenabozho inevitably prevails.

Such is the conceit employed here by Waasaagoneshkang to effect Nenabozho's victory over his brother, Hewer of His Shins. Reveling in the glory of his victory, Nenabozho races four times to his fallen opponent and kicks him, establishing the practice for time immemorial as the ultimate act of military valor. He then beheads his victim and sets off to share his marvelous inventions with humans, culminating in a scheme to draw attention to himself and his handiwork that has a decidedly undignified character. He teaches people the arts of war. Only on returning to his grandmother and listening to her wise counsel does he come to understand the tragedy he has wrought. There are timeless lessons here in thinking through the ultimate effects of one's inventions and in the relationship between personal creativity and deeper social wisdom.

Suggested Reading

Translations of Ojibwe traditional tales, including extensive Nenabozho myths, can be found in Barnouw (1977). Blaeser (1993) and Vizenor (1993) both provide excellent introductions to various aspects of the Ojibwe trickster/culture hero. Louise Erdrich's *Tracks* (1988) is an artful employment of the character of Nenabozho within a contemporary milieu.

Barnouw, Victor. 1977. *Wisconsin Chippewa Myths and Tales and Their Relation to Chippewa Life*. Madison: University of Wisconsin Press.

Blaeser, Kim. 1993. "Trickster: A Compendium." In Lindquist and Zanger 1993, 47–66.

Erdrich, Louise. 1988. *Tracks*. New York: HarperCollins.

Lindquist, Mark A., and Martin Zanger, eds. 1993. *Buried Roots and Indestructible Seeds: The Survival of American Indian Life in Story, History and Spirit*. Madison: University of Wisconsin Press.

Swann, Brian. 2004. *Voices from Four Directions: Contemporary Translations of the Native Literatures of North America*. Lincoln: University of Nebraska Press.

Vizenor, Gerald. 1993. "Trickster Discourse: Comic and Tragic Themes in Native American Literature." In Lindquist and Zanger 1993, 67–83.

THE ORIGIN OF WAR

Told by Waasaagoneshkang
Translated by J. Randolph Valentine

I

And such was what Nenabozho did.
Well, once again he went searching for his grandmother,
and he went and lived with her once more.

And once again he said that he intended to go searching for a brother,
and he was told this by his grandmother:
  "You can't kill him,"
    he was told by his grandmother.
  "He is guarded by a vast host.
  That's what will prevent you.
  But listen, I'm going tell you what you are likely to see,
  should you still decide to go.

  Now, on an island lives the one called
    Hewer of His Shin,
  and all about the island, there in the midst of the water,
    pitch floats as you come near.
  You won't be able to pass through,
    even though you have a canoe.
  Because your canoe will be mired there.
  Well, that's the first obstacle you will encounter.

  And even if you are able to safely get through,
    you'll see yet another barrier,
  and you'll think it to be a row of pines.
But it will be the dorsal fins of the Great Pike that you are seeing.
  And you won't be able to get around them.
  So that will be another obstacle lying in your way.

  And if you are able to negotiate that,
  you will come in sight of where your brother lives.

And when you paddle closer,
    you'll see a host of snow geese,
and you won't be able to get past them,
    even though you might seek to paddle around them.
It's they who guard the one you're seeking.
But this you must say to the snow goose,
whichever among them it might be that first makes a sound,
    you will say to it:
'Shay! Look, here is in token a white potato.'
And when you offer it the potato,
    this is what the snow goose will say:
'The other's robbing me of my white potato!'
    that snow goose will say.

And even if you succeed in passing through that obstacle,
then you shall disembark there where your brother lives.
But as you go up from shore,
    a blue jay will call out.
It will come racing toward you,
    and this you will do:
    you will offer it an acorn.
And then it will say:
    'The other's robbing me of my acorn!'
    that blue jay will say.
And at that point the one who lives on the island will arrive."

And this he was told by his grandmother:
  "In the very center of the island
  lives he whom you seek.
  In a long lodge he lives."

II

So, at that point he began to prepare,
    and he made himself a boat,
and when he had completed it,
he set off looking for an animal that was rich in fat.
And from it he made oil,
and then he made a store of everything he planned to use.
And next he went looking for a white potato.

And then he looked for acorns.
And when he had completed these tasks,
he started making arrows.
And when he had finished the arrows,
he said to his grandmother:
"Well, the time has come for me to set off."
And this he said to his grandmother:
"I'm setting off for war,"
he said to his grandmother.
And this he said to her:
"I will be four days in making passage across Gichigami.
And so the length of time that it will be calm will extend to four days,"
said Nenabozho.

III

And so he set off, boarding his canoe.
And truly, at some point as he paddled across Gichigami,
indeed he saw something lying across his path.
"Well," he had been told by his grandmother regarding this,
"You shall most certainly not be able to pass through."
His grandmother had told him.
And when he approached the pitch,
he oiled up his canoe with the fat,
and his paddle as well.
And when he drove his canoe into it,
not a speck of pitch adhered to his canoe,
nor to his paddle.
And from time to time he would add more fat
to his canoe and his paddle.
And thus he was able to pass through the pitch.

And so he paddled on,
and then again as he journeyed,
most certainly he saw something that must be pines,
he thought.

And as he came near,
it was indeed the Great Pike.
And this he said to it when he reached it:

"Please lower the fins of your back!"
he said to the Great Pike.
And truly, after the Great Pike has done so,
he accordingly passed over them.
And then he came in sight of the place
where he was bound,
and when he got a closer view of it,
most certainly he saw a snow goose.
And he was spotted by the snow goose,
so it called out.
So "Hiss!" he said to it,
and then he offered it the white potato.
And it came racing toward him.
"Hiss! What is the matter with you!"
said the manitou coming to it.
"Well, that snow goose is stealing a white potato from me,"
said the snow goose.
And this the manitou said:
"Why is he not able to get one for himself?"
the snow goose was told.
Now indeed, while the manitou was proceeding back,
Nenabozho hid.
And so he was able to continue on.

And when he went ashore,
he left behind all his equipment.
And truly he went walking along.
And then he was seen by a blue jay.
And the blue jay seeing him
began to cry out.
So he offered it an acorn,
and so it ceased to cry.
And once again another manitou came running.
"Hiss, what is the matter with you?"
it said to the blue jay.
And the blue jay said:
"He's robbing me of my acorn!"
And the blue jay was told:
"Why can't he get his own acorn?"

And when the manitou went back,
  Nenabozho came out of hiding again.

IV

And soon upon his way he went,
  and he came in sight of where his brother lived.
Indeed it was a very long lodge.
And as he came up near him,
  he could hear the other pounding on something
  there within his dwelling.
And when he looked within the dwelling,
lo, it was on his shins that the other was hacking!
And so he watched him, but the other did not look toward him.

And presently when the other began to rise to his feet,
  his legs were bent;
and when he had risen,
  his legs wobbled terribly as he walked:
they were on the verge of breaking,
and he would have fallen
  had he not steadied himself by holding on to something.

And this he said as Nenabozho watched him:
 "Someone is watching me!"
  he said.
And he spoke again,
  and this he said:
 "Someone is watching me for some purpose!"

And again he started hacking away at his shins.
And when he stood up, he legs were bending, and as he walked
  beside the hearth, he fell over.
"Somebody is watching me!"

And when he looked about,
  he saw Nenabozho peeking in, and he said to him:
 "Wait a bit, and then come in,"
  he said to him.

And so after Nenabozho had watched him awhile,
he was addressed again: "Okay, come in now,"
he was told.

And so truly he went in.
Well, he had made a cushion there for Nenabozho to sit on.
And as he sat there, this he was told:
"There is no doubt, Nenabozho, but that you are a manitou,
because you were able to make your way to me.
And I suspect that it is not for nothing that you have come,"
he was told.
And this Nenabozho said to him:
"I have come with no purpose in mind,"
Nenabozho said to him.

"You have *not* come without purpose!"
he was told.

Naturally he tried to deny what the other was saying:
"I am merely coming for no particular purpose,"
he said to him.

"Most certainly you are a manitou,"
he was told.

Well, then they quietly conversed together for awhile.
And this Nenabozho said to him:
"What do you fear that might kill you?"
he said to him.

"Aha, it is not to no purpose that you have come!"
he was told.

"Not," he said to him, "for such a long time would I merely be watching you,
had I some design,"
he said to him.

"Well, yes," he said to Nenabozho, "by means of a small blue
point on an arrow,

with a piece of flint fastened on for a spear—by means of
this might I be killed.

Well, that's all I'm going to tell you.
But how about you, Nenabozho, what is it that can kill you?"

And this Nenabozho said to him:
"Were my foot to be touched gently by cattails,
then I would be killed."
But he was only deceiving him.
He wouldn't die;
that was not what might kill him.
"Now that's all I have to say to you!"

V

And so Nenabozho rose to his feet and left,
going back to his canoe.
Then immediately he began preparing what the other had said would kill him.
So he made arrows.
And when he had finished,
he made the whoops of war and fell upon the wigwam.

"You worthless dog!" the other said to Nenabozho.
"Now it's clear that he's come to wage war on me," he said to Nenabozho.
But the moment that Nenabozho had departed,
he had gone out to gather cattails
and had brought them into his lodge.
And when Nenabozho approached the wigwam,
he came racing out.

And so Nenabozho shot him in the back,
squarely in the middle of the back he hit him.
And after the other had pulled the arrow out,
then Nenabozho retreated.
And then it was Nenabozho's turn to be pursued,
and he himself was shot in the middle of the back.
And he as well simply pulled the arrow out of his back.

And there he forgot his heart; he had not put away his heart anywhere.
Well, after a while he remembered to put his heart away somewhere.
And then he raced to the attack,
    and when he had overtaken his foe,
    he shot him.
And then it was his turn to flee,
and too he was overtaken and shot.
And he did what he had done before,
    pull out the arrow.

And then it was his turn once more to charge,
    and to overtake and to shoot.
And then the other pulled out the arrow.

And then once more it was his turn to be chased,
    and again he was shot.

And now it was getting to be dusk.

And evidently he thought this:
  "It seems that he may vanquish me,"
    he thought.

Well Nenabozho chased him,
    and shot him again.
And he did the same,
    pulling the arrow from his back.
And then he came pursuing again.
So Nenabozho began to cry.
Because he had only two arrows left,
    and that made him very afraid.

But he was spoken to by the Red-Headed Woodpecker,
    who said to him:
  "What's wrong with you?"
    the Red-Headed Woodpecker said to him.
  "Is it possible that you are really crying, Nenabozho?"

"Yes, because I shall soon die, my younger sibling."

"Why is it that you should die?
    Just do this:
You can't kill him by shooting him on the body.
    Listen, you have to shoot him at the base of the hair knot."

And that's indeed what Nenabozho did.
And so when he overtook him again,
    he shot him,
    and he nearly hit the wrap of his hair knot,
    and indeed, he almost fell down.

And this he was told:
    "What's the target you're trying to hit, Nenabozho?"
"Yeah," Nenabozho said to him.
    "In many places arrows will fall during the course of a battle."
And then he turned and fled.

Well, now he had only a single arrow remaining,
    and it was for this reason that he ran a long way off.
But again he was shot,
    because indeed the other still had an abundance of arrows.
So then he rose up against him again,
    and he came up close to him,
    and he shot him in his small headgear.
And so the other fell, and Nenabozho gave a whoop of victory.
And when he fell, Nenabozho ran up to him and kicked him,
    and then he ran back.
And again he charged him and kicked him,
    and again ran back;
and then again he charged him,
    and again ran back;
and again he charged him
    and kicked him again;
"Thus shall humans do as long as the earth shall last;
    thus it is four times will they kick their opponent;
    it is that many times by which they shall obtain honor
    when they engage in battle."

VI

And then he commenced to skin the vanquished's head.
    And then he dried the head.
And when the head was dry,
    he set off homeward.
And once again he set off across Gichigami.
But no more did he see the blue jay or the snow goose.
So he set straight out for deep water.
And no more did he see the Great Pike nor the pitch.
Indeed, he encountered no difficulties on his entire trip home.

And when he came near home, he thought:
  "This is what humans shall do until the end of the world,"
    he said.
And when he was arriving home,
  "I wonder whether I should go over there," he thought.
He saw a place where some people had a settlement,
    and so he headed straightaway to meet them.
But then he turned back.
Because he had no banner by which to draw attention to his arrival.
Well, at last it dawned on him that he could make a flag of his soiled
    loincloth,
    and dangle it on a pole in front of him.
And so he straightaway set sail for where the people were.
And as he went along, he sang, for he thought:
  "What might lift up the spirits of the people?
    This is what will lift them up;
    this will lift up every living soul!" he said.

And so now he saw the people quite close,
    and so he began to sing,
    and this is what he began to sing,
    and it was to his soiled old loincloth that he began to sing:

"What is it, what is it, which suspended from two corners hangs so limp?
    Yay aha ho yo ween jah
What is it, what is it, which suspended from two corners hangs so limp?
    Yay aha ho yo ween jah."

Well, the people then spotted him.
"That must be Nenabozho," said the people.
"What could it be that he has hoisted on a pole?"

"I think it's his old soiled loincloth that he's got lifted up!"

"But look, there below, there's something else that he's got on the staff."

And lo, when Nenabozho drifted to shore,
it was a human head that he had lifted up on the staff.

"Lo, by this shall you all be stirred to feelings of joy, people."

And that is indeed what happened.
Not for a moment did they sleep
while they were being taught the things that they would do.

And this said Nenabozho:
"Even though they be greatly sad of heart,
yet shall people find consolation in this,
and cease from their sadness.
Thus shall the people do until the end of the world."

VII

And then he set off to find his grandmother;
and when he came to where she was, he said:
"Well, my grandmother, relieve me of this, my grandmother!"

And truly, that's what the old woman did.
And then Nenabozho said:
"Thus shall the people do for each other until the end of the world;
oh, so truly will the people love this till the end of the world;
even though they be grievously sad,
yet will their sadness lift when they see the human head!
No matter what may their concerns be,
nonetheless they shall find joy in these doings of mine.
Truly from their cares will the people be delivered," said Nenabozho.

And this he was told by his grandmother:
"Vast harm have you done to humanity by having them do this to one another.
Listen to the reason why I say this.
Listen, when you attacked your brother,
that in attacking him so should all people come to do so to one another,
This is what I have to say to you about this:
it's the *children* upon whom you bring harm.
That's the way I see it,"
he was told by his grandmother.

"Yes," Nenabozho said to her.
"Alas, I have not succeeded in doing a good thing.
Well, I have completely erred in what I've done,"
he said to his grandmother.

"It's because I'm so foolish, being a child myself,"
Nenabozho said.
And he said: "Obviously I didn't think it thoroughly through.
You are so right, Grandmother, in what you say,"
he said to his grandmother.

That's what he said initially to his grandmother.

And then he set off, setting off from there,
and he roamed about, doing all sorts of deeds.
He wandered over this entire earth.
And behold the many things he's done here on the earth.

That Way We Should Be Walking

Introduction by Mary Magoulick

Oogima Ikwe, an Ojibwe/Nishnaabe woman from the eastern Upper Peninsula of Michigan, broke into performance mode during our tape-recorded interview session while I was doing fieldwork in her community in the mid-1990s. Her speech reflects themes and styles of her ancestors, even while offering a very contemporary message and feel. Today, as in the past, acceptance in a Native community and identity as a Native American are complicated by outside influences and pressures. Many contemporary Native Americans are worried about losing either their identity (through too much sharing or assimilation) or their control over their identity (as in the case of outsider appropriation of ceremonies). That these concerns are legitimate is demonstrated partly by parallel concerns in earlier generations, for whom assimilation was very immediate and real, manifesting itself in boarding schools, missionary activities, and laws prohibiting traditional ceremonies, religions, and languages.

Mirroring her ancestors' struggles to maintain culture, Oogima Ikwe ponders here how to revive culture, to remember what was forgotten, to find what was once considered "lost." In spite of disconnection from ancestral ways (even for generations), a renewed, revived culture, along with related attitudes about cultural authenticity and tradition, emerge here. Many Native American people today partake in vital and dynamic cultural renewal, refashioning their perspectives, values, and lifestyles after centuries of oppression and attempted assimilation. In places like the eastern Upper Peninsula of Michigan, such rejuvenation occurs in English, the dominant language spoken by most Nishnaabeg there.

Studying and speaking words or phrases in Ojibwe (Nishnaabemowin) often mark one's involvement in the cultural renaissance, yet few residents of the region have acquired sufficient communicative competency to make Ojibwe a viable primary means of cultural transmission. Although English predominates, many Ojibwes manipulate or transform it when transmitting cultural values or messages. Oogima Ikwe's discussion of the outward trappings and inner life of being Native today, through a traditionally modeled oratorical performance (in English), projects an intuitive understanding of the transitory and fluid nature of all cultural knowledge and symbols. This performance during our discussions reflects traditional oratory when tradition is realized as a dynamic process.

Often the most poignant and artful performances in English among Native people today, like this one, revolve around events and feelings connected to issues of identity and cultural renewal, such as sobriety, powwows, spiritual ceremonies, or teaching circles. Native people in the eastern Upper Peninsula of Michigan today connect to the past and try to focus on "that good way of life" while living in the present and facing the future. They are reshaping traditions to change their lives for the better. Many speak of the power of Native spiritual and cultural renewal in changing lives, staying sober, and feeling hopeful.

Oogima Ikwe's passionate performance bears witness to the success and significance of the renewal of culture in which she participates. Her speech emphasizes that people *are* all "those things" that are really important to culture. Oogima Ikwe understands that culture is a matter of worldview, internal knowledge, lifestyle, and not outward trappings (all viewpoints embraced by contemporary scholars of culture and folklore as well). She feels very strongly that the spirits will provide whatever the people will need for culture to continue. She portrays metaphorically a view of culture as emergent and dynamic, teaching her ways of living, thinking, and communicating. Culture, she affirms, is a way of living and being, not a catalog of outward trappings or props. She avoids the trap of reifying culture, to which even some scholars succumb.

Oogima Ikwe, like many Native people, learns about and connects to her culture from community events like powwows or spiritual ceremonies, through seeking out "elders" or knowledgeable members of the community who practice culture, through structured learning environments like the tribal college, or through personal dreams, visions, and other experiences. The most valued and widely acknowledged way of connecting to tradition remains elders. Additionally, however, some younger members of Native communities in the Upper Peninsula find themselves relying on personal visions and dreams as means of learning and reviving culture. For instance, Oogima Ikwe discusses and practices receiving teachings from dreams/visions as a means of learning and growing.

In spite of her expression of faith in the spirits to provide for her people, and of people to maintain a meaningful ethnicity through visions and a good relationship with the spirits, Oogima Ikwe's speech reveals that she sometimes longs for the symbols and trappings of her ancestors, like many of her cohort. Her moment of insight in this speech was spurred by her longing to find a feather to enhance beautiful regalia to wear at powwows. She participates in ceremonies, sweat lodges, and powwows, but in realizing that outward trappings and ceremonies are not the equivalent of culture, she negotiates acceptance of culture as a process and anticipates satisfaction with whatever manifestations of culture her generation can stimulate, imagine, and maintain. She may want, enjoy, and learn from ceremonies and other concrete expressions of culture, "But, we don't need them. . . . We won't need those things, / 'Cause we'll be those things." She affirms culture as an ongoing, emergent process involving people and ways of living, thinking, and being, a matter of consciousness or spirit rather than of biology or material goods.

Because this utterance is eloquent, passionate, interpretable, and intentionally delivered in a measured rhythm, I transcribe it according to the performance theory (or "ethnography of speaking") insights of Dell Hymes, Dennis Tedlock, Barre Toelken, and Richard Bauman. This attention to textuality emphasizes it as a poetic speech event. Performance theory requires greater focus on both the artfulness of oral performances (in terms of how they are represented as written text) and attention to context, particularly in terms of the local culture. I break lines according to the rhythm of her speech and indicate relevant gestures or other vocalizations, intonation, and emphases. To better understand the speech, we will also examine contextual information from Oogima Ikwe's own explanations of her philosophy and lifestyle.

THE WAY WE SHOULD BE WALKING

Told by Oogima Ikwe

But, you know, people are too ritualistic.
I said to a friend one day,
I said, "What happens if all the pipes were gone?
Creator just took all the pipes away?
No more eagles,
No more eagle feathers,
No staffs,
No pretty regalia,"
    [an aside] What the hell is that anyway, regalia?
    I don't even know what that word means.
    I'll have to look it up someday.
"No pretty regalia,
No fans,
No breastplates,
No nothing."
"Oh, God!" [in mock worried tone]
"Are we not Indian anymore, Maanii?" [laughing].[1]
"Where's my identity lie?" you know.

And then, oh, I was sitting by the water one day,
And the water says,
    And this was a teaching from the water I got,
    But I've heard it from other people since, though,
    You know,
Because at that time I was looking for an eagle feather,
And I was looking for that medicine,
And I was looking for that pretty regalia,
And I was like,
"Oh help me get some buckskin so I can have a nice buckskin outfit,
And oh, me, me, me, me, me, me!"

1. Maanii is the author's name in Ojibwe.

I put my tobacco in the water and stirred it up like that
And the water took it and said,
"Hmm" [she laughs],
"We have a problem here" [she laughs more].
And so they told me,
"Well what would happen if everything went away?"

And I was sad.

I was thinking, "God, that would be a real drag!"

And the water said,
"Why?
You *are* the pipe,
You *are* the drum,
You *are* the feather,
You *are* the buckskin,
You *are* the Earth,
You are *all* these things.

All these things are is a reminder,
A tool,"
You know.

"But there are many tools.
These mean *nothing* really."

"Ooh!" [intakc of breath]

God, don't say that in a circle either!
[in a mock serious tone]

But they really do mean nothing [sincerely]
Okay,

That spirit of that eagle
Isn't limited to that feather,
Or we would never dream about 'em.

That spirit of that pipe
Is not limited to that pipe
You know
Or else that pipe wouldn't be able to talk to you from fifty miles away
You know

It's the thing behind that.

My spirit is not limited to this body,

So we are all those things,

We don't need those things

And someday we won't have those things.

Mary: You believe that?

Oogima Ikwe: Yeah.
I believe someday we won't have those things,
We won't need 'em.
We never needed them before.

[with passion]
So is the legend of how the pipe came to the people,
How the sweat lodge came to the people,
How the eagle feather fell to the people,
How the drum came to the people,

Because we had gotten away
From where we were over here,
As spiritual beings,
And needed reminders.

We needed to see something,
Because we had lost our faith.

So the drum had to come to us,
BOOM, BOOM, heartbeat of Mother Earth.
Now we can hear it again.

So the pipe came to us
Okay,
That stone from that earth,
That balance with that wood,
That female,
Now we can see it,
We believe it,
We know what it does.

And so those eagle feathers came to us,
So they could remind us about what that eagle is there for,
Okay,
And those warriors that died,
What did they fight for?

Well, we never needed these things.
They all came to us.
You know

The sweat lodge—
The people were sick.
We never used to be sick!
So we didn't need any healing,
Any sweats.
But now we do,
So plink!
Creator brought that down for us.

And they're all good things
Don't get me wrong,
And they serve a good purpose,
But, we don't need them.

If we were really walking in that way we're supposed to be walking,
Or should be walking,
Or hopefully will get to that point again walking,
We won't need those things,
'Cause we'll be those things.

Oogima Ikwe's speech harkens back to Ojibwe oratory of times past. Scholars and the general public in the past often appreciated Native oratory, but principally as evidence of social stratification. David Murray asserts that discussions of oratory are most often used to promote a particular view of Native Americans as noble savages who fit a historical scenario of the disappearing Indian (Murray 1991). In such cases, the speech as a fragment, relic, or translation, in other words a "pale imitation," only heightens its appeal. The arrogance and ignorance of the dominant culture in its praise of speeches emerges in that "[w]hat Indians say in private, or to each other, is seen as less expressive of their true selves than what they say in public to whites" (Murray 1991, 42).

Nora and Richard Dauenhauer have worked among Tlingit people to correct what they see as a lack of sufficient scholarship on oratory. They demonstrate that for Tlingits oratory ties the community together and draws out and actualizes major values of the culture (1990). They also note more generally, in regard to Native American oratory and poetry: "Songs are often the revelations, if not the manifestations, of the spirits themselves, and they evoke the spirits when sung. Oratory employs the spirits in ceremonial use, especially for healing, removal of grief, and prevention of harm" (1990, 146). Thus oratory served a crucial purpose traditionally and continues to do so in some communities.

In his discussion in *Native American Verbal Art*, William Clements notes that Henry Rowe Schoolcraft, Indian agent in Sault Sainte Marie, Michigan (the very community where Oogima Ikwe grew up), during the first half of the nineteenth century, and collector of Ojibwe folklore, was surprised by the richness of Indians' verbal art (Clements 1996, 116). Schoolcraft, like many others, often saw this oratory as evidence of the primitive nature of the Indian. Clements notes that he grudgingly admitted that it had poetic qualities. Schoolcraft nonetheless notes some interesting characteristics in regard to this verbal art. Clements discusses Schoolcraft's presentation of qualities in Ojibwe oratory such as "great simplicity," "occasional strength of an Indian's thoughts," "figures and epithets of beauty," "[being] surrounded by all the elements of poetry and eloquence—tempests, woods, waters, skies." He also shows Schoolcraft's romantic bias: "His very position—a race falling before civilization, and obliged to give up the bow and arrow for the plough—is poetic and artistic" (Schoolcraft [1851], in Clements 1996, 121). This attitude that the Indian was a child of nature who thereby had access to fundamental elements of poetry, along with the perspective that the Indian was "falling before civilization," adds a hint of melancholy. Thus Schoolcraft concludes that we might understand the Indian's propensity for basing his figurative imagery on nature and for including elements of mystery and a hint of melancholy (Clements 1996, 121). Such an attitude underscores Murray's message that speeches were typically praised only as part of the larger ethnocentric perspective of seeing Native Americans as a primitive, vanishing race.

Beyond recognizing their skills in creating imagery, Schoolcraft also notes of Ojibwe orators:

> They appear to have an accurate ear for the rythm [*sic*] of a sentence, and a delight in rounding off a period: the language affords great facilities for this purpose, by its long and stately words, and multiform inflections (1857) . . . no unity of theme, or plot, unless it be that the subject, war for instance, is kept in the singer's mind . . . both the narration and description, when introduced is [*sic*] very imperfect, broken, or disjointed (1848). (quoted in Clements 1996, 122)

Some of this apparent praise is diminished when we realize Schoolcraft also considered Indian verbal art a "shapeless mass" until worked on by Schoolcraft's poetic aesthetic (Clements 1996, 122). Both Clements and Dell Hymes have demonstrated well that Schoolcraft's translations and refashionings are not improvements from a contemporary perspective (see Hymes 1981, esp. "Some North Pacific Coast Poems").

Clements quotes the significant passages in which Schoolcraft describes the salient aspects and elements of Ojibwe oratory:

> He excels in that rapid, continuous flow of utterance, in which it seems to be the object of the speaker to go on, without a pause, as long and as vehemently as possible. In listening to this kind of outpouring of words, it seems as if a thousand syllables and words were amalgamated into one, and as if to pause in the middle, or at any intermediate point, would be to break the harmony, or to mar the sense. (Schoolcraft [1828], in Clements 1996, 125)

> Nothing is more characteristic of their harangues and public speeches, than the vehement, yet broken and continued stream of utterance, which would be subject to the charge of monotony, were it not varied by an extraordinary compass in the stress of voice, broken by the repetition of high and low accent, and often terminated with an explanatory vigor, which is sometimes startling. It is not the less in accordance with these traits that nearly every initial syllable of the measure chosen is under accent. This at least may be affirmed, that it imparts a movement to the narrative, which, at the same time

> that it obviates languor, favors that repetitious rhythm, or pseudo-parallelism, which strongly marks their highly complex lexicography. (Schoolcraft [1837], in Clements 1996, 125–26)

Schoolcraft finds the rhythm of Ojibwe oratory particularly fascinating, and he characterizes it as "pacing." He notes the rapid flow, the vehemence, and the length of speeches, which he finds marked by unusual accentuation, repetition, and parallelism. Realizing the tradition of long, heartfelt, rhythmic "outpourings of words" helps us appreciate Oogima Ikwe's speech as continuing a long-standing tradition among her people, albeit within a very new framework and to a new audience—English speakers with a different attention span and expectation for oratory.

Oogima Ikwe's speech is distinctive from traditional Ojibwe oratory in some obvious respects. It is composed in English (her language), and she is a woman. Typically orators were men according to Murray (1991), though this may be our perception because collectors ignored women's verbal art. Oogima Ikwe's speech is innovative as well in its forward-thinking emphasis; in other words, she doesn't dwell on a culture dying (a typical subject of nineteenth-century speeches), but is inspired instead by the image of cultural rebirth or renaissance. Yet overall, the rhythm, length (although her speech is relatively short, in a modern conversational context its length is noticeable), parallelism, continuous flow, vehemence, and harmony of her speech (all qualities Schoolcraft noted among her people's oratory 150 or more years ago) suggest that she has indeed revived a traditional form of expression of her ancestors.

The qualities of her speech that inspire its transcription as poetry flow from a general cultivation and understanding of the poetic mode; Oogima Ikwe enjoys writing poetry. She explained to me that she typically composes her poetry in dreams or reveries, and she quickly records them upon regaining consciousness. Cultivating her dream life and her sense of poetry establish her connection to her culture's traditions. She explains:

> Sometimes I write stuff down so, 'cause my mind is so full. If I didn't have to think about everything else, like rent and this and that and the other thing, I think I'd be able to remember more things. But they say you remember what you're supposed to remember anyway. But some of the best teachings, just from the water talking to me, you know, have come during those times I sat down by the water, long before I thought, you know, I thought I was picking up this path and then come to understand I've already, I've always had it, you know. I've always walked it. I just didn't know that.

One of the most interesting aspects of Oogima Ikwe's oratorical message is its forward-thinking hopefulness. But in subsequent discussion, Oogima Ikwe makes it clear that she also tries to honor the past and traditional ways of learning from elders. In most Native cultures, elders today hold much authority, and their words usually hold rhetorical power to teach, remember, or shape culture. But Oogima Ikwe asserts and affirms the possibility of learning directly from the spirits as an equally authentic and significant means of learning and participating in culture, thereby empowering her generation, as she explained to me during our conversation. Her vision involves what she calls "a new hoop" coming:

> But the new hoop is the young people, it's gotta be that eighth fire, you know. And it's coming strong. It's also a shifting of powers where mostly it was men who had a lot of power in some tribes. It's been a shift to the women and children. The women and children are going to be the seers and the people who go out and find the answers during that third shaking of the earth or after or before or whenever. It'll be all around that kind of time zone and, ah, the new hoop is kind of like, it's going to be kind of like this [twining her two fingers together], like two fingers locked together, you know. And back here on the left side of your one finger is the old hoop, the old, old, old way, long time ago. And then over in this way is the evolution from that old way. And it's all the things in history and time when the pipe and everything were just talked about, and then right here, is total chaos and confusion [light laugh] 'cause it's right where the new and the old meet, and there's going be a lot of head butting. . . . but when we get over here, we'll be almost back like where we were here. But only, lot of people, they understand the new hoop, but they really haven't come to that understanding yet either. The new hoop is really the old hoop, see. It's just different. And it'll be different, but it'll be the same.
>
> Mary: Where did you come across this idea?
>
> Oogima Ikwe: In my own mind, and then I started, um, picking up on things. I didn't call it the new hoop, but I perceived it like that, and, ah, from Creation, and I didn't understand things, so I, I talked to the Creator, said, I recognized that something was flowing, something was happening, you know, that young people were coming up with more wisdom than old people. And old people were acting like children without any wisdom, without any focus or understanding or compassion or tolerance, and it was the young people coming up who were having the dreams. It seemed like the old people never dreamt any-

> more. But the young people were dreaming and they were seeing the future which was like the past. . . .
>
> They won't have the elders to go seek things out, you know, and, ah, to get guidance or understanding. It'll be part of who they are, already, they'll have that within themselves, even as very young people. You can see that, but it's got, it's kind of not in its pure enough state yet, but you'll see, you can see that in young people. They act older, they have, uh, in, a wisdom about themselves, you know that they never had when they were younger. They were very naive and innocent of things, and now they're very much thinking of grander things, the earth, the environment, their future, you know. And these are very young people, Native, non-Native, spiritual, nonspiritual, because that's, that's given to them by the Creator now, you know. That was something that was given to the elders through experience and through teachings, a lifetime of teachings, then they gained that wisdom. But we can't afford that luxury anymore. So now it's just been handed to them, from the Creator to the young people as a gift. (taped interview)

Many times during our discussions, Oogima Ikwe confirmed the importance of elders, stating she wants to learn from them whenever possible, but she also looks to the spirits for guidance, as here where she discusses the new hoop envisioned by her son and confirmed, as she says, "in my own mind."

Oogima Ikwe details an apocalyptic vision of fire and change that seems dramatic (only partly revealed here). Yet her overall philosophy (as her speech emphasizes) concerns the idea of cultural change and adaptation more than a specific physical apocalypse. Her philosophy is that young people can carry on the culture. They are "a new hoop," a new way of living and organizing the world, as seen when she says they are "almost mirroring" the old ways, but the reflection also shows a new world. So the hope comes not only from elders, from whom Oogima Ikwe continues to seek knowledge and guidance, but also from the younger culture members. With all ages working together, there is indeed a possibility for real change, metaphorical if not actual fire, and cultural rebirth, whether through more peaceful means or actual revolution. Regardless of whether the prophecy comes true, the mind-set that change can come and traditions can be maintained at the same time is exciting and bodes well for the cultural revitalization underway.

That dreams and visions should play such a key role in Oogima Ikwe's experience and understanding of the refashioning, or renewal, of culture, is another marker of her connection to traditional Ojibwe values. Frances Densmore notes the importance of dreams traditionally, which have long been cultivated and attended to in Ojibwe culture:

> An aged Chippewa said: "In the old days our people had no education. They could not learn from books nor from teachers. All their wisdom and knowledge came to them in dreams. They tested their dreams, and in that way learned their own strength." The ability to dream was cultivated from earliest childhood. "Try to dream and to remember what you dream," was a frequent admonition to children when they were put to bed. Thus the imagination was stimulated, and there arose a keen desire to see something extraordinary in sleep. . . . The dream thus secured was of greatest importance in the life of the individual. . . . The Chippewa say that in their dreams they often returned to a previous state of existence; also that they saw things which no Indian had seen at that time, but which they themselves saw and recognized in later years, such as sailing vessels and frame houses. (1979, 78–79)

Thus even though Oogima Ikwe's earlier words stress the coming of a new hoop in which elders might not play such a significant role as young people, she is not breaking with tradition. She still respects elders, as seen in her frequent invocation of them to empower her own words throughout her discussions, in which she, like many others, lends authority to her words by prefacing statements with the phrase "the elders say." She is respectful and mindful of tradition but cultivates as well another traditional value within her culture, the power of dreams to shape lives and culture itself. And in this sense she faces the future. Shaping the future while realizing (intentionally) continuities with the past defines tradition conceptually.

Other Native people whom I interviewed also discussed the importance of dreams and visions in their lives. While many people recognize the significance of dreams and visions to the revitalization in their community, most others seem to foster visions and dreams especially within contexts such as fasting and ceremonies and don't emphasize them as a primary means of rebuilding the culture (except within these ceremonies). Some elders in the eastern Upper Peninsula use visions to reestablish traditions such as names and clans. Among the consultants with whom I worked, Oogima Ikwe most strongly emphasizes and uses "spirit teachings" as a means to understand herself and her culture, but her experience is only a more intense example of a widespread faith in visions.

While visions may contain original teachings or confirmations of what the elders say, those visions that challenge the status quo are not unanimously welcomed. Oogima Ikwe realizes that the visions she receives might offend elders or others when she says in her speech that the outward symbols of being Native mean nothing really. Then in an aside she jokes: "God, don't say that in a circle either!" She knows her assertion would not be well received by all because too many people rely on those outward symbols of culture as measures of identity. While she fulfills the accepted norms of valuing elders, she also believes in the potential of a "new hoop" envisioned by a younger generation.

The kinds of things Oogima Ikwe learns from her dreams include her clan, her name, how to dress, that she can have a pipe, and so on. Such knowledge today is typically the domain of elders (who often recover such information as a service to tribal members, sometimes for a fee). In fact, an elder gave Oogima Ikwe her name, which she later changed (shortened) based on a vision. That same elder only hinted at her clan, which she herself knew from dreams. Furthermore, she has her own idea about the importance of outward symbols of culture like pipes, drums, and the traditional Ojibwe language based on her visions (not based on what the elders tell her), and she expresses herself according to spirit messages from dreams. All of this indicates her willingness to accept personal responsibility for shaping her culture and affirming the possibility for cultural revival, regardless of authoritative voices (of, for instance, elders) in establishing authenticity.

She confirms that learning from visions is authentic and important when she affirms that although her understanding is imperfect, it is appropriate and true:

> It seems like whenever I was really distressed about things, I would always come home and I would always come by the water. Or I'd go to the woods, camp out in the woods. And for some reason I was always looking outside of that, 'cause I thought you found religion in some kind of church or some organization, you know. And kind of forgetting, the teachings of my father were kind of buried. They didn't, they weren't really in the forefront of my mind, you know. Or my aunts and my uncles, you know.
>
> So when I came back and I was talking to [a friend who is very spiritual] and the more she would talk to me about her Native beliefs and stuff, the more I would think in my mind that "I already know this, I already know this, I already know this." So then it dawned on me like [snapping her fingers] *could have had a V-8* [louder] "I ALREADY KNOW THIS!" [laughing] you know. This is inside of me, you know. This is, has always been here, it will always be here. You know, I can't run here and I can't run there. I can't run away from it, 'cause it's always here.
>
> So the more I heard, the more I understood that this's always been the way I've thought, but I've just been looking for other people who've thought this way. So I had to come home and find the root of it all, more or less, you know,

> I could see the tree but I didn't know where the roots were. So the more she talked to me, the more I realized this is what I've been looking for, and it's been where I've gone all the time and it's been what I've done all the time, but I've never really understood it, you know, or where it came from.
>
> So I had to come back by the water [laughing lightly]. I always come back to the water. And, uh, we, even when we lived in Detroit, every other weekend I was up here fishing or swimming, had to be because of the water you know. It's very healing, and course I always knew that, but I, I didn't know any teachings with it. I always knew that when I sat by the water I felt better, you know, or I would talk to the water, and it would feel like something would be lifted from me, like away. But I never understood that there's spirit associated with the water. That the water is the lifeblood of Mother Earth. It's very cleansing and healing, you know. I never understood all that, but yet I was doing it.
>
> So I think that stuff is always, always inside of you.

She receives "teachings" from spirits, in moments of reverie, or from other moments of life. She suggests here that being Native is less a matter of "picking up this path" than of something intrinsic to her being: "I've always had it, you know. I've always walked it," she says, and she also asserts, "So I think this stuff is always, always inside of you" and "I ALREADY KNOW THIS!" Such confirmations of various teachings integrate her experiences into a coherent and livable worldview, clarifying her identity.

Nonetheless, Oogima Ikwe credits friends recognized as elders for encouraging her practice and involvement in cultural renewal. Strong community relationships based on sharing culture are common. The fact that her internal sense of knowledge reverberates with her community makes her visions harmonious and authentic in her own sense of those terms. Overall, Oogima Ikwe's message is one of hope for her generation. Being Native is positive and healing, environmentally and emotionally sound. But she is nonetheless concerned for the burden it places on the young generation (see her discussion of the new hoop). Oogima Ikwe articulates both the potential and the need for the young generation to carry on whether or not enough elders are left to teach them, as seen when she says:

> That was something that was given to the elders through experience and through teachings, a lifetime of teachings, then they gained that wisdom. But we can't afford that luxury anymore. So now it's just been handed to them, from the Creator to the young people as a gift.

What elders had uniquely was time and experience, "a lifetime of teachings." But times have changed. Without that "luxury" of time, people and culture must also change. Old people "should have" the knowledge, but if they don't, and if young people do, that is okay.

Oogima Ikwe's affirmative view realizes and embodies the dynamism and fluidity of all culture and tradition. Her speech resonates with oratory in the spirit of her ancestors while reflecting the current climate of cultural rejuvenation in her community. N. Scott Momaday states: "We are all, I suppose, at the most fundamental level what we imagine ourselves to be. And this is certainly true of the American Indian" (1998, 4). Like the best of us in any culture, she imagines life with beauty and strength of spirit that affirms humanity in the spirit of Momaday's words.

References and Suggested Reading

Bauman, Richard. 1984. *Verbal Art as Performance.* Prospect Heights IL: Waveland Press. Originally published 1977.

———. 1986. *Story, Performance, and Event: Contextual Studies of Oral Narrative.* Cambridge: Cambridge University Press.

Clements, William H. 1996. "'All We Could Expect from Untutored Savages': Schoolcraft as Textmaker." In *Native American Verbal Art: Texts and Contexts,* 111–28. Tucson: University of Arizona Press.

———. 2002. *Oratory in Native North America.* Phoenix: University of Arizona Press.

Dauenhauer, Nora Marks, and Richard Dauenhauer, eds. 1990. *Haa Tuwunáagu Yís, for Healing Our Spirit: Tlingit Oratory.* Seattle: University of Washington Press.

Densmore, Frances. 1979. *Chippewa Customs.* Minneapolis: Historical Society Press. Originally published as the Smithsonian Institution's *Bureau of American Ethnology Bulletin,* no. 86 (1929).

Evers, Larry, and Barry Toelken, eds. 2001. *Native American Oral Traditions: Collaboration and Interpretation.* Logan: Utah State University Press.

Hymes, Dell. 1981. *"In Vain I Tried to Tell You": Essays in Native American Ethnopoetics.* Philadelphia: University of Pennsylvania Press.

Kroeber, Karl, ed. 1997. *Traditional Literatures of the American Indian: Texts and Interpretations.* 2nd ed. Lincoln: University of Nebraska Press.

Momaday, N. Scott. 1998. "Native American Attitudes to the Environment." In *Stars Above, Earth Below: American Indians and Nature,* ed. Marsha C. Bol, 3–11. New York: Roberts Rinehart, for Carnegie Museum of Natural History.

Murray, David. 1991. *Forked Tongues: Speech, Writing and Representation in North American Indian Texts.* Bloomington: Indiana University Press.

Tedlock, Dennis, trans. 1978. *Finding the Center: Narrative Poetry of the Zuni Indians.* Lincoln: University of Nebraska Press. Originally published 1972.

Three Tales

Introduction by Laura Buszard-Welcher

During the historical period, the people known as the Potawatomis lived in the upper Midwest, in the territory close or adjacent to Lake Michigan and stretching eastward across southern Michigan. They were closely allied with the Ojibwes and Ottawas, forming together the "Three Fires." The languages of these groups are also closely related, with Potawatomi being the most divergent, largely due to later contact with the Fox Indians. The English word "Potawatomi" derives from the self-designation Bodéwadmik, although it is more common for the Potawatomis to refer to themselves and closely related tribes as Neshnabék.[1]

As a result of a series of treaties made with the United States government, and the federal policy of removal, the Potawatomis live today throughout the Midwest, with communities in Michigan, Wisconsin, Kansas, and Oklahoma. Many fleeing removal found refuge among the Ottawas across the Canadian border. Although some eventually returned to live in the United States, many stayed; thus there are people of Potawatomi heritage living on Ottawa reserves in Ontario today.

Removal, which isolated Potawatomi communities; government policies aimed at assimilation; and the external pressures of being increasingly engulfed by American society, culture, and language led to a gradual shift in which speakers increasingly used English to the exclusion of Potawatomi. Today Potawatomi is a critically endangered language. There are only a few elderly fluent speakers, and the speech community has shifted to using English almost entirely. On the positive side, many tribally sponsored programs as well as grass-roots groups are working to revitalize the use of Potawatomi within heritage communities. The three stories provided in translation here are part of a larger project to make Potawatomi narratives available in the language of their telling.

The Transcriptions

The stories were first transcribed in the early 1940s, when Jim and Alice Spear, Neshnabék who were living on the Prairie band reservation in Kansas, told them to linguist Charles Hockett. He was working on his dissertation, a grammar of the Potawatomi language, and made several trips to Kansas to work with the Spears. The narratives, about fifty in all, formed the corpus that he used to analyze the structure of the language. Although he never published the narratives as a set, he included two of them in a series of articles he published on Potawatomi grammar.

The language sessions were not recorded by a mechanical device, as we might use a tape recorder nowadays; rather the Spears dictated and Hockett transcribed word by word, using a phonetic script. The stories therefore retain much of the vividness of their original telling. They are unedited, except in the sense that they were part of the narrators' repertoires and were therefore practiced performances.

Many of the stories were given partial translations, usually in the form of glosses for individual Potawatomi words, when these were known. For a few narratives, each sentence was given a colloquial translation, probably based on translations given by the Spears. These provide a very useful guide today, in some cases, overriding what might seem to be a more likely translation.[2]

The Narratives

The three narratives given here belong to the *yadsokanen* genre, a traditional distinction that includes stories about a mythological time or that involve mythological elements, as opposed to *yajmowen*, narratives about modern events, activities, and recent history. *Yadsokanen* commonly feature animals as characters, although there are often people who interact with them as well.

Stock characters, such as Rabbit, Raccoon, and Wolf, are representative of behaviors that are either esteemed or censured by the community. Rabbit, although he may be destructive, is sympathetic as an underdog that gets out of tricky situations by using his wits. Raccoon and Wolf are commonly juxtaposed in stories to contrast the foresight and moderation of the raccoon with the opportunistic and gluttonous nature of the wolf. Cleverness, foresight, planning, and moderation are all traits that contribute to the success of life in a harsh northern environment, where resources are often scarce and the possibility of starvation very real.

Sometimes characters represent a character type. For example, many narratives feature a small boy (often the youngest child) as a protagonist. This child is frequently paired with an elderly adult, and together they suffer adversity until the child, through cleverness, luck, or magical ability, raises both their fortunes. In "Crane Boy," the protagonist, a young crane, is initially presented as an example of how excessive or reckless behavior can bring about misfortune (the narrator says it is a story about "Crane misbehaving"). However, very soon we are introduced to an old woman, who finds the abandoned crane and takes him home to be her "grandson." We then know we are dealing with stock character types. For the listening audience, this sets up expectations about the rest of the narrative. As anticipated, we learn that in return for her benefaction, the crane brings good fortune to the old woman's home by ridding her first of a bully, then of a pesky big wooden spoon that steals her food.

I have chosen these three stories and presented them in a particular order to highlight another theme that emerges in such a presentation: that of the changing nature of Neshnabék life in contact with Chemokmanek (European American) society. The first story, "Crane Boy," takes place in mythological time when the boundaries between people and animals are blurred: people talk and interact with animals, and animals talk and behave like people. One has the sense of a certain nostalgia when Alice Spear describes the old woman's traditional home, filled with woven mats and *jak zhe na gégo Neshnabé zhechgéwen*, "all kinds of Indian things." In the next story, the Neshnabék live in settlements, and homes have fireplaces, gardens, and wells; these artifacts of contact and the presence of alcohol allude to a more modern setting with increased pressure on traditional ways of life. The third story is situated in recent times, perhaps the time of the narration, and features white people as the only human characters. Yet the Neshnabék are still very much present, represented by the raccoon and the wolf. Although the story takes place after a considerable period of contact with Chemokmanek, the world of Raccoon and Wolf is still very much as it ever was: the clever raccoon is still plotting ways to trick the wolf, and the wolf, hungry and opportunistic as ever, still falls for them. The story also alludes to traditional life by incorporating themes such as the importance of planning ahead and moderation. Much of the drama takes place under the noses of the white people, who are humorously ignorant of it all. It is a kind of celebration of the Potawatomi world, an assertion that it continues to exist and thrive in the face of external pressure from Chemokmanek society.

Pronunciation

The orthography used here was developed in the 1970s for use in second-language teaching. It is a phonemic system in which each letter or digraph (such as *ch* or *zh*) represents a single contrastive sound.

There are five Potawatomi vowels:

a as in f*a*ther, p*a*sta
é as in b*e*t, s*ai*d
i as in s*ee*, l*ea*ve
o as in b*oa*t, r*o*pe; in southern Michigan, the sound is pronounced more like s*ou*p.

e like English schwa, with slightly different pronunciations based on its environment in a word. Before *n*, it sounds like the underlined vowels in the words tin, print, mitt. When *e* occurs before ', *k*, *g*, or at the end of a word, it is pronounced like sun, cub, and ton. Elsewhere, it is like *a*bout or in the unstressed pronunciation of the words *a* and th*e* (as in *a* car, th*e* car).

Consonants found in the Potawatomi words used here are pronounced as follows:

g as in *g*o (never a "soft" *g* as in *g*iant)
ch as in *ch*oose
j as in *j*ust
sh as in *sh*ine
zh as in gara*g*e, azure

Notes

1. The term Bodéwadmik is usually translated as "fire keepers." Although there are etymological problems with this translation, it is in keeping with the traditional Potawatomi role in the Three Fires alliance. Neshnabék, usually translated as "first people" or "original people," is a Potawatomi term that has varied use. It can mean Potawatomi people or more broadly Three Fires or other Algonquian people. In contrast with Chemokmanek, "Americans" (literally, "big knives," apparently from the bayonets Americans used on their guns), Neshnabék can mean more generally Native American people.
2. See, for example, "A Rabbit Tale," in which the word *bzhew* for the native "bobcat" is translated instead as "tiger."

Suggested Reading

Buszard-Welcher, Laura. 1997. "Language Use and Language Loss in the Potawatomi Community: A Report on the Potawatomi Language Institute." In *Papers of the Twenty-eighth Algonquian Conference*, ed. David Pentland, 34–43. Manitoba: University of Manitoba.

Clifton, James A. 1998 [1977]. *The Prairie People: Continuity and Change in Potawatomi Indian Culture, 1665–1965*. Iowa City: University of Iowa Press.

Edmonds, R. David. 1978. *The Potawatomis, Keepers of the Fire*. Norman: University of Oklahoma Press.

Hockett, Charles. 1948a. "Potawatomi I: Phonemics, Morphophonemics, and Morphological Survey." *International Journal of American Linguistics* 14:1–10.

———. 1948b. "Potawatomi II: Derivation, Personal Prefixes, and Nouns." *International Journal of American Linguistics* 14:63–73.

———. 1948c. "Potawatomi III: The Verb Complex." *International Journal of American Linguistics* 14:139–49.

———. 1948d. "Potawatomi IV: Particles and Sample Texts." *International Journal of American Linguistics* 14:213–25.

———. 1939. "The Potawatomi Language." Ph.D. diss., Yale University.

Landes, Ruth. 1970. *The Prairie Potawatomi: Tradition and Ritual in the Twentieth Century.* Madison: University of Wisconsin Press.

CRANE BOY

Told by Alice Spear
Translated by Laura Buszard-Welcher

Once when it was getting close to autumn, cranes were preparing for spending the winter in the south. At first they talked to one another about when they would start, as was customary, and they stored things away that they would eat while they moved. It must have taken four days for them to get ready, packing their food to eat.[1] When they were finished getting ready, they planned to leave very early.

That evening the boys were excited about leaving. As they were fooling around, one boy broke his arm. His parents told him they would have to leave him behind all winter. The boy cried and cried. "What will we do with you if you cry all night?" his parents said to him. "You did this to yourself; you don't listen when you're told—you are too naughty." Sure enough, the boy cried all night.

Morning came, and the cranes were leaving. One rabbit was put in the boy's sack for him to eat for the entire winter.[2] He didn't take it, though. As the cranes flew up, the boy jumped and jumped, but he couldn't fly away because his arm was broken.

After a while he stopped crying, and the boy stood around there by the lake. An old woman was standing nearby and heard something, like someone crying, she thought. "Who could it be?" she said to herself. "Maybe I will be blessed by a child," she said.[3] So she went straight toward where the sound was coming from. As she came to the big lake, the boy had just started to walk off. "What's the matter, boy?" she said. The boy was so scared, he fell back. "My parents left me behind with nothing, and they won't come back until the springtime," said the boy. "Don't be sad," said the old woman. "All through winter you shall work for me. You'll have company, and you'll be my grandchild." The boy was very happy to have a place where he would spend the winter.

1. Four is a significant number in Potawatomi cosmology. The four days of preparation seem to underscore the importance of this annual event for the cranes.

2. The parents provision the boy with a token rabbit, but likely it is also all that could be spared. They leave, fully expecting that the boy will succumb to the harsh northern winter.

3. In traditional Potawatomi culture, grandparents would often raise a grandchild, who is both a comfort as well as a help to them.

So he went with his grandmother, and soon they came to where her house was. The old woman lived in a mat house.[4] Everything was all done the Indian way—the boy saw that the mats were good and spread out all around.

At night his grandmother told him stories and about things that would happen. Afterward she told him, "There is one other boy I take care of. He's a bad young fellow, he talks back, and he drinks a lot," said the old woman. Sure enough, later on when they were going to sleep, they heard someone whooping. "That's him all right, coming yelling," said the old woman.

After a while he came tumbling in, "I'm a man, Grandma," said the boy, and he kicked a pail.[5] So the crane boy picked him up and threw him outside. "Where did he come from, Grandma?" said the bad boy. "You go away, now, Grandchild," said the old woman. "That's right; you go on, behaving any old way. I've already raised you, and I can't make you listen any more. Go on and take care of yourself, now; you're big enough. You talk back too much, so you will never know your parents. That's why this will happen to you: you will always be called turtle. You'll never have any smarts, because you talked back too much," he was told. And that's why the turtle doesn't know his parents.[6]

So the little crane kept working, and he took care of his grandmother all winter. Usually in the morning, the old woman would tell him what she would cook for dinner. "Fetch water, Grandchild," she would say to the boy. "I'll cook dried meat and corn for us to eat," she said. The boy would always wonder, "Why does she do that? Why does she tell me what she's going to cook?"

Well, it must be that someone would always talk to the boy when he went out to fetch water, asking him what they were going to eat. When the boy came back, his grandmother would ask him, "Did you see someone, Grandchild?" "No," said the boy.

So once the boy thought, "I must know why he asked me what it is we're going to eat." So in the morning, once again, he went to fetch water, and he heard, "What are you going to eat, little crane?" "You sure bother me, always asking what we're going to eat. Well, I'll tell you: squash, with a little pork mixed in," said the boy. So now the boy wanted to know what would happen.

Something happened, all right! Just as the old lady was almost through cooking, in came a big spoon. "Yaa! Grandchild!" she exclaimed. "You told! Now we'll be hungry!"[7] Sure enough, they were hungry all day, and so the boy knew what it

4. A *pekyegen* is a traditional dwelling made with rush mats.

5. "I'm a man" is a common boast, also made by Rabbit near the end of the second narrative.

6. The old woman is somewhat mystical in this story. Here she acts as a kind of culture hero, creating the creature we know today as the turtle.

7. The narrator isn't explicit but implies that the big spoon stole all their food.

was like to be hungry. When it was night, his grandmother told him, "Don't say anything else about what we will eat." So the boy kept in mind what happened.

"Okay, Grandchild," he was told again in the morning, "today, don't tell him what we're going to eat: I'm going to make corn soup." "I'll certainly keep that in mind today," said the boy. When he went out, again someone spoke to him, "What are you going to eat, little crane?" "What are you going to do?" said the crane boy. When he returned, sure enough, his grandmother asked him, "Well, Grandchild, did you tell?" "No, Grandma, I didn't tell. I was hungry, so that's why I didn't tell," said the boy.

They picked up fish that the waves had washed to the shore, and the old woman would roast them. The boy gathered lots of wood, because they would always roast fish. And usually when they were going to sleep, his grandmother would teach him.

Once, when he was lying down at night, the boy heard something that sounded like frogs. "What's happening, Grandma?" said the boy. "What's the matter, Grandchild?" said the old woman. "Seems like I hear frogs," said the boy. "Oh, Grandchild, now soon it will be spring," said the old woman. "Always look there, toward noon.[8] If spotted clouds come, your parents will be leaving to come back," said the old woman. The boy was very glad.

After he woke up in the morning, he kept looking toward noon, and just barely, every once in a while, there would be white clouds. The boy came flying in and told his grandmother, "Every once in a while, I see spotted clouds, Grandma!" "Your parents are starting to leave," said the old woman.

So the boy took his pail to get water. "Be careful, Grandchild; don't tell what we're going to eat: I'm going to cook yuccapans with bear meat mixed in," said the old woman.[9] That really sounded good to him. "For sure, I won't tell," thought the boy.

Sure enough, just after he dipped into the water, that man asked him, "What are you going to eat, little crane?" When he returned, his grandmother asked him, "Well, Grandson, did you tell?" "No, I did not, Grandma," said the boy. So they had a good meal, and the boy once again thought of what his grandmother had said. "That's right; the spotted clouds will come," thought the boy. "I'll wake up early and look for the spotted clouds. So now must be the time my parents will come," he thought.

So he took his pail again, and he was told, "Grandchild, I'll cook corn and mix

8. If you face the sun in the northern hemisphere at noon, you will be facing south.

9. The translation has "yuccapans." Native speakers aren't sure from the original or the translation what type of food this is.

in some deer meat." But he was so happy about seeing his parents that he didn't remember his grandmother's warning. When he came to the river, sure enough, someone asked him, "What are you going to eat, little crane?" "Boy, you certainly have a way of abusing your fellow creatures. You're dependent and snatch away what your fellow creatures would eat. She's going to cook a little corn mixed with dried meat, whatever you may do about it." So the boy once again did wrong.

So as his grandmother was cooking, he would ask her every once in a while, "How soon until it is ready?" "Almost," the boy was told. "I'll sit by the door, Grandma," said the boy. He sat hiding with a big stick. "What's the matter, Grandchild?" she asked him. "Don't you know, Grandma? It's hot here, Grandma. Seems like you would know. It's getting to be spring, you said, Grandma. That's why it's getting to be hot," said the boy. So then the old lady took up her kettle. That big spoon came reaching in. So the boy grabbed the stick and split that big spoon.

Then the boy ran outside. He left for the place where he had come from with the old woman. When he arrived, he sat down and looked up—and there were spotted clouds! He began to hear something, and he stood up and faced that way—for sure, a black cloud was coming. "It must be the cranes!" said the boy. Soon, sure enough, the cranes arrived, and once again the little crane jumped up and down. Soon his mother and father were looking for him. "Ah, my son, we are very glad you are still alive," said his parents. "If it weren't for Grandma, I wouldn't be—I couldn't live on just that rabbit you left behind for me," said the boy.

So that is as far as the story goes, about little Crane misbehaving.

A RABBIT TALE

Told by Jim Spear
Translated by Laura Buszard-Welcher

Once there was a village, and someone was destroying their gardens and wells. So they had two scouts watch out for whoever might be doing that. Later, sure enough, someone came along. They saw him pulling out beans and doing all kinds of things. It was Rabbit.

Early in the morning they told the leader what Rabbit was doing. The chief said, "Tomorrow at noon we'll have a meeting and decide what to do about him." Since the rabbit belonged to the village, they couldn't kill him as they pleased; they would have to get something more on him in order to kill him.

During the council, one of them said, "I might know how to get him. We will have him go get a sackful of ants."

So they told Rabbit, and Rabbit said, "That's easy." He picked up a sack, put in some sugar, and left.

When he got to the anthill, he talked to the head ants and told them, "I've made a big bet. Those people say you won't be able to eat up all the sugar. I say you will." So the ants started to crawl into the sack. Soon the sack was filled. The rabbit tied it good, took the sack, and gave it to the chief. "Here," he said to him. And the chief said, "Hmph."

So the council about him went on again. While they were talking, another man said, "Tiger told me that he could kill the rabbit."[1] So they talked to the tiger.

So there by the rabbit's trail, the tiger played dead. Soon Rabbit came along. Rabbit sat and watched him awhile. Finally he spoke to the tiger. "This is the second time I've been to one of your funerals. When your father died, I was there. Well, today you're dead, and here I am. But you're lying differently than your father did. Your father died with his legs sticking up in the air." So the "dead" tiger lifted

1. The word used here is *bzhew*, which usually translates as "bobcat." The bobcat is found throughout the continental United States, although its range is somewhat spotty over the central Midwest. Jim Spear likely knew that this word referred to the bobcat, although he apparently chose to translate it as "tiger," perhaps in consideration of his audience. I follow his usage here.

his legs. Then the rabbit laughed at him, "Ha ha! No one ever dies with his legs sticking up." So Rabbit ran away from him and into a hollow tree.

Then the tiger went back and told the chief's attendants, "I couldn't kill him." Then the chief said, "Maybe I am the only one who would know how to kill him. I'll give it a try. I'll ask him to kill that lion. This lion is killing piglets and sheep. If Rabbit doesn't kill that lion, then he will be killed."

So the rabbit was told what the lion was doing, and the chief said, "If you don't kill him, you will be killed." "Oh, that's easy," Rabbit told him. So the rabbit looked for the lion. As he started to walk, he saw an old well with a little water in it. He looked in and saw himself. Then he made a noise and the sound came back to him, and he knew right away how to kill the lion.

He found the lion close to the pig pasture. When he came to the lion, he said to him, "Brother, I'm very scared! I'm running away from someone. He sure looks awesome. You look awesome—but him, even more so. Let's go over there; he sure is scary." Lion said, "Let's go and take a look at him." Rabbit told him, "Be careful."

When they arrived at the well, Rabbit said to the lion, "Hurry up, look in." So the lion looked in, and someone in there sure looked mean. Then rabbit said to him, "Hurry now, roar!" So the lion did. The lion heard the echo, and he really thought there was someone in there. Lion roared three times, and then he got mad. He got so angry, he jumped into the well.

Then the rabbit ran to the chief and told him, "I killed the lion." The chief said, "Hmph, my attendants will go over and take a look." When the attendants got there, sure enough, he was in there struggling. When the attendants got back, they told the chief, "The lion is dead for sure."

So the chief said, "I will test him once more; I have a scheme. There on a hill is a big snake. I will tell the rabbit that I want the teeth. I'll ask him to get them." So the attendants called the rabbit. "The chief wants you to get that snake's teeth for him." So he went, and the chief told him what he wanted. And then the rabbit said, "Oh, that's easy."

The rabbit left. He got an axe and chopped off a stick. He sharpened it and made a mark on it. Then he went to the snake and told him, "I've made a big bet. If I win, you can have some of it. See this mark? Those people said that you won't be able to swallow up to it, but I said you will." So the snake said, "That's easy!" As the snake opened his mouth to swallow the stick, the rabbit shoved in the stick up to the mark, then pulled it out again, killing the snake. Then he took the teeth to the chief and said, "Here."

The chief took them and said, "Hmph." So he said, "Come back tomorrow; I have another difficult thing for you to do." So the rabbit left.

On his way back that night, the rabbit ran across some young men. They were drinking something. These young men gave the rabbit a drink, and he got just about drunk. Feeling pretty good, the rabbit started for the chief's house.

When he arrived, he told him, "Chief, you know I am smart; you know it. No one here can kill me. You have been trying everything to kill me." Then the attendants charged at him, grabbed him, and told him to keep quiet.

Well, there must have still been a fire in the fireplace at the chief's house. Rabbit said, "I'm a man; I could even go through this fireplace." So the attendants tried to hold him but couldn't keep him back. Rabbit escaped, ran into the fire, and started to climb the flue. Finally he smothered.

Then the chief said "Rabbit sure is smart. He killed himself."

So that's the end of this rabbit story.

RACCOON AND WOLF

Told by Jim Spear
Translated by Laura Buszard-Welcher

This story is about the raccoon running about.

While Raccoon was running along, he saw a beehive hanging from a tree. He had been going about, stealing pork rind from someplace. Raccoon said to himself, "I'll bet I'll meet my brother Wolf, and like always, he will be hungry."

Sure enough, he met the wolf. "Brother, do you have anything to eat?" he said to the raccoon. "Not much; I just have a little for my own dinner," said the raccoon. So the wolf asked him, "What do you have?" "Just a little meat rind," said the raccoon. Wolf said, "Oh, please, let me have that rind." So finally the raccoon gave it to him. "Where did you get it from?" asked the wolf. "I stole it from the white people," said the raccoon.

So he took the wolf to the place. When they arrived he told the wolf, "This is it. There's lots of pork." And the wolf said to him, "Let's come here tonight." "Wait until it's getting to be morning," said the raccoon. He added, "You know, when I was going along, I saw a sack of meat hanging up. I am too small, so I couldn't reach it. But I made a few jumps, anyhow. You're big, though; you could make it. If you can do it, give me half."

When they arrived there, the wolf saw it and thought, "Sure enough." So they went back a ways in order to jump at it. Raccoon made the first jump but couldn't make it. So then the wolf tried—and that meat sack was full of bees! The wolf got stung all over. The raccoon was high in a tree and saw the wolf get badly stung. That wolf didn't get mad, though; he kept his mind on the meat—he wanted to go back and steal that pork.

After midnight they returned to the place where the pork was. Just as it was getting to be morning, they entered the storehouse. The raccoon judged the situation carefully and took only one piece of meat out of the storehouse to eat it. But the wolf stayed and filled himself up. Then the wolf was too stuffed to go back out where they had crawled in.

So, early this white man went to get some pork and found the wolf stuck in the storehouse. He caught the wolf and took him to his house. At noon he called some councilmen. They must have laid the wolf on top of a table. Well, the wolf was so full, he couldn't move away while they talked over what to do about him. One man said, "Let's finish talking about him at one o'clock."[1]

While the men were eating, the wolf got up and left and so was gone when they got back. So those men who were deciding over the wolf said, "From now until forever, the wolf will be punished, as long as the world stands." And the wolf is still being punished today.[2]

So that's the end of this story about the wolf.

1. This "council" over the wolf is reminiscent of the council held over the rabbit in the second story, although here it is clearly a farce—the white people humorously stop at noon for a lunch break, just after starting the meeting, giving the wolf the opportunity to slip away.

2. From 1915 to 1941, the federal government placed a bounty on the wolf, paying up to five dollars per hide for wolves trapped and killed on federal land. In addition, some states enacted their own wolf bounty programs.

Louse and Wide Lake

Introduction by Richard J. Preston

The story you are about to read is an Eastern Cree narrative of a conjuring contest, from the eastern Subarctic region of Canada, where ever since the melting of the great Wisconsin glacier, thousands of years ago, small groups of indigenous peoples have hunted for their living over a wide expanse of land, rivers, and lakes. Crees still go to the bush to hunt and trap today, though few families spend the entire winter. The Cree language continues to be spoken by many thousands of people, and along with Ojibwe and Inuktitutt, is considered to have a very secure future in Canada.

The storyteller was George Head, a fine old man who told stories to me and to others who were respectfully interested in learning about the "old ways." George said that this story is a *tipachiman* (Preston 2002), meaning that it is not one of the stories from time out of mind (not what we call a myth), but rather it describes a more recent—and local to the region—set of events. In addition to many stories, George also sang the traditional Eastern Cree songs, quiet yet exuberant expressions of hope for getting a living in the northern "bush."

George narrated "Kawichkushu" ("Louse") in 1969 at the community of Fort George, Quebec, when it was translated by Gerti Murdoch of Waskaganish, Quebec, and recorded by Richard J. "Dick" Preston. The recounting was not done in a "traditional" bush camp, but George had recorded stories for non-Crees at Fort George on other occasions and was quite comfortable with the setting. Commentary on the story was recorded in Waskaganish in 1974 by Dick Preston in conversation with John Blackned, who was born in the 1890s and hunted inland up the Eastmain River, Quebec. Translation and comment was provided by Albert Diamond, a young university-educated Cree of Waskaganish. The session took place in John's house.

Of all the many Cree stories I have recorded, the story of Louse and Wide Lake's conjuring struggle against each other is the one that struck me most forcefully for its wealth of extraordinary images. When I first read through it, I wrote on the transcript, "ever metaphorical!" My enthusiasm set off in my mind an uneasy sense of caution, and this led me to ask the anthropologist's question. Was I imposing my own culture's notions of metaphor on this traditional Cree story? The short answer is "yes". But what were the Cree notions or habitual sense of "fit-ness" regarding the use of trope in language? When I asked Gerti about the Cree use of metaphor, she thought a while and replied that she thought that there were no metaphors in Cree. I had a problem.

I reread the story, this time to try to discern which of the "metaphors" might almost certainly be something like a metaphor in Cree. I found only one for which I could feel confident, where the conjuring power rises, "like a wave". But perhaps even here my interpretation was misplaced or an artifact of translation from Cree to English. The wave was not a metaphor; it was deadly power. The rest of the images were probably to be taken literally, or as dream images, or perhaps something else. I had stumbled upon a profound problem in translating images of power. I had to discover how words were serving to communicate Cree meanings within an ethos and structure of knowledge that was the cultural context of this story and the rest of the oral tradition.

I needed to ask the experts, beginning with the one from whom I had recorded the story, but George Head had died a few years after the recording, so I brought my question to John Blackned, who had been my mentor during the 1960s. The transcript of this conversation is included at the close of the story.

I also looked for experts who have written on the topic of metaphor. I found the most help in Terence Hawkes's little book on the history and types of metaphor (Hawkes 1972). But the problem did not yield very easily. What were those waves, really? How could a man cause another's arm to swell enormously, without more physical contact than touching a bit of seaweed? How could a sorcerer travel underground, then move invisibly up a thin tipi pole, move across on a thin pole serving as a drying rack, and then cause a cloud of steam by spitting in a fire? Was this an image of striking an adversary in his very hearth and home? How could separate bits of bone blind both of a man's eyes at the same time? How could the blind man, standing in a canoe, use a bow and arrow to shoot a seal? What is the story telling us about conjuring power? What are we being told about the consequences of interfering in other people's lives? The story opens up the whole domain of stories, worldview, ethos, the nature of human relationships, the agency of conjuring power, and more. Since I was particularly interested in conjuring (Preston 2002), my attention focused on this aspect, especially in the follow-up discussion with John Blackned.

Conceptual Perspective

I want to begin with Edward E. Evans-Pritchard's thoughts, late in his career, on the problem posed to anthropologists and others, that in all known cases in culture history, people have had some kind of spiritual beliefs. He wants to clarify the question of how we may best understand them.

> My answer to the question that I have asked [in *Theories of Primitive Religion*] must be that while the problem posed is, wide though it may be, a real one, the answers are not impressive. I would propose instead that we do some research into the matter. (1965:119)

> Perhaps, also, field research into this particular topic demands a poetic mind which moves easily in images and symbols. (1965:112)

Let us, then, try to move more experimentally in images and symbols, in allusions and intuitions. To begin, let's take Evans-Pritchard's example of how a missionary to the Eskimo or Inuit peoples of the Arctic in the nineteenth century could translate the biblical phrase "Feed my sheep." Translating into Inuktitutt words, he might try "Feed my seals." But this does not convey the allusion to a shepherd who protects and nurtures his flock. An Inuk hunter is not interested in herding and nurturing seals, but in nurturing one seal's acquiescence in being found and then killing it to nurture his family. The ideology of an Old Testament pastoralist is radically different from the ideology of an Arctic hunter. And so the translation of the spiritual idiom requires us to look beyond the translation of words, to translation of images and cultural systems of images (Geertz 1973).

It is helpful and historically accurate to view metaphor, as we understand and use it today, as a much more specialized and deliberate use of word images than what was practiced as recently as only a few hundred years ago in our own literate tradition. That is, the use of imagery in modern English has only recently involved the deliberate use of metaphors that we are familiar with today (Hawkes 1972). Extending this "proto-metaphoric" characteristic to the Cree, I will beg the question by claiming that for our own traditional ancestors and for the Cree's traditional ancestors, there was neither concept nor notion of a crafted metaphorical use of word images. Following on this, we will not look for evidence of a class of deliberate, cognitive, "special" cases of trope but rather for evidence of experience that is both intuited and expressive, more than it is intellectual and literal minded. For an example of the intuitive and expressive in our own storytelling tradition, here is Shakespeare on man's glassy essence:

> But man, proud man!
> Drest in a little brief authority,
> Most ignorant of what he's most assured,
> His glassy essence, like an angry ape,
> Plays such fantastic tricks before high heaven
> As make the angels weep.

A literal and intellectual approach to this passage would miss the point. This is expressive literature, and it asks us to try to intuit what human pride and folly means. I would like to believe that Shakespeare's "glassy essence" was pointing us at the multifaceted, fragile, and deceptive ambiguities of "seeing through a glass, darkly," not at the literal clarity of looking in the mirror. In the glass, the seer may apprehend a clouded microcosm of the world where one may sometimes be allowed to see beyond the normal restrictions of time and place and sense an aesthetic (though not necessarily beautiful) unity in life's experiences. This would involve the formulation of images of our nature as humans but would not involve more abstract (and possibly reflexive) intellectual symbols.

The next step is to consider some Cree images, with the proviso that these images, too, may not be essentially cognitive, but rather intuitive and spiritual, dreamlike and emotional. If we can get a grasp of imagery at this level, we will have achieved a fair understanding of Cree imagery as a whole (Preston 2002) and perhaps some ideas about a tacit Cree theory of language. The story is unusual in my experience for the degree that it involved direct "quotes" of the persons, moving us right into the action. Most stories, most of the time, refer to the persons speaking by an identifying third-person pronoun ("then he said"), rather than giving a first-person account. Rather than create paragraphs, and thereby changing the emphases of the narrative, I have tried to space the printed form of the statements in a way that represents the timing of the storytelling and the pacing of the thoughts that are being conveyed (Toelken 1969, 1987; Tedlock 1983). Following this story, with its allusions to extraordinary and powerful events, we will hear another Cree storyteller's thoughts about what the story is telling us.

Suggested Reading

There are some useful and authoritative guides to reaching further insights into this story and similar stories. For the larger sample and context of Eastern Cree stories, conjuring, and some insight into one storyteller, see my book *Cree Narrative: Expressing the Personal Meanings of Events*, 2nd ed. (Montreal: McGill-Queen's University Press, 2002). For an introduction to the deeply held convictions of peoples in nonliterate cultures, a small but excellent introduction is Edward E. Evans-Pritchard, *Theories of Primitive Religion* (Oxford: Oxford University Press, 1965). For the landmark in theorizing the anthropological experiments in thinking in images and image systems, see Clifford Geertz, *The Interpretation of Cultures* (New York: Harper & Row, 1973). On the history of the use of metaphor, another small but excellent book is Terence Hawkes's *Metaphor* (London: Metheun, 1972). For the discussion of how to best represent the spoken word in printed form, see

Dennis Tedlock, *The Spoken Word and the Work of Interpretation* (Philadelphia: University of Pennsylvania Press 1983). Barre Toelken has worked wonderfully (I use that word thoughtfully) with Navaho myths, especially interesting for his revisiting of one trickster myth, delving more deeply beyond the surface of apparent events to the moral discourse and below that, to the connectedness of words and power in the universe. Four of his papers should be read in sequence: "The 'Pretty Languages' of Yellowman: Genre, Mode, and Texture in Navaho Coyote Narratives" (*Genre* 2 [1969]: 211–35); "Life and Death in the Navaho Coyote Tales" (in *Recovering the Word: Essays on Native American Literature*, ed. Brian Swann and Arnold Krupat, 368–401 [Berkeley, University of California Press, 1987]); "Ma'ii Joldlooshi la Eeya: The Several Lives of a Navaho Coyote" (*The World and I* 5 [1990]: 651–60); "From Entertainment to Realization in Navaho Fieldwork" (in *The World Observed: Reflections on the Fieldwork Process*, ed. Bruce Jackson and Edward D. Ives, 1–17 [Urbana, University of Illinois Press, 1996]).

I have had a look at some recent thinking on metaphor, because I have a point to make and don't want it to founder on the criticism of intellectual obsolescence. I have the benefit of an anonymous reader who is quite current, and it's useful to see another person's reaction, in this case with a cutting edge but presentist approach to the problem of metaphor. If this were the 1970s, the reader would have wondered how I could possibly have missed the opportunity to do a structural analysis.

It may be that I am "confusing metaphor with allegory or even just fantastical actions," as the reader noted, but my intention is to withhold judgment on what is in the mind of the narrator that might look to us like metaphor, allegory, or fantastical action. The task that worries me is to find a comfortable fit for the reader's perspectives with an ethnographer's respect for the Cree idiom. I had found Hawkes historical view the least likely to lead to imposing an inappropriate theory on the Cree, because I feel that he is reaching back to a use of words that is close to what was, until a few centuries ago, probably a baseline.

Rereading the reviewer's comments, I tripped over his certainty—"you can't take myths literally"—and wonder at this person's range of experience and intellectual hubris. Perhaps she or he would learn something if she or he would try telling this "can't" to someone who takes the Bible as the absolute word of God. Or to an old Cree storyteller who deeply believes in the truth of the story he is recounting. That is to say, you CAN take myths literally, for some people do. I am not a "literalist," but neither am I easy with the view expressed by the reviewer that you "can't."

My approach has been that, as an ethnographer and a friend of the storyteller, I do the very best I can to understand it from the storyteller's point of view. So first, I try to see it from a literalist stance, and only then do I back off and try to interpret that stance into the generalized readers' frame of mind.

I strongly commend Barre Toelken's four articles and am thrilled by his depth —nothing at all like the shiny new structural apparatus I was enjoined to use in the 1970s, or the brave certainty regarding imagery I am now enjoined to use— Barre goes humanly deeper.

LOUSE AND WIDE LAKE

Told by George Head
Translated by Gerti Diamond Murdoch

The man's name was Louse—Kawichkushu.

He is a dangerous old man. He is going to have a fight with another man.

He is going to try to beat this other old man, Pikawgami (Wide Lake), who has power too, but a different type. This Pikawgami had something, in a little power bag, that he hangs under his cache, and if anyone gets too close, he dies, and the bag transmits a noise to Pikawgami, and then he knows that someone got killed.

So one day Kawichkushu said, "I'm going to see Pikawgami. I'm going to trade him some caribou skins for his fishnet."

He said that because he just wanted to go to see his power, to test it.

So he went off to Pikawgami's place and took the caribou skins with him, and when he arrived at Pikawgami's tent, he said, "I've got some caribou skins here that I want to trade to you for a fishnet.

So Pikawgami said, "Oh, sure, I'll take the caribou skins. I won't be able to give you an old net. I'll give you a brand new one. I need the skins."

The reason he did this was to make Pikawgami mad. So Kawichkushu went back with his net and left the skins.

The next day he went back to Pikawgami's camp and took the net back and told the old man, "I brought this fishnet that you gave to me. I heard that you weren't satisfied with the skins, so I brought the net back."

Pikawgami said, "No, I didn't say that. Somebody must have been joking. I'm satisfied with the skins."

"Anyway," he said, "I want my skins back." So Kawichkushu went back, with his skins.

Nothing happened. Pikawgami was mad but didn't do anything.

Kawichkushu thought, "I would like to make that old man mad, to see how powerful he is. If there is some way to make him mad. I'm going to go there. I'm going to use my own power, too, and have my power ready."

So as he came close to Pikawgami's tent, Kawichkushu saw the cache with the little bag hanging under it.

"I took my spear with me. I drew two straight lines close to the cache, between myself and the cache.

"I went under the cache and walked back and forth. The bag didn't move.

"Then I started to walk back and forth again, under the bag, and it started to move. Then I ran back of the second line."

When it moved, it sent the signal to Pikawgami, and he sent his full power back to the bag to attack the one that walked close. When the bag transmitted to Pikawgami, he told the woman, "Go and see who is killed under the cache. There is somebody killed out there."

And the woman replied, "I don't see anybody dead, but I see Kawichkushu over there."

When Pikawgami heard this, he started to use his power again. It came back to the ground from the bag, like a wave, and then it rose and came to the first line, and slowed, but rose (again, like a wave) and came toward the second line.

Kawichkushu took his spear and stuck it at the second line. When the wave of power came to the second line, it stopped there; the power failed.

"So I went back home, but I didn't feel anything at all. I knew that he was going to do something with me, so I was ready for it."

Later Pikawgami sent his power to Kawichkushu, and he wasn't expecting it. Kawichkushu told his younger brother, "Let's go out and visit our fishnets."

When they got down to their canoe, one of the paddles was missing and they thought one of the kids was playing with it, and it floated away.

So, he told his brother, "Let's paddle around anyway. Maybe we'll find the paddle floating."

(But the power of Pikawgami is in the paddle.)

The paddle was floating in the water, and Kawichkushu picked it up. There was a bit of seaweed on the end of the paddle. He tried to wash it off by passing it in the water, but it did not come off.

So he tried to flick it off with his fingers, and the power, which was in the seaweed, went up into Kawichkushu's hand.

His fingers felt peculiar, and then he knew it was too late. He has to control himself now.

"My fingers felt like they were burning now, and worse, when I got home."

It started to swell. He made a tourniquet to keep it from going up his arm. But each time he put it on, it got so bad he had to move it up. Finally it was to his shoulder, and there was no way to tie it.

Finally he fell into a coma, and he started to talk, but he didn't know what he was saying. "The only thing that will help me is the skunk *widui* (musk)".

They sent the men out (and dogs, too) to look for skunks.

Finally, all day, the men came back with nothing. There were still some dogs out.

The last dog to come back, late in the night, had a skunk.

Kawichkushu said, "I hear them talking about skunks. I feel a little bit better. That is the medicine I need." The men started to rub the *widui* on his arm.

So in the morning his arm was back down to normal again.

"The next night, when I went to sleep, I tried to find out why it had been like that. I tracked it, and I saw Pikawgami going up my arm to my shoulder, but there was a giant skunk there, and Pikawgami turned back.

"So I thought to myself, 'It's my turn to do something to Pikawgami.'

"So I looked around, and I couldn't find anyplace where I could reach him; his power was all around.

"Then I thought to myself, 'I don't think he has power underground.'

"So I went underground and came out right at the entrance to his tent.

"He was lying at the back of his tent, and he didn't know me.

"So I came up the pole and across and sat on the pole, and still Pikawgami didn't see me.

"There was an open fire under me. I spit on the fire, and the steam came bigger and bigger.

"At last it burst.

"While it was bursting, I grabbed Pikawgami by the throat and took him out. By the time I got him out, Pikawgami could hardly move.

"So I didn't take any chance. I just killed him right there.

"Pikawgami's power was gone just like that.

"So I am the only one left who can be the leader now.

"So at last Pikawgami died, and I had no more problems.

"So that was the end of it. I lived with the people!"

Pikawgami had a brother, who was upset and mad when he heard that.

He said, "I only wish Kawichkushu would get into trouble, and after all he has caused trouble to other people."

Kawichkushu didn't know what the brother was saying. So they traveled and hunted and nothing happened to them.

Finally they got a lot of caribou. Kawichkushu was told to stay at home one day to grind the bones.

So while he was working on the bones, hammering them, the pieces flew up and stuck in his eyes.

He tried to take them out, but he couldn't.

The women tried, but they couldn't get them.

So they had to leave them.

So he couldn't see anything at all.

He had a brother somewhere. He told his friends to go get his brother, because his brother lived with his old grandmother, and he thought his grandmother could do something about it. So finally the brother arrived with his grandmother, and they were fed with caribou meat, and he told them what happened.

The old grandmother couldn't do anything, too.

So he told his grandmother that he feels sorry that he couldn't see his children, couldn't do anything at all.

The grandmother didn't say anything at all.

When the grandmother got ready to go home, she said, "Sorry, Grandson, I can't do anything to you. The old man that used to feed me and help me you have killed.

"You will have to help yourself."

That's the last time she ever saw Kawichkushu.

So Kawichkushu thought, "I guess there is nothing much I can do, just wait."

He told his friends, "There is one thing you can do for me. That is to make me a canoe.

"When the sea opens in the spring, I'll paddle around.

"And make bows and arrows.

"And when it is finished, take me down to the sea, and I will float away.

"I'll float around the sea.

"I'll hear the seals coming out from the water.

"I will take my bow and arrow, and I will shoot where I hear the noise.

"And I will hear my arrow stuck in the seal's head,

"And I'll go and get the seal and make a big meal. I'll make a big supper.

"And in the fall I will start setting rabbit snares. I will use the seal fat to fry the rabbit meat."

And that was the last word, and he died.

CONVERSATION OF JOHN BLACKNED, DICK PRESTON, AND ALBERT DIAMOND (translating)

Dick: Well, I'm not clear what's happening . . .

(John says he is not sure he remembers the story, so Dick recites it, as well as he remembers it.)

Albert to John: He wants to ask you a few questions concerning this story. I don't know if you will be able to answer them. Did you hear this story before?

John: I heard this story before. It's like someone dreaming. I remembered parts here and there. The way he tells it sounds like the way I heard it. When I was told this story, I wasn't really listening. I was too restless. I'd only listen to parts of it. And as I got older that's when I started to listen to these stories. (John laughs.)

Dick: There sounds like there is quite a lot of meaning behind the words. Towards the end of the story, there, because if you were to take it literally, it's not likely that a blind man could shoot a seal with a bow and arrow. Also, he's preparing himself for all these things he is going to do, but he dies right there. And also, where he is going after Wide Lake, he is going underground and coming up on the tent pole. It doesn't sound like he could be taking his body with him. It would have to be his spirit, or maybe spirit is not the right word. And what I want to know is, how is he doing that?

Albert to John: In the story, when he was blind, why did he ask for these things, like the canoe and also when he said he would kill the seal?

John: Maybe, it's the fact that he wants to kill those things last.

Dick: Would you ask him if it's possible that he is talking about after he leaves this world?

John: It's possible, when a person leaves here, the things he likes most doing here, he'll probably do up there.

Dick: So, I wondered when he says to make him a canoe . . . Is there a word in Cree for metaphor? (asked of Albert) . . . Anyway, it seems like when he says to make him a canoe that there's something behind the words there, that's like, "prepare me for leaving this world," and he is telling them what he is going to be doing.

Albert to John: When he (Louse) asked "make me a canoe," do you think that there was a reason why he told him this before he died?

John: Yes, he knew that he was going to die soon; that's what he liked doing the most. Maybe it was because he liked traveling by canoe; that's why he wanted that made.

Dick to Albert: You wouldn't really call that a metaphor, would you?

Albert to Dick: No, the way I put that question to him, I couldn't really say metaphor (in Cree), so I told him, "When he asked for the canoe, do you think he was trying to convey a message, not directly but indirectly, to the people that he is leaving?"

Dick to Albert: Well, we can go back to the other part where he is going to go under the ground. This is where he is going to come in his tent.

Albert: Now, the one that they call Louse, when he was ready to see Wide Lake, why did he go underground? How did he do this when he went underground?

John: That skunk he asked for. That's who he used. That's what I heard; that's all I remember. The skunk made the tunnel for him, and he followed it. I forgot the rest.

Dick: It was his whole self then—he was taking his body, too?

Albert to John: When he went under the tunnel . . .

John: Louse went where the skunk went, when he went to see Wide Lake, so that Wide Lake would not see him. That's what I heard. I don't remember it all.

Dick: The reason I want to ask that is that I wondered if, when a person is very powerfully conjuring, his mind or spirit can leave his body and do something. I thought maybe that was what was happening when he went underground. That's . . . the same, if he goes and he's out on this pole and he's spitting into the fire. I thought, he can't be very big now, because it's not a big hole, maybe?

Albert to John: "This is what I thought," Dick says, "when he went underground and also when he climbed the pole, that he wasn't too big." Dick didn't hear the part when the skunk helped him.

John: The reason why Louse died is because when the bones were put in his eyes, they worked their way down into the heart.

Dick: Did he say if it would be possible for this self or other person to leave the body and conjure like that?

Albert to John: Could it be possible for this to happen that when someone *goosbtum*, this person can make it look like someone else is doing the thing, but actually he is the one that is doing it?

John: Yes, that could happen.

Dick: One of the stories I got from John is about Meskino going to his *mistabeo* and killing a woman and also a kid. . . . I was wondering, when they speak of the conjuror going like that, if he is leaving his body behind.

John: When he conjures, he doesn't send his own self, but his *mistabeo*, or his helper. (And here we get a sense of the story's imagery as telling us about actions unseen, or not ordinarily seen, or perhaps seen in a dream.)

Albert to John: Do you think that this is what happened to Louse? Did he go himself, or did he send someone else?

John: Oh yes, he sent someone else. He used the skunk as his helper; that's why he asked for him.

Albert to John: Did he go himself?

John: Yes, he went himself. (And here we are given a merger of self and his helper.) Sometimes they kill each other by making things.

Dick: What kinds of things?

John: Like a rock. He aims at the person when he's not looking. He blows on the rock; it falls on the man, and it makes its way to the heart. It goes off like a bullet when he blows it.

Dick: Can you draw out that object before it gets to the heart?

John: Some people know how to stop it. When they see him do it, he uses an axe to stop it, by knocking it away. It's the same thing with Louse, when he had those bones. That's a way to kill someone. Also with the porcupine quills, they use that a lot. They don't blow it like they do with the rock. They put it in the fire, and they aim it at the person. It's just like shooting someone, and it works its way to the heart and then (the person) dies. The devil was helping them when they did this.

Dick to Albert: There's nothing like a metaphor, but there's a meaning where you can be saying something and meaning something underneath it? Ask John.

Albert to Dick: I'll try. (Here Albert tries to approximate a Cree equivalent of metaphor.)

Albert to John: When someone knows that he's dying, especially, if they don't know that he's dying. He's just about ready to tell them that he's dying, but he wants to tell them in another way. Can that happen?

John: Yes, that can happen. Before he's ready to die, he's telling them that he's going to die.

Albert: Is he telling them right out that he's going to die?

John: Yes, he's telling them that he's not going to be on this earth, and that he will not be walking around. One way you can know is through dreams. A man can dream when he is ready to lose his wife. He dreams that she is walking and she is not turning back. She just keeps on walking.

Dick: It's like a metaphor then? Not the same? (Albert leaves this question alone.)

John: It happens to some women too; they dream about their husbands. She dreams he's going hunting, and he's taking everything. She sees him walking away until he disappears. Not everyone knows that her husband is going to die. Usually she's feeling very unhappy that this is going to happen. That's when some people know that something is going to happen. She doesn't even tell them. It's not until it actually happens that she tells others that she dreamt this.

John: (laughs) I guess she's getting tired of waiting for you. (He is referring to Dick's wife, Sarah, who is waiting in the same room.) She's probably wondering if they'll ever run out of words to say. (And so our enquiry is closed.)

Concluding Comments

What can we understand from the story and the discussion of it with John? I can offer only my educated guess. Albert was fluently bilingual and bicultural, and he adroitly put my queries to John, but was not able to ask John about a "metaphor" because there was no Cree way to word such a question.

Louse provokes the anger of Wide Lake to try to prove himself the more powerful shaman. He feels the power of Wide Lake, coming through the covert agency of a bit of seaweed, enter his finger tips and make its way powerfully—visibly—up his arm. He is saved by his helper, the skunk, whose powerful scent is rubbed on the swollen arm and saves him from death. To confirm his apperception of the situation, Louse then sees—experiences in his mind's eye—the power of Wide Lake coming up his arm, until at the shoulder it reaches Louse's own power, manifested in the agency of the skunk.

Louse's ability to stop Wide Lake is a sign of his power for the ending of the contest. The consequent foray into Wide Lake's tipi was made by the skunk, serving as Louse's helper or "vessel" for his power—a kind of small Trojan horse whose powerful scent overcame Wide Lake.

Later the retaliation comes in small bits of bone, blinding Louse in a way that his grandmother declines to remedy.

In the end Louse asks his group to prepare his way to the afterlife, creating for him the practical implements he will need to hunt. But this is a speech that ends with his death, not a set of directions for their practical action.

A Pair of Hero Stories

Introduction by Susan M. Preston

These stories are two of many recorded by Richard J. Preston, my father, during the 1960s in Waskaganish (then Rupert House), Quebec. They were told by his Cree mentor, John Blackned, who was in his seventies at the time. John had heard the stories from his grandmother at the outset of the twentieth century, when his family—like most others—lived by subsistence hunting and trapping within a vast traditional family hunting territory. The stories were translated during the telling by Anderson Jolly, one sentence at a time. Anderson was about the same age as John, and his English was vernacular rather than academic, learned through having been raised by a fur-trading-company family.

The recordings were later transcribed by a young Cree high school graduate who conscientiously worked to improve the accuracy of the English translation. Even so, a few details were missed, so I have retranscribed from the original recordings and inserted only items that were clearly omitted in the earlier work. John's careful use of brief sentences and repetition add narrative tension, so I have respected that stylistic quality in this transcript, in an attempt to retain the rhythm of the telling in Cree.[1] In some instances I have made minor grammatical changes for clarity but have refrained from imposing the use of English words that imply conceptual structures more characteristic of a Western cultural way of thinking than of Cree. Sometimes the distinction appears subtle, but in terms of culture, the change in meanings can be quite significant. The result may seem a little stilted, but its effect should be understood as a conscious and intentional part of the narration.

Both of the stories are part of a tradition of unknown duration—the Eastern Cree have lived in the James Bay region for about five millennia. Within this tradition are *atiukan*, which might be described as ancient myths or legends; *tepachiman*, or old stories believed to represent the history of persons now long dead; recent historical events and life histories of the narrator or persons known to him or her; and hunting songs. When considered as a whole, the stories and songs reveal much about the traditional experience of subsistence life in the Subarctic, including a detailed depiction of the cultural relationship to—and understanding of—landscape.

Landscape

The Western idea of landscape or environment does not have an equivalent concept in traditional Cree culture; instead what we might consider "landscape" for them consisted of the land, waters, topographic features, climate, animals, spirits, and humans. It is an integrative, holistic concept from both an ecological and a *social* perspective, which is to say that, as the Crees understood it, all these elements of the landscape were *active participants* in a set of relationships with one another that were predicated on mutual respect and associated expectations for the behavior necessary to maintain equilibrium and continuity throughout the whole. All have the status of "persons."

When trying to understand the meaning and representation of landscape in this tradition, I found that it was bound up in the context of the relationships and actions of persons. For the Cree families whose subsistence activities occurred inland from the coast, it was a life of near constant movement corresponding with the cyclical patterns of movement of the various animals they hunted. To be successful at living, one had to understand the language of the landscape and the life within it.

The legends "The Birds That Flew Off with People" and "How the Wolf Came to Be" encompass most of the major symbolic landscape themes that I have discerned.[2] These include a heightened tension in activities that occur on water, often associated with conjuring power; water is also often the locus of species transformation, both literal and symbolic. Islands and mountains are like topographic and narrative punctuation marks—they are places apart from everyday experience and are often associated in the stories with exceptional creatures or activities. The land itself is rarely if ever mentioned; instead the reference is to the tracks left by persons—typically in the surface of the snow.

The representation of tracks is another key theme in understanding landscape. Tracks are critically important in the subsistence life way and are the most prevalent indicator of cultural activity in the landscape. Tracks have several experiential and narrative functions: 1) tracks are directional: they are maps; 2) tracks are language and text: they convey information of great complexity, they confirm the nature of circumstances and events, they are linked to dreams and metaphors, and they can be used intentionally to assist, deceive, or redirect activity; 3) tracks have a temporal function: their condition reveals the time that has lapsed since their imprint, and they anticipate future events; and 4) tracks are carriers of the fundamental cultural values of endurance and competence.

Finally, the depiction of interspecies relations is central to representing landscape, reflecting the values of reciprocity and respect that inform the hunter's worldview through familial relations. Extending this worldview is the notion of multispecies perception—particularly when persons demonstrate their competence in their ability to experience the landscape through the mind of others. Cross-species transformation is the ultimate manifestation of this concept and can be literal, symbolic, or implied.

The Stories

I think of these two legends as hero stories, which in the Eastern Cree tradition are subtle. In both cases heroism is manifested in a young man's ability to understand the landscape and interact with it to overcome great adversity, gaining knowledge and with it, a degree of authority. They are set in the context of traditional life ways, reflecting on ways of knowing the landscape through its form, the cues created by the activities of others, and the relationships among different species within it.

Structurally the stories have important parallels; in both cases the hero is a young man who has been orphaned early in the story. In his vulnerability the hero is confronted by the perplexing lack of information about what has happened to his family and by an antagonist determined to kill him. The antagonist is described as bad or cruel and is in effect someone who is disrupting the balance or equilibrium of relations in the landscape. Both heroes respond by drawing on their own skills and self-control to overcome the challenge and restore balance. Their competence is demonstrated through skill in psychic ability, social relations, and traditional craftsmanship. In each case the hero offers to make for his captor a gift—a new nest and a new canoe. The captors are pleased and overconfident, not realizing that the gift is to be the vehicle of their own destruction. The events function as a rite of passage for the young heroes, and having overcome where many before them did not, they attain authority manifested as knowledge and "right behavior" consistent with maintaining the greater balance. One of their final deeds in the stories is to dictate the moral code of appropriate social behavior to new participants in the landscape who have been created through the events of the heroes' challenge. Finally, both stories have an etiological component, explaining the current size and location of certain bird species and the origins of wolves.

Notes

1. With the financial assistance of the Cree School Board in 1999, and under the initiative of my father, I began the painstaking task of preserving the original

acetate recordings by transferring them to CD-ROM format. The result of the first round of work was a twenty-six-volume set titled *Eastern James Bay Cree Oral Tradition Series.* Minor editing focused on improving ease of listening—entailing removal of excessive background noise such as crying children, coughing, and interruptions. The intent was to preserve the sound of the spoken word in both the Cree and the initial English translation, for use in the Cree school system as well as by scholars. In addition, the beauty and craftsmanship of traditional objects is preserved and shared through the use of photographs on the CD jewel-case covers. Copies are now in each of the nine Eastern Cree communities for school use, as well as being housed in various archival and research collections in Canada, including the Rupert's Land Institute in Winnipeg and the Canadian Museum of Civilization in Ottawa/Hull. Inquiries should be addressed to Dr. Richard Preston, Department of Anthropology, McMaster University, Hamilton, Ontario, Canada.

2. This introduction reflects a major research initiative focusing on landscape meaning and representation in Eastern James Bay Cree oral tradition, begun in 1998. Several articles have been published in conference proceedings, the most detailed of which is in the *Papers of the Thirty-first Algonquian Conference* (see "Suggested Readings"). The complete study is presented in my forthcoming book *At Last He Could Walk No Further: Landscape Experience and Symbolism in Eastern James Bay Cree Oral Tradition.* Thanks are due to R. J. Preston for introducing me to the world of Cree narrative and culture and for sharing many insights.

Suggested Reading

On Eastern Cree oral tradition and this collection:

Preston, Richard J. 2002. *Cree Narrative: Expressing the Personal Meanings of Events.* 2nd ed. Montreal: McGill-Queen's University Press.

On Eastern Cree worldview:

Feit, Harvey. 2001. "Hunting, Nature, and Metaphor: Political and Discursive Strategies in James Bay Cree Resistance and Autonomy." In *Indigenous Traditions and Ecology: The Interbeing of Cosmology and Community,* ed. John A. Grim, 411–52. Cambridge: Harvard University Press.

Preston, Richard J. 1978. "Le Relation Sacree Entre les Cris et les Oies." *Recherches Amérindiennes au Québec* 8:147–52.

———. 1982. "Towards a General Statement on the Eastern Cree Structure of Knowledge." In *Papers of the Thirteenth Algonquian Conference,* ed. William Cowan, 299–306. Ottawa: Carleton University.

Scott, Colin. 1996. "Science for the West, Myth for the Rest? The Case of James Bay Cree Knowledge Construction." In *Naked Science: Anthropological Inquiry into Boundaries, Power, and Knowledge*, ed. Laura Nader, 69–86. New York: Routledge.

On Eastern Cree landscape interpretation:

Preston, Susan M. 2000. "Exploring the Eastern Cree Landscape: Oral Tradition as Cognitive Map." In *Papers of the Thirty-first Algonquian Conference*, ed. John D. Nichols, 310–32. Winnipeg: University of Manitoba.

On Aboriginal cultural landscape interpretation generally:

Feld, Steven, and Keith H. Basso, eds. 1996. *Senses of Place*. Santa Fe: School of American Research Press.

Hirsch, Eric, and Michael O'Hanlon, eds. 1995. *The Anthropology of Landscape: Perspectives on Place and Space*. Oxford: Clarendon Press.

Ingold, Tim. 1996. "Hunting and Gathering as Ways of Perceiving the Environment." In *Redefining Nature: Ecology, Culture and Domestication*, ed. Roy Ellen and Katsuyoshi Fukui, 117–55. Oxford: Berg.

THE BIRDS THAT FLEW OFF WITH PEOPLE

Told by John Blackned
Translated by Anderson Jolly

Just prior to telling this story, John made a point of drawing attention to the significance of the references to something strange or surprising happening in the story. This is understood to be quite serious, referring to the sense of being suddenly confronted by something astounding. The reference occurs repeatedly at the beginning of the story for emphasis and is reinforced again at the end.

This is an old Indian tale about the birds that flew off with people. Once they lost a man, suddenly, just as if he had flown away; that's what people thought. And when they followed his tracks, they found what he had been carrying, and his trail stopped at the same place. They didn't know why they lost him like that, just the same as if he had flown away. He had been on his way home at night. Nobody ever knew anyone who lived up in the air, these people long ago, and they didn't know who could have taken this man from his trail, leaving everything he was carrying behind.

There was a woman who disappeared too, on her way home after checking traps with her husband. He did not find her, and he did not see where someone could have killed her. She was lost.

Another man had been out checking traps with his wife. When they came home in the evening, the woman started cooking the beaver. It was dark outside when the woman went out. Suddenly, she could hear someone up in the air singing to a baby, as if they were trying to put it to sleep. So she called out to her husband, "Come quick! Listen!"

They could both hear what sounded like a woman up in the air singing a baby to sleep, passing by in the sky. At last they could hear what she was singing, "Goodbye! A large bird is flying away with me! You, people, down there with your fire burning!" as she could see their fire from up above. "Goodbye!"

After they went into their tent, the man said, "I guess that's the one who has been flying away with people, like the man who was lost."

When a person disappears, their tracks are very clear in the snow until they end suddenly, as if they had just flown away from the ground, and whatever they were carrying was there, at the place where the tracks ended. And he told his wife, "It must be a big bird to fly away with people like that. It probably carries people away like it does rabbits. Someday someone will figure it out."

There was a young man who was an only child, living with his mother and father. One night, his father did not return home. They had plenty of food. His mother said to him, "I wonder what happened to your father; he did not return home, yet."

The young man dreamt about his father; he dreamt he was following his path, and at last he saw someone pick him up as he walked along. In his dream, he was thinking that his father was carried away by a very large bird. "I guess that's what I'm going to find, what I saw in my dream," he thought.

He decided to follow his father's tracks to see if his dream was true. At last he saw the signs at the place where his father had killed two porcupines along his trail, but he didn't see the porcupines. His father had left from the side of their wigwam and was circling to go home. He wasn't very far from it, and the young man was wondering how he could have lost his father so close to home. "My father seems to have been on his way home," he thought.

They were camping near a lake, and already he could see the lake through the bush. He thought his father must have starved before he reached the lake. But his father's trail went halfway out across the lake and then stopped, suddenly. There they found his bow and arrows, and his axe too, but not the porcupines. The young man went home and told his mother, "This is where I lost my father, on this lake not far from here. I found his bow and arrows and axe there, at the end of his trail."

So it was just the two of them living together then, the mother and son. The young man started to hunt in the area, like his father had. He didn't know to be scared to walk around at night. He didn't think about how his father might have been killed by something that comes out in the night. He didn't know that there was a large bird up in the air taking people away at night to eat them up.

One day the young man and his mother were out hunting for beaver, and he told his mother to haul the ones he had killed back on the sled. It was getting dark already when his mother went home, and their wigwam was very close. She would have to walk in the open across a frozen lake to get there. The young man thought to himself, "I guess my mother is cooking now, and she will probably have some beaver ready for me." So he came back home too, but his mother wasn't there. He wondered what happened to her, so he turned back again to have a look around for her, but couldn't find her.

The next morning when he got up, the young man went back out again to look for her. As he came across the lake, all he could see was the end of her trail, but she wasn't there. So he started to look around on the lake, and at last he saw something small and black. Here were the beavers his mother had been pulling on the sled, and they looked as if they had fallen down from the sky.

The young man made up his mind to find out how his father and mother had been lost. So that day he started to talk, saying, "I wish that creature who carried my father away would come to see me."

All that day he talked that way, to make the creature hear him and appear. Then he started to dream, and he dreamt that he had a big bird as his grandfather. All that day while he was sitting in the tent he was saying, "My grandfather, come to see me."

Long ago people did not have very good axes to cut firewood, so they used long logs and sticks that reached all the way from the fire to outside the wigwam door, and they would just shift the wood further into the fire as it burned.

Finally, he could hear someone, flying by very fast and heavy. He started to talk through the door of his wigwam, saying, "If you are a bird, start moving my firewood logs and sticks that are lying partly outside."

As soon as he said that, the wood started to move. He started to open his door. Standing there was a very large bird, and it spoke to the young man, saying, "My grandson, I am not the one who ate your father or your mother. I did not eat them. Your grandmother ate your father and mother. Your grandmother does not fly by day but by night. When she sees a person walking around in the night, she picks them up and flies away with them to kill and eat them. I eat the same kind of food you eat," he told the young man. "Since you wanted to see me, try not to let your grandmother fly off with you. You are never to walk when it is dark because your grandmother will fly off with you if you do. We have two young birds, and they eat like their mother. We live at the very top of a big mountain. But I do the same as you—when the sun comes up in the morning, I start to hunt. So be careful. I am leaving you now." The bird turned around and started to fly away.

The young man continued to hunt, always remembering what the big bird told him. As soon as the sun would start to set in the evening, he would head for home, before it got dark. Sometimes he used to talk to himself, saying, "It's my grandmother who is going to kill me." He lived by himself for a whole winter and never forgot what the big bird told him. If he was walking at night, he did not cross the lake but went around it.

One evening he came upon a small lake where he had walked earlier, as he was following his trail home. He thought he would be safe from his grandmother because it was a small little lake, saying to himself, "My grandmother will never fly off with me here." So he started to run over it, and just about halfway across, he could hear someone coming after him. He was carrying an ice chisel. He could feel someone grabbing him, and he started to talk to her, saying, "Grandmother, don't put your claws through me. Don't, don't."

The bird flew off with him and took him toward the mountain. She began knocking him against the rocks, and when he knew that she was going to try to kill him that way, he positioned his chisel to protect himself from the rocks. Without the chisel, he could not have saved himself, and the big bird would have knocked him down on the rock and killed him.

At last she took him right to the top of the mountain and let him go. The bird who came to see him at his wigwam was sitting there and said to him, "What are you doing, my grandson? I told you not to let your grandmother carry you away. I told you to be careful."

The young man didn't say anything.

The next morning his grandfather flew away. His grandfather had told him that they called themselves eagles. While the young man was sitting there, the young birds started pecking at him, trying to eat him, so he hit their noses with a stick to stop them.

His grandfather was not gone long and returned with a deer. He said to the young man, "Now we can eat, my grandson. I guess you will have to stay with us."

So the young man stayed with them, but he thought he could not live up there very long or he would be very lonesome.

He used to see his grandmother bringing men up there, killing them and smashing their heads off. On one side at the top of this mountain, he could see bones of many people she had killed. His grandfather kept the bones from his food in a separate place. Sometimes his grandmother would fly home with women too, but not very many children. When she got them near the top of the mountain, she'd knock them against the rocks and kill them that way.

At last the young man was very angry at her for killing all the people, and he thought she would kill all the people on earth eventually if she kept on that way. He wondered how he could kill her. He thought, "I think I will ask if I can build them a nice, new, big nest." There were some small trees up on that mountain, not very big and all dried up from the sun—that's what they used to make their nest. He asked his grandfather first, saying, "I'll make a nice one."

"Sure, make one," the bird told him.

After the grandfather came back from his hunt with a deer one morning, all the eagles started to eat. His grandmother ate the people in the morning, and then she would sleep all day. The young man started building the nest, using very dry twigs and grasses, and he looked for bushes and branches that were very dry and would burn easily. It was quite large and very high all around.

Finally, he was finished. He said to his grandfather, "I am finished with our new home, Grandfather." He also built a door. He said to him, "Now, you can sleep, if you want to sleep in it."

Then in the night his grandmother flew away and came back with someone to eat. In the morning his grandfather would fly away and come back with a deer every time. They had very big hands with heavy claws. All four of the eagles ate, and then they started to sleep.

The young man built a fire away from the nest to cook himself a meal from the meat that his grandfather had brought. Then he took some of the fire and set it right at their door and all around the nest, even underneath. The flames rose up and up, right around, and at last the fire closed around the whole nest.

When she saw the flames, the grandmother started to call out, "We got burned! Our nest is burning!"

All the birds tried to get out but went into flames as they stood up. His grandmother and the two young birds were all on fire. All he could see was fire around them. At last they couldn't move.

The young man pulled his grandfather out of the nest just before it all burned up. He could see axes lying around that had belonged to all the people who had been killed there. So he took an axe and started to chop the bodies into small pieces. He started to throw the pieces over one side of the mountain, but not all around. Wherever he didn't throw them, there are no eagles in that part of the country now, but on the side where he threw the pieces, there are some eagles. As he was throwing the pieces, he called out, "These birds will eat and hunt like my grandfather. There will be no more birds that will eat human beings."

The top of the mountain was very, very high, and it was rocky down below. He had not cut up the body of the grandfather, only the grandmother and the young birds. Now he cut open the stomach of his grandfather and pulled the guts out. He decided to try to go down the mountain inside his grandfather's body. So he pulled it near the edge of the mountain and climbed inside. Before he entered, he started talking to the body, saying, "Grandfather, fly me down." He shook himself, and the big bird fell down from the mountain.

At last he managed to get down. He started to break the body into pieces and throw them in the same direction as the others. As he was cutting up the pieces, he told them, "You are only going to be this big, my grandfather."

The young man started walking around on the earth again. At last he found other people. He had saved one of the eagle's feet and its beak to show people how big they were. When he found people, he asked them, "Did you ever hear of anyone who was lost? A person who disappeared, and his tracks ended, suddenly?"

The people answered him, "Yes, yes," they told the young man. "We found that often long ago. We lost someone from their tracks. We all wondered about them.

We thought it was very strange to disappear suddenly, and see the person's tracks end."

He said to the people, "I guess you will not believe the story I'm going to tell you." And he told them his father got lost that way, "Someone flew away with him, and the same with my mother; I lost her that way too." He had kept the bird's foot and beak in his bag and brought them out to show the people. Then he started to tell them the story, all about the eagles.

"There will be no more of these big birds flying around here for a while. They flew away with me too," he said. He told them the story of when the first bird came to see him. "The bird who came was my grandfather, and he told me all about my grandmother. It's my fault that she flew away with me." He told the whole story to them, exactly what he did. He said to them, "I did not stay with them very long, but my grandmother sure flew back with a lot of people. You should see on top of the mountain; there are a lot of human bones. You can tell how many people she and her children ate. They were growing rapidly. But the male bird didn't eat people, just deer meat. It is a good thing that the young ones were not fully grown; otherwise they could have helped their mother fly off with people too. There will be no more birds that size in this country," he told them.

Before the young man did that, no one knew how it was that people got lost— that the eagles were flying off with them. They could only wonder, and thought it was a person or a creature walking on the earth. On one side of the country, the Indians had not heard about or were not bothered by this bird. She only flew around the other side of the country. The story spread, and now they knew who was killing all the Indians. Other Indians heard about people disappearing, and they all wondered, "If the creature ate the Indians on the spot, why did it not leave any parts or stains?" If a person carried a baby on their back, the baby also disappeared. After the young man had finished telling the story to them, they knew what it was that was killing them.

HOW THE WOLF CAME TO BE

Told by John Blackned
Translated by Anderson Jolly

Once there was a man who had two sons. One of his sons was a very small little boy, and one was grown up. This man would hunt around, and many times he would go paddling in the canoe with his wife, leaving the older boy to watch after his younger brother.

One day the man and his wife did not return home after paddling. The two boys started to search for their parents every day. The younger son started to cry for his mother and father. Their mother always warned them when they used to cry that a wolf would hear them crying. The older boy started to make toys for his little brother so that he would not miss their parents so much. But there was nothing that could make him stop crying, even when he had a lot of toys made by his older brother. At last the older brother made a whistle that made a sound when he blew on it.

The older brother would go down to the shore, still waiting for the return of his parents. He thought they would be back. At last, when they didn't come home, the older brother was sure they must have died. The boys didn't know what could have happened to them. They thought maybe they had drowned or someone had killed them. They could not go looking for them on the water, as their mother and father had taken their only canoe. And the older brother couldn't go very far when he was walking around because he couldn't leave his brother alone, crying all the time.

This young man had heard that there were some Indians quite a distance away, and another man not very far from them who had a lot of daughters. He heard that he had sons-in-law for a short time; then he killed them. The young man heard that this was a very cruel old man.

Just the same, he kept going down to the water to look for his parents. One day he saw someone coming in a canoe. He saw it was not his parents. The person came paddling to the shore and asked the young man, "What are you doing staying here?" It was a very old man and he was alone.

The young man told the story. "My father and mother went away and never returned after paddling, and all I have is my younger brother with me, and he is always crying." While he was talking to the old man, he was holding his young brother's favorite toy, the whistle. He showed it to the old man and said, "This is the only toy that helps him stop crying."

The old man asked him, "May I see it?" After he finished looking at the toy, he threw it to the front of his canoe, way at the end. The young man told him to bring it back.

"Take it."

The water was very deep, so the young man climbed in the canoe for the toy. As soon as he was in, the old man quickly pushed his canoe out, and he jumped in before the young man could get the toy. The young man said, "My brother is going to cry himself to death. Take me to shore! Take me to shore!" But instead of taking him to shore, the old man started to paddle very heavily. At last, they were very far from his young brother.

Finally, the old man said to him, "We are very close to my wigwam." Then the young man saw a wigwam and three girls there with children. When they reached the shore, the old man said to him, "Come on; come on up."

After he entered the wigwam, the old man said to him, "That's my daughters, the three of them. You can have one of them as your wife. You can marry the one you want."

The young man started to talk to the girls. He started to tell them, "My mother and father went out paddling but never returned home. We left my brother over there, where we lost our parents. I guess he will die from crying so much."

The girls warned the young man, "Our father always kills our husbands. You will not be able to stay with us very long. You might as well be sure that he will kill you."

The young man was very angry when the old man paddled away from his brother. He whispered to the girls, "Are you going to be glad if I kill your father?"

There were three sisters; two of them wanted him for a husband. The girls said to him, "Those are all our children. After our babies are born, our father kills our husbands."

He asked them again, "Would you be glad if I kill your father?"

They answered him, "We would be glad as we would be able to stay with you for a longer time."

The young man's father had taught him how to build a canoe. He said to the girls, "Tell your father I am going to build him a canoe."

The girls told their father, "The young man wants to build you a canoe."

The old man thought, "He only wants to build a canoe for me," not realizing that the young man was going to try to kill him. He thought, "He must be pleased because I gave him a wife; that is why he wants to build a canoe for me."

The young man started building the canoe. He tried to build it very quickly. He asked the girls, "Ask your father if he has any gum or glue from a sturgeon for the canoe."

The old man said to his daughters, "The last time I had gum or glue from a sturgeon was long ago, before your mother died. There are sturgeons in this lake where we can go and get some."

The young man's wife whispered to him, "If you go with him, I think my father is going to kill you."

"Never mind," he said, "I am going out with your father."

She replied, "Make sure you return."

The two men went out. The young man started to try to kill his father-in-law. When they got to the first rapids, he said to the old man, "Let us play in the rapids. Here are very dangerous looking rapids. Let us go and play." He knows that the old man is able to use a bird that sings in the winter, called a whiskey jack, as a helper to conjure against people. The old man pretends he's a whiskey jack. The young man also pretends he is a small bird. They went to a very dangerous part of the rapids. He asked his father-in-law, "I believe you have a bird—where is your bird?" Suddenly, a whiskey jack landed right in front of them. The young man said, "It's my turn. Come and fly here, small bird." Then, a small bird landed beside the whiskey jack.

The water of the rapids was falling down and splashing up, making a lot of spray, and it looked very dangerous. The young man said to the old man, "Look, I am going to fly." Through the small bird, the young man started to fly. He crossed the rapids, circled around and returned, landing again. "You try it," he said to the old man. "It's your turn."

The old man sent the whiskey jack to fly, but he wanted to land and rest on the other side of the river. The young man yelled to him, "Don't, don't land." He was halfway where the rapids looked very dangerous. The young man started shouting at the whiskey jack. It fell down into the rapids and died. The young man asked, "What happened, you could not make it across?" He said to the old man, "Now, let us go to where the sturgeons are." This old man didn't know he was close to dying already. He was still thinking he could kill his son-in-law before the end of the day.

Now, the young man's father had told him that if someone ever tried to kill him in the water, he should imagine he was an otter, and he would never be killed. The two men went out in the canoe. The old man said to him, "Here it is. This is where the sturgeons are speared." The old man handed him a spear and told him, "You will look for them since you are younger." The young man stood up. When he saw his son-in-law getting up inside the canoe, the old man told him, "You know these crosspieces on the canoe; that's where I stand when I am looking for sturgeon to spear, right up on the last one at the end, right on the top." The old man was trying to kill his son-in-law. He thought it would be easy, that he would sway the canoe and the young man will fall into the water.

So the young man started to stand on top of the smallest thwart. Finally, he saw a sturgeon way under the water. It was a very big one. He speared it, and as soon as he did, the old man started to sway the canoe, knocking him into the water. The young man pulled the spear from the surgeon and held onto it. He remembered what his father had told him, to pretend he was an otter when someone tried to kill him in the water. He traveled under the water, holding onto the sturgeon. Finally, he reached the shore, hiding himself from the old man and secretly watching him. The old man was very still in his canoe, looking around in the water. Finally, he pulled in the spear that was floating in the water using a stick. He put the spear in his canoe.

The young man started running way up into the bush, to go home with the sturgeon. When he reached her, he did not tell his wife what her father had done to him. He said to her, "Hurry up and cook the sturgeon. Tell the children to look for the return of their grandfather."

Finally, it was very dark. The children came home saying, "Our grandfather is coming in his canoe."

The young man told his wife, "Give the children some cooked sturgeon, and let them eat it when they meet their grandfather down on the shore." He said to one of the children, "Eat the sturgeon." This was not his own child, but one belonging to another son-in-law whom the old man had killed.

When the old man came to shore, he asked the children, "What is that you have, my grandchildren? What are you eating?"

The children were very small, and they thought the young man was their father. They answered their grandfather, "Our father brought a sturgeon home."

He scolded them, saying, "You don't make any sense. Your father is being tossed back and forward." This was how the old man told them their father was dead, that he was being tossed about in the waves.

They went up to their wigwam, and the old man entered. Here was his son-in-law sitting. The son-in-law was sitting, thinking, and staring at him. The old man wondered how he had managed to return. The last time he saw his son-in-law, he was way under the water, and he thought he was drowned.

So the young man continued to build the canoe for his father-in-law. He also made new paddles, and he put something in the canoe that made a noise like a whistle. This thing he put in the canoe will destroy the old man. At last it was finished, but he did not give it right away. He waited until the old man lived with them for a while.

One day he said to his wife, "Tomorrow morning I am going to kill your father. Are you sure you will be glad if I do it?" He was sure that his father-in-law would not be able to kill him, no matter what he did. He was still very angry at the old man, as he was sure that his young brother was dead by then.

The next morning he went out, and it was a very calm day. They were staying along the coast. He said to the women, "Ask your father to try out his new canoe and paddles. If he can't paddle with his new paddles, I will make new ones for him. Also, if he doesn't like his canoe, I will make him a new one."

The old man said, "Yes, I will try out my new canoe." He was banging on his old canoe, saying, "What a rotten canoe I had." He went out in his new canoe.

As he pulled a paddle, there was a whistling sound: cho-c-o-o-o-o. The women yelled to their father, "Oh, Father, your canoe sounds good. Why don't you paddle around here." So, the old man was paddling with a cho-c-o-o-o-o sound.

Then the women yelled at their father, "Why don't you paddle farther out in the water?"

At last their father was far out in the water. He was very, very far away. Suddenly, there was a heavy fog, and he couldn't see anything. After a while they could hear him calling out, "My daughters, where are you?"

The young man told them not to answer the old man. Finally, they could hardly hear him, he was so far out in the sea. He did not know where he was going. At last a storm came. The man said to the women, "Your father is drowning now."

The women were very glad about their father's drowning. They thought, "We can live with this young man for a long time." Sure enough, the old man did not return because he drowned.

The young man started to build another canoe for himself, but he could not build it very rapidly. He realized he could not make it to where his young brother was in his father-in-law's old smashed canoe. When he was finished and his new canoe was ready, he started to hunt for food so they would have some when they went to find his younger brother. At last they left. He had all the women and their children with him. He thought about his brother, "At least I can give him a burial," as he was sure he was dead.

When they went close to the point where they had left him, they saw someone come running along close to the shore where they were. This person said to him, "My brother, I am a wolf now." It was his young brother.

In their younger days, their mother told them many times that a wolf was going to hear them when they start crying. "You will become wolves if a wolf hears you," she had said to them.

The young brother said, "Now I am a wolf, older brother. A wolf heard me crying and that is why I am a wolf."

"I guess you will have to live as a wolf. I don't want you to eat any people; you will only eat like people do," his brother replied.

"Yes, yes, yes, older brother."

The Indians of long ago said this was how the wolf came to be.

When they reached the shore, he collected all his father's belongings, also his mother's belongings. He gave all his mother's belongings to his wife and kept his father's belongings. Then he said to the women and children, "Let us now return." They all returned to his father-in-law's hunting grounds, where the young man began to hunt.

Omushkego Legends from Hudson Bay

Introduction by Paul W. DePasquale

The following stories were originally told in Omushkego, or Swampy Cree, by elder David Sutherland (ca. 1880–1963) and were retold and recorded in English by Aboriginal historian and storyteller Louis Bird (Pennishish).[1] A member of Winisk First Nation who lives in Peawanuck, Ontario, Bird has collected over 340 hours of audiotaped material, the majority in Omushkego, recording his people's *aatanoohkana* (legends or sacred stories) and *tipaachimowina* (news, gossip, and stories, including oral history). This collection is the largest known corpus on traditional and contemporary Aboriginal culture, literature, spirituality, and worldview and is housed at the Centre for Rupert's Land Studies (CRLS), University of Winnipeg, Manitoba, Canada. Begun in June 1999 with funding from the Social Sciences and Humanities Research Council of Canada, the Omushkego Oral History Project (OOHP) is directed by Louis Bird and consists of faculty and student researchers in anthropology, history, English, and religious studies. The OOHP has its first book, *Telling Our Stories: Omushkego Legends and Histories from Hudson Bay*, in preparation with Broadview Press and was recently awarded a significant grant from the Canadian Heritage Canadian Culture Online program to build a world-class online resource of digitized Cree cultural and historical materials. The goal of the Web site (www.ourvoices.ca) is to give community members, scholars, students, and other interested learners access to a fully searchable digital library of Omushkego materials, with sound as well as text files, in both Cree and English. The initiative meets recommendations established by the 1996 Royal Commission on Aboriginal Peoples that records of Aboriginal history need to be "collected, preserved and made more accessible to all Canadians before it is too late" (Government of Canada 1996, 88). The project will also fulfill Bird's own goal of passing down to future generations the stories that his grandparents, parents, and elders have told him (OOHP, Mission Statement).

Louis Bird has traveled throughout Canada, the United States, and the Netherlands as an invited storyteller. He was born in 1934 about sixty miles northwest of the village of Winisk, Ontario, renamed Peawanuck after it was destroyed by a flood in 1986, located on the west coast of James Bay. Other than the four years he had to spend at Saint Anne's Residential School in Fort Albany, Bird spent the first twenty years of his life receiving a traditional Omushkego education, listening to his people's stories and legends and learning how to fish, hunt, trap, and survive in the bush. Bird recalls that his fascination with Omushkego history began as a baby, when his mother told him traditional stories, and continued as a young man, when he would eagerly ask his elders to tell him stories that their grandfather's grandfathers used to tell. Initially he didn't have a recording device and memorized these stories to write down later in his own hand (OOHP, "Louis Bird Biography").

Jobs as a tractor operator, line cutter, economic development officer, and translator took Bird to various communities throughout the Hudson and James Bay Lowlands and provided opportunities to meet elders and learn their stories. Around 1965 he saw that many of those born in the last two decades of the nineteenth century—those most familiar with the traditional stories and way of life—were passing away, and that their knowledge was not being passed on to members of the next generation as it had in the past. This is when Bird actively set out to record the voices of his elders. "My intention was only to keep their voice alive," he explains. "That is when I seriously thought of recording any kind of their stories about their culture and their Legends or any other cultural stories. The oral story was the only way they pass on their knowledge to the next generation" (memo written by Louis Bird, addressed to the OOHP team, February 21, 2002).

Bird purchased his first tape recorder in the early 1970s, but while he did manage to record some members of his community, he soon discovered that many were shy about having their voices recorded on the machine. "Unfortunately some elders did not want to be recorded," says Bird. "Most of them did not want to be recorded. . . When they are recorded they are very careful what they say; they do not mix jokes in their stories. But when there is no recording or no note taking they are free to speak" (CRLS tape 1, "Louis Bird's Autobiography"). For this reason Bird developed a system, as he calls it, for listening to elders, asking questions, memorizing details, and later recording the information in his own words. Some of these stories he wrote out, but unfortunately this material was destroyed in the 1986 flood (February 21, 2002, memo). Other stories he recorded on tape in careful detail in his own voice, in Omushkego and English, and this became his primary method of preservation.

I was introduced to Louis Bird shortly after joining the English department at the University of Winnipeg in 2000. I had recently completed my doctoral work on representations of Native Americans in early modern colonial writings and was hired to teach in this area and in the area of Aboriginal literatures. I became interested in Bird's work in large part because of my own ties to a First Nations community, the Six Nations of the Grand River in Ontario. I had seen in my own family how assimilationist strategies such as residential schools and relocation incentives had contributed to a loss of pride and a sense of shame about being Indian. Few of my relatives spoke Mohawk, told traditional stories, or practiced the traditional culture. So when I met Louis Bird and heard him talk about how his own language and culture have been eroded since first contact with Europeans, I understood the value of his work and was pleased to be able to participate in it.

Bird works mostly in the Omushkego language and has—to his surprise—taught himself how to use a computer in order to transcribe his stories in syllabics. Although he believes that today Aboriginal peoples need to learn English in order to live effectively in the modern world (Bird n.d., 1), the main reason that Bird has felt compelled to record some material—about 15 percent of his collection—in English is that he has had little support to work in Cree. Many Aboriginal scholars and authors whose first language is not English have complained about having to produce work in the colonizer's language, and Louis Bird is no exception. Translation is a difficult exercise, yes, but more, it is one that, because of fundamental differences between the two languages, fails to capture the most vital aspects of Omushkego culture:

> The language you call "Cree" and that I call *ininiimowin* is full of action words—verbs. But English is different. It's full of nouns. When I tell a story in my language the words I use are like moving pictures of activities in the bush. The stories are full of verbs that describe action. The stories are also very visual. That's the way my language works. When this is translated into English the Omushkego traditional way of life is blotted out. That's why it's important to write these stories in the Omushkego "Cree." (Bird n.d., 1)[2]

The need to preserve an Omushkego point of view as much as possible, even when working in English, is illustrated by "blind spots" in the most comprehensive collection of Swampy and Moose Cree stories, C. Douglas Ellis's *Cree Legends and Narratives* (1995). Louis Bird and anthropologist George Fulford recently discussed this important collection (Bird and Fulford 2001, 276). "That book doesn't talk much about our original culture," observes Bird. Absent, he explains, are those aspects of the culture that relate to *mitewiwin* (or "shamanism," as it is often called). According to Bird, any treatment of Omushkego culture must involve *mitewiwin* because the traditional spiritual practices account for between 50 and 75 percent of Omushkego culture (e-mail to George Fulford, forwarded to research associates, July 11, 2002). The blind spots in Ellis's collection are due not only to the fact that Ellis is an Anglican priest, as Fulford suggests, but also to the impossibility of an outsider, even one who respects the culture and peoples, fully capturing in English the nuances of traditional Aboriginal spiritual practices.

The following legends fall into the category of Omushkegowikiskinomaakewina, or "traditional Omushkego teachings." They are examples of *aatanoohkana*, "legends or sacred stories." Bird arranges Omushkegowikiskinomaakewina chronologically, he says, "to reflect the Omushkego theory of creation—what scientists call 'evolution.' These stories tell the story of the emergence of humans from a world in which only animals previously existed." These basic teachings are familiar to other Crees of the Hudson and James Bay Lowlands and include, according to Bird's order: 1) Giant Animals, stories about creatures who once roamed the earth, believed to be dinosaurs; 2) Giant Skunk, about animals that in the past were all *mitew*, or "shamans," who killed the Giant Skunk and predicted the arrival of humans; 3) Sinkipiis, about a diving bird who is dull and homely, unlike his handsome brother the loon; 4) Ehep, about the emergence of the first humans, who were lowered in a basket to the earth by a spider from the world above; 5) Wemishoosh, about a powerful *mitew* who abuses his abilities; 6) Ayaas, another legend about a powerful *mitew* who errs by taking two wives; 7) Wiissakechaahk, the famous trickster figure, another *mitew* who exists between the world of animals and that of humans; 8) Chaahkaapiish, also a *mitew* who desires power and ends up traveling to the moon; 9) Mahikan wiihtiko, a story about an old man who ignores his daughter-in-law's warnings about a rabid wolf; 10) Paaskwaachi pawaachikanak, about a woman who has sexual relations with her dream helpers, not a good thing; 11) Wihtiiko, stories about spring time *wihtiiko*, "windigo or cannibal devil," and *ketastotinehwan* (a cannibal who was killed by another cannibal); and 12) Paastahowin, legends about blasphemy and retribution (Bird n.d., 2–3).

For many contemporary Aboriginal artists, the trickster figure, the subject of Bird's legends about Wiissaakechaahk, is a highly complex and dynamic figure at the center of a mythological universe (see Ryan 1999). For Cree author Tomson Highway, whose celebrated works include *Rez Sisters*, *Dry Lips Oughta Move to Kapuskasing*, and *Kiss of the Fur Queen*, the trickster is as fundamental to Cree spirituality as Jesus Christ is to Christian mythology, a precept the author explains in a headnote to each text. She or he is a modern-day shape shifter, confidently negotiating a space between human and supernatural worlds, provoking thought and transformation in both internal characters and readers. In the novel *Kiss of the Fur Queen*, this trickster appears as Miss Maggie Sees, a "Las Vegas show queen," or as she herself declares, "Miss Maggie-Weesageechak-Nanabush-Coyote-Raven-Glooscap-oh-you-should-hear-the-things-they-call-me-honeypot-Sees, weaver of dreams, sparker of magic, showgirl from hell" (Highway 1999, 234). In the cosmic landscape of Highway's text, Miss Maggie Sees is a powerful *okiskenohama*, or teacher, whose playful sarcasm, sexual freedom, and adaptability enable the troubled protagonist, Jeremiah, to see, on some unconscious level beneath the comedy, the truth of her instruction. For Gerald Vizenor, himself a prolific author of contemporary trickster narratives, the comic spirit that the trickster exhibits is *the* defining feature of contemporary Aboriginal literature that gives writings a sense of cultural truth or what he has called in an interview with Joseph Bruchac "mythic verism" (quoted in Ryan 1999, 5).

The trickster in Louis Bird's legends is a traditional prankster who behaves very much according to his name, Wiissaakechaahk, which Bird translates as a "pain in the neck or even worse." He is a subversive figure who, like other traditional tricksters, breaks taboos about sexual practices and religious institutions (Sullivan 1987, 168). Indeed, his lascivious behavior even makes him offensive to some readers, as I recently discovered when I introduced a draft text of "Wiissaakechaahk and the Foolish Women" to a group of senior undergraduates in my Aboriginal literatures course. Some were offended by Bird's title for the story, particularly given that the female characters—described as "nursing people and doctors," who, with their special knowledge of plants and herbs, are able to cure most diseases—are depicted as intelligent people, with perhaps naiveté as their downfall. Some students were also disturbed, understandably, by the suggestion early in the narrative that Wiissaakechaahk had even considered committing rape to satisfy his sexual urges. As Bird told me, however, any sense of "dirtiness" might again be a problem of translation. "There are no swear words in my Omushkego language. Nothing is dirty. It [the story] is much easier to say in Cree; it is not harsh, not dirty." The character Wiissaakechaahk performs the valuable function of helping young listeners prepare for life's important events:

> The teenagers question about many things. So the *Wiissaakechaahk* there is showing them what can happen. The old people don't speak to the teenagers. They let the *Wiissaakechaahk* show their youngsters. For example, most teenagers want to know about sex. How? Why? When? They cannot ask their parents directly and the parents do not have the answers. It's not proper to talk about these things as a parent. But it's possible through the elders. . . . They know the young people. So they created the legends which will explain things about life to the young people. (Bird and Fulford 2001, 282–83)

One of the roles of the traditional trickster is that of the fool who attempts to trick others but is himself tricked in the end. The Lakota story about the trickster spider Iktomi is a good example. One day Iktomi is about to eat his dinner of prairie chickens when he sees something he thinks is a woman swimming in a river. Deciding to pull a prank on her, he changes into a man and then extends an enlarged penis to her. The prank backfires when his large organ gets stuck, and he realizes that the woman he thought he was having sex with is actually a couple of trees. Meanwhile, while Iktomi is attempting to gratify his sexual desire a coyote comes along and eats all his food (St. Pierre and Long Soldier 1995, 51). Interestingly, while we might expect a similar retribution in "Wiissaakechaahk and the Foolish Women," Wiissaakechaahk succeeds in having his way with the women and then moves on, unscathed, to his next adventure. Of course, the same cannot be said of him in the second legend presented here, "Wiissaakechaahk and the Geese," a popular story with versions also appearing in Ellis's *Cree Legends*. Here Wiissaakechaahk, because he has punished his rear end, is almost made to starve to death, but he is saved, as he always is, by his indomitable spirit.

The legends of Anwe and the Cannibal Exterminators represent traditional teachings about the *wihtiiko*, the "windigo or cannibal devil." Windigos are Algonquian monsters, supernatural creatures thought insane and cruel enough to consume human flesh, although humans could be transformed into windigos by witchcraft or extreme starvation (Brightman 1988, 337). Voyageurs who came into contact with Algonquian-speaking peoples, including Menominees, Montagnais (Innu), Naskapis, Ojibwes, Ottawas, Potawatomis, and Crees, often heard tales of the dreadful creatures, Algonquian equivalents, according to anthropologist Richard Preston (1978, 63), of Satan in Christian tradition. Louis Bird says that his legends about *wihtiiko* fall into the subgenre of *mahtawachimowina*, or "mystery stories." Prior to contact with Europeans, Omushkego peoples were disturbed by very few diseases or illnesses, the most serious of which were arthritis and rheumatism, brought on in old age by a life lived in extreme weather conditions without protective clothing like boots. Bird also details several types of communicable diseases caused by contact with animals. Starvation was the only cause of widespread illness, in times of drought or when animals were scarce. People suffering from the extraordinary pain of starvation would become insane and begin to eat human flesh. As Bird observes, prior to contact it was widely known that those who ate human flesh often became very ill:

> If a person ate the human flesh which had died because of starvation, the flesh itself became a poison and the person who ate it became puffed up and an insane state developed. The brain, probably damaged already by starvation, never regained its former state of proper consciousness. Therefore, if a person began to eat human flesh, it had a habit of needing to eat again. . . . The canni-

> bal itself, once it became inhuman—an unnatural human person—by wanting to eat some more human flesh—they could not digest the normal food items. Thus they became cannibals. (Bird 2001)

These legends about Wiissaakechaahk and about the *wihtiiko*, like all *aatanoohkana*, were originally told as a means of instructing Omushkego peoples how to survive the challenges of both life and land. *Aatanoohkana* are stories about actual events that occurred long ago. "They actually happened," explains Bird. "We remember the story, but we forget [the historical person's] name. So we insert that name 'Wiissaakechaahk,' . . . 'Chaahkaapiish,' . . . [and] 'Wemishoosh.' These people existed way before the time of Europeans, maybe 10,000 years ago. So actually the legends are real happenings from way past" (Bird and Fulford 2001, 277).

The stories printed here were recorded in the early 1990s, before Louis Bird began working with researchers at the University of Winnipeg. He told me that he had no specific audience in mind when he taped these stories. The fact that they are recorded in English, combined with the use of vivid details about Omushkego culture and traditions, suggests that he taped them for audiences unfamiliar with the traditional culture, which could well include members of his own community, particularly the younger people often raised watching television in English instead of listening to traditional stories in Cree.

Bird credits his parents and grandparents for many of the stories he has recorded and includes the elder David Sutherland among his strongest influences. "I bet most of what you heard I have heard from David Sutherland," he explained recently when I asked about the sources for these two stories. Bird remembers hearing "Wiissaakechaahk and the Foolish Women" from Sutherland three times, first when he was about eight, then at eleven or twelve years of age, and then in an adult version when he was about twenty-two. David Sutherland was of the same generation as Bird's grandfather, John Pennishish, and was the brother of Bird's grandmother, Maggie Sutherland. Bird talks about Sutherland with the utmost respect and admiration; he remembers that the elder was always telling fascinating and entertaining stories, always in Cree, the only language he knew. Sutherland was one of three signatories of the Treaty Nine "adhesion" around 1930, an extension to the original treaty of 1905, by which Attawapiskat, Winisk (present-day Peawanuck), and Fort Severn, as well as a few other neighboring areas, surrendered title to the lands, according to the Crown, and "received treaty." In 1957 Sutherland was recorded by missionaries Father Pepin, Brother Gagnon, and Father Morin, who interviewed the old man in Winisk about his experiences, including the treaty signing. According to Bird, the original reel-to-reel tapes in Cree were destroyed sometime after the Winisk flood, but his English translation of the interview is part of his oral history collection.[3]

Wanting to work more in his own language, Louis Bird is less concerned with working on his English recordings and has left the question of how to represent his voice and work in print largely up to me. I have chosen an ethnopoetic line presentation for his work. Although this format may not be suitable for Bird's *tipaachimowina*, it does seem useful and appropriate in the case of his legends. Working with verbatim transcriptions, I have presented the text according to conventions used by Julie Cruikshank, Dell Hymes, Dennis Tedlock, and others who use line breaks to indicate a pause or breath and a line space to denote a longer pause. I have deleted only repetitions and false starts, maintained Bird's idiom and grammar throughout, and have included in brackets my own words to clarify or to indicate possible alternatives where the wording is unclear. My hope is that the resulting text gives readers an accurate sense of the sound, texture, and style of Louis Bird's distinctive storytelling voice.

Notes

1. I would like to acknowledge the support of the Six Nations of the Grand River Post Secondary Education Office during my undergraduate and graduate studies. The Social Sciences and Humanities Research Council of Canada, the Canada-U.S. Fulbright Program, and the University of Winnipeg have also supported my research. My thanks to students in my Aboriginal literatures course at the University of Winnipeg (class of 2002–3 and 2004), members of the Omushkego Oral History Project, and research assistant Kelly Burns for offering feedback on earlier versions of this introduction and text versions of the legends. George Fulford and John Long helped me with details about the Treaty Nine "adhesion" and the 1957 interview with David Sutherland. Thanks especially to those people whose knowledge and values are reflected in Louis Bird's words.
2. For details on the Omushkego language and the need to preserve it, see Louis Bird's conclusion in *Telling Our Stories: Omushkego Legends and Histories from Hudson Bay*, ed. Jennifer S. H. Brown, Paul DePasquale, and Mark Ruml (Toronto: Broadview Press, forthcoming).
3. John Long, Faculty of Education, Nipissing University, tells me he was given a transcription of the tapes by George Hunter, then chief of Winisk First Nation, when he began working for the Mushkegowuk Council (e-mail to author). Long discusses treaty making at Winisk and the 1957 interview with Sutherland in "Who Got What at Winisk, Treaty Making, 1930."

References and Suggested Reading

Bird, Louis. 2001. "Ancient Worlds—Legends—History." Audiocassette recorded April 20, 2001, available at CRLS, University of Winnipeg, Winnipeg MB.

———. n.d. "A Narrative Description of Mr. Louis Bird's Project Proposal." Funding grant proposal to the Canada Council.

Bird, Louis, and George Fulford. 2001. "The Omushkego Oral History Project." In *Pushing the Margins: Native and Northern Studies*, ed. J. Oakes, R. Riewe, M. Bennett, and B. Chisholm, 270–89. Winnipeg MB: Native Studies Press (University of Manitoba).

Brightman, Robert A. 1988. "The Windigo in the Material World." *Ethnohistory* 35 (4) (Fall): 337–79.

Government of Canada. 1996. *People to People, Nation to Nation: Highlights from the Report of the Royal Commission on Aboriginal Peoples.* Ottawa: Minister of Supply and Services

Highway, Tomson. 1999. *Kiss of the Fur Queen.* Toronto: Doubleday Canada.

Long, John. 1995. "Who Got What at Winisk, Treaty Making, 1930." *The Beaver* 75 (1): 23–31.

Omushkego Oral History Project (OOHP). "Louis Bird Biography." http://www.uwinnipeg.ca/academic/ic/rupert/bird/bio2.html.

———. Mission Statement. December 2000. Available at the CRLS, University of Winnipeg, Winnipeg MB.

Preston, Richard J. 1978. "Ethnographic Reconstruction of Witigo." In *Papers of the Ninth Algonquian Conference*, ed. William Cowan, 61–67. Ottawa: Carleton University.

Ryan, Allan J. 1999. *The Trickster Shift: Humour and Irony in Contemporary Native Art.* Vancouver: UBC Press; Seattle: University of Washington Press.

St. Pierre, Mark, and Tilda Long Soldier. 1995. *Walking in the Sacred Manner: Healers, Dreamers, and Pipe Carriers—Medicine Women of the Plains Indians.* New York: Touchstone.

Sullivan, E. Lawrence, ed. 1987. *Native American Religions: North America.* New York: Macmillan.

LEGEND OF WIISSAAKECHAAHK

Told and Recorded by Louis Bird (Pennishish)

Wiissaakechaahk and the Foolish Women

Wiissaakechaahk is a wanderer, an adventurer,
and he is also a single man—he's not married.
They say he appear from the west part of this country—
    from this Hudson and James Bay.
He was expected to pass through the country;
he was expected to come from the east
and move towards the west.
He lives in the territory, the district;
he stays a while,
stays with people, stays on the land;
he knows all the rivers and all the lakes and all the places—
    the bay areas, wherever the Native people enjoy most.
He would participate in the seasonal activities;
he would also go amongst the people wherever they have festivities,
wherever they gather, he would also go in there.
After knowing all the people in all the districts and territories and river
  systems,
he move to the next section.
And that's what it means;
he came from the east doing the same thing
and he move on towards west,
until he come to the end of the land.
That's what the story says.
By doing this,
the people around in Hudson and James Bay area
knew that he would be passing through
that he will be staying amongst the people;
he will be the neighbor, or he can be a hunter, fisherman, or anything.
Or sometimes he would join the animals.

He was able to do that.
He was apparently around this area
when he was traveling through,
because he doesn't stay with any one family at length
probably stay with family for a season
then move on to the next family or
other areas for the next season,
he's a loner type of person but very adventurous and very mischief [mystic?].
When he wants something, he will play trick on people or animals in order to get his way.
I guess that's why people call him "trickster";
he fits the description anyway,
and besides that, he's a shaman—he can do anything.

Now, once upon a time, Wiissaakechaahk
was traveling.
It's been a long time since he'd seen a man,
and he's kind of lonely for a human being.
So he decided to search for a family on the land.
We don't know for sure exactly where,
but we think it's between James Bay or Hudson Bay area.
There were lots of people then;
people were scattered all over; there was no villages;
the people live wherever they can find life.
So he wanders off—where he knew the people would be staying.

Since he is a man and has a man's emotions,
and he had the same desire as man;
he needs female companionship.
He wants sex, to be clear.
And he has it in his mind, because he hasn't seen human for some time,
especially he wanted to see a woman.
So he sets off to find some people.
He knows the family—they were not far away from where he is
so he travels towards there;
he knows there were a family there
they were about two families at least.
He know that there was an old lady, and there was daughters,

and a daughter married,
and he knows there was some single people.
Anyway, he knew that there was single women, so he went.
That's exactly what he was interested in anyway,
so he went searching for the family.

And sure enough, a few days later, he came upon the camp.
He saw the trail, the tracks of the people, men hunting.
He knows the direction where their camp would be.
So he investigate the trails, the tracks,
where they lead to mostly,
to pinpoint the site where the camp would be.
Finally he figured it out, and he walks towards it.
This was close to the evening.
The sunset would be very soon.
But in the right timing—he was really hoping to do something.
Because he was so—shall we say, so horny?—he wanted sex right away.
So he has to figure out, you know,
how to get sex very quickly without so much fuss.
Not necessarily rape. People, anything, woman.
So he decided to use a trick to get what he wanted.
So he think about it as he was walking, how would he do it?
How would he accomplish his wishes?
So finally, as he investigate the tracks leading to one center,
he knows that that will be [where] the camp is located.
By this time he already formed his plan, and what he's gonna do.

So he decided to play a trick on those women.
He knows that men would not be home yet,
because men always out hunting in the daytime
and don't usually get home till sunset or maybe late after sunset,
and that's why he know for sure the men will be away,
and only the women will be home,
and that's what he wanted.
So he had a plan.
He was certain that it would work; he would make it work anyway.
The closer he got to the camp, now he was getting excited.
He figured it would be just the right timing before the sunset.
He knows the wind wasn't in his favor,

because the wind was from the west sort of thing.
Sometimes the wind is gusting in this time of the season;
this is spring season—
early or middle of April thereabouts, just when all the animals are beginning to stir and mate—
he too, as a human, he begin to feel that.
So anyway, he has all the time in his mind;
all he has to do now is put it into action.
So finally he came upon the camp.
It's a large camp, which usually hold about three families.
He wasn't sure yet whether these were the right people he come to.
He knows that there will be women—single women—and all that;
that's why he come to this camp.

The traditional way to let people know you are arriving is to hit a tree with an axe.
Sure enough, as soon as he hit the tree, the youngsters came out,
and they say: "He is a stranger."
Older children came, then the teenagers, and finally the mother,
and the grandmother showed up later.
So he walks in, takes off his snowshoes,
and puts down his axe and his personal possessions,
which he carries only in his pack. He hung it there outside.
After the greeting and all that usual stuff,
the women, as a tradition, always invited strangers, said:
"We have some soup"—
soup is the only thing they used to offer; there was no tea then. Soup was always available, however they made it.
We don't have to go through that because we want
to get to the story.
So they says:
"Come in and have soup, hot soup, you must be tired."
And he says:
"Yes, I will do. I'm sort of hungry," and right away he said: "But I can't stay"—
because it was almost sunset—so he says: "I can't stay longer because I have to make a distance."
And that's all he says for the time being just to let them know he's not going to stay.

Because usually when a stranger arrive in the evening before sunset the usual
thing was to offer him a place to sleep in the home.
So that's why he said right away: "I can't stay."
That was strange also,
why a person wants to travel late in the evening when it's time to stop
unless there is an urgency, so the women figured.

Inside, there was an old lady, about sixty years old.
Her daughter was about thirty-five or forty,
and there were the daughter's children, sons and daughters.
There were only a few girls;
one was about twenty and the other probably a teenager.
So he looked them over and all that stuff, you know,
him and his desire to have them.
So he looked them over, you know,
as they move around and do things
when they prepare food and everything;
so he wants them.
So he just judge them and all that stuff.
Really, sex is all that he has on his mind—never mind the food—
but they were busy arranging the food to feed him, as usual,
as a tradition.
So finally they offer him the food.
So he says:

"Thank you very much," and he eats, and he try to eat very fast; he seem to be in a hurry.

So the middle-aged woman asks, you know:

"Why are you in such a hurry? What is so urgent?"

He says:

"Well, I can't stay. I didn't want to tell you this.
I can't stay here; I want to go on.
I may not be good to you; I may have a disease."
"What kind of disease?" they say.
Now the ladies are getting excited;
they getting serious; they get anxious;
they want to know what is wrong with him.

Usually when a stranger come, he would be happy to spend the night or stay a while unless there's something wrong.

They did not know the man was Wiissaakechaahk.

Wiissaakechaahk says:

"My sisters, I am sorry; I didn't want to scare you.
There is a disease coming. The epidemic, it's very bad.
Kills people. There's no cure for it, they say.
So I was just trying to move ahead of it."

By this time the old lady and the ladies are getting very curious—because the women are the medicine people.

The women are usually the nursing people and doctors for the family because they have all the knowledge about the herbs and plants they can use to cure almost any disease they used to have.

That's why they were so curious;
they wanted to know how does the disease affect anyone,
and how do you cure the disease? They want to know.

But Wiissaakechaahk say:

"Well, I don't know, I really don't know.
I never really ask, because I never really saw it;
I just hear about it.
I just met people on my travels,
and they said that there is that disease which kills,
and very contagious, and there is no cure for it really."

So the ladies are really getting worked up now,
so they constantly ask him:

"Can't you think of any cure at all for this disease?" and
"How do they describe it?" and "How do they feel?"

He said:

"I can't tell you; I really can't tell you what.
It's a very strange kind of thing."

By this time he was finished eating,
and it was almost sunset—

I guess it was sunset already because it was getting dark inside—so he said:

"Well, I have to go; I don't want to get caught in this thing.

That's the only thing I can do is to warn you that it's coming and if there's any way you could avoid it or cure it and see if you have anything. But there isn't much I can do."

So they says:

"Okay." They were very anxious, wringing their hands and all that stuff, and they don't know what to do.

At last, as he goes out they ask him again:

"Can you think of anything? Can you suggest anything to do?
Did you hear anything at all,
how to prevent or cure this disease?"
So he says:
"Well, I didn't want to tell you this,
because it's embarrassing."
So they says:
"Tell us anyway."
"Some men told me," he says, "that the only way they can prevent it is to stick their head into the ground,
and lift their rear end up."
So the women say:
"Strange, really.
Is it contagious because of the air we breathe?"
"Yes," he says,
"that is why you must put your head down in the ground,
not to inhale."
"How do you know when it's coming?" they say, the women.
"Well," he says, "it travels with the wind,
because this wind seems to travel with this disease.
There is usually a gust of wind which brings the disease."
The ladies now begin to formulate their defense,
or prevention or whatever.
Wiissaakechaahk says:
"Goodbye, goodbye, good luck to you."
The women asked:
"How far behind is it?"
He says:
"I don't know; it could be very close.
It was only yesterday that I met a man that tell me he had it,
so I moved away from there.
It could come anytime; just prepare for it."

The men folks are still out, and it was after sunset.
Soon the men folk will be in, and he knows that.
So he took off, not far from the camp,
and turned right around and went towards
where the wind is coming from.
What he did was he cut the branches or willows, tied them together,

and he begin to run towards the camp.
And those tied willows and everything that he drags sounds as if the wind
was coming.
And that's exactly what he wanted the women to think.
As soon as he reached the camp, he can hear the women say:
"Well, there it is, there it is. There is a wind."
I guess what he did was, you know,
he run around the camp dragging the branches,
something that makes sounds as if the wind is moving with the trees,
and as soon as he run around twice
and soon as he get in front of doors,
he take off his snowshoes and left the door flap open and look in
and here were the women,
putting their heads in the ground and stick their bums up.
So all he did was, you know, just walked right in,
and he has his way,
and he has his sex as he had planned to do.
So anyway.
After he has his way, then he walks and travels off again.
Grab his snowshoes and those tied willows he was dragging,
drag them off as if the sound goes away.
When he goes away,
back to the tipi, inside the *wikwam*,
we can see these women are talking to each other.
They say: "Did you get it?"
And somebody says: "No, not me."
And all those women, too, they say: "No, I don't feel a thing."
Nobody says anything.
Finally there was one girl who said: "Yes, I get it."
"How does it feel?"
She says: "It feels good." (Laughs)

Anyway, that's the end of that story.
Once again the Trickster, Wiissaakechaahk, had his way.
And this is to put it mildly, the story.
That's very mild; it's not even humor.
But amongst the men, sometimes it's very funny.
But just amongst the men—the way they describe that woman.
But it is always said in a little different way,

the way I have just said it,
very mildly put together,
for the sake of the young people and the young children,
so they wouldn't ask questions.
But the elders, the older women and the older men,
they understand exactly what it means.
They would giggle,
or at least give a little smile, if there is a children,
so this is the way the story goes.
It made that way.
The stories are very flexible that way.
So that's one part of the story about Wiissaakechaahk.
So he went on, he had his way, he had tricked some people.
But it doesn't say what happened to him after that.

Wiissaakechaahk and the Geese

The story picks up again, only later.
That once again, he was by himself.
And this time he was hungry.
This was in the middle of August, somewhere thereabouts,
August or September,
just when the geese are beginning to fly in the coastal regions and all that stuff in the Hudson and James Bay.
And this time he was traveling by himself again, as usual.
And he was hungry.
Really desired to have a special cooked goose and goose dinner would be nice, he thought.
He was very hungry; he hasn't eaten very well.
As he was thinking, he just travels, wanders off—
he was hunting actually—
all he has is a bow and arrow, tomahawk, probably a very rough knife.
He usually had a sling too also, a sling.
You know, for a stone?—the rope sling?—he has that.
[With] all these things,
even the bow and arrow, even if you are an expert,
you only get maybe one or two geese.
And the sling will give you only one chance, one shot.
Unless you can do something,
unless the geese were still moving,

that's the time you can get as many as you want.
But seeing that he was a wise man, besides being a trickster,
he never kill more than he needs.
He has to eat everything that he gets first—
    if he ever does eat anything.
And this was one of those days that he wanted to have a feast;
he wanted to take care of himself;
he wanted to satisfy himself with food,
and that's what he was thinking, he says:
    "Why not? I never have a feast by myself."
Once in a while he does that.
Once in a while he'll kill an animal and probably caribou or moose and he would stay there,
just cook the way he likes and
preserve the food, and he used all the animal,
just like the way it should be.
And he wouldn't leave that there until he finish.
So it's one of those wishes that he wanted to do.
It was now for the geese.
So anyway.
He was thinking about that, and he went to look around for the place where the geese usually hang around.
So he remembered this special small river, more like a creek,
that used to be a place there where the geese always eat,
Canada geese, snow geese, and any other geese—
    one of those lake type of thing.
    Lake, inlet, and outlet and everything.
So he went there.
As he was going up the river, walking on the shore,
all of a sudden he hear the geese,
a whole bunch of geese; he can hear them; they were eating.
He went up slowly, sneaking up the river of the creek.
And soon enough there was a open water there,
quite a large size of a lake—a pond, I should say, not the lake—
    that is only about three hundred feet long, maybe,
    and probably one hundred feet wide, two hundred feet wide,
    but very shallow with lots of grass around.
    Just the type where the ducks and geese likes to eat.
So he sneaks there and look over it,

and sure enough there were Canada geese in the middle, swans,
and all kinds of them, even some moose in there.
So anyway.
He went back, put himself back, and decided what to do.
So he began to plan:
    "What could I do with these birds?
    Not to get only one, but to get a lot.
    How do I do it, so I would have a feast?"
    Finally he decided to trick them—
    "I wonder if it'll work," he thought.
He knows that Canada geese and snow geese and some other ducks and all that stuff, usually they want to know what they saw.
They curious, especially the Canada geese in the springtime;
they're very curious;
they have that nature.
They're wise; they want to know what they saw;
they want to make sure that it's safe and okay.
So he knows. Wiissaakechaahk know all these things about birds.
So he uses that, he uses their curiosity to trick them.
Instead of him hiding from them, he decided just to come in the open.
So he did.
Before he expose himself in front of them,
he had a bag, you know, the ordinary backpack;
there's not much in it, just a little utensils maybe,
just something that he used to eat with,
and even the clothes, because he never has any clothes that much.
So decide to put lots of moss in this bag,
pack it and tie it and put stones in too,
to make it look like he's carrying something very heavy
and bulky inside.
The ordinary man wouldn't look like that;
the ordinary hunter wouldn't carry anything like that unless he has had a successful hunt.
Anyway, he walks.
Soon as he expose himself then the geese and ducks saw him,
but he did pretend not to look at them.
He just walked on shore; it was nice shore.
Sandy shore and on the north side because north side is a
favorable place for the people to camp,

usually on the shores of the river.
On the north side it's always nice,
so the sun can shine into the shore;
that's why they do that in the middle of the summer,
so they always favor that place.
So he has the same instinct that any other people have.
So he walks there. And on south side of the pond was wide open muskeg,
and all the birds are eating on the muskeg.
He knows all this area.
So as he walks over there,
and the Canada geese were the closest one to where he walks.
Since that he pretend not to bother them, not even lookin' at them,
the Canada geese, you know, just wondered why.
So they call him:
    "Hi, Wiissaakechaahk."
And then he says:
    "Hi, *nishim*"—*nishim* means "my brother"—but he didn't stop,
    just kept on walking.
So they say:
    "What's wrong with him? Wonder what he's got in his bag?
    Let's ask him."
So the ducks and the geese come in, and they say:
    "Really strange, yeah, I wonder what he's got."
So then they call him again, they said:
    "Hey, Wiissaakechaahk, tell us what you got in your bag."
And then he didn't stop; he still walks. He says:
    "Nah, nothing of your interest. My possession."
    "But what's in it?"—
    they knew that human doesn't carry that big of a bag
    in a simple travel; no, humans don't do that, especially men.
    So they were more curious, and lots of them came in,
    land close by, and said: "You tell us what's in it."
So he get their attention very closely now.
That's what he want.
So finally he says:
    "Well, if you want to know that bad,
    what I carry in my bag is my secret and my private possession."
    "What is it? Tell us."
So he says:

"It's my songs."
So the ducks and geese and swans say:
"Songs?"—how a person can carry a songs in a bag?
The ducks and geese they do not carry songs.
So they begin to say:
"How does he carry songs?" So they ask him:
"How you carry songs in a bag?"
So he says:
"I have my way. And you guys had your songs,
and you have them in your mind.
Mine, I carry them."
So that they find very strange.
So finally, finally they said:
"Well, sing us a song."
He says:
"No, no, no, this is a private thing.
I don't sing them any anytime;
it has to be a special, special arrangement.
There better be a stage if I want to perform in front of the audience,
and I have to have that stage or place
where I could sing."
They said:
"Well, why don't you create it right now? We'll all wait for you.
The daylight is still high; I'm sure you can do it."
So he stop, and he says:
"Well, are you serious that you want to hear my songs?"
They says:
"Yes, yes, we will wait; we will come;
we will get some more people to come, more of us to come."
That's what he wanted; he wanted as many as he can.
So he says:
"Okay, you have to give me time."
And right where he was standing there was a nice sandy beach right there, few rocks.
And then over the bank there was a nice white moss ground.
And beyond it, away from the river there were lots of trees,
the kind of trees that people use for making *wikwam*, or tipi.
So he says:
"I have to make a large *wikwam*.

> There's quite a few of you; I have to fit you in,
> and [have a place] where I could sit.
> Because I do not give performance for just anyone," he says,
> "you have to be invited."

So they said:

> "Okay." They are all excited; they haven't heard him sing.
> He must be very special to carry songs in a bag;
> that's what they wondering.
> So they says: "Okay, go ahead;
> we will just have to continue eating here
> and call us when you are ready."

So, "Okay," he says. So he went into the bush, and he says:

> "I'll be right here."

And ducks and geese went back into their busy schedule and eating.
Feeding their youngs and all that stuff.
And you can hear in the bush there crashing sound and all that stuff.
And this was Wiissaakechaahk making a large tipi, large *wikwam*.
He was making a makeshift *wikwam*, but they has no covering,
and he didn't want to make a moss house,
but he just wanted to have enclosure
so that nobody can peek in.
So he uses lots of poles, and then
he uses a parts to cover around it and
just halfway was good enough.
But you know, the geese have wings, they've been flying,
so that's why he uses only few poles.

Usually when somebody makes a *wikwam* or tipi,
usually you need about twenty sticks;
that's at least twenty sticks or even twenty-four.
The four sticks to control the wind flap
and the twenty to put them around.
But he has to put them about four inch apart
so he needed a lot of sticks, lots of poles.
And that's what he did,
and all the parts, he created the parts.
He skinned the trees and the parts he put them on the lengthwise on the bottom and right up, like a shingles.
Whatever he does, you know, it works, for him.

And also at the same time he take out the roots,
the tree roots, any kind of roots,
the roots are just like a rope for them in those days—
    that's the only kind of rope they used to have.
    I mean, makeshift rope.
So he pulled lots of those, lots of them, and he put them around the tipi, around the base,
and covered them with the branches and everything.
In the middle he let the ground stay as it is.
At the back there, the back door,
that's were he put his seat, and also he has created a drum—he has made a drum which seems to fit above this bag.
He made it so he said to the ducks that this was what he was carrying.
He use this to sing, this little drum.
So that's what the geese and ducks were so anxious to see;
what does it look like, his songs?
Actually, it was a drum.
But he didn't carry the drum; he made the drum,
because he can make a drum.
Probably, naturally—remember, he has a shaman power—
he can do tricks.
So anyway, which makes it more impressive for the ducks and geese and all that.

So finally when he finish, when he thought of everything,
so he calls them, he says:
    "Hey there, brothers and sisters, I'm ready, I'm ready to sing"—
    in those days the only musical instrument they had was the drum.
    There were no electric guitars, saxophones.
    But they did used to have some kind of flute and the drum.
    I don't think they ever created any string instrument.
    They did have rattles they used sometimes when they sing.
    So Wiissaakechaahk has a drum, and that's what he used to sing.
By this time all the ducks and geese had come into the shore
and saw this impressive tipi, big enough to fit them. Very big.
So they all rush in.
Wiissaakechaahk is sitting in the back and says:
    "Make yourself at home, make yourself at home.
    Crowd around as close as you can."

They did manage to fit them all in.
There were lots of Canada geese, and swans, black ducks, mallards, pintails, teals, and diving ducks. Even the loon.
And of course there were male and female.
All the females wanted to dance.
He says to them:
"You are going to participate in these songs.
You will dance as I sing, and sometimes I will give you instructions how to dance.
And you must follow my instructions.
Whatever I say when I sing, you will do so."
So they said:
"Okay"—they were very eager, very eager to dance.
He begins to sing and start his drumming.
Because he was a shaman, he made them enjoy.
The ducks and geese they step to the music.
They get lost in dancing.
He sang for many different songs, and they were enjoying themselves.
Sometimes they take a break.
They ask him again to dance.
And he danced.
And then in one song, he says:
"This song is for you to all dance together"—
something like waltzing—
"so you listen to my instructions."
So he begin to dance and drumming, and halfway through he says:
"Now put your heads together"—
you know how the geese they got a long neck,
and the swans and the ducks.
So he says:
"Put your head together."

So by this time all the ducks and geese were dancing very freely;
they're not aware of anything but amongst themselve.
They were totally enjoying themselve.
And then once again Wiissaakechaahk give instruction and he says:
"Now close your eyes."
And they begin to close their eyes and dance together and
all the swans and Canada geese and snow geese

winding their necks to each other.
Then again he says:
"Now move around. Go around."
And then they go move around together.
And by this time Wiissaakechaahk was preparing, as he sing,
because the ducks and the geese are so busy dancing and enjoying themselve.
And then he pick out those, Wiissaakechaahk pick out those ropes that he place around the tipi.
He use it as a rope.
He had make the loop of them;
all he did was as they pass,
throw it over their neck and tie it quickly,
amongst the geese and swans first.
And he just choked them
and throw them over the side, as he sang,
and everybody was busy, nobody knows what happening
because all they hear was the feathers rustling as they dance,
so they didn't notice much; they didn't know it.
Until the loon begin to be aware of something,
that dance place was not as packed as it used to be,
begin to move around very easily, and he noticed that there was
not as full as it was.
And Wiissaakechaahk kept on tying those necks together and throw them aside, as he sing.
Then for sure some of the ducks also aware that the room was getting empty.
And the loon, being sneaky as he is,
opened one eye and to see what's going on.
And as he open his eyes, right away he saw Wiissaakechaahk
tying the geese together and throw them aside.
And he scream, and he says: "Wiissaakechaahk is killing us," he says,
and as soon as he say that then every other remaining ducks and geese they opened their eyes,
and here he was, killing; they were killed.
And they screamed and rushed out to the door and
because of the loon who had screamed—
he's not a very good walker on the ground—
he was very slow, and he was tramp over by the door.

And by this time Wiissaakechaahk had killed half of them anyway.
He stepped on the loon, stuck by the door,
as he tried to drag himself out.
Step on his back—
    that's why we see the loon today, he has a very bad back, squashed like;
    that's why he cannot walk on the ground.
And now Wiissaakechaahk thanked his lucky stars that he was able to get all kinds of geese and ducks,
and he said to himself: "Now I am going to feast."
By this time all the remaining ducks and geese have take off into the river and really get scared.
So there was no geese or anything around in the lake anymore.
Wiissaakechaahk was by himself.
Once again he has succeeded, tricked the people.
His trick has work again.
Now he begin to decide, now how am I going to cook these things?
[What is] the best way to have my feast?
Usually when you have the ducks and geese,
they would be plucked and cooked.
But him, since that he wanted to cook special way,
cook them at one time,
he decided to do a special way.
There's a way to cook a geese once and a while when there's no pots or anything.
He could pluck them all and roast them or even smoke them or even many other ways.
Since that he didn't have a pot, he decides the next best thing.
So he said to himself, "Well, I'm going to cook them in the sand,
    roast them in the sand."
First of all, people used to pluck the geese, leave the feet in,
or sometimes not necessarily leave the feet in,
after taking the guts out, wrap it in leaves, some kinds of leaves you can find on the lakes—
    I think they call them lily pads or frog pads, they call them,
    and some of them are underground, underwater,
    they are very wide leaves—
usually that's what people used to wrap the geese around and put them in the sand.

Some people do it differently.
Some people make a large fire over the sand;
after the sand has been heated right down to maybe a foot or so,
they would just make a hole in there and put the geese in and bury the goose in there.
Usually after an hour or two the goose will be cooked very nicely.
But Wiissaakechaahk, because he was so greedy [and] hungry,
after deciding what to do,
he didn't bother to pluck the geese; he just put them right in.
What he did was, he dig a sand,
and then he make a fire in the sand, a large fire.
And heated the sand, and shifted over again, and all that,
and after he satisfied there was enough heat,
then he put all the geese in,
head first and stick out the feet; he didn't pluck them.
So he buried them with this hot sand,
very hot sand, and he left them there.
Nobody says how many he got, but there were lots.
And after he buried them and
he left them there, and he says:
"It should take a long time to cook. Meanwhile," he says,
"I might as well take a nap."
So he did that.
In order for him to sleep,
he knows that there will be some animals traveling by or anything and they may steal.
He's aware that there will be foxes; there will be something, even human.
So he decided to sleep for a while.
Where he chose the place to sleep was right on top of the riverbank.
The riverbank was not that high really.
So he decided to have a guard.
Somebody should keep an eye on his cooking.
So he talks to his rear end, and he says: "Well, you watch."
He laid down his bum to the riverside, and he says:
"You watch, and let me know
if anybody steal my food."
And it so happens he fall asleep;
it's late in the afternoon.

And so happen that there were some human around;
there were some people around there.
They too were looking for some food—they were hunting.
This was a famous place for them to hunt—that's why they were traveling
this small river, small creek.
There were about two canoes, maybe three.
What the Native people used to do in those days were they used to
drift along the river, and then if they see the ducks or geese
on the river, they would stop.
And then they would sneak from the shore
and shoot the geese with the bow and arrow.
That's what they were doing;
they were sort of drifting down the river and
the guy that sit in front of the canoe always look ahead
so if they see a geese then they back up;
then they will go into the shore and sneak up on the geese,
and this is what they were doing.
The leader of the canoe just keeping his eye open, and then
this is a famous place here—there usually lots of geese—and slowly coming
down, they don't even move, just very slowly,
and the man kept looking on the water; there's nothing;
the lake, the pond, was empty—there's nothing.
Except that he saw somebody sleeping on the bank;
somebody was laying there.
The bum side was exposed and he watch.
Then all of a sudden he recognize—gave a sign to back down, to back up to
the shore—and he says:
"There's nothing there, no geese, no nothing.
The only thing I saw there—I'm sure is—somebody sleeping up there.
You see his bum stickin' out."
"A bum stickin' out?" they say. "But why?"
So they begin to talk to each other, and who would do such thing?
So they know there was Wiissaakechaahk around;
he always does something unexpectedly.
Could be Wiissaakechaahk, so they says:
"Why would he do that?"
They begin to wonder, and they talk about why would he do that and
why there's no geese there now; they say:

"He must have kill a geese. There's nothing left there now.
Let's take a look again."
This time this guy just went ahead by himself,
look at this person laying there, on top of the bank;
his bum is bare,
and as he expose himself he can see that this man is going to fart,
and he backed down,
went back to his group, and he says:
"You know, this person sleeping, and every time I expose myself, you know, he wants to fart."
So they says:
"That's him all right; he must be using his rear end as a guard. What shall we do?"
"We will sneak behind him, and you stay here,"
they say to one person.
"Just pretend that you are here and you're not going there. Try it.
Walk towards him and if he wants to fart, sign it, give a sign.
If he doesn't fart, that means we beat him."
So they tried it, and Wiissaakechaahk didn't fart.
They know it is Wiissaakechaahk.
In the meanwhile, they take all the geese from the sand and cut the feet off and
throw the geese—I don't know whether they were cook already but
they stole his geese—but they cut the feet off and stick it back into the sand.
They rearranged the sand so they won't show any tracks,
and after they finish,
this person who was taking care of this rear end,
stay put there and walks away until they all went down the river.
Finally they take off.
So they have stole his geese.

In the meantime, Wiissaakechaahk just slept.
It was towards the evening now, and by the time he woke up—he woke up all of a sudden, well rested and everything—and the first thing he think about was his geese, his cooking, so he says:
"Oh, man, I'm sure I overcooked my cooking."
So he talks to himself, and he says:
"Is there anyone coming? No nothing."

He jump up and grab his stick, you know, to take out one [goose], nothing
 there.
He says: "Oh, yes, I did overcook."
He pull another set of feet, same thing,
until he begin to [become] aware there's nothing attached to it.
He begin to dig, and there's nothing—
 all the feet have been cut from the body of the geese.
He begin to realize that while he was sleeping some human must have
 steal—
only human can do that, animal would have [dragged off the whole bird].
He went to the shore, the water;
on the shore, the sand, there was no sign of footprint or anything.
But at the water level, there is a sign; there's a footmarks, and canoe marks,
so he was very certain that he's been robbed,
so he was very mad.
He doesn't know where those people are now; he knows they will be far
 away.
So there was nothing else he can do;
all he can do is [be] mad at himself—
 mad at his rear end because it didn't give him any warning.
So he talks to his rear end—shall we say, his asshole—says:
 "Why didn't you warn me? I told you to keep watch."
And finally all he can do is eat those feet that's leftover,
but he's still mad at himself. He talks to himself:
 "I'll fix you," to his rear end, "because you didn't give me no
warning."
And there was still a fire there burning,
so he recandles the fire, and he heat up a stone
and when the stone begin to get hot,
he sits on it—that's to punish his rear end for not warning him.
[After a while] he decided that's enough punishment.
That's the end of the story at that moment.

It's said he move on to other section of land
and was hungry, because he had lost his food.
That well-planned feast he wanted to have, it didn't turn out,
and that was his mistake;
for once he was paying for his tricks to the animals that he did kill;

he didn't have all that feast. He realized that.
So he traveled places and all that stuff.
Then all of a sudden he notice, when he was trying to sneak on a ducks or whatever he wants to hunt,
he begin to fart when he moves a little bit;
every time he want to sneak up on an animal, anything, he would fart,
and he would scare the animal away.
First he thought it was very funny;
when he walks, he would fart, you know, with the short steps,
and they were very short farts, quick ones,
and he'd take a long stride and there was a long sound coming out from his rear end.
Soon enough he was getting very, very hungry
because he hadn't eaten,
and he begin to starve, because he couldn't hunt anything,
because of that.

Finally the day came that he was starving, truly;
the end seems to be just few more days,
and there was nothing to eat.
That's the end of the story about him starving,
but there is a bit to it that doesn't sound too good.
I'm gonna leave that out,
so that's the end of that part.
[. . . and he travels on] and has forgotten his mistake, his greediness,
he still carries on his tricks
to anyone that he can beat . . .

ANWE AND THE CANNIBAL EXTERMINATORS

Told and Recorded by Louis Bird

I will not talk about the different tribes of people,
but I will talk about
which has been passed on to me by the Cree language only.
It has happened here—
    right here where I'm sitting on this river, Winisk River.
In the area of the Winisk area band.
And also in James Bay and further up to the York Factory area.
This area was covered by the Cree people,
and they have intermigrated amongst each other.
There was no place on the land that was not known
and who lives there, and what families are living there.
Everybody known to each other because the word—the news—traveled fast, related to one another into another band.

This was, of course, when there are too many cannibals existed on the land;
the elders of the ordinary people—
    those who did not become the cannibals
would seek the solution to these problems—
to the area problem or territorial problems which begin
the territory problems amongst them.
So they have to have a decision made
because this unnatural behavior amongst the groups amongst them
or amidst of them.

It was said in the times when this happened,
in this particular story which I listen to my grandfathers
say that when—once upon a time when—the cannibals were too many,
there was a cry for a solution from the area people.
So the elders and the wise men amongst the group got together
and discussed the situation, and seek solutions,
and then make resolution that they must seek help

from amongst the methods possible
or amongst other tribes, if it was possible.

Most of the elders had acquired some shamanism.
The communication part of their activities was a shaking tent.
So it was decided to set up a shaking tent to communicate outside help or to communicate [to an] outside tribe
[to seek] somebody with the shaman power capable of overcoming
their problem, the area problem, overcoming the cannibals,
because the cannibals were once ordinary people with the shaman power.
Once they became cannibals,
they became most feared people in the area,
so they were not easily get rid of because they had the power also.
So some expert has to be found in the area or outside of the area,
and therefore the wise men—the wise shamans—have to
apply their skill to seek help, the outside help.
This particular story I am going to tell is called "Anwe."
Anwe was the name of the person that was found amongst other tribes.
Apparently, it was in the area of the Plains Cree.
Whichever province today he [Anwe] was located,
he was contacted through the shaking tents
or by a runner or a communicator or liaison person amongst the tribes
to contact such a person and asked or begged
to come to the area to get rid of these cannibals,
for the people in the area.

And so the guy was found by the name of Anwe.
He was an expert exterminator of cannibals.
That was his profession amongst the Indian tribes.
Therefore he agreed to come, I guess with some pride [prize?].
I don't know what his fees was,
but he agreed to come to the area where this problem existed amongst the tribes.
So he came in, well prepared with his expertise
and contacted the Natives who required his assistance,
and he went around and talked with the elders
and asked them how many groups are they and
where would they be located?
And all the information Anwe required was readily made available to him, and from then on he decided strategies,

what [how] to go about eliminating these cannibals.
So the story goes
that he did his job and eliminated all the cannibals in the district.
And therefore, the Crees, or whatever tribes there were,
lives normally after that.
And that's the end of the story about the cannibalism,
one part of cannibalism story.

Another cannibalism story that was very peculiar was that
once upon a time—
    it was probably before the *Anwe* story;
    Anwe is a person, the exterminator,
    the professional exterminator, amongst the tribe.
    Whether it was before this or after,
    once upon a period,
    in the past amongst the Indian people there existed a band of cannibals, a Native, whether they were Cree or other tribes,
    it [the story] doesn't say.
But these particular groups were very fantastic.
They were more fearsome than the ordinary cannibals that we just mentioned.
These particular cannibals, it's said, were hard to get rid of.
Many a times
a proposed exterminator of the cannibals
had failed to get rid of them because he simply couldn't kill them.
These cannibals have acquired somehow to take their heart out of their body, and somehow preserve them.
And the heart pulses separately from their body.
And it is said that they had a special scaffold where they camp;
a special basket was made containing down feathers
very warm and well insulated, and this is where the hearts are kept.
And they lived around the scaffold,
and they lived just like an ordinary person.
But they do eat human beings, beside eating the ordinary animal food.
They look to be exactly like the normal people, but they are not.
Whenever it's necessary, whenever they want to eat human flesh—
    which has been a habit to them—
they would kill the next-door neighbor or whatever it is if it's happen to be living with them without their knowledge.
Of course, the cannibals knew,

but the ordinary person without shaman power would not know readily—
he would think that these people were just ordinary people.
And so happened, the story goes on, it existed for some years.
Finally the rest of the groups of families and clans, whatever it is,
restricted their movement,
and appointed the area where those people are
camping or located and they have a certain distance to certain areas where they stayed
they do not associate with the ordinary people, as I say before.
But they were well known amongst the tribes,
and they could not be killed.
Once again the situation was getting so tragic and fearsome.
Once again the elders and wise men of the tribes has to gather and have council.

The council of elders and shaman were gathered amongst the ordinary people and discussed the situation.
And therefore decided
to eliminate these extraordinary cannibals.
There is a special name for these cannibals.
It's something to describe as "people who left their hearts apart from their body."
They say that if you kill one with an arrow or with an axe or anything, you would inflict the damage all right,
but later on it would get up and walk away,
alive, because you did not actually kill it.
Its heart was still alive;
its body mend itself.
And that is why so fearsome about them.
And therefore there existed a man.
It was not Anwe;
it was a young man
who was an orphan and had acquired powerful shaman skills,
and was asked to take over responsibility of exterminating
[the cannibals] for the benefit of the district tribes,
whatever they are.
And then he agreed to proceed and to kill them.
What he did was very fake—more like a fiction, the way he did it.

It was said he went right up to their camp
and turned himself into a small baby,

a baby that crawls on the ground.
He walked into the camp when the young men were hunting around.
These people act as normal people—
    they hunt, they trap, they kill animals and all that
    for everyday life, but they usually venture out and just special hunt for human being for them to eat once a month or once a week or whatever it is whatever the period they required to do so.
This young man studied their habit, and he find out most young men
were out and only the old people live.
And the old person's usually the leader of the groups,
and he went directly into the heart of the problem.
He went to visit the elders.

When he went to this camp, he found an old man and his wife,
and there were no young men; they were out hunting.
This exterminator first had studied the surrounding of the camp,
and he know that the old man and his sons were out hunting.
Only the women were at camp and the old man who was actually a leader,
a director, for the group, only [him and] his wife.
So he walked in, crawled in as a baby.
As those two elders were sitting in their home, in roll in the baby, a crawling baby.
And they so startled they just grab the baby,
    the old man [and woman].

[The remainder of this oral recording is lost. The following is based on a transcription of the original recording by George Fulford, (Anthropology, University of Winnipeg).]
This old man, the old leader of the cannibals,
when he saw the baby crawling,
apparently he was seeing the illusion from the power of the exterminator.
The cannibal exterminator had this power to appear himself as a baby.
As he had already contacted the old man in his mind,
he already beat him in his mind—with the mind power.
Therefore the elder and his wife seemed to think they saw a baby crawl in.
Actually it was the exterminator,
who have appeared himself as a helpless baby,
fat and chubby and very tender to eat—very tempting.
Thus the cannibal could not help himself to grab the baby and extinguish its life.
Readily, just as if it was a fat piglet or chicken.

The Indian habit of having so hungry and
when he want to eat so quickly he would usually roast the animal or bird.
Put it into a roasting stick and put it into open fire and roast it.
This way is a delicacy.
It's the fastest way and very easy to cook.
With this gift from somewhere,
the old cannibal and his wife act the same.
Naturally, they just kill the baby and with no question,
automatically grab the roasting stick, put the little baby over it,
and lean it over against an open fire.
Turn it once in a while, quickly cook it and everything.
Once it was nicely cooked, brown and everything,
because the exterminator overpower the old man,
that caused him to change his mind and set aside readily prepared food and put it out on the scaffold.
Hang it over there to cool.
And that was a foolish thing to do.
He was already beaten, consciously.
The baby itself was a man, and he make the elder to take him over to the scaffold,
where the hearts were prepared and stored and pulsing.
Here he was drawn on top of this scaffold covered with material,
shoved under, and then the old man forgot everything.
Just forget completely and walk in and continue his daily existence inside the *wikwam*.

Meanwhile, the apparent baby took himself off the roasting stick,
take the roasting stick, and became a man and set out to uncover the secret place where the hearts are preserved and kept.
He opened a container and saw those fluffy down feathers
and see those pulsing heart sitting there.
There were at least seven of them.
He touched each one very lightly with the roasting stick.
He didn't hear anything.
He knows if he touch the right one, the one of the old man,
he will hear him.
And as he began to touch each of them, finally one of them,
he can hear the old man, just a little way from the scaffold,
exclaiming: "Ahhhh!" That's all he could say.

At that moment he just let it go.
Then he got down from the scaffold, according to the story, and walk into the tipi as a man.
And the elder and his wife were so startled they couldn't do anything but act naturally,
as if they have been visited by a stranger.
And they offered him tea, make him set at the best spot,
and treat him very cordially and respectfully.
By this time the elder was totally beaten with the will power of the exterminator.
His wife too.
Then he start to tell a story about his sons.
His eldest son, who was out there hunting with his brothers.
And there were about three or four tipis around.
And he says:

"My oldest son"—there were seven sons—"is out hunting with his brothers. They should be back this evening."

By his story, the exterminator knew well the other sons—
the cannibals—
would be home soon.
So he left, went back up to the scaffold, and started jabbing those hearts, pulsing hearts, one at a time.
Then finally the old man.
As he stabbed them, wherever those cannibals were, they dropped dead.
So that's that.
The exterminator had done his job.
There is no story about what he did to the females,
whether he killed them after he killed the men.
Once again there is peace amongst the area people; they relax.
They continue to live on for the next generation or so.

That is a part of the story which is very interesting for me.
This story reminds me of today's horror movies about vampires,
vampires that go to sleep, walk around at night as ordinary people.
And you can't kill them.
The only way you can kill them is to drive a stake through the hearts in the daytime.
This story is very similar to this one I just talked about.
Now that is another story.

The next one (the same type of story) is about a story a long time ago. This doesn't say it was before the cannibals who left the heart
 or had been eliminated by enemy.
I think this one is more ancient than the others.
Or maybe it is more recent.
I think it is more recent.
It is more recent because it is said that before this story the people used to have a *wiitiko*.
A form of human being that killed off the Natives of this country,
or any other part of North or South America.

The story goes on to say that animals would emerge and kill off the people.
Sometimes in the form of a giant wolf or bear or any other animal.
And there was no stopping these things.
More frequently by human form, which they call *wiitiko*.
Wiitiko is actually a person who does not exist as a human person,
which can be very fearsome.
Its mere existence around normal human being would be felt.
His usual habit of killing would be his voice,
which affects the mind of human being.
Sort of numbed them, and passed out.
After that he would just kill them off.
Hit with whatever he's got—a club, stone, or stick.
And begin to eat.
And this kind of *wiitiko* is not a cannibal—
 it's just a kind of being that existed all of a sudden from nowhere.

Other stories say that he is a cannibal.
One time he would have been a human person,
but being cannibal for so long, [and] so extraordinary,
combined with mystic powers,
the inhuman beast becomes a prey to ordinary people amongst the Indian tribes.
This happens, they say, more often.
It is said amongst the ordinary elders and shamans [that] there
existed a prophet sometimes amongst them.
A prophet that has such powers to cure or do feats not accomplished by the ordinary shaman.
He would just be a shaman who can foretell future.
The main threat amongst Indian people—in time past before European—

was that it is *wiitiko* that is actually a threat to the Indian people.
This *wiitiko* is something like a disease that emerges and
kill off the Indian people if there was not a starvation.
And therefore, because of this, there was a lady—

seems to be an ordinary lady who was married to an ordinary man who was a good provider, a good family, so it seems—

And the lady had acquired the shaman power to control the events, whatever it is.
Maybe she is a prophet to alter nature's ways amongst the tribes across the land.
And this so happened, this lady was married to the ordinary man
and also had three small children with her husband.
Maybe more than three.
As we know, the Indian people used to have the children, in their prime years, every second year.
Therefore the children, if they were three or four,
they would be very small.
It so happened that this lady had an extraordinary dream as a young girl. And the dream was so powerful and so realistic
that it actually seemed to happen in her lifetime.
In the time when they were in their daily activities, following their culture traditions, migrating on the land,
she had this extraordinary dream.
Apparently she was the orphan; she didn't have no parents.
She was an orphan as a young girl and thus acquired some strange shaman powers, so she can visualize ahead.
And was so fateful, she actually prepare for it,
and prepare her husband and her children,
so that when time comes they won't be terrified.
And one day, before her husband left for his daily activities as a hunter, she told him:

"Do not be afraid if you see an extraordinary trail of a human kind, leading towards our camp, because that will be my father.

My father will be coming.
He is not ordinary person; he is *wiitiko.*
I have dreamt he will stay with us.
He will not be a threat.
He will live amongst us until the time comes that he has to
take away those ancient happenings among our people.
He will take all the cannibals and *wiitiko* that have lived among our people.
He will lead them to another part of the country."

So the man shrugged his shoulders, and he left.
Sure enough, days pass.
But the man was prepared.
He knows cannibals existed in the land.
But he never encountered anyone.
But he heard stories that they were cannibals, *wiitikos*,
killing off the people some other part of the country.
Strange animals appearing that possess extraordinary power.
Their nature is to kill people off.
And the man had been out hunting.
He had encountered other bands, other families,
and visit them before coming back to his own territory.
One day as he traveled home towards evening, he saw a human track—
    which was extraordinarily large, not an ordinary person.
Right away he remembers his wife's warning that one day her father will come to visit her
in the form of the *wiitiko* and that he should not be afraid.
With this preparedness he was ready to face this extraordinary thing.
As he got home, he met his wife and he said:
    "What?"
And his wife said:
    "He has arrived! My father. He is inside."
And his wife was busy taking the larger poles to make a tipi.
She was taking those to extend the tipi to accommodate this person.
And therefore she asked her husband to help her.
Sure enough, the man cooperated.
And they extended the tipi large enough to accommodate the person
who was coming to their home.
And they extended one side of the tipi, the *wikwam*,
for this person to stay.
Sure enough, the thing came in.
The human form, it is ugly and stinks.
It crawls and greet him as a son-in-law.
And the man greets him as his father-in-law.
And the children greet him as their grandfather.
So they live.
But the man never faces the fire.
He always faces the wall and talks just like an ordinary grandfather.
Talks to his grandchildren, to his daughter, and to him.

But he doesn't talk to him directly.
He talks to him by way of his daughter.

After staying with him for a month or so—
    not eating so much of ordinary food—
the man begins to worry about what he is going to do for his father-in-law. He decided to hunt for his father-in-law,
to bring something of food value to this person.
So one day, he told his wife:
    "I'm going to bring something for your father."
The wife understood immediately and says:
    "Okay. Not to worry."
So he visit the next neighbor—
    a neighbor which is not too far away,
    probably a day's walking distance in return travel.
So he went to visit and asked the man to come and help him along the way—towards his home.
Close to his home he killed the man and carried him the rest of the way and left him outside.
He came into the home, like an ordinary day, and prepared to have dinner with his family
and whispered to his wife:
    "You can tell your father that there is something out there for him to have."
And the wife understood immediately and communicated the news to her father.
And then the *wiitiko* says:
    "Thank you. I shall go outside because I do not wish to splash anything on my grandchildren. I will make a fire,
    make preparation, outside."
So he crawled out and went outside—
    you can hear all the crash as he was breaking the trees and making the fire.
And it was late at night when he started to cook whatever it was that he was cooking—which was actually the human being.
Then he ate.
It took him almost all night to eat.
Then he crawled back to his place in the *wikwam*.
And he was okay for the next month or so.
Finally, after a few months pass, the man knows his father-in-law might be hungry.
So he scouted around for more people.

Sure enough, he found about five families.
He knows that his grandfather, this *wiitiko*, would eat a lot.
So he went home and tell the story to his wife:

"I found people out there. Not too far away.

If your father wishes to have something else to eat, then he can go. See what he thinks."

Sure enough, the wife relates the message and he [her father] says:

"Thank you. I shall go. But tomorrow I want you to change camp.

I want you to leave this place and travel for two days. I wait for you. Because I do not want to knock my grandchildren down when I attack my food"—he means human beings.

So the next morning the man and his wife and his children prepare to go. They travel for two days, and then towards the evening of the second day they hear the person shouting.
That's the *wiitiko*.
That's when he was attacking those camps amongst the people.
That was it.
The young people almost drop to their knees,
because of this fearsome voice which usually the *wiitiko* is associated with, before they shout down the human being before they kill him—

that is the usual way for the *wiitiko* to kill his prey.

Anyway, the week passed.
Finally the *wiitiko* came back to their camp.
He carried something on his back, and he left it away from the camp.
And he came in very content to live with his daughter and grandchildren.
Anyway, towards spring, after the ice gone away,
he told the story what's going to happen.
He told his daughter somebody is going to visit them.
The other *wiitiko*, which is going to be way bigger than him.
And he is the final *wiitiko* in the land. He normally kills off all of the people. And he is going to take him [the old man] away.
So he says:

"When he comes, I am going to get up and run around the tipi.

When I run seven times, you run inside and stay with the children and your husband.

When I run around the camp the seventh time, that will be the last time. I will say that I am leaving.

At that time I shall be going away towards the east.

At that time you will instruct your children, my grandchildren, to get outside and sing this song."
And he instructed them in this song.
I forget the wording of the song, but it went something like:
"My grandfather has taken away all the *wiitikos* of the land.
Never again will the Indian people experience such fearsome things in this life,
because I am taking away the *wiitiko* to another land."
And you can hear the shocks of the land as these giants run around,
and the shocks seem to fade away to the east.
And ever since then, there were never any more *wiitikos* of that size
to be so fearsome among the tribes.

That must be the fiction stories of the people among the land of the Mushkegos, or Swampy Crees.
If it only belongs to the Swampy Crees, or the Ojibwe tribes, much more inland from the bay area.
These were some of the stories I heard as a boy.
These stories were not legends.
They seemed to be fiction stories.
But fiction stories are similar to the legends.
But these ones seemed so real.
Everything that has happened a long time ago is associated there.

Culture-Hero and Trickster Stories

Introduction by David J. Costa

Miami-Illinois

Miami-Illinois is an Algonquian language originally spoken in what is now Indiana and Illinois. In Indiana the groups speaking this language included the Miami tribe proper (*myaamiaki*, "downstream people"), along the Wabash, Maumee, Mississinewa, and Eel rivers; the Weas (*waayaahtanooki*, "whirlpool people"), along the middle reaches of the Wabash River; and the Piankashaws (*peeyankihšiaki*, "torn ears people"), in the southwest of the state around present-day Vincennes. The two main groups speaking the Illinois language were the Kaskaskias (*kaahkaahkiaki*, "katydids") in the southwest of the state near the Mississippi River, and the Peorias (*peewaaliaki*; etymology unknown) to the north, along the Illinois River. The closest neighbors and linguistic relatives of the Miami-Illinois people were the Kickapoo, Mascouten, Fox, Sauk, Potawatomi, and Shawnee Indians.

By 1832 pressure from European settlers and warfare with neighboring tribes had combined to force the various Miami-Illinois-speaking groups to abandon the Illinois area. After spending a few decades in eastern Kansas, they were eventually settled in what is now Ottawa County, Oklahoma. The Weas and the Piankashaws were likewise forced out of Indiana in the early nineteenth century, eventually merging with the Peorias and the Kaskaskias as the modern Peoria Tribe of Oklahoma. In 1846 about half of the Miami tribe proper were forced out of Indiana. After a stay in Kansas, they too relocated to Indian Territory, settling next to the Peorias. Their descendants live there to this day, as the modern Miami Tribe of Oklahoma. However, many other Miamis managed to stay behind in Indiana, and to this day their descendants mainly live in the northern portion of that state, as the Miami Nation of Indiana.

There are no longer native speakers of Miami-Illinois in either Oklahoma or Indiana, although efforts to revitalize the language are underway in both states. In Oklahoma the last fluent speakers seem to have been born during the tribes' stay in Kansas and probably passed away in the first half of the twentieth century, though a few speakers with limited fluency lived a few decades past that. In Indiana the language seems to have ceased being passed on to children around the last decades of the nineteenth century, with the last speakers surviving into the early 1960s.

The Miami-Illinois language is documented over a timespan of more than two hundred years. Old Illinois is well attested in at least four major documents surviving from the French missionary period of the late seventeenth and early eighteenth centuries, including three dictionaries and a prayer book. Extensive documentation of the modern Miami-Illinois language began in the late nineteenth century. From the 1890s through 1916, the speech of the last generation of fluent speakers was documented by Bureau of American Ethnology linguists Albert Gatschet and Truman Michelson and by Jacob Dunn, a lawyer and avocational linguist from Indiana. Although perhaps four dialects of modern Miami-Illinois were documented in this time period—Peoria, Wea, Indiana Miami, and Oklahoma Miami—the different dialects of Miami-Illinois are in fact all extremely similar and fully mutually intelligible, generally showing only very modest lexical differences.

The texts presented here were originally elicited in Oklahoma in 1895 by Albert Gatschet from two speakers, George Finley and Elizabeth Vallier. Born in 1858, George Finley was actually a full-blood Piankashaw by birth, but grew up among the Peorias and spoke that dialect. Born in Kansas, by age twelve he had moved to northeast Oklahoma, where he lived the rest of his life. He seems to have grown up in a culturally very conservative family, but as an adult in Oklahoma, he successfully integrated into the white world, traveling as a young man with the Sells Brothers Wild West Show, serving as an interpreter, frequently visiting Washington DC as a representative of the Peorias, converting to the Baptist Church, and eventually even becoming a Master of the Royal Secret of Scottish Rite Masonry in 1917. He was also an excellent speaker of Peoria, with a very large vocabulary and conservative grammar, largely uninfluenced by the syntax and word patterns of English. Perhaps in recognition of his command of his ancestral language as well as his ease in getting along in white society, Finley worked with more linguists than any other speaker of Miami-Illinois: he worked extensively with Albert Gatschet in 1895, Jacob Dunn in 1909, and finally Truman Michelson in 1916. He passed away in 1932, probably one of the last speakers of Miami-Illinois capable of giving connected traditional texts of such quality.[1]

Regrettably, much less biographical information is available on the other Miami-Illinois speaker included here, Elizabeth Vallier.[2] Vallier was born in Indiana, probably in the 1830s. She evidently lived in Indiana until she married a Peoria man, whereupon she moved to Kansas and then Oklahoma, living among the Peorias the rest of her life. She appears to have passed away sometime around

1900. In 1895 Albert Gatschet worked with Vallier, obtaining a considerable amount of vocabulary and seven texts, two of which are presented here. Vallier's dialect is basically Miami, though with some Peoria influences. Given that Vallier was apparently unable to speak English (C. Dunn 1937, 37), it is perhaps not surprising that she was an extremely conservative speaker, her speech showing even more archaic features than Finley's and no discernible influence from English grammar or sentence patterns.

All the Miami-Illinois stories here are from Albert Gatschet's original field notebooks at the National Anthropological Archives. In addition to these original first versions, the NAA also has reworkings of these texts done a few years later by Gatschet, as well as still later re-elicitations by Jacob Dunn. Gatschet's later versions show many small changes in word choice, inflection, and syntax when compared to the earlier versions. In turn, Dunn's later re-elicitations of these texts are clearly derived from Gatschet's second versions, only very seldom deviating from them in word choice or grammar. I have made the decision here to hold as close as possible to Gatschet's *first* editions of these texts, since there is good reason to believe that these versions are the truest to the stories as Finley and Vallier actually gave them and show the least corruption from either re-elicitation with other speakers or misanalysis on Gatschet's or Dunn's part. That said, I have felt free to consult all the different versions of these texts in my effort to understand them. However, neither Gatschet nor Dunn ever gave free translations of their texts, at most only providing fairly loose word-for-word glosses. Thus, the translations given here are my own, based not only on Dunn's and Gatschet's interpretations but also on my own study of Miami-Illinois grammar and vocabulary. By and large, my translations adhere quite closely to the original Miami-Illinois. However, since the original texts can be rather terse, I have taken the liberty of adding small amounts of clarifying material, usually just more explicit indications of who is saying what to whom during sequences of dialogue. I have not attempted to translate every one of the extremely common discourse particles Elizabeth Vallier uses, since they usually do not translate well into English. For example, in Vallier's Wissakatchakwa story, she uses *neehi-'hsa*, "and then," a total of eighty-three times; since rendering this as English "and then" every time would be painfully repetitive and add nothing to an understanding of the story, I have included it in the translation rather sparingly.

All the Miami-Illinois texts presented here are what is called *aalhsoohkaakana* (roughly pronounced AAHL-sooh-KAA-kon-a; plural *aalhsoohkaakanaki*), a term often translated in Algonquian studies as "sacred story."[3] One of these is a short story by Vallier about Wilaktwa, a Miami trickster; the other two, told by Finley and Vallier, are about Wissakatchakwa (*wiihsakacaakwa*, pronounced WEESsock-ah-CHAW-qua), the Miami-Illinois "culture hero." The Miami-Illinois word *wiihsakacaakwa* has no known etymology, though since it has cognates in several other Algonquian languages, it must be reconstructed for Proto-Algonquian. The Wissakatchakwa stories given by Finley and Vallier are not single "stories" so much as rather loose assemblages of free-floating episodes; the two texts do not share many scenes in common, though no doubt they both represent just a small part of what centuries ago was a much larger Wissakatchakwa story cycle.

Finley's and Vallier's Wissakatchakwa stories are entirely typical of Great Lakes Algonquian legends. Virtually all the scenes in both stories have parallels in stories from neighboring tribes, especially Fox and Kickapoo. Vallier's story has much in common with the Kickapoo story "When Wīza'kä'a Went Visiting" (in Jones 1915, 5–8); for example, Wissakatchakwa tying white cloths around his children's necks to make them look like Kingfisher (*kíhkamanhsia*, KEEH-com-MON-see-ah) in the Miami story is paralleled in the Kickapoo story by *wiiθahkeeha* (his Kickapoo counterpart) painting white stripes on his wife and children to make them look like Skunk.[4] Both stories share the episode of Beaver (*amehkwa*, a-MEH-quah) feeding Wissakatchakwa with flesh from his own child, followed by Wissakatchakwa throwing the bones into the water. When Beaver then visits Wissakatchakwa in turn and Wissakatchakwa attempts the same trick Beaver performed, in both versions Beaver successfully brings Wissakatchakwa's child back to life when Wissakatchakwa himself cannot. The scene in which Wissakatchakwa ties fake bills on his family members in anticipation of a visit from Pileated Woodpecker (*kwaahkwa*) is paralleled in Kickapoo by *wiiθahkeeha* doing the same thing when Kingfisher visits. Likewise, the Kickapoo "Wīza'kä'a and Buzzard" (Jones 1915, 9–13) shares the scene of Wissakatchakwa falling a long time and landing in a hollow tree. The scene ends there in Vallier's version, though a version of this story that Finley told Truman Michelson twenty-one years later shares with the Kickapoo version the subsequent scene of Wissakatchakwa having his pubic hairs sticking out through a hole in the tree and thus being mistaken for a bear. Oddly, in the version Finley gave Gatschet (presented here), this is replaced with Wissakatchakwa landing on a catfish, then cutting the fish open to reveal a bear sitting inside. Additionally, Vallier notes in her version that all of Wissakatchakwa's hair rotted off while he was trapped inside the fish's belly, and that this explains why white men are bald; while the notion of the culture hero being a white man is not common among the Great Lakes tribes, this equation is commonly seen in Plains tribes, both Algonquian and otherwise.

There are also many parallels between the Miami-Illinois Wissakatchakwa stories and the Fox culture hero *wiisahkeeha*. "Wīsa'kä Visits the Beaver" (Jones 1907, 228–35) is especially close to Vallier's version, including Beaver killing his child to feed Wissakatchakwa, Wissakatchakwa being caught hiding the child's little finger in his mouth, Wissakatchakwa killing his own child when Beaver visits in turn, and Beaver once again being able to revive Wissakatchakwa's dead child when Wissakatchakwa himself cannot. And again, in "Wīsa'kä Goes to Visit the Kingfisher," *wiisahkeeha* puts a fake bill on his nose in anticipation of Kingfisher's visit (Jones 1907, 267). In Vallier's apparently rather terse version, the significance of Wissakatchakwa hiding the little finger of Beaver's child in his mouth is not explained, though the Fox version (Jones 1907, 231) notes that since this little finger was missing when the bones of Beaver's child were thrown into the water, this explains why the claws on beavers' paws are shaped the way they are, with a missing joint on their little fingers.

The Miami Wissakatchakwa story also has many parallels in stories of the Menominee culture hero Mɛʔnapos (Bloomfield 1928, 186–213). For example, in "Me'napus Visits His Little Brother, the Woodpecker," Mɛʔnapos wears a fake bill in anticipation of Woodpecker's visit, as also happens in Vallier's story. In Vallier's story, when Fox Squirrel (*oonsaanikwa*) visits Wissakatchakwa, in an attempt to get "nut meats" to feed Fox Squirrel, Wissakatchakwa pierces himself, though only blood comes out. No doubt out of propriety, Vallier left out any explicit reference in her story to the fact that Wissakatchakwa was in fact trying to puncture his testicles to feed Fox Squirrel, though it is clear from his notes that Gatschet understood this. However, this fact is made clear in the Menominee "Me'napus Goes Visiting" and "Me'napus Visits His Little Brother, the Squirrel," where Squirrel pierces his own testicles in a successful attempt to feed Mɛʔnapos wild rice (Bloomfield 1928, 191–93 and 206–7).

In contrast, most of the parallels one can find with the Wissakatchakwa story George Finley gave Gatschet are actually *not* found in "culture-hero" stories in neighboring languages. The basic setting of Finley's story, where two blind men living together are led astray by someone moving the ropes they use to fetch water, is from the frequently seen "Deceived Blind Men" motif, as seen in the Menominee story "Raccoon's Pranks" (Bloomfield 1928, 346) as well as the Kickapoo text "A Chief and His Son" (Jones 1915, 78–81; see also Thompson 1929, 59). Moreover, the seven-headed manitou has a vague parallel in the ten-headed monster in the Kickapoo story "A Young Man and His Pets" (Jones 1915, 44–53) and an even closer parallel in the seven-headed "dragon" in the Ojibwe story given by Thompson (1929, 201–5), though Thompson ascribes this motif to European influence.

A mention should be made here about the "manitou," or, in Miami-Illinois, *manetoowa* (mon-ET-OO-wa), of George Finley's Wissakatchakwa story. In telling this story to Albert Gatschet, Finley variably translated *manetoowa* as "monster" or "devil," no doubt because he knew of no real English equivalent for the word. In my translation of this story, I have rendered this word as "manitou" (itself from the Ojibwe cognate), a word that has long been familiar in the literature, since I thought it best to avoid the misleading associations clinging to words such as "monster" and "devil." By the nineteenth and early twentieth centuries, *manetoowa* was sometimes used to render the English word "devil," but the connotations of this word in the pre-Christian period were very different. In the early eighteenth-century Illinois dictionary attributed to Jacques Gravier, this word is translated simply as "espirit, Dieu," with no negative connotations. In the traditional belief systems of the Algonquian peoples, "manitous" generally denote any number of various powerful spirits or supernatural beings, potentially either good or evil. No doubt due to the decidedly "pagan" connotations of this word, when the Miami-Illinois speakers came to be Christianized, the *manetoowaki* became demonized as either the Christian devil, demons, or sometimes amorphously frightening "monsters," and another word, *keešihiwia*, literally "creator," came to be used for the Creator god of more monotheistic forms of belief.[5]

Perhaps most interestingly of all, the dwarves (*páyiihsaki*; pronounced pie-EES-sock-ee) in Finley's Wissakatchakwa story have their parallel in the Fox "Little Creatures of Caprice" (Fox *apaya·ši·haki*), the "boy heroes of the Fox Lodge-Boy and Thrown-Away cycle" (Goddard 1994, 33).[6] Although Jacob Dunn (n.d.) once defined Miami-Illinois *páyiihsa* as "a small supernatural who is supposed to guide departed spirits to the happy hunting ground," in the Peoria story here the *páyiihsaki* are malevolent creatures who attack Wissakatchakwa as he sleeps next to a river. Miami-Illinois *páyiihsa* is clearly the origin of the word "Piasa" (pronounced PIE-a-saw), the name given to the manitous painted on the sides of cliff faces along the Mississippi River north of Saint Louis in early French colonial times, evidently identified as depictions of monsters who destroyed and swallowed up people traveling along the river in canoes (see Goddard 1985, 51–54). This etymological connection with "Piasa" is even clearer when one compares it with early French spellings such as "paillissa" (where French ll is evidently meant to be pronounced like English *y*), found on Nicolas de Finiels's map of 1798 (see Wood 2001, plate 13A).[7] Although the monsters in the Piasa drawings sound as if they did not in fact depict actual *páyiihsaki*, but more likely the underwater panther (Illinois *araamipinšia*, modern Peoria *lénipinšia*), it is nevertheless significant that both creatures represent supernatural beings who attack river travelers.

The other Miami-Illinois story included here, much shorter than the others, is "The Story of Wilaktwa," told by Elizabeth Vallier.[8] "Wilaktwa" (in Miami, *wilakhtwa*, pronounced wil-OCK-twah) is a Miami trickster and seems to be a typical such figure among the Algonquian tribes. Although Wilaktwa is known only from this one story, there were doubtless other Miami stories about him, and it is a shame more was not recorded about him. He is an extremely anarchic, malevolent character, without any of the humorous bumbling seen in either of the Wissakatchakwa stories or the Shawnee Little Jack story given here.

Shawnee

Shawnee is a central Algonquian language, most closely related to Sauk-Fox-Kickapoo. In earliest contact times, the Shawnees seem to have been primarily located in what is now Ohio, though in the wake of the disruptions of white contact, Shawnee bands were soon found throughout the eastern United States. By 1870 the various Shawnee bands had all relocated to Indian Territory, coalescing into the three recognized tribes known today: the Absentee Shawnees, in central Oklahoma, centered around the towns of Shawnee and Norman; the Loyal Band Shawnees (sometimes known as the Cherokee Shawnees), in northeastern Oklahoma, centered in Vinita and White Oak; and the Eastern Shawnees, in the northeastern corner of Oklahoma, in present-day Ottawa County (next to the Miamis and the Peorias). Despite their great degree of geographic scattering during historical times, Shawnee represents a single language with minimal dialect variation. At present the Shawnee language has the most speakers among the Absentee Shawnees; there are probably fewer than ten speakers among the Loyal Shawnees, while the language is no longer spoken among the Eastern Shawnees.

Perhaps the most important documentation of the Shawnee language was undertaken by the linguist Carl Voegelin in 1933–34. Working with about ten or twelve speakers, Voegelin elicited an enormous amount of vocabulary and twenty-six notebooks' worth of texts.[9] Voegelin's Shawnee texts are an incredibly rich resource, though they are still largely unexamined. He seems to have intermittently worked on these texts to prepare them for publication, though by the 1950s he appears to have abandoned the project about halfway through, and they remain unpublished to this day.[10]

The Shawnee text presented here is the trickster story "Little Jack," chosen for its comparability with the Miami trickster and culture-hero stories.[11] The narrator refers to this text as a "winter story," Voegelin's usual English translation for Shawnee *hatθohkaaka* (pronounced hot-thoh-KAA-kah; plural *hatθohkaakanaki*).[12] "Winter stories" are defined by Voegelin (1938–40, 430) as those stories specifically concerned with people who lived before the flood released on the earth by the Grandmother's grandson (Voegelin 1936, 9–10). Thus, the category of winter stories does not include more ordinary stories, such as historical accounts, personal anecdotes, or autobiographical narratives. *hatθohkaakanaki* are called "winter stories" because traditionally it was only permissible to tell them during the winter; if this taboo was violated and a winter story was told during summer, it was believed that it would attract snakes that could devour the person who was responsible.

It is not certain who gave this story, though judging from the texts surrounding it, it was probably Frank Daugherty, a Loyal Band Shawnee from whom Voegelin obtained many texts. This text seems to exist only in a typed version with free translation. In keeping with Voegelin's usual method, the English translation given for this text is extremely literal; while this is very helpful in analyzing the original Shawnee of these texts, in an English-only, printed edition, such a hyper-literal translation is not terribly readable. Moreover (much like Elizabeth Vallier's Miami culture-hero story), the Shawnee original of this text is quite terse, no doubt because the meaning of the text was clear to the original Shawnee-speaking audience. Thus, in this edition, the translation has been smoothed out somewhat, both to make it less stilted and, again, to make it clearer who is saying what to whom.

"Little Jack" and "Crazy Jack" are the usual English names for the Shawnee trickster.[13] In the story presented here, he is called "Little Jack," or, in the original Shawnee, *čeekiiθa* (chay-KEE-thaw), clearly a loanword from English "Jack."[14] The Little Jack story here seems to show more European influences than the Miami Wilaktwa story. Moreover, Little Jack seems to show more in common with Wissakatchakwa than with Wilaktwa, in that Little Jack is more a benign, bumbling character, with most of the humor deriving not only from Little Jack's pranks, but also from his lack of common sense, inability to follow directions, and disregard of usual social norms.

Notes

1. Additionally, Finley also told a few short stories in English to the folklorist Jessie E. Baker (1931), presumably sometime in the 1920s.
2. Also known as Elizabeth Valley.
3. In the present work, the correct, phonemic spellings of Miami-Illinois and Shawnee words are given in italics; the equivalents of these spellings given in roman with hyphens are intended only as an *extremely* rough guide to the pronunciation of these words for readers unfamiliar with Americanist and linguistic symbols. Any reader interested in a more accurate description of Miami-Illinois pronunciation can consult Costa (2003).
4. In this paper, the symbol *θ* is used in the writing of Kickapoo and Shawnee words for the *th* sound of English "thin."
5. This same word has undergone some interesting permutations of meaning in other Algonquian languages over the past few centuries as well: its original

meaning seems largely intact in Ojibwe and Cree, but in Shawnee, *maneto* has come to mean "snake, supernatural power, creator." In Fox *maneto·wa* most often means "snake." In Menominee *mane·tow* means "game animal (other than a bird)." Munsee Delaware *manə́to·w* and Pequot *manto* both simply mean "God" now, while Mi'kmaq *məndu* means "devil." Additionally, a variant of this word, *manetwa*, is the Miami-Illinois word for "snow (when falling)." I will not presume to offer an explanation for this.

6. The Miami-Illinois word *páyiihsa* also has cognates in Ottawa *pahiins*, "elf, leprechaun" and Potawatomi *paʔis*, "fairy." This word is also attested as *païssa* in the anonymous Illinois dictionary in the Archives des Pères Jésuites de la Fontaine at Saint-Jérôme, Quebec (n.d.). It is not glossed there, though it is given in the midst of a list of several terms naming different types of supernatural beings and animals.
7. This word appears three times in de Finiels's map: "Hauteurs de paillissa," "R[ivière] de Pallissa" (*sic*), and "I[le] de Paillissa." I thank Duane Esarey for bringing this map to my attention.
8. The name "Wilaktwa" is also of unknown etymology.
9. Voegelin's Shawnee materials are now archived at the American Philosophical Society in Philadelphia.
10. Voegelin's goal seems to have been to replace his original handwritten texts (with only word-for-word glosses) with typed texts with fairly literal free translations but no word-for-word glosses. Very regrettably, Voegelin seems to have often discarded his original texts when the typed versions were complete, so about half the texts in Voegelin's notebooks are the handwritten originals and the other half the retyped versions. Additionally, most of the texts in Voegelin's notebooks are not identified for speaker, making it very difficult to make generalizations about dialectal or idiolectal differences.
11. This story is text 66, in notebook 6 in Voegelin's papers. I have yet to find evidence for a Shawnee culture hero comparable to Fox *wiisahkeeha* or Miami-Illinois *wiihsakacaakwa*.
12. Shawnee *hatθohkaaka* is the cognate of Miami-Illinois *aalhsoohkaakana*.
13. Crazy Jack is also an English name sometimes used for the Delaware trickster (see Voegelin 1945 and Bierhorst 1994).
14. *čeekiiθa* is also a Shawnee word for "donkey," though this is obviously a later development. The probable original Shawnee name for the Shawnee trickster is *naasiiθeki* (pronounced NAW-SHE-theck-ee; of unknown etymology), seen in various other texts Voegelin collected.

References and Suggested Reading

Baker, Jessie E. 1931. "Piankishaw Tales." *Journal of American Folklore* 44:182–90.

Bierhorst, John. 1994. "Tales of the Delaware Trickster." In *Coming to Light: Contemporary Translations of the Native Literatures of North America*, ed. Brian Swann, 489–94. New York: Random House.

Bloomfield, Leonard. 1928. *Menomini Texts*. American Ethnological Society Publications 12. New York: G. E. Stechert.

Costa, David J. 2003. *The Miami-Illinois Language*. Lincoln: University of Nebraska Press.

Dunn, Caroline. 1937. *Jacob Piatt Dunn: His Miami Language Studies and Indian Manuscript Collection*. Prehistory Research Series 1, no. 2. Indianapolis: Indiana Historical Society.

Dunn, Jacob P. n.d. Various Notes on Miami. Manuscripts at the Indiana State Library, Indianapolis.

"French-Illinois Dictionary." n.d. Manuscript in the Archives des Pères Jésuites de la Fontaine, Saint-Jérôme, Quebec.

Gatschet, Albert. n.d. Notes on Peoria. Various manuscripts at the National Anthropological Archives, Smithsonian Institution, Washington DC.

Goddard, Ives. 1985. *Reflections of Historical Events in Some Traditional Fox and Miami Narratives*. In *Papers of the Sixteenth Algonquian Conference*, ed. William Cowan, 47–62. Ottawa: Carleton University.

———. 1994. *Leonard Bloomfield's Fox Lexicon*. Algonquian and Iroquoian Linguistics, Memoir no. 12. Winnipeg: University of Manitoba.

Gravier, Jacques, S.J. n.d. "Illinois-French Dictionary." Manuscript in Watkinson Library, Trinity College, Hartford CT.

Jones, William. 1907. *Fox Texts*. American Ethnological Society Publications 1. Leiden: E. J. Brill.

———. 1915. *Kickapoo Tales*. Trans. Truman Michelson. American Ethnological Society Publications 9. Leiden: E. J. Brill; New York: G. E. Stechert.

Rafert, Stewart J. 1996. *The Miami Indians of Indiana: A Persistent People, 1654–1994*. Indianapolis: Indiana Historical Society.

Thompson, Stith. 1929. *Tales of the North American Indians*. Bloomington: Indiana University Press.

Trowbridge, Charles C. 1938. *Meearmeear Traditions*. Ed. Vernon Kinietz. University of Michigan Museum of Anthropology, Occasional Contributions 7. Ann Arbor: University of Michigan Press.

———. 1939. *Shawnese Traditions: C.C. Trowbridge's Account*. Ed. Vernon Kinietz and Erminie W. Voegelin. University of Michigan Museum of Anthropology, Occasional Contributions 9. Ann Arbor: University of Michigan Press.

Valley, Dorris, and Mary M. Lembcke. 1991. *The Peorias: A History of the Peoria Indian Tribe of Oklahoma*. Miami OK: Peoria Indian Tribe of Oklahoma.

Voegelin, Carl F. 1936. *The Shawnee Female Deity*. Yale University Publications in Anthropology 10. New Haven CT: Yale University Press.

———. 1938–40. *Shawnee Stems and the Jacob P. Dunn Miami Dictionary*. 5 parts. Prehistory Research Series 1:63–108, 135–67, 289–323, 345–406, 409–78. Indianapolis: Indiana Historical Society.

———. 1945. "Delaware Texts." *International Journal of American Linguistics* 11:105–19.

———. n.d. Shawnee Texts. Unpublished manuscripts at the American Philosophical Society.

Wood, W. R. 2001. *An Atlas of Early Maps of the American Midwest*. Part 2. Illinois State Museum Scientific Papers 29. Springfield: Illinois State Museum.

WIIHSAKACAAKWA AALHSOOHKAAKANA

Told by George Finley
Translated by David J. Costa

Wissakatchakwa was walking along next to a river when he came upon a Frenchman. "Bon jour, bon jour, bon jour!" he said. He was going around to trade some merchandise.

Wissakatchakwa asked him, "Where are you going? Can I go with you in your boat?"

The Frenchman answered him, "Yes, come along!"

Wissakatchakwa replied, "Wait for me a bit! First, I have to kill a raccoon and then dry it."

And then he built a fire to dry the raccoon skin. And then after he dried it, he counted the number of rings going around its tail. "For each ring going around the tail, I'll be given one item," he thought. "A cape, a blanket, a gun, gunpowder, and some bullets. But it's not enough! I'll kill another deer."

And so he killed a young buck with spots all over it. "Ha, ha! I'll get a lot for this deerskin when I trade it off, what with these spots all over it." He laughed. "Now I'll take off in your boat!"

And so they headed off toward the trading post. And then Wissakatchakwa lay down in the boat and started singing. The Frenchman said to him, "Be quiet, my friend! The man-eater lives nearby. If he hears you, he'll catch us!" Wissakatchakwa made like he didn't hear him. He sang to the end.

Sure enough, the seven-headed manitou heard them. He caught them, and they were sucked into his den. The Frenchman wept. But Wissakatchakwa just took a look at everything. He kept saying over and over again, "How much? How much?" The manitou wouldn't answer him. He was a little afraid of the manitou.

After a while Wissakatchakwa got hungry. "Hungry! Hungry! Damn it, my friend, the storekeepers ought to feed people!"

Then the manitou said, "Cover your faces!" And they all covered themselves with blankets. Wissakatchakwa secretly watched them from a hole in his cover. But a number of the people in there were starving. The manitou ate the people up. And then, after he ate, he continued: "Uncover your faces!"

After a while the manitou became sleepy. He lay down. Soon Wissakatchakwa thought, "He's asleep." Wissakatchakwa rose with a bound. He shook all seven of the manitou's heads. It didn't wake the manitou up. Then Wissakatchakwa opened up some gunpowder in a keg and poured it out onto the manitou's heads. He told all the captives to get out. Some were almost starving. They couldn't get out.

Wissakatchakwa grabbed as much as he wanted of everything. Then he rubbed some gunpowder into a rag and strung it out away from the manitou's heads, toward the door. As he was leaving he lit the fuse. Then he got out of there. He went up on a hilltop to watch the manitou blow up. Then, after he blew him up, the water boiled up for many years.

Finally the water cooled off. And Wissakatchakwa went back in and took possession of the manitou's home. Now he owned it. Wissakatchakwa threw out all the corpses' bones and the manitou's bones. He cleaned it out and made it nice, so that he could live there.

And so one day Wissakatchakwa came out and lay down, sunning himself on a big rock. Then he saw some dwarves. They were coming from around a bend in the river. Wissakatchakwa pretended to be asleep. "I wonder what they'll do?" he thought.

And then the dwarves said to one another, "There's Wissakatchakwa, asleep on a rock. Let's scare him!" And they dove into the water. They came up near the rock. Then one of the dwarves said, "I'll shoot him!"

Wissakatchakwa heard him. "Hold on, damn it! If you want the cave, just ask me for it. I'll give it to you!"

The dwarves replied, "We want it!"

"So why didn't you tell me, instead of shooting? I'll give it up to you, and then I'll go away."

And so the dwarves became its owners. You can still see the footprints of the dwarves quite clearly there.

And so Wissakatchakwa was walking around, when he came across two old blind men. They were sitting down, shaking hands with each other.

Wissakatchakwa quietly slipped into their lodge and hit one of the old men with his hand. The old men let go of each other. Then he started hitting the other old man with his hand over and over again.

Then one old man said to the other one, "My friend, why are you hitting me?"

"You hit me first!" the old man replied.

So they both jumped up and started fighting. After a while one of them got tired. "Damn it, hold on a minute, my friend. I think our grandchild is in here!"

And so one old man said, "Let the door slam shut." And it slammed shut, and Wissakatchakwa was locked in. The old men punched around for him.

Finally Wissakatchakwa got tired. He was cornered. "Stop it! My grandfathers, don't kill me! I'll wait on you and cook for you if you don't kill me!"

Then the old men said, "Why didn't you say so? You made fun of us for no reason. We're poor and helpless, Grandchild," Wissakatchakwa was told. "Yes, you must cook for us, Grandchild."

And so Wissakatchakwa stayed there, living with the old men and taking care of them. But after a while, he got tired of the old men and wanted to leave them. The old men had stretched ropes toward the water, so that they wouldn't get lost when they went to fetch water. So Wissakatchakwa stretched out the ropes in the other direction, to where there was a steep bank. And then he went away and left the old men.

After a while, the old men became hungry. And one said, "My friend, fetch some water. Let's cook something. It looks like our grandchild has deserted us." So the old man went to get water, following the ropes. Sure enough, he fell down the cliff and couldn't climb back up. And he shouted to his friend. He came. And he said, "Be careful, you'll slip and fall! Our grandchild has rearranged the ropes in the other direction."

After a while the old man down in the hollow found the ropes and grabbed onto them. And then he crawled back out. They both went back into their lodge.

And then one of the old men said, "Let's draw our grandchild Wissakatchakwa by smoke!" So they filled up a pipe. One of them lit the pipe. He said, "My friend, draw our grandchild near. We have to throw him far away. It's our turn to fool Wissakatchakwa." Sure enough, Wissakatchakwa circled back and returned.

The old men said to him, "Why did you move the ropes on us?"

Wissakatchakwa said, "I forgot to put them back the same way before I left!"

And so Wissakatchakwa lived with the old men a little while longer. Then one of the old men asked Wissakatchakwa, "Grandson, why don't you go and catch us a bunch of birds out on the lake?"

Wissakatchakwa replied, "How am I supposed to catch them?"

"Peel a bunch of basswood bark off the trees. Then dive into the lake and tie the basswood bark to the birds' feet. After you've tied it to the feet of several of them, tie them to your belt. Then come to the surface in the middle of the lake. Then you must tell the birds, 'You can't all keep on living here!'" That's what the old men told Wissakatchakwa.

And so Wissakatchakwa did as the old men told him. All kinds of ducks, brants, geese, swans. He tied their feet all together. Every time he had tied two of them together, for a short time he would come up with only his nose out of the water, floating behind their tails. And then he would take another breath. And after he tied them all, he came up in the middle of the lake. He did what the old men told him. He said, "You can't all live here!"

And then the birds all flew up. Wissakatchakwa meant to catch them, but instead he was lifted up in the air. He was carried far away.

After a while he got tired. "I wish the pieces of bark would break!" said Wissakatchakwa. And sure enough, the strings broke and Wissakatchakwa fell. While he fell, he said, "I hope I land in deep water!"

And then Wissakatchakwa landed on a catfish. He killed it when he fell on it. Wissakatchakwa took it out from the river and cut it open. To his surprise, he cut into a bear sitting inside.

So Wissakatchakwa lived there several months. After a while he ate up the bear and the catfish.

That's as far as Wissakatchakwa goes.

WIIHSAKACAAKWA AALHSOOHKAAKANA

Told by Elizabeth Vallier
Translated by David J. Costa

Wissakatchakwa was living at a place, and he had a wife.

Once he went to see his friend Fox Squirrel. There he was fed nut meats. "Take some!" Wissakatchakwa was told. "Take the leftovers back to your children!"

And then Wissakatchakwa told Fox Squirrel, "Likewise, my friend! We eat stuff just like this. You must come and visit me some time."

And so Fox Squirrel went visiting. He went to see his friend. Wissakatchakwa said to Fox Squirrel, "Come in, my friend! Sit down!"

Then Wissakatchakwa tried to feed him nut meats, but he couldn't cut a hole in himself. Instead, blood just poured out. He meant to get nut meats out, but he failed. He gouged himself for no good reason. He would try anything he saw anyone else doing and fail. So Fox Squirrel went back home when Wissakatchakwa couldn't feed him.

Then Wissakatchakwa said to his wife: "I'm going to visit Fox Squirrel's friend. I'm lonely." And so he went to visit Bear.

Then his friend Bear said, "Here comes my friend Wissakatchakwa! Come in, my friend!" Then Bear said to his wife, "Spread something out where my friend Wissakatchakwa can sit! What shall we feed your brother-in-law?"

"Turn around!" Bear told his wife. And then Wissakatchakwa closely watched what Bear did.

Bear cut the tenderloin out of his wife. When Bear finished cooking it for him, Wissakatchakwa was fed with it. Then Bear pierced his wife's heel. Grease poured out. Bear fed his friend tenderloin and grease.

"Take the leftovers with you," Wissakatchakwa was told. "Maybe your children will eat it."

"Ho! Just like this! As for me, we eat stuff just like this, my friend," Wissakatchakwa said. And then, in the same way, Wissakatchakwa said to Bear, "You must come and see us, my friend." Then Wissakatchakwa headed home.

Then it was Bear's turn to come visit. Wissakatchakwa said to his wife, "Ho! Here comes my friend Bear! Let's spread something out where he can sit down!"

"Come in, my friend!" Wissakatchakwa said to Bear. And then Bear sat down.

"What shall we feed your brother-in-law?" Wissakatchakwa asked his wife. "There isn't anything to feed him with." Then he said to her, "Give me a knife!"

"What will you do with it?" his wife asked him. It was as if she didn't know what he was going to feed him.

"Turn around!" he said to his wife.

"What are you going to do?" his wife asked.

"Sit down, and turn around."

And Wissakatchakwa cut into his wife's back, so as to cut out her tenderloin. She cried and cried as he cut out her tenderloin. After he cut it out, Bear gathered up ashes and tossed them onto the place where Wissakatchakwa had cut her tenderloin out. Then Bear rubbed in the ashes. It healed back up from where he had cut it out. Wissakatchakwa failed to feed his friend. He just fed himself again.

"How did you do it, my friend?" Bear asked.

"I did it the same way you fed me!" Wissakatchakwa said. And so Bear went back home.

The next day Wissakatchakwa again went off, to visit his friend Woodpecker.

Then Woodpecker said to his wife, "Here comes my friend Wissakatchakwa! Spread something out where he can sit down. Come in, my friend! Sit down, my friend!" said Woodpecker and his little woodpecker children. Then Woodpecker asked his wife, "What will we feed your brother-in-law, Wissakatchakwa? Spread something out over there by the shellbark hickory."

And then Woodpecker started to climb the tree. Then, as Woodpecker's wife held a wooden dish, Woodpecker climbed up and knocked down cracklings. He told his wife they should feed him cracklings instead of grub worms.

Then Woodpecker said, "Eat, my friend! What shall I feed you? This is the only thing we eat. Take the leftovers back to your children. Your children will eat it!"

"We eat the same stuff. We eat it," Wissakatchakwa said to Woodpecker. And then, as Wissakatchakwa started to head home, he said to Woodpecker, "Come and see me, my friend."

Then Wissakatchakwa went off and cut a stick. He went back home. As he walked along, he whittled the stick. He carved woodpecker bills out of the stick.

Then, in the morning, his friend Woodpecker was coming. Wissakatchakwa fastened the fake bills onto the noses of his children and his wife, and himself. He fastened them to their noses.

"My friend Woodpecker is coming!" Wissakatchakwa said to his wife. "Spread something out where he can sit down! Come in, my friend! Sit down! Why aren't you cooking something?" he said to his wife.

"What will I put on to cook?"

"Over yonder near the tree, spread something out," Wissakatchakwa replied.

And then Wissakatchakwa climbed up the tree. "Bring a dish!" he said to his wife. Then Wissakatchakwa pecked at the tree, shoving the fake bill onto his nose. Then he fell down, and blood ran out from his nose.

Then Woodpecker ran out, and he knocked out some cracklings and fed his friend in return. Wissakatchakwa said, "I used to do things this way, but now I fail. What's wrong with me?"

And so Woodpecker headed back.

And then Wissakatchakwa said, "I'm going to visit my friend Beaver next."

"Here comes your brother-in-law!" Beaver said to his wife. "Spread out something where he can sit down! Come in, my friend! Sit down!" Beaver said to his friend. "What will we feed your brother-in-law? Hang up the kettle!" Beaver said to his wife. And Beaver called one of his sons. And then he killed his son. He cooked the child.

And so Wissakatchakwa was fed with the young beaver. Then Beaver said, "My friend, put all the bones here in this wooden dish." Then Wissakatchakwa put all the bones there, except for one he kept in his mouth.

Then Beaver went to the river to throw the bones out and then called up his son. "Come, little beaver!" he said. Beaver's son came back, but he was crying. Beaver said to him, "What is wrong with you?" Then, to Wissakatchakwa, Beaver said, "My friend, what have you done to hurt my child? One joint of his little finger is missing!" Wissakatchakwa felt around in his mouth. He found it and took it out. He gave it back to his friend. And as he began to leave, he said to his friend Beaver, "Come and visit me sometime." Then Wissakatchakwa left.

So then Beaver went to visit his friend Wissakatchakwa. "Here comes my friend Beaver! Let's spread something out where he can sit down," Wissakatchakwa said to his wife. "Come in, sit down, my friend. Make a fire! Aren't you going to cook something for your brother-in-law Beaver? What shall we feed him?" Wissakatchakwa asked. So the woman hung up the kettle.

After some water had boiled, Wissakatchakwa called for his son, Little Wissakatchakwa.

"What are you going to do?" Little Wissakatchakwa asked. It seemed as if he didn't know what was going to be done.

Then Wissakatchakwa killed his son and put him on to cook. While he cut up his son, his wife cried and cried. "My son, my son!" she cried. "I'll never see my son again!"

And so Wissakatchakwa fed his friend Beaver. He set down a wooden plate there. "Put the bones there, my friend," he said to Beaver. And then Wissakatchakwa threw the bones away into the water.

And then Wissakatchakwa said to his wife, "Call our son!" The woman was weeping. She couldn't call him. So he did not come. Then Beaver called Wissakatchakwa's son. This time he came. Then Beaver went home.

And so the next day Wissakatchakwa went to see Kingfisher. Kingfisher said to his wife, "Here comes my friend Wissakatchakwa! Spread something out where he can sit down! Come in, sit down, my friend. Make a fire! Hang the kettle up! What shall we feed him, then?"

And so Kingfisher went to the river and called a fish. A pike came. Kingfisher dropped into the water and caught the pike and pulled it ashore. He put the fish on to cook and fed Wissakatchakwa with it. Of what he had left, he said, "Take it along to your children. Maybe they will eat the fish, just like we eat, my friend."

"You must come and see me next, my friend," Wissakatchakwa said to Kingfisher.

So then Wissakatchakwa went home.

The next day Kingfisher set out to visit Wissakatchakwa. Wissakatchakwa put white cloths around the necks of his children and his wife and himself. Then he said to his wife, "Here comes my friend Kingfisher! Let's spread something out where he can sit down." He greeted Kingfisher: "Come in! Sit down, my friend!" He told his wife, "Cook something!"

His wife was already scared. "What will I put on to cook?"

"Make a fire! Hang up the kettle!" Wissakatchakwa answered.

And then Wissakatchakwa ran out to call up a fish. A pike came. Wissakatchakwa jumped toward it, trying to catch the pike. But the fish came with its mouth open and swallowed up Wissakatchakwa.

Time passed. Then Wissakatchakwa's wife became frightened. She cried. She said to Kingfisher, "Brother-in-law, what can have become of Wissakatchakwa? He's gone forever!"

Then Kingfisher rushed over to the river. Then Kingfisher called up a fish and caught it and took it out of the water. He cut open the fish's belly. There Wissakatchakwa sat, inside the fish, and his hair was all rotted off. That's the reason why white men have bald heads.

And so Wissakatchakwa felt ashamed. He locked his children up in a tent. "Don't look at me!" he said to his children and wife. "I'm ashamed of myself. I'm going to leave you all."

And so Wissakatchakwa headed off toward the sky. "Don't look at me!" he said to his children and wife. His wife wondered what he would do. She secretly raised the edge of the tent and watched her husband. He just went up and up. But then he fell back and fell into a big hollow tree full of leaves. That's the reason why Wissakatchakwa got his name, from always doing like he saw others do. So then Wissakatchakwa said, "As long as the earth remains and as long as man is alive, my grandchildren will talk about me and tell stories about me."

That's as far as the story goes.

WILAKHTWA

Told by Elizabeth Vallier
Translated by David J. Costa

Wilaktwa was out on a hunt. He brought along his wife, and a big kettle, a wooden spoon, some parched corn, and some beef tallow.

Once he was cooking. Then some warriors were coming. He put the parched corn on to boil. When it was almost done, he put some of the tallow in the water. Then he heard the warriors give the war whoop.

Wilaktwa then said to the warriors, "Come in, sit down! Just hold on a bit, please. If you don't mind, we should eat first; then I'll go with you."

Then, when the corn soup was done cooking, Wilaktwa threw it at the warriors. He blinded them all and then beat them all to death.

And then some more people were coming, on the side of those whom Wilaktwa had killed. So then Wilaktwa went up on a hill. Then the warriors arrived and captured Wilaktwa's wife and took her away. She was led away crying. Wilaktwa knew that she was being abducted.

And so Wilaktwa killed a buffalo and put blood on the bladder. Then he put the bladder on his head like a hat. He then laid down there on the road where the warriors were about to pass by.

Then the warriors found him. They examined him closely. Then Wilaktwa quickly jumped up and let out a groan. He scared them all. They fainted, and he killed them all.

And so then Wilaktwa took his wife and started heading back. When he got there, he died and he was buried. Four days later they dug him back up, but he was gone. Instead, there was just a hole in the ground where he had been put.

That's as far as it goes.

ČEEKIIθA

Told by an unknown Shawnee speaker (Frank Daugherty?)
Translated by David J. Costa

For my winter story I will talk about the one known as Little Jack. He had a mother. At that time his younger brother was small.

Once Little Jack was told by his mother, "Go buy a kettle!" Little Jack went and bought one. He packed it on his back as he walked home. Then his back became tired. He put down the kettle. Then Little Jack saw that the kettle had three legs.

"Well!" he told the kettle. "There's no reason for me to be carrying you. You have three legs, but I only have two!"

Then Little Jack said to the kettle, "Let's race each other. Whoever wins brings himself to the house." Little Jack took off his hat. "When I have counted to three, then you must run," he told the kettle. Then he counted to three, and he ran up there.

When Little Jack got to the house, his mother asked him, "What's the matter with you? You haven't brought it! You were supposed to bring it like I told you."

"Didn't he get here?" Little Jack asked.[1]

"Who's supposed to get here?" his mother replied.

"The kettle. He has three legs; I only have two. He must have outrun me," Little Jack told his mother.

"You're crazy!" Little Jack was told. "How is a kettle supposed to run?" she asked.

1. An ambiguity important to the humor of this passage, which cannot be easily rendered in English, is that Shawnee *hahkohkwa*, "kettle," is animate, which means that it would take the same pronominal reference as a human. This is behind the momentary misunderstanding between Little Jack and his mother here.

A stick was picked up, and Little Jack got a whipping. "Go out of here, crazy one!" she said to him.

And so Little Jack wandered around in the wilderness all day long. At night he came back and spoke nicely to his mother. Finally a place where he could sleep was fixed for him, and he slept.

In the morning Little Jack was again given a task. "You must go buy needles," his mother told him.

Little Jack bought needles, but he didn't have them wrapped—he just went and took them with him.

As he was walking along, he saw some boys off in the distance. They were handling wheat straw. "Come along with us!" they said to him, "Let's play!" He went with them.

They played on the wagon. He stuck himself a little bit with his needles. "Just a moment," Little Jack said, "I need to get rid of these." He put the needles in a hole in the straw. He dropped them down there. "Well, now, that's that," he told them.

They played and churned about that straw with their feet. When he looked for his needles, he couldn't lay his hands on them, since he didn't know where he kicked them. At that point he went home.

Little Jack's mother asked him about the needles. "Did you bring them?" she asked him.

"I lost them," he said.

"Little Jack, you are just completely crazy!" his mother replied. He got a whipping again.

Then, the next morning, Little Jack's mother spoke to him. "I can't give you any chores to do, since you're so crazy. Just take care of your little brother at home. I'll go look for the needles. However, don't let your little brother get bitten by a mosquito. Kill the mosquito for him if he gets bitten."

So, at one point, when Little Jack looked at his younger brother, he saw that a mosquito was biting him. "Little brother, hold still for just a second. I'll get an axe and stun that mosquito," Little Jack said. Then Little Jack hit him. He stunned both the mosquito and his younger brother.

Little Jack then became frightened. Under cover a goose was setting on some eggs. Little Jack crawled in there and stunned the goose. Then Little Jack poured out some molasses and ripped open a feather bed. Then he laid down where he poured the molasses and then got inside the feather bed. When he came out of it, he was all covered with feathers. After that he sat there, pretending to be the goose.

When Little Jack's mother came back, his younger brother was lying there dead.

"You, Little Jack, what are you doing? Why is the goose scolding under cover? You're annoying me!" his mother said. "Maybe it's really you, Little Jack, and not the goose who's scolding under cover!" she said. Then his mother took up the fire poker and chased Little Jack out from under cover. "Get out of here!" she said to him. "I don't care if the wolves eat you!" Then Little Jack went away.

Finally, when it was night, Little Jack was afraid. They were keeping a cow, and Little Jack killed it. Then Little Jack thought, "I'll climb with this cowhide. I'll stretch it out on the branches of a tree. I'll sleep there, and the wolves won't kill me."

Then Little Jack found a tree, and he climbed up with the cowhide, holding it in his mouth. As he climbed, he heard some people coming. "Maybe they'll kill me," Little Jack thought.

But directly beneath Little Jack was some money, which some people had apparently stolen. They were going to divide among themselves what they had stolen. The men were saying, "This is for you; this is for me." However, while they did this, Little Jack got tired of holding the cowhide in his mouth.

Little Jack let go of the cowhide. "What is there for me?" he said, frightening them. They ran away, and he came down and gathered up their money.

Little Jack took the money to his mother. "Let me in!" he said to her.

"Go away, crazy!" he was told.

"But I've brought you something, Mother!" he said. "Open the door just a little. Let me show you what I've brought."

That's how he acted toward his mother. She saw all the money. Then she let him come in.

Then early in the morning, Little Jack went to where the chief lived. He had borrowed a half-bushel container, and he pressed his money into the tallow lining the container. The money left a trace in the container. Then he took the half-bushel container over there. When the chief looked at it, he said, "Where did you get the money? It's left a trace here."

Little Jack replied, "For one thing, you know we have a cow. I killed him, and I went and sold his skin. That's how I got this money."

"Couldn't I get money that way, too?" the chief asked.

"Easy. You have a lot of cows. You should be able to get a lot of money," he told the chief.

Then the chief killed his animals and went to sell the cowhides. He hardly sold one. At that point the chief got mad at Little Jack. "I'll kill you!" the chief told him.

"But you never know what might happen," Little Jack told him.

"Next morning I'm coming after you!" the chief replied.

The next morning the chief hitched his cattle on the sled, since they always did the pulling. There was a big sack there. "You crawl in here," Little Jack was told, "in that sack!" Then Little Jack was tied up at once. "Now I must take you. Little Jack, I'm going to go drown you!" the chief said.

When the chief got into town, he stopped a moment and went in the saloon. Right away somebody came along talking. He was driving along cattle, sheep, and pigs. "What are you doing there?" the man asked Little Jack.

"This is what our chief did when he couldn't persuade me to marry his daughter! Now he's going to take me by force. I don't want to be his son-in-law!" Little Jack said.

"I'd like to!" the man with the animals said. He untied Little Jack. Next Little Jack tied up his friend. Then Little Jack went home, driving those animals.

Later, when the chief came, he took the one who drove those cattle to the river. He then told him: "You've harmed me enough, Little Jack! Now I must drown you!"

"Don't!" the man replied. "I'm not Little Jack!"

"Yes, you are!" the chief said and threw him into the water and drowned him. Then the chief went home.

The next morning when the chief woke up, he heard somebody. He heard Little Jack in the direction from where he was staying. He went to look for Little Jack. When the chief got up there, he was standing there. Little Jack had a whole bunch of cows, sheep, and hogs. The chief asked Little Jack, "Where did you get these animals?"

"You know where you threw me, or you should know. Just over on the other side it is deeper. A great many more animals are there," he said to the chief.

"Couldn't I do that too?" the chief said.

"Certainly!" Little Jack replied. "As for me, I know where a great many more animals are. That's where I will throw you," he told his chief.

Little Jack carried him there. He drowned his chief.

That's all.

Winter Stories

Introduction by Ives Goddard

Presented here are translations of two Meskwaki winter stories, "The Ice Maidens" by Sakihtanohkweha and "Has-a-Rock" by Charley H. Chuck.[1]

Sakihtanohkweha and Chuck wrote these stories, in the Meskwaki language, for Truman Michelson of the Bureau of American Ethnology. The originals are in the collection of nearly twenty-seven thousand pages of Meskwaki manuscripts assembled by him that is in the Museum of Natural History of the Smithsonian Institution.[2] Sakihtanohkweha's story is on loose sheets of lined yellow foolscap, the standard U.S. Government notepaper of the time, which Michelson passed out to Meskwaki writers in the first few years of his fieldwork, beginning in 1911. It was probably written in 1914, the date on the accompanying translation. Chuck's story is the second of four he wrote in a school tablet, a kind of paper that Michelson provided later on. On the inside of the cover, Chuck wrote (in Meskwaki): "This is the whiteman's book, for anyone to write an old story, and also if they tell a winter story."

The Meskwakis

The Meskwakis (also called the Fox) have lived since the mid-nineteenth century on the Meskwaki Settlement, in Tama County, Iowa. Their land is not a federal reservation but was purchased by them over the years. There were approximately twelve hundred tribal members at the beginning of the twenty-first century and about three hundred speakers of Meskwaki, an Algonquian language nearly identical to Sauk and differing slightly from Kickapoo.

Meskwaki Writing

The traditional Meskwaki writing system derives ultimately from the Roman alphabet as used to write French, but the shapes of some letters and combinations have evolved.[3] Word dividers are indicated, though often omitted, but there is no punctuation separating sentences or marking quotations, and vowel length and preconsonantal h, which often distinguish meanings in Meskwaki, are not indicated. As a result, Meskwaki can be difficult to read, even for native speakers, but by the same token it is easy to write. The stories are written fluently, and it is clear that the written versions essentially reproduce the way they would have been told in an oral performance. For example, writers who discover that they have omitted something or said the wrong word typically correct themselves as they would in speaking, using the repair markers *ne·pehe*, "Oh, I forgot," and *=we·na*, "or rather."[4]

Note: The reader may wish to read the stories before reading the following discussions, which give away some of the surprises.

Winter Stories

Winter stories (Meskwaki *a·teso·hka·kanaki*) are myths traditionally told only in winter. Many winter stories, like these, describe the deeds and adventures of legendary heroes, and for several hero tales the collection has multiple versions written by different speakers. These two, however, are unique: the adventures of their nameless heroes were recounted by no other Meskwaki writer or teller. At the same time, they well represent the generic type, though they illustrate two quite different styles of storytelling.

To some extent these and other winter stories can be seen as a concatenation of motifs and episodes, a characteristic that reflects the basic technique of the oral composition that is never far below the surface, even when some concatenations have jelled into a conventional sequence. The stories presented here, though unique as wholes, incorporate a number of such conventional motifs. Among those found elsewhere in native North American oral literature are the moccasin switch, the inexhaustible kettle, and the feigned dream.[5] Familiar from other Meskwaki stories are the orphaned brother and sister living alone; the footrace for power; white or albino animals as the object of the quest; the magically swift return trip; and the restoration to life and health by sweat bath (effective only if the pleas of the patient to be let out are ignored). Stock figures that appear are Old Lady Manoneha, who lives alone and welcomes and aids the hero, and, in both stories, Elder Sister, who is typically vain, mean, and jealous.

Meskwaki stories, as commonly in North America, are greatly concerned with personal relationships. They tend to consist of dialogue combined with minimal scene setting and summary accounts of action and events. Detailed descriptions not crucial to the plot are rare, and when they appear, as in the eight lines devoted to the ice garments of the oldest of the Ice Maidens, they have special impact. But these relationships exist within a world that is still in its primeval state, dominated by powerful creatures both humanoid and not, having not yet been made safe for the people to come. The first-time listener trying to understand what is going on is drawn into a world where the characters face similar but more exigent perplexities. Familiar expectations and any reluctance to yield to the flow of the narrative without being at every step in a state of complete enlightenment must be suspended. Listeners must "sit as children," in the Meskwaki phrase, respectful and attentive, unquestioning but mentally active.

Among the relationships of interest in stories are, of course, those that involve difficulties. Both stories may be said to deal metaphorically with the risks taken in seeking a wife and acquiring in-laws. In addition, the central factor in "Has-a-Rock" is the betrayal of the normally inviolate bond of solidarity between uncle (*nešise·ha*, "my mother's brother") and nephew. The norms of traditional Meskwaki behavior require an uncle and nephew to defend each other to the death against all others. But the uncle in the story seems to have spent a good part of his life plotting against his nephews. In contrast, Meskwakis view the relations between brothers as fraught with potential conflict, but in the story the brothers' loyalty to each other is absolute, and one takes great risks, against the other's fearful pleas, to ensure his brother's well being. As a foil to the norms of human relationships, "Has-a-Rock" exhibits a sort of native exoticism in its presentation of the kinship relations of the characters. The albino bear and otter are brothers to the uncle but apparently not related to the nephew. The hero and his brother and the girls he wins as wives for the two of them are nephews and nieces to the old man and even brothers and sisters to each other, a relationship that is never spelled out but that would seemingly violate Meskwaki incest prohibitions.

Narrative Devices

Meskwaki differs from English in its grammar, in the structure of its sentences, and in the types of stylistic devices employed by its speakers in narratives, features that are often interdependent. For example, because Meskwaki verbs are inflected for both subject and object, nouns are much less frequent than in English. Demonstrative pronouns are typically used to signal a shift in the referent rather than the continuation of the same referent. The use of a noun to refer to an established character almost always has some special significance, such as signaling the end of an episode. In the racy, dramatic style used by Chuck, quotations follow one after the other with only occasional indication of who is speaking or spoken to. We can imagine that, in performance, such dialogues were fleshed out with distinguishing voice mannerisms and characterizations.

A major transition, especially an exit line, may also be signaled by an expression like, "That's what he did," or, "That's what happened to them." Certain repetitions also serve this function, as in "The Ice Maidens" when the description of the hill owner as turning into a vulture is given twice, on successive lines. In the same story, the episode with the evil mother-in-law begins after she is portentously named twice in two successive lines that describe her anger at the killing of her evil daughter.

Among the narrative techniques used by Meskwaki storytellers and evident in these stories is overlay. An event is briefly described and then reprised in more detail, or the reverse. For example, after giving the hero's thoughts when he decides to seek a wife, Sakihtanohkweha then jumps back to, "He was hunting," and recaps the event from an external perspective. After describing Elder Sister as burning the moccasins, the narrator returns to before this event to describe the hero's actions. Similarly, Chuck twice recounts the resumption of speed by the pursuing bear and how the hindquarters monster stuffed itself to capacity, and after describing the uncle's sister as swallowing the otter's head, he goes back to report the threat that preceded this.

An overlay typically ends by moving the narrative forward. In this it differs from repairs and asides, which can usually be bracketed off in the edition and translation, but the distinction is not always sharp. Also, the possible conscious use of false repairs after witting omissions further complicates the typology of nonlinear narrative devices and the task of annotating them for the reader. For example, at the end of Chuck's story the overlays, repeats, and repairs follow with such rapidity that the chronological sequence is thoroughly obscured in the headlong narration, but the confusion works to heighten the drama of the climactic scene.

A device used in Meskwaki narratives but nearly impossible to replicate in English is the proximate shift. If two characters are interacting, the nouns, pronouns, and verbal inflections referring to one will be marked as being in the proximate category, and those referring to the other will be marked differently, for the obviative category. The proximate character is foregrounded and determines the point of view taken by the narrative, while the obviative character is backgrounded. A skilled narrator, however, moves the characters in and out of these categories. A secondary figure may be shifted from obviative to proximate to take center stage for a while, and a primary character may be shifted to the obviative to indicate that the action is viewed from the point of view of another. For example, in "The Ice Maidens," after the hero finally defeats the owner of the hill, the vanquished man is shifted into the proximate, and his physical exhaustion and dispossession are recounted as if from his point of view, heightening the pathos. Later, when the evil mother-in-law meets her end, she is shifted into the proximate for the last five lines of the episode, while the hero disappears from direct reference, and the killing is recounted in the passive voice.

Another feature of Meskwaki grammar that may be exploited in the telling of myths is gender. All nouns belong to either the animate (or high) gender or the inanimate (or low) gender, with all living things and many that are not living classed as grammatically animate.[6] The word *oši·kani*, "his hindquarters," is inanimate, so describing the activities of the hindquarters monster in "Has-a-Rock" presents problems. At one point the narrator shifts the pronominal inflection for the monster from inanimate to animate for three lines. This variation introduces no clarity, but the ostensible uncertainty over how to articulate the description seems emblematic of the bizarre and ambiguous nature of the creature.

The Translations

These translations render the Meskwaki originals closely, in the sense that they start with an attempt to translate every word. There are a few systematic exceptions. The enclitic hearsay marker ='pi, "they say," has not been translated except to mark some lines that are presented as author's comments outside the stream of narrative. The mild expletives =*ni·hka* (used by men) and ='*škwe* (used by women) are also usually not translated, following the practice of native speakers, except for an occasional "damn" and "darn."

Declarative statements in Meskwaki narratives mostly have verbs inflected in what is called the aorist conjunct mode, which is also used for a range of conjoined and subordinate clauses, translatable as "and," "that," "as," "when," and the like. It is often uncertain how to divide into sentences a series of clauses having aorist verbs. As a rule of thumb, an aorist is taken as the verb of an independent sentence to the extent that it is accompanied by other words, especially certain sentence particles, while one that is the only word in the clause is interpreted as coordinate or subordinate. To replicate the effect of the serial aorists in a colloquial narrative style, many sentences are translated with "And" as the first word. The absence of a sentence-initial "And" where there otherwise might be one indicates a larger break.

A number of features of Meskwaki discourse and narrative style are kept in the translation. Rather than recasting whole sentences and, in effect, whole narratives as if they had been told from the outset in English, traces of these devices are left in the translation to convey an explicitly exotic style to the narrative. This subtly alien voice may serve to alert readers that learning to interpret these devices will heighten their experience of the tales and deepen their understanding of what is different about how they work their charm.

The translation usually follows the Meskwaki text in using pronouns instead of nouns. In a few cases, where the lack of a noun would be burdensome on the English reader, it has been supplied. Similarly, the omission of quotative verbs has generally been followed in the translation of Chuck's dialogues. To help indicate the intended reading of the English, commas have been used strictly to indicate breaks, and words to be stressed (usually on a high pitch) are in small caps, with intermediate pitch indicated by italics. One artificial distinction introduced into the dialogues in "Has-a-Rock" is to translate the vocative *nesi·hi*, literally "O my younger brother," as "little brother" when used to the hero by his older brother, but as "my brother" when used by the uncle to his animal kin. Also, the uncle's animal brothers are referred to as "he" or "it" in dialogue, depending on the speaker's attitude, but only as "it" in the narrator's voice.

The translation of interjections and imitative words has often been a matter of conjecture. Even where more or less conventional interjections are involved, the underspecificity of Meskwaki spelling may make identification uncertain. For the imitative vocables that Chuck used exuberantly for sound effects, the problem is even greater. They seem often to be his own ad hoc creations, Meskwaki spelling is completely inadequate for representing them recognizably on the page, and English is little better. One especially doubtful case is treated in a textual note.

The presentation on the page employs a phrase-line format in order to follow the phrasing of the original and to reflect the slower pace of oral delivery. It is hoped that this format will "elicit a form of readerly attention slower and more intense than that invited by prose."[7] If not read aloud, the translation should at least be read with an internal speaking voice. And, in any event, the text should be approached not as expository prose, but more as the dialogue and stage directions of a play, to which such tales may usefully be compared.

A new paragraph is typically indicated where the Meskwaki text has a proximate shift or certain delimiting words, expressions, or grammatical forms. A paragraph is also marked at the start of each direct quotation, except in a few cases where a quote continues after a quotative verb. Within a quotation a new paragraph may also indicate a shift in addressee or the beginning or end of an aside. Closing quotation marks directly followed by another quotation indicate a shift of speaker. The section divider (≈) indicates a break larger than a paragraph, typically corresponding to the passage of time or a change of location. Repairs are set off by dashes used as brackets, and narrator's asides, especially if they break the flow of the narrative, are placed in parentheses or, if lengthy, set off as a separate section.

Where the idiom of the two languages diverges, I have been guided by advice and suggestions from native speakers on equivalents. The translation has benefited greatly from my review of selected words, lines, and sections with the late Adeline Wanatee and with an anonymous Meskwaki elder. Renderings of some words were taken from a free translation of Sakihtanohkweha's story dictated by Harry Lincoln to Truman Michelson in 1914. There is no translation of Chuck's story in the collection

Specific interesting or problematical cases of translation are commented on in notes.

Sakihtanohkweha

Sakihtanohkweha (*sa·kihtanohkwe·ha*) was born in 1875 and died in 1957. Her name is of the Water clan. She never had an English name and was referred to in English as Bill Leaf's wife or Mrs. Bill Leaf, after the last of her husbands. She was skilled in the making of traditional craft items, including mats, bags, beadwork, and yarn belts (finger-woven sashes).[8]

Sakihtanohkweha's stories tend to be carefully told, but with an occasional playfulness. She may violate the listener's expectation or poke fun at the repetitive diction of the tales by using a conventional or repeated expression in an incongruous context. For example, in "The Ice Maidens," after the hero receives each of his blessings he looks for who has spoken to him and sees, in turn, his arrow, his bowstring, and . . . his eye.

Chuck

Charley H. Chuck's full English name is a riff on the nickname Chuck derived from his Meskwaki name, *ča·kehta·kosi·ha*, which is of the highest lineage of the Thunder clan. He was born in 1867 and died in 1940 when he was struck by a train near the settlement. He was for a number of years the tribal secretary, making written records in Meskwaki of official meetings and other activities, and was for a time also the tribal policeman. In 1905 he rewrote some of his personal archive and writings in an alphabet that used English letter values, and this collection was published, in Meskwaki only, by the State Historical Society of Iowa.[9]

Chuck is remembered as a lively storyteller, whose performances featured voice characterizations and oral sound effects. Various more or less conventional patterns of expressive and emphatic intonation are implied in his dialogue sections, but as these cannot be indicated in writing they can be recovered only by reviewing the texts with speakers. For example, a different intonation may turn a statement into a sarcastic remark with the opposite meaning. All these features present challenges to the interpretation and translation of the written text.

"The Ice Maidens"

The Meskwaki name for this story is *pepo·natesi·hkwe·waki*. This was written at the top of the first page by the writer's husband, Bill Leaf, and appears twice in the narrative itself. It is formally the plural of the feminine equivalent of *pepo·natesiwa*, the name of the Winter God,[10] and might thus be translated literally as "Winter Spirit women." This feminine form is apparently not found elsewhere.

The English translation used here for this name is, of course, borrowed from Hans Christian Andersen. The general characteristics of the Meskwaki Ice Maidens and the fatal difficulties men face in courting them justify the appropriation of the familiar and convenient label. It remains to be seen whether there is any further significance to the vague parallels found in Andersen's tale and in the Grimm brothers' tale of the Snow Queen. The ice bridge and the ice garments of Eldest Sister among the Meskwaki Ice Maidens recall the crystalline Otherworld of European myth,[11] but exact parallels have not been found.

The general plot of "The Ice Maidens" and the entirety of the opening and closing episodes match closely the Meskwaki story of *we·pene·me·ha*, "Turkey-Owner," of which there are several versions in the Michelson collection, including one by Sakihtanohkweha. The core tale about the Ice Maidens themselves, however, from the hero's arrival at Manoneha's house to his departure for home, is, except for a few incidental motifs, unique. This core tale contains the only occurrence in attested Meskwaki oral literature of the widespread motif of the Vagina Dentata (toothed vagina).[12] It thus serves as a caution against taking as conclusive the absence of a motif or tale type from an attested tradition. A motif found in an oft-told tale or tied to a major character in one tradition may play a minor role in another and thus easily be at risk of being overlooked.

"Has-a-Rock"

Chuck's name for this story was *we·to·seni·me·ha*, which literally means "the one who has a stone or rock," here rendered "Has-a-Rock." Other names of Meskwaki myth characters made on the same pattern include *we·to·če·ka·me·ha*, "the one who has a fisher skin," and *we·pene·me·ha*, "Turkey-Owner," already mentioned. It is noteworthy that Has-a-Rock is not the hero of the story, who has no name, but the hero's uncle and antagonist.

An unusual feature of this story is that it begins in medias res, with part 2, in effect. The listener is in the position of trying to deduce what happened in part 1 as the story goes along. This is gradually revealed by the hero's older brother, whose pitiful condition and its connection with the earlier events also become clear only gradually: he speaks from high up and is described as standing and sitting but not as moving or doing anything else, and he can aid his younger brother only by shouting insults at his pursuers from afar. His brother stands while speaking with him. Well into the story we learn that his name is *ki·škesita*, "Cut-Off." It turns out that he was cut in two by their uncle's arrow, with his upper half landing atop a tree and his hindquarters becoming a voracious monster that stalks the easternmost wastes of the earth.

A close parallel to the Meskwaki story "Has-a-Rock" is the first part of the Menominee tale of the hero Wäwapikuahsemit.[13] The name Wäwapikuahsemit (to use Bloomfield's early spelling), later written technically as *wɛ·wa·pekuahsemet*, means "one who has (a or some) *wa·pekuahs-*," which is clearly "small white something-or-other," perhaps "small white feather."[14] Wäwapikuahsemit's antagonist is an evil grandfather that raised him, rather than an uncle, and it is the enchanted sisters who cut his older brother in two, sticking his top half on a stump and giving his hindquarters to the sky spirits of the east and west as a plaything. The hero marries both girls and makes his brother whole. But the Menominee tale, at least in the two tellings we have of it, does not have the same impact as the Meskwaki one, since the condition of the older brother is fully explained at the outset.

On one point, though, the Menominee version clarifies an allusion in the Meskwaki one. Twice the uncle in the Meskwaki story refers to hummingbirds being worn as earrings, without specifying their significance or even exactly who is wearing them. The Menominee hero Wäwapikuahsemit also wears birds as earrings. They are referred to as "little birds called Masanakoka" in John V. Satterlee's translation, which leaves them otherwise unexplained, but in the telling by Josephine Satterlee, John V. Satterlee's daughter-in-law, they are specifically hummingbirds (which are called something else in Menominee) and are a source of his power. The Menominee story thus makes it certain that the hummingbird earrings in the Meskwaki tale were worn by the hero. For Meskwakis, hummingbirds traditionally represent speed and endurance and are the source of the spiritual power of ceremonial runners (*aška·pe·waki*), as they are the ceremonial runners of the birds.[15] In the Meskwaki tale, then, the hummingbirds give the hero extraordinary powers as a runner.

While Chuck's "Has-a-Rock" resembles the first half of the Menominee tale "Wäwapikuahsemit," the second part of "Wäwapikuahsemit," in which the hero goes to rescue two sisters,[16] closely parallels the Meskwaki tale "Turkey-Owner," which, as already discussed, matches the framing narrative of "The Ice Maidens." From such comparisons the modular construction of such stories in general is evident, reflecting the way winter stories were told, one after another, night after night. Tellers would suture together different stories with nameless heroes, and in time some combinations became conventional.

A man who is half tree also appears in an Eastern Sioux tale retold by Schoolcraft: "[T]his man, who had the looks of great age, was composed of *wood* from his breast downward, and appeared to be fixed in the earth."[17] He gives advice to the hero, White Feather, who has been raised in isolation and kept in ignorance by his grandfather, but the stories are otherwise quite different. Even more different is a Teton Sioux tale in which a man is made to grow a tree base by a vengeful sister he had branded for tricking him into unwitting incest.[18] A faint echo is in the Oklahoma Wyandot tale "The Old Bear and His Nephew," in which the hero is called to by "A uki . . . sitting high up in the tree-top. His name was 'The-one-with-bare-loins-and-without-lower-limbs'." The uki (manitou) comes down from his tree to converse.[19] The striking agreement between the name of the hero in the Eastern Sioux tale and a possible interpretation of the name of the hero in the Menominee tale suggests that a search for versions of the Sioux and Algonquian stories that share more than the motif of the tree man might be fruitful.

Notes

1. I am grateful to Lucy Thomason and Charlotte I. Goddard for helpful comments, and to Dan Zwiener for sharing his knowledge of Native American corn varieties and for his suggestions about the possible identity of the corn served by Manoneha in "The Ice Maidens."
2. National Anthropological Archives manuscripts nos. 2662 (Sakihtanohkweha) and 2737 (Chuck).
3. Goddard, "Writing and Reading Mesquakie (Fox)"; Walker, "Native Writing Systems," 168–71; Kinkade and Mattina, "Discourse," 274, fig. 13.
4. All Meskwaki words in italics are in a technical phonemic orthography. Short vowels are pronounced approximately as in Spanish or Italian; long vowels (marked with a raised dot) are pronounced roughly as in German; *š* is English *sh*; and *č* is English *ch*. The double hyphen (=) marks enclitics, words that must be pronounced together with a preceding word and therefore cannot occur at the beginning of a sentence.
5. For some references, see Thompson, *Tales*, 325, 330, 335.
6. Goddard, "Grammatical Gender."
7. Ruth Moore, in *The Times Literary Supplement*, August 9, 2002 (no. 5184), p. 5.
8. Torrence and Hobbs, *Art of the Red Earth People*, 121, 127 (nos. 16, 97).
9. Cha kä ta ko si [Chuck], *A Collection of Meskwaki Manuscripts*; Purcell, "The Mesquakie Indian Settlement in 1905," 52–54. Few Meskwakis have been able to read the odd spelling used in this publication, and this may account for the reported belief that, when Duren J. H. Ward obtained the copies of Chuck's writings from him, Chuck "did not take the assignment too seriously" (Purcell, 54). There is reason to believe, however, that Chuck made verbatim copies of his papers for Ward and did not alter them for publication, except for prudent omissions, though he did not provide a comprehensive tribal history of the sort Ward appears to have thought he was getting. His manuscript is in the State Historical Society of Iowa, Iowa City.
10. Also translated "Spirit of Winter," "Winter Spirit," and more freely "North Wind," "Cold Weather," and even "Santa Claus." The name is derived from *pepo·wi*, "winter; it is winter" (compare Kickapoo *pepoonwi*) by a suffix *-(a)tesiw*

that makes several names of nature gods and the like, including also *ni·petesiwa*, "Harvest Spirit" (compare *ni·penwi*, "it's the time when the garden crops are ripe").

11. Patch, "Some Elements," 608 n. 23 and 610 n. 30.
12. Thompson, *Tales*, 309 n. 115.
13. There is an English version of this in Skinner and Satterlee, "Folklore of the Menomini Indians," 317–324, 524, and a Menominee version told by Josephine Satterlee in Bloomfield, *Menomini Texts*, 468–77.
14. The unattested but implied word *wa·pekuahs-* contains *wa·p-*, "white," and the diminutive suffix *-hs*, but the medial portion has no known meaning or obvious analysis (Bloomfield, *Menomini Language*, 234, 403). It is possible, however, that *-ekuahs* is an archaic fusion of the attested element *-ekon*, "feather," and the diminutive suffix *-hs*. If so the name would mean "one who has a small white feather (or feathers)."
15. Michelson, "Ceremonial Runners," 9, 23–35.
16. Skinner and Satterlee, "Folklore of the Menomini," 324–27; Bloomfield, *Menomini Texts*, 476–83.
17. Schoolcraft, *Algic Researches*, 76.
18. Deloria, *Dakota Texts*, xiii, 177–78.
19. Barbeau, *Huron-Wyandot Traditional Narratives*, 33, 199.

References and Suggested Reading

Barbeau, Marius. *Huron-Wyandot Traditional Narratives in Translations and Native Texts*. National Museum of Canada Bulletin no. 165. Ottawa: Canada Department of Northern Affairs and National Resources, 1960.

Bloomfield, Leonard. *Menomini Texts*. American Ethnological Society Publications no. 12. New York: G. E. Stechert, 1927.

———. *The Menomini Language*. New Haven CT: Yale University Press, 1962.

Callender, Charles. "Fox." In *Northeast*, edited by Bruce G. Trigger, vol. 15 of *Handbook of North American Indians*, general editor William C. Sturtevant, 636–47. Washington DC: Smithsonian Institution, 1978.

[Chuck, Charley H.] "Cha kä ta ko si." *A Collection of Meskwaki Manuscripts*. Iowa City: State Historical Society of Iowa, 1907.

Deloria, Ella. *Dakota Texts*. American Ethnological Society Publications no. 14. New York: G. E. Stechert, 1932.

Goddard, Ives. "Writing and Reading Mesquakie (Fox)." In *Papers of the Twenty-seventh Algonquian Conference*, edited by David H. Pentland, 117–34. Winnipeg: University of Manitoba, 1996.

———. "Grammatical Gender in Algonquian." In *Papers of the Thirty-third Algonquian*

Conference, edited by H. C. Wolfart, 195–231. Winnipeg: University of Manitoba, 2002.

———. "Meskwaki: Two Winter Stories." In *Voices from Four Directions*, edited by Brian Swann, 423–67. Lincoln: University of Nebraska Press, 2004.

Jones, William. "Episodes in the Culture Hero Myth of the Sauks and Foxes." *Journal of American Folklore* 14 (1901): 225–39.

———. *Fox Texts*. American Ethnological Society Publications no. 1. Leiden: E. J. Brill for the American Ethnological Society, 1907.

———. "Notes on the Fox Indians." *Journal of American Folklore* 24 (1911): 209–37.

———. *Ethnography of the Fox Indians*. Edited by Margaret Welpley Fisher. Bureau of American Ethnology Bulletin no. 125. Washington DC: Smithsonian Institution, 1939.

Kinkade, M. Dale, and Anthony Mattina. "Discourse." In *Languages*, edited by Ives Goddard, vol. 17 of *Handbook of North American Indians*, edited by William C. Sturtevant, 244–74. Washington DC: Smithsonian Institution, 1996.

Michelson, Truman. "Notes on the Ceremonial Runners of the Fox Indians." In *Bureau of American Ethnology Bulletin* no. 85, pp. v–vii, 1–50. Washington DC: Smithsonian Institution, 1927.

Patch, Howard R. "Some Elements in Mediæval Descriptions of the Otherworld." *Publications of the Modern Language Association of America* 33 (1918): 601–43.

Purcell, L. Edward. "The Mesquakie Indian Settlement in 1905." *The Palimpsest* 55 (1974): 34–55.

Schoolcraft, Henry R. *Algic Researches*. New York: Harper & Brothers, 1839.

Skinner, Alanson, and John V. Satterlee. "Folklore of the Menomini Indians." In *Anthropological Papers of the American Museum of Natural History* vol. 13, part 3. New York: American Museum of Natural History, 1915.

Thompson, Stith. *Tales of the North American Indians*. Cambridge: Harvard University Press, 1929. Reprint, Bloomington: Indiana University Press, 1966.

Torrence, Gaylord, and Robert Hobbs. *Art of the Red Earth People: The Mesquakie of Iowa*. Seattle: University of Washington Press, 1989.

Walker, Willard B. "Native Writing Systems." In *Languages*, edited by Ives Goddard, vol. 17 of *Handbook of North American Indians*, edited by William C. Sturtevant, 290–323. Washington DC: Smithsonian Institution, 1996.

THE ICE MAIDENS

Written by Sakihtanohkweha
Translated by Ives Goddard

And then there were two other people, living in a single lodge,[1]
Indians,[2]
a young brother and sister.
Their lodge was the only one there, far off in the wilderness.
No other Indians lived nearby.
They were all by themselves.
And then at some point the man had a thought:
"Well, why don't I go out and look for a wife.
At least then my sister would have someone to talk to whenever she's left at home.
"I mean, what else are we going to do for the rest of our lives!" the man thought.
Without further ado, he then went back,
going to tell his sister.
He was hunting.
And then it suddenly dawned on him,
and he told her that.
"But don't just go, though.
You must first do some fasting," she told him.
"The creatures called 'women' are hard to get," she told him.
And then the next morning he fasted.
And before the full number of days had passed, that fellow received a blessing.
And he told his sister.
"That won't do it," she told him.
"Women are hard to get, I tell you," she told him.

1. The introduction of the characters as "two other people" indicates that the writer was writing out more than one story at the same time and transitioning between them in the same way as if she were telling the stories in sequence.

2. "Indians" translates the plural of *neno·te·wa*. This word generally means "Indian," especially "Meskwaki Indian," but in winter stories and ceremonial texts it may be used generically for "human being." For consistency, and because the exact intended nuance is often unclear, it is always translated in these stories as "Indian," the meaning it has for contemporary speakers.

And then he began fasting again,
and he received yet another blessing,
and again he told his sister.
"You definitely have to do some more," she told him.
"You still haven't gone long enough," he was told.
And he then fasted yet again.
And yet again he told his sister.
So, then he was told, "Go, if you wish, as you now are, without full gear."

≈≈≈

And then he departed.
And having gone over the hill he came out in the open again.
And on the hill someone else came into the open.
They came out at exactly the same time.
And at exactly the same time they said, "Hello!" to each other.
Well, it seems every time they spoke they both said the same thing.
After a while they got their conversation straightened out right.
And then they could challenge each other to a race.
And they gave each other their word.
They ran the circuit of the whole earth,
and that Indian lost the race.
(Now, it turned out that the one who made the challenge was the owner of that big hill.)
He lost all his clothes on the bet,
and even his dream power.
He was beaten out of all his blessings as well.
That fellow was beaten out of all of them as well,
and he went back naked.

≈≈≈

After he got back to his sister's place,[3]
he stood outside
and asked for something he could wear.
It was handed out to him,
along with a scolding.
His sister lost no time in giving him a big scolding.

3. "His sister's place" translates *otehkwe·meki*, the local form of the word for "his sister"; this not an odd expression in Meskwaki, since dwellings are usually the property of women.

"That's why I told you,
it's hard to go somewhere else," the man was told.

≈≈≈

Now, the one that beat him had said,
"Come back and challenge me again,
whenever you want to come and challenge me."
And he had said he would.

≈≈≈

And now he lost no time in starting to fast again.
And before the fast was over he received a blessing.
"Cease your weeping.
I am, without a doubt, the fastest in the whole wide world," said the voice of someone speaking to him.
And when he looked at whoever might be speaking to him,
why, here he found that what was speaking to him was his own arrow!
"Gee, so THAT'S what it was!" thought the Indian.
He set to weeping loudly all over again.
And he didn't eat anything.
After a few days someone spoke to him again.
"All right, cease your weeping.
I am, for sure, the fastest in the whole wide world," said the voice.
And when he looked at whoever might be speaking to him,
why, here he found that it was his bowstring!
And he recommenced weeping loudly
and recommenced fasting strictly.
And again he received a blessing.
The voice told him the same thing as before.
And when he looked at whoever might be speaking to him,
why, here he found that his eye, his very own eye, was what had blessed him!
In other words, he could run at speed as far as he could see.
No matter.
He thought that that as well was not enough.
And he did not cease his weeping.
He kept on as before, weeping and weeping.
And AGAIN someone blessed him.
"All right, cease your weeping.
I bless you.

That guy that outran you doesn't AMOUNT to anything![4]
But I am actually, for sure, the fastest in the whole wide world," the voice told him.
"Look at me," the other told him,
and he looked at him.
Why, here he found that his heart, his own heart, was blessing him!
"Hey, now I'm in business!
It's really true," he thought.
"Truly there's no stopping me now," he thought,
and he left for home.
When he got back to his sister's place, he ate a meal.
"It's done," he said to his sister.
"I'm going to go race," he told her.
"Why, go ahead," he was told,
and he left.

≈≈≈

He went and ran out into the open over on that hill.
And over there, after he ran out, in no time at all the same man as before again came running out towards him.
"Hello," they said to each other.
"Do you challenge me?" they said to each other.
Every time they spoke they said the same thing.
Quite some time later they got their conversation straightened out right.
"Are you here to challenge me now?" the Indian was asked.
"Yes," he replied.
"Oh! Why, it's quite up to you, of course," he was told.
And they began to strip down.[5]
And they told each other, "Go!"
And they took off.
And he left him an overwhelmingly great distance behind.
He ran at the speed that his heart beat.
The other man was left really way far behind.
Now HE was slowing down from exhaustion.
He came running up slowly.

4. Sarcastic; to be said with declining pitch, the lowest pitch on the stressed word "AMOUNT," before rising slightly at the end.

5. "To strip down" translates *peninawi·-*, which means "get undressed, take one's clothes off"; it would be understood, however, that they stripped down to just their breechclouts.

He barely made it back, so far was he left behind.
And then he began to pay off his bet.
Everything he was wearing was won from him.
He really lost a great deal,
and his dream power was won from him with the rest.
He turned over everything.
"That's it," he said.
"You are truly really fast," he told him.
"What's more, no one else has ever beaten me," he said.
"So you've now beaten me for the first time," the man who had been outraced told him.
He even ceased to be a human being and turned into a turkey vulture.
He ceased to be a human being, they say.
And as for him, he arrived back loaded down with things.

≈≈≈

And then he again set out from there.
NOW he went a-courting.
And on and on that young man walked.
When nightfall overtook him, he built a small fire by a river.
And he killed a deer.
Then after his meal he slept a bit.
When he woke up, it was early,
and he started walking,
setting out.
He just started walking whatever way he was going, with no particular destination.
That evening he again arrived over at a river,
where he killed a single deer,
and he roasted it on a spit.
After cooking it, he ate it.
And after eating, he slept.
When he woke up, he set out.
Quite late he again came to a river over somewhere,
and he killed a deer.
Then after eating something he slept.
And when he woke up he set out,
going to seek a bride.
Over somewhere he again came to a river,
and he went hunting

and killed a deer.
Again, after waking up, he set out without bothering to eat.
He did not need to eat in the morning.
All he ever did after waking up was set out.
That's what he did.

≈≈≈

And thus, over yonder, he then came to a village,
an Indian village.
And he went into a certain little house,
where there was a little old lady living all by herself.
"Goodness me! It's my grandchild," she said to him,
and she cooked a meal for him, Old Lady Manoneha did.[6]
"Why, I don't think I can get my FILL, with her cooking so LITTLE!" thought the fellow.
"Mercy me! My grandson is challenging my kettle," said the old lady.
"Whoops! Darned if she doesn't know what I'm thinking," the fellow thought.
And he tried as hard as he could not to think about anything else.
Soon she finished her cooking.
And he watched her serving the corn into a little wooden dish.
Well, it was half a small kernel of white hominy corn and half of a little currant.[7]
She fanned it to cool it off,
and the amount of it grew steadily larger.
"Eat!" he was told.
And he set to eating.
Soon he could eat no more.
He was unable to finish his plate.
"That's all I can do," he said.
"You challenged my little kettle," he was told.
"And now you've failed to avoid being unable to finish your plate," the fellow was told.
After he was through eating, his grandmother instructed him.

6. "Old Lady Manoneha" translates *mano·ne·hi-metemo·he·ha*, literally "Manoneha little-old-woman," a somewhat elaborate designation for Manoneha *mano·ne·ha*, a stock character in winter stories. The name has no meaning.

7. "White hominy corn" is a conjectural translation of *otepimina*, literally "brain corn," a designation that probably refers to its appearance; "currant" translates *pekomini*, following Harry Lincoln.

"There are some young maidens that come to this place," she said.
"What's distinctive about them is that a little old lady always comes last of all.
SHE's the young maiden of the lot.
The ones further to the front are actually older," she said.
"So, SHE is for sure the youngest of them all," his grandmother said.

≈≈≈

Why, soon someone was coming.
Sure enough, it was some women.
A bunch of them were seen coming,
and a camp was made.
And he saw a little old lady come walking last of all,
using a cane.
That night he and a lot of other guys went to sneak in with the girls.[8]
Except that the visitor went to sneak in with the little old lady.
And the other young folks made fun of him for sneaking in with an old lady.
Then did he make the old lady his wife.

≈≈≈

The very next day they left,
and went back.
When they camped over yonder, the women made a lodge.
Every one of them had a husband.
So there were really a lot of them living together when they all got there.
That night, Elder Sister burned all the moccasins.[9]
But that Indian KNEW that she was going to do that.
And a short time into the night he switched his moccasins from where he had hung them up,
hanging up HER moccasins instead in the place where HIS moccasins had been.
Then Elder Sister had inadvertently burned her own moccasins along with the rest.

≈≈≈

8. "To sneak in with girls" translates *no·tehkwe·we·-*; this verb applies specifically to the common method of courtship by sneaking into a girl's sleeping place at night, and perhaps even snuggling under her blanket, usually chastely, like the colonial American practice of bundling.

9. "Elder Sister" translates *mači·hkiwesi·hkwe·wa*; this word is treated here as a proper name, since she is a stock character in winter stories, though translation as a common noun is also possible. The listener would understand that everyone's moccasins had been hung up to dry before the fire.

As if nothing at all were amiss she said, "This IS the Planting Moon."[10]
"Hey! Don't take my moccasins down!" she was told.
"Those are MY moccasins, as you can see," she was told.
"Oh my! Why, where did they go, then?" she said.
That woman had really made things hard for herself,
for there was a lot of snow, which she had to contend with.
And as for those other sons-in-law, every one of them was without footwear.
Meanwhile, Elder Sister wrapped her feet with a little blanket.
And those other sons-in-law were told by the Indian, "Go back!
"And I'll give you these things to wear," they were told, meaning as footwear.
Now, it was all kinds of animals—
a buffalo, a bear, a lynx, a wolf, a mountain lion—
all kinds of animals.
And they all turned back.
"And I'll bring your wives back to you," the ones turning back were told.

≈≈≈

He was the only one who continued the pursuit.
And remember, there was really a lot of snow.
There was so much it came up to their knees.
But that fellow was really powerful, as well.
When they set out every time, he would say words,
for the weather to stay warm.
They say those women would really get worn down by the heat when the weather was warm.
That's how much that man was in control of things.
And as for Elder Sister,
she would lie down without even eating supper,
as she was just too tired.
But in the case of the man,
whenever he got tired he would bar the path of the others.
He would hang up his blanket, then, wherever he'd gotten to.
That's where the other woman would drop her load,[11]

10. "The Planting Moon" translates the name of the month of the Meskwaki lunar calendar that is equated very approximately with May.

11. "The other woman" translates *i·na ihkwe·wa* (with vowel elision in the text), literally "that woman." Such an expression implies a reference to a woman other than the one just mentioned, so here it must refer to the youngest sister.

where she would drop the things she was carrying on her back.[12]
Right away that other woman would set to making a lodge,
while that man, for his part, went and killed a deer.
Then he would bring it back,
and then they would cook it.
Much later in the night the woman Elder Sister would walk up.
And before eating anything at all, she fell asleep,
lying there dressed in the full outfit of clothes she was wearing.[13]

≈ ≈ ≈

Over yonder they arrived at a river,
and there was a bridge.
He could see it was all ice.
It was enveloped in solid ice.
But come to him, he braved it,
clambering up the last.
Those wives of his, on the other hand, went running on up, as if there were nothing to it.
But HE was expected to meet his end right there,
when he would slip.
And he did not suffer the expected fate.
And he did not slip.
As if there were nothing to it, he climbed on up.
And he did not fall off.
He still arrived over where those Ice Maidens lived.

≈ ≈ ≈

Elder Sister could be seen dressed in finery.
She had ice for earrings,
wearing it like those long dangler earrings that shimmer.
And the woman also wore bracelets of it,
and just everything.
And even her leggins were of it,

12. From the reference to "the things she was carrying on her back," the listener can deduce that, as in other stories, Manoneha has made a formal gift of fancy clothing to her grandson's bride.

13. This whole line translates *e·h=kekiki·kehčina·hkwapiso·ne·šino·hiniči*, a word of amusingly bizarre complexity, a verb that incorporates a noun derived from a compound verb.

and besides all that she also wore a blanket of ice.
She had quite a costume of finery, indeed.

≈≈≈

But when those women got back
the older women were glad,
at the prospect of killing that young man.
And ONE of those women never went anyplace.
So, whenever the others brought sons-in-law to the family,
they say, SHE would sleep with them first.
And she would kill them then.
She would reportedly weep when they didn't sleep with her.
But he knew ahead of time that she did that, they say.
So, they say, that fellow already had a rock with him.
And sure enough, then, that woman announced, "I shall sleep with our husband first."[14]
They say that woman's vagina had teeth.
And when anyone had sex with her,
she would bite off his penis.
So, as she lay there yielding, then, that fellow stuck the rock into her.
Suddenly, early in the night, she was heard to cry out.
"His thrusting broke all my teeth off," she said.
And right away she died,
early, early in the night.
And the old lady was angered,
as the daughter of the old woman had been slain.

≈≈≈

And then she used an entirely different tone of voice.
"I shall give a ceremonial feast," said the old lady.
"And you shall serve as my attendant for it," the old lady told her son-in-law.
"All right, I will," he replied to her.
And he served her as ceremonial attendant.
And she gave a Grand Medicine feast with chopped-corn soup.
After she sang some songs,
she told him, "Okay now, I'm going to sing dancing songs."

14. "Our husband" translates *nena·pe·mena·na*, specifically "our (exclusive) husband," that is, "ours but not yours," referring to the speaker and her youngest sister.

"All right," her son-in-law answered her.

"And you must DANCE," she told him.

"All right, I will," the man told her,
and he stepped outside for a moment.

And he put a rocky crag on his back.[15]

This time the old lady was sitting there with a war club.
And when her son-in-law danced past her,
she took the war club and struck him on the back.
And failing to snap his spine,
all she did was make the rocky crag resound from her blow.

"Gosh!" she said,
and she was frightened.

After she broke off singing,
"Now me," she was told.
"I actually have just the right medicine for that, too.

"We're supposed to take turns singing when we do this," declared the son-in-law.

"All right," his mother-in-law replied to him.
And he began to sing.
He sang any old way at random.

After he finished singing,
"Okay now, you must DANCE," she was told.
"Now it's your turn."

"All right, I will," said the old lady,
and she danced.

"Why don't I do just what I saw you do!" she was told.
And the war club was at the ready on the sidelines.
And when she danced directly in front,
the old lady was struck with that war club,
and she was killed.

≈≈≈

Those whose mother she had been hauled their things outside.
And after taking them out of the lodge, they burned it up along with everything in it,

15. "Rocky crag" translates *ši·kona*, which is both "rocky crag, cliff, outcrop" and "whetstone"; for the intended purpose, however, a whetstone would be rather feckless even in real life, let alone in a winter story.

along with their mother.
They burned her up as well.
And also that thing she somewhat prayed to they burned her up with, too.
And as for that man, "Get ready to travel," he said to those ten girls.[16]
"We're going to leave.
"Wait, I have to work on you first," he told them,
and he had them sit in a straight line.
"Bare your knees," he told them.
And he grazed them on the knees with the shot of an arrow.
Every one of them had their knees twisted sideways by it.
So, then women were fixed,
so they would not have stamina,
so they would tire pretty easily.
Before that was done to them, they really had stamina.
So, now, since that time, they tire pretty easily,
after that was done to them.

≈≈≈

Then they left to go to where the man came from.
—To where he was married, rather.—
They only slept once on the way.
And the next day they arrived over where the women's husbands were.
And the women were dropped off.
They say that's what happened to the Ice Maidens at the time they were fetched back.
Only, first their mother had to be killed.[17]

≈≈≈

And then that man and his wife lived there at Manoneha's house.
For quite a few years in all, that man hunted for his grandmother.
And after a while, then, they had a baby,
a little boy.
And then at some point that man informed his grandmother of his plans, telling her that he would be leaving.

16. "Get ready to travel" translates *nana·hi·hta·ko*, literally "get dressed," but idiomatically this implies getting everything ready for the trip.

17. "Only . . . had to be" corresponds to *še·ški*, "only, nothing else but"; the translation follows Harry Lincoln, whose rendering was: "They had to kill their mother before they got there."

"Why, go right ahead and DO that!" the old lady told him.
Only, he first cut great loads of wood for her.

≈≈≈

After they had cut loads and loads of wood for her, they left her,
going to his sister's place.
After arriving over at a river,
all they did was go to sleep.
And eating a deer the next day,
they then arrived over where his sister was.
And when they came walking up a short distance off,
they noticed that their house had no smoke coming from it.
"Uh-oh! What could have happened to my sister!" he thought.
And when they got to the door,
here they found it shut.
And he spoke to her.
"Hey, what's wrong with you?" he asked her.
And here what she said was, "Here they are, back again!"
And she said to them, "Mind you, you're always making me mistake your voices."
"I promise you it's US," he told her.
"See, that's what you always say to me," she said.
"And what's more, here's your nephew.
Feel his hand," he told her.
She went over there,
and she felt his hand.
And sure enough, she found her hand in contact with the little hand of a baby.
It turned out that foxes had been abusing her,
always throwing ashes in her eyes.
That's what they did.
Those foxes had made that woman's eyes turn inside-out from the burning.
And then that man just kept hunting.
That's the end of the story about them.

HAS-A-ROCK

Written by Charley H. Chuck
Translated by Ives Goddard

This uncle and nephew, as it turns out, were living wherever it was.
One time, "Nephew," said the one to the other,
"if I have a nightmare, you must use my rock.
You must hit me with it, if I have a nightmare."
And one time his uncle was moaning,
and he hit him with it.
THUNK!
"Yow-ow-ow-ow!
You hit me too hard, Nephew."
"Come on, I just rolled it over that way a little."
"Listen, Nephew, I saw a vision of a bear,
for me to put on a ceremonial feast with.
He's white, apparently.
In the south, not far off,
that's where he is, apparently.
So, he's the one you must go get for me,
for me to put on a ceremonial feast with."
"Okay, I will.
Sure, I will go after him.
I'll leave tomorrow morning," he told him.

≈≈≈

When it was daylight he left.
And at some point as he was walking on, someplace over that way,
someone spoke to him from somewhere.
"Gee, it's my little brother," said the other to him.
He kept looking around for the place where the speaker might be.
And high up, there he saw him sitting.
"Where are you going, little brother?"
"Has-a-Rock sent me to get something so that he can put on a ceremonial feast with it."

"Listen, little brother, I will tell you.
Stand there a while.
"Now our uncle is making plans for you.
That's the reason you see ME like this.
This is where the blow launched me to, when our uncle shot me.
Though I did bring the creature to him.
It's a pretty fast runner,
but me, I outran it,
and another one as well.
I outran them.
I ran faster than both of them.
"So here's what you must do.
After you have killed it, and after our uncle has had a look at it,
he will say, 'Say, that's terrific!
This will make a splendid tobacco bag for me,' he will say.
"You must walk over to pick up a firebrand,
and pick up the creature on the way.
You must whoop four times
and throw it in the fire.
"Me, I went different places doing what he wanted.
And so that's the reason I'm the way I am.
That's why it was easy for him to do me in.
"So, don't you believe him.
"Oh, say, I forgot, when you pick up the firebrand:
'You might have made a slip of the tongue about yourself.
I mean, really, don't you think you would have said, "I had a vision of a creature
I'm to make a tobacco bag out of."
Don't you really think you would have said that at the outset.
What you did say, remember, was, "For me to put on a ceremonial feast."'
"And after you have put it all in the pot,
you must cook it uniformly to perfection.
His sister will rush to take a spot down there in the entranceway.
And so she's the one you must serve the head to.
And also you must tell her, 'This is what he's praying to here:
his war club.[1]

1. "War club" translates *mi·si·hikani*, literally "instrument for causing to defecate by striking"; probably this is the same as what is elsewhere called *pehkwiki·hi*, a heavy, ball-headed war club.

And this is what, I imagine, you should be praying to as well,' you must tell her.
You must set it standing in front of her.
'This is what he prays to,
as it is hungry.
So any dawdler I imagine I'm supposed to club to death with this war club.'
That's what you must tell her,
so she will eat.
"Well, he will have a toothache.
The moment you walk over to take up the firebrand
is the exact moment our uncle will develop a toothache.
"That's it.
"Now go on ahead," his elder brother told him.

≈≈≈

Sure enough, when he arrived over there,
the bear was lying about.
There was none but a small bit of black on it,
and he shot it in the hollow of its throat.
And as soon as he let fly the arrow, he took off running.
—Say, I forgot, what his older brother instructed him to do:
"There are guards over there.
So you must toss tobacco to them.
And again further on.
Those are the kind that are really ravenous.
'Don't cry out,' you must tell them.
And then a little further on is where it's lying."
So then that's what he did.
He offered tobacco to those creatures each time he came out of the forest,
so they wouldn't cry out.
So then he got to the place where it lay.—
And when he took off,
he ran really fast.
And with that, sure enough, he could sense it coming behind him.
And with that, sure enough, every thrust of his feet
was followed instantly by the sound of the snapping of its teeth.
CLACK! CLACK! CLACK! CLACK!
He ran really fast.

≈≈≈

And he came running back to where his older brother stood.
"Bravo! Run fast, little brother.
You're outrunning the red-eyed one.
"So, what does he LOOK like as he comes?
His eyes are RED!
Isn't he ASHAMED of himself for always CHASING people around!" he said to the bear.
And after it ran right by him:
"And what kind of a BUTT does he have going by?
Why, he's got a really big brown bunghole!"[2]
The bear in its anger twisted sideways as it ran.
And after it had gone past, again:
"So, what sort of heels does he have running off?
Why, his heels are really chapped," he said to it, once more,
angering it by his insults.
But meanwhile his younger brother had already run on a considerable distance,
so much had he distracted the bear.
The bear went running off atwist for quite some distance,
and took off.
After it had gone a good distance past,
it took off again,
running after its prey.

≈≈≈

Before it could manage to catch up with him again,
they came running out of the forest back at the house he shared with his uncle.
Now, the old man had barricaded himself in the house to a fair-thee-well.
He stopped up all the holes,
so there was no way the other fellow could dash in through someplace.[3]
And he closed up all the little cracks.
And then every now and then he looked to try and see them.
And suddenly they came running out of the forest.

2. Chuck wrote the equivalent of: "Why, really (expletive) (emphatic)," omitting a verb, presumably by oversight. The insult has been supplied here from another of Chuck's stories, "When Raccoon Was Smart."

3. "The other fellow" is supplied in the translation because it is clear from later references that the old man is concerned specifically about his nephew. In the Meskwaki there is no overt subject, only a verb that could be translated with "he" or "they" (or, unlikely in this context, "it [animate]").

"Bravo! Run fast, my nephew!
You're outrunning him.
"Run fast, my brother!
You're definitely catching up with him.
Fling him headlong![4]
"Run fast, my nephew!
You're definitely outrunning him.
"Fling him headlong! Fling him headlong!"
And they came rushing up.
"WHUMP! WHUMP!" was the noise they made.[5]
"Phew!"
"Oh my!
Well, my younger brother IS quite a runner!
"Oh, why did you have to face hummingbird earrings![6]
"Well, my younger brother DOES run fast!"
Suddenly he was aware of him quivering his arrows.
Now, he was kneeling at the door,
gripping the door in his hands.[7]
And just as he looked, he saw him quivering his arrows.
"Uh-oh!
Well, I always DID tell my nephew to fast.
Well, my nephew IS a swift runner."
And he opened the door and looked at him.
"Terrific! By golly, Nephew!
This will make a splendid tobacco bag for me to wear when there's a celebration, Nephew."
He walked over and picked up a firebrand.

4. "Fling him headlong!" translates *anika pakiši* (plural *anika pakinehko*), following William Jones. This is a conventional encouragement to deadly pursuers in winter stories.

5. "WHUMP!" renders an imitative sound effect written in Meskwaki as "kwa," which I interpret as *kwah*. In the three episodes the number of WHUMP!'s always corresponds to the number of runners, and the verb used in the present case, *inwe·we·šin-*, "to make such a noise," indicates that the sound is caused by physical action and not oral. I take these vocables as representing the sound of the runners colliding with the barricaded door of the house, but the interpretation of such expressive words is always conjectural.

6. Literally "Oh, why does (did) it have to be that hummingbirds are (were) worn as earrings!" Since the hero must be the one with the magic hummingbird earrings (as explained in my introductory essay), the uncle must here be anguishing over the uncertain fate of the bear.

7. The door would naturally be a skin door flap.

"Say, you might have made a slip of the tongue about yourself.
I mean, really, don't you think you would have said at the outset, 'I had a vision of a creature I'm to make a tobacco bag out of.'
What you DID say, remember, was, 'For me to put on a ceremonial feast with.'
You might now have made a slip of the tongue about yourself."

He was holding the bear by the leg.

"Yohohoho! Yohohoho! Yohohoho! Yohohoho!"
He whooped.
After he whooped four times, there was a joyful shout from the people.[8]
And he threw it in the fire
and singed the hair off it.

"They're in on it with that scoundrel.
Woe is me, my poor brother! Woe is me, my poor brother!"

After singeing the hair off, he brought it back
and set to butchering it.

"What shall I do now?
You're not keeping on with your instructions to me."

"Actually, I'm bothered by a toothache, Nephew.
Just any way will do.
You be in charge of how to butcher it yourself.

"Yow-ow-ow! Yow-ow-ow! Yow-ow-ow!
My poor brother!"

"Why, you really keep making the most inappropriate outcries!"

"Actually, it's just because the worms are biting me every which way—
that's the reason for the way I keep on crying out, Nephew.

"Yow-ow-ow-ow! Yow-ow-ow!

"Don't pay any attention to me, Nephew."

After putting it in the pot,
he barely let it boil at all.

"All right, now here this is clearly all overcooked."

"Well, okay, Nephew, invite people.
Now you must go outside and give the call.
Namely, you must tell them they're invited to eat.

And he went outside.
"You must tell them they're invited to eat!"

"You said exactly what I said."

"Well, that's what you told me to say.

8. From the other lodges.

So that's the reason I said it."
And he went out again.
"You are invited to eat!"
He shouted then for real.
And the other people trooped in.
And then, after they had all filed in:
"This here is what this man prays to,
as it always eats at that time.
'It's probably hungry,' he says.
Actually, he's bothered by a toothache.
So this war club of his is what he prays to."
And he stood it up in front of them.
"Anyone who doesn't completely finish everything I'm supposed to club to death.
As each of us finishes our plate we're supposed to sink into the ground," he told them.
After serving it out to them, he told them, "Pitch in!"
In no time they were sinking into the ground one after the other.
And last of all was the old lady,
last of all, at her wit's end,
unable to chew the severed poll.[9]
"Why, now I suppose I must club this one to death," he said to her.
But concluding there was nothing else for it, she swallowed that head in a gulp,
as the war club was being aimed at her.
And with that she went sinking into the ground, barely in time.
"You were frightening the old lady," the other told him.

≈≈≈

"All right, Nephew, you must hit me with my rock again,
if I come to in my sleep, Nephew."
"Okay, I will."
And again at some point he moaned.
He even sprang up in the air a bit.
He threw it hard,
and the blow he struck against him went, "THUNK!"
"Yow-yow-yow-yow!
You hit me too hard, Nephew."

9. "The severed poll" translates *opehkwa·tepi*, a rare word for a head by itself, detached from a body.

"Why, and here I only rolled it over that way a little.
I wonder what kind of a noise you'd make if I DID hit you hard."
"Listen, Nephew, again I had a vision that I am to give a ceremonial feast.
A bit further on from where you went to get the other one there's an otter, apparently.
It's white, apparently.
So, that's the one I want you to get for me."
Again he told him, "Okay, I will.
I'll go early tomorrow morning."

≈≈≈

The next day he left.
And he went by where his older brother was.
"All right, little brother, try your hardest.
This time he runs even faster.
But once you outrun him, you shall outrun him.
Though I DID outrun that one as well.
So, once you outrun him,
you must do the same thing you did to the other one.
You must do exactly the same thing as before.
And on your way there, as well, you must do exactly what you did as you went on your way before.
Exactly the same as what you did before is what you must do," his older brother told him.
And he went on.

≈≈≈

And he arrived over there.
But he did the same series of things that he had done as he went along before.
When he got there, here he saw it facing him from the hillside opposite.
And he shot at it.
And as soon as he let fly his arrow,
he took off running.
And with that, sure enough, every thrust of his feet
was followed instantly by the sound of the snapping of its teeth, coming behind.
Then he really ran fast.

≈≈≈

And he came running to where his brother was sitting.

Then, HE, as before, hurled insults at the otter.

"What are his eyes like as he comes running?
See, his eyes are really red.
Or is it when he's running fast?
His eyes must just be red like that when he's running, apparently,
the one who apparently has no shame," he said to it.

It turned its head the other way as it ran
and ran by.

But meanwhile his younger brother had already dashed on a considerable distance.

After it had gone past, it took off running again.

≈≈≈

But as for the old man,

"Which way do you suppose that guy runs in through?" the old man was muttering.

And sure enough, at that he came running into view.

"Bravo! Run fast, my nephew!
You're outrunning him.

"Run fast, my brother.
He has killed your older brother.
Fling him headlong, my brother!

"Run fast, my nephew.
You're outrunning him.

"Fling him headlong, my brother!
Fling him headlong."

And they arrived there on the run.

"WHUMP! WHUMP!"

"Phew! Phew! Phew!"

"Oh my!
Well, the younger brother IS quite a runner!

"What's going on?

"Don't think you didn't grieve me no end in killing my younger brother!"

And he said to the other one, "Why did you have to face hummingbirds in the ears!"

At some point he was aware of him quivering his arrows.

"Uh-oh.
Well, I DID egg my nephew on.

I always DID tell him to fast.
My nephew IS quite a runner.
That's the reason why I told him to fast."
And he opened the door.
"Say, that's terrific!
This will make a splendid tobacco bag for me, Nephew,
when there's a celebration.
You realize my tobacco bag would be a unique standout."
"Wouldn't you have said, 'I had a vision of the one I will have as my tobacco pouch.'
But BEFORE you clearly said, 'This time I had a vision of the one I will make a ceremonial feast with.'
You might now have made a slip of the tongue about yourself," he told him.
And he walked over and picked up a firebrand.
"Woe is me! My poor brothers!
Woe is me! He has now killed both my younger brothers.
"Yow-ow-ow-ow, Yow Ow-ow-ow, Yow Ow-ow-ow.
Woe is me! My poor brothers!"
He whooped four times,
and a joyful shout could be heard.
"They're in with that rascal on the killing of both my brothers.
"Woe is me! My poor brothers!"
He finished singeing the hair off it and brought it back.
"What the . . . ! I must have a toothache again."
"It's darned inconvenient for you to start having a toothache every time you're about to give a ceremonial feast.
Talk about bad timing!
I mean, here you had a vision that you would give a ceremonial feast."
He set to putting it in the pot.
"Why, now here this one's bones have clearly come loose in the boiling."
"Evidently, you could try to invite people to eat, now."
"Yes, I could."
"Now you must go outside and give the call.
Namely, you must say what you said before.
"Yow Ow-ow-ow, Yow Ow-ow-ow."
And he stepped out.
"You must say what you said before."
And he stepped back in.
"'It's US. You're invited to eat,' you must tell them."

And he went out again.

"'You are invited to eat,' you must tell them."

"You must say just what you said."

"Well, that's what you told me to say."

He shouted for real.

"You're invited to eat!"

The other people kept coming in.

After they took their seats, he began serving them.

And that old lady was again the one he served the head.

"All right, this time now this same thing is again what he prays to.

So this time now it will want to be fed.

It's exactly the same thing again we did before.

Again we must eat it bones and all.

As each of us finishes our plate we're supposed to sink into the ground," he told them.

"Pitch in!" he told them.

There was nothing but CHOMP, CHOMP, CHOMP, CHOMP, CHOMP, CHOMP, CHOMP, CHOMP.

One after the other they sank into the ground as they finished their plates.

Last of all the little old lady was wondering what to do with the head.

She had no teeth, you see.

But eventually she swallowed it whole.

"All right, here I go, I'm going to club this one to death," he said to her, as he stood there taking aim at her.

"You're definitely frightening the old lady."

She just barely sank into the ground in time.

≈≈≈

And then, after they had finished their doings, his uncle again lay down.

"Again you must hit me if I have a nightmare," he told him.

"Nephew, you must hit me with my rock."

"You must be keen to have a toothache again.

And also, I'm always hitting you too hard."

"No, it's okay to hit me."

At some point he saw he was having a nightmare.

And he said, "Apparently this guy has a fearfully hard head," and hit him as hard as he could.

THUNK!

"Yow Ow-ow, you hit me too hard, Nephew."

"Why, I just pushed it over there a little."
"All right, Nephew, I had a vision that I would have daughters-in-law living here.[10]
A bit beyond where you went after the others is a place where there are women.
So those are the ones you must go after."
"Sure, I'll go tomorrow."

≈≈≈

The next day he left.
And he went by where his older brother was.
"All right, little brother, now, they run really fast.
Try your hardest!
"Once you do outrun them, here's what they'll do:
Once you do the business with those women,
then you'll meet your ruin.
"Try your hardest!
"Myself, I did the business with Elder Sister.[11]
And consequently that's why this was done to me.
"And once, by some chance, you get through,
then what's there is the thing.
A stone-headed arrow with a cedar shaft is there.
And that's what you must use.
You must tell him, 'This is our arrow, the girls' and mine.'
And what he'll tell you is, 'Use this,' referring to HIS arrow.
Don't listen to him.
"He'll shoot at you twice.
And if he does that and misses you, then you will shoot.
And you must hurriedly set a fire under him while he's up in the air.
If you don't do that to him, however,
he'll get back in it.
You must take the firewood there on the run, hurriedly.
Only then will you kill him.
That's what you must do, little brother.
Try your hardest!

10. In the Meskwaki kinship system, a man applies the term *nesemya*, "my daughter-in-law," to the wife of a nephew.

11. "Elder Sister" is the translation of *mači·hkiwesi·hkwe·wa*, the name of a stock character in winter stories; translation as a common noun is also possible.

"And here's the thing: those women will press you hard to do the business with them.
But don't, little brother.
Believe what I'm telling you now."
The other finished speaking to him.
And he went on, then.
He went the same way he had gone the times before.

≈≈≈

When he got over there, here he saw there was a little dome-shaped winter lodge.
And he snuck up on it,
and peered in through a crack.
They were on opposite sides, making yarn belts.
"Well now, someone is peering in at us," said one.
And he took off running.
When he came rushing up to where his older brother was,
"Bravo, run fast, little brother!
You're definitely outrunning them.
"And, what kind of bodies are they coming with?
Well, there's my old shafting hole in the older one.[12]
So, what kind of bodies are they coming with?"
The women covered themselves with their hands.
And after they had gone by,
this time he said to them, "And what kind of rear ends are they going away with?"
They ran off atwist.
And then at some point he saw them take off again.
In a short time his younger brother was caught up to.
And when they caught up, they stopped running a bit.
"Oh, the woman is in love," thought Cut-Off.[13]

≈≈≈

Meanwhile, the old man had barricaded himself in the house.
And here they came, running out of the forest.

12. Here and later in the story "older one" translates *mači·hkiwesa*, taken as a common noun. Usually this is the name of the stock figure Elder Brother.

13. "Cut-Off" translates *ki·škesita*, literally "the one who is cut off." The elder brother's name appears here for the first time in the story.

"Bravo! Run fast, my nephew!
"Bravo, you two! Fling him headlong!
He HAS killed both our younger brothers, both your brothers.
Fling him headlong!"
WHUMP! WHUMP! WHUMP!
"Phew! Phew!" he heard someone say.
"Oh my! My nieces DO run fast.
They're definitely pretty good runners."
Suddenly he was aware that they were taking their clothes off.
"Uh-oh!
Actually, I always DID tell my nephew to fast.
Oh my! My nephew is definitely quite a runner," he said of him.
Now, that skin had an arrow hole in it,
and that's the hole he would rush in through.
And then the old man made gifts of bridal clothing,[14]
handing broadcloth blankets out the door.
After they had come in,
"All right, my nieces, four days.
"All right, my nephew, you must hit me if I have a nightmare.
"Four days, my nieces."
"Mercy on us, what in the world is he talking about?"
At some point he saw him rousing in his sleep,
and he hit him.
THUNK!
"Yow Ow-ow-ow!
"What gives, my nieces?"
"Well, what in the world is it that he keeps talking about?
That he would be putting us at the end of the line, apparently."
"I frankly don't believe you, my nieces.
I think you're fibbing me.
I'll start over in four days again.
This time for certain.
"All right, Nephew, if I rouse in my sleep,
you must hit me with my rock, Nephew."
—Say, I forgot, back when he slept with the other two the first time,
the man slept in the middle.

14. He would make the gifts as the uncle of the man, welcoming his daughters-in-law; a man's family traditionally made gifts of fancy clothing to his bride.

And the older one pressed him hard,
as she would wrap herself around him.

And her younger sister said to her, "Really now! You realize the one you're getting in with killed them both!"

I forgot that's what they did first.—

And then this time again they did the same thing, too.
And they paid no attention when the uncle roused in his sleep.

After four days, "Darn it all, try and hit him as hard as you can!"

"Well, obviously that's my practice.
I always hit him as hard as I can," he told them.

And he hit him as hard as he could.

"Yow Ow-ow-ow.

"I think you egged him on, my nieces."

"Really the only thing he did was kick it over there as we were occupying his attention," he was told.

"Listen, Nephew, I had a vision that we would try to shoot each other, Nephew.
We must try to do it right now," he said to him.

"Okay," he told him.

Right away he found himself being made to stand in place.

"Hold him firmly, my nieces," he told his nieces.

(Understand, he was being held by both arms.)

And after he was held,
he shot at him at a spot a little below his navel.

And as soon as he let the arrow fly,
he was pushed down,
and the uncle's shot missed him.

KSHEEOOO!
Its sound was heard going by.

≈≈≈

And Cut-Off,
"Ee! I wonder what happened to my poor brother.
Oh dear, I hope he gets to shoot," said Cut-Off.

"Now he'll be shot at one more time,
if, by some chance, the shot missed him."

≈≈≈

"All right, THIS time, my nieces.
You definitely pushed him down.

You're in with him, I think.
After all, this fellow killed both your brothers, my nieces.
Hold him firmly!"
"But, can't you see, he almost knocked us over," they answered him.
"Maybe we can NOT hold him."
"No, my nieces.
DO hold him," he told them.
"Now!"
And he took his stance.
"You must jump up in the air," the women told him.
As soon as the uncle's shot came off the bow,
they jerked him up in the air.
Now, this fellow shot a little below the height of his knees,
in order to hit him if he threw himself down again.
KSHEEOOO!
And he missed him.

≈ ≈ ≈

And again Cut-Off,
"Well now! The shot must have missed my brother.
And then, once he shoots, that'll be that," he said,
and he kept listening for the sound.

≈ ≈ ≈

And then again he said to them, "All right, my nieces."
And after taking his stance he told them, "You must push him down."
"All right, Nephew, here's our arrow, yours and mine."[15]
"Oh, well here's OUR arrow, THEIRS and mine.[16]
And this is what I will use."
"Gee, but with that you won't be able to shoot me,
if you were to use that one."
"Oh, well this is the one I'll use."

15. "Our arrow, yours and mine" translates *ki·pena·ni*, "our (inclusive) arrow," that is, "belonging to us, including you".

16. "OUR arrow, THEIRS and mine" translates *ni·pena·ni*, "our (exclusive) arrow," that is, "belonging to us, excluding you"; stressed pronouns are used in the translation to bring out the contrast between the inclusive and exclusive forms for "our arrow" that Meskwaki distinguishes with different inflectional prefixes.

"Down, my nieces.
For, if you go in with HIM, that'll be that.
Don't forget, he killed both your brothers."
The arrow was loosed at him.
KSHEEOOO!

≈≈≈

Cut-Off made his tree rock with his whooping.

≈≈≈

Meanwhile, the others made a large fire.
And after making a large fire, they could hear the sound of him getting closer.
Whereupon he landed in the middle of the blaze
and burned.
They burned him up.
After they burned him up, they left.
"We'll go camp over yonder where her husband is,
so they can talk together."

≈≈≈

And they arrived over where he was.
"Hey, I've brought you your wife,
so you can talk with each other and see each other."
And they built a house.
And after they built it, Elder Sister was told, "Well, this will be your spot.[17]
And you can see each other across the lodge, directly up through the smoke hole."
"Well now! That's excellent, little brother.
"That WAS how I was expecting you to get through, little brother.
All I've been thinking here is, 'If only he, by some chance, gets through.'
So now I'm really pleased that you got through
and overcame our uncle.
That's what pleases me.
And also that you brought me this old lady.
And, that's where she and I can talk together, at least."

≈≈≈

17. In a traditional lodge, every person or married couple (except the baby) had a permanent, delimited section along the wall for sitting, sleeping, and storing belongings.

And one fine day some time later on he asked him,
"By the way, big brother, where's your bottom half?"
"Gee, don't, little brother.
It's very dangerous.
Don't do it.
What do you care about it, that you would talk about it?"
"I DON'T.
It's really just so I'll know that I'm asking you.
But not to do anything with it."
"Well, it stays far off toward the sunrise.
Where its territory begins, right there human life ends.
When anyone smokes,
it immediately attacks them.
That's the nature of it.
Our uncle's arrow is the same thing.
That's its tooth.
It's very dangerous, little brother.
What do you care about it, that you would be talking about it?"
"Oh, I see. Actually, I was just asking you for the heck of it."

≈≈≈

And at some point they said to Elder Sister, "All right, we're going to gather Indian hemp to fix."

"By the way, where have our younger brother and sister gone to, Wife?"

"Well, they announced they were going to gather Indian hemp to fix," she told him.

"Look OU-UT! I'm 'onna *chop you* DOW-WN!"[18]

"Gee, don't, Wife.
I mean, as it is we're having pleasant conversations.
Understand, I won't LIVE if I fall down.
Anytime I ever fall, I will die for real."

"Well, I'm STILL going to chop you down!"

"Don't be cruel to me, Wife."

He was really hard pressed by her, to have her chop him down.

"Well, perhaps she really WILL chop me down sometime," he thought about his wife.

18. To be read in singsong as a mock threat, with pitch rising to the words in small caps, then falling on two notes.

When his younger brother came back,
"Little brother, could you SPEAK to your *sister-in-law.*[19]
She will deal me a cruel fate if she ever chops me down.
As it is now, we have pleasant conversations when we're talking.
I mean, it's not as if I have to live the life that the rest of you live.
And once I fall down, that very moment will be the end of my life, little brother.
So, it would be good if you spoke to your sister-in-law.
I think she's going to chop me down sometime.
You see, if we're left by ourselves, that's what she makes me worry about.
When we're at home by ourselves, she's always after me to chop me down."
"Listen now, that's right.
Never say things to him.
You might make him worse if you keep saying that to him.
Only be talking with him.
Don't say that," Elder Sister was told.
But these others gathered Indian hemp all day long, day after day.
They went off every day.
"Wife, by the way, where's our younger brother and sister?
What could they possibly want with always picking Indian hemp?
You must ask our brother and sister when they come back what they're going to do with it."
"Okay, I WILL ask them when they get back.
But you mean, YOU don't know what it's used for?
Women braid string with it in the winter.
That's some of the work they do.
So I guess that's probably why they're picking it."
When the others got back, "That other fellow up there wants to ask you what you're going to do with that stuff.
For that matter, I don't know what HIS concern with it would be," the woman was asked.
"Well, it'll be for me to be making string with this winter when there's no work for me to do,
and also to be passing the time when it's nasty weather.
Do you understand about it?"
"Yes, I understand about it.
Actually, I'm just asking for the heck of it.
It's nothing, little sister."

19. To be said in a pleading tone, with declining pitch.

≈≈≈

And there came a time, after they had finished a great deal of it,
two whole large bags of it,
and when they then left,
that, as time went by, his younger brother never came back.
Next day, "Where have our brother and sister gone, Wife?"
"What's supposed to be your concern with them,
that you're forever talking about them,
always the same old story about them?
They've gone to hunt for your bottom half, apparently."
"Oh no! My poor brother!
What was the use of him making it through all those dangers!
Now my little brother is going to die.
In fact, from this moment on we shall see neither our brother nor our sister again.
Oh no! The poor guy!
What was the use of my little brother making it through all that!"

≈≈≈

Meanwhile, those others could suddenly see bones lying around.
"Oh, here is probably as far as it comes," said the man.
And they set to stringing the Indian hemp along the ground to be in place.
And after they set it up, they smoked.
"Let the wind blow to the east," he said.
Sure enough, with that it came into view,
going, "CLACK! CLACK! CLACK!" as it came.
And they stood up.
And the creature[20] made a beeline for the point where that Indian hemp was strung from
and then immediately began devouring it.
And it ate and ate till its mouth was full.
The thing[21] ate and ate till its mouth was full.
And abruptly it stopped

20. "The creature" translates, not a Meskwaki noun, but a shift to animate gender. Up to this point the monster has been referred to with inanimate inflection, inanimate being the gender of *oši·kani*, "his hindquarters," but here it switches to animate gender for three lines.

21. "The thing" translates the shift back to inanimate gender. There is no noun in the Meskwaki.

—when here it couldn't get any more hemp in its mouth.[22]

And at that point they rushed at it.
And they knocked out its teeth using a hatchet.
They had killed it.
And they started back with those hindquarters, carrying them home on their shoulders.

≈≈≈

That night they got back to their house.
First thing the next morning, "My wife, have our younger brother and sister come back?"
asking her.

"Yes, they're right here."

"Golly, little brother, your sister-in-law was really scaring me with what she said.
She's not being nice by saying that to me all the time.
Whenever I ask her a question she always says things to me."

"My stars! Every time, as soon as they're gone,
every time, you ask about them.
Right away, every time, you say, 'Where have our brother and sister gone?'
So that accounts for what I keep saying to you."

"All right, go cut some small lodgepoles."

The others made a sweat lodge.
And he went after a sweat-lodge stone
and made a fire under it when he brought it back.

When he almost had the stone heated up all the way,
"All right, now chop him down," the other's wife was told.

"Hey! Here I CO-OME! I'm 'onna *chop you* DOW-WN!"

"Gee, don't!

"Gee, is she really chopping me down?

"Oh no, tell your sister-in-law not to!

"Oh no, tell your older sister not to!

"I will *not* SURVIVE if I fall down.

"You deal me a cruel fate.

22. Up to this point the monster, whether animate or inanimate, has been referred to with obviative forms, indicating that it is presented in the narrative as viewed by the human observers. Here, as indicated by the new paragraph in midsentence, it shifts to a proximate form, the equivalent of taking center stage or appearing in a cinematic close-up.

"Oh my! Now is when I die, apparently."
And he began to fall.

≈≈≈

And then his parts were set against each other.
And water was poured on the sweat-lodge rock for him,
and he moaned.

The second time, he was bouncing off the walls.
"Open this up for me!"[23]
And he also begged them with, "What was the use of you putting me back in good shape!"

Soon he fell silent.

—Oh, I forgot, the woman kept making attempts to open up the lodge for him and was repeatedly thrown aside.—

And when he fell silent, bitterly did Elder Sister weep.
For, of course, she was desperate to open the lodge for him.
But it was no use.
She was held fast,
and she was also admonished.
And yet she was insistent that she would open it up for him.
It came to where she was in a shoving match with her brother-in-law,
as he held her back.

After water was poured on for the fourth time, he fell silent.
"WAA-HAA! You've KILLED him!" said Elder Sister,
and she threw her blanket over her head,
and wept in the entranceway.

Suddenly the other's voice was heard: "Hey, come on, these things have all gone cold."
He handed him something to use as a breechclout.
"All right, so what's the matter with you?" the woman was asked.
"Go ahead and *open it* UP for him!"[24]
"You're missing your big chance to open it for him," Elder Sister was told.

She rushed forward and opened up the sweat lodge for him.
And here was this extremely handsome man.

23. "Open this up for me!" translates *pa·hkeniko*, literally "open or uncover me (you plural)"; the sweat lodge must be uncovered from the outside in order for the man to be able to get out.

24. To be said with a tone of mock impatience, the pitch rising to "UP," then dropping.

He immediately went tearing out
and took a leak.

And Elder Sister saw.

Now they had restored him to health.

That's the end.

Three Winter Stories

Introduction by Lucy G. Thomason

This introduction assumes that the reader has already read "Winter Stories," by Ives Goddard, in this volume.

Presented here are translations of three Meskwaki winter stories: "The One Whose Father Was the Sun," by Maggie Morgan; "Golden Hide," by Pearl Leaf; and "The One Whose Eye Was a Bear's Eye," by an unknown author. All three stories were written in the Meskwaki language for Truman Michelson of the Bureau of American Ethnology.

These stories are impossible to date precisely. However, both "Golden Hide" and "The One Whose Eye Was a Bear's Eye" were written on yellow foolscap. They must have been produced during Michelson's first few years of fieldwork. This is confirmed by the fact that Pearl Leaf had very little time to write for Michelson: she died in May 1913, within two years of Michelson's first visit to the Meskwaki Settlement, which began on July 1, 1911.

"The One Whose Father Was the Sun" was written on a school tablet and must postdate both "Golden Hide" and "The One Whose Eye Was a Bear's Eye." Most probably it was written in 1914, the year that Maggie Morgan wrote two other texts for Michelson.

All three authors have highly individual and highly expressive styles, and it is a great loss to posterity that we have only a few stories from their hands. Michelson's corpus contains only three texts by Maggie Morgan. It contains five texts wholly or partly by Pearl Leaf. It contains two texts by the unknown author (referred to as Anonymous 5), one of at least thirteen unidentified authors whose work appears in the corpus.

Maggie Morgan (*te·pasa·ke·hkwa*) was born in 1873 and died in 1921. Her name is of the Thunder clan. Pearl Leaf (*ma·ta·ši·hkwe·ha*) was born in 1893 and died in 1913. Her name is most likely of the War Chief lineage of the Fox clan.[1] We do not have a certain identification even of the sex of the unknown author, much less of this author's name, clan, or date of birth.

My translations follow the texts fairly closely. However, in many places, as an aid to English speakers who lack the proximate/obviative distinction of Meskwaki, I've added a noun phrase in the translation where none existed in the original. These are always marked by brackets.

Note: The following discussion gives away many of the plot devices of the three stories.

Manitous

The three stories contained in this chapter are all winter stories, sacred stories that, in accordance with a cross-continental ban, should be told only when snow is on the ground and the spirits are asleep. In "The One Whose Father Was the Sun," there is a conventional play on the fact that, for the spirits, summer and winter are the equivalent of the human day and night: spirits wake during the summer and sleep during the winter.[2]

It's a near-universal belief that time runs very differently for mortals and immortals. Many cultures have conventional tales involving cross talk and misunderstanding when words like "day" and "night" are used. Consider, for instance, the ancient Irish tale of the fairy mound at Newgrange, the Síd in Broga, which was leased by its original owner under the misimpression that "a day and a night" meant one round of the sun, rather than all eternity.[3] This story is clearly linked to the belief, which has persisted through the centuries, that humans who enter fairy mounds stay for a single night of dancing and reemerge bent and aghast into a world in which many years have passed.

The North American version of the belief that years pass like days underground is based straightforwardly on the observation that many spirits, unlike humans, hibernate for the winter. And since spirits, like humans, are likely to resent having their names bandied about too freely, it's safest and politest to tell stories about them only when they are asleep.

Spirits—to give them their Algonquian name, manitous—are much-mentioned in all three of the stories in this chapter. In Meskwaki tradition, a manitou can be either a spirit or a human with spirit powers. Humans with manitou powers can often take the form of an animal. In rare cases, and irreversibly, they can take the shape of a rock, a tree, or a star. Manitous proper usually appear as an animal, a rock, a tree, a star, or a sun, but can also take human shape.[4]

Pearl Leaf's story "Golden Hide" has examples both of humans temporarily taking animal shape and of a manitou passing for a human so successfully that not until the end of the story is he recognized for what he is.

Relations between Manitous and People

There is a very strong sense, made explicit in Pearl Leaf's story, that manitou powers ought to be used for the good of the community. The human manitous in "Golden Hide" turn into animals—an otter, a beaver, a swan, and a helldiver, respectively—in an attempt to save a kidnapped child on behalf of the whole village. And the thunderer manitou in "Golden Hide" turns into a human in order to kill a monster that has plagued the village and in order to feed the monster to his manitou kin.

The monster in question is itself a manitou. By perverting its powers to selfish and antisocial purposes, it makes itself outcast among both manitous and men. When its lake is destroyed, it seeks refuge with all the other underwater manitous in turn, only to be chased away as a child killer.

Pearl Leaf's story points up the enmity between the thunderers, eaglelike manitous that live in the sky, and the underwater manitous, snakelike manitous that live in lakes. Their antagonism is ancient, widespread, and widely renowned in North America. In Pearl Leaf's story, both the sky dwellers and the lake dwellers have fearsome qualities from the human point of view, but each is bound by its own web of social and moral laws, and each has ties to the human community. The water manitous repudiate one of their number who would kill human children, and the thunderers come when invited by the villagers to eat the carcass of the monster and leave the villagers the tallow in return.

A similar theme of reciprocal obligation between humans and manitous is at the core of the anonymous author's tale of "The One Whose Eye Was a Bear's Eye." The hero of this story spends his whole youth offering all his hunting trophies, with each day a new bow and arrows thrown in, to whatever manitous might want them. As a result, when he is killed in battle, the manitous join together to restore him to life. Those among them who—unthinkingly, rather than maliciously, in this case—transgress this sacred bond are severely reprimanded.

The main manitou character in "The One Whose Father Was the Sun" is actually half-human and half-manitou. In a motif familiar from stories from around the world, the hero's mother, who lives isolated from other humans, is impregnated by the sun one day while going about her daily chores.[5] In Meskwaki lore, the offspring of such unions, no matter how well or ill intentioned, inevitably pose a threat to human and manitou communities alike.[6] In Maggie Morgan's story, the Sun Child changes from a harmless infant in his mother's care to a dangerous adult raised by the rogue manitou who kidnaps him. In the end, after reverting to his mother's care and undergoing rigorous fasting and penance in the cause of rescuing his uncles, he becomes a harmless infant again.

In the Sun Child's intermediate state, the story hints, he's a monster who hunts and kills humans and manitous both. He comes close to killing his own mother. The manitou people who help his mother in her quest to find him are terrified of him and beg her to reconsider and go home. In two of the four places where she seeks counsel, her manitou helpers warn her that her son has iron rods projecting from his elbows. This motif is never further elaborated in Maggie Morgan's story, and her story is the only place in the Michelson corpus, so far as we now know, where it occurs. However, three groups with whom the Meskwakis were in fairly close contact in the recent historical period—the Ojibwes, the Iowas, and the Winnebagos—give a prominent place to monsters that have awls or knives projecting from their elbows. In Iowa tradition, the Sharp Elbows are the monsters that kill the hero brothers' mother. In the Meskwaki tradition, the hero brothers' mother is killed by cannibal giants. In both cases it's clear that her death is accomplished by monsters that are completely inimical to humankind.

The moral of human and manitou dealings in this story, like the moral of human and manitou dealings in Pearl Leaf's story "Golden Hide," seems to be that everyone suffers when there are individuals wandering around who are not safely embedded in a dense web of social connections among their own kind. The offspring of human and manitou connections are perhaps dangerous exactly because they have a foot in two worlds, with resultant confusion in their morals and their loyalties. The same confusion is evident in manitous or humans who are isolated, willingly or not, from their communities. Golden Hide, in Pearl Leaf's story, lives alone in its lake with a pet dog; it tries to expand its family by stealing a human baby, but has such an unnatural absence of affection for its adopted child that it kills it rather than let it be rescued. The woman in Maggie Morgan's story, bereft by her brothers' deaths and left alone in the wilderness, is exposed to her strange conjunction with the sun. Her sons, kidnapped by Toad Woman and raised on deceits and dark magic,[7] are exposed to the worst lawlessness of their own nature. Only after the woman's brothers are restored to their home can the entire family resume normal, healthy relations. The scene at the very end of "The Ice Maidens," in the preceding chapter—a scene that occurs in one form or another in many Meskwaki winter stories—has a similar theme: the sister lives an unnatural and danger-fraught life until her brother comes home with his bride and his son, and it's not when her brother first arrives and speaks to her but when she first takes hold of her nephew that things begin to revert to normal. There is now a true community in her home, a web of interdependence that involves more than just two people.

Relations between Kin

All three of the stories in this chapter place a great emphasis on familial love, and especially on love in the shape of a favorable judgment made by the village, the tribe, the larger community. "The One Whose Father Was the Sun" concludes with the statements that the Sun Child's uncles love him dearly (the Meskwaki verb stem is *tepa·n*, "love, cherish, prize"), and that his brother the dog is loved too. The introduction to "Golden Hide" places tremendous emphasis on the fact that the baby is loved by the entire village (again, verb stem *tepa·n*) and near its close observes that Spotted Shins has gone from being generally despised to being generally admired (*tepa·n* again), now that he has shown that he is a stalwart member of the community. The main point of "The One Whose Eye Was a Bear's Eye" is that the Meskwaki and his sacred pack come to be highly valued by the Kickapoos. The summing-up of this story gives greater prominence to the fact that the pack is now prized (stem *tepa·ta·te·*, a derivative of *tepa·t*, which is the inanimate-object version of *tepa·n*) than it does to the fact that the Kickapoo mother's son has been brought back to life.

In all these stories, devotion to family members is very strong. The brothers in "The One Whose Father Was the Sun" and "The One Whose Eye Was a Bear's Eye" risk their lives to save each other; the sister in "The One Whose Father Was the Sun" fasts hard to find her brothers and risks her life to regain her sons; her sons undergo the most rigorous fasting imaginable to find their uncles and succeed where their mother failed. The villagers whose baby dies in "Golden Hide" are devastated. So are the Kickapoo mother and son when the younger son dies in "The One Whose Eye Was a Bear's Eye." The elder brother in this story even stops eating or speaking or moving at all until his brother is brought back to life.

The most interesting case is that of the Sun Child and his would-be mother. Upon witnessing two proofs that Toad Woman is not his real mother—actually trading on her affection for him in order to establish the fact—he instantly transfers his devotion and allegiance to his real mother and turns on Toad Woman and kills her with all her brood.

People who act selfishly in these stories are never rewarded. Toad Woman, Hill Owner, and Golden Hide all come to bad ends. The good characters, by contrast, agonize about making decisions that will affect their relatives. So, the Sun Child's mother presents her case to him as a series of tests that will prove the truth of what she says, and the Meskwaki hero of "The One Whose Eye Was a Bear's Eye" presents his marriage proposal obliquely, as an arrangement that would greatly benefit his stepsons. His wife-to-be frets silently about whether or not she should marry, until her sons notice that something is wrong and coax a confession from her.[8]

Outsiders in general have to earn the respect of the community. Both Spotted Shins among the Meskwakis and the Meskwaki man among the Kickapoos must prove their loyalty and worth. Spotted Shins, in "Golden Hide," retains his primary loyalty to the world of the thunderers, and eventually returns to his native land. The case of the hero of "The One Whose Eye Was a Bear's Eye" has to be handled much more delicately by its author, in order to mitigate an apparently intolerable conflict of loyalties. Although the hero of this story will never be Kickapoo himself, he has clearly chosen to live with the Kickapoos for good. The only way this can be made at all acceptable, as a moral conclusion to a Meskwaki story, is for his Meskwaki family not be mentioned at all (a bare obviative pronoun followed by a bare indefinite pronoun is used to mark whichever relative it was who made him his bows and his arrows when he was a boy) and for the Meskwaki community to have wronged him in some profound but unspecified way. The interest is then in how he attaches himself to his new family.

Structure of the Texts

"The One Whose Eye Was a Bear's Eye" has no major plot elements in common with any other story attested in the Michelson corpus—not the blessing by all the animals, not the reassembly from various animal parts, not the sacred pack that by itself unassisted can restore life, not the defection to the Kickapoo country, not the proposal to wed the widow and her sons. The motif of mismatched eyes (one from a bear and one from a cougar) is widely attested elsewhere in North America but is not developed in the anonymous author's story. The story is composed of two basic parts: the events that lead to the creation of the pack, and the events that lead to its first use and first renown. Each part has at its core a death in battle followed by an unlooked-for resurrection.

Pearl Leaf's "Golden Hide" has several partial cognates in the Michelson corpus. The closest is "Bareshins," by Anonymous 6, which has a version of the baby's theft and attempted rescue and a version of Bareshins' (Spotted Shins') destruction of the monster responsible, but which entirely lacks the thunderer subplot. Alfred Kiyana's "Lazybones" has Lazybones (Spotted Shins) kill a lake monster but lacks both the baby's theft and rescue and the thunderer subplots. Jack Bullard's "Meshwakaha," or "The One with the Arrowshot Hole," has a version of the story of the baby's theft and rescue but springs off from there into an entirely different tale.

The thunderer subplot changes Pearl Leaf's version of this story considerably. It adds an extra episode, describing the disposal of the monster, to the basic two-part division into a story about the baby's theft and the abortive attempts to rescue it, culminating in an eleventh-hour "rescue" that results in the baby's death, and a story about the monster's flight and the abortive attempts to kill it, culminating in an eleventh-hour attack that results in the monster's death. It also gives a kind of explanation for Spotted Shins' peculiar conduct. As a thunderer, he is bound to behave differently than an ordinary human being and is also the mortal enemy of monsters of Golden Hide's ilk. The three independent parts of Pearl Leaf's story are thus knit together in a highly satisfying way. This is a good example of the kind of modular storytelling described in the introduction to "Winter Stories" in this volume.

Maggie Morgan's "The One Whose Father Was the Sun" is also an example of modular storytelling—the stitching-together of subplots that elsewhere combine with still different subplots or else stand on their own. Maggie Morgan's story parts are not merely strung end to end but are combined together in such a way as to form an interrelated and interreferring whole. Maggie Morgan's story-within-a-story, which could stand on its own, describes how a lone woman in the wilderness conceives by the sun, loses her two children, and subsequently regains them. The first half of the framing story describes how ten brothers set out few by few—two, then three, then four, then one—and are killed one after the other by an ogre who later hangs them in his larder. The second half of the framing story describes how the Sun Child fasts in order to find out what's become of his uncles, then kills the ogre who killed them, and then restores his uncles to life.

The framing story in "The One Whose Father Was the Sun" is composed of two main components, which elsewhere occur separately: Hill Owner, in which the hero is challenged to a contest by a man who meets him on the brow of a hill, and the Ogre's Larder, in which the hero kills an ogre (male or female) who keeps a larder of human meat, afterward resurrecting the ogre's victims.

Hill Owner can stand by itself. It usually involves (nonfatal) foot-racing contests, as in the first part of "The Ice Maidens," in the preceding chapter. The Ogre's Larder can be grafted onto various stories but often occurs in combination with a plot in which ten or more men go seeking wives at the same time (as in "The Ice Maidens," in which, however, the larder theme does *not* occur). Maggie Morgan, in "The One Whose Father Was the Sun," blends these three motifs into a single story and combines them with the story of the Sun Child. The Sun Child has two partial cognates elsewhere in Michelson's corpus: Alfred Kiyana's "The Man Whose Father Was the Sun, and His Older Brother a Dog" and Jack Bullard's "The One Whose Father Was the Sun." These have considerable overlap with Maggie Morgan's story-within-a-story, but entirely lack the Ten Brothers, Hill Owner, and Ogre's Larder frame. No three of these four themes—Sun Child, Ten Brothers, Hill Owner, and Ogre's Larder—occur together anywhere else in Michelson's corpus.

Maggie Morgan's story, like the anonymous author's and Pearl Leaf's, consists of two basic parts with a similar structure at their core: the first part treats the woman's loss of her brothers and their ultimate restoration to life, and the second part treats the woman's loss of her sons and their ultimate restoration to their nonmonstrous selves.

In the anonymous author's and Pearl Leaf's stories, the two hinged halves of the story are consecutive. In Maggie Morgan's story they are nested.

Maggie Morgan's and Pearl Leaf's stories are made up of largely familiar themes with a few elsewhere unrepeated details (such as the sharp elbows in "The One Whose Father Was the Sun" and the metal manitou in "Golden Hide"). The anonymous author's story is made of largely unfamiliar themes with a few elsewhere repeated details (such as the manner in which the mother broaches the subject of her proposed marriage to her sons). All three authors manage to compose the different parts of their stories into a self-contained whole, and to achieve a similar moral climate that promotes loyal and loving family ties, respectful performance of extrafamilial obligations, implacable punishment of transgressions against blood kin, placable punishment of transgressions against extrafamilial friends, and submergence of the individual good in the good of the larger family.

Notes

1. The genealogical list in BAE Bulletin 125 gives Pearl Leaf's clan affiliation as "War Chief (?)." She probably belonged to the War Chief lineage of the Fox clan, the lineage of her adoptive father.
2. See the description of the boy's and dog's fast toward the end of "The One Whose Father Was the Sun."
3. See pp. 134–35 of John Koch and John Carey's *Celtic Heroic Age* for Carey's translation of De Gabáil in t-Sída, "The Taking of the Hollow Hill," from the Book of Leinster.
4. The manitou in Pearl Leaf's "Golden Hide" is made of metal, which counts as a rock in Meskwaki taxonomy. In Meskwaki the verb stem fragment meaning "metal" and the verb stem fragment meaning "stone" are one and the same.
5. Motif T521, "impregnation from sunlight," in Stith Thompson's index in *Tales of the North American Indians*. Compare "Stone Child," by Anonymous 6, in which the father is a spirit rock, and Alfred Kiyana's "When Wisahkeha Killed the Cannibal Giant," in which the father is a spirit tree.
6. For a translation of "When Wisahkeha Killed the Cannibal Giant" and a fascinating analysis of the role the cannibal giant plays in Meskwaki cosmology, see Ives Goddard, "Two Winter Stories," in *Voices from Four Directions: Contemporary Translations of the Native Literatures of North America*. The giant is both a benefactor of the human race and a great danger to continued human existence. Consider also the case of Furry in Patches, from the Red Leggings story cycle, who is a terror both to his bear kin and to his human kin; and the case of Stone Child,

whose innocent but deadly idea of fun destroys all the animal children; and the case of the Apayashis, the Meskwaki hero brothers, whose depredations among the manitous culminate with nearly killing the sun, and dueling with the Culture Hero, and causing the Great Manitou considerable distress.

7. See an Ojibwe partial cognate of this story, story 51 in Jones's *Ojibwa Texts*: "Old-Toad-Woman steals a Child." In this story, the boy is wholly human rather than half-manitou, and he has two dogs, which are pets, rather than one dog brother. Old-Toad-Woman raises him overnight from an infant to an adult by feeding him her urine.
8. This is a common motif in Meskwaki winter stories. More typically it involves a young man who hesitates to tell his sister or his father that he wants to seek a wife.

References and Suggested Reading

Anonymous 5. "The One Whose Eye Was a Bear's Eye." National Anthropological Archives, Truman Michelson ms. 2794.21.

Anonymous 6. "Bareshins." National Anthropological Archives, Truman Michelson MS 2794.13.

———. "Stone Child." National Anthropological Archives, Truman Michelson ms. 2794.35.

Bullard, Jack. "Meshwakaha." National Anthropological Archives, Truman Michelson MS 2794.1.

———. "The One Whose Father Was the Sun." National Anthropological Archives, Truman Michelson MS 2123.1.

Callender, Charles. "Fox." In *Handbook of North American Indians*, vol. 15, *Northeast*, edited by Bruce G. Trigger, 636–47. Washington DC: Smithsonian Institution, 1978.

———. "Kickapoo." In *Handbook of North American Indians*, vol. 15, *Northeast*, edited by Bruce G. Trigger, 656–67. Washington DC: Smithsonian Institution, 1978.

———. "Sauk." In *Handbook of North American Indians*, vol. 15, *Northeast*, edited by Bruce G. Trigger, 648–55. Washington DC: Smithsonian Institution, 1978.

Dahlstrom, Amy. "Narrative Structure of a Fox Text." In *Studies in Honour of H. C. Wolfart*, edited by John D. Nichols and Arden C. Ogg, Algonquian and Iroquoian Linguistics Memoir 13, 113–61. Winnipeg: University of Manitoba, 1996.

Goddard, Ives. "Aspects of the Topic Structure of Fox Narratives: Proximate Shifts and the Use of Overt and Inflectional NPs." *International Journal of American Linguistics* 56 (1990): 317–40.

———. "The Obviative in Fox Narrative Discourse." In *Papers of the Fifteenth Algonquian Conference*, edited by William Cowan, 273–296. Ottawa: Carleton University, 1984.

———. "Some Literary Devices in the Writings of Alfred Kiyana." In *Papers of the Twenty-first Algonquian Conference*, edited by William Cowan, 159–71. Ottawa: Carleton University, 1990.

———. 2004. "Two Winter Stories." In *Voices from Four Directions: Contemporary Translations of the Native Literatures of North America*, edited by Brian Swann, 423–67. Lincoln: University of Nebraska Press, 2004.

———. "Writing and Reading Mesquakie (Fox)". In *Papers of the Thirty-second Algonquian Conference*, edited by John D. Nichols, 164–230. Winnipeg: University of Manitoba, 1996.

Jones, William. *Ethnography of the Fox Indians*. Edited by Margaret W. Fisher. Bureau of American Ethnology Bulletin 125. Washington DC: Smithsonian Institution, 1939.

———. *Fox Texts*. Publications of the American Ethnological Society 1. Leiden: E. J. Brill, 1907.

———. *Ojibwa Texts*. Edited by Truman Michelson. 2 vols. Publications of the American Ethnological Society 7. Leiden: E. J. Brill, 1917–19.

Kiyana, Alfred. "Lazybones." National Anthropological Archives, Truman Michelson MS 2984.3.

———. "The Man Whose Father Was the Sun, and His Older Brother a Dog." National Anthropological Archives, Truman Michelson MS 2653.

———. "When Wisahkeha Killed the Cannibal Giant." National Anthropological Archives, Truman Michelson MS 2688.

Koch, John, with John Carey, eds. *The Celtic Heroic Age: Literary Sources for Ancient Celtic Europe and Early Ireland and Wales*. Malden MA: Celtic Studies Publications, 1955.

Leaf, Pearl. "Golden Hide." National Anthropological Archives, Truman Michelson MS 2024D.1.

Morgan, Maggie. "The One Whose Father Was the Sun." National Anthropological Archives, Truman Michelson MS 2790.

"The One Whose Eye Was a Bear's Eye." National Anthropological Archives, Truman Michelson MS 2794.21.

Radin, Paul. *Winnebago Hero Cycles*. International Journal of American Linguistics Memoir 1. Baltimore: Waverly Press, 1948.

Shapochiwa. "Elm Tree Owner." National Anthropological Archives, Truman Michelson MS 2664.8.

Skinner, Alanson. 1925. "Traditions of the Iowa Indians." *Journal of American Folklore* 38 (150) (1925): 425–506.

Thomason, Lucy. "The Assignment of Proximate and Obviative in Informal Fox Narrative." In *Papers of the Twenty-sixth Algonquian Conference*, edited by David Pentland, 462–96. Winnipeg: University of Manitoba, 1995.

———. "The proximate and obviative contrast in Meskwaki." Ph.D. diss., University of Texas at Austin, 2003.

Thompson, Stith. *Tales of the North American Indians.* Cambridge: Harvard University Press, 1929.

Trigger, Bruce G. *Northeast.* Vol. 15 of *Handbook of North American Indians.* Washington DC: Smithsonian Institution, 1978.

THE ONE WHOSE FATHER WAS THE SUN

By Maggie Morgan
Translated by Lucy G. Thomason

Well now, they say ten men were living somewhere.
They had a single sister.
At some point it seems it snowed a little, at night.
When they woke up in the morning, one of them went outside.
Why, here he saw the tracks of a ceremonial runner[1] going by.
He had left tracks in the new snow right at their door.
"Hey, wake up!" he said to his brothers, they say.
"A game animal has gone past leaving tracks!" he said.
And they all woke up.

≈≈≈

And then the oldest brother said, "We two must follow it."
The next oldest went with him.
They belted on their clothes, getting all decked out in crow skins,
and went trailing the game.
They kept cresting the tops of the hills,
the entire day long.

≈≈≈

1. Maggie Morgan unmistakably wrote ".a cka be wa ni." = *aška·pe·wani*, "ceremonial runner," a young man with special ritual functions, rather than ".a ya be wa ni." = *aya·pe·wani*, "buck." "Buck" would seemingly make much more sense here: three lines later, the man who saw the tracks of the "ceremonial runner" informs his brothers that a large game animal has left tracks in the snow. This oddity is compounded by another: a little later in the text, the two brothers who set off in pursuit of the large game animal inform Hill Owner that they are tracking some people who came by tracking game. Since later sets of brothers are actually tracking people (their brothers) who set off tracking game, it's possible that Maggie Morgan has simply made two small mistakes, writing "cka" for "ya" in the first case and skipping ahead of herself in the second. However, I have let the textual oddities stand.

At some point, as evening was coming on, they ran out into the open at the top of a steep hill.
Why, here came a man walking toward them.
"Oh, are you going somewhere, boys?" he said to them.
"Oh, we're following the tracks of some people who just went by.
They came past trailing game yesterday," they told him.
He was all decked out, decked out in a crow skin.
He was holding a flat-faced war club, and a knobbed war club too.
"Oh, they probably caught up with it someplace," he told them.
"And then dusk overtook them wherever it was that they caught up with it.
They probably slept there," he told them.
"Oh, off with you then, boys," he told them.
"Or night might overtake you," he told them.
As they turned around, they were struck on the nape of the neck with the knobbed war club,
and were hauled away right then and there.
Their snowshoes were set up on the cliff,
set upright facing back the way they had come.

≈≈≈

Back at home, that night, their brothers said,
"They must be barely able to move beneath their load of game."
The youngest sat up until morning.
And in the morning, the next three [brothers] prepared to set out.
"Now, make certain you return today!" [the youngest] told his older brothers.

≈≈≈

And they set out.
They tracked them all day long.
As evening was coming on over there,
they said, "All right, one more time, let's run to the top of the next hill!"
When they ran out into view, why, there were two people standing over [on the next hill],
and they shouted out to them.
"Hey, what's the matter with you?" they asked them.
"You've been off trailing game for quite some time now, you know!" they said to them.
And they ran down the hill.

≈≈≈

When they got to the top of the next hill, why, here came a man walking toward them.

"My, what a noise you're making as you go, boys!" he said to them.
It was that same man as before.

"We're calling to the two men standing over yonder," they told him.
"They've been tracking game for quite some time now," they told him.

"Oh, off with you then, boys, go on!
Or dusk might overtake you," he told them.

As soon as they turned around, they were struck with a knobbed war club.
They were knocked on the head, one after the other,
and hauled away.

When they were carried to that same spot, their snowshoes were fixed in position,
and they were set upright in a group of five.
They never came back.

≈≈≈

Back at home, the youngest brother [sat up] until morning again.

In the morning, again, "Why, what can have happened to them?" he said.

"Well, it's your turn," he told [his remaining brothers].
"The four of you should go," he told them.

"But you must make certain you return today," he told them.
"It might be that someone has been killing them," he told them.

"Do your very best!" he told them.

≈≈≈

And they set out, four of them, this time.
[They kept on] for more or less the whole day.

In the evening, they said, "All right, for the last time, let's run to the top of that next hill!"

When they ran out into view, why, there stood [their brothers] over [on the next hill],
standing in a group of five.

"Hey, you'd better start back!
What could be the matter with you, that you didn't come home right away?" they asked them.
And they broke into a run.

≈≈≈

When they ran out into view, why, here came a man walking toward them.
"My, what a noise you're making as you go!" he said to them.
"Yes.
We're calling to those men standing in a row over yonder, calling them to come here," they told him.
"They made haste following tracks to this place, the tracks of some game animals that went by recently," they told him.
"I see," he said to them.
"Why, they must have killed them," he told them.
"They must be toiling beneath their load of game," he told them.
"Jeez, off with you then, boys.
Or dusk might overtake you," he told them.
As they turned around, they were knocked on the head, one after the other, and were hauled away right then and there.

≈≈≈

Back at home, night came again.
"Well, it's pretty certain that someone has been killing them," [the youngest brother] said to his sister.
"Well, it's my turn tomorrow," he said to his sister.
"Well, but if I see anyone, I'll attack him," he said.
[Next day] he set out, heading the way they had gone.

≈≈≈

(Now, they all dressed the very same way.
For his part, he was carrying a knobbed war club and a flat-faced war club.
He was outfitted exactly the same way [the others] had been outfitted, in fact.)

≈≈≈

That evening, when he ran out into view,
why, there they stood, standing in a group of nine.
"Why, you're standing there without a care in the world!" he said to them.
And he shouted to them.
"Get a move on, and come home right away!" he said to them.
And he broke into a run.

≈≈≈

As he was going, why, suddenly here came a man.
"My, what a noise you're making as you go!" he said to him.
"My, what a noise you're making as you go!" he replied to him.
"Oh, you're really in a temper," he said to him.
"Oh, you're really in a temper," he replied to him.
And he said to him, "Those men standing in a row over yonder came this way in a big hurry trailing game."
"Hm, they must be toiling beneath their load of game," [the man] told him.
"Well, off with you then, boy," he told him.
"You must be in a big hurry now," he said to him.
As he turned around, he was knocked on the head,
and he was slung across the man's back.

≈≈≈

Back at home, where their sister was, night came again.
And then morning came again.
"Why, it must be that someone has been killing them," she thought.
And by golly, she started fasting.[2]
(Now, their house was a longhouse.
The quivers were hanging up, hanging directly above each of her brothers' spots in the house.
And so happens they really had a lot of meat.)
The woman stayed around there, fasting.
Eventually she ate part of their food.
Gradually there was less and less of it.
And at some point she ate it all.
And then she just dug up potatoes all day long, day after day.

≈≈≈

One time she was digging potatoes in a ravine.
(They say it was completely still and quiet, by the way.)
Suddenly the wind blew and blew her skirt up.
It blew her rear end naked as she was standing there.
She began to have a strange sensation as she was standing there.
She went home right away, they say, and stayed around the house.
At some point she realized she was pregnant.

2. She's fasting in the hope of finding out from the manitous what's become of her brothers, and how she may help them.

And at some point she gave birth.
She gave birth to a baby boy and a puppy together.
And she continued to stay around the house.
Gradually [the boy] got bigger and bigger.
And gradually the puppy got bigger.

≈ ≈ ≈

At some point, "I'm going to fetch some firewood," she told him.
"You must rock your younger brother," she told the puppy.
And she tied a rope to the baby swing.
The puppy rocked the swing.
He ran back and forth from the one side of the house to the other, gripping the rope in his mouth.
[The baby]'s cradleboard was decorated with wampum beads.

≈ ≈ ≈

Meanwhile, Toad Woman[3] peeped in from the far end of the lodge.
Why, there she saw someone running around unattended, rocking a swing.
She went on in and started taking down the cradle baby.

≈ ≈ ≈

The baby's older brother yelped.
He barked his head off at her when [his brother] was taken away,
and he bit her,
snapping off the tip of her underbelly.
Toad Woman left a trail of blood as she went off.
The dog went yelping after her, a little behind.
It was toward the east that his younger brother was taken.

≈ ≈ ≈

Meanwhile, when their mother got home,
what should it be but her children were gone!
She cried out and fell into fits of wailing, there in her house.
After some time had passed, she stopped crying and looked around.
Why, she saw something there.
A bit of raw flesh was lying on the ground,

3. Toad Woman is a stock wicked character in Meskwaki winter stories.

and it looked like it had bumps on it.[4]
She stopped crying and started making moccasins.

≈≈≈

When she was done making them, when she was done making her moccasins,
she started tracking where the trail of blood led.
She went due east.
And she got a long way off in the course of one day,
keeping on until shortly after dark.

≈≈≈

Late at night, she looked about for a place to sleep.
At some point she saw a hut, and she peeped inside.
"Hey, come on in, Granddaughter!" [someone] said to her.
"You're acting like you're up to no good," she said to her.
It was Manoneh whose house she had come to.[5]
And she cooked for her.
She merely stuck her hand into the dark space against the wall and dipped up water.
When she was done cooking for her, she asked her, "You're walking around for some reason?"
"Yes," she answered her.
"My son has been stolen from me," she said.
"I suspect that the one who stole him from me was a toad," she told her.
"He has a pet puppy," she told her grandmother.
"I don't have any knowledge of him, Granddaughter," her grandmother told her.
"But the ones who live over yonder, your grandmother and your granddad, must know about him," she told her.
"You should go straight to them," she told her.

≈≈≈

First thing in the morning she gathered firewood for her.
After gathering firewood for her, she set out.
She went due east.

4. Toad skin.
5. Manoneh is a stock benevolent character in Meskwaki winter stories.

≈≈≈

Sometime that evening she again looked about for a place to sleep.
At some point there was another hut with smoke coming out of it,
and she went in.
"Goodness, it's my granddaughter!" they said about her.
They were seated on opposite sides of the lodge.
She sat down at the far end of the lodge,
and [her grandmother] cooked for her.
She merely stuck her hand into the dark space against the wall and dipped up water.
When she had eaten, her grandmother asked her, "Is there some reason that you're walking around?"
"Yes," she answered her.
"I've lost my son.
He has a pet dog," she told her.
"I see," [her grandmother] said to her.
"I suspect that the one who stole him from me was a toad," she told her.
"We don't have any knowledge of him," [her grandmother] said to her.
(But she was just saying that to her.
She really did know about him.)
In the meantime, she was told, "Your grandmother will fill you in.
You should go straight to her tomorrow," she was told.

≈≈≈

First thing in the morning she gathered firewood for them.
After gathering firewood for them, she set out.

≈≈≈

At some point it was evening where she was again.
Late in the evening, she looked for a place to sleep.
At some point there was another hut with smoke coming out of it,
and she peeped in.
"Come in, Granddaughter!" she said to her.
"You're acting like you're up to no good," she said to her.
She was warming her back at the fire.
She went in and sat down at the other side of the lodge,
and [her grandmother] cooked for her.
She did exactly as had been done before.

She merely stuck her hand into the dark space against the wall and dipped up water.

When she had eaten, her grandmother asked her, "Are you going around walking about for some reason?"

"Yes," she answered her.

"I've lost my son," she told her.

"He has a pet puppy," she told her.

"Goodness, Granddaughter, it would be much too much if that guy was your son!" she said to her.

"'He's really dangerous,' is what is said about that boy," she told her.

"'He has an iron rod attached to his elbow,' is what is said about that boy," her grandmother told her.

"No, Grandmother, it sounds as if it IS my son," she told her.

"The ones who live over yonder, your grandmother and your granddad, really know about him," she said to her.

"They're the ones who will fill you in," she said to her.

≈≈≈

First thing in the morning she gathered firewood for her.

After gathering firewood for her, she set out.

She went east.

She went east every time.

≈≈≈

At some point dusk overtook her again, and she looked about for a place to sleep.

Why, here was a hut with smoke coming out of it,

and she went in.

They were warming their backs at the fire on opposite sides of the lodge.

"Goodness, it's my granddaughter!" her grandmother said.

And she cooked for her.

She did as had been done before.

When she was done cooking for her, she asked her, "You're walking around for some reason?"

"Yes," she told her.

"I'm tracking my son," she told her.

"He's been stolen from me," she told her.

"Goodness, Granddaughter, it would be much too much if that guy was your son!

He's really dangerous," she said to her.

"No, Grandmother, it sounds as if it IS my son," she told her.

"He's really dangerous," she said to her.

"All right, Granddaughter, here's what you must do.
At the time when you're going to milk your breasts, you must make little birch-bark bowls, two of them," her grandmother told her.

"But he's really dangerous," was said to her.

"And then, whichever side you nursed him on is the side where you must set it down," was said to her.

"And you must climb a white pine tree, the tallest one there is," her grandmother told her.

"He's really dangerous.
He has iron rods attached to his elbows," she was told.

"But see, he's my son," she said.

≈≈≈

Next day she set out.
When she got there, she milked her breasts.
She put [the bowls] on the left side, where the dog would drink.
The left side is where she suckled the dog.
After putting them there, she climbed the tallest tree.

≈≈≈

At some point, at noon, he came running,
the dog came running back and forth on top of the water.
At some point he ran right toward her.

"Twa, twa, twa, twa, twa, twa!" the boy said to him.
And the dog got bigger and bigger.

"Hey, my son!
It's ME, my son!" the woman said to him.

"Twa, twa, twa!" he was told.
He grew as tall as the very top of the tree.

"It's ME, my son!" she told him.

At some point the dog paid attention to what she was saying.
He lunged at the milk, and it tasted good.

And then the boy tried it, in turn, and liked it.

"Come on, climb down!" he told their mother.

≈≈≈

After the woman climbed down, she related to her children what had befallen her.
"Well, my son, you were both stolen from me," she told him.
"A sign you may know it by is that your cradleboard is decorated with wampum beads," she told him.
"So here's what you must do.
You must pretend to be sick.
'Only after I've seen my cradleboard will I get well,' you must say to her.
'And also, only when you jump across me,' that's what you must say to her," she told him.
"She must have a scar," she told her children.[6]

≈≈≈

The dog was really happy.
And they went home.
Lo and behold, the dog went off running back and forth on top of the water.
The dog arrived first, butting in ahead at a run, so happy he was.

≈≈≈

When he got there, he rushed in, and Toad Woman hit him.
"This guy threw away my son!" she said about him.[7]
The dog yelped.
"Ow, ow, ow, ow, ow!" he said.

≈≈≈

Meanwhile, the boy heard his dog being made to cry out,
and he went on in.
"Ow, ow, ow!" he said.
"He was really badly injured.
You've hurt my dog!" he said.
"Ow, ow, ow, ow."
Toad Woman couldn't think what to do with him.

6. A scar from where the dog snapped at her underbelly. Toad Woman, though a toad woman, wears skirts. Some authors play around quite a bit with the animal-or-human ambiguity of anthropomorphized manitous and monsters, but Maggie Morgan, in this text, takes for granted the juxtaposition of entirely toadlike qualities with entirely humanlike qualities.

7. The Meskwaki verb stem *pakin* has a wide range of meanings: drop on purpose, throw away, throw down, divorce, disown, release by ceremonial adoption. Toad Woman is accusing the dog of negligence for coming home without his master.

"Ow, ow, ow, ow!
If I saw my cradleboard I would get well.
Ow, ow, ow," he said.
"Here it is!" he was told, about an awful cradleboard.
"Ow, ow, ow!
I don't think so," he said.
"Or I would be well, wouldn't I," he said.
After a while it was taken out and shown to him.
But it was no good.
He was still sick.
"Ow, ow, ow!
Why not jump across me, Mother?" he said to Toad Woman.
"Mother, you don't hate me, do you?" he said to her.
"Ow, ow, ow."
"Well, why don't I," the old lady said.
And she jumped across him.
"Ow, ow, ow, ow!
Another way, now!" he told her.
At some point, in a flash, she flew above his eyes.
Why, sure enough, she had a scar.
He sprang to his feet.
"Damn these vermin!" he said about them.
And he clubbed them all to death.
And by golly, they were toads.

≈≈≈

And they went home.
When they got to where their mother was,
"Well, my son," she said to him,
"Don't do anything bad to the people we're going to be visiting," she told her son.
And they set out.
That evening they got to their grandmother's place.
The old woman was afraid of him.
With a distinct lack of enthusiasm, "Goodness, Granddaughter, you've brought your son," she said to her.
"But I went to get him, after all!" she told her grandmother.
Still and all, the old woman was afraid of him.
In the morning, after they ate,

"Well, Granddaughter, when do you want to get there?" she asked her.
"Tomorrow," she told her grandmother.

≈≈≈

A moccasin patch was shriveled in the fire for them, and they set out.[8]
At noon they reached the third set of people she had visited,
and they went inside their house.
The old people shrank back.
"He won't do anything bad to you," she told them.

≈≈≈

In the morning, after she gathered firewood for [her grandparents], they set out.
That evening they arrived over at their house.
And they just stayed around there.

≈≈≈

At some point the boy was sitting around there,
looking at the quivers that hung all in a row.
"Hey, who do these belong to?" he wondered as he sat there.
At some point, "Hey, Mother, who do these belong to?" he asked her.
And she cried out.
"Ow, ow, ow, my brothers!" said his mother.
She was weeping.
And he sat there the whole time with his head bowed.
After considerable time had passed, his mother stopped crying.
"That's how many uncles you used to have," his mother told him.
"I see," he told her.
"Soon I'm going to try to find out about my uncles," he told his mother.
"I'll do a four-day fast," he said.
And he lay down, along with his dog.

≈≈≈

8. This is a stock motif in winter stories. It's sympathetic magic. People with special powers can put a piece of leather (patch, sinew, rawhide strip) into the fire, and as the leather contracts, so does the beneficiaries' journey. In the Ojibwe story "Old-Toad-Woman steals a Child," it's actually Toad Woman who shrinks her journey by shrinking her leather skirt.

(Now, when he said, "I'll do a four-day fast,"
four years at a time is what he meant, when he was going to do a four-day fast.)[9]

≈≈≈

And he fasted.
They rolled over in midwinter.
And when it was midsummer again, at the end of four years, he woke up.
Then, "Mother, I've learned about my uncles," he told his mother.
"All right, first let's have a meal," he said.
And before doing anything else they looked for something to eat.

≈≈≈

At some point, near a small hill, "All right, here's a fat one!" he told his dog.
"Twa, twa, twa!
Roust it out!" he told his dog.
And a great big bear was tossed out for him.
After [his dog] rousted it out, he carried it home on his back.[10]
When he got there with his load, he singed the hair off.
When he was done singeing the hair off, he put it in the pot to boil.
When he was done cooking, he forked it out onto willow sticks, half for himself and half for his dog.

≈≈≈

"Well, Mother, cover up!" he told her.
"I'm going to have my meal first," he told her.
The woman covered up, and her son shouted.
After shouting four times, he ate his meal in no time.
There was even a whizzing sound as the bones went flying.
"Done!" he said.[11]

≈≈≈

9. This is a recurring motif in Meskwaki stories. Manitous, when they speak of days, mean years.

10. This motif appears in other stories. Ordinary mortals can't carry bears on their backs.

11. The covering-up of bystanders, the four shouts, the whizzing bones, and the rapidly disappearing large game animal make up a stock motif that is usually associated with thunderers' meals. In Shapochiwa's story of Elm Tree Owner, when the hero peeks, he sees the thunderers eating so fast that the bones are shooting out of both sides of their mouths. Afterward, they explain that they call bears "squirrels."

"Now it's your turn," he told his dog.
"Wait a while longer," he told his mother.
And then the dog had his meal, in turn.
They say that he was even faster.
They say that the bones even embedded themselves in a tree.
"Done!" [the boy] told his mother.

≈≈≈

"Okay, I'll set about going to see my uncles," he told his mother.
"All right, you must keep an eye on this," he told her, referring to a shell.
And he put water in it.
"If I'm in any kind of a fix, the sign you will know it by is that the water will quiver," he told his mother.
"And if something bad happens to me, [the shell] will turn upside down," he told his mother.
And he set out.
He walked around here and there, going just anywhere.

≈≈≈

At some point, as evening was coming on, he worked up his dog.
"Twa, twa, twa, twa!" he said to him.
And [the dog] shook himself.
"Twa, twa, twa, twa!" he said to him.
At some point a hound came yelping toward them.
It was also fairly big, they say.
At some point they met.
Speaking together, they said to each other, "Oh, how you're having your dog come crying!"
They kept on uttering the same words at the same time whenever they said anything.
Eventually the owner of the hound got angry.
"Oh, are you really challenging me for real?" the owner of the hound declared.
"Are you challenging me to wrestle with you?" he asked.
"I don't wrestle," [the boy] told him.
"No?
Well, are you challenging me, then?" he asked him.
"No, I'm not," he told him.
"Well, to fight, then?" he told him.
"Oh yes," he answered him.

"Perhaps our dogs (should go) first," he said to him.
And he worked up his dog.
"Twa, twa, twa, twa!" he said to him.
And he grew to the height of a tree.
"All right, why not be that big!" he told his dog.
Oh, and as for the owner of the hound,
[his pet] was considerably smaller.
And they went for each other.
They fought for a long time.
They say that the hound kept being made to squeal.
They fought all over under the earth.
At some point, "Twa, twa, twa!
Come on, kill him!" he told his dog.
And the hound was killed.
And then they went for each other, in turn.
At some point the boy grew angry, and he made [the man] roar again and again.
They fought all over on the earth's surface, and also up in the sky, and under the earth.

≈≈≈

Back at home, the woman was keeping an eye on the shell.
At some point the water in it quivered.
Then she really kept a close watch on it.
"My son is in a hard-fought match!" she thought.

≈≈≈

At some point, "Get ready, I'm going to throw him now," he told his dog.
"You must attack him," he told his dog.
And he threw him.
The dog made a pounce.
And by golly, they killed him.

≈≈≈

After he'd rested, he headed for the [man]'s house.
When he got there,
why, good gracious, there were serious numbers of people hanging head downward.
Some of them looked very fresh.
"Oh my!" he thought.

Some of them looked ancient.
"Well, I'll work a cure on them," he thought.
He looked for certain special reeds,
and found some, and began to pick them.
He carried a great bundle of them on his back.

≈≈≈

When he got back there, he started laying them out in a row.
After laying all the reeds out, he crumbled them into powder.
After laying them all out, he set them on fire.
"Hey there, we're under attack!" he said to [the people].[12]
And they sprang to their feet one by one.
"Hello!" they said.
"Oho, so that's it, you're men, it seems!" he said to them.
As it turns out, the ones who spoke like men were his uncles.

≈≈≈

Then he said to them, "Well, help me!"
And they helped him.
They gathered reeds for a second try and brought them back on their backs.
And then they crumbled them again.
And then they set them on fire again.
"Hey there, we're under attack!" he said to [the people].
And a good several more sprang to their feet.
"Oho," he said to them.
"So that's it, you're men, it seems!" he said to them.
"It looks as if you didn't get your revenge," he said to them.

≈≈≈

Some of the bones had done nothing more than fly together.[13]
When he set [the reeds] on fire for the fourth time, they all came back to life.
"All right," he told them, after he had brought them all back to life,
"Now you can depart for the places you came from!" he told them.

≈≈≈

12. The idea is that the combined threat of fire and war should shock the ogre's victims back to life.

13. These are the ogre's earliest victims.

For his part, he headed home then.

And they say that some of them, the ones that had been killed a very long time ago, didn't know where to go.

But for his part, he headed home then, and many men followed after him. As it turns out, they were his uncles.

And they all arrived back at the house.

And then he changed all the way back to his former tiny size, they say.[14]

And then his uncles really doted on him. He was passed around the whole house, being held by one after the other.

And his dog was doted on, too.

So the story is told of him. "The sun is his father," is what's generally said about him. That's more or less what I've heard. That's all.

14. He turns back into a baby.

GOLDEN HIDE

By Pearl Leaf
Translated by Lucy G. Thomason

What happened to the Meskwakis long ago.[1]
Well now, some people had a village.
And a certain married couple had a little child.
They had only one child, a baby that was still in a cradleboard.
And they were the only ones that had a baby.
None of the others had children.
And they doted on that baby.
Everyone doted on it.
That baby was adored.
Women kept going to fetch that cradle baby,
doting on it.

≈≈≈

Then at some point the mother of the child went to do her washing.
She did her washing on a sand bar over at the water's edge.
And she put the baby a little ways off.
And then she went to hang her laundry on top of the bank.
When she got back, she didn't see the cradle baby, her child.
"They must have fetched it away," she said,
"The women," she said.
She wasn't frightened.
She went on doing her washing without thinking twice about it.

≈≈≈

After some time had passed, she went home.
When she got there, "Who fetched it home?" she said,
she asked.
At some point she told the people, "I've lost it!"

1. The title of this story was written not by Pearl Leaf, but by Sam Peters, her coauthor for the fourth story in the tablet.

"No one brought it back," she was told.
Only then did she realize that she had lost it,
and only then did she get frightened.
"That must be it, someone has seized it from me!" she said.

≈≈≈

And then the people were called to assembly.
They assembled at the chief's lodge,
and they held council about what they could do to get that [baby] back.
At some point one man filled up his pipe
and went along offering a smoke to the people who were holding council.
No one accepted his pipe.
He knocked the ashes out of it and filled it up again.
And again he started walking, going around and offering them a smoke.
After a long time, one man accepted it.
When he got back to his starting place, he knocked the ashes out of his pipe
and filled it up again.
And again he started walking, offering a smoke.
After another long time, one man accepted it.
When he got back to his starting place, he knocked the ashes out of his pipe
and started filling it up again.
And again he started walking, offering a smoke.
Someone accepted it again.
Then he was finished,
the requisite number, four, having accepted that pipe of his.[2]
There was now the right number of men to fetch back that child.
"Now, this is why I accepted it," one man said.
"Because of what I was blessed to do when I fasted," he said.[3]
"I'll act like an otter," he said.
And one said, "As for me, this:
I'll act like a beaver," he said.
And one said, "And I, a swan."
And one said, "And I, a helldiver."[4]

2. One of the four has been omitted in the telling.

3. The four volunteers are all manitous—humans with spirit powers. They must have fasted when they were young in order to get these powers. See the discussion of manitous in the introduction to this chapter.

4. A country term for the pied-billed grebe.

"All right then, hurry!" they were told.
And they set out.

≈≈≈

The entire village headed for the place at the water's edge where [the baby] had been lost.
The mother of the child showed the way.
And then the helldiver went into the water with a splash.
A very short time later he came back out.
"It's no good," he said.
And next the beaver went into the water with a splash.
When he got to midstream, he couldn't go under the water,
and he came back.
"It's no good," he said.
And next the swan set out, diving under the water.
When he got close to that place,
—I forgot: he was tagging along with the otter.
The swan was swimming a little behind.—
The otter told the swan, "All right, turn back!"
The swan just barely made it back.
"Alas!" he said.
"It's no good," he said.
"But HE kept right on," he said,
"The otter," he said.
"He told me, 'Turn back!'" he said.

≈≈≈

That route they took was like a road.
But it was water racing along.

≈≈≈

When the otter got close,
they say he succeeded in reaching that place.
When he got there, he peeped in at Golden Hide, the one that had stolen the baby from before from them.[5]
Why, there was the one he had come to fetch lying propped against a wall.
[The manitou] also had a pet dog.

5. An actual manitou, a water monster made of metal.

And they say it was black.
It was a chicken dog that it had for a pet.
They say that that dog promptly caught sight of him as he was peeping in.
He peeped in only a little bit.
But still it saw him, they say.

≈≈≈

And then he went inside,
and he saw that Golden Hide's house was of very thin stone.
He selected a place where he struck it,
and that whole stone house broke into pieces.
Before doing anything else, [the manitou] punched a hole in the baby's head.
Then the otter tipped over its bowl.
There must have been water in it.
And that was why there was a lake there.
That was the end of it.
After he tipped [the bowl] over, the lake dried up.

≈≈≈

And then the dog rushed out ahead of [its master].
And then Golden Hide crawled out, the evil manitou.
Then all the people from before came running,
and they struck at it over and over again as it made off.[6]

≈≈≈

And there was a certain man who had an eccentric nature.
"Hey, you're not bestirring yourself at all!" was said to him.
As if nothing out of the way were happening, he was just warming his shins at the fire,
and his shins were spotted from the heat.
Taking his time about it, he was working up to a full battle rage.
"They didn't summon me in any great hurry, you know," he said.
"Well, hurry up!" he was told.
"Dammit!" he said.
"They're in a terrible fix.
It's nearly gotten away from them," he was told.

6. Golden Hide's name literally means "made of yellow metal." Their weapons are bouncing off its hide.

"Dammit, you just won't lay off me!" he said.

Taking his time about it, he went and hacked off a basswood bough.
He hacked it off, and shaped it with his axe, and made a war club of it.
He took his time curing it in the fire.

"Hey, hurry up!" he was told.

"Nearly done," he would answer.

≈≈≈

In the meantime, over in the other place, they were striking it with axes again and again,
without being able to kill it.

≈≈≈

Then he went out, and he took off at a run,[7]
making for that Golden Hide.
When it had almost reached another lake,
when it was up to its waist in the water,
that man struck at it.

Now, he had never worked a day in his life.
And he had never fasted.
He was widely disliked.
But as it happens, he was a manitou.

—Hey, I forgot: he chopped that [evil manitou] in two,
chopping it in two right at the waist.—

And then he took its hindquarters to the village.

Now, the underground manitous hated that [evil manitou].
It went around visiting those manitous one after the other,
but they kept on driving it away.

And then it managed to get inside a stand of cattail reeds.

Now, that child had died.
Golden Hide had killed it.

—Hey, I forgot, those manitous told him, "Go away!

7. The passage that follows is riddled with artistic use of overlay. For a discussion of this device, see the introduction to "Winter Stories" in this volume. The chronological sequence here is: the baby dies; Golden Hide seeks refuge with all the other underground and underwater manitous; they drive it away as a child killer; it crawls inside a bed of reeds; Spotted Shins catches it as it is about to enter the water, and cuts it in two; he takes the bottom half back to the village.

Or else you might ruin my children," the manitous told that Golden Hide.—
It had been cut in half, and it was all bloody.

≈≈≈

And over in the other place those people, the villagers, held council again.
"All right, fortify your houses!" the women were told.[8]
—Hey, I forgot: that man who had killed Golden Hide now was doted on, for a change,
and he no longer was hated.—
And then they finished fortifying their houses.
And then they began carving the hindquarters, Golden Hide's hindquarters, into pieces.
They got a fire going, making a long bank of coals,
and they hung a kettle over it.
And they put that [manitou] into a big wooden bowl after they carved up its hindquarters.
And then they put it into the pot piece by piece,
and they held a clan feast.
And some of the people asked for the tallow.
"Wait!" they were told.
"Let's see what those who will eat this [manitou] will do," those who asked for [the tallow] were told.
"If they want to give it to us, the sign you will know it by, obviously, is that they won't eat it," they were told.
And then it was finished cooking.
"All right!" the attendants were told,
"Take it out!" they were told.
And they served it out into big wooden bowls.
Four bowls full is how much of that evil manitou there was.
And then they put the oil into a tiny wooden bowl,
one of those attendants did.

≈≈≈

And then that one man made a speech,
inviting the thunderers to eat that [evil manitou].[9]

8. A strong wind is coming.

9. Thunderers are storm spirits. They are winged manitous, somewhat like eagles, but much

And then the thunderers arrived.
Terrible-looking weather rolled in,
and the wind blew,
and the sky turned very green.
The sky even came turning over and over, as the wind blew.
And then when the wind ceased to blow, the attendants went out.
Why, there was nothing there but bones scattered around.[10]
They had eaten up that Golden Hide, it seems.
And the oil hadn't been eaten.
Then and only then was it given to those who had asked for it.
That's what befell one group of people long ago.
—Hey, I forgot: that man who had killed Golden Hide was not until then known to be a manitou.
That man with his shins all spotted from the heat was a thunderer, it seems.—[11]
Then he went back up to the sky.
"Or else I might eventually cause some damage," he said.[12]
That's the end of the story about those people of long ago.

---

more terrifying. They are the mortal enemies of water manitous and often hunt them and eat them.

10. This is the thunderers' meal motif again. Compare the boy's and dog's meal toward the end of "The One Whose Father Was the Sun."

11. This explains why Spotted Shins has manitou powers, even though he never fasted. He's a real manitou, a thunderer, in human shape. As a thunderer, he's a fit nemesis for the evil water manitou.

12. Thunderers are closely associated with storms.

THE ONE WHOSE EYE WAS A BEAR'S EYE

By an Unknown Author (Anonymous 5)
Translated by Lucy G. Thomason

And then long ago [someone] made a bow and arrows for a certain Meskwaki boy.[1]
Whenever he killed anything, any birds, that boy put them in a certain place, along with his bow,
leaving them as food for pretty much any kind of manitou.
He put his bow there, too, and the arrows as well.

He did the exact same thing every time.
And every time, new bows and arrows were made for him.[2]
Still, whenever he killed anything, that boy put it in that same place.

Then later, after he was grown, after he had started killing deer,
each time he killed a deer, he would put it in a lonely place, in that very same way, they say,
along with his clothing, and his bow and arrows besides.
They say that Meskwaki boy did that exact same thing every time.

≈≈≈

Then at some point there was a going-out of war parties, they say.
And he went along.
Then he was killed over there.

And he never lost his awareness.
He had his senses the whole time.
But his body was incapable of movement.

At some point after the fighting ended, eagles and crows began to alight,

1. This story is missing an introduction. It begins in midstream, as if tacked on to the end of a different story. An unidentified relative of the boy's, here referred to only with an obviative pronoun, has made a bow and arrows for him.

2. Some still-unspecified relative of the boy's, here referred to only with an indefinite pronoun, keeps making new bows and arrows for him.

and began to eat the slain.[3]

And he never lost his awareness.

Creatures of every description ate of them, raccoons, skunks, wolves,
and all kinds of animals, in fact.

Then at some point, when they had started on our hero, right after his eyes had been pecked out,
someone arrived,
after his eyes had already been eaten.

"Hey!" the animals who were eating him were told.
"It seems you didn't know," those animals who were eating them were told.

And then, they say, the chiefs of the animals who eat people were summoned:
the chief of the wolves, and the chief of the bears, and the chief of the skunks, and the chief of the raccoons, and the chief of the eagles.
The chiefs of all the different animals were summoned, in fact.

"Hey!" they were told.

And he never lost his awareness.
Also he understood everything that they said when they spoke to each other.

"It seems you didn't know," the animals who were eating him were told.
"For this is the one who, when he was still a boy, used to please us by making offerings to us," was said.

"Now then, let's cure him!" those animals were told.
"We must all help him to come back to life," those animals were told.
And every one of them consented.

"Each of you must tell the way in which you'll help him," was said.

"For my part, I'll give him my eye," said Bear.

"That is to say, just one of them.
Or why not, here's what I'll do:
why don't I give him both," said Bear.

"So be it!" he was told.

"Oh, me too," said Cougar.
"I too will give him one of my eyes," said Cougar.
"But one of my eyes I'll keep," said Cougar.

"Oh, your turn now, the rest of you.

3. The passage that follows is rife with artistic use of repetition and overlay. For a discussion of these devices, see the introduction to "Winter Stories" in this volume. The chronological sequence here is: animals come to eat the dead; a latecomer scolds them for eating their benefactor; the chiefs of each kind of animal are summoned; the chiefs restore the hero.

Speak up!" the others were told.
"Oh, I'm in," one of them said.
"If someone helps me, I'll raise him up," he said.
"Hold on!" he was told.
"Better do that after someone gives him some hair," he was told.
"Give him some, one of you!"
(He had been scalped, by the way.)
"Oh, I'll do it," said Buffalo.
"So be it!" he was told.
Then the one who'd said, "If someone helped me, I would raise him up" was told, "All right, time to raise him up!"
And it was Wolf who raised him up, with Golden Eagle helping.[4]
And then he was brought back to life.
"All right, time to instruct him!" was said.
He was really and truly brought back to life.
And they began telling him how each of them had blessed him.
He was given some medicine, and he made a sacred pack.[5]
"Even if someone has died, he will come back to life if you treat him with this medicine," he was told.
And he went back home to where the Meskwakis were.

≈≈≈

Then at some point he got in a rage.
It seems that the Meskwakis said something that greatly incensed him.
Then he went away,
and he went to stay in the Kickapoo country,[6] together with his sacred pack.[7]
He stayed on and on in that place, for a very long time.

4. Other Meskwaki stories also suggest that wolves and foxes have a special power to resurrect the dead.

5. Sacred packs are made when a manitou (in this case, manitous) bestows a blessing consisting of detailed instructions regarding the pack's composition and use.

6. The Meskwakis and the Kickapoos are closely related. Their languages are more than mutually intelligible: Meskwaki, Sauk, and Kickapoo are considered dialects of the same language. See Callender's articles in vol. 15 of *Handbook of North American Indians*, pp. 636–67, for a brief history and ethnography of the Meskwaki, Sauk, and Kickapoo peoples.

7. Sacred packs are great treasures. A pack of such power as this one can avert catastrophe for individuals or for the entire community. It's a disaster to lose one. The Meskwakis' loss, in this case, is the Kickapoos' gain.

≈≈≈

At some point he became fond of a woman who was a widow released from strict mourning.[8]
She had two boys.
—That is, they were young men, rather.—
Then at some point he addressed that woman.
"I want to marry you.
And I'm fond of your sons," he told her.
"They could be cured at least once by my sacred pack," he told her.
And she rebuked him sharply.

≈≈≈

At some point that woman thought seriously about what he had said.
She would lie reflecting on it.
Some time later, that woman's sons noticed something different about her.
"What's the matter?" they asked her.
"Perhaps you've thought of something bad.
At some point you began to behave differently," she was told.
"Not so!" she said.
"If it's that you've thought of something bad,
or if someone has said something bad to you,
tell us!" her sons said to her.
So then she told her sons.
"It was a Meskwaki, and he said to me, 'I'm fond of your sons,'" that Kickapoo woman said.
"'I thought to myself, "If they had a sacred pack, I believe they would take good care of it,"' that Meskwaki said," she told her sons.
"Good Lord, you can't have turned him down!" she was told.

≈≈≈

Some time later, that Meskwaki pressed his suit with her again.
He was accepted,
and he married that Kickapoo woman.
Then those young men gave real clan feasts every so often.[9]

8. Kickapoos, like Meskwakis, traditionally observe four years of strict mourning after widow(er)hood.

9. Since they now have a sacred pack, they can hold real clan feasts.

≈≈≈

At some point, a while later, the Kickapoos went on the warpath.
And those young men went along.
At some point, over there in a faraway place,
some Sioux had recently gone by, it seems,[10]
moving camp as they went, it seems.
There were marks where the poles had been dragged,
with horses dragging them along.
[The war party] immediately went off someplace, it seems, to some place close by.
And those two young brothers were sent to have a look at where [the Sioux] had camped,
and they started tracking them.

≈≈≈

Now, at the time when those Sioux camped over there in some faraway place,
"All right, go back and keep a watch on the route we came by!" was said.
And they kept a watch on the way they had come when they moved camp.

≈≈≈

Now, sure enough, the Sioux saw two people come walking toward them,
and they hid themselves.

≈≈≈

The boys, meanwhile, [thought they had] crept up unobserved on a man whose head was showing.
"Pretend you don't see him!" they exhorted each other.
Very slowly they went to turn back.

≈≈≈

As soon as they turned around, [the Sioux] charged at them,
and they broke into a run.

≈≈≈

The elder brother stopped to wait for his younger brother.[11]

10. The Woodland Sioux are the traditional enemies of the Meskwakis, but *not* of the Kickapoos.

11. The gap between this sentence and the sentences that precede and follow it is a little

(Now, they were carrying that sacred pack.)
At some point his younger brother was all but overtaken.
At the very instant that an axe blow was leveled at his younger brother,
he decided there was nothing for it but to go back for him.
When he looked back, a head was being thrust out at him.
It was his younger brother's head.

≈ ≈ ≈

And then he really fled all out.
He went straight home.
When he got there, he threw himself facedown at the far end of the lodge.
(Now, he always wore that sacred pack across his shoulder.)

≈ ≈ ≈

The woman, meanwhile, when her Meskwaki husband got home, hit him on the shin.
"'It will cure them at least once,' is what you said before about that sacred pack of yours!"
"I DIDN'T tell you, 'You must hit me on the shin,'" the Meskwaki told his wife.

≈ ≈ ≈

He immediately summoned the attendants
and gave a clan feast.
Then the next night he slept.
And the night after that he gave another clan feast.
After he gave the second clan feast,
the next night he gave yet another clan feast.
After he gave the third clan feast,
the next night he gave yet another clan feast.
After he gave the fourth clan feast,
early the next day, in walked the boy who had been killed.

≈ ≈ ≈

---

unexpected from the perspective of canonical English narrative. This passage involves lots of overlay again. The chronological sequence here is: the brothers run for their lives; the younger brother is nearly overtaken; the elder brother notices that his brother has fallen behind; the younger brother is actually overtaken and killed; the elder brother turns around just in time to see his brother's severed head.

Now, the elder brother had been lying in the same position for four nights.
At the time when his younger brother came in, then and only then did he get up.
And also at that time the elder brother ate a meal, they say.

So then the one who had been killed came back to life.

So then that sacred pack was prized, they say.
That pack must have remained there in the Kickapoo country.

And this story is the truth about what that man did long ago.
It's a real story of very long ago.
Before the white man came is the time of this tale.

But that's all that's said about this particular Meskwaki.
And he doesn't have a name.
The person who told the story didn't know what he was called.
He's the one whose eye was a bear's eye, and who was given a cougar's eye, and who was given a buffalo's hair.
After he died, he came back to life.

The Origin of the Spirit Rock

Introduction by Marianne Milligan

This version of the Spirit Rock story was told by Charles Dutchman (Naehcīwetok) to Leonard Bloomfield in 1920 or 1921 and was originally published in both Menominee and English in his 1928 *Menomini Texts*.[1] Bloomfield stayed for several weeks with Dutchman and his wife, Louise, who lived on the Menominee Reservation located in northeastern Wisconsin. In the preface to the texts, he states that they "were my chief informants and became my close and parental friends" (xi). He goes on to say that Naehcīwetok was "a man of abounding vitality and humor, yet given to philosophic speculation" (xi).

Versions of this story can be found in several collections of Menominee tales. Bloomfield's texts include two versions of the story. The one that Bloomfield titles "The Origin of Spirit Rock" (I will refer to this version as B1) is significantly shorter than the one presented here, titled "The Origin of Spirit Rock: Second Version" (B2). A version of the story with the title "The Search for Maeqnapos" is found in Walter Hoffman's *The Menomini Indians*.[2] In addition, there are two versions in Alanson Skinner and John V. Satterlee's *Folklore of the Menomini Indians*, titled "The Men Who Visited Maeqnapos" (SS1) and "The Legend of Spirit Rock" (SS2).[3] The story of Spirit Rock is a story that is still told by elders and is often taught in schools on the reservation.[4]

The main plot of the story involves a group of young men who go to visit Maeqnapos, the culture hero. SS2 differs slightly in that it is Maeqnapos's brother whom they visit. In all the versions except one, they go because Maeqnapos comes to one of the young men in a dream or a vision and asks the young man to visit him and bring along some friends. If they come, Maeqnapos promises to give them whatever they ask for. In SS1 the young men ask that Maeqnapos renew the power of the medicines that he had given human beings long ago since the medicines had lost their potency. In the Hoffman version and B1, they ask for hunting medicine. In B2 and SS2, the young men ask for different things: to be a good hunter, to be a fast runner, to learn the power of medicines, to be a war leader, and to be attractive to women. In each version, the last young man (or last two in SS1) asks to live forever. Maeqnapos changes this last one into a rock, called a Spirit Rock, since it is the only thing he knows that will last as long as the earth.

In SS1 as well as B2, kettles of food and tobacco magically appear in Maeqnapos's house while the young men are there. The young men and Maeqnapos eat and drink their fill and then smoke the tobacco. The narrator in SS1 says that the offerings made by members of the Medicine Lodge appear in Maeqnapos's house. In B2, the narrator simply says that any offering made on earth by human beings comes to Maeqnapos's house.

All the versions begin and end in much the same way except SS2. It begins with the statement that there is a Spirit Rock on the reservation and no one "passes it without depositing an offering of tobacco" (487).[5] The narrator then gives three explanations for the existence of this Spirit Rock. First, he says that when the Menominee first came to their reservation, one of the chiefs noticed that when he passed a certain rock at night, it made noises as if haunted by a spirit. This rock was identified as the Spirit Rock. The second explanation is that there once was a man who was tired of his mortal existence even though he was a good hunter. He discovered that he could live forever if he became a rock, and he did. The third, which the narrator identifies as the most widely accepted explanation, is the story of the men who go to visit Maeqnapos.

One thing to note while reading the story is that Maeqnapos is the nephew of human beings. Therefore, he usually addresses people as his aunts and uncles, and people usually address him as their nephew. However, "aunt" and "uncle" are also used as general terms of address to someone older, and "niece" and "nephew" are used for anyone younger. In this story, Maeqnapos is older than the young men, and three times one of the young men calls him "uncle" and twice Maeqnapos calls one of them "nephew."

As mentioned, Bloomfield published the texts in both Menominee and English. However, he made some changes to the stories when he published them. This can be seen by comparing the Menominee version found in his original field notes, housed in the National Anthropological Archives at the Smithsonian Institution, to the texts. For the retranslation of this story, I have used the version found in his field notes.

Traditional storytelling is an oral art form. Bloomfield and his contemporaries translated these stories into prose as was the norm at the time. However, I have retranslated this story using ethnopoetic methods, which attempt to capture the oral quality of the original by treating the text like poetry rather than prose.[6] The organization of the text into lines, stanzas, scenes, and acts is based on both linguistic elements and meaning. For example, each line of the translation roughly corresponds to a clause in Menominee (I have left a relative clause that is the subject or object of another clause on the same line), and the lines are usually grouped into stanzas based on meaning. One of the linguistic elements that provide important clues to the internal structure of the text is initial particles, such as *eneq*, "it was then/there/that," and *nahāw*, "well, then." In this text, Naehcīwetok often places a noun before the initial particle, which places emphasis on that noun. I have, therefore, given such nouns a separate line to indicate that the syntax of the original is different and also to capture the focus in the English translation. Although it is impossible to recreate the experience of hearing a story in person, I hope that this translation captures some of the feel of the original.

Notes

1. I would like to thank Monica Macaulay and Ives Goddard for their help and comments and the tribe for giving me permission to do this work. This material is based on work supported by the National Science Foundation under grant no. 0132926, and by grants from the Endangered Language Fund, the Smithsonian Institution, and the Graduate School of the University of Wisconsin-Madison.
2. Note that Hoffman uses the spelling Mä·näbūs for the Culture Hero, Maeqnapos.
3. Note that Skinner and Satterlee use the spelling Mänäbus for the culture hero, Maeqnapos.
4. Menominee is an extremely endangered language with only thirty to forty fluent speakers left. The tribe is actively working to revitalize the language and passed a tribal ordinance in 1996 that mandates the teaching of Menominee in all schools on the reservation as well as the development of a curriculum. Classes in Menominee are taught in all the schools on the reservation, including Head Start, the public schools (K–12), the tribal schools (K–8), the College of the Menominee Nation, and NAES (Native American Educational Services) College. The tribe's Language and Culture Commission also offers free classes for community members, and there have been several mentor-trainee immersion programs.
5. The practice of leaving an offering of tobacco at the Spirit Rock is still observed by the Menominee.
6. Hymes, "Discovering Oral Performance and Measured Verse in American Indian Narrative"; Hymes, "Particle, Pause and Pattern in American Indian Narrative Verse"; Hymes, "Some Subtleties of Measured Verse."

References and Suggested Reading

Bloomfield, Leonard. 1928. *Menomini Texts*. Publications of the American Ethnological Society 12. New York: G. E. Stechert.

Bright, William. 1984. "A Karok Myth in 'Measured Verse': The Translation of a Performance." In *American Indian Linguistics and Literature*, 91–100. New York: Mouton.

Hoffman, Walter J. 1896. *The Menomini Indians*. Bureau of American Ethnology Annual Report 14, 1–328. Washington DC: GPO.

Hymes, Dell. 1976. "Louis Simpson's 'The Deserted Boy.'" *Poetics* 5:119–55.

———. 1977. "Discovering Oral Performance and Measured Verse in American Indian Narrative." *New Literary History* 8:431–57.

———. 1980. "Particle, Pause and Pattern in American Indian Narrative Verse." *American Indian Culture and Research Journal* 4(4): 7–51.

———. 1985. "Some Subtleties of Measured Verse." In *Proceedings of the Fifteenth Spring Conference of the Niagara Linguistics Society*, 13–57. Buffalo NY: Niagara Linguistics Society.

Keesing, Felix Maxwell. 1939. *The Menomini Indians of Wisconsin: A Study of Three Centuries of Cultural Contact and Change*. Philadelphia: American Philosophical Society.

Skinner, Alanson B., and John V. Satterlee. 1915. *Folklore of the Menomini Indians*. American Museum of Natural History Anthropological Papers 13, no. 3. New York: Trustees. Also cited as Anthropological Papers of the American Museum of Natural History 23:217–546.

THE ORIGIN OF THE SPIRIT ROCK

Told by Charles Dutchman (Naehcīwetok)
Translated by Marianne Milligan

Act I: The Dream

Scene 1

Some Indians lived somewhere.
One young man
    it was then that he was fasting.

One time, just when he had become a young man,
    it was then that Maeqnapos called him.

"Well, then, come, Uncle!
I'm the one who invites you,
    to come here to my house.
As for me, I'll give you what I have.

And with you will go along nine young men who are clean,
    who have never been with girls;
        that's the kind [of young man] you will bring here to my house."

So Maeqnapos said to this young man,
    talking to him
        as he slept.

Scene 2

Now, when dawn came,
    the young man carefully thought it over,
        "And I wonder how I might reach [the place] where Maeqnapos invited me;
            maybe I can't get there."
    So thought the boy.
And so, all day long,
    while he was at their house,
that was his thought.

Now, when night came again,
    when he was sleeping,
        it was then that he heard him again;
Maeqnapos spoke to that young man.

"Yes, Uncle, you will arrive there at Maeqnapos's house;
    it's really me who invites you!"
        he again said to him there [in his dream]
            as he slept.

Scene 3

Now, it was then that he woke up.

"Well then, I'll try to do it.
    That's what I'll do.
If I can convince the young men,
    I'll take them with me to Maeqnapos's house."
So thought the young man
    as he lay there.

When dawn came,
    it was then that he sought out one young man.
When he had found him
    he told him about it:

"Well, then, my friend, I'm going to go to Maeqnapos's house.
You should come with me;
    we'll go to Maeqnapos's house."

"All right, I'll go with you,"
    the young man said to him.

Now, it was then that he sought out another young man.

Now, when he saw him:

"How are you, my friend?
Won't you go with me?
    I'm going to Maeqnapos's house.
        I'm going to take nine young men with me;
we'll go to Maeqnapos's house."

"All right, I'll go with you,"
he answered him.

It was then he had found two young men.

Now, it was then that he found another one:
"Well, then, my friend, let's go to Maeqnapos's house!"

"All right, I'll go with you."

Now, it was then that he had found another young man:

"Now, I'm going to Maeqnapos's house;
you must come with me."

"All right, I'll go with you."

It was then that he found four of them.
And he found nine young men in all,
and it was then, with him, they were ten.

"All right, in ten days,
it's then that we'll set out,"
he said to his young friends.

Scene 4

And so, it was then that he told his father and mother:

"Now, Father, over here while I was fasting,
Maeqnapos asked me to go to his house;
and he told me to take along some young men.
And this is what I have now finished;
I'm going to take nine young men with me,
and with me we'll be ten in all,"
he said to his father.

And so, for a long time the old man didn't speak,
greatly marveling that they were going to [the place] where
Maeqnapos lived.
After a long time had passed,
it was then that the old man spoke.

"Well then, Son, be on your guard!
Whatever you may have come to know,
it must be done properly.
That is the warning I give you,"
he told his son.

It was then that the young man made an elm-bark canoe,
gathering his young friends.
They all had told the old men,
the young men, and the old people.
The old men marveled at the news.

"If it's truly as this young man says,
it will be good;
surely they will bring something back,"
the old men said,
as they talked together.

That's how they were content with it;
they gave their sons permission
to go there.

Act II: The Journey

Scene 1

So it turns out that when ten days had passed,
it was then that they got into their elm-bark canoes,
to cross this small sea.
They traveled and traveled;
then it was
that they came to land.

From there where they had set out,
they had traveled nine days.
And on the tenth day of traveling by canoe,
when it was noon,
it was then that they saw land.

A river—
    it was there that it flowed by;
about as far as a man can jump
    was the distance of the other side.
It was then that the land moved;
    it was here that the ground moved from side to side.

"Don't look down!"
    the leader said to his young friends;
"Like I move,
    that's how you should move!"
        he said to them.

"All right!"
    the young men said.

One man—
    it was then that he jumped;
        he stood on the far side.
Soon another one—
    it was then that he too jumped over it.
All of them—
    it was then that the young men did so.

Just as the last young man was going to jump,
    it was then that he looked down below at the water.

"Oh, no! Don't look there!"
    the leader said to him.

Then again, as he was going to jump,
    it was then that he looked at the water;
        it was then that he almost fell.

"Oh, no! Our friend!"

All the while, the ground was shaking,
    moving like this,
        moving side to side.

Now, all at once the young man made up his mind;
    it was then that he jumped.
It was then that falling short, he fell;
    it was then that he died,
        falling there where the ground moved from side to side.

"Oh, no, our friend! Well, then he'll fare so,"
    the leader said.

Scene 2

After they had started again,
    when it was evening,
        just as the sun had set,
it was then that they came in sight of a wigwam.

Arriving at the door,
    it was there that they stopped.
It was then, the story goes, that someone spoke from inside.

"And why, Uncles, don't you come in?
    Come in, Uncles!
Thank you for coming to me!"
    Maeqnapos said to his nephews.

When they had entered,
    a man sat there.

"Now, sit down, sit down, sit down, Uncles!"

The young men sat down somewhere.

Act III: The Visit

Scene 1

And so, when the young men were all seated,
    a kettle hung over his hearth.
        Maeqnapos started to take down his kettle.
A large wooden bowl was Maeqnapos's bowl;
    and a large wooden spoon was his spoon.
He took up his bowl and spoon.

That kettle was completely full of corn, sweet corn;
    half of it was venison,
        with which he had cooked it.
It was then that he placed it in the bowl,
    and he fed them.

"Well, then, Uncles, eat!"
    he said to them.

It was then that the young men ate,
    oh my! They ate everything in that large bowl,
        the young men all going at it together.
After they had finished eating,
    they moved the bowl.

Scene 2

"Well, then, Uncles, thank you for coming to me!
It was I who invited you,
    here where I live
        to come.
And it's good
    that you've come to me.
After four days pass
    you will go home,"
        Maeqnapos said to them.

"You'll stay here four days.
It's then that I'll be satisfied.
Uncles, I'll cooperate with you.
I will give you
    whatever you ask for, Uncles,"
        Maeqnapos, their nephew, told those young men.

Now, then, the young men were glad
    to hear
        Maeqnapos talking to them.

Scene 3

Then while they were there,
it was then, the story goes, that a kettle came into Maeqnapos's house.
Just imagine! Someone must have boiled meat, splendid!
Truly—
that was good meat.
Tobacco also came along into the house.

"Now, Uncles, eat what's in this kettle.
We're being given food
we can eat;
and we'll smoke
the tobacco that's here,"
their nephew Maeqnapos said to them.

How was it? Well, then, the young men truly—
it was then that they ate a lot;
they ate the meat.
When they had finished eating,
and, it was then that the young men also had a good smoke.

And so it is that as a person gives a feast here,
making an offering of tobacco;
it's then that the person's feast offering along with the tobacco come into Maeqnapos's house.

That's how the young men carried on,
eating and eating.
Maeqnapos never cooks;
when someone gives a feast,
it's then that it all goes to Maeqnapos's house.

And this is what the young men ate and ate,
all the time there were there.

Scene 4

And four winters—
that's how long the young men were there;
but Maeqnapos calls four years four days.
And truly, those young men only slept four times
during those four winters.

It was just four winters,
  when they had slept four days.
When it was morning,
  it was then that he told them:

"Now, Uncles, it is time for you to go home.
When morning comes,
  you will start off,"
    he said to them.

It was then that he asked the young man who had taken along his young friends:

"Now, then, Uncle, and what do you want
  that I can give you?"

And so, the young man thought it over.

"Well, then, Uncle, too often do I go hungry
  where I come from.
That I may know how to skillfully kill deer and game,
  that's what I ask you
    to give to me,"
      he said to his nephew Maeqnapos.

"All right, Uncle, I will give it to you.
  That's how you will be;
you will easily overcome game animals,
  when you arrive at the village you come from,"
    Maeqnapos said to his uncle.

And now another one—
  it was then that he also asked him a question:

"Well, then, and you, Uncle, what do you want?"
  Maeqnapos asked his uncle.

And so, this young man too—
  it was then that he thought it over.
Then—
  it was then that he too spoke to him.

"Well, then, as for me, I want
    to know how to fight well;
        so I may be a war leader;
  that's what, as for me, I ask for from you, Nephew,"
    the young man said to his nephew Maeqnapos.

"All right, Uncle, that's how you'll be,
    as you want.
  You'll be good at fighting;
    you'll be a war leader,
        whenever you seek other people,
            there in the village you come from,"
    Maeqnapos said to his uncle.

Well, then, it was then that he had already finished with two of his uncles.

Now,
"Now, and what do you want, Uncle?"

"Well, then, Uncle, the medicines that are good,
    perhaps you could teach me."

"Oh, all right, Uncle, I'll tell of them."

Medicines—
    that's what he told him about.

"Now, it's this, Uncle, that you will be a good doctor,"
    he said to his uncle.

And so, it was then that he had finished [granting that wish] too.

"Now, and you, Uncle?"

"Now, to be a fast runner—
    the other young men always leave me way behind in a race—
        that is what, for my part, I want."

"All right, it will be that way;
    this thing that you ask me for,
        I will give you."

And so, it was then,
now, as for the next one, to be a good hunter,
he asked him,
and another to be a good hunter
that's what he asked for.
Now, and another [asked] to be a good fighter.

And, now, the next one also:

"And now, as for you, Uncle, what do you want?"

"Well, then, Uncle, all the young women dislike me.
That they like me,
that's what I ask you for,"
he said to his nephew.

"All right, Nephew, I will give it to you;
the young women will like you
it will be that way."

"All right!"

And so, that's how it was.

And now, one more,
and this last one:

"And now, Uncle, what for you?"

"Well, then, Nephew, for my part, I want
to live forever;
that as long as the earth exists,
I will live.
That's what, as for me, I want."

"Oh, all right, I'll give it to you.
As long as the earth exists,
you will live,"
Maeqnapos said to his uncle.

He stood up;
    getting hold of him by the shoulders,
        it was then that he lifted him up;
and by the door
    it was there that he set him down.
When he had set him down,
    a Spirit Rock was there.

"Now, Uncle, it's here that you will always be;
    as long as the earth exists,
        you will live."

And it was so.
A Spirit Rock was there by the door.
And still,
    it's there that the young man sits.
Well, then, he asked
    that as long as the earth exists,
        he would live.

Scene 5

It was then that Maeqnapos had finished [giving gifts to] all his uncles.
And it was then that they slept.

After they woke up in the morning,
    after they had eaten,
it was then that hot embers—
    it was then that he took them out
        and this is how he laid down the hot embers;
            he spread out the embers by the wall of his house.

It was then that he took out a deerskin.
After he had spread it out,
    it was then that he placed it over the embers.

And so, as that deerskin burned—
    here's how big it was—
        it shrunk in the heat.
It was then that he put it somewhere.

"Now, Uncle, you will sleep once on the way,
after it's day,
after it's evening,
you will arrive,"
their nephew said to them.

It was then that he had scorched the earth,
when he burned that deerskin.

Act IV: The Return Home

Scene 1

After it was day,
after it was evening,
the young men arrived
at the village from which they had started out.
The old men had given up all hope of their children.

"It's been four years,
they aren't coming,
something must have happened to them somewhere,"
the old people thought.

Just imagine! When their sons arrived,
truly
it was then that the old people were glad.

They were big men.

When he went hunting,
the one who had asked for game animals,
nearby,
it was there that he would kill a bear.
Truly,
it was then that they always ate well.

And, now, the one who asked for medicines,
when he doctored sick people,
he cured them all.

And, now, the one who asked
    to be a good fighter,
wherever there was fighting,
    he was truly the person everyone relied on.

And, now, as for the one who was going to be a fast runner,
    no one ever outran him.
And he was also good at killing game animals,
    since he ran fast there.

And now, as for the one who asked
    that the girls like him,
oh my! When they came to their village,
    whenever he walked anywhere,
        right away young women came running at him,
            to talk to him.

That's how he occupied himself,
    talking to young women;
at last, truly, he had legs like a grasshopper's,
    having reduced himself to ruin
        being with young women this way.

That is all.

3 West

Pine Root

Introduction by Stan Cuthand

"Pine Root," or "Wa ta pi wi yin," is one of the myths my father used to tell us when we were children. My father was a Plains Cree storyteller and told us many stories in the winter months, which was the time to tell stories. I was born in 1918 on Little Pine's Reserve in Saskatchewan. Growing up in the 1920s, I knew many elders who were storytellers. Some of these men had fought the Canadians at Cutknife Hill during the rebellion of 1885 in Saskatchewan, and some had fought the Blackfeet. I became a storyteller myself when, teaching at the University of Manitoba in the mid-1970s, I came across Leonard Bloomfield's book *The Sacred Stories of the Sweet Grass Cree* and found some of my father's stories in it! (Bloomfield had come to the Sweet Grass Reserve in 1925).

"Pine Root" is a "long-ago" story, or *atayohkewin*, and its function was to teach the role of different age groups. Grandfathers, for instance, are supposed to be knowledgeable in weaponry, hunting, and spiritual power for survival. A grandmother is a kindhearted woman who has wisdom and power. Kinship relations are often the central theme in these stories.

Much of the content of this story focuses on spiritual beliefs concerning the forces of creation, which we call Atayohkanak, or the First People. The Atayohkanak were numerous and lived together for ages in harmony. But in some mysterious fashion they changed as they developed, and eventually differences were sufficient to cause conflict, so they split into two camps. From the good camp originated different kinds of foods. They established institutions, arts, games, amusements, dances, and religious ceremonies for the coming race. They felt the approach of friends or enemies from a distance. For instance, Pine Root's grandfather says, "I am alarmed that someone will come for you." They knew what others thought in their hearts. If one of these beings expressed a wish, it immediately happened. The bad camp was cunning and deceitful and had harmful powers. The two sisters come from the bad camp and try to destroy Pine Root, who comes from the good camp. They mock him, calling him "sweetheart." There were great conflicts between these two camps until all in the bad camp were turned into things, animals, vegetable, and mineral. These things are either helpful or harmful to humankind, and thus Creation is accomplished. For instance, the old woman, after she is defeated by Pine Root, becomes a dead stump. Thence came the custom of shredding a rotten stump to make a moss bag, which kept an infant warm and dry.

I have chosen to translate the story in short sentences, using the Cree style of telling. When I translated the spoken word to the page, I broke the lines where I did because I liked the way they appeared, seeming to create tension and energy, slowing down and quickening up the pace.

Some parts of the story might need explanation. For instance, some men had more than one wife, and sometimes they married two sisters, who addressed each other by a term translated here as "sister-wife." In olden times, when a man took a woman home, they were accepted as married; the same if a woman came home with a man. Also, it was taboo to speak to or touch your mother-in-law, and so Pine Root hits her with a stick to wake her. The part about naming shows each person trying to defeat the other by the spirit of the name. A person's name is a guardian spirit. Some are more powerful than others. The "dart" is a throwing stick, or atlatl, flat and pointed at one end.

PINE ROOT

Written and Translated by Stan Cuthand

There was an old man
and his grandson, a young man,
who lived by themselves.
And the old man was
very fond of his grandson.
He was always hunting.
Then one day: "Now, my grandson,
I will try and kill something
that you may use as a hat."
That's what he said to his grandson.
"Yes," answered the other.
"I am alarmed that someone
will come for you," the old man
said to his grandson.
He killed a jack rabbit
and skinned it.
"Now then, Grandson,
I will try to kill another one
for your hat,"
he said to his grandson.
"Yes," said the other.
And so he killed a raven
and skinned it.
"Now, my grandson,
as I hunt each day,
if someone arrives
do not look at him or her."
That's what the grandfather said.
"Grandfather, try and kill a partridge.
I will have it for my tobacco pouch,"
the young man said.
"Certainly, my grandson.

What you say is good.
I will supply it for you.
In it put this stone, an arrowhead,"
he said to his grandson.
Then the old man made a set of darts.
"Now, my grandson,
don't forget to take these darts
as you leave. They are for your use,"
said the grandfather.
"Yes," he said.
"And now, my grandson, sit here," he said.
And he blew his breath on him.
There appeared a stone, sitting.
"Now I am leaving you too weak.
Perhaps someone will overcome you,"
his grandfather said to him.
"Grandson, allow me, lie down,
lie down flat on your back,"
his grandfather told him.
He blew his breath on him repeatedly,
as roots appeared from all sides,
roots coming from deep underground,
until he was firmly secured by the roots.
"My grandson, this will be your name,"
he said. "Pine Root Person is your name.
Do not look at anyone," his grandfather said.
"Try to remember to grab these darts.
I will tie them on the door-flap frame.
All these things I give to you,
and also your tobacco pouch,"
his grandfather said.
"Do not look at anyone
who is to come."
"Yes, Grandfather," he replied.
Therefore he refused to look
at anything at the door. He lay uncovered.
He wrapped his head with his blanket.
Suddenly a ringing sound approached.
When he heard it he covered his head.

Someone came laughing cheerfully.
"These are women," he thought.
"These are the ones my grandfather meant," he thought.
They came in right away.
"Oh, so this is where he sleeps,
he who will not look at us, our sweetheart,"
they said.
"Surely they must be beautiful," this young man thought.
And so they kept talking to him,
saying all kinds of things to him.
He would not speak to them.
"Our sweetheart, Pine Root, really hates us,"
they said.
"Go on, let us go home," they said.
But it happened one stayed to peek in
while the other laughed as she left.
"They have left by now," Pine Root thought,
"so I'll look at the doorway now
there is no one to see." Thinking this,
he uncovered his head
and immediately looked toward the doorway.
"Oh, so he is not sleeping at all,
he who will not look at us!" she said.
And she went on her way, laughing.
Pine Root jumped to his feet,
breaking all the pine roots
as he moved with force.
Those things his grandfather prepared
he took with him.
He followed the women at the same distance all the time.
He carried those things made for him,
his hat, his tobacco pouch, and his darts.
Finally he arrived at a lake.
Land was not visible in the direction
one of the women was leading them.
"Hey! Sometimes it is customary to tell:
What is your name, sweetheart? Pine Root?" she said.
"Wait now—I will not be the first
to tell my name! You first,

tell me your names!" he said to his sweethearts.
"Yes, sister-wife, you first," one girl said
to her younger sister. "You first.
Tell our sweetheart your name."
"All right. As far as that point of land, that far,
Snowfall of Awls I am called."
"Then lead on," he said to them.
And it became slippery, on the ice.
He took his dart, supporting himself with it
like a cane. He took another.
He attached an arrowhead to it.
He walked on the great expanse of ice.
Though awls were falling on his head
yet he continued to walk.
When they reached the point of land,
yes, they were still accompanied by Pine Root.
"Now it is his turn to amuse us.
Now it is his turn.
Let him name himself."
"Oh no," said Pine Root. "You first.
You will tell me your names."
"All right. As far as that point of land, that far,
Blown on Ice Walker is my name," she said.
And he will be swept away on the smooth ice
by the wind.
The lake was not frozen in the middle.
The wind was to blow him there.
And as they headed out
there came a great wind.
This young man took out his darts,
and he leaned on them as canes.
Although it was windy,
he kept on walking. Finally they arrived.
"Oh, our sweetheart is still with us.
Now it is his turn to name himself."
"Yes, my sweethearts," he said.
"I have two names. Not far over there,
at that point, that far,
Hot Rainwater is my name.

As far as that point."
"Then off you go, sweetheart.
We will follow you."
As soon as he started out,
it began to rain.
Like boiling water,
that's how hot it was.
And they said, "Oh, I am scalded!"
The women touched themselves
all over, walking with great difficulty.
"Oh," they said, "our sweetheart
has a difficult name.
Let him name himself again."
"All right," said Pine Root.
"Now your little cabins are in sight,
as far as that house, there,
Walking Backward Stooped Skirts Pulled Up
is my name."
And so these women
pulled up their skirts like this,
walking backward and stooped.
Now the old woman was on the lookout
for her children.
When she saw them she said,
"What on earth makes you act in this silly way?"
"Get away! We are learning
our sweetheart's name," they cried.
"We must walk this way until
we touch your house."
They walked backward
with their dresses up
until they bumped into their house.
Then they stopped.
The old woman said, "Now, my children, sit over there,
on my son-in-law's bed.
I have nightmares so often that
I might accidentally bump into my son-in-law."
When darkness fell, they went to bed.
Before dawn, suddenly

this old lady was crawling about.
She had an awful nightmare.
At last her son-in-law hit her with a stick
to wake her up. Then she sat up
and said: "My children, that lake over there,
there is a big beaver there.
I ate its head and tail,"
the old woman said.
"That is when I stopped dreaming.
Tomorrow my son-in-law should kill it,"
she said.
The young man heard all this.
Then when daybreak came,
he went out very early.
He took his axe and his darts.
When he reached the lake,
he chopped the ice in the middle of the lake.
He chopped a big hole.
"Oh, my grandfather, come out!"
he said. "I came to feed you this,
something you like."
Suddenly a big beaver appeared
with its mouth wide open.
He struck it with his dart
and killed it.
He took the head and the tail.
He took them home.
He threw them into the house.
"Here are the things your mother
wanted to eat!"
The old woman cried out.
"My dream spirit! My dream spirit!" she sobbed.
"Oh, it was as foretold.
Go and feed them to the people.
They will eat these things,
and that which is killed
let them fetch it.
They will eat it."
Again night came.

They went to bed.
And once again
this old woman had a nightmare.
When she woke up:
"I dreamed that my son-in-law
killed a big deer.
When he killed that deer
that is when I stopped dreaming,
when eating the head," she said.
Then in the morning
voices were heard by the people
saying, "There he goes!"
He jumped out of his house.
There, passing by, was a deer
leaping as it went.
He threw a dart at it.
He killed it.
He only took its head.
He flung it into the house.
"Here is what your mother wants to eat!"
he called to them.
And again the old woman cried out:
"My guardian spirit is killed!
I am grieving for that," she cried.
"Now, my children,
go and feed the people."
"Yes," they replied.
Then the other people ate it.
Then night fell.
Again the old woman had a nightmare.
"Now, my children,
I dreamed that an elk ran by here,
and I ate its head.
That was the end of my dream," she said.
In the morning Pine Root was told.
"I will not kill it this time," he thought.
Then someone said,
"There goes the elk! It is huge!"
and he went out, taking only one dart.

He threw this dart at it
as it ran past.
And off it went with his dart
in its belly.
The young man went home.
He took all his darts, his hats,
and followed it.
He kept coming to where it had sat.
Soon it was afternoon.
It had sat down now more frequently.
Presently he came to a lovely stand of trees.
There were willows round about.
It was beginning to snow.
"It will not die far from here, whatever happens.
I will sleep here.
I will have a fire.
I will keep a fire going," he thought.
It was a big stand of mostly young poplars.
So he cleared away the snow
and made a fire.
It grew dark.
Close by was a tree,
a dry poplar tree.
"I shall put this on my fire,"
he thought, and started to take it down.
But as he did so, "Oh, oh!" cried the tree.
He left it alone
and moved away. On the other side of the fire
he spread willows and grass.
But he could not sleep.
It was very windy,
and it began to snow.
Suddenly, on the lee side
the young man heard something.
He looked up in surprise.
There was a person stumbling along,
coming with her leggings
all fallen down.
She had not tied them up.

"Oh," said Pine Root, "Grandmother!
My dear grandmother will freeze to death!
Now, Grandma,
sit over there.
I was chasing an elk.
I wounded it, and I am tired
trampling over the deep snow.
Tomorrow I shall kill it, Grandma.
We will eat some meat."
"My grandson," she said,
"I am very hungry. Over there is a camp.
The people are moving to that camp.
They went off and left me behind.
Now I am lost."
"Don't worry, Grandma.
I will take you home
to the camp tomorrow,
after I kill the elk.
I will take you home.
You are too cold."
He pulled up her leggings
and tied up her moccasins.
He was very kind to his grandma.
"Now, Grandma, I am going to sleep.
Try to keep the fire going," he said.
"Yes, Grandson," she said. "If I am able
I will put wood on the fire."
And so Pine Root went to sleep.
But he did not really go to sleep.
He wanted to deceive her,
for he thought, "This is my mother-in-law."
After a while, the old woman said,
"Grandson, I am cold." But, despite this,
he pretended to be asleep. "Argh, argh,"
he snored. The old woman sat up.
"I will add him to my trees!"
she said. But the young man was listening.
Then she untied something,
a medicine bundle.

"No, no," she said, "not this one!
This is the restorer."
She put it down.
She untied another bundle
and took out another medicine.
"Yes, this is it!" she said.
Then the old woman chewed a twig.
She touched the medicine with it.
"This is the medicine
with which I make trees," she said.
Then she held it up to Pine Root,
intending to touch him with it.
But he grabbed her arm.
"Why, you stinky-breath beast!"
He seized the twig.
"Grandson, Grandson, wait a moment!
You have defeated me! Now, wait.
The time will come when people
will multiply. They will take
decayed wood with which to keep
a child warm and help him grow up.
I too will assist a child
to grow up.
I will dwell in the land
of the setting sun.
When a person says,
'I have dreamed of the old woman,'
he will speak the truth.
So now, Grandson; touch me."
He touched his grandmother
with that same medicine,
and there appeared the trunk of a tree.
Thus the old woman became
a dead stump.
Then he took the medicine
of which his grandmother had said,
"This is the restorer,"
and with it he touched a tree.
Lo, there appeared an elderly man.

"Oh", he said, "I am weary with standing."
Then with the twig Pine Root touched a tree close by.
It was almost daybreak.
Lo, there stood a young man.
"Now," Pine Root said to the elderly man,
"don't stop touching these trees
with this thing my grandmother
called 'the restorer.'
I am going to kill this elk,
and the women will pack it
for you to roast.
If I live two nights
I will, return," he told the women.
"All right," they said.
Then he took off.
And soon, there, not far away was the dead elk.
He took the head.
He brought it home
and brought it into their house.
He threw it in at the doorway.
"Here is what your mother wanted to eat!"
The young women were weeping,
mourning for their mother.
They were certain
she was defeated.
When night came,
they went to bed.
Suddenly the older sister
had a bad nightmare.
Pine Root shoved her aside.
And when she woke up,
she told her dream.
"I dreamed that our sweetheart
stayed one night in that empty house.
That is when I stopped dreaming," she said.
He went there in the morning.
He gathered a lot of wood
and brought it into the house.
At nightfall as he sat in the house,

the doorway disappeared.
The logs became solid.
It was very cold.
He warmed himself at the fire,
but at last the wood was gone.
So he went to bed.
To a big rabbit he said,
"Come now, my hat, warm me."
But the rabbit grew cold in a short time.
He took it and blew his breath on it.
"I told you to warm me."
Again it was cold in no time.
He took it again.
And again it became cold.
He didn't take it again.
He took his other hat.
"Now, my grandfather,
flap your wings," he said.
And the raven croaked,
and it beat the walls,
which were covered with ice.
But the raven was quickly overcome by the cold.
"Perhaps I'm going to freeze,"
Pine Root thought. So he took his dart
and threw it at the fire.
There was a big fire.
The dart blazed high,
but quickly the flame died down.
The raven lay there freezing.
Pine Root took another dart.
Again he threw his dart at the fire.
That too blazed up.
He held the raven near the fire.
By now it was almost daybreak.
The fire went out.
He took another dart
and again threw it at the fire.
It made a great blaze.

Eventually, as it was dying out,
he took his tobacco pouch
and slammed it on the ground.
"Flap your wings, my pouch!" he said.
Then he took his hat
and blew his breath on it.
Lo, the partridge was alive.
And to the partridge he said,
"Flap your wings!"
And suddenly this partridge was running about indoors,
flapping his wings and calling,
"Summer! Summer! Summer! Summer!" again and again,
while the raven croaked without ceasing,
and the rabbit threw itself
here and there and everywhere.
Pine Root's dart was still blazing.
"Grandfather, let my dart blaze higher,"
he prayed. "I have no more darts."
He was addressing the grandfather who cared for him.
And soon there was no snow
in the house.
The fire blazed higher,
and the partridge ran around
making summer indoors,
calling for leaves,
serving his grandson.
Then before dawn
everywhere leaves sprang forth,
and inside on the floor
berries grew, strawberries,
because the partridge never stopped calling "Summer!"
Pine Root stripped
to his waist, as if in a contest,
and sat eating strawberries.
It was very hot inside.
And in the morning
when the sun was up, one of the women said,
"Now, my sister-wife, go

and throw out our sweetheart.
He will defile our storehouse."
So one of them went over there.
She heard the raven croaking over and over.
She heard the partridge too.
When she looked inside, he was picking berries.
"Oh, my dear, can you give us those strawberries
you are eating?"
"Last night I had a dream
that you and your older sister
ate all these berries.
That is when I woke up."
"Well, that won't be hard to do," she replied
and went back home.
"What's going on now, Sister?
What's he up to?"
"If we eat up all the remaining strawberries,
then our sweetheart will not have nightmares,"
she said.
So they went back.
"Now, my sweethearts," said Pine Root,
"when you've eaten up all of these,
then we can all leave."
These silly women were very glad,
so they ate all the berries.
But when they ate all the berries from one place,
the partridge would run over and the strawberries
would be back on the stalks.
After a while the women just sat back,
for they had eaten too much.
"Ooh, my sweetheart, you have defeated us.
Push us over toward the direction
of the noonday sun.
We will certainly be kind.
When mortal people multiply
and say 'I dreamed of a silly woman,'
they will be telling the truth.
Come, sweetheart, be quick!"

And they went on their way,
talking as they went,
on their way to a new home after their defeat,
these evil ones.
That is the end of this story.

Ghost Dance Songs

Introduction by Jeffrey D. Anderson

Between 1890 and 1893 James Mooney collected at least seventy-three Ghost Dance songs in his extensive fieldwork among both the Northern Arapahos of Wyoming and the Southern Arapahos of Oklahoma (1896, 653–54).[1] At the same time, as both tribes became the leading cultural movers of the Ghost Dance from the Great Basin onto the Plains, many of their original, trance-inspired songs in the Arapaho language became the life force of the dance itself in other tribes. Mooney observes that Arapaho songs were the "favorite among the tribes of Oklahoma" (1896, 958). Alice Fletcher also mentions that "[f]rom the Sioux delegation visiting Washington in February, 1891, [she] learned that the songs sung at the dance were in the Arapaho tongue" (1891, 58). Given the centrality of Arapaho musical creativity in the Plains version of the Ghost Dance, it is remarkable that there has been no intensive return to the linguistic features and cultural context of those songs. Informed by the more abundant ethnographic and linguistic evidence available today, retranscription and retranslation of Mooney's original song texts will provide a ground for further interpretation to clarify distortions and reveal heretofore ignored details and dimensions of the songs.

From his own archival manuscripts (Voth n.d.) at Bethel College, it is clear that H. R. Voth, with the assistance of Southern Arapaho informants, completed most, if not all, of the original translations and transcriptions of the song texts appearing in Mooney's work. A number of drafts in the making are available in his handwriting and in the orthographic style he used elsewhere in notes on Arapaho language, compiled from his research during ten years (1883–93) as a Mennonite missionary among the Southern Arapahos. Thus, it appears that Mooney recorded the songs and then solicited Voth and Southern Arapaho informants to transcribe and translate them, though clearly the accompanying commentaries and interpretations belong to Mooney.

Though the original translations are remarkable for their time and the transcriptions roughly decipherable to anyone with a background in the Arapaho language, subsequent linguistic material collected by Alfred Kroeber (1916), Truman Michelson (ca. 1910), and Zdenek Salzmann (1983), along with the author's own field data, can lend much to more precise retranscription and retranslation. From a contemporary perspective, Mooney's transcriptions employ a cryptic orthography predating the systematicity of descriptive linguistics and include some very old forms of Arapaho usage no longer familiar to modern speakers. Though the majority of texts for the other songs have been retranscribed and retranslated, the twenty-five songs included here represent those for which the entire texts can be presented with a high level of reliability and validity. The Arapaho versions are presented in the modern orthography accepted by the Northern Arapaho tribe and based on the original system proposed by Salzmann (1983) for the first dictionary project. Salzmann's works on Arapaho grammar were also employed to reconstitute inflections and derivations (1965a, 1965b, 1967). Lexical and grammatical evidence was also drawn from the author's own field research (1989–2002) among the Northern Arapahos and materials compiled by the Arapaho Language and Culture Commission.

Since the publication of Mooney's classic monograph, much distortion and confusion has come to surround the Ghost Dance. As Michael A. Elliott argues (1998, 213–14), one contributing factor is the almost exclusive attention given to the first two-thirds of Mooney's text, titled "The Narrative." Another source is the still murky field of identifying the origins, diffusion, and causes of the Ghost Dance, often without systematic attention to cultural content (see Kehoe 1989; Hultkrantz 1981). In this body of literature, the concept of the Ghost Dance has taken on a generic definition that often ignores variation among cultural and historical contexts. More particularly, scant attention has been paid to what the Ghost Dance became for Arapahos, who are often treated as a passive cultural conveyer of the movement or of interest only as a causal link for other events elsewhere.

Ironically, Mooney's greatest ethnographic contribution via Arapaho fieldwork of songs has been set aside. The "Songs" section has been entirely ignored, in large part because the texts of the songs seem impenetrable or undecipherable for analysis to those with only a modest background in the languages or cultures involved. At the same time, Mooney's connections of song elements to linguacultural contexts have largely eluded careful and critical reexamination. Without further explicating the ethnolinguistic background to the songs and without understanding Arapaho centrality in the movement, knowledge about the Ghost Dance as a cultural form has advanced little since 1896.

Characterizations of the movement based on the narrative section generally focus attention on the "doctrine," then trace divergences from the original among the various tribes that came to embrace it. For Arapahos, the doctrine is indeed a crucial part but not all of what shaped Arapaho experiences of the dance and what was expressed in the songs. The Ghost Dance was a religious movement but not one paralleling Western messianic reform movements in which a code, message, or doctrine embodied in an oral or literate text becomes the ground for consensual belief (see DeMallie 1982, 387).

Rather, Wovoka's prophecy and message provided Arapaho people themes for improvisation through trance experiences and songs composed from them. Mooney offers a remarkable—albeit unsystematic and at times misplaced—array of linguistic and cultural connections for appreciating the creative depth of the songs and the dance itself. A retranslation and more thorough reinterpretation of the Arapaho Ghost Dance songs open our understanding to the multiple layers and artistic creativity participants engaged. In other words, the Ghost Dance was less about blind adherence to a new moral order than about the unleashing of imaginations.

Ironically, few if any studies have followed Mooney's recognition that "[t]he Ghost-dance songs are of the utmost importance in connection with the study of the messiah religion." The dances themselves inspired an unprecedented efflorescence of creativity through trance and song: "There is no limit to the number of these songs, as every trance at every dance produces a new one. . . . Thus a single dance may result in twenty to thirty new songs." Out of these, some were transient; others endured: "While songs are thus born and die, certain ones, which appeal especially to the Indian heart, on account of their mythology, pathos, and peculiar sweetness, live and are perpetuated." Among all the tribes who adopted the dance, Mooney further notes, "First in importance, for number, richness of reference, beauty of sentiment, and rhythm of language, are the songs of the Arapaho" (1896, 953).

While Mooney acknowledges their central involvement in the movement and his research, Arapahos have been largely overlooked in studies of the Ghost Dance. For many reasons beyond the scope of this study, the turn to the causes, eventful history, or doctrine of the movement has detracted attention from the creativity of the Ghost Dance and the place of Arapahos in it. Only occasionally in larger works on the movement, one of the Arapaho songs or one of Mooney's original illustrations is inserted to stress the tragic background of deprivation and suffering behind the movement. That context was indeed tragic, but all meanings for the movement cannot be reduced to an expression of historical conditions or political realities. To do so is to dilute the creative breadth of the songs produced by imaginations at play in a time of crisis.

Furthermore, despite the reputation of Mooney's classic monograph, many of the original cultural and linguistic connectivities he wove for translation and interpretation of the Arapaho Ghost Dance songs remain at times loosely tied or thinly sketched. While surveying many other cultures, Mooney supplied the first serious ethnographic account of Arapaho culture and language, but subsequent research has supplied a rich ethnographic base for a more elaborate study. One essential step toward excavating deeper layers of meaning and creativity is to retranscribe and retranslate the original song texts with the aid of accumulated ethnographic, linguistic, and archival evidence.

Surviving much longer than the doctrine itself among the Northern and Southern Arapahos, the songs were the most durable element of the movement, a pattern consistent with the few studies of the songs in other Plains cultures. Åke Hultkrantz observed performance of the Ghost Dance among Wind River Shoshones during his 1948–58 field research (1981, 273). As central to Judith Vander's extensive research (1997), the Naraya (i.e., Round Dance/Ghost Dance) songs predated the Ghost Dance of 1890 and survived into the 1980s among the Eastern Shoshones, neighbor tribe of the Northern Arapahos. Among the Kiowas, as Benjamin Kracht describes (1992), the dance and songs persisted through social dances, much longer than previously realized. Likewise, Alexander Lesser (1978) has shown the enduring Pawnee cultural revitalization through the hand game that evolved out of the Ghost Dance. Alice Kehoe similarly documents the survival of the dance among the Dakotas of Saskatchewan as late as 1950 (1968, 298–302). Amid all of this though is the clear evidence that the form of the dance and accompanying songs preceded the 1890 Ghost Dance in various forms and has endured to the present in various permutations. In all, music and dance tended to be the most adaptable cultural form among Plains cultures, largely because it is an aesthetic expression with value and meaning transcending religion, societal consensus, and historical vicissitudes.

By reducing the Ghost Dance to a doctrine, a historical event, or a social form, scholars tend to reify order and function where there was none. Moving in another direction, there is sufficient evidence to examine the real experience of the movement as poetically polysemous and imagistic. Human creativity as a current for enlivening sociocultural reality is not entirely dependent on consensual interpretations attached to single functions, whether it be needs, crisis resolution, "making sense" of the world, or political problem solving. Neither do the elements always coalesce as into galaxies of shared meanings, since much of what is expressed in the songs dissipates, eluding interpretation despite the aesthetic power they retain.

Both isolated and recurring elements in the Arapaho songs have multiple meanings irreducible to a single gloss or connotation. Drawn from trance states, many song elements remain ambiguous while retaining aesthetic form and affect. Further, the linguistic and poetic form of the songs lent much to their depth of expression in ways that defy simple referential meanings or reduction to the linguistic code. As Mooney appreciated, some songs were more resilient than others because of their depth and synergy of mythical allusions, musicality, mood, and prophetic elements.

The images themselves creatively bridged old familiar forms, new invented elements, and individualized meanings. As such, the songs both conformed with and broke from past culture. For the Ghost Dance songs more than for any other evidence of Arapaho culture, the sense of dialogue between mythical past and prophesied future is rich and complex. On one level are the deep mythico-ritual continuities with Arapaho tradition. On a second, there are indeed elements conforming to the so-called doctrine of the movement, at least as Arapahos learned it from Wovoka or Ghost Dance leaders. On a third plane are elements that express the unique images individual participants experienced through alternative states of consciousness often linked to their life historical contexts or unique orientations to the world. Reanalysis will thus illuminate junctures of both cultural continuities and discontinuities in Arapaho experiences of the Ghost Dance, as well as the interconnections among them activated by creative imaginations at play. The ultimate aim, only sketched out here, is to explicate the immense complexity of the songs' connections to other cultural and linguistic forms.

To begin with one example of the complexities of retranslation, song 1, included here, was an opening song created among the Northern Arapahos and then borrowed by the southern tribe in Oklahoma (Mooney 1896, 958). The opening line refers to "another of your pipes" offered apparently by Heisonoonin, "Our Father." The meaning of this reference to another pipe is difficult to establish. Kroeber later collected a replica of the "new" Flat Pipe in his study of Arapaho decorative symbolism a decade later. An old Southern Arapaho man, who had never actually seen the original, made the pipe, as directed in a dream or vision and apparently carried it in the Ghost Dance (1983, 359–60). It thus does not resemble the sacred Flat Pipe itself, which is now as since the beginning of time held among the Northern Arapaho by a family of the Beesowuunenno' (Wood Lodge People), an ancient subtribe. As long as the Flat Pipe is cared for, the Arapaho people and the earth will survive. The implication of both song 1 and this evidence is that at least one man and perhaps a group received a message that they would receive a new pipe separate from the original as part of the renewal of the earth, human lives, and material culture.

The last line refers to events in the Arapaho origin myth to be perhaps reenacted in the coming of the new earth. In the beginning, Flat Pipe took the dirt returned in Turtle's claws from beneath the deluge and then expanded or moved it to create land (Dorsey and Kroeber 1903, 1–19). Homologous with the mythical beginning and renewal theme, the pipe precedes all other actions in ritual; thus it is logical that the pipe would be central in the opening song.

An equally striking combined continuity and discontinuity involving the Flat Pipe appears in song 2. Talk of or appeals to the Flat Pipe outside the Offerings Lodge, pipe ceremonies, age-grade lodges, and women's Buffalo Lodge deviates from what was and is accepted practice. It was not only the most sacred and powerful object but also a person in Arapaho terms; the pipe often spoke to the people about where to move camp or of coming dangers, but only to the pipe keeper entrusted with its care. That the song refers to someone other than the pipe keeper receiving direction is a break from traditional practice.

As I discuss elsewhere (Anderson 2001a), there are two sides or phases in Arapaho ritual movement: first, to contain and concentrate on suffering or life-negating things, then, to release or discard them for lighter life-generating movement. Overlooking the cultural details of this process, many works have cited song 28 to emphasize the historical conditions of suffering addressed by the movement in some generic sense. Most interpretative frames for this song follow Mooney in stressing the tragic break from traditional subsistence to deprivation in reservation life. As Mooney relates, "This is the most pathetic of the Ghost-dance songs. It is sung to the plaintive tune, sometimes with tears rolling down the cheeks of the dancers as the words bring up thoughts of their present miserable and dependent condition" (1896, 977). However, crying while singing or praying conforms to the Arapaho tradition of containing and expressing suffering, or pitiable conditions, in the ritual process. Here, retranslation and recontextualization recognize the level of continuity with all Arapaho prayers, supplications, and mythology. The song does not just refer to the current hardship, because the term for thirst, *nookooyei-*, in Arapaho also means "to fast." "Pity" in the Arapaho verb stem *hoowouu-*, expressed through fasting and crying, is at the center of all Arapaho petitions to sacred beings above. Pity is further connected with senses of difficult movement, as in carrying a heavy burden, which can be released through song, dance, or ritual sacrifice into a lighter and easier life movement (Anderson 2001, 261–66). One vows to relieve one's own hardship or that of another, then makes sacrifices to seek the pity of sacred beings beyond or on the earth. There is thus no break from past tradition in use of verb forms for pity, crying, and fasting. For this reason mainly, as Mooney observes, the song affected Arapaho people deeply. The songs were not necessarily direct expressions of sorrow for the historical moment, but really a means of transvaluing that state into a ritualized sorrow and thus a condition that could be discarded and from which release is possible.

Arapahos are and were one of the most religiously conservative Plains groups, but the Ghost Dance inspired individual trance states without precedent in Arapaho culture or any other group that followed the movement before them. Arapaho Ghost Dance followers broke from traditional ritual process, for Mooney does not record that any of the traditional forms of preparation, exchange, or vows were required for participation. The words of the songs were in many cases expressions of trance or dream experiences, and themselves helped trigger the trances that culminated in the Ghost Dance performance. The side-step dancing, the feather waving by dance leaders, and the power of the songs combined in synergy to effect release and even flight to another world. Compared to the ritual among other groups that followed the movement, the trance was most central and prolific in the Arapaho Ghost Dance.

Thus, Ghost Dance songs involved direct relations to sacred beings outside the age-ranked system or appeals and prayers. In particular, prayers to Our Father above were generally reserved for the oldest men, such that older age groups mediated on behalf of younger participants. Furthermore, trance states were limited to individuals who had been purified and prepared. The Ghost Dance thus anticipated a trend to follow in Arapaho religious practice toward more general, collectively accessible ritual forms, open to all regardless of age or preparedness.

Within the songs themselves, the appeal to Heisonoonin, "Our Father," throughout the songs is remarkable but not unambiguous. Similar recurring forms are *neisonoo*, "my father," and *neixoo*, "Father!" the vocative form used for direct address. Conversely, when songs take the voice of "Our Father," the term *neniisono'*, "my children," is used. Mooney (1896, 59) interprets this relationship as that between Wovoka as "Father" and Ghost Dance followers as children. Though this is one connection, the relationship deserves further elaboration. The Our Father addressed throughout all Arapaho prayers and songs is the Creator, referred to alternatively as Hihcebe' Nih'oo3oo, "Whiteman Above," though not connoting non-Indians, called by the same term *nih'oo3oo* (*nih'oo3ou'u*, plural). The Creator is also called Beeteet, a term translated as "Great Mystery," but also referring to any medicine man (Hilger 1952, 144). However, forms other than Our Father rarely appear in prayers, songs, or other ritual supplications. Two intercultural paths also converge in the Our Father usage. One is from the tradition Arapahos share with Algonquian traditions in which the Creator is referred to as Father. The other is from the Great Basin and in particular Eastern Shoshones co-residing with the Northern Arapahos at Wind River in Wyoming. Prior to and separate from the Ghost Dance of 1890, the Shoshones performed a Father Dance, a round-dance form held in the fall to petition for blessings of food, good weather, and continued life (Hultkrantz 1981, 276). As in their appropriation of Christianity (see Anderson 2001b), Arapahos tended to embrace introduced parallel religious forms as revealing what they had known all along while rejecting the less familiar elements. What is remarkable about the songs is the direct appeal to Heisonoonin outside the Arapaho age-graded order of prayer and ritual authority in which only the most senior men were allowed to make such an appeal on behalf of others.

There are indeed elements of the songs that reflect the doctrine of earth's destruction and renewal, reunion with deceased kin, and regeneration of the land, the buffalo, and the culture. However, there are forms without precedent either in the Great Basin or in Arapaho tradition. Within the new mythical epoch, the fifth world in the Arapaho cosmology, Crow is a sacred being originating in the Arapaho dance and songs but subsequently borrowed by other Plains groups. Insignificant in Arapaho mythology, Crow (*houu*) figures as mediator and creator in Ghost Dance songs. Crow's presence remains polysemous and ambiguous. In future prophetic time, he takes on roles paralleling those of other traditional beings of the mythical past, while also denoting the Christian God, Jesus, and Wovoka, as well as the Arapaho Crow Dance performed prior to the Ghost Dance. As Mooney adds, in song 40, Crow addresses the people of this world gathered on the border of the earth waiting to meet the people of the other world likewise gathered at the border of their land to the west. According to prophecy, with a piece of earth from his beak he creates first a mountain, then a land bridge between the two worlds, one of the living, the other of the afterworld (1896, 983). In this manner, Crow's power parallels the mediating role of Turtle in the earth-diver tradition of the original creation myth and the transformative role of the trickster Nih'oo3oo (see Dorsey and Kroeber 1903). Like the turtle in the last creation, he supplies the part for generating the totality of the earth. In this sense, Crow is the new creator of the new earth as the doctrine holds. From this context, the term *houu*, for Crow, has become a modern alternative form in Arapaho for Creator or "God." *Houusoo*, meaning "offspring of Crow," seems to have referred to Wovoka originally but also came to refer to Jesus in common usage. In general, Jesus, Our Father, Crow, and Wovoka are intermingled as the addressee or speaker in the songs. One common thread tied to the trickster Nih'oo3oo, too, is that all died and came back to life. Like the trickster, too, Crow has unrestricted mobility and power to transform the world. In myth, Nih'oo3oo himself changes from a mobile being into the unmoving Hihcebe' Nih'oo3oo, the Creator above. Crow's role in the Ghost Dance seems to anticipate this metamorphosis, but more needs to be done to understand the rich connectivity of Crow.

The songs also address a number of enduring and immediate questions or contradictions about Arapaho–non-Indian relations. These go beyond literally political resistance to raise and redress ontological, moral, and existential contradictions posed from a distinctly Arapaho perspective. Why do whites have so much wealth since they show no or little pity to Indians? And, why does the Creator not pity Arapahos for their deprivation at this tragic time in history? The answer is placed in the prophecies of the future built up from vision experiences. Several songs here and throughout the collection confront the irony of relations with Nih'oo3ou'u, Euro-American people. The term *nih'oo3oo* refers also to the spider, for which the connection was made originally. The irony is based on the implied or explicit contrast between the original moment of "pity" showed to whites, such as "giving them fruits" in song 3, followed only by the realization that "whites are crazy," the final line of song 23, in which Indians "render whites sad," placing them in a pitiful condition and reversing the current relation between whites and Indians. Any being described as crazy is both foolish and powerful. Children are crazy, as is the trickster figure in myth, also called Nih'oo3oo. One reading, then, is that Arapahos showed whites pity at first, treating them as persons, but in the end non-Indians proved to be less than persons.

As Mooney explains, Left Hand created song 4 from a Ghost Dance vision in which he saw that all things the Father gave originally to whites out of pity for them would be given to Indians. In a vision paralleling the millenarian side of Melanesian cargo cults and the Shoshone Father Dance, Left Hand saw that Indians would receive the orchards and the fruits referred to collectively as *koh'owootino*, a term now used to refer to all canned goods, but that once perhaps referred only to fruits belonging to whites. In the end, the song embodies a larger prophetic vision narrative in which the Creator revokes his pity for whites and places things in their right balance. Overall, the songs express an ironic tension between and continuity of tradition and renewal that breaks from the past.

Another dimension to be foregrounded by reanalysis encompasses the unique poetic and musical formal properties of the songs. As George Herzog recognizes (1935, 403), the "paired progression" of repeated lines only characterizes Ghost Dance songs and hand-game songs. The latter accompany the progress of guessing and hiding tiles in the hands in a traditional gambling game, with roots in the Plateau and the Great Basin. This repetition is perhaps linked to the hypnotic effect of the songs, in the Ghost Dance for inducing trance visions and in the hand game to distract the guesser.

One of the poetic features of the songs is effected through the linguistic complexity of Arapaho verb compounding and the indigenous play of images it generates. One measure of virtuosity in Arapaho speech performance is the ability to improvise novel combinations of two, three, or even more verb stems or modifiers in one construction. Song 27 contains a present tense verb construction *touheteinih'ohunoo* compounding three stems followed by the first person suffix *-noo: touh-*, "yell"; *-hetei-*, "roar"; and *-nih'ohu-*, "fly." The first two are interesting together since the first connotes an abrupt sound, such as a yell or thunder (e.g., *neniitouht*, "he/she thunders") and *hetei-* referring to a sustained roaring sound, as in a variant *heteiniicie*, "roaring river" for the Wind River in Wyoming.

Song 29 contains other verb compounds with aesthetic effect. The first two repeated lines contain a verbal construction combining a modifier for "yellow" (*neniihoon-*) and the verb "flying" (*nih'ohu-*), while the second pair combines three elements: "wild rose" (*yeneisitii-*), "wearing in hair" (*-nookuu-*), and "flying" (*-nih'ohu-*). Yellow predominates in Ghost Dance songs among the four main Arapaho colors, including also red, black, and white. Yellow is the color of east, dawn, childhood, and all new beginnings (see Anderson 2001a, 191–96). Based on a trance-induced vision, both song 27 and 29 contain the common motif of flight combined with aural and visual imagery, a recurrent theme in the Ghost Dance songs for rejoining deceased kin. Flight operates on multiple levels of meaning. It is indeed an archetypal motif of dreams and vision states, but also pervades many American Indian subconscious reactions to specific confinement on reservations, in boarding schools, or in other exiling asylum contexts.

Song 39 illustrates reduplication in verb construction, another function of Arapaho morphology for effecting poetic form, in this case, a unique parallelism. In *Nonoononoo'ooteinoo houu* the initial vcvcc- combination of *nonoo-* in the stem form *nonoo'oo (e)t-*, "to circle," is repeated to denote present, repeated action of indefinite duration. Repeated or replicated actions, events, or references in space or time can be marked by reduplication. Recognizing this level contributes much to a more involved understanding of the multifaceted complexity of repetition and its effect generated in the songs.

Thus, song images cannot just be examined referentially, or even solely as metaphors or other analogical devices, which preoccupy Western poetic readings. Song elements are particularly imagistic and exceed singular glosses or one-to-one poetic associations. Most central to them is the piling of layers of homologous motion, rhythm, and stress. For example, songs invoke circularity paralleling the motion of the dance itself, such as in songs 17 and 39.

The prosodic musicality of the songs is the most difficult to regain from the translations and render in written form. For instance, Arapaho speech lends itself to a rhythm and rhyme of recurring final sound combinations, especially *-oo*, *-t*, or glottal-stop endings. As each line is repeated, this lends a parallelism approaching rhyme. To suggest some interesting patterns, each line of song is generally preceded or followed by vocalic forms to extend the line and mark the breaks, usually, if Mooney's orthography is consistent for these, as *-ei-*, *-o(o)-*, and glottal stop. In one simple song (6) the high back-vowel orientation of *'eiyeihei* follows low back-vowel sounds moving to a frontal *u* sound in *wonooyou'u*. Finally the stress of the songs has been left out of the retranslations, because Mooney did not mark them. As Salzmann has analyzed (1956), stresses combined with raising or falling register mark differences in meaning and give what some speakers described as the unique sing-song nature of Arapaho language to songs. To give one example, the line of song 67 with stresses would appear as *nenééninoo tihnóokuuninoo nookóóxuu*. These stresses in turn define the contours of singing, though this needs further research beyond the limits of this study.

Some songs contain conspicuously novel grammatical forms. For instance, song 26 uses two conjunct constructions in the specific and habitual past tense as *tihne'etiitoonehehk* (when there was life) and *niiteehehk* (it was he). First of all, these are rare examples of the conjunct in the past tense. The conjunct order is generally reserved for present or future states comparable to a subjunctive mood, such as in "if" statements. Second, reference to mythical events, such as in this text, are usually framed in the narrative past tense.

Morphologically, almost all verb constructions in the songs are phrased in the past, future, or present tense, without employment of the narrative past tense marked by the prefix *he(e)'ih-* denoting the speaker's temporal and epistemic distance from events presented in the third person. It thus functions as an evidential modality for placement of events in a mythical time. By contrast, all the songs are presented as direct experiences in the present or near past, even though many recount images from visions or trance states inspired by the dance itself and accompanying songs.

Connected and also missing here are the musicality and the kinesthetic motion of dance. Mooney offered musical transcriptions of eight songs and commented that "[t]heir religious nature has led them to take a more active interest in the Ghost dance, which, together with the rhythmic nature of their language, has made their songs the favorite among the tribes of Oklahoma" (1896, 958). Arapaho music is distinctive and preferred in the old style of Plains music, for its low, plaintive, and slow qualities. The music was shaped also by the distinctive dance step, now recognized as a "round-dance" form in Plains Indian social dancing. The song form and accompanying dance style clearly predate the Ghost Dance in the Great Basin and Plateau by an indeterminable period of time.

Arapahos thus merged the syncopated rhythm of the round-dance form with their own low timbre and plaintive tone. The iambic cadence of the step infuses the music with a mournful but uplifting affective tone:

> When all is ready, the leaders walk out to the dance place, and facing inward, join hands so as to form a circle. Then, without moving from their places they

> sing the opening song, according to previous agreement, in a soft undertone. Having sung it through once, they raise their voices to their full strength and repeat it, this time slowly circling around in the dance. The step is different from that of most other Indian dances, but very simple, the dancers moving right to left, following the course of the sun, advancing the left foot and following it with the right, hardly lifting the left foot and following it with the right, hardly lifting the feet from the ground. For this reason it is called by the Shoshoni the "dragging dance." All the songs are adapted to the simple measure of the dance step. As the song rises and swells the people come singly and in groups from the several tipis, and one after another joins the circle until any number from fifty to five hundred men, women, and children are in the dance. When the circle is small, each song is repeated through a number of circuits. If large, it is repeated only through one circuit, measured by the return of the leaders to the starting point. (Mooney 1896, 920)

The poetic prosody of the songs combined with the kinesic syncopation of dance likely generated a collective effervescence without precedent in Arapaho culture. Holding hands in a dance open to everyone—and even hundreds—who wanted to participate irrespective of age and gender only occurred in social contexts outside the core ceremonies of the *beyoowu'*, including the Sun Dance, men's age-grade lodges, and women's Buffalo Lodge, all becoming extinct or threatened at the time of the Ghost Dance. The contradictions and possibilities of Ghost Dance songs, too, allowed individuals to participate by contributing new songs. For participants, "revitalization" was in and of the dance, the trance, and the songs themselves, not in a future world.

The texts of the songs must be placed in an aesthetic moment not just framed by the millenarian doctrine or its history but radiating with unprecedented creativity and sociality. Songs were the medium of feedback for the unique poetic creativity circulating in the dance. They both inspired and resulted from trance states within a social context and scope unprecedented in Arapaho culture before or after. Prior to the reservation period, vision states from individual fasts or participation in the lodges inspired songs with individual power for medicine but rarely would these become collective songs readily shared with others. In this way the songs are still part of an uncanny history, given that Arapahos were and still are among the most conservative ritual practitioners on the Plains. As Fowler (1982) demonstrates, Northern Arapaho age structure remained very strong as a system for maintaining traditional authority and tribal consensus. Still to be fully studied, though, is the other equally essential side of Arapaho culture through which prolific creativity flowed through individual imaginations at play in dreams, visions, invention, and songs. Though it is impossible to return to the immediacy of their performance, it is possible to get closer to some of the images and some sense of how the songs were experienced.

At a time of confinement the songs offered release but also reincorporation in the social. While non-Indian society was confining Arapahos to generic, even racial terms, Arapahos came together in a new sociality that allowed expression of individual creativity. While agents of assimilation were trying to liberate individualism from primitive communism, authors of the songs were released by trance and dream into novel paths of creativity. The promised or prophesied new world was really already experienced in the moments of dance, songs, and visions they engendered. I hope that the beginnings of retranscription and retranslation provided here will open eyes to the immediacy of the songs and Arapaho experiences expressed through them.

Orthography

Contemporary Arapaho orthography is as follows: *b* is pronounced as in English, except at the end of words, when it sounds like *p*; *c* is like a *ch* in English (e.g., "church"), but voiced like a *j* sound at the beginning of words; *e* sounds like the *a* in English "cat," and when written double *ee*, is held longer; *h* is like the English *h*, but always also pronounced at the end of a syllable or word; *i* is similar to the short *i* in English "bit," but in the long double form written as *ii*, it sounds like the long *e* in English (e.g., "meet"); *k* is usually produced like the *k* in English, but voiced as a *g* sound at the beginning of words; *n* is the same more or less as in English; *o* is almost the same as in English "got," and in the long form rendered as *oo*, it sounds like the vowel sound held longer in the pronunciation of "caught"; *s* is the same as in English though never voiced as a *z*; *t* is a voiceless alveolar stop much like English *t*, but voiced as a *d* sound at the beginning of words; *u* is like the *u* in English "put," and in the long form, written as *uu*, it is held longer like the long *u* sound in English "cute"; *w* is the same as in the English word "water," but also pronounced as voiceless at the end of words; *x* is most like the rough *ch* as in German *ich*; *y* is similar to the English form but also pronounced as voiceless at the end of words; *3* is a voiceless dental fricative as in English "thin" or "three" (thus, the symbol) but never voiced as in English "than"; ' is a glottal stop in which the glottis at the base of the throat is closed. The vowel combination *ou* sounds like the long *o* sound as in "boat." The *oe* diphthong sounds like the long *i* sound in English "bike." The *ei* combination is just as in English "reins." Triple-vowel forms are pronounced longer yet than their double-vowel counterparts but with a double stress as in *éeé* or *óuú*.

Note

1. Several songs are also available in Densmore (1936) and Curtis (1934).

References and Suggested Reading

Anderson, Jeffrey D. 2001a. *The Four Hills of Life: Northern Arapaho Knowledge and Life Movement.* Lincoln: University of Nebraska Press.

———. 2001b. "Northern Arapaho Conversion of a Christian Text: The Our Father." *Ethnohistory* 48 (4): 689–712.

Curtis, Natalie. 1934. *The Indians' Book.* New York: Dover.

DeMaillie, Raymond J. 1982. "The Lakota Ghost Dance: An Ethnohistorical Account." *Pacific Historical Review* 51 (4): 385–405.

Densmore, Frances. 1936. *Cheyenne and Arapaho Music.* Los Angeles: Southwest Museum.

Dorsey, George A., and Alfred L. Kroeber. 1903. *Traditions of the Arapaho.* Repr., Lincoln: University of Nebraska Press, 1998.

Elliott, Michael A. 1998. "Ethnography, Reform, and the Problem of the Real: James Mooney's Ghost Dance Religion." *American Indian Quarterly* 50 (2): 201–33.

Fletcher, Alice C. 1891. "The Indian Messiah." *Journal of American Folklore* 4 (12): 57–60.

Fowler, Loretta Kay. 1982. *Arapahoe Politics, 1851–1878: Symbols in Crises of Authority.* Lincoln: University of Nebraska Press.

Herzog, George. 1935. "Plains Ghost Dance and Great Basin Music." *American Anthropologist* 37:403–19.

Hilger, M. Inez. 1952. *Arapaho Child Life and Its Cultural Background.* Smithsonian Institution, Bureau of American Ethnology Bulletin 148. Washington DC: GPO.

Hultkrantz, Åke. 1981. "The Changing Meaning of the Ghost Dance as Evidenced by the Wind River Shoshoni." In *Belief and Worship in Native North America,* ed. Christopher Vecsey, 264–81. Syracuse NY: Syracuse University Press.

Kehoe, Alice B. 1968. "The Ghost Dance Religion in Saskatchewan, Canada." *Plains Anthropologist* 13 (42): 296–304.

———. 1989. *The Ghost Dance: Ethnohistory and Revitalization.* New York: Holt, Rinehart, & Winston.

Kracht, Benjamin R. 1992. "The Kiowa Ghost Dance, 1894–1914: An Unheralded Revitalization Movement." *Ethnohistory* 39 (4): 452–77.

Kroeber, Alfred L. 1983. *The Arapaho.* Foreword by Fred Eggan. Lincoln: University of Nebraska Press. (Orig. pub. in three parts in 1902, 1904, and 1907).

———. 1916. *Arapaho Dialects.* University of California Publications in American Archaeology and Ethnology vol. 12, no. 3, pp. 71–138. Berkeley: University of California Press.

Lesser, Alexander. 1978. *The Pawnee Ghost Dance Hand Game: Ghost Dance Revival and Ethnic Identity.* Madison: University of Wisconsin Press.

Michelson, Truman. ca. 1910. Field Notes. Smithsonian Institution National Anthropological Archives. Washington DC.

Mooney, James. 1896. *The Ghost-Dance Religion and Sioux Outbreak of 1890*. Fourteenth Annual Report of the Bureau Ethnology, 1892–93. Part 2, pp. 641–1110. Washington DC: GPO.

Salzmann, Zdenek. 1956. "Arapaho I: Phonology." *International Journal of American Linguistics* 22:49–59.

———. 1961. "Arapaho IV: Interphonemic Specification." *International Journal of American Linguistics* 27:151–55.

———. 1963. "A Sketch of Arapaho Grammar." Ph.D. diss., Department of Anthropology, Indiana University–Bloomington.

———. 1965a. "Arapaho V: Noun." *International Journal of American Linguistics* 31:39–49.

———. 1965b. "Arapaho VI: Noun." *International Journal of American Linguistics* 31:136–51.

———. 1967. "Arapaho VII: Verb." *International Journal of American Linguistics* 33:209–23.

———. 1983. *Dictionary of Contemporary Arapaho Usage*. Arapaho Language and Culture Instructional Materials Series, no. 4. Fort Washakie WY: Northern Arapaho Tribe, Wind River Reservation.

Vander, Judith. 1997. *Shoshone Ghost Dance Religion: Poetry Songs and Great Basin Context*. Urbana: University of Illinois Press.

Voth, H. R. n.d. H. R. Voth Collection. Bethel College, Mennonite Library and Archives. Newton KS.

Wallace, Anthony F. C. 1956. "Revitalization Movements: Some Theoretical Considerations for their Comparative Study." *American Anthropologist* 58:264–81.

THE SONGS

Translated by Jeffrey D. Anderson

1

'Eiyeihei! neniisono'
'Eiyeihei! My children.
'Eiyeihei! neniisono'
'Eiyeihei! My children.
Hinee ceese' hetiicooninoo Hei'eiyei!
There is another of your pipes. Hei'eiyei!
Hinee ceese' hetiicooninoo Hei'eiyei!
There is another of your pipes. Hei'eiyei!
Nohooni ne'nii3eetouhunoo Hei'eiyei!
Look! Thus I shouted. Hei'eiyei!
Nohooni ne'nii3eetouhunoo Hei'eiyei!
Look! Thus I shouted. Hei'eiyei!
Biito'owu' tihno'oobenowoo Hei'eiyei!
The earth, when I moved it. Hei'eiyei!
Biito'owu' tihno'oobenowoo Hei'eiyei!
The earth, when I moved it. Hei'eiyei! (Mooney 1896, 958)

2

Se'iicooo hei'towuuneinoo—Eiyohei'eiyei
Flat Pipe is telling me. Eiyohei'eiyei.
Se'iicooo hei'towuuneinoo.—Eiyohei'eiyei
Flat Pipe is telling me. Eiyohei'eiyei.
Heisonoonin—Yohei'eiyei
Our Father. Yohei'eiyei.
Heisonoonin—Yohei'eiyei,
Our Father. Yohei'eiyei,
Hootnii3oowuce'woohonoteino'—Eiyohei'eiyei
We shall surely be put together again. Eiyohei'eiyei!
Hootnii3oowuce'woohonoteino'—Eiyohei'eiyei
We shall surely be put together again. Eiyohei'eiyei!
Heisonoonin—Eiyohei'eiyei,

Our Father. Eiyohei'eiyei!
Heisonoonin—Eiyohei'eiyei,
Our Father. Eiyohei'eiyei! (Mooney 1896, 959)

3

Hee, teebe tih'owouunonou'u, neniisono'
Yes, at first when I pitied them, my children.
Hee, teebe tih'owouunonou'u, neniisono'
Yes, at first when I pitied them, my children.
Nih'oo3ou'u
The whites.
Nih'oo3ou'u
The whites.
Nihbinou'u koh'owootino
I gave to them, fruits.
Nihbinou'u koh'owootino
I gave to them, fruits. (Mooney 1896, 961)

6

Eiyeihei! Wonooyou'u—
Eiyeihei! They are new.
Eiyeihei! Wonooyou'u—
Eiyeihei! They are new.
Hookouno
The bed coverings.
Hookouno
The bed coverings. (Mooney 1896, 963)

8

Neniisono', neniisono'
My children, my children.
Hee, Neniiniibeineese' wookuuno'
Yes, it is singing wind, the head feathers.
Hee, Neniiniibeineese' wookuuno'
Yes, it is singing wind, the head feathers.
Neniisono', neniisono'
My children, my children. (Mooney 1896, 965)

10

Neniisono', neniisono'
My children, my children.
He'ne'nowouunou'u nih'ei'towuunono'
Thus I pity them, those who have been instructed.
He'ne'nowouunou'u nih'ei'towuunono'
Thus I pity them, those who have been instructed.
Tihce'inih'oniitowoo3i'
When they again were ambitious.
Tihce'inih'oniitowoo3i'
When they again were ambitious. (Mooney 1896, 966)

13

Hohootii niiboot—Eiheiyei
Cottonwood song. Eiheiyei.
Hohootii niiboot—Eiheiyei
Cottonwood song. Eiheiyei.
Neniibootowoo
I am singing it.
Neniibootowoo
I am singing it.
Heiyeyo'oheiyei!
Heiyeyo'oheiyei! (Mooney 1896, 967)

14

Eiyeihei! Hee, nii'ehiisoono'
Eiyeihei! Yes, the young birds.
Eiyeihei! Hee, nii'ehiisoono'
Eiyeihei! Yes, the young birds.
Hei'ei'e'eiheiyuhuuyuu!
Hei'ei'e'eiheiyuhuuyuu!
Hee, boh'ooni'ehiisoono'
Yes, the young thunderbirds.
Hee, boh'ooni'ehiisoono'
Yes, the young thunderbirds. (Mooney 1896, 968)

15

Hee, heisonoonin neyoooxetihi'
Yes, Our Father little whirlwind.

Hee, heisonoonin neyoooxetihi'
Yes, Our Father little whirlwind.
He'ne'nihi'koohunoo
Thus, I run swiftly.
He'ne'nihi'koohunoo
Thus, I run swiftly.
Heisonoonin he'ne'noohowo'
Thus, I saw Our Father.
Heisonoonin he'ne'noohowo'
Thus, I saw Our Father. (Mooney 1896, 970)

16

Hee, heisonoonin neyoooxet
Yes, Our Father, the whirlwind.
Hee, heisonoonin neyoooxet
Yes, Our Father, the whirlwind.
Woow ce'ni'iinookuunit houno'
Now, again he can wear a crow headdress.
Woow ce'ni'iinookuunit houno'
Now, again he can wear a crow headdress. (Mooney 1896, 970)

17

Nonoo'onih'ohunoo
I am flying in circles.
Nonoo'onih'ohunoo
I am flying in circles.
Biito'owu' heneiisei'i
The earth's boundaries.
Biito'owu' heneiisei'i
The earth's boundaries.
Heeneihȝi' ne'nih'ohunoo
They are long (feathers), as I fly.
Heneihȝi' ne'nih'ohunoo
They are long (feathers), as I fly. (Mooney 1896, 970)

18

Hoho'nookoowuunen beniineinoo
Rock man is giving to me.
Hoho'nookoowuunen beniineinoo

Rock man is giving to me.
Hinowun koononeinoo
His paint—he washes me.
Hinowun koononeinoo
His paint—he washes me. (Mooney 1896, 971)

21

"*Iiyeihei! hee, neniisono'—'Uhiiyeheiheiyei!*
Yes, my children. 'Uhiiyeheiheiyei!
'Iiyeihei! hee, neniisono'—'Uhiiyeheiheiyei!
Yes, my children. 'Uhiiyeheiheiyei!
'Iiyeihei! hootowouuno'—Eiyei'oeyoheiyuu!
We render him sad. Eiyei'oeyoheiyuu!
'Iiyeihei! hootowouuno'—Eiyei'oeyoheiyuu!
We render him sad. Eiyei'oeyoheiyuu!
Nih'oo3ou'u hohookeeni3i'—'Oheiyuheiyuu!
Whites, they are crazy. 'Oheiyuheiyuu!
Nih'oo3ou'u hohookeeni3i'—'Oheiyuheiyuu!
Whites, they are crazy. 'Oheiyuheiyuu! (Mooney 1896, 972)

24

Ho(h)'onookee, ho(h)'onookee
The rock, the rock.
Teneesokuutowo'
I am standing on it.
Teneesokuutowo'
I am standing on it
Heisonoonin he'ne'noohoowo'
Thus, I see him, Our Father.
Heisonoonin he'ne'noohoowo'
Thus, I see him, Our Father. (Mooney 1896, 973)

26

Hee, teebe tihne'etiitoonehehk
Well, just when there was life.
Hee, teebe tihne'etiitoonehehk
Well, just when there was life.
Niiteehehk be'enoo neeceeheiht
It was turtle who gave this gift.

Niiteehehk be'enoo neeceeheiht
It was turtle who gave this gift.
Biito'owu'
The earth.
Biito'owu'
The earth.
Tihtowuuneinoo neisonoo
When he told me this, my father.
Tihtowuuneinoo neisonoo
When he told me this, my father. (Mooney 1896, 975)

27

Neneisono', neneisono' neneeninoo touhnoo ne'nih'ohunoo
My children, my children. It is I. I yell-thunder; thus I fly.
Neneisono', neneisono' neneeninoo touheteinih'ohunoo
My children, my children. It is I. I yell-thunder-roar-flying. (Mooney 1896, 976)

28

Neixoo nehcih'owouunoni
Father, have pity on me!
Neixoo nehcih'owouunoni
Father, have pity on me!
Woow, biixonokooyeinoo
Now, I am wailing-fasting-thirsting.
Woow, biixonokooyeinoo
Now, I am wailing-fasting-thirsting.
Hoowuuni bii3itii
There is no food.
Hoowuuni bii3itii
There is no food. (Mooney 1896, 977)

29

Neniihoonih'ohunoo
Yellow I am flying.
Neniihoonih'ohunoo
Yellow I am flying.
Yeneisitii'inookuunih'ohunoo

Wild roses I wear on my head, I fly.
Yeneisitii'inookuunih'ohunoo
Wild roses I wear on my head, I fly.
Hihcebe'—Hei'ei'ei!
Above. Hei'ei'ei!
Hihcebe'—Hei'ei'ei!
Above. Hei'ei'ei! (Mooney 1896, 977)

39

Nonoononoo'ooteinoo houu
Crow is circling and circling me.
Nonoononoo'ooteinoo houu
The Crow is circling and circling me.
Tohce'noȝeinoo houu
Because he Crow is coming after me again.
Tohce'noȝeinoo houu
Because he Crow is coming after me again. (Mooney 1896, 984)

40

Hee, neniisono' Ei'ei'yei!
My children. Ei'ei'yei!
Hee, neniisono' Ei'ei'yei!
My children. Ei'ei'yei!
Hiiyou heeȝeibenowoo
Here it is; I hand it to you.
Hiiyou heeȝeibenowoo
Here it is; I hand it to you.
Biitoh'owu', Ei'ei'yei!
The earth. Ei'ei'yei!
Biitoh'owu', Ei'ei'yei!
The earth. Ei'ei'yei! (Mooney 1896, 984)

48

Beih'ineniinootee' niitobeenoo
Everything, I hear. I hear well.
Beih'ineniinootee' niitobeenoo
Everything, I hear. I hear well.
Neneeninoo houu

I am Crow.
Neneeninoo houu
I am Crow. (Mooney 1896, 993–94)

51

Niicie'iizeti'
Beautiful, good river.
Niicie'iizeti'
Beautiful, good river.
Ciinohootiini'
Where there are no trees.
Ciinohootiini'
Where there are no trees.
Kouun boh'oonibino zii'ookou'u
But thunder-berries are standing.
Kouun boh'oonibino zii'ookou'u
But thunder-berries are standing. (Mooney 1896, 995)

63

Niinoo'oekoohuwoo ciibeet
I am walking around the sweat lodge.
Niinoo'oekoohuwoo ciibeet
I am walking around the sweat lodge.
Heinootee' beii zi'eyoone'
The shell is lying there on the mound.
Heinootee' beii zi'eyoone'
The shell is lying there on the mound. (Mooney 1896, 1001)

72

Hee, neixoo nookooxuu
Yes, Father! Morning star.
Hee, neixoo nookooxuu
Yes, Father! Morning star.
(hii) noohoobei niinoho'ookeenohowoono'
Look at us, we dance (habitually) until dawn arrives.
(hii) noohoobei niinoho'ookeenohowoono'
Look at us, we dance (habitually) until dawn arrives. (Mooney 1896, 1011)

73

'Ohouyuu heeɜeinoo heisonoonin houu
Our Father the crow says.
'Ohouyuu heeɜeinoo heisonoonin houu
Our Father the crow says.
Yooɜon heetih'useebe
Five times may you walk.
Niiɜeinoo heisonoonin
Says Our Father.
Niiɜeinoo heisonoonin
Says Our Father. (Mooney 1896, 1011–12)

Three Stories

Introduction by Andrew Cowell

The three stories presented here were all told in Arapaho on a single occasion by Richard Moss (born 1933) on the Wind River Reservation in Wyoming in November 2000. They were performed for a high school Arapaho language class at Wyoming Indian High School. All those present were Arapahos, but except for Richard Moss, only the teacher was a native speaker and able to fully understand the stories. The stories were videotaped by the students for inclusion in a video on Arapaho storytelling traditions (funded principally by the Wyoming Council for the Humanities), which was completed in collaboration with Andrew Cowell. They were transcribed by Alonzo Moss Sr., who is cochair of the Northern Arapaho Language and Culture Commission and Richard Moss's younger brother, and translated by Alonzo Moss and Andrew Cowell. Cowell wrote this introduction, in part based on discussions with Alonzo and Richard Moss.

The stories are presented in the order in which they were told. The storytelling was preceded by a lecture by Richard Moss (in Arapaho) on the importance of the old ways, the necessity of continuing to learn the Arapaho language, and a lament about how Arapaho is being replaced by English on the reservation. Though we have not included that lecture here, it forms an important context for the stories. Once the lecture was completed, Richard Moss told the stories without intervening commentary.

Richard Moss has lived his entire life on the Wind River Reservation, in the town of Ethete. He is regarded as one of the best remaining Arapaho storytellers. He learned these stories from his father, Paul Moss (1911–94), who himself heard them as a young man in the "chief's tepee" (where such stories were often told) in the early twentieth century. The storytelling tradition continues on the reservation today, in both Arapaho and English, but since the youngest native speakers are now in their fifties, fewer and fewer occasions arise for Arapaho-language stories. The narrative tradition more generally is also declining, and few younger people know many of the stories, even in English.

Presentational Format

There are many ways in which one can choose to reproduce a verbal narrative on the printed page. The most important thing to remember about these choices is that they are all incomplete—the full range of gesture and vocal effects can never be reproduced from the actual telling, for example, and the surrounding context of the narration also crucially influences how it is received by those actually present—who is present, when they laugh or nod their heads, and so on. In addition, the subtle clues about poetic organization and meaning that are picked up by individuals fluent both in the language and in the performance traditions of the speaker can never be captured fully by outsiders.

We have chosen three different strategies to present the three different stories. Different strategies highlight different aspects of the narration, obviously. We hope that readers of the three stories can get a sense from the different presentations how the various features of Arapaho narrative might combine to produce their full effect in an actual storytelling session. For all three stories, we have tried to respect the original language and oral character of the narratives as much as possible, at the expense of sometimes awkward English. Richard Moss often switches perspectives as he narrates, for example, moving abruptly from "there" to "here." This switch is made clear by gestures during the telling but can seem jarring when read. Likewise, he sometimes starts a sentence, pauses, and then starts a new sentence, abandoning the old one. We have retained this feature of the narration in our translation.

For the first and third stories, we have tried to capture the linguistic structure of the story—that is to say, the way in which the literal content or semantic component of the narration is organized into a form of poetry. Many scholars have noted this form of organization within Native American stories. This regularity of structure shows up especially well on the printed page. "The Captive" has been arranged into stanzas and lines. A "line" can be defined in two main ways in the context of this collection. First, the narrator typically uses a special verbal prefix *he'ih-* on the verb. This prefix indicates that something "is said to have happened." The use of this prefix typically occurs only once in a sentence and never with subordinate clauses. It can be used to define an Arapaho "line," which roughly corresponds to a grammatical sentence. Often appositions are added on to a sentence, as in "they went that way, over there, toward the river," generating very long "lines" of verse. Where such lines run over the length of a line on the page, their continuation is indented within the stanzas.

The second way by which a line can be defined is simply a complete grammatical sentence. Within a story, the narrator will often shift from the past tense to the present tense, to heighten the immediacy of the story. When he or she does this, the use of *he'ih-* is dropped. Where this occurs, we have simply determined each complete grammatical sentence to be a "line." The same thing occurs when the narrator switches into the voice of a character. Thus the use of the prefix *he'ih-* is the first determinant of a line, and where this is not used, grammatical sentences are used as a secondary definition.

Stanzas are typically defined by the initial word *wohei* (which we have left untranslated, and which can mean variously "so," "well," "okay," "now then," "next," and such). This word is also, incidentally, a third determiner of poetic lines and always comes at the beginning of a line. Shifts from narration to direct quotation also typically indicate the beginning of new stanzas. Using just these two automatically applied rules, along with the rules for defining lines, one can generate a large number of stanzas with an average length of four lines. The most common variant to this number is three or five lines.

Arapaho narrative is not simply mechanically regulated by automatic rules, however, like a European sonnet would be. With just the rules given here, one finds a great deal of irregularity in the structure of a narrative. However, if one then adds a somewhat more subjective series of criteria (knowledge of four lines as a kind of target length for stanzas; the use of shifts in content in the narrative to break up especially long stanzas and define shorter, more coherent ones; and the presence of a few other common narrative prefixes such as "and," "and then," "then," "thus," and "that's how/why/when," etc.) to define either lines or shifts to a new stanza, then one can generate a fairly regular text of stanzas with median lengths of four lines. Not coincidentally, the most sacred number in Arapaho culture is the number four.

Of course, one could also look for more global organizing features as well—scholars often speak of "scenes" and "acts," which might include several stanzas. These structures are typically far less clearly defined and more subjective than lines or stanzas, however. Whereas in "The Captive" we have provided a minimal organizational structure, in "The Eagles" we have divided the story into larger units that we call simply "parts." We have also italicized key phrases that are repeated in two or more parts (the English translation sometimes partly obscures these repetitions as they exist in the original Arapaho). For each repetition, we have put in brackets a reference to the stanza in which the phrase first appears. This is intended to show how repetition is used in the narrative to tie the multiple parts together through a complex series of cross references to parallel events and attitudes. Note that while this presentational format provides clearer guidelines for the reader, it also necessarily imposes a particular, limiting interpretation on the text. Were one to define repetition more loosely, a much denser series of such cross references could easily be established, though with the choice of which repetitions to emphasize again constituting a form of interpretation.

Listening to—as opposed to reading—the stories reveals that many of these orderly patterns are broken up for the listener by pauses, shifts in the volume and tone of voice, and so on. Thus, one should not mistake the organization presented here on the page for "the" organization of the text, or even the most salient organization for the listener at many points. In the second story, we have presented a more oral-based organization, which focuses on showing pauses, changes in volume and tone of voice, speed of delivery, and so on. In that story, lines are based on pauses in narration (typically of approximately three-quarters to one second). Stanzas are indicated by double spacing and are defined by longer pauses of two seconds or longer. A louder vocal emphasis is indicated by small capitals. Drawing out of words is indicated by hyphenated vowels, as in "lo——ong." A higher tone of voice is indicated by the use of italics. This higher tone is always used with direct speech in narratives by Richard Moss, but I indicate only especially marked occurrences. The tone resembles an English tone of surprise, as when one is reporting animatedly on an unexpected event: "I saw my long-lost cousin last week!"

Meanings

Alonzo Moss Sr. comments that virtually every word of these stories could be discussed at length. The stories use a traditional vocabulary that is heavily laden with deeper connotations. Much of this vocabulary is common to a wide range of stories, and elements of it are also important in prayers, rituals, and ceremonial life, as are subjects such as "the old men" ("the old man" is a name used for the Arapaho sacred pipe) and the eagle. The many ways in which all three of these stories are embedded in Arapaho culture and ideology are too complex to treat here. We can note briefly, however, a few evocative facts.

The golden eagle is seen as the most powerful and sacred of all birds and animals by the Arapahos, and its soaring flight is considered to bring it closer to the heavens and the power and wisdom that derive from the heavens. The number four is also considered to be the symbolic, sacred number of greatest importance. In other versions of "The Eagles," the transformation of the boy is linked to the origins of the Thunderbird—the mythical figure responsible for thunderstorms, lightning, hail, and summer weather more generally, as well as for keeping watch over the Arapaho people. Thus while "The Eagles" seems to be about transgression and punishment, its underlying moral implications are far richer and more ambivalent.

"The Second Thought" is a relatively rare instance of completely traditional poetic organization, vocabulary, and moral themes combined with a clearly newer, reservation-era content. It lacks what non-Arapaho readers would call a supernatural element and instead focuses on the tension between Arapaho and white ways (represented in the person of the work boss and the restaurant waiter). On one level, the story seems to mock the Indian unfamiliar with white ways. But it also seems to mock the Indian who seeks to enter the white world, suggesting that this attempt will lead to problems of reintegration into the Arapaho world. The (supposed) knowledge and money that can be gained from white society turn out to be of little use back on the reservation. The Arapaho protagonist avoids catastrophe by finally recalling the traditional wisdom he received before he departed the reservation (literally "all the things that one uses," both material and intellectual) and by putting aside the excess suspicion he brings from the white world. Yet the story clearly recognizes the new economic realities of reservation life (including the paternalistic authority of the whites) and is finally perhaps a meditation on the inevitable problems of integrating the two, just as the story itself formally integrates Arapaho and white narrative technique and content. Richard Moss says that he heard the story as a young man from an Arapaho named "Strong Bear," so he is not the sole creator of the innovations in this story.

"The Captive" is one of many examples of stories in which humans receive help from superhuman sources, which they then use for the benefit not of themselves but of the whole tribe. The coyote is a common source of such help; the coyote does not coincide with the trickster figure for the Arapahos the way it does for many tribes. Note that the young man learns four key skills—finding water, finding food, making fire, and finding his way safely home. There are several accounts of historical Arapaho conflict with the Apaches, and Arapaho placenames for areas within Rocky Mountain National Park refer to a battle there with the Apaches. There are also a number of other Arapaho "captivity" narratives, involving both other tribes and whites.

Finally, it should be noted that all three of these stories are considered by the Arapahos to be "true," as opposed to mythical stories, trickster stories, or other genres of verbal narrative. Alonzo Moss Sr. stresses that they all are primarily moral lessons, not just "entertainment," and that they were not just told "for no reason." We offer them here in that spirit. The three stories are connected by many themes and motifs that underline these messages: the importance of listening to advice, as well as the difficulty of correctly interpreting that advice in various situations; the importance of both travel from and return to the camp circle, with its metaphorical relationship to identity formation; the related way in which each individual Arapaho, though armed with a shared cultural knowledge, must confront problems as an individual, and find his or her own individual solutions within the context of tradition; the problem of "recognition" when the changed individual returns to the tribe; the importance of learning, reflection, and second chances; and the importance of respecting superiors and elders, whether human or nonhuman. (The Arapahos, incidentally, call themselves *hinóno'éí*, a word that cannot be analyzed linguistically.)

Suggested Reading

For general information on Arapaho language, culture, and history, see Jeffrey Anderson, *The Four Hills of Life: Northern Arapaho Knowledge and Life Movement* (Lincoln: University of Nebraska Press, 2001) (on the historical conflicts between Arapaho and Euro-American culture, ideology, and modes of social organization); Loretta Fowler, *Arapahoe Politics, 1851–1978: Symbols in Crises of Authority* (Lincoln: University of Nebraska Press, 1982) (on social and political history primarily of the reservation era); Alfred Kroeber, *The Arapaho* (Lincoln: University of Nebraska Press, 1983) (on culture and ceremony of the nineteenth century); and Virginia Cole Trenholm, *The Arapahoes, Our People* (Norman: University of Oklahoma Press, 1970) (on general history, especially prereservation). For more narratives, in English, see George Dorsey and Alfred Kroeber, *Traditions of the Arapaho* (Lincoln: University of Nebraska Press, 1998). *Hinóno'éínoo3ítoono/Arapaho Historical Traditions*, a bilingual anthology of Arapaho narratives, edited by Andrew Cowell and Alonzo Moss Sr., will be published by University of Manitoba Press in 2005.

THE EAGLES

Told by Richard Moss
Translated and edited by Andrew Cowell and Alonzo Moss Sr.

Introduction

1. Wohei, listen carefully.
This is *a story that was told* . . . that *the old men told us*.
I remember, it was my father who told this story.

Part One: In the Camp

2. The Arapaho were staying here—they used to move camp all about.
They were staying in a big camp.
All those who know, the young men, they went hunting,
and the old men, the old women, the children, they stayed behind.
3. Wohei, this one boy went pretty far, way over there to the mountains.
That's when he would bring home eagles—the ones with the white rump, black eagles.
4. "Wohei," they said to him, "*we're going to warn you*.
Don't . . . *don't do it* anymore.
Just one or two times, that's okay.
Four . . . *four times*, once you're to that point,
I don't know how things will turn out."

Part Two: From the Camp to the Eagles

5. But *this young man isn't listening to them*, isn't listening.
He thinks differently.
Well, he's going back to the nest where he can find the eagles.
And you see, it's very steep.
He slid down the slope to where a rock was sticking out a little bit, where the nest was.

He sees something white there.
Maybe the eagles had just hatched.
6. "Wohei, *I'm going to try and get them.*"
He's going to make a rope.
It's a long way down to the ground there.
He tied the rope to a tree,
and *he's lowering himself downward* with the rope.
Now he's just almost reached it, the nest where the eagles are,
and that rope broke.
7. Wohei, he was by himself,
and then that rope broke,
and there was no way whatsoever for him *to get back down* to the ground,
so he had to stay with those eagles.
And their mother, she brought them . . . brought them rabbits, snakes,
various things.
He ate them up.
8. Wohei, rainwater, somewhere, a puddle, that's where he drank.
That's how it was.
He's living with them.
Finally, these eagles got big.
He's not hungry; he's eating well, even though the meat is totally raw.

Part Three: From the Eagles to the Camp

9. Wohei, these eagles—*the two of them*—they're growing up quickly.
When they were big, they got feathers, which made them strong.
Then he took them . . . they would shake their feathers,
and they flapped their wings.
Now they're almost ready to fly.
10. "Wohei, *I'm going to try and hold on,*" [6] the young man said,
and he took one by its legs.
It shook its feathers,
and then it leapt down . . .
these eagles tried to fly here . . . where . . . and *they're slowly descending.* [6]
Right *down to the ground.* [7]
11. Then their mother flew to the eagles, her children.
Then she called to the young man, "It's okay.
You're going to get back down. [7]

These children of mine are helping you.
They're doing you a favor."

12. "Wohei, I'm going to give you some advice, kind of *as a warning to you.* [4]
Birds, when you eat them, *whatever kind of birds*, there's one part . . .
Don't eat it, don't eat it! [4]
If you eat it, we'll come for you."
That's what she said to him.

Part Four: In the Camp Circle Again

13. Then he went home.
Everyone was happy when he got home.
Then he told them where he had been:
"The eagles *brought me back down."* [11]

14. Wohei, the way they lived, they killed things for themselves, including turkeys, grouse, various things, pheasants, *different sorts of game birds of various types.* [12]

15. "Wohei, *I was warned* [4, 12] that there's one thing I can't eat.
If I eat it, then they'll . . . they'll come for me." [12]

Part Five: From the Camp to the Eagles

16. Wohei, it happened that the others, since they didn't know about this one part,
they prepared a meal.
Well . . . then they fed him,
and he accidentally *ate that part.* [7]
"Aie! *I was warned,* [4, 12, 15] and now I've eaten it."

17. "Wohei," he told his relatives,
"You put up a tepee, and that's where I'll sit.
They're going to come for me." [12, 15]

18. And then he went there, into the tepee.
In front, everyone is sitting, and they watched him.
After a little while, well . . . then *two eagles* [9] came circling in the air, and landed nearby.
Then they went into the tepee:
that's how they came for him there. [12, 15, 17]

19. Wohei, now it's open, that door.
The eagles came out.
There were three eagles.
Then they flew away: they took him away.

Conclusion

20. That's it. Things can be done *four times.* [4]
If you go beyond this, then it's dangerous.
That's what the old men said. [1]
21. Wohei, then when this young man, this child . . .
because *he didn't listen* [5] and he wanted to go out on his own . . .
that's where it's dangerous.
Maybe that's still the way it is.
We still have wisdom and power.
We still live according to our customs.
22. Wohei, that's it.
They told us [1] about this eagle.
That's how it is,
That's the way this story goes.

THE SECOND THOUGHT

Told by Richard Moss
Translated and edited by Andrew Cowell and Alonzo Moss Sr.

1. Lo——ong ago,
the STRIving life,

2. the ways they lived, VARious ways.

3. A YOUNG man, it was like this,
when he was first married,
thereabouts where they were living,
there was no work:
there's no work anywhere;
it was full.

4. And that's how it was,
his life. He'd been married for maybe several months.

5. WOHEI! "Wohei," he said to his wife.
"I'm going to set off. I'm going . . .
to look for work."

6. "If I find it somewhere, I'll work there.
I'll make money."

7. Wohei, here's his wife, preparing him.
She put all his clothes, his various things, everything he would use, in a bag.

8. Wohei, then when he was ready,
"Wohei," he told his wife. "Here's your home. Watch over it!
Watch over it!
Sometime, I'll come back."

9. "I'm going to look for work."

10. *Wohei, then this man set off.*
Wa——ay far away.
Way off over there he went to ask for work. There's NONE.
"The last one . . .
just got here. I just hired the last one.
Wohei, he's going to work for me. Now we're full up, already full"

11. WherEVER he went, that's what he was told. *He kept pushing fa———arther onward.*

12. Wohei then,

13. WherEVER he asked for work, then he was told.
"We're full too. I'm not . . . I'm not looking for any more workers."

14. Wherever he arrived, *they'd* JUST *filled the last opening.* Here he is, arriving,
"Here I just hired the last one. Now we've got enough.
There, farther down that ways,"

15. "He's looking for workers. Right away! Go see him!
Go see him right away! Right away! Head over there right away!"
Wohei, I guess he didn't find him there. Then he set on off. He arrived over there.

16. He went on in to see this white man. "I'm trying . . ."
"Wohei, what are you looking for?" "*Work. I'm going to work.*" *"Yes."*
WOHEI, *he came along* JUST *at the right time.*
"You, you're the last one to arrive. I'll hire you.
You'll work for me."
That's what he told him. That's where he's going to work, doing various things.
Then he started working.
He told his boss, *"Most of my money, I want to put it away in the bank."* He put it in there when he got paid. "I'll buy things for myself, the things I need, shoes, socks, shirts, and the various things."
Wohei, that's what happened. Everything that he got ahold of, he saved it up.
He saved up a lot from all his work. Well . . .

17. After a long while, maybe twenty years since the beginning. Wohei, then he thought about it. "Maybe now there's enough, my money, what I've saved.
Might as well go on back home now."

18. WOHEI, THEN he told his boss.
"Before I go, I'm going to tell you."

19. "I'm going to take my money home. I'm heading back home.
So you can look for whoever's going to . . .
replace me around here."
And that's how it went.

20. Wohei, now the time has arrived, the time when he'll set off.
Wohei, his boss,
someone had arrived to replace him there.
"I'm going to tell you what you will do."
Wohei, then his boss arrived with the bag.
"Wohei, here's you money. It's all inside here.
I'm going to give YOU some ADVICE.
There where you're going, where you're going, when you're going back home,
DON'T *look around at anybody!*
Don't talk to anybody!
Whenever you arrive in a town where you're going to eat,
the waiter, tell him what you want to eat.
When you've finished, put down some money. A little extra, more than it costs [as a tip]." Then he set off. That's what he did.
Wohei, sure enough he arrived at a town, and he went to a restaurant.

21. He looked around to see what he would eat.
Then he told
the waiter. *When he'd finished, he put down some money, a little extra.*
He got up. He went outside, SET off.

22. After a while, he heard someone running toward him; there was someone running toward him. Well right away, he took off.
"Wait, wait, I'm not going to hurt you. I won't . . . Wait! Stop!"

23. So he just stopped. The man came running to him.
"Here's your bag. You forgot it."

24. "Wohei, I'm going to give YOU some ADVICE.
Don't talk to anyone. Don't . . . If you do that, they will GET you.
They will . . .
get all your money. *They will try . . . You might get killed.*
I'm warning you about this. Just keep right on going."
And that's what he did.
It's still a long ways to where he's going.
Finally, he was getting there.
There was still a hill to cross to get to where his house was.
Now it's getting DARK.
He climbed up on the ridge. His house was lit up. "*I guess maybe . . .*
apparently . . .
my wife is maybe still there.
She's still around waiting for me to bring something home."

25. That's just what he thought.
He headed on down there.
He got to his house.
To the fence, to the gate, he opens it, goes on into [the yard].
WOHEI, there's a window.
Wohei, *he's looking inside.*
His wife is sitting there, and a young man. He saw him.
And here he is, hugging and kissing her!
Right away, he got real angry.
He's going to get a gun.
"I'm going to SHOOT them both with it" he thought to himself.

26. "WOHEI, no, no, don't go right away and . . . don't do that,"
he thought to himself.

27. He will THINK about it CAREFULLY,

28. How he was told to think with all his mind, all the things that he uses.
Once he's thought about it carefully, then his mind starts to go straight again.
"If it's LIKE THAT, then I'll shoot them."

29. He goes RIGHT to the door. He knocks.
That young man opened the door.
"Who is that that I see there?" asked his mother.
"Mother, is this man my father? Mother." "Yes, he's your father. Look at your father."
Look! If he hadn't put his thinking skills to use,
he would have shot his wife.
That's how this story is.
You must use all your capacities to think. Consider things carefully.
THAT's the way it is.

THE CAPTIVE

Told by Richard Moss

Translated and edited by Andrew Cowell and Alonzo Moss Sr.

1. Wohei, a story that I was told.
Long ago, that's . . . that's how life was.
They moved all around various places,
all about . . . they moved camp all about,
toward the north, or the east, southward.

2. Wohei, "the rising lands," as they called the west,
all about, everywhere, that's how they camped.
Wherever they found buffalo, that's where they went.
They would follow them, kill them.
They made jerky.
And when the fruits were ripe, they picked them.

3. Various places, down south, somewhere over there,
they were attacked by the Apaches.
They were attacked.
Well, the Apaches seized a young man, they captured him.
When they had seized him, they took that child, that young man home with them.

4. That's where he stayed: he's living with them, playing with them;
And their language, soon he knows their language,
and how they live there where it's hot, where the Apaches live,
where they find their various foods, where water is.

5. Wohei, they go out on the warpath.
He takes part; this young boy is involved in everything.
And then this young one, however old he is, maybe almost . . .

6. "Wohei," they said to him, "we're going to let you go.
We won't do anything to you; we'll just take you over here.

You'll accompany us here.
We'll prepare you here.
We'll . . . we'll put meat in your bag, food, and water."
They prepared him.

7. Wohei, then the day arrived when they would let him go.
"Wohei, over that ways, where your people are over that ways,"
they only pointed this way.
"You'll only get home if you go straight.
Somewhere there, you should avoid that.
The direction where you're facing, go that way.
Just try to recognize it.
You will recognize it."

8. Wohei, he set off.
At first, he ran this way, and his moccasins were all worn out.

9. Wohei, then he ate up all his food; there was no more water.
There where it's real hot, where it's dry, there was no water, no water.
He's searching all around, looking all around, this boy, and well, there's no water; rivers: none; streams: none.
He keeps walking.

10. Wohei, he's getting tired from traveling; he's hungry; he's thirsty.

11. Wohei, maybe now his tracks will come to an end.
"Maybe now I'm finished," he thought to himself.

12. Wohei, then he found a place with a little shade.

13. Wohei, then he lay down.

14. "Wohei, here, this is where I'll die," he said. It was hot.

15. Wohei, as he was lying there,
there was something else.
He saw a coyote.
It was sitting there; it's speaking to him.

16. "Wohei, friend, what are you doing?"
"I was a captive with those people,
they kept me;
and then released me,
and I just have to go home here where my people are.
That's what they said to me."

17. "Wohei, I don't have any food.
I used up the water that they gave me.
I'm hungry.
I'm thirsty.
Maybe this is just . . . this is as far as I go."

18. "Yes," Coyote said, "I will help you.
You'll get back home.
I'll help you.
I will teach you things.
You'll have things of value.
I will give you things.
You'll have power, as it's called."

19. "Wohei, first of all, water.
I will show you where to find water.
Come on!
A short stick: here, take it!
Here, come on."

20. So the young man went on,
and then suddenly he stopped:
he saw this green, shady place.

21. "That's where water is.
Dig there.
Wohei, in that direction . . . you won't . . .
if you can find damp ground is, you'll know that's where there's water.
Then you start digging."

22. There was damp ground.

23. Wohei, then water appeared.
That's what happened.
Soon he had drunk his fill of water,
and that's how he was able to drink again.

24. "Wohei, I've given you this:
You will be able to find water no matter how dry it is.
You'll know where to find water.
You won't be thirsty."

25. "Wohei, come on!
Here, I'll teach you how to eat again.
Get a long stick, fairly long, with a fork in it,
and when it's ready, come on over here to where it's rocky."

26. Then he climbed up there.
There were rabbits.
They all started running away,
and they ran underground, where their dens were . . .

27. "Wohei, put that stick in there under the ground.
If you touch one, then you twist it.
You'll be able to get one out."

28. That's what he did.
He dragged out rabbits,
and then he cut off the heads of several of them.

29. "Wohei, I've taught you how you can have food again.
Others . . . I'm going to tell you what you have to . . .
This game will be bigger.
You'll kill it for yourself."

30. "Wohei, come on,
I'll show . . . how to cook with fire.
Fire, I'll show you how to do it.
You'll start a fire for yourself."

31. But there were no flints—none.
"I'm going to start a fire.
There's nothing.
I'll show you."

32. "Wohei, watch me.
Pile up these sticks, these ones.
Watch me!"

33. He jumped over the pile.
Again he jumped over it.

34. Wohei, from here, again he jumps over there.

35. Wohei, four times he's jumping over the pile.
Then he slapped the pile with his tail,
and it lit up,
then it slowly started to burn.

36. "Wohei, blow on it!"

37. "Wohei, I'll also give you the rock lying there.
You will take a stick,
you'll start to spin the stick on the rock.
You'll . . . until . . . that's how you'll start a fire."

38. "I do it like this too.
You can use this method too.
If you get too cold, this is how you can start a fire for yourself.
I'm giving you this too."

39. Wohei, home, he went homeward,
and this coyote led him.
This coyote went way over thataway hunting.
He came running back.

40. "We'll . . . we'll take a different route in that direction.
Enemies are around here.
We'll take a different route,

over there, on top of the hills, is where they are.
We almost went the wrong way."

41. "You're alone . . . if you had been alone, you would have run into them,
we'll avoid them,
we'll keeping going in that direction."

42. Wohei, they came to a little stream.
That's the place where one swims across.

43. Wohei, there in the vicinity are some lakes, somewhere there.
They went through there,
toward where it's mountainous, this way.

44. Wohei, good . . . he's going along good.
He's using the things that he's been taught.
And coyote brought him more game to cook.

45. Wohei, here's how far they walked, here to a ridge.
They climbed up that way.

46. "Wohei, see, it's way over there, where the ridge is.
Over the ridge, a stream flows.
Across it, that's where" . . . that's where his relatives are, the Arapahos.
That's where they are.
"After a while, we'll go over there."

47. They're setting out for the camp.
Boy, it's getting dark!
They're climbing up the last ridge.
Down below, it's lit up, some kind of fire, there was a camp.
They're still making dinner.
And there's lots of talking:
They didn't know that this young man had . . . had arrived.

48. "Wohei, just cross the river.
After you cross the river, go in where the Arapahos are,
then you'll be reunited with them."

49. And that's what he did.
He went on across that river,
on to where everyone was sitting about,
and then he came to a stop.

50. But the other young men at first said,
"We've never seen this one before."

51. Then he came a little closer:
"He resembles, a little bit—our son!
I wonder if it might be him.
Go check him out," the man's wife said.

52. "Kind of near his heart, by his stomach, there's a dark birthmark.
If it's there, then he's our son."

53. Then he went to him,
"Where have you come from?"
"I've come from far away."

54. Wohei, then he lifted his shirt up,
He lifted it a little bit,
and there it was.

55. "You, you're my son.
Over there is your mother."

56. Wohei, that's how he was reunited.
And that coyote, as soon as he saw that he had found his mother and father again, all the other coyotes who were around there, he started howling to them.
He's telling them:

57. "I brought that young man back.
Now he's found his parents again."

58. Wohei, they started howling all around—they were happy about it.
And that's how this story goes.

The coyote brought him back,
and that's how he got his power.

59. Wohei, now he's back home with the other children.
Eventually he became a chief.

60. Wohei, that's the story, that's how it is.

Scarface

Introduction by Theresa Schenck

The Blackfeet are a group of confederated tribes: the Siksika, or Blackfoot; the Kainaa, or Bloods; and the Pikuni, or Piegans, who are further divided by the forty-ninth parallel into Northern and Southern Piegans. Their territory, which once extended from the North Saskatchewan River in Alberta to the Missouri River in Montana, is today reduced to three reserves in Canada and one in the United States. The term Blackfeet refers to the inhabitants, mostly Southern Piegans, of the Blackfeet Indian Reservation in Montana. The Blackfeet speak a language of the Central Algonquian stock, although it differs greatly from the others of the same stock. The number of Blackfeet who speak the language fluently in the United States is now estimated to be fewer than one hundred, but the language is currently being taught in the public schools on the reservation and in the Blackfeet Community College in Browning, Montana, and it is hoped that soon a new generation of native speakers will emerge. A private school in Browning, the Piegan Institute, is also contributing to the revival of the Blackfeet language through its program of total immersion.

The Scarface story is at the very heart of Blackfeet culture. It explains the origin of some of the practices that are central to our spiritual life: purification, cleansing, and renewal through the sweat; healing, sacrifice, and thanksgiving through the Medicine Lodge; and the sacred role of women in Blackfeet society.

Because it is a living story, there have been many versions of the Scarface myth, none of them definitive. One of the earliest is that of George Bird Grinnell in *Blackfeet Lodge Tales*, published in 1892. He does not identify the specific source of this story but rather mentions all his informants in his introduction. Clark Wissler and his Blackfeet collaborator David Duvall included two versions of the myth, one by a Piegan man, the other by a Piegan woman, in their *Mythology of the Blackfoot*, published in 1908. Walter McClintock's narrative, titled "The Legend of Poïa, the Christ Story of the Blackfeet," was related to him by his adoptive father, Mad Wolf, and published in 1910 in *The Old North Trail*. More recently, Percy Bull Child has devoted a whole section to an expanded version of the Scarface story, "Honoring Creator Sun," in his book *The Sun Came Down*, published in 1985.

Scarface, the young man disfigured by a scar across his face, represents man in his most pitiful state. He is poor and alone; he is poor because he is alone, without relatives or kin. But most of all he is weak, in need of help. Rejected by the beautiful girl he wants to marry, he then turns to the Sun, who has the power to heal. All versions of the story mention the young man's offensive smell and the Sun's response: to smudge him with cedar. This is the first step toward cleansing and becoming whole. But the Sun does not look favorably on this earthling. It is his wife, the Moon, who intercedes for Scarface, and thus it is through her influence that the Sun pities the young man and agrees to help him. The Sun's heat is the power that can not only cleanse and purify, but also heal, and the Sun's instrument is the Sweat Lodge, whose heat removes the scar and transforms Scarface into the image of Morning Star, son of the Sun.

Scarface becomes companion to Morning Star and on one of their hunting expeditions, saves him from seven vicious birds by killing all of them. In gratitude the Sun gives Scarface that most sacred of all ceremonies, the Medicine Lodge, with instructions on how to perform it, and especially on the role of his wife in all the essential aspects of the ceremony. He also gives him a bundle containing the suit he will wear in the ceremony, decorated with seven black stripes on the sleeves and leggings and a disk representing the Sun. For his wife there is an elkskin dress and two black raven feathers, Raven being recognized as having great wisdom and power coming from the Sun.

It is no accident that the Sun describes a special role for the woman who will become the wife of Scarface. Just as the Sun listens to and honors his wife, the Moon, so must Scarface share his power with his wife. On his return to earth by way of the Wolf Trail (the Milky Way), he goes first to his future wife and offers her the gift of the raven feathers. It is only then, when both are endowed with special power from the Sun, that they are able to bring the Medicine Lodge to the people.

The Medicine Lodge of the Blackfeet is a ceremony given to honor the Sun in fulfillment of a vow by a holy woman, one who has never been with a man other than her husband. In every version of the Scarface story, this is stressed from the very beginning and in the Sun's instructions to Scarface. The woman of the Medicine Lodge belongs to the Sun.

The version here was written by Pauline Running Crane and told to her by one of her grandfathers, John Little Blaze. It contains many of the essential elements of the traditional story, yet differs in that it also stresses many Blackfeet values not found in the other myths: the interdependence of humans and animals, gratitude for gifts and favors, respect for property, fidelity to promises, and the importance of honesty and a good heart over outward appearances. It is, perhaps, these values that Little Blaze wanted to teach his granddaughter, by working them into a story already familiar to all Blackfeet children. It is interesting that the explanation of the Sweat Lodge does not figure strongly in this story, although it is hinted at when Scarface "was treated with warmth from the Sun." Traditionally, Blackfeet women do not enter a sweat lodge.

Suggested Reading

Bullchild, Percy. *The Sun Came Down.* San Francisco: Harper & Row, 1985.

Grinnell, George Bird. *Blackfoot Lodge Tales.* Lincoln: University of Nebraska Press, 1962.

McClintock, Walter. *The Old North Trail.* Lincoln: University of Nebraska Press, 1968.

Wissler, Clark, and D. C. Duvall. *Mythology of the Blackfoot Indians.* Lincoln: University of Nebraska Press, 1995.

SCARFACE

Written and Translated by Pauline Running Crane

A long time ago there was an orphan boy who lived with his grandmother among the Blackfeet. All the other children in the camp made fun of him because he had a mark on his face, and he was poor. This boy, called Pawakksski, or Scarface, spent a lot of time with the animals and birds in the forest; this is how he came to speak their language. They were the brothers and sisters he never had, for he was an only child.

The chief had a beautiful daughter. All the young men were trying to win her, but she did not like their bragging and smart ways. She never liked the way they acted. Scarface fell in love with her, but he did not want to speak to her because he was poor and his face was scarred. All the other young men made fun of him after they found out that he was in love with Soo-tah-ih-ki, which means Singing in the Rain. They told him, "Maybe she will give her heart to the one who is poor and ugly." They kept after him and saying things to hurt him. Eventually one evening by a creek Scarface found the courage to speak to her. Soo-tah-ih-ki knew he was a kind-hearted young man and an honest person. She never saw the scar on his face. She told Scarface, "I would marry you, but I already made a promise to the Sun, Na-to-sii. You have a good heart, and you are honest. It does not matter that you are poor. I would marry you, but I have promised the Sun never to marry."

Scarface was sad over what she had told him. He said to her, "You make me happy; then you make me sad. Could you not be free from the promise?"

Soo-tah-ih-ki told him, "If you go to the Sun, he may free me from my promise."

"I will go then," said Scarface. "I do not think the Sun wants his children to be unhappy."

The beautiful girl asked Scarface if he knew where to go. "All I know," he replied, "is that he lives past the Great Waters. There will be someone to help me find the way."

In the days before he left to find the Sun, his grandmother sewed him some extra moccasins and crushed some dried meat with berries and fat so he would have food along the way. She felt very sad for him. After he left, he found many trails leading toward the Great Waters, but he did not know which one to follow. It was already snowing all around, and he knew his people never came to this place. It was the Wolf, Makoyi, that helped him follow the right trail. All the animals knew about Scarface because he was friends with all the animals in the woods. They knew he was nice to all animals, and everyone knew about him.

The Wolf told him, "I do not know of the Sun's place, but you can go through this trail. The left path is the one to follow." Then he came to a place with more paths, and the snow was falling harder. He saw a mother Bear and asked for help. He asked for help from the Bear. She told him which way to go, and he thanked his friend, the mother Bear and her little ones.

After a long time he came to a place where no one had ever been. There was so much snow, everything looked white. He saw the snow white owls and asked them for help. The owls said, "Our cousins speak of you. We fly close to the Great Water, but we have never seen the Sun's place." They took him to the edge of the trees and water. He also thanked them.

Scarface looked far out over the water, but he could not see the end. He began to wonder how he would cross the great expanse. He then spent three days and nights praying. When the fourth day came, a road showed up on the Great Water leading toward the Sun's home. On this road he went across the Great Water, knowing that he was close to the Sun's home. Then he found a path very much used, and he followed it. It seemed to be a happy place. He saw a bag of arrows, but he did not touch it. Then a handsome young man met him and asked if he had seen his arrows. Scarface told him they were where he left them. This man was wearing a beautiful beaded outfit of buckskin and asked Scarface who he was. "I am Scarface," he answered. "I have come to see the Sun."

"I am Kii-pi-so-waahs, Morning Star," he replied. "My father is the Sun, and my mother is the Moon." Then the two young men went to get his arrows. Afterward they went to the Sun's home, where Scarface met the Mother Moon and told her he had come to see the Sun. He was invited into the lodge, but he was ashamed to say why he came. She fed him and gave him water. When the Sun came back, he was treated with warmth from the Sun and was praised for his honesty, and the Sun heard of his troubles.

He was then warned not to go to a certain mountain where there were savage birds. He said he would not go to this place. Still, he wondered how he could ask the Sun to let Soo-tah-ih-ki off her vow, because they were so kind to him. He did not want to make the Sun angry, so he kept his secret to himself. After going with Morning Star to different places in the Sun's realm, he was glad and sad of the beauty around him and also knew of the beauty of Soo-tah-ih-ki.

Morning Star had a secret desire to meet and battle with the savage birds Scarface had been told to avoid. One morning Scarface realized that Morning Star was missing. He knew where to find him. He had gone out to fight the birds, and they were trying to kill him. Scarface helped Morning Star kill the birds. They rested, and then started for home. Sun got after Morning Star and praised Scarface for saving his son. The Sun told Scarface he would grant him whatever he wished for. The Moon spoke and said, "You are our son; anything you want you will have." It was then he spoke of the maiden back at his village. She had made a vow to the Sun that she would never marry. "I am asking you to free her so I could marry her." The Sun smiled and said, "We will not deny your heart's desire. I release the maiden from her promise, but in return you are to make a Medicine Lodge so that the people may honor me. Return to her and claim her as your wife." It was then that the Sun touched Scarface and his scar disappeared. He gave him two raven feathers and gifts of rich clothing and taught him how to make a Medicine Lodge in his honor. He gave him songs and everything that is to be used in the Medicine Lodge. But first he had to build a sweat lodge to cleanse himself in order to be pure enough to build the Medicine Lodge. Then Morning Star took him to the end of the sky and showed him a shorter road to earth called Ma-ko-yooh-so-koyi, or Wolf Road.

The maiden was always waiting for Scarface. When she saw him coming she ran to meet him. He showed her where the Sun had touched him and healed his scar, and explained that she was now free to marry him and that together they would give a Medicine Lodge for all the people to honor the Sun. He gave her the two raven feathers, and they got married the next day. Together they gave the first Medicine Lodge. He was never teased again, and his new name was Ist-tsik-ski, Smooth Face. He gave some of his gifts to his grandmother.

My grandfather told me this is how the Medicine Lodge began and was finally built here on the reservation. Before doing a Medicine Lodge, the people doing it fast for four days. They are camped directly west of where the Medicine Lodge is to be made. Both the woman and the man are to be pure and true about what they are doing. There are many songs and dances used in the ceremonies of the Medicine Lodge. They pray for the good of everyone on earth and all animals and birds. They pray to all the animals on land and in the water to help everyone.

The Rolling Head

Introduction by Wayne Leman

The Cheyennes live in Oklahoma and Montana. Originally they lived near the Great Lakes, but they moved westward as they experienced pressure from other tribes in the area. After they obtained horses, they were able to sustain a nomadic lifestyle on the Great Plains, hunting buffalo and eating berries and other food that they were able to find.

Today the Cheyennes in Oklahoma are part of the same tribal organization with the Southern Arapaho. There are approximately eight thousand enrolled members of the Northern Cheyenne tribe on their reservation in southeastern Montana.

The story of a rolling head has traditionally been told in Cheyenne, Cree, and likely other Algonquian languages. The version in this book was narrated in the Cheyenne language by Laura Rockroads in February 1975. At that time Rockroads had been bedridden with arthritis for a number of years. We do not know the circumstances of the recording, but it is quite possible that the recordist was Ray Mueller, audiovisual specialist of Busby School, operated by the Northern Cheyenne tribe, which was located a couple of blocks from the home of Laura Rockroads. We do know that Mueller collected a number of Cheyenne stories from Rockroads to preserve them for future generations of Cheyenne children. We are all in her debt for recording these stories since today they are seldom told to Cheyenne children, especially in the Cheyenne language, which is no longer learned by most Cheyenne children. The stories recorded by Laura Rockroads were published in the large volume of Cheyenne texts, *Náévâhóó'ôhtséme / We Are Going Back Home: Cheyenne History and Stories Told by James Shoulderblade and Others* (listed in the "Suggested Reading" section). This entire volume of Cheyenne texts was dedicated to Rockroads as follows: "Dedicated to the memory of Mrs. Laura Rockroads (1910–1979) who wanted Cheyenne young people to know how to live and so left us her teachings. Nea'eshemeno, Sóena'hané'e (Thank you, Kills Through the Enemy Woman)."

Typical of indigenous legends, the story of the rolling head is told from the viewpoint of the Algonquian worldview. To those who are not familiar with the Algonquian worldview, a number of elements in the story may not make sense until some background information is provided to explain the culturally implicit information assumed by those who narrate the story in its traditional form. We provide such background through footnotes at appropriate points in the story.

Cheyennes are aware that non-Indians feel a certain amount of revulsion when they encounter the story of the rolling head. But they respond by pointing out that there are traditional stories in European folklore that, similarly, have elements which can cause revulsion. One such story mentioned by Cheyennes is Little Red Riding Hood, in which a wolf eats the grandmother of Little Red Riding Hood, the heroine, and in some versions, also eats the heroine.

Laura Rockroads's version of the rolling head story was transcribed into the modern Cheyenne spelling system by linguist Wayne Leman and Cheyenne language teacher Josephine Stands in Timber Glenmore, daughter of the tribal historian, John Stands in Timber. Josephine Glenmore also helped Leman translate the Cheyenne transcription of "The Rolling Head" to English.

Typical of the narration of traditional legends, a number of slightly different versions of the story of the rolling head have been told in Cheyenne. Another version of the story, which linguist Leman has published (1980), was told by Albert Hoffman, a Cheyenne who lived in Oklahoma. The Rockroads version of this story was previously published in Cheyenne, with interlinear English translation, in the book *Náévâhóo'ôhtséme / We Are Going Back Home*, mentioned earlier.

A particularly interesting aspect of the Rockroads version of this story is the way that Laura Rockroads inserts herself into the narrative, using traditional Cheyenne exclamations for what occurs at various points in the story. At the beginning of the story, Rockroads provides a person comment about what the value of this story might be. Such personal comments on the story expand the length of this version of the story over the shorter versions, which simply state the action within the story itself.

Cheyennes often point out that their stories and humor do not sound nearly as good in English as they do in Cheyenne. This, of course, has much to do with the fact that things that are said in life are usually most meaningful in one's mother tongue. Also, there is an important cultural connection between the original language of a narration and many elements of that narration, cultural elements that have traditionally been expressed through the native language. These cultural associations are not nearly as strong in a translation as they were in the original-language version of a story. Nevertheless, we present this English translation of this traditional Algonquian story for non-Cheyenne speakers to read and appreciate the forms of storytelling and cultural elements of those who originally told this well-known story in their mother tongues.

"The Rolling Head" begins with the typical Cheyenne text opening, "I'm going to tell a story about," and ends with a typical closure, "And that's the way the story is," literally, "And that's the way the story lies."

The main plot of the story involves a man who discovers that his wife has been having an affair with a water monster. He kills both the water monster and his wife and decapitates his wife. He abandons his children, an older daughter and a young son, accusing them of his wife's death to the rest of the tribe. The decapitated head of his wife chases the children as they flee.

On four different occasions (four being a sacred number to many Native Americans and the number of times many things occur in Cheyenne legends), this rolling head almost catches up to the children. But the older sister has special powers she uses to create an obstacle for each of the four occasions (wild rose bushes, bearberry bushes, wild plum bushes, and a crevasse in the earth) to keep the head from catching them.

In the end the children are reunited with the rest of their tribal group, and their father is killed by the children's pet bears.

Suggested Reading

Grinnell, George Bird. 1923. *The Cheyenne Indians: Their History and Ways of Life.* 2 vols. Repr., Lincoln: University of Nebraska Press, 1972.

———. 1926. *By Cheyenne Campfires.* Lincoln: University of Nebraska Press.

Hoebel, E. Adamson. 1978. *The Cheyennes: Indians of the Great Plains.* 2nd ed. New York: Holt, Rinehart & Winston.

Leman, Wayne. 1979. *A Reference Grammar of the Cheyenne Language.* Busby MT: Cheyenne Translation Project.

———, ed. 1980. *Cheyenne Texts: An Introduction to Cheyenne Literature.* Busby MT: Cheyenne Translation Project.

———, ed. 1987. *Náévâhóó'ôhtséme / We Are Going Back Home: Cheyenne History and Stories Told by James Shoulderblade and Others.* Memoir 4. Winnipeg MB: Algonquian & Iroquoian Linguistics.

———, ed. Cheyenne Language Web Site. http://www.geocities.com/cheyenne_language. Includes materials to read on Cheyenne oral literature, language, and culture; Leman publications in this list are available through this Web site.

Stands in Timber, John, and Margot Liberty. 1967. *Cheyenne Memories.* Repr., Lincoln: University of Nebraska Press, 1972.

Weist, Tom. 1977. *A History of the Cheyenne People.* Billings MT: Montana Council for Indian Education.

THE ROLLING HEAD

Told by Laura Rockroads

Translated by Wayne Leman and Josephine Stands in Timber Glenmore

I am going to tell a story about when some children were chased by a head. I'm going to tell it. I don't know how anyone would learn anything from this story, but perhaps they could learn something about that woman or the man or how the children were taken care of.

This man and woman had camped. They were camped by themselves. And they had two children. They would move camp off by themselves as a family. They would go around looking for meat.

Then they camped somewhere. Naoo,[1] that man would bring in a lot of game! They made dry meat.

Each morning after they had eaten, this man would braid his wife's hair and paint her face red.[2] Then this man would leave and go hunting. They lived this way for some time.

After the man would hunt for some time, when he would come home, the red paint that he had put on his wife would just be all gone. It would be completely gone. "What does she do?" he would wonder about her.

Then one day he said to her, "Eaaa, every time I put red paint on your face and on your hair. But what do you do when I'm gone, because when I return the paint is all gone?"

"When I'm working, for instance, when I'm tanning, I sweat, and I guess I just wipe it all off," she told him.

But he didn't believe her. He was suspicious of her.

So one morning he left early and hid behind a hill close to where they were camped. He lay down to watch his wife. But she just stayed home. He watched like this for a few days.

Then one day his wife came out of the tepee. They were camped close to a lake. That's where they would go to fetch water. His wife went over there to the

1. *Naoo* (or *Nooo*) is a Cheyenne exclamation that may only be said by females. It may be translated as "Wow!" or "Oh, my!"

2. That's what the men would do for the women in the old days.

lake. Her children remained in the tepee. Her husband snuck up so he could lie there watching her. She stood at the water's edge. "I have come," she called out. "I have come again." Nooo, after awhile big waves began to appear on the water, and the man realized something was swimming toward his wife. She just stood there. Naoo, it came closer, and, here,[3] it was a water monster! It swam to where she was standing. It started to lick her head, all over her face. She just stood very still. And all the time her husband was watching, lying down, watching her.

When it finished licking her, the woman left. All the red paint her husband had put on her had been licked off. As she started back home, naooo, her husband attacked her. He killed her quickly, then dragged her away, and cut her head off. He threw it away and sliced some meat from her body. Then he walked back to camp from a different direction.

When he reached the tepee, here, his children were there. The girl was in her teens; the boy was younger. "Has she come back yet?" their father asked.

"She's been gone a long time. We don't know where she went," the children replied.

"Well," the father said, "I just brought a small piece of meat. I'm going after the rest of it. You do the cooking," he told his daughter.

"Eat, and when I return, perhaps she'll be back by then," their father told them.

Then he left. That's when he abandoned his children.

Nooo, the girl fixed the meat. They roasted it. After it was done, they ate. They tried to wait for their mother, but they went ahead and ate without her. As they ate the meat, the boy said, "Eaa, older sister, my mother used to taste like this when I nursed on her."

"Nooo, just hurry up and eat!" his sister replied. "What on earth is he saying? We're eating deer."[4]

They finished eating. Naoo, suddenly a head came rolling in! It must have been their mother's head that came rolling in. It chased them around inside the tepee. Nooo! The girl grabbed her little brother by the hand. "You ate me," the head called out. "You did something terrible! You ate me!" it screamed, as it chased them all about.

3. "Here" translates the Cheyenne *hotahtse*, which indicates something unexpected.

4. In the first sentence, the girl is actually speaking to the boy but refers to him in the third person, a common narrative device in Cheyenne that creates a culturally appropriate social distance. Since it is culturally inappropriate for Cheyennes to criticize or compliment someone too directly, the sister probably uses the third person here so she does not sound too harsh to her brother.

The children dashed outside. They ran and kept on running, and all the time the girl had her brother by the hand.

Nooo, the head rolled out of the tepee and started chasing them again. They ran and ran, a long way. Nooo, all the time the head was screaming, "Wait for me! Wait for me!" as it rolled after them.

Nooo, soon the boy became tired. "Older sister, I'm tired," he said.

"Yes, I know," she answered.[5] "Somewhere near here where I used to play there was a hedge of wild roses. They were red, sharp, and thorny. I couldn't get through them." Nooo, suddenly, a hedge of rose bushes appeared. They were red, sharp, and thorny.[6] So the children sat down and rested on the other side of the hedge.

But after quite some time, the head rolled up. Nooo, it rolled back and forth, but it could not get through the rose bushes.

Then the boy woke up. "Let's go!" he said.

So they ran and ran. When they had gone quite a ways, they heard the head screaming again. It had almost caught up with them. "Wait for me! Wait for me!" it was calling. But they kept on going.

The boy got tired again. "Older sister, I'm tired," he said.

"Yes, I know," she replied. "When I used to play near here, there were bearberry bushes that were red, sharp, and thorny. I couldn't get through them." Nooo, bearberry bushes just then appeared as a hedge. They were red, sharp, and thorny. Again the head tried but could not get through these bushes either.

Then the boy got rested again. He said, "Older sister, let's go!" So they ran off again. Apparently they knew where the people were camped and tried to run in that direction. Nooo, they ran and ran.

But again the boy got tired. "Older sister," he said, "I'm tired again."

"Yes, I know," she replied quickly. "When I used to play near here there were wild plum bushes that were red, sharp, and thorny. I couldn't get through them." Nooo, so wild plum bushes appeared as a hedge. Again, the head was stopped by the bushes. So the children rested again. After a while they left again when they had gotten rested.

They went a long way, until the boy said, "Older sister, I'm tired again."

"Well, when I used to play near here," she said, "the earth would crack open and I could not get across." Nooo, at once, the earth just cracked open right in front of them. But the head was still coming after them. So the girl looked around

5. The Cheyenne is simply *heehe'e*, meaning "yes," which is an appropriate Cheyenne response in this situation. Here and later in the narrative, I have added "I know," which makes the rhetorically implicit meaning clearer for the English reader.

6. Here we see the girl has powers. Just by speaking about something, it can happen.

for a piece of wood.[7] She found one and laid it across the opening in the ground. She held on to her brother, and they both walked across.

Nooo, the head came rolling up. The children were standing on the other side of the opening in the ground. "Help me across!" it called to them. So they girl laid the stick back down, and the head started to cross. Naoo, the girl turned the stick over, and the head fell down into the hole.

The ground closed back up. Then the children set off again.

They got near the camp and sat down on a hill near it, looking down at the camp. Naoo, their father must have recognized them—perhaps he had always been looking for them. He gave a bad report about them to the other people: "Those children you see coming here ate their mother. What they did was terrible!" he said.

Nooo, so some people ran up and grabbed the children and began tying them up. Hurriedly the people in that encampment moved their camp. They couldn't wait to get away from the two children who had done such a terrible thing, so they took them off into the brush and tied their hands and feet with thongs and staked them down. But an old dog was there, and it had seen where they were tied up. It felt sorry for them and carried some things in its mouth that would be useful for the children. And then the old dog hid in the brush near them.

Nooo, they were abandoned by the whole camp. They were going to die because they had done wrong by eating their mother.

When evening fell, the dog came out of the bushes. It was almost toothless. It came up to the girl and started to pull the thongs loose; it freed up her hands with its mouth. It chewed on the thongs so much that they became white. And that's how, with her thongs loosened, the girl got free and then freed her little brother.

Then the dog left. But, here, it soon returned with those things in its mouth that the children could use.

The next morning the children were just sitting there. Then the girl got up and started walking around. Nooo, it was really pretty there, with green grass. She said to her brother, "Nooo, I would like to have a big tepee right here some day. We would camp here. And this dog would have the place of honor in the tepee.[8] I would lie here on one side, and you would be on the other. And we would have pet bears. They would guard the doorway there."

Then she turned around. Nooo, then the boy looked again—and there was a large tepee. "Older sister, older sister!" he called out. "Look over there! The tepee you wished for is already here!" His sister looked over there—and there it was!

7. Literally, "a stick."

8. The place of honor is at the back of the tepee, directly opposite the door.

Nooo, they became very happy and ran over to the tepee. They looked into it, and exactly as she had said, that's how it was. Their bedding was there, just as she had wished. Everything was the way she had wanted it, even the bears sitting on either side of the doorway.

The children sat near the doorway. The looked toward the hillside. Buffalo were climbing up the hill, two of them. "Older sister," he said, "look at those buffalo that are going up the hill."[9]

"Nooo, even if I looked at them they would not die," she said.[10]

"Quick! Just look at them!" the boy said. "They are almost out of sight; they're almost out of sight!" He tried to get her to hurry and look. So then she looked. Nooo, both buffalo fell over and died. The children climbed up there to look at the buffalo. Here, they were certainly dead. So they butchered them. It took a long time. They carried all the meat down the hill. The girl sliced it for jerky. Nooo, she sliced a lot!

Then, after she had cleaned everything up, the next morning her brother said, "Older sister, look at all those deer that are coming into sight! There's two of them."

"They wouldn't die," she said.

"But hurry! Just look over there!" he said to her.

So she looked, and both deer fell down dead. "They've dropped out of sight," the boy said. "Let's go look for them." So they went and cut up all the meat. Nooo, so then they had a whole lot of meat hanging to dry.

Meanwhile, the people who had moved away, nooo, they were very hungry there where they had set up a new camp. The men hunted and hunted, but with no success. They never found anything. Not a thing. And still they hunted. And those people got hungrier and hungrier.

There was a crow where the girl and boy were. The girl said to the crow, "Take some of this dry meat and fat to the middle of their camp. Make a lot of noise so the people notice you. And when they have seen you, drop this meat and fat. Say this to those people: 'Those you abandoned have plenty of meat.'"

So the crow flew off and soon reached the camp. He did exactly as he had been told. Nooo, the people fought over that fat and dry meat. Then they quickly moved camp back to where they had abandoned those children whom they had once considered bad. Everybody went to where the brother and sister sat inside the tepee. The girl had already explained to her pet bears what they were to do.

9. The boy wants his sister to look at the buffalo, believing that if she looks and wishes for them to die, they will, and there would be fresh meat.

10. But here it seems the girl doubts her powers are strong enough.

When their father entered the tepee, he said, "Eaa, my children must be living here."

Right then the children said to the bears, "That's him!" Nooo, so the bears tossed him out of the tepee and killed him. Then people took him and buried him somewhere.

And that's the way the story is. That's it.

Contributors

Jeffrey D. Anderson is an associate professor of anthropology at Colby College. He is the author of *The Four Hills of Life: Northern Arapaho Knowledge and Life Movement* (2001), *One Hundred Years of Old Man Sage: An Arapaho Life* (2003), and various articles on Arapaho language, culture, and history.

Jennifer Andrews is an associate professor in the Department of English at the University of New Brunswick. Her coauthored book, *Border Crossings: Thomas King's Cultural Inversions*, was published by University of Toronto Press in 2003.

John Armstrong (ca. 1824–ca. 1900) was a native speaker of both Munsee and Seneca. Of Munsee, Seneca, and English descent, he was a principal keeper of Munsee tradition at the Cattaraugus Seneca Reservation in western New York.

John Bierhorst is the author-editor-translator of more than thirty books on Native American literature, including *Four Masterworks of American Indian Literature* (1974), *Cantares Mexicanos: Songs of the Aztecs* (1985), and *Mythology of the Lenape: Guide and Texts* (1995).

Omushkego, or "Swampy Cree," historian and storyteller **Louis Bird** (Pennishish) is a member of Winisk First Nation, located on the west coast of James Bay in Peawanuck, Ontario, Canada. He has been recording his people's stories and legends since about 1965. Bird directs the Omushkego Oral History Project at the University of Winnipeg, in Manitoba, Canada, and is the author of *Telling Our Stories: Omushkego Legends and Histories from Hudson Bay* (Broadview Press, forthcoming).

John Blackned (Eastern Cree) was born in the 1890s, lived in Waskaganish, Quebec, and hunted inland up the Eastmain River, Quebec. Scholar Richard J. Preston relied heavily on John Blackned for his knowledge of Cree culture, history, language, and storytelling.

Julie Brittain is presently an assistant professor in the linguistics department of Memorial University of Newfoundland, Canada. She began research on the dialect of Naskapi spoken at Kawawachikamach (Quebec) in 1996 and continues to work on this and related dialects. She is the author of *The Morphosyntax of the Algonquian Conjunct Verb: A Minimalist Approach* (2001) and has written numerous articles on the structure of Cree, Innu-aimun, and Naskapi.

Jennifer S. H. Brown is a professor of history at the University of Winnipeg, Manitoba, Canada. She has written and edited several books and numerous articles on Algonquian and Metis ethnohistory and on European-Native relations in the northern fur trade.

Laura Buszard-Welcher is a postdoctoral researcher on the EMELD project (Electronic Metastructure for Endangered Languages Data) affiliated with The LINGUIST List, Wayne State University and Eastern Michigan University. The EMELD Web site (www.emeld.org) houses a working version of a Potawatomi dictionary that was chosen as a test lexicon for the FIELD software tool. Besides the dictionary, Buszard-Welcher's current research on Potawatomi includes a grammatical description and a set of glossed and translated texts.

Alma Chemaganish is a member of the Naskapi Nation of Kawawachikamach. She works for the Naskapi Development Corporation as a Naskapi translator and proofreader. She has contributed to the translation and editing of a collection of Naskapi stories and legends and serves as the main copyeditor for all corporation documents in Naskapi. Alma is a cotranslator of John Peastitute's story *Umâyichîs: A Naskapi Legend from Kawawachikamach*, which appears in Brian Swann's *Voices from Four Directions: Contemporary Translations of the Native Literatures of North America* (2004).

Charley H. Chuck (ča·kehta·kosi·ha), a member of the Meskwaki community, was born in 1867 and died in 1940 when he was struck by a train near the settlement. A member of the Thunder clan, he served as the tribal secretary and was for a time also the tribal policeman. A lively storyteller, in 1905 Chuck rewrote some of his personal archive and writings in an alphabet that used English letter values, and this collection was published, in Meskwaki only, by the State Historical Society of Iowa.

David J. Costa has worked on Miami-Illinois since 1988 and Shawnee since 1992 and also studies southern New England Algonquian languages. He is the author of several articles on Miami-Illinois, Shawnee, and historical Algonquian linguistics, as well as the book *The Miami-Illinois Language* (2003). He is currently preparing an annotated collection of Miami and Peoria texts. He works in Native language revitalization and is a third-generation northern Californian.

Andrew Cowell is an associate professor at the University of Colorado. He teaches both medieval European literature (focusing especially on oral performance traditions) and Native American traditional narrative. He has published articles on Arapaho language, culture, and storytelling traditions, many in collaboration with Alonzo Moss Sr., and has just finished a book-length bilingual anthology of Arapaho narratives, also in cooperation with Alonzo Moss.

Reverend Stan Cuthand grew up on Little Pine's Reserve in Saskatchewan, Canada. An accomplished writer, translator, and storyteller, he worked for the Saskatchewan Indian Cultural Centre as a writer and translator in the curriculum department and research department. Now retired, he is working on a translation of the Bible into Cree for the Canadian Bible Society.

Nora Thompson Dean (1907–84) was raised east of Bartlesville, Oklahoma. She attended many of the traditional Lenape ceremonies with her family and was raised speaking the Lenape language. In her later years, especially after the death of her father in 1964, she began her tireless efforts to preserve the Lenape language and culture.

Paul W. DePasquale is a Mohawk member of the Six Nations of the Grand River in Ontario. He is an assistant professor of English at the University of Winnipeg, where he works in the areas of Aboriginal literature and early modern European colonialism. He is a coeditor of *Telling Our Stories: Omushkego Legends and Histories from Hudson Bay* and *Aboriginal Contexts for North American Native Literatures*, both forthcoming from Broadview Press.

Charles Dutchman (Naehcīwetok) was a Menominee who worked with the linguist Leonard Bloomfield in the early 1920s.

Phil Einish Jr. was chief of the Naskapi Nation of Kawawachikamach for two terms, since 1997. He serves as the full-time administrative translator for the Naskapi Development Corporation, a position he has held for over fifteen years. He translates both from Naskapi to English and from English to Naskapi, working in the Naskapi syllabic script directly onto computers. He is forty-nine years old and has a vision for improving the lives of the people in the Naskapi community, by both his leadership and work in preserving the Naskapi language and culture.

George Finley (1858–1932) was a full-blood Piankashaw who grew up among the Peorias and was one of the last traditional speakers of the Miami-Illinois language.

He was born in Kansas but as a child moved to Miami County, Oklahoma, where he lived the rest of his life. Often a representative for the Peorias in Washington DC, Finley shared stories and his knowledge of the Peoria language with linguists Albert Gatschet, Jacob Dunn, and Truman Michelson.

David A. Francis is a lifelong resident of Sipayik in Perry, Maine. A fluent speaker of Passamaquoddy, he is recognized by generations of scholars for his linguistic abilities. He helped develop a writing system for Passamaquoddy-Maliseet and has translated stories, songs, chants, and prayers from oral tradition to writing. He worked with Joseph Nicholas to establish the Waponahki Museum at Sipayik, where he is currently working with Robert M. Leavitt on a dictionary of Passamaquoddy-Maliseet.

Michael William Francis (1923–95) was born on the Mi'kmaq reserve of Big Cove in New Brunswick, Canada. He was highly respected in his community for his knowledge of Mi'kmaq history and culture. He was an accomplished storyteller, visual artist, and musician. His paintings were featured at Expo 67, among other venues, and have been sold nationally and internationally. Together with Franziska von Rosen, he coproduced *Jipuktewik Sipu* (1992).

Josephine Stands in Timber Glenmore (1920–90) worked closely with researcher Wayne Leman for many years, teaching him the Cheyenne language and helping translate Cheyenne stories, develop a Cheyenne topical dictionary, and produce other materials in the language.

Ives Goddard is senior linguist in the Department of Anthropology in the National Museum of Natural History, Smithsonian Institution. He has been conducted fieldwork on Meskwaki since 1990. He has written extensively on Native North American languages, cultures, and ethnohistory, particularly that of the speakers of Algonquian languages. He edited volume 17, *Languages*, of the *Handbook of North American Indians* (1996).

Alex MacKenzie Hargrave is an independent scholar who is currently completing his "Dictionary of Algonquian Etymology" begun over fifteen years ago. He grew up in the Finger Lakes district of New York in the epicenter of the Seneca Nation, an area infused with Iroquois place names. His interest in the study of indigenous languages was initially drawn by the obvious similarity between Iroquois and Algonquian toponyms.

George Head was born at the turn of the twentieth century. He grew to adulthood, married, and spent most of his hunting career in the vicinity of Lake Caniapiscow, Quebec. A member of the Caniapiscow band of inlanders until they merged with the north coasters and south coasters of the Fort George band, he told many fine stories and sang traditional songs for appreciative audiences.

Oogima Ikwe (Lindel Clement) was born in 1961 in the poorest section of Sault Sainte Marie, Michigan, and was raised by loving parents of Italian, Scottish, French, and Native American (Ojibwe) descent. She teaches at the charter Bawating School (run by the Sault tribe). She strives to live in balance with all of Creation, ever mindful of her interconnectedness to all things. Her favorite quote comes from a humble man who once said, "Be the change you want to see in the world" (Gandhi).

Anderson Jolly (Eastern Cree) lived in Waskaganish, Quebec. He worked as translator with John Blackned and Richard J. Preston in the 1960s.

Pearl Leaf (*ma·ta·ši·hkwe·ha*) was born in 1893 and died in 1913. She was a member of the Meskwaki nation and most likely of the War Chief lineage of the Fox clan.

Robert M. Leavitt is a professor in the Faculty of Education at the University of New Brunswick, where he is director of the Mi'kmaq-Maliseet Institute. He is coeditor of the forthcoming *Passamaquoddy-Maliseet Dictionary*, regular updates of which may be searched at http://www.lib.unb.ca/Texts/Maliseet/dictionary/.

Wayne Leman descends from the Russian-Alutiiq family that founded the little Alaskan fishing village of Ninilchik, where he grew up. Since 1975, at the invitation of Cheyenne elders, he has been working for the Cheyennes, assisting them in various language projects. He and his wife, also a linguist, live on the Northern Cheyenne Indian Reservation in southeastern Montana.

Philip LeSourd is an associate professor of anthropology at Indiana University, Bloomington. He is the author of *Accent and Syllable Structure in Passamaquoddy* (1993), as well as a number of articles on Algonquian linguistics, and is the editor of *Tales from Maliseet Country: The Maliseet Texts of Karl V. Teeter* (Nebraska, forthcoming). He was first introduced to the Maliseet language and its speakers by Karl Teeter while he was studying linguistics at Harvard and MIT.

Willie Longbone (1869–1946) was born in Indian Territory (later Oklahoma) and grew up speaking the Lenape language. He was respected as a singer and drummer at the old Lenape ceremonial functions. In 1939 he worked with linguist Carl Voegelin at the University of Michigan, where he recorded some old Lenape stories.

Marguerite MacKenzie teaches linguistics at Memorial University of Newfoundland and works with speakers of Cree, Innu (Montagnais), and Naskapi on dictionaries, grammars, and language training materials. She is coeditor of the *East Cree Lexicon: Eastern James Bay Dialects* (1987) and the *Naskapi Lexicon* (1994). She is presently involved in a collaborative research project investigating the formal properties of Labrador Innu-aimun. An integral part of the project is to publish a substantial audiotape archive of Innu oral narratives from Labrador.

Mary Magoulick is an assistant professor in English and interdisciplinary studies at Georgia College and State University. As part of her dissertation research for a doctorate in folklore from Indiana University, she did fieldwork from 1994 to 1996 in the eastern Upper Peninsula of Michigan. She lived in Sault Sainte Marie while studying Ojibwe language and teaching in the English department at Bay Mills Community College (a tribal college).

Marianne Milligan is a graduate student in the linguistics department at the University of Wisconsin-Madison. She is writing her dissertation on the metrical structure of Menominee and works with the tribe on issues of language preservation.

Lewis Mitchell (1847–1930) served as the Passamaquoddy representative to the Maine state legislature in the 1880s. His 1887 speech to the legislature concerning Passamaquoddy treaty rights remains a landmark in aboriginal land claims. A fluent speaker of Passamaquoddy, he transcribed many songs and stories from oral tradition and translated them into English. He collaborated with the linguist John Dyneley Prince to produce the series of *Passamaquoddy Texts*. Mitchell was the great-great-grandfather of contributor Wayne A. Newell.

Maggie Morgan (*te·pasa·ke·hkwa*) was a member of the Meskwaki nation and belonged to the Thunder clan. She was born in 1873 and died in 1921.

Alonzo Moss Sr. is a native speaker of Arapaho who has lived on the Wind River Reservation, Wyoming, since his birth. After a long career as a logger and construction worker, he learned to read and write Arapaho when an orthography was developed in the late 1970s. He subsequently began teaching the language at Wyoming Indian High School in Ethete, Wyoming, and later at the college level as well. He is cochair of the Northern Arapaho Language and Culture Commission and a widely admired singer of country and gospel music, in both Arapaho and English.

Richard Moss (born 1933) has lived his entire life on the Wind River Reservation, in the town of Ethete. He is considered one of the best remaining Arapaho storytellers.

Gerti Diamond Murdoch was born in 1946 and was the first high school graduate from Waskaganish. She lived with Richard J. Preston's family in Lancaster, Pennsylvania, for two years, during which she transcribed his tapes of stories. She has served as community education administrator, band councilor, justice of the peace, maker of wedding dresses, leader of a dance troupe, and helper of many people for many years.

Silas Nabinicaboo is a member of the Naskapi Nation of Kawawachikamach. He is trained as a Naskapi translator and works for the Naskapi Development Corporation as a Naskapi language editor and technician. He is the editor of the *Naskapi Hymn Book* (1999) and has collaborated on a number of Naskapi language projects for the corporation. He is a cotranslator of John Peastitute's story *Umâyichîs: A Naskapi Legend from Kawawachikamach*, which appears in Brian Swann's *Voices from Four Directions: Contemporary Translations of the Native Literatures of North America* (2004).

Wayne A. Newell is director of bilingual education for Indian Township at Motahkomihkuk and has documented Passamaquoddy culture for decades. He received an Ed.M. from Harvard University and is an Ed.D. candidate at Boston College. A fluent speaker of Passamaquoddy, he has assisted scores of outside scholars researching Passamaquoddy culture as well as writing and contributing to many publications.

Joseph A. Nicholas was born at Sipayik in Perry, Maine, where he currently resides. He has held the office of Passamaquoddy representative to the Maine state legislature for several terms. A fluent speaker of Passamaquoddy as well as an accomplished singer and dancer, in the 1960s he helped establish a Passamaquoddy dance group dedicated to maintaining the traditional songs and dances and to presenting public cultural programs. Nicholas helped establish the Waponahki Museum at Sipayik and was director of bilingual education. In recognition of his efforts, he was awarded an honorary doctorate by the University of Maine at Machias.

David M. Oestreicher has for years conducted ethnographic and linguistic research with the Lenape (Delaware) Indians of Oklahoma and Ontario. He holds masters degrees in anthropology and Hebraic studies and has a doctorate in anthropology from Rutgers University. In 1995 Oestreicher attracted international attention by demonstrating that the Walam Olum, long believed by many to be an authentic Lenape Indian migration epic, is in fact a hoax.

Charlie George Owen (Omishoosh) was a highly respected member of the Ojibwe community at Pauingassi, Manitoba. His grandfather, Fair Wind (Naamiwan), was a renowned medicine man. Fluent in the Ojibwe language, Charlie George Owen died in 2001.

Peter Lewis Paul (1902–89) was born in Benton, New Brunswick, but lived most of his life on the Maliseet reserve at Woodstock, New Brunswick. A noted baseball player in the 1920s, he played on a semiprofessional team based in Saint John. The father of nine children, he made a living for his family during the Depression as a cooper and a skillful trader. Widely recognized in his community as an expert on Maliseet traditions, he also served as a consultant and advisor to several generations of historians, anthropologists, and linguists. In recognition of his contributions to the preservation of knowledge of the traditional culture of the Maliseet, he was awarded an honorary doctorate by the University of New Brunswick and was elected to the Order of Canada.

John Peastitute, Naskapi elder and storyteller, was born circa 1890 and died circa 1981 in Matimekosh, Quebec. He was a respected community member and a skilled teller of stories, and he had extensive knowledge of the traditional Naskapi life. His children and grandchildren still live in Kawawachikamach. His stories, audio recordings of which are now available to the Naskapi community, are much loved by all generations. An English translation of his story *Umâyichîs: A Naskapi Legend from Kawawachikamach* appears in Brian Swann's *Voices from Four Directions: Contemporary Translations of the Native Literatures of North America* (2004).

Captain Pipe (Tauhaugeeacaupouye) was chief of the Sandusky Delawares, along with Moonshine, George Ketchum, William Montuer, Isaac Hill, and Solmon Journeycake, in 1833, when the tribe left Sandusky for Kansas. The Sandusky Delawares were one of the last Indian splinter groups to join the Kansas Delawares.

Richard J. Preston was born in 1931. He began his sojourns in the James Bay region in 1963, mentored by John Honigmann, and spent most of his academic career at McMaster University, Hamilton, Ontario. He has continued research and teaching as professor emeritus.

Susan M. Preston, Ph.D., is a scholar of environment and culture. Her work focuses on the importance of environmental experience in the formation of shared values and collective identities and the implications of these experiences, values, and identities in community, cultural, and environmental integrity. Her research addresses landscape symbolism and meaning in Eastern James Bay Cree oral tradition, and modern narratives and dynamics of landscape meanings in conservation planning for Ontario's Niagara Escarpment World Biosphere Reserve.

Jim Rementer grew up in southeastern Pennsylvania and developed a great interest in the Lenape, as they were the original inhabitants of the area, and many of their placenames are still used there. In 1962 he moved to Dewey, Oklahoma, to study the Lenape language. He was adopted into the Thompson family by James H. Thompson, who was one of his earliest tutors in the language.

Laura Rockroads (1910–79) was a member of the Northern Cheyenne community. She gifted her people by passing on traditional Cheyenne stories that she had heard from her ancestors.

Roger Roulette is an Ojibwe linguist and translator with Aboriginal Languages of Manitoba, Inc., and a professor of Ojibwe language at the University of Manitoba. He writes and speaks widely on issues of Aboriginal language survival and heritage.

Pauline Running Crane, the daughter of Paul Running Crane and Jenny Guardipee, has three children and ten grandchildren. She is a Blackfeet language instructor at Heart Butte Elementary School on the Blackfeet Reservation and serves her community also as an emergency medical technician.

Sakihtanohkweha (Meskwaki) was born in 1875 and died in 1957. Her name is of the Water clan. She was skilled in the making of traditional craft items, including mats, bags, beadwork, and yarn belts (finger-woven sashes).

Theresa Schenck is a member of the Blackfeet Nation and assistant professor of American Indian studies at the University of Wisconsin-Madison. Her publications include *The Voice of the Crane Echoes Afar* and an edited volume, *My First Years in the Fur Trade*, by George Nelson, which she coedited with Laura Peers.

Lorne Simon, a nephew of Michael William Francis, was born in 1960 on the Big Cove Reserve in New Brunswick, Canada. He was a graduate of En'owkin International School of Writing, where he received the Simon Lucas Jr. Award (established by

Dr. David Suzuki) for being the top graduate student. Lorne's first book, *Stones and Switches*, was published in 1994 by Theytus Books. He died that same year in a car accident at age thirty-four.

Bessie Snake (1896–1999) was raised near Anadarko, Oklahoma, and both she and her husband spoke the Unami dialect of the Lenape language. Bessie was a highly respected elder and worked with several linguists to help preserve her language. She also worked with anthropologists and historians to help preserve knowledge of Lenape ways.

Blanche Sockabason has been the lead singer for the traditional dances at the Sipayik Ceremonial Day for ten years. She has contributed to several commercially available recordings of Passamaquoddy music. Sockabason has taught and performed in local, state, and federal traditional arts programs, and her singing has been featured in exhibitions at the Abbe Museum in Bar Harbor and the Downeast Heritage Center in Calais, Maine. A fluent speaker of Passamaquoddy, she taught bilingual and cultural classes at the Motahkomihkuk school and has advised many outside scholars.

Alice Spear lived on the Prairie Band Potawatomi Reservation in Kansas. Her tellings of stories in Potawatomi were recorded by the linguist Charles Hockett in the early 1940s.

Jim Spear, together with Alice Spear, dictated approximately fifty stories in Potawatomi to the linguist Charles Hockett during Hockett's field research in the 1940s.

Ann Morrison Spinney is an ethnomusicologist currently working in Maine and the Boston area. She has taught at Harvard University, Franklin & Marshall College, Brandeis University, and Boston College. Her 1997 dissertation on Passamaquoddy ceremonial songs was undertaken with the assistance of David A. Francis, Wayne A. Newell, Joseph A. Nicholas, and Blanche Sockabason, among others.

Brian Swann is the author of many books of poetry, short fiction, and poetry in translation, as well as books for children. He has edited a number of volumes on Native American literature, including *Coming to Light: Contemporary Translations of the Native Literatures of North America* (1994) and *Voices from Four Directions: Contemporary Translations of the Native Literatures of North America* (2004). He teaches at the Cooper Union for the Advancement of Science and Art in New York City.

Lucy G. Thomason is an employee of the Department of Anthropology in the National Museum of Natural History, Smithsonian Institution. She has an A.B. in folklore and mythology from Harvard-Radcliffe University and a Ph.D. in linguistics from the University of Texas at Austin. She has spent parts of each summer since 1982 assisting the Bitterroot Salish and Pend d'Oreille peoples of northwestern Montana with their language work and has spent summers and winters since 1992 doing translation, analysis, and dictionary work on the Meskwaki language.

J. Randolph Valentine teaches in the linguistics department and in the American Indian Studies Program at the University of Wisconsin-Madison. His research interests focus primarily on Ojibwe linguistics and literature, and he has authored a grammar of Nishnaabemwin, the dialect of Ojibwe spoken on the shores of Lake Huron and regions to the east.

Little is known about the life of **Elizabeth Vallier** (1830s-ca. 1900). A Miami Indian by birth and language, she grew up in Indiana, married a Peoria man, and eventually came to live in Oklahoma. A monolingual speaker of Miami, she served as a linguistic consultant to Albert Gatschet in the 1890s.

Franziska von Rosen is a documentary filmmaker and an adjunct professor at Carleton University. She has done extensive fieldwork among First Nations communities in Canada. Her films *Jipuktewik Sipu* (1992), *River of Fire: Celebration of Life* (1994), and *Mi'kmwesu* (2000) are all based on stories told her by the Mi'kmaq elder Michael W. Francis. She is also a coauthor of *Visions of Sound: Musical Instruments of First Nations Communities in North America* (1994).

Waasaagoneshkang was an Ojibwe storyteller who shared many tales with anthropologist William Jones at the beginning of the twentieth century. Little is known about his life; he apparently grew up on Rainy River, Rainy Lake, and the Lake of the Woods.

Index

Abbot, Charles Conrad, 8
Ahenakew, E., 123
alcohol, 57
The American Nations, 4, 6, 8, 18
Andersen, Hans Christian, 326–27
Anderson, Jeffrey D., 448, 463, 477
Andrews, Jennifer, 72
animal stories: bird, 235–40; crane, 206–9; eagle, 478–86; Eastern Cree, 235–46; Naskapi, 121–58; Passamaquoddy, 72–83; Potawatomi, 206–14; rabbit, 210–12; raccoon, 74–75, 81–83, 213–14; turtle, 72–74, 77–80, 105–7, 455; wolf, 213–14, 241–46; wolverine, 121–58
Anishinaabeg, 161, 165–69
The Arapaho, 477
Arapahoe Politics, 1851–1978, 477
The Arapahoes, Our People, 477
Arapaho Indians: Captive story, 487–94; contributions of James Mooney to translation of stories of, 448–51; Eagles story, 478–86; and earth's destruction and renewal, 455; geographic location of, 448; Ghost Dances as doctrine of, 449–51; Ghost Dance song texts, 463–71; imagery in Ghost Dances of, 452–53; meanings in stories told by, 475–76; orthography, 460; presentational format of stories told by, 472–75; relations with non-Indians, 455–56; Second Thought story, 482–86; and songs' linguistic structure, 456–58; spirituality of, 450, 453–55; texts of songs of, 459–60; translations of stories told by, 448–49
Armstrong, John, 62–66, 69
arrival of Europeans in North America: Lenape accounts of, 49, 51–52, 55–61; Ojibwe account of, 160–69
Âtalôhkâna nêsta tipâcimôwina: Cree Legends and Narratives from the West Coast of James Bay, 123
At Last He Could Walk No Further, 233n2
authenticity of texts, 3–6, 23n2, 23–24n5

Baraga, Frederick, 44
Bering Strait, the, 14–16, 17–18
Bierhorst, John, 62
Bird, Louis, 256, 279; background of, 247–48; first meeting with Paul W. DePasquale, 248–49; stories told by, 249–54; translation work of, 249
bird stories, 235–40
Black, Glenn, 5
Blackfeet Indians, 495–500
Blackfeet Lodge Tales, 495
Blackned, John, 215, 216, 226–29, 230, 235, 241–46

Blalock, Lucy, 21
Bloomfield, Leonard, 123, 411, 412, 431
Boas, Franz, 170
Bobbish-Salt, Luci, 130
Brinton, Daniel G., 5; acceptance of Rafinesque's translation, 17, 20; on American Indian migration to North America, 6, 8, 9–10; on migration of the Snake tribes, 13; translations by, 15, 28–29n16, 31–32n22; Walam Olum Song III translation by, 39–40
Brittain, Julie, 121, 141, 150
Brown, Jennifer S. H., 159
Bruchac, Joseph, 251
Bull Child, Percy, 495
Bulletin of the Archaeological Society of New Jersey, 23–24n5
Buszard-Welcher, Laura, 201, 206, 210, 213

cannibal stories, 252–53, 279–91
Captive story, 487–94
Cartier, Jacques, 85, 160
Cass, Governor, 51
Cattaraugus Seneca Reservation, 62–63
Ceekiiθa story, 315–19
ceremonies, Algonquian, 42–43; songs, 84–98
Chemaganish, Alma, 122, 141, 150
Chemaganish, George, 136n8
Cheyenne Indians: cultural worldview of, 501–2; geographic location of, 501; language, 501; Rolling Head story, 502–9
Chuck, Charley H., 320, 326; Has-a-Rock story told by, 327–29, 345; narrative devices used by, 322, 323
Clements, William, 192, 193–94
Cook, Captain James, 160
Costa, David J., 292, 303, 308, 314, 315
Cowell, Andrew, 472, 478, 487
Crane Boy story, 206–9
Crania Americana, 8
creation stories, 62–71, 455–56
Cree Legends and Narratives, 249
Cree Narrative: Expressing the Personal Meanings of Events, 218
cultural renewal, 185–87
culture-hero stories, 295–98, 411–12; Wiihsakacaakwa Aalhsoohkaakana, 303–13; Wilakhtwa, 314
Curtin, Jeremiah, 62–66
Cuthand, Stan, 431, 433

dances: Passamaquoddy, 84–85, 88; social and ceremonial, 84–85, 88; women's, 91–93
Darwin, Charles, 8
Dauenhauer, Nora, 192
Dauenhauer, Richard, 192
Daugherty, Frank, 299, 315
Dean, Nora Thompson, 52, 61
Death and Rebirth of the Seneca, 63
de Buffon, Comte, 11
Delaware Indians: creation stories, 62–71; Munsee language, 62–66; of western Oklahoma, 60. *See also* Lenape Indians
de Mortillet, G., 8
Densmore, Frances, 196–97
DePasquale, Paul W., 247
Desbarats, Peter, 122, 136–37n11
Diamond, Albert, 226–29
Dorsey, George, 477
dreams and visions in Native American culture, 196–99

Dry Lips Oughta Move to Kapuskasing, 250
Du Halde, P., 27n12
Dunn, Jacob, 293, 294
Dutchman, Charles, 411, 415
Dutchman, Louise, 411
Duvall, David, 495

E, Qanute story, 87–91
Eagles story, 478–94
Eastern Cree Indians: Birds That Flew Off with People story, 235–40; conceptual perspective, 216–18; conversation between John Blackned and Dick Preston on, 226–29; guides to reading literature of, 218–20; hero stories, 232; How the Wolf Came to Be story, 241–46; landscape concepts and, 231–32; Louse and Wide Lake story, 215–16, 221–25; metaphor in stories told by, 215–16, 217–18, 219–20; translation of stories told by, 215–16, 230, 232–33n1
Eastern James Bay Cree Oral Tradition, 232–33n1
Eastern Seaboard Community, 42–48
Einish, Noat, 136n8
Einish, Philip, 122, 141, 150
elders, Native American, 195–96, 197–98, 199–200
Eliot, John, 44, 46n4
Elliott, Michael A., 449
Ellis, C. Douglas, 123, 160, 249–50
Espons: Raccoon story, 74–75, 81–83
Europeans: arrival in North America, 49, 51–52, 55–61, 160–69; Indians mistrust of, 59–60; Lenape stories about, 49, 51–52, 55–61; Ojibwe stories about, 160–69; predictions about the arrival of, 61; relations with Arapaho Indians, 455–56; repeated trips to North America, 57–59; weapons, 57–58, 166
Evans-Pritchard, Edward E., 216–17, 218

Fair Warning story, 47–48
family history stories, 112–13
feast councils, 42–43
Finley, George, 294–95, 296, 297, 303
The Four Hills of Life, 477
Fowler, Loretta Kay, 459, 477
Francis, David A., 93, 95, 96n15, 97n16
Francis, Michael William, 112–14, 116
Francis, Peter Andrew, 112
Fulford, George, 249

Gatschet, Albert, 293–94, 295, 296
Geertz, Clifford, 218
General History of China, 27n12
Ghost Dances. *See* Arapaho Indians
Glenmore, Josephine, 502
Glenmore, Timber, 502, 504
Glooscap Legends, 72
Goddard, Ives, 50, 320, 332, 345, 375n6
Golden Hide story, 397–403
Grammar, 16–17, 18, 19–20
Grammar of the Language of the Lenni Lenape Indians, 4
Great Being stories, 55–57, 455–56
Great Fire story, 113–18
Greeting Chant, 87–91
Grinnell, George Bird, 495
Guanish, Joe, 136n8

Hale, Horatio, 5, 8–9
Hallowell, Irving, 159, 160

hand-game songs, 456
Hargrave, Alex Mackenzie, 42
Harnois, Anna, 101
Harrington, M. R., 5
Has-a-Rock story, 327–29, 345–67
Hawkes, Terence, 218, 219
Head, George, 215–16, 221
Heckewelder, John, 4, 28n15; story of Europeans' arrival related to, 51, 55–58
hero stories, 232
Herzog, George, 456
Hewitt, J. N. B., 62–63
Highway, Tomson, 250
Hockett, Charles, 201
Hoffman, Albert, 502
Hoffman, Walter, 411
Houlton Band of Maliseet Indians, 100
How the Wolf Came to Be story, 241–46
Hudson Bay Company, 161, 162
Hultkrantz, Åke, 451
Hymes, Dell, 193

The Ice Maidens story, 326–27, 332–44
Ikwe, Oogima: on dreams and visions, 196–99; on elders, 195–96, 197–98, 199–200; language of, 185–87; narrative of, 188–91; oratory style of, 192–94
The Interpretation of Cultures, 218

Jack-in-the-Pulpit story, 107
James, Edwin, 27n12
Jancewicz, Bill, 122, 136n7
Jensen, Hans, 6
Jolly, Anderson, 230, 235, 2416
Jones, William, 170–71

Kawichkushu, 215–16, 221–25
Kehoe, Alice, 451
Kiss of the Fur Queen, 250
kitahikan, 13–16
Koluskap: and Baby, 108; Jack-in-the-Pulpit story, 107; Maliseet Indian tales of, 99–111; Passamaquoddy tales of, 72–83; power of, 72–74, 102; and Turtle, 72–74, 77–80, 105–7; Wishes Granted stories, 108–11
Kroeber, Alfred, 477
Kwâhkwâchâw stories, 123–25

Laderman, Ezra, 5
landscape represented in Algonquian literature, 231–32n2, 233n2
languages, Algonquian: Arapaho, 449; Cheyenne, 501; Maliseet, 100, 103; Menominee, 413n4; Meskwaki, 320–21; Miami-Illinois, 292–93; modern, 51; Munsee Delaware, 62–66; Naskapi, 121–22; Ojibwe, 159–60, 185–86; Passamaquoddy, 72–98; Pidgin talk, 50–51; pronunciation guides, 52, 94, 103, 125–27, 203–4, 324–25, 460; root stems of, 43–44; Shawnee, 298–99; spelling in, 45; transcription errors in, 16–18, 24–25n6–7; translation of, 5–10, 16–18, 18–22, 23n3, 37–41, 43–44, 64–65, 99–100, 121–23, 136n4, 138n25, 201–2, 215–16, 230, 232–33n1, 249–50, 299–300n5, 300n6, 324–25, 448–49; variation in dialects of, 49, 87, 123–24, 138n21; word division in, 45
Leaf, Bill, 326

Leaf, Pearl, 368, 369–70, 371, 373–75, 397
Leavitt, Robert M., 72, 77, 81, 84
Legends of the Micmacs, 99
Leland, Charles G., 99–100
Leman, Wayne, 501, 502, 504
Lenape Indians, 3–6; accounts of Europeans' arrival in America, 49, 51–52, 55–61; first encounters with the Dutch at New York Island, 55–58; migrations of, 6–13, 26–28n12; mistrust of Europeans, 59–60; predictions about the arrival of Europeans, 61; storytelling, 49–50
LeSourd, Philip S., 105
Lesser, Alexander, 451
Lilly, Eli, 5
Lincoln, Harry, 325
literature, Algonquian: animal stories, 72–83, 105–7, 121–58, 206–14, 235–46, 478–86; Arapaho, 448–94; arrival of Europeans described in, 49, 51–52, 55–61, 160–69; Blackfeet, 495–500; cannibal stories, 252–53, 279–91; ceremonies portrayed in, 42–43, 84–98; Cheyenne, 501–9; creation stories in, 62–71, 455–56; culture-hero stories, 295–98, 303–13, 411–12; Eastern Cree, 215–46; Eastern Seaboard community, 42–48; errors in transcription of, 16–18, 24–25n6–7; fake, 3–22; family stories told in, 112–13; hero stories in, 232; Koluskap figure in, 72–83, 99–111; landscape represented in, 231–32, 233n2; language root stems in, 43–44; Lenape, 49–61; Maliseet, 99–111; manitous and, 369–71; Menominee, 411–28; Meskwaki, 320–410; metaphor in, 215–16, 217–18, 219–20; Miami-Illinois and Shawnee, 292–319; Mi'kmaq, 112–18; Munsee, 62–66; narrative devices, 322–24, 472–75; Naskapi, 121–58; Ojibwe, 159–200; Omushkego, 247–91; on the origin of war, 170–84; Passamaquoddy, 72–98; Plains Cree, 431–47; Potawatomi, 201–14; reduplication as a narrative device in, 127–28; relations between kin in, 371–73; speeches in, 42–48, 192–96; spirituality in, 55–57, 216–17, 431–32, 450, 453–55; storytelling in, 49–50, 412–13; trickster figures in, 123–25, 170, 250–52, 294–99, 314, 315–19; verbal art and, 192–95, 412–13; winter stories, 49, 321–22, 326–29, 334–410
Little Blaze, John, 496
Little Pine Tips dance, 91–93
Long, John, 254n3
Longbone, Willie, 51, 59–60
Louse and Wide Lake story, 215–16, 221–25

MacKenzie, Marguerite, 121, 141, 150
Magoulick, Mary, 185
Maliseet Indians: Koluskap stories, 99–111; language, 100, 103; traditional world view of, 101–2; translation of stories of, 99–100
manitous, 369–71
Mannitto, 55–57
Matthews, Maureen, 159
McClintock, Walter, 495
McCutchen, David, 6
Mechling, W. H., 99

Menominee Indians: culture hero stories, 411–12; language, 413n4; Origin of the Spirit Rock story, 415–28; translation of stories told by, 411–12
The Menomini Indians, 411
Menomini Texts, 411
Meskwaki Indians: Charley H. Chuck of, 320, 322, 323, 326; geographic location of, 320; Golden Hide story, 397–403; Has-a-Rock story, 327–29, 345–67; Ice Maidens story, 326–27, 332–44; manitous and, 369–71; narrative devices, 322–24; Ojibwe stories and, 376n7; One Whose Eye Was a Bear's Eye story, 404–10; One Whose Father Was the Sun story, 379–96; relations between kin and stories of, 371–73; Sakihtanohkweha of, 326; structure of texts by, 373–75; translation of stories told by, 324–25; winter stories, 321–22, 368; writing, 320–21
metaphor, 215–16, 217–18, 219–20
Metaphor, 218
Miami-Illinois and Shawnee Indians: Ceekiiϕa story, 315; culture-hero stories, 295–98, 303–13; language, 292–93; trickster stories, 294–98, 314, 315–19; Wilakhtwa story, 314; Wissakatchakwa stories, 294–98, 303–13
Michelson, Truman, 293, 320, 325, 368, 448
Micmac Storyteller: River of Fire, 112
migration of American Indians: across the Bering Strait, 14–16, 17–18; portrayed in Walam Olum, 6–10, 26–28n12; Snake tribes, 10–13, 28–29n16
Mi'kmaq Indians: Great Fire story, 113–18; types of stories told by, 112–13
Milligan, Marianne, 411, 415
Mitchell, Lewis, 72, 77, 81, 93, 95, 100
Mitchill, Samuel, 26n12
modern Lenape language, 51
Mooney, James, 5, 448–51, 453, 456, 458–59
Moore, Mary, 86
Morgan, Maggie, 368, 370, 371, 373–75, 374, 379
Morton, Samuel G., 8
Moses, Leo, 122
Moskim, 64–66, 69–71
Moss, Alonzo, Sr., 472, 475, 476, 478, 487
Moss, Paul, 472
Moss, Richard, 472, 473, 478, 487
motewolon, 93, 101–2
Mueller, Ray, 501
Munsee Delaware Indians creation stories, 62–66
Murdoch, Gerti, 215, 221
Murray, David, 192
Mythology of the Blackfoot, 495

Nabinicaboo, Silas, 122, 141, 150
Náévâhóó'ôhtséme/We Are Going Back Home, 501, 502
Napora, Joe, 5
narrative devices: Arapaho, 472–75; Meskwaki, 322–24
Naskapi Indians: pronunciation guide, 125–27; reduplication as narrative device used by, 127–28; subgroups of, 135n1; translation of stories

told by, 121–23, 136n4; Wolverine and the Ducks story, 128–31, 141–49; Wolverine and the Geese story, 131–35, 150–58

Native American Verbal Art, 192

Nenabozho stories, 170–71, 173–84

Neptune, Estelle, 101

Newell, Wayne A., 86, 90, 96n15

Nicholas, Joseph A., 86, 91

Nuttall, Thomas, 26–27n12

Oestreicher, David M., 3

Ojibwe Indians: cultural renewal among, 185–87; Meskwaki stories and, 376n7; origin of war stories, 170–84; stories about arrival of Europeans in North America, 160–69; That Way We Should Be Walking story, 188–91; translation of language of, 159–60; verbal art, 192–95; Waabitigweyaa stories, 161, 165–69

The Old North Trail, 495

Omushkego Indians: cannibal stories, 252–53, 279–91; formal preservation efforts of stories of, 247–49; stories of, 250–54; translation of stories told by, 249–50; trickster figures in stories of, 250–52; Wiissaakechaahk stories, 251–54, 256–78

Omushkeogo Oral History Project (OOHP), 247

The One Whose Eye Was a Bear's Eye story, 404–10

The One Whose Father Was the Sun story, 379–96

The Origin of the Spirit Rock story, 415–28

On the Origin of Species, 8

orthography. *See* Pronunciation guides

Owen, Charlie George, 159–62

Papers of the Thirty-first Algonquian Conference, 233n2

Parkhill, Thomas C., 99–100

Passamaquoddy Indians: animal stories, 72–83; Cihkonaqc: Turtle story, 72–74, 77–80, 105–7; Espons: Raccoon story, 74–75, 81–83; geographic location of, 84; Greeting Chant, 87–91; social and ceremonial songs, 84–98; spiritual songs, 93–94; women's dances, 91–93

Passamaquoddy Texts, 100

Paul, Peter Lewis, 100–102, 105

Pearson, Bruce, 60

Peastitute, John, 121–23, 130, 131, 132–33, 134, 135, 141, 150

Pennishish, John, 253

Peters, Sam, 397n1

Pidgin talk, 50–51

Pilgrimage, 27n12

Pine Root story, 433–47

Pipe, Captain, 51, 58–59

Plains Cree Indians: Pine Root story, 433–47; spiritual beliefs of, 431–32

Polchies, Carole, 101

Polchies, Peter, 101

Potawatomi Indians: Crane Boy story, 206–9; geographic location of, 201; pronunciation guide, 203–4; Rabbit Tale story, 210–12; Raccoon and Wolf story, 213–14; transcription of stories told by, 201–2; types of stories told by, 202–3

Preston, Richard J., 215, 226–29, 230, 232–33n1

Preston, Susan M., 230
Prince, John Dyneley, 72, 93, 96n15, 97n16, 100
pronunciation guides, 52, 94, 103, 125–27, 203–4, 324–25, 460
Purchas, Samuel, 27n12

Rabbit Tale story, 210–12
raccoon stories, 74–75, 81–83, 213–14
Rafinesque, Constantine Samuel, 3; on American Indian migration to North America, 6–10; on the migration of the Snake tribes, 10–13; transcription errors by, 16–18; translation authenticity of, 18–22, 24–32; on translation of the word *kitahikan*, 13–16; Walam Olum Song III translation by, 37–38
Rand, Silas T., 99
Recovering the Word: Essays on Native American Literature, 219
The Red Record, 6
reduplication as a narrative device, 127–28
Rementer, Jim, 60
Rez Sisters, 250
Rich, Matthew, 122
Rockroads, Laura, 501–2, 504
Rolling Head story, 502–9
Roman Catholic Church, 86–87
Roulette, Roger, 159, 160, 161
Running Crane, Pauline, 496, 498

The Sacred Stories of the Sweet Grass Cree, 123, 431
Sakihtanohkweha, 326, 332
Salzmann, Zdenek, 448, 449, 458
Sandy, Thomas, 136n8
Satterlee, John V., 411
Savard, Rémi, 121, 122, 129, 131
Scarface story, 495–96, 498–500
Schenck, Theresa, 495
Schoolcraft, Henry Rowe, 192–94
Second Thought story, 482–86
Seneca Indians, 62–66
Shawnee language, 298–99, 315
Sign, Symbol, and Script, 6
Simon, Jesse, 113
Simon, Lorne, 114, 116
Sipayik Ceremonial Day, 85
Skinner, Alanson, 411
Smithsonian Institution, 5
Snake, Bessie, 60
Snake tribes, 10–13, 28–29n16
social and ceremonial songs, 84–98
Sockabason, Blanche, 86
Song of the Drum, 93–94, 95–96
songs: Ghost Dance, 448–60; social and ceremonial, 84–98
Spear, Alice, 201–2, 206
Spear, Jim, 201–2, 210, 213
Speck, Frank G., 5, 63
speeches, 42–48, 192–96
spelling of Algonquian words, 45
Spinney, Ann Morrison, 84
spirituality, 55–57, 216–18, 431–32, 450, 453–55
The Spoken Word and the Work of Interpretation, 219
Squier, E. G., 4–5; acceptance of Rafinesque's translation, 17, 19; on American Indian migration to North America, 6, 8, 10; on migration of the Snake tribes, 10–11, 13; translation of the word *kitahikan*, 14–15; Walam Olum Song III translation by, 38–39
Stands, Josephine, 502, 504

storytelling, 49–50, 202–3, 412–13
The Sun Came Down, 495
Sutherland, David, 247, 253
Sutherland, Maggie, 253
Swampy Cree Indians. *See* Omushkego Indians
sweat lodges, 496–97

Tanner, John, 27n12
Tedlock, Dennis, 219
Teeter, Karl V., 100, 102
Telling Our Stories: Omushkego Legens and Histories from Hudson Bay, 247, 254n2
That Way We Should Be Walking story, 188–91
Theories of Primitive Religion, 218
Thomas, Cyrus, 5
Thomason, Lucy G., 368, 379, 397, 404
Toelken, Barre, 219, 220
Traditions of the Arapaho, 477
treaties made by Algonquian tribes, 42–43
Trenholm, Virginia Cole, 477
trickster figures in Algonquian literature, 123–25, 170, 250–52, 294–99, 314, 315–19
Trowbridge, C. C., 51, 58–59
Tuhtuwas dance, 91–93
Turner, Lucien, 123
Turtle stories, 72–74, 77–80, 105–7, 455

Valentine, J. Randolph, 170
Vallier, Elizabeth, 293–94, 293–95, 297, 308, 314
Vander, Judith, 451
verbal art, Native American, 192–95, 412–13
Vizenor, Gerald, 251
Voegelin, Carl F., 5, 6, 10, 59–60; on migration of the Snake tribes, 11; Shawneee translations by, 298–99, 300n10; story of Europeans related to, 51–52; translation of the word *kitahikan*, 15–16; translation of the word *nakopowa*, 20–21, 31n21; Walam Olum Song III translation by, 40–41
Voegelin, Erminie, 5, 16,*Voices from Four Directions*, 170, 375n6
Volney, C. F., 27n12
Voth, H. R., 448

Waabitigweyaa, 161, 165–69
Waasaagoneshkang, 170–72, 173
Wabanaki Indians: animal stories, 72–83; social and ceremonial songs, 84–98; translations of stories of, 99–100
Walam Olum: American Indian migrations portrayed in, 6–10, 26–28n12; authenticity of, 3–6, 23–24n5, 23n2; Snake tribes portrayed in, 10–13; Song III translations, 37–41; transcription errors in, 16–18; variations in translations of, 5–22, 18–22; the word *kitahikan* in, 13–16
Walam Olum, or Red Score: The Migration Legend of the Lenni Lenape or Delaware Indians, 5
Wallace, Anthony F. C., 63
Wampum ceremonies. *See* Passamaquoddy Indians
Wanatee, Adeline, 325
war, origin of, 170–84
Warren, William, 170
weapons of Europeans, 57–58

Weer, Paul, 5
Weslager, C. A., 5
What They Used to Tell About: Indian Legends from Labrador, 122
Wiihsakacaakwa Aalhsoohkaakana story, 303–13
Wiissaakechaahk stories, 251–54, 256–78
Wilakhtwa story, 314
Williams, Roger, 44, 45n3
winter stories, 49, 368; Golden Hide, 397–403; Has-a-Rock, 327–29, 345–67; The Ice Maidens, 326–27, 334–44; manitous and, 369–71; Meskwaki Indians, 321–22; The One Whose Eye Was a Bear's Eye, 404–10; The One Whose Father Was the Sun, 379–96; relations between kin in, 371–73; structure of, 373–75
Wissakatchakwa stories, 294–98, 303–13
Wissler, Clark, 495
wolf stories, 213–14, 241–46
Wolverine, 123–25; and the Ducks story, 128–31, 141–49; and the Geese story, 131–35, 150–58
women's dance songs, 91–93
Woodbury, Anthony C., 122
word division in Algonquian language, 45
The World Observed: Reflections on the Fieldwork Process, 219

Zeisberger, David, 4, 16–17, 18, 19–20, 22, 26n11, 29–31nn17–19

RY
MA 02116